THE PEOP

THE PEOPLE'S PEACE

Britain Since 1945

Fourth Edition

KENNETH O. MORGAN

OXFORD
UNIVERSITY PRESS

OXFORD
UNIVERSITY PRESS

Great Clarendon Street, Oxford, OX2 6DP,
United Kingdom

Oxford University Press is a department of the University of Oxford.
It furthers the University's objective of excellence in research, scholarship,
and education by publishing worldwide. Oxford is a registered trade mark of
Oxford University Press in the UK and in certain other countries

First published as *The People's Peace* 1990
First issued as an Oxford University Press paperback (with corrections and additions) 1992
Second edition 1999
Third edition published as *Britain Since 1945* 2001
Fourth and revised edition 2021

Impression: 1

Published in the United States of America by Oxford University Press
198 Madison Avenue, New York, NY 10016, United States of America

British Library Cataloguing in Publication Data
Data available

Library of Congress Control Number: 2020950280

ISBN 978-0-19-884107-4

Printed and bound by
CPI Group (UK) Ltd, Croydon, CR0 4YY

CONTENTS

PREFACE TO THE SECOND EDITION

This new edition essentially follows the text of the original version published in 1990. However, it takes the story on from the fall of Mrs Thatcher to the end of the first year of the Blair administration in May 1998. I have also taken the opportunity to make some small emendations and corrections, and to update the Bibliography.

K.O.M.

Long Hanborough
September 1998

PREFACE TO THE THIRD EDITION

This new edition takes the story on from the end of the first year of the Blair government in May 1998 to the general election of June 2001. I have made some small changes elsewhere, and also revised and updated both the Conclusion and the Bibliography.

K.O.M.

Long Hanborough
June 2001

PREFACE TO THE FOURTH EDITION

In this updated edition, the story of modern Britain is continued from 2008 to the Brexit settlement in March 2019. I am particularly grateful for the advice of my daughter, Katherine.

K.O.M.

Long Hanborough
June 2021

LIST OF PLATES

1. VE Day celebrations: rolling out the barrel, Piccadilly Circus, 8 May 1945 (Keystone/Hulton Archive/Getty Images).

2. Lord Mountbatten discussing Britain's plans for the transfer of power in India with Pandit Nehru, Lord Ismay, and Mohammed Ali Jinnah, 7 June 1947 (Keystone-France/Gamma-Rapho via Getty Images).

3. The worst of austerity: housewives queuing for horse-meat, 1949 (Popperfoto via Getty Images/Getty Images).

4. The Earls Court Motor Show, 21 October 1952: a Sunbeam Talbot 90 coupé admired by girls from the Windmill Theatre (Fox Photos/Getty Images).

5. The first CND Aldermaston March on its way through Maidenhead, 13 April 1958 (Keystone/Hulton Archive/Getty Images).

6. Harold Macmillan and Nikita Khrushchev at Moscow airport, 21 February 1959 (Keystone Press/ Alamy Stock Photo).

7. Symbols of the Permissive Society: the Beatles in concert, 1965 (Patrice Habans/Paris Match via Getty Images).

8. Bobby Moore, England's captain, holding aloft the World Cup, June 1966. Others in the picture are Jack Charlton, Stiles, Banks, Ball, Peters, Hurst, Wilson, Cohen, and Bobby Charlton (Trinity Mirror/Mirrorpix/Alamy Stock Photo).

9. Kenyan Asian immigrants arriving at London airport, 26 February 1968 (Topfoto).

10. 'Bloody Sunday' in Londonderry, 30 January 1972: a demonstrator chased into custody by a soldier from the Parachute Regiment (Sputnik/TopFoto).

I

The Era of Advance
1945–1961

1. *The Façade of Unity*

———

'NATIONAL unity', declared Sir William Beveridge in 1943, was the great moral achievement of the Second World War. It rested not on party bargains or formal coalitions but on something far more deeply rooted—'the mutual understanding between Government and people'. It stemmed from 'the determination of the British democracy to look beyond victory to the uses of victory', to follow a people's war with a people's peace.[1] To much of British opinion at the time of Beveridge's remarks, the Second World War was seen as a climacteric of British experience. Observers as varied as Harold Laski and Harold Nicolson, rationalist planners like Patrick Abercrombie or Julian Huxley, artists like Henry Moore, populist communicators like J. B. Priestley agreed that the war years were creating a vast cultural transformation in the British as a people. In place of the illformed rhetoric of 'reconstruction' of the First World War, with its bitter aftermath and the sense of class betrayal that followed Lloyd George's election pledges in 1918, there was now a genuine sense of unity rooted in the social and cultural realities of wartime. The lion would lie down with the lamb, as in Henry Moore's sketches of the London population huddling together in *ad hoc* sleeping arrangements on the platforms of the underground railway during the blitz. Here truly were to be seen common sacrifice, common purposes, common objectives. Beveridge quoted the Prime Minister, Winston Churchill, on the Treaty of Ryswick in 1697, writing in his life of Marlborough of how the British

———

[1] Sir William Beveridge, *Pillars of Society* (London, 1943), 109.

invariably threw away the fruits of victory after a successful war.[2] This time, though, it would be utterly different. The past would be exorcized and the future transformed.

Since that time, almost all subsequent interpretations of the history of Britain after 1945 have viewed it as a time of decline or eclipse, both external and internal. Yet the heady impact of the Second World War long exercised its magnetism on a variety of commentators. Across the political spectrum, they saw the experience of Britain between 1939 and 1945 as offering a last, fleeting vision of national greatness. Mrs Thatcher, Prime Minister throughout the 1980s, made frequent attempts to evoke the spirit of Winston Churchill, a symbol of great-power status and indomitable resolve. The fact that the real Churchill was a paternalistic 'one-nation' Whig of romantic disposition, concerned after 1951 to recapture aspects of the social reformism of his younger days, was set aside. For the right, the war embodied constructive patriotism and the will to victory. For the centre-left progressive, it rather implied social cohesion, Keynes-style budgetary management, economic planning, the human version of social citizenship embodied in the Beveridge Report in 1942. It offered the intellectual and historical underpinnings of the post-war consensus. Further to the left, politicians like Michael Foot or even (at times) Tony Benn would look back to the war as a crucible of social revolution, as George Orwell had done in *The Lion and the Unicorn*, achieved in the classless sacrifice of the Blitz and military service, and taken much further by the Labour government of Attlee after 1945. Michael Foot, then Labour's leader, spoke in these terms during the general election campaign of 1983.

In a variety of ways, often instinctively felt, the Second World War supplied images that were satisfying and self-confirming. It was crucial to Britain's usable past, as Americans and others interpreted it. By the 1980s, the late war was almost as much a

[2] Beveridge, *Pillars of Society*, 115.

part of a thriving 'heritage' industry as were Tudor manor houses or medieval cathedrals. Tourists queued up to view the War Cabinet's subterranean quarters in central London. The successive volumes of Martin Gilbert's biography of Sir Winston Churchill attracted massive publicity, while the fiftieth anniversary of the outbreak of war in 1989 launched a huge flood of literature of all kinds. Wartime films such as *Brief Encounter* or *In Which We Serve* retained their popularity. The monarchy, following the crisis of Edward VIII's pre-war abdication, gained new strength through memories of George VI's wartime tours of bomb-ravaged cities, while the Queen Mother lived on as a surviving, ever-popular heroine of the Blitz. Enthusiasts for the arts looked back to the origins of wartime state patronage through the work of the Council for the Encouragement of Music and the Arts (CEMA) and the image of cultural solidarity conveyed by Myra Hess's piano recitals in the National Gallery. On a popular level, Vera Lynn's ballads about the White Cliffs of Dover and 'Meeting Again' made her 'the forces' sweetheart' for ever. Conversely, young hooligans, travelling to support the England football team overseas, expressed themselves through anti-German chants dating from the propaganda operations of Hugh Dalton at the Ministry of Economic Warfare during the war— even if, oddly enough, they were combined with Nazi-type salutes and raucous racist sympathy for the National Front. It was not unknown in Britain in the late 1980s for social workers to discover German schoolchildren beaten up in British schools they attended, even if the causes or course of Anglo-German hostilities were quite unknown to either assailant or victim. Both were stereotypes of an ideal of national greatness on which the post-imperial sun refused to set. As late as July 1990, a Cabinet minister, Nicholas Ridley, gave vent to fierce anti-German sentiments and evoked comparisons with Hitler in discussing present-day German attitudes towards the European Community. On this occasion, however, Mrs Thatcher, who was thought to share many of these sentiments herself, was compelled to ask him to resign.

The decades that followed the Second World War produced, and continued to produce, a wide array of diagnoses of the course of modern British history. Almost all of them, in some sense, originated from perceptions of the Second World War and what it was supposed to have meant for modern Britain. The most fashionable interpretation was that of 'consensus', a somewhat ambiguous and deceptive concept, which broadly saw the war as enshrining welfare democracy as the dominant national creed. Several features were seen as central to this process. In economic terms, Keynesian demand management was enthroned by the work of the Economic Section of the War Cabinet secretariat, including notable Keynesians such as Meade and Stone, with monuments such as Kingsley Wood's budget of 1941 and the 1944 White Paper on Employment policy, largely the work of James Meade. Chancellors, from Cripps in 1947–50 to Heathcoat-Amory ten years later, used a variety of techniques, mainly fiscal but also to some degree monetary, to produce sustained growth without undue damage, it was hoped, to the balance of payments or domestic inflation. From around 1961, more direct forms of governmental intervention were adopted, but the broad premisses of Keynesian expansion survived until the economic crises of the mid-1970s. In industrial terms, the war meant a mixed economy, with some significant measures of nationalization introduced by the Attlee government after 1945 and largely retained by the Conservatives in 1951–64. Economic policy was kept on the move, not by Monnet-style indicative planning, but rather by corporate negotiations between government, business, and a hugely expanded trade union movement, itself clearly one of the victors of the war. Dr Keith Middlemas has well described the 'package' contained in the 1944 White Paper on Employment and the enduring system of pluralistic bargaining that it implied.[3]

Socially, the war consensus was taken to mean common citizenship and newly framed social rights. They stemmed from the

[3] Keith Middlemas, Power, *Competition and the State*, vol. i, *Britain in Search of Balance*, 1940–61 (London, 1986), chap. 3.

1942 Beveridge Report with its philosophy of 'cradle to grave' comprehensivism, and were taken much further after the war by the Attlee government, notably through Aneurin Bevan's National Health Service. This basic core of economic and social 'middle-way' moderation survived, even during the traumas of the Wilson–Heath period of 1964–76. Even in the manifestly different climate of the Thatcher government in the 1980s, vigorous debate over the future of the Health Service or attempts to remodel the Social Security system to the disadvantage of some poorer groups or of working-class children showed how the legacy of 1939–45 continued to cast its long shadow. Meanwhile, the short-lived Social Democratic Party, founded in 1981, was a rally by post-1945 Keynesians to fortify past achievements and to defend them against the extremism of the Bennite left or the Thatcherite right.

There were, however, alternative interpretations of the wartime experience. To the new-model Conservatives of the 1980s, the war provided a vision not of centrism but of extremism. In the face of the increasingly disconsolate apostles of the Keynes/Beveridge consensus, the new right saw the war as inaugurating national decline. Even under the regime of the venerated Churchill, the war launched a destructive pattern of state intervention, uneconomic full employment policies, institutional rigidities, and that expansion of the money supply which became the basis of the British disease. There were echoes of this kind of critique intermittently in the 1950s. The Chancellor of the Exchequer, Peter Thorneycroft, called for cash limits and a pegging of public investment. In January 1958, along with his Treasury team of Enoch Powell and Nigel Birch, he resigned from the government on broadly monetarist grounds.[4] This was the first, abortive challenge to the orthodoxy of statism, rising public expenditure, and social balance. But not until the IMF crisis of late 1976 was a serious attempt made to curb the money supply. A Labour Prime

---

[4] See below, pp. 171–5.

Minister, James Callaghan, could tell his disbelieving comrades that: 'You cannot now, if you ever could, spend your way out of recession.'[5] Even so, in the view of the new Conservatives, this partial rejection of the post-war orthodoxy was nullified by the pressure for higher expenditure created by the institutional mass of the trade unions and other sectional pressure-groups, and by the continued existence of an inflated public sector with much interference in the market mechanism by the Enterprise Board and a myriad of other agencies of central government. In the 1980s, the Thatcher government, for all its Churchillian rhetoric after its victories over the rival challenges of General Galtieri and Arthur Scargill of the Mineworkers, was attempting to dismantle the inheritance of the Second World War. It pounced on the self-doubts of Keynesian economists and patrician technocrats to undermine statist planning in the interests of market enterprise, even if much of manufacturing industry was to be sacrificed in the process. Like the Keynesian centrists, the new Conservatives (sometimes christened 'neo-Liberals')[6] saw the war years as providing a mask of unity. But it was only a façade that concealed a rotting fabric of economic degeneration and endemic inflation from the foundations up.

For Mrs Thatcher and her followers, the war could then be seen as a saga of wrong turnings and missed opportunities. So, too, it was viewed by many on the far left. There was broad agreement here, somewhat on the lines of George Orwell in *The Lion and the Unicorn* or Harold Laski's *Reflections on the Revolution of Our Time*, about the way it presented new opportunities through its potential for social revolution. Some saw Britain in 1945, as did the young E. P. Thompson, newly returned from service on the Italian front, as on the verge of a socialist transformation on the Leninist model.[7] Denis Healey, Labour

---

[5] *The Times*, 1 Oct. 1976.

[6] A term coined in David Marquand's excellent work. *The Unprincipled Society* (London, 1988).

[7] E. P. Thompson, *The Guardian*, 3 Mar. 1984.

candidate for Otley, called at the pre-election Labour Party
conference in 1945 for Britain to take the lead in fostering similar
uprisings in continental Europe. The Marxist playwright Trevor
Griffiths, in his play *Country* (1981), was to depict Britain in
1945 as on the verge of social revolution with *jacqueries* of
rebellious peasants pulling down squirearchical stables. Years
after the event, Tony Benn claimed to see the Attlee government
(in which his father, Lord Stansgate, was a Cabinet minister) taking
that revolution further. The glories of 1945 were compared with the
betrayals of 1964 in terms of socialist expectations.

But by the 1980s, the left-wing critique focused rather on how
little had changed. Benn in 1988 denounced the Attlee government now as 'Stalinist'. In its foreign policy, a favoured target for
far-left criticism,[8] Britain after 1945, under Labour and Tory
governments alike, maintained an unrealistic and imperialist
overseas posture, with a covert nuclear defence programme, fierce
opposition to Communism and colonial liberation movements
from Malaya to Cyprus, and Cold War links between government, right-wing union bosses, and capitalist industry. As 'Sagit-
tarius' put it in the *New Statesman*:

> The Red Flag hangs above the Whitehall camp
> But folded like a Foreign Office gamp.[9]

At home, the left placed emphasis on the evident failure to
remodel the class system after 1945, on the limits of redistributive
tax systems especially on wealth, and the intolerance shown to
genuinely socialist critics like Zilliacus or Platts-Mills, 'Labour's
conscience'. Aneurin Bevan, the one figure of stature who
emerged as leader of the left in the early 1950s, betrayed his
followers, according to this view, by his commitment to British
nuclear weaponry, by crawling into partnership with Gaitskellites
and the Labour right, and, at crucial periods, detaching

---

[8] See e.g. John Saville, *The Labour Movement in Britain* (London, 1988), 88ff.;
Peter Weiler, *British Labour and the Cold War* (Palo Alto, Calif., 1988).
[9] Ian Mikardo, *Backbencher* (London, 1988), 102.

himself and failing to give a lead. The cultural critics of the 1950s, vocal in the novels and plays of the period, were one kind of response. A more formidable one was the growing tide of working-class protest against wartime corporatism in the 1960s and 1970s, culminating in the grass-roots explosion against incomes policy in the 'winter of discontent' in 1978–9. Coincidentally, postwar Britain also meant authoritarian excesses by central government and the bureaucracy, with assaults on civil liberties ranging from legal curbs on traditional union freedom to internment without trial in Northern Ireland and the censorship of suspect literature such as the book *Spycatcher*. To left-wing critics of post-war Britain, it was all too probable that the secret services built up during wartime might have led to the mysterious death of the reformist Labour leader, Hugh Gaitskell, as reflecting the long arm of the Russian KGB. They might have then plotted to destabilize the next Labour government, even one as manifestly unsocialist as that of Harold Wilson.

These views of post-1945 British decline may be characterized as unduly political or even polemical. But there have also been technocratic and academic critiques increasingly to the fore, picking up themes outlined first in analyses of the British economy in the late-Victorian period. There has been a variety of diagnoses of the 'what went wrong' kind, which captured the public imagination perhaps in the 1961–4 period for the first time, and largely retained it ever since. One form of historical backing was provided by the American historian Martin Wiener,[10] writing in the late 1970s, which related Britain's continuing decline in industrial productivity, technical innovation, and scientific adaptation to an ancient preference for gentlemanly traditions and humane disciplines rather than for scientific values. The entrepreneurial spirit gave way to the cult of respectability. Even during the war, J. B. Priestley propagated support

[10] Martin Wiener, *English Culture and the Decline of the Industrial Spirit, 1850–1981* (Cambridge, 1981).

for Merrie England. A vigorous exponent of this conclusion, though with very different explanations, was Correlli Barnett in a controversial work, *The Audit of War* (1986).[11] This located Britain's subsequent economic decline specifically in the failure of the modernization and re-equipment of industry during the Second World War. Barnett's thesis was clearly not one conceived in terms of *laissez faire*. On the contrary, it implied an injection of vigorous Prussian interventionism in the economy in place of sentimental utopianism and woolly models of voluntary partnership. It drew on Barnett's earlier work as a military historian. Barnett's thesis was criticized for placing exaggerated hopes in the potential of business, the unions, and, indeed, government itself for directing resources in a pluralistic, libertarian country like twentieth-century Britain. Barnett may well have been wrong in linking industrial decline with the alternative policy of investing heavily in welfare-type social spending according to 'new Jerusalem' nostrums. In fact, more successful industrial rivals such as Western Germany or Sweden devoted higher proportions of their gross product to public spending (including heavy subsidies for public services) and to social welfare. Even so, Barnett provided a powerful account of how the reality of declining British productivity and scientific skills was masked by the achievements of wartime, themselves heavily dependent on American aid.

The evidence suggests, it can be argued, that what the war did was to galvanize British manufacturing production to new levels of output, but on the basis of existing structures and with little heed for post-war development. It marked the last effective gasp of the late-Victorian and Edwardian economy, given deceptive

[11] Correlli Barnett, *The Audit of War: The Illusion and the Reality of Britain as a Great Power* (London, 1986). There is a shrewd critique of it by Paul Addison, 'The Road from 1945', in Peter Hennessy and Anthony Seldon (eds.), *Ruling Performance: British Governments from Attlee to Thatcher* (Oxford, 1987), 19–24. Also see articles by Correlli Barnett, Paul Addison, T.C. Barker. Sir Alec Cairncross, and Margaret Cowing in *Contemporary Record*, 1, no. 2 (Summer 1987).

vigour after 1945 because economic rivals such as Germany and Japan were defeated and prostrate. By the mid-1950s, the increasingly outdated nature of the British economic structure was painfully apparent. The debates of the 1950s—sterling's role as a reserve currency, British wariness towards the European idea or the aspirations of the Treaty of Rome, orchestrated 'chutzpah' in rebuilding the relations with the Americans after Suez—diverted the people from this underlying reality. To critics like Barnett, interpretations of the wartime achievement have been largely misconceived. The 'guilty men' were not Macmillan and Lloyd in the Tory eclipse of 1961–4, nor again Wilson in the turmoil of the 1960s, nor the Heathite corporatists or the Callaghan-style immobilists of the seventies, but the ministers of the Churchill government of 1940 and their civil service advisers and the pressure groups to which they were emotionally and personally attached. The architects of victory in 1945 were in truth the national grave-diggers.

Clearly, the Second World War left an ambivalent legacy. The elements of unity and of division were both present. At a variety of levels, of course, it was the symbols of national unity and consensus which gained most attention. Important studies by historians such as Paul Addison and Arthur Marwick have explained how this mood became the conventional wisdom after 1945.[12] Addison has termed it 'Attlee's consensus'. But the most powerful personal symbol, of course, was the wartime prime minister, Churchill. Personally an erratic, often depressive figure cast into enervating gloom, whose pre-1939 career was a catalogue of crises and failures, during the war he struck a consistent public pose of courage and resolve. In dark periods such as the loss of Singapore and then of Tobruk in early 1942, in the later march to victory, and especially in international conferences with other allied leaders from Placentia Bay to Yalta, Churchill embodied an uncomplicated national determination.

---

[12] Paul Addison. *The Road to 1945* (London, 1975) and Arthur Marwick, *Britain in the Century of Total War* (London, 1968).

No one at home seriously challenged his ascendancy apart from a brief flurry in favour of Sir Stafford Cripps in 1942 which was soon suppressed. Labour and Liberal leaders, along with the unions, worked with Churchill in relative harmony, in marked contrast to the intrigue and press warfare that scarred Lloyd George's presidential style of premiership in 1916–18. Churchill's mystique endured for years afterwards in a highly personal, visible way. Even when, quite astonishingly, he compared the intended activities of his recent Labour colleagues with the operations of the Gestapo in an election broadcast in 1945, Churchill's personal stature seemed relatively undiminished, despite his disastrous showing at the polls. At the official Victory celebrations in 1946, there seemed a determined nationwide effort to emphasize that his electoral defeat was not intended personally and that his historic stature remained undiminished.

The kind of unity that Churchill embodied, however, was traditional and highly limited. He was, of course, still unpopular in working-class communities, notably in South Wales where his activities, real or alleged, during the 1910 Tonypandy riots and the 1926 General Strike, were rooted in popular folklore. Aneurin Bevan's assaults on him in the Commons did not cause the shock in Ebbw Vale that they did in Westminster. Churchill took only a transient interest in the domestic aspects of total war. When he did intervene it was usually in a conservative direction, as when he opposed the costliness of the Beveridge Report, or aspects of Willink's proposed national health service, or when he resisted the nationalization even of the discredited privately owned coal industry. Churchill's war leadership was geared to visions of imperial greatness, related to an Empire of which (including India) he had remarkably little firsthand knowledge, and which the events of war were making dangerously outmoded. He forced inter-allied strategy into imperial ends, on the lines of the 'secret treaties' of 1914–18, by making the preservation of Egypt and the North African littoral a priority over an attack on Nazi-held Europe, and by intense concern to uphold the Indian Raj for all the known resistance of the Congress movement. Churchill flared up in 1942 when Roosevelt sought to apply the lessons of the American War of Independence to India. The Prime Minister declared that he could not 'abandon our responsibility and leave [India] to anarchy or subjugation'.[13] In military discussions, Churchill argued vehemently against a Second Front and successfully pressed for priority to be given the 'Torch' invasion of North Africa rather than the 'Overlord' assault on Europe in 1942–3. Lack of military preparedness was much cited. But the Prime Minister's emphasis was also on the preservation of imperial greatness, especially perhaps in the eastern Mediterranean and the Middle East, a region with which he had been much involved as Colonial Secretary after the First World War. The wartime debates between British strategic planners such as Alanbrooke and Tedder concerned matters of military detail rather than long-term change. In which specific role this heady vision of enduring national greatness could be best deployed— in an already fragmenting Commonwealth, in a one-sided partnership with the Americans, or an ill-defined 'United Europe'—was never clear. Churchill's concept was Whiggish, misty, and romantic. But down to VE Day it appeared sufficient for many of his people. Twenty years later, at his funeral at Bladon church, Oxfordshire, in 1965, a left-wing commentator, T. R. Fyvel, noted the symbolism involved.[14] The warrior king's burial gave renewed strength to the sense of national identity and destiny.

No other member of the government offered any clear alternative vision. The only one who came near to doing so was Ernest Bevin, General Secretary of the Transport Workers and now Minister of Labour. His role as Minister brought the unions into direct corporate relationship with the government, in industrial relations, manpower policy, regional planning, welfare, and much else besides. In 1944 Bevin was a central figure in the

[13] William Roger Louis, *Imperialism at Bay* (Oxford, 1975). 149–50.
[14] T.R. Fyvel, *Intellectuals Today: Problems in a Changing Society* (London, 1968), 77.

bargain between the unions, private industry, and government to sustain industrial growth along with free collective bargaining after the war. Bevin was the most prominent of Labour's war-lords, the massive embodiment of the social patriotism of 1940. In the 1945 general election he was a major asset to his party, especially since he seemed to stand above the mêlée as a non-partisan representative of the interests of productive industry. He was sometimes touted as the head of a putative postwar coalition.

But Bevin's corporatist view of national unity had its problems, too. It rested on broad structures of national negotiation through central union officials with entrées to the administration. *The Economist* even saw him as proposing a managed economy that would bypass the parliamentary system, almost a benign form of fascism.[15] It contrasted with the pattern of decentralized shop-floor plant bargaining that the wartime growth in the number and power of shop stewards tended to encourage. Bevin entered Attlee's government in 1945 not just as Foreign Secretary but also as the founding General Secretary of Britain's largest union. He was the most important and influential trade-unionist alive. Yet he was necessarily becoming increasingly detached from the rank and file, and to prove something of a divisive force as a union leader as well as a Foreign Secretary. Years after his death, the Donovan Commission was to show how the processes of wage bargaining had moved beyond Bevin's central-ized procedures, including amongst the shop stewards of his own transport workers. Shortly after the war, they led to a rash of 'unofficial strikes' which forced the Attlee government, with Bevin's endorsement, to have recourse to 'states of emergency' and strike-breaking procedures that dated from Lloyd George's coalition in 1920. They testified to the difficulty of translating a vision of coherent industrial partnership into firm policies that

---

[15] Alan Bullock, *The Life and Times of Ernest Bevin*, vol. ii. *Minister of Labour, 1940–1945* (London, 1967), 275–6, citing various extracts from *The Economist* in 1942–4.

commanded the loyalty of local producer-groups and satisfied pressures for industrial democracy. Bevin's England, too, was moving into an autumnal phase.

The most convincing statements of national harmony in policy terms came from the planners, those assorted economists, social engineers, and technocrats who came to the fore during the war. They paraded their creed proudly in the famous 'planning' issue of Edward Hulton's *Picture Post* in early 1941.[16] We have already noted Beveridge for his passionate advocacy of the ethic of unity at this time. The huge sales of his report on the social insurance system in November 1942 led him to believe that his ideas had captured the popular imagination. His later experience was less promising, and his star began to wane after 1943. His hopes of becoming a kind of Minister of Reconstruction were dashed, and he found himself at odds with Churchill over the White Paper on employment in 1944, which he regarded as a timid compromise.[17] Churchill regarded him as a semi-socialist; yet Beveridge was also distant from the Labour movement. In the 1945 general election, somewhat humiliatingly, he lost his seat as Liberal MP for Berwick-on-Tweed, partly because local nonconformists in the far north suspected an élitist Oxford-based technocrat. Beveridge proved to be no People's William. Even so, his vision of a comprehensive social insurance system, binding private philanthropy and state provision into a uniform system, came close to embodying a national consensus about the purposes of the war. For all his personal disappointment, Beveridge was the often unacknowledged legislator of the world.

Maynard Keynes's war was even more satisfying. He had no clear public role. His membership of the Chancellor of the Exchequer's 'consultative council' and governorship of the Bank of England were his only formal commitments. But the war gave him both a forum for applying economic ideas worked out by him in their complete form only in the *General Theory* in

[16]   *Picture Past*, 4 Jan. 1941, entitled 'A Plan for Britain'.
[17]   José Harris, *William Beveridge: A Biography* (Oxford, 1977), 434ff.

1936, and for advocating broader views about economic management and money which he had elaborated for a quarter of a
century. His adroit methods of personal contact and private
diplomacy gave him access to channels of decision-making over
a wide front, including (through Brendan Bracken and others) the
occasional ear of Churchill himself. Keynes was thus personally
involved in most key aspects of wartime high policy from the
details of national fiscal policy and assessment as embodied in
Kingsley Wood's budget of 1941, to external planning for the
post-war period with the Americans. He was a crucial figure in
the Bretton Woods Agreement of 1944, including the decision to
maintain sterling as a reserve currency which contributed to
stable exchange rates but which also gave so much trouble in
later years.[18] But the new economic thinking, naturally, extended
far beyond the personal influence of Keynes, considerable though
that was. Economic theorists like James Meade and Richard
Stone in the Cabinet's Economic Section, planners like Sir Richard Hopkins (a particularly close ally of Keynes's), joined later by
the independent-minded figure of Richard ('Otto') Clarke, at the
Treasury, occupied key positions. At a different level, young left-
wing economists like Hugh Gaitskell, Evan Durbin, Douglas Jay
at the Board of Trade, Harold Wilson at the Ministry of Fuel and
Power, embodied the economics of Keynes, while rejecting much
of his politics and his sociopsychology. The Keynesians, though,
were far from a homogeneous group. The extent of budgetary
management was a source of fierce controversy. Income restraint
was another.[19] There were many critics of employment policy for
its compromising attitude towards the private market. But what
was largely agreed was that, in the determining of post-war
patterns of investment and employment, the state must assume
wide new responsibilities. This belief, embodied in such wartime

[18] Richard Gardner, 'Bretton Woods', in Milo Keynes (ed.). *Essays on
John Maynard Keynes* (Cambridge, 1975), 202ff.
[19] See Douglas Jay, *Change and Fortune: A Political Record* (London, 1980),
113.

measures as the 1945 Distribution of Industry Act, went far beyond the impact of Keynes himself or indeed any other individual.

The united outlook implied in wartime socio-economic policy was something broader than the ideas of the Keynesians. It embodied an ethic of planning and social direction widespread throughout the professions and the mandarin class of administrators. In the 1930s, the planners had been searching for a role. Active in bodies like PEP, they felt frustrated by the control of the Treasury and the hostile attitude of the National government towards regional policy and much else besides. Now in the war years architects and town planners, for instance, found themselves to be honoured and valued figures after the reports of Barlow on the geographical distribution of industry and of Uthwatt and Scott on town and countryside development. Architects like Abercrombie and Maxwell Fry were caught up in schemes for the redevelopment of London, and many other urban planning projects. The creation of a Ministry of Town and Country Planning in 1943 was a notable portent. The British Medical Association worked in close association with the Ministry of Health in pursuit of the idea of a national health service, while educationalists were similarly active in building up the secondary and further education system. In the arts, W. E. Williams of CEMA commented proudly on the eighty public exhibitions of the visual arts put on in 1940, at the height of the Battle of Britain. He listed (with mathematical precision) the 804 publicly sponsored symphony concerts put on during the war years.[20] The professional journals in 1939–45, indeed, were full of the cry for planning, public investment, and social development. In fact, the war years are unique in British history for the adventurous, self-confident vitality surging through the middle-class intelligentsia and their representatives in the civil service. Even as non-political a book as Professor Lancelot Hogben's best-selling *Mathematics*

[20] W. E. Williams, in *Seventeenth Annual Report of the Arts Council*, 1961–2, 5ff.

for the Million slipped in observations about the social need for planning, calculation, and rationality. Through their blueprints, they hoped, the intellectual middle classes were giving a sense of direction to the nation as a whole after the numbing despair of the 1930s.

To some degree, indeed, this unified ethic percolated through-out society more generally. Mass military conscription and the privations of sacrifice and collective regime implied in ration books, identity cards, and the like, expressed a kind of common identity. But these had existed during the First World War also without achieving a similar result. They had produced emotional rhetoric about a land fit for heroes, followed by a mood of collective disillusion and 'goodbye to all that'. For most people, the unity this time seemed more genuine and more openly arrived at. Industrial relations, with some exceptions in the mining indus-try like the Betteshanger dispute in Kent and the 'boys' strike' in South Wales, were conducted more equitably, without the injust-ices of the Munitions of War Act of 1915. Within the armed services and the various auxiliary services at home—'fire-watch-ing' and the like—divisions of rank and status visibly diminished. The ABCA (Army Bureau of Current Affairs) discussions of politicial issues, amongst the army overseas, may not have been those philosophical Putney debates of popular legend; but it is still remarkable that such exercises in public communication existed at all, and that they were so popular. Ministry of Information briefings, launched during the Blitz in 1940, testified to a cheerful, tolerant people, quietly convinced of the righteousness of their cause, happy to endure privations collectively until the appointed victorious outcome duly arrived.

The received images of the Second World War, then—images faithfully relayed to promote national solidarity in the years of the Labour government after 1945—are of unity and common endeavour. There was a new civic morality which extended even to the intimacies of family life and of private conversation. After all, as the poster had it, 'Careless talk costs lives'. Hugh Dalton launched the slogan, for the benefit of housewives and mothers,

'More darns on your socks mean more bombs on the Germans'; this, too, was apparently well received. But a determining factor of British history after 1945 was that these images and slogans conflicted in crucial respects with the social reality. It was clear, for instance, that the belief that the British class system dissolved or was basically modified during the war is a total myth. Britain in the 1930s had been governed in terms of social division, with the thriving middle-class suburbs and shopping precincts in the Midlands and southern England, on which the Conservative ascendancy was based, carefully segregated from the working-class 'tribe apart' in Labour-run South Wales, the North of England, and industrial Scotland.[21] The public order troubles of the thirties, the vigorous and sometimes ruthless way in which the police put down marches of the unemployed, Welsh 'stay-down' miners, and the like, reinforced this sense of polarization on which Neville Chamberlain's regime rested. The population movements of the decade, which saw Welsh mining families transplanted to Cowley and Scottish steel-workers to Corby, did not greatly alter this social division. Tawney spelt it out memorably in terms of the differential standards of nutrition, health, and survival dictated by the British 'religion of inequality'.[22] Tawney's Halley Stewart lectures in 'Equality' were delivered in 1929 but things were little different ten years later.

The purpose of wartime social policies, no doubt, was to promote a genuine sense of solidarity and 'pulling through together'. In practice, evacuated children from inner-city slums in London or Liverpool found themselves all too often confronted by uncomprehending or disapproving middle-class communities in rural areas or seaside towns, concerned about fleas or lice-ridden hair. This was the more disagreeable side of 'Mrs Miniver'. Many evacuees could not wait to return to their own shabby homes, Blitz and all, and large numbers of them did so within twelve months. The wartime schemes for social insurance,

---

[21] The phrase appears in Barnett, *Audit of War*, 190ff.
[22] R. H. Tawney, *Equality* (London, 1931), 24ff.

urban planning, and the rest inspired less than whole-hearted public enthusiasm, according to Mass Observation finds or the Nuffield survey organized by G.D.H. Cole[23]—certainly much less than government-sponsored documentary films might suggest. They were superimposed on a divided society with a tender concern for private provision, savings, and home ownership, and a fear of bureaucracy. Indeed, accounts of the looting of bombed properties and the vigorous life of the 'black market' to evade wartime rationing suggest widespread exceptions to the perceived civic culture of the time. Often it was officials in the public service—ARP wardens, auxiliary firemen and so on—who were the culprits in Britain's so-called 'finest hour'. In 1941, there were no less than 4,585 looting cases in London alone, many of them from bomb-ravaged homes.[24]

In some ways, the war hardened rather than dissolved social distinctions. Much has been made of the way in which the wartime years promoted the freedom of women in terms of job opportunity as factory workers or 'land girls', and even advanced leisure and recreation facilities as well.[25] In fact, much women's work during the war was deliberately low-level and routine. The assumption was that, especially for married women, their work would be wound up when peace and normality returned. Married women still found barriers against their advancement, or even to being hired at all, for instance in the civil service. Equal pay in the professions was still far off: the National Union of Teachers was sometimes derided for being mainly a union of women state teachers. Amongst male workers, the corporate arrangements under Bevin's aegis tended to favour the big

[23] José Harris, 'Did British Workers want the Welfare State? G. D. H. Cole's Survey of 1942'. in J. M. Winter (ed.), *The Working Class in Modern British History* (Cambridge, 1983), 200ff.

[24] Geoffrey Pearson, *Hooligan: A History of Respectable Fears* (London, 1983), 241.

[25] For an excellent discussion of this aspect, see H. L. Smith, 'The effect of the war on the status of women', in Smith (ed.), *War and Social Change: British Society in the Second World War* (Manchester, 1987), 208ff.

battalions of organized workers rather than smaller or more dispersed groups of the unskilled or 'dilutees'.

One notable area is public education. The 1944 Butler Act, as is well known, divided the secondary school population between grammar schools for an educated élite, secondary moderns for the unskilled majority, and a small fringe of technical schools for the residue. Such an outcome could have been foreseen. The act resulted from the appointment of the Norwood Committee in 1943, under the chairmanship of the president of St John's College, Oxford, a classicist who had previously been headmaster of Marlborough and Harrow public schools.[26] Norwood was a deeply committed Christian, and much time was taken up with the representations of the churches on religious instruction conducted in school hours. Norwood himself accepted almost uncritically the findings of psychologists on the tripartite division of the 'child mind': in large measure this was based on the supposedly scientific 'IQ' tests used by the later discredited psychologist, Cyril Burt. Such works as Burt's *Backward Child* (1937), later seen to be inadequate on scholarly and statistical grounds, were during wartime treated almost as holy writ by educationalists. Norwood's committee duly found that secondary education should be moulded so as to fit, not only into the intelligence spectrum but also the social hierarchy. No one seriously argued the cause of the multilateral school, let alone the need for more technical training. It is one of the mysteries of the wartime period that the 1944 Butler Act, of which Chuter Ede, a Labour minister, was a major architect, became regarded as a bold, egalitarian measure. It is even more strange that the Attlee government after 1945, with a famous left-wing figure, the flame-haired 'Red' Ellen Wilkinson of Spanish Civil War fame at the Education Department, concentrated on enshrining the 1944 Act as the permanent base of the educational system. Meanwhile the public schools and the universities of Oxford and Cambridge,

[26] Brian Simon, *The Politics of Educational Reform, 1920–1940* (London, 1974), 327–9.

with their massive closed scholarships, huge private endowments, and overwhelmingly public-school intake, along with a heavy bias in favour of the humanities (including compulsory Latin until 1970) remained sacrosanct against change.

The course of wartime policy, indeed, met with rather more challenge at the time than is commonly inferred. On the right, there was the famous work of Professor Friedrich August von Hayek, *The Road to Serfdom* (1944) with its passionate protest against creeping state control as illiberal and its attack on planning as a self-defeating illusion. This was much influenced by the currency inflation and socialism of 'red Vienna' in Austria before the war. In 1944, Hayek seemed almost to be laughed out of court by the public mood. Evan Durbin, one of his students at the London School of Economics much influenced by Hayek's views on the trade cycle, criticized his old mentor for his lack of faith in (or, perhaps, knowledge of) the robust patriotism of the British people.[27] It was a patriotism which Durbin himself had hailed in romantic, quasi-Elizabethan terms in his own *Politics of Democratic Socialism* (1940), an influential treatise in favour of revisionist social democracy. In an election broadcast in 1945 Clement Attlee poured derision on the German Hayek (whose Christian names were carefully spelt out in full), as the Labour demonology's answer to the Tory bogy of the Jew Laski. Nevertheless, Hayek's criticisms even at the time struck a chord amongst many who questioned the omnicompetence of the central state apparatus and the certainty with which statist planning was put forward. The famous Fabian, Barbara Wootton, set out to demolish Hayek's arguments; but she found much difficulty in doing so and had to rely on counter-assertion. His economic views on the trade cycle retained their appeal even among Labour economists like Gaitskell. The Hayek view of economic freedom, consumer choice, and the primacy of the market mechanism was buoyant in the mid-1950s, long before it was

[27] Review by Durbin in *The Economic Journal*, 1945.

appropriated by the monetarist Tory Policy Group in the 1970s.
But it was a product of the Second World War in origin.

Yet it was the left-wing critique of wartime policy which was
much more cogent at the time. Its major exponent was Harold
Laski. A highly influential writer and political theorist, and a
famous teacher at the London School of Economics, his political
impact was dissipated by tactical naïvety on the Labour National
Executive. He led a vain assault on Attlee's leadership in 1944–5
which the party leader deftly brushed aside. Laski as a political
figure was not a great success. But as an author he was a communicator of much skill and influence. His *Reflections on the
Revolution of our Time* (1943), in which old libertarian ideas
going back to John Stuart Mill were yoked with a more recently
acquired form of Marxism, called for the socialist ownership of
all means of production.[28] It drew a contrast between a real
socialist policy of economic ownership and direction and the
compromise system of 'control' favoured by Attlee, Morrison,
Bevin, and other Labour members of Churchill's coalition. On
the party NEC, Laski made himself the advocate of doctrinaire
socialism. He asserted that the war had radicalized the British
people; it had produced another 1789. With some effect, he
accused the party leadership of flirtation with capitalism under
the guise of the unity needed to defeat Hitler. A similar line of
attack in parliament and in the weekly journal *Tribune* came
from Aneurin Bevan, a particular critic of Ernest Bevin and other
Labour ministers for their dictatorial and illiberal approach
towards industrial protest. Bevan's venomous tract, *Why not
trust the Tories?*, written under the pseudonym 'Celticus' in
1944, pointed out the dangers of following the coalition line
on employment, housing, industrial relations, and much else.
He urged Labour to be on its guard against a betrayal of the
workers such as had happened after 1918. Bevan's truculence

---

[28] Harold Laski, *Reflections on the Revolution of our Time* (London, 1943);
see Kenneth O. Morgan, 'Harold Laski', in *Labour People: Leaders and Lieutenants, Hardie to Kinnock* (Oxford, 1987), 91ff.

towards his leaders almost cost him the party whip in mid-1944: he was truly *mauvais coucheur* at this time. But soon afterwards he was elected to the constituency section of the party's National Executive as a forceful advocate of socialist policies, In July 1945, after a quiet election campaign, he could be muzzled no longer, and Attlee had to promote him to the Cabinet. Ernest Bevin was supposed to have told Attlee, 'He can be awkward sometimes but he's got his head screwed on'.[29]

The belief that the Coalition, far from expressing a united programme of social advance, was really delaying the progress of socialism in our time was widespread throughout the labour and trade union movement. It was pointed out that distinctive socialist policies on health care and secondary education had been worked out, by the Socialist Medical Association and the National Association of Labour Teachers, in the 1930s, but were ignored by the Coalition. Also, Labour had evolved its own approach to social insurance and family allowances before Beveridge's White Paper ever saw the light of day. Many constituency parties rebelled against the constraints of the wartime electoral pact. This criticism took the form of vigorous attacks on Coalition foreign policy, notably the endorsement by Bevin and other ministers of Churchill's intervention on the side of the royalist right in the Greek Civil War in 1944. The left's most celebrated triumph came with the so-called 'Reading resolution', moved by Ian Mikardo, candidate for Reading South, at party conference in December 1944. Here, an anodyne NEC motion, moved by Philip Noel-Baker, calling for state control of economic policy was swept aside, without even a vote, by a floor resolution calling unambiguously for the nationalization of all key industries, including the difficult one of iron and steel. After all, public ownership of the joint-stock banks and of land had vanished altogether during the war. Many delegates felt that

[29] John Campbell, *Nye Bevan and the Mirage of British Socialism* (London, 1987), 151.

public ownership as an aspiration should not be allowed to disappear totally. The passage of the Reading resolution thus forced the party leadership to adopt a wide-ranging policy of nationalization as main priority. Mikardo recalls how he left the Methodist Central Hall in a daze after his triumph. Morrison then put a hand on his shoulder. 'Young man, you did very well this morning... but you do realise, don't you, that you've lost us the general election?'[30]

Quite apart from these movements within the rank and file, the Cabinet Reconstruction Committee in 1943–4 had shown lively antagonism between Labour and Tory ministers, with the former much better briefed and gaining the upper hand in argument. The notion that there was a cross-party consensus over the main forms of post-war social and economic policy is often much exaggerated. On nationalization, full employment, economic controls, a National Health Service, housing, taxation, and much else in domestic policy (not to mention India, Egypt, and other aspects of external policy) British political opinion was clearly polarized in Westminster and throughout the land.

There is another point to be made here. Programmes for industrial planning or budgetary management were not monolithic or hermetically sealed off from the surrounding culture. The social policies of the war had somehow to be harmonized with a wide range of sectional groups with a pluralistic, or purely selfish, ethic. The social policies of the war had not merely invoked general principles of solidarity. They had also reflected a rich variety of pressure groups, many of them deeply entrenched. The idea of a National Health Service was conceived partly in terms of the professional self-interest of the British Medical Association, deeply hostile to the idea of a salaried medical profession under state control. Henry Willink's moderate proposals for a national health service foundered ignominiously in

[30] Mikardo, *Backbencher*, 77; *Report of the Forty-Third Annual Conference of the Labour Party*, 11–15 Dec. 1944, 160ff.

1944 for this very reason.[31] Education was a theme inseparable
from an immense array of vested interests, public and private,
local and central, secular and religious. Beveridge-style social
insurance had to be accommodated to highly profitable industrial assurance companies, the friendly societies, and a myriad of
other 'approved' bodies including the trade unions. Industrial
modernization ran up against not only the rigidities of older
firms buttressed against change by tariff protection since 1932,
but also a myriad of small-scale private firms, the privileges of
the professions and the implacable pluralism of the trade unions.
The very unity of the United Kingdom had to be measured
against the renewed sense of Scottish identity released under
Tom Johnston's aegis at the Scottish office, and some signs of
similar forces at work in Wales with pressure for devolution
from the Welsh Reconstruction Committee and major advocates
of a Welsh Secretary of State.[32] The war, in short, had promoted
fragmentation as much as it had fostered coherence.

In a less obvious way, the war had also challenged national
cohesiveness in external policy. Britain fought the war as a great
imperial power, as of historic right. As has been noted, Churchill
gave that sense of imperial destiny the maximum of rhetorical
support. Yet in many ways the experience of 1939–45 also
began to free the British from their sense of world ascendancy
without replacing it with anything more positive. The prevailing
image of the war for Britain was national, indeed insular. The
Battle of Britain, with the courageous spirit of Spitfire and Hur-
ricane pilots and the nation fighting alone in the face of defeatism, treachery, and the military failures of the French, Dutch,
Norwegians, and others, provided a dominant symbol. It offered
a compelling vision of isolationism. The fact that the Americans

---

[31] See Charles Webster, *The Health Services Since the War*, i (HMSO, 1988)
57–71. Also see *British Medical Journal* from September 1944 onwards. *The
Lancet*, the specialists' journal, was much more sympathetic.

[32] Tom Johnston, *Memories* (London, 1952). 147ff.; Kenneth O. Morgan,
Rebirth of a Nation: Wales 1880–1980 (Oxford and Cardiff, 1981), 299ff.

remained formally non-belligerent until after Pearl Harbor in December 1941, while the British fought their corner through sea power as they had done since the days of the Spanish Armada, encouraged still further a sense of inward retreat. The British had engaged in scarcely any significant public debate on foreign policy from the end of the First World War down to the time of Munich and the guarantee to Poland. The National government which had to resist Hitler in 1936–9 was composed of men returned to high office to meet solely domestic needs back in August 1931. Little enough debate on foreign policy took place during the wartime years either. Linking Britain to some kind of integrated Europe, however defined, hardly made sense, given the ideological divisions and military defeat of most of continental Europe. The handling of sensitive European leaders in exile like General de Gaulle was no testimony to the British regard for European sensibilities. The flight of liberal or leftish Europeans from Nazi persecution aroused relatively few echoes of solidarity in Britain. The Labour Party, taking its cue from the ferociously 'anti-Hun' Dalton, was notorious for its lack of comradeship towards the German Social Democrats who had fled to Britain.[33] Discussions of a post-war settlement of the German question always brought up the insistence that Britain could not give future pledges of entanglement in the diplomatic or military affairs of the continent. The guarantee to Poland in 1939 could not be repeated. The relationship with the Americans was always tense and resentful, as the wartime conferences showed beneath the mid-Atlantic clichés. Christopher Thorne has shown how the diplomatic postures of the war were at variance with endless tensions between Britain and the United States over China, Persia, Palestine, Egypt, and Britain's general approach towards liquidating the colonial heritage.[34]

---

[33] See Anthony Glees, *Exile Politics During the Second World War* (Oxford, 1982).

[34] Christopher Thorne, *Allies of a Kind: The United States, Britain and the War against Japan, 1941–1945* (London, 1978).

Roger Louis's powerful works have documented how, at the end of the war, US policy was already fully geared to promoting British decolonization.[35] Even in the Middle East, where most British diplomatic enterprise (and money) had been devoted to building up secure positions in Persia and Iraq, there was a sense of 'an empire at bay'. The Commonwealth remained, of course, but the wartime image simply reinforced Britain's dominance within it. Commonwealth leaders like Smuts in South Africa and Mackenzie King in Canada were viewed basically as 'friends of Britain'. The wartime operations of the sterling bloc, including the future disposal (or non-disposal) of the sterling balances with African and Asian countries were worked out to British advantage, and the future of the Commonwealth in trading terms was largely seen as colonial territories providing cheap raw materials for a metropolitan country. Even Labour's colonial thinking, stemming largely from the Fabian Colonial Research Bureau and the writings of Rita Hinden, concentrated on imperial partnership and development rather than on decolonization.[36] It ignored such problems as the fact that the Commonwealth 'dollar pool' disadvantaged colonies like the Gold Coast or Malaya from using surplus dollars gained for their cocoa or rubber to buy goods outside the sterling area. It was generally believed that there was a special relationship between the British liberal left and the Indian intelligentsia, many of whom had studied or worked in Britain between the wars. But the abject failure of the 'Cripps offer' of 1942 showed the wide gulf that persisted between British political leaders of most shades and the Congress movement, let alone the Moslem League. The war years saw the latent erosion of the imperial system without any alternative vision to take its place. At least Lloyd George in 1919 had a clear view of Britain as a major force for international stability

---

[35] William Roger Louis, *Imperialism at Bay* (Oxford, 1977) and id., *The British Empire in the Middle East*, 1945–1951 (Oxford, 1984).
[36] P.S. Gupta, *Imperialism and the British Labour Movement*, 1914–1965 (London, 1975), 278ff.

with obligations to intervene abroad to preserve political harmony, relieve Franco-German rivalry, revive trade, and promote world disarmament and disengagement from the Russian steppes to the west of Ireland. It was partly because the British government then did offer an intelligible, if controversial, vision of world leadership that Keynes's rival approach in *The Economic Consequences of the Peace* made such an extraordinary impact. To quote Bonar Law in 1922, the British had no wish to be 'policeman of the world'. There was no room, or need, for another Keynes in 1945 to voice the cause of withdrawal. No coherent scenario presented itself to Britain's peacemakers at Potsdam in 1945 other than the vague notion that Britain, with its empire and sterling bloc, was truly one of the 'Big Three'.

The war years, then, left a complex and untidy heritage. There were pressures for an expression of national unity based both on military success and vigorous reform programmes on the home front. There were also forces of disunity and division, based in part on the background of pre-war social divisiveness, in part on the new transformations and choices of total war. Both aspects came out strongly in the political circumstances that resulted from the war in 1945.

In the 1945 general election, all major parties were agreed that an early appeal to the people was necessary.[37] There was some political finessing that came about when Churchill offered Labour ministers the prospect of continuing until the defeat of Japan, perhaps well on into 1946, an offer which appealed to Attlee, Bevin, and Morrison, but not to the party at large. Nevertheless, any continuation of something resembling the Lloyd George coalition of 1918–22 of ill memory was unthinkable. There would be no 'hard faced men' in the saddle this time. Once Labour's party executive and conference endorsed an immediate withdrawal from the coalition in May, all politicians, including Churchill, threw themselves into the battle with zest.

---

[37] See Henry Pelling, 'The General Election of 1945 Reconsidered', *Historical Journal*, 23, 2 (June 1980), 339ff.

Any suggestion of emulating the Popular Front regime in France, ranging from de Gaulle to Maurice Thorez and the Communists, was unthinkable. In the campaign that followed, the themes of unity and of sectional conflict came out in vivid contrast.

All the parties harnessed the sense of patriotism for their own purposes. Even the Liberals offered their own variation with Beveridge as a popular hero and his insurance scheme as their unique contribution to total victory. Churchill, naturally, exploited his own special role as military and strategic leader, the voice and inspiration of the people in the darkest of days. Tory posters urged the voters to 'Vote National', perhaps an unwise reminder of the pre-war days of Baldwin and Chamberlain. Churchill, however, was to draw a delicate contrast between his own independent role and the formal stance of the orthodox Conservative party against which he had been a vehement rebel on behalf of causes good and bad throughout the thirties. His choice of mavericks such as Brendan Bracken and Lord Beaverbrook as personal confidants during his disastrous election campaign underlined the distinction. He had very little connection with Anthony Eden, for instance, another rebel of the thirties, partly admittedly because Eden was withdrawn after the sad news of the death of his son in an air crash, but more because of policy differences, especially over eastern Europe.[38] Eden thought the tone of Churchill's election broadcasts to be appalling.

Labour concentrated on the 'people's war' theme of emphasizing housing, social insurance, and full employment. Allied to this was the need for modernization and central planning instead of the acknowledged waste of the industrial stagnation of the thirties. In addition, for once in its history, Labour could uninhibitedly play the patriotic card. Ministers like Morrison, Bevin, and Dalton had been well to the fore in highly visible positions on the home front, though Attlee himself remained relatively obscure to

[38] Robert Rhodes James, *Anthony Eden* (London, 1986), 297ff.

the public at large. The loyalty of the trade union leaders, even a Communist like Arthur Horner of the Mineworkers, was beyond question. On foreign affairs, Labour need not be timid about proclaiming a major external role, nor about accepting the need for strong national defences. After all, it was the Conservative Party, not Labour, which was tarred with the brush of Munich, appeasement, and 'peace in our time'. More controversial or abrasive Labour figures such as Aneurin Bevan or Emanuel Shinwell were given less prominent roles in the campaign.

Yet it was a highly partisan election, also. The extent of political polarization, of barely suppressed anger, was much noted by foreign observers. The quiet, dull mien of Attlee, clipped and prosaic in speech, modest in manner, could not disguise the clear commitment of his party to a form of socialism with widespread state intervention. Churchill's supra-political status did not muffle his attacks on Labour as quasi-Communist and reckless over national defence and the preservation of empire overseas. The 'Gestapo' broadcast which became so notorious was hardly an aberration. Labour won a huge election majority, with 394 seats to the Conservatives' 210, and over 200 gains. These included large numbers of suburban and commuter constituencies, cathedral cities, and other unlikely strongholds of socialism.[39] But the expectations of these constituencies and their voters showed a rich variety as the very vagueness of Labour's proclaimed 'socialism' implied. The election was fought in a mood of 'never again' amongst electors who sought guarantees that the unemployment, stagnation and defeatism of the thirties would not return. There was much utopianism in the air, especially amongst middle-class intellectuals of the *New Statesman* type. But nostalgia was almost equally present. Social change would result in the old order and stability being retained. The presence of Attlee in Downing Street, a far more conventional figure in social philosophy and

[39] I include in the Labour total Wing-Commander Millington, elected for Chelmsford as Common Wealth candidate, who joined Labour shortly after the election.

personal tastes than the romantic, swashbuckling Tory who had preceded him, testified to the sense of national contradiction or perhaps self-deception. In its pursuit of the New Jerusalem, Labour looked to the past, through the eyes of relatively conservative, conventional leaders. Perhaps Britain in July 1945 was simply too exhausted by war to offer any alternative prospectus. Amidst the very euphoria of victory in 1945, the nation offered not a triumph of the will but a suspicion of change and the paralysis of self-doubt.

2. *Labour's High Noon*

1945–1947

'THE Socialist advance continues', proclaimed the Labour Chancellor of the Exchequer, Hugh Dalton, in May 1946.[1] The cause of this exultation was the relatively humdrum one of the public ownership of cable and wireless. It was already a service with a large element of state participation, through the Post Office, going back to before 1914. But it was, to Dalton and his colleagues, part of a broader floodtide of collective economic advance and change launched by Labour's election victory in July 1945. In the eighteen months that followed. Britain appeared to undergo a massive transformation unique in her history. Over 20 per cent of the economy was taken into public ownership or was well on course for it. The framework for a welfare state was boldly set out, with the National Health Service Act passed in May 1946, along with a National Insurance Act that enacted the Beveridge proposals, and new drives for publicly subsidized housing and advance in elementary and secondary education. Labour enthusiasts wrote of Britain's 'middle way' of democratic socialism, an inspiration for the peoples of western Europe and for the third-world nations of Africa, Asia, and the Caribbean. Overseas, the most dramatic change had come with the appointment of Lord Mountbatten in place of Wavell as Viceroy of India in January 1947 with powers to negotiate a rapid settlement with the leaders of the Congress and the Muslim

[1] *Parl. Deb.*, 5th ser., vol. 422, 201 (21 May 1946).

League, so as to grant independence to the people of the subcontinent. The transfer of power in India and Pakistan duly came in August 1947; 450 million people, over two-thirds of the entire population of the Commonwealth, received their freedom. In overseas policy, Britain under Bevin took a bold, often belligerent, lead in generating a strong western response to a perceived Russian threat. By mid-1947, for all its economic difficulties, Britain was acknowledged as the main force behind Western European union and the restructuring of the industrial, commercial, and monetary policies of the non-Communist world.

For many people, therefore, it was an exciting, eventful time. It was certainly so for the policy-making élite, if not for the mass of the community cast into austerity, controls, and rationing from the end of the war. Labour Britain was a laboratory of social engineering and reconstruction. Planners stepped in boldly to construct new towns and remodel ancient institutions. Civil servants in the Board of Trade generated a stream of ideas to relocate new industry in formerly stagnant regions, to re-equip ailing industrial giants such as the textile and shipbuilding industries, and to promote new forms of corporate development councils. The Treasury itself, a consistent voice of caution in the thirties, was galvanized into life through new young planners such as 'Otto' Clarke and Alec Cairncross, along with James Meade, Richard Stone, and Robert Hall in the Cabinet Office Economic Section. Most of these came from a radical or socialist background: Meade, for instance, had been a very active Fabian who had written extensively on a socialist credit and pricing policy. At the same time, development economists and investment strategists flocked to the Colonial Office. The Barlow Committee at the end of 1945, including such eminent scientists as Appleton, Blackett, and Zuckerman, called for a doubling of the annual output of scientists from colleges and universities and a considerable expansion of higher education, especially on the scientific and technological side.[2] Not since the Washington of

---

[2] *Scientific Manpower: Report of a Committee appointed by the Lord President of the Council* (Cmd. 6824), P.P., 1945–6, XIV, 22.

the early New Deal in 1933, the heyday of 'the man in the grey flannelled suit', had the governmental agencies in a democratic country been so caught up in experimentation and social advance. The gentleman from Whitehall, the titan of post-war reconstruction, dominated the collective ethos. Lofty mandarins like Edward Bridges or Norman Brook stood at the apex of a powerfully efficient policy-making machine. Even the most cursory reading of Sir Alec Cairncross's magnificent book, *Years of Recovery*,[3] ostensibly a prosaic academic account, confirms how the social engineers and bureaucrats of that fleeting era felt themselves to be the chosen of the earth.

Nor were their benevolent activities confined to practical matters of getting and spending. There were new councils to promote scientific research and development with a new breed of scientist/civil servant like Appleton and Cockroft. The formation of the Arts Council in 1945, soon after VJ day, testified to the wider involvement of central agencies, backed by state funding, in matters of the mind and the spirit. A quarter of a century later, Lord Goodman, a characteristic representative of this post-war Fabian mood, recalled the basic principles, reflecting the language of the time.

I believe that the last thirty years in this country has demonstrated a profound social change. Within our society there is now a widespread feeling that the provision of drama and music and painting and culture in all its broadest aspects is no longer to be regarded as a privilege for a few but is the democratic right of the entire community.[4]

Similarly, in the popular dissemination of numeracy, Lancelot Hogben, an associate of Harold Laski at the London School of Economics, wrote of how mathematics were 'for the million' and science was 'for the citizen'. He even pressed the cause of an international language which he called 'Interglossa'.

---

[3] Alec Cairncross. *Years of Recovery: British Economic Policy*, 1945–51 (London, 1985), Sir Alec served at the Board of Trade, 1946–9.
[4] Introduction to the *Twenty-Fourth Annual Report of the Arts Council, 1968–9*.

Some of the recipients of this planning activity, naturally, were less than gratified. The novels of Evelyn Waugh and, in a different vein, Ivy Compton-Burnett in the immediate post-war period implied a deep revulsion, in part of the literary world at least, towards the encroaching tide of state direction and control. In any event, the extent to which such cultural enterprises as the Edinburgh Festival or the reopening of Covent Garden Opera in 1945–7 were in any meaningful sense popular activities is open to much doubt. But, for some while, writers like Evelyn Waugh, along with right-wing commentators like Colm Brogan, T.E. Utley, or the ex-socialist, W.J. Brown, had a strong feeling of swimming against the tide. They met with little enough comfort from the political opposition in challenging Attlee's chosen instruments of intervention. The Conservatives themselves, with their leader, Churchill, long a virtual absentee and mainly concerned with world affairs, turned to planning and direction, too. The revival of the Conservative Research Department, under the command of R. A. Butler, at the end of 1945 was a recognition that the party's disastrous performance at the polls was the result of its having no credible stance towards the need for social reconstruction.[5] So, too, was the attention paid to 'political education' through the newly formed Conservative Political Centre, led by C.J.M. Alport. The most important product of this Tory rethinking, perhaps one somewhat exaggerated in later accounts, was the Industrial Charter of 1947, in which the party unambiguously accepted the principle of the mixed economy, including much state involvement in public investment strategies and a recognition of the much higher profile of the trade unions since the war. Other 'charters' on agriculture and social policy followed much the same drift. Almost all the leading Conservatives in the post-war period—Butler, Eden, Macmillan, Woolton—along with youthful back-room planners like Maudling, Macleod, Alport, and Enoch Powell, worked hard to reduce the

[5] See John Ramsden, *The Making of Conservative Policy since 1929: The Conservative Research Department* (London, 1980).

gap between public stereotypes of their position and the prevailing 'Labourist' ethos. While the Conservatives recovered their confidence sufficiently to harass the government over some of its measures in 1946, even to the extent of voting against the second and third readings of the National Health Service Bill, their opposition was largely based on tactics and administrative detail rather than principled hostility to the idea of an expanding state and a client citizenry.

For the bulk of the population, the immediate post-war years were a time of continuing drabness and shortages in their daily lives. Bread rationing was introduced in July 1946, while a vast panoply of physical and other controls over materials and manpower remained from the wartime years. People travelled in ancient, draughty, and overcrowded trains; buses had 'standing room only'. Certainly, traditional pleasures improved public morale. Professional football and test matches resumed; the dance hall, the seaside holiday camps, and especially the cinema added to public cheerfulness. The year 1946 saw the record attendance for British cinema-going with over 1,600 million attending; teenage girls, deprived of perfume or 'nylons', would go to their local Gaumont, Odeon, Ritz, or Regal three or four times a week. But the general mood was one of restriction and continuing crisis. New clothes, cars, currency for foreign travel, luxuries of all kinds were in desperately short supply. Things seemed little improved 'now the war was over'. Middle-class people in particular were heard to complain of their declining standards of living in absolute terms, especially for those on fixed incomes. Some took the option of migration to the Commonwealth, with Southern Rhodesia a particular magnet; perhaps 50,000 British migrated there between 1946 and 1952. Canada, Australia, and New Zealand attracted other emigrants, while tens of thousands of 'GI brides' went with their servicemen husbands to the lush pastures of the New World.

Yet if there was drabness in the community at large, the decisionmakers in Westminster and Whitehall were excitedly carrying out their presumed mandate for blueprints of reform.

Thus, between the autumn of 1945 and the summer of 1947, six great measures of public ownership were carried through—the Bank of England, cable and wireless, civil aviation, coal, electricity, and road and rail transport; gas and iron and steel were scheduled to follow. Over a fifth of the economy went into public hands, with the Cabinet's Socialization of Industry Committee acting as a conveyor belt.[6] In the 1980s, especially after 1983 when the privatization of such nationalized concerns as British Telecom and British Gas made rapid headway, the principle of public ownership found relatively few defenders. Even the Labour Party showed little inclination to defend it, especially after the election of 1987. On the far left, *Marxism Today* and some of the followers of Tony Benn called for an end to the 'monolithic and bureaucratic' public ownership of the type favoured by Herbert Morrison after 1945.

At the time, though, most of the nationalization measures of the Attlee government were carried through in a matter-of-fact way with only limited controversy. They seemed the logical outcome of the planned economy introduced during the war. The state ownership of the Bank of England, Labour's demon of 'bankers' ramp' legend in 1931, was especially uncontroversial. Even Churchill found it hard to defend its role in the 1930s, and the Conservatives did not oppose the measure. In some cases such as civil aviation or electricity there had long been much corporate involvement by the state, directed by Conservative-led governments in the 1930s or even the 1920s. Neville Chamberlain's government, for instance, had created the British Overseas Airways Corporation in 1939. Bipartisan inquiries such as the McGowan Report for electricity or the Heyworth Committee on gas in late 1945 had already urged the cause of public ownership on grounds of technical efficiency and an integrated service on the pattern of the national grid. In some cases, such as gas again,

[6] CAB 134/687–8.

the principal of municipal ownership was already long established, and there was believed to be an overwhelming case for a centralized system on the grounds of 'co-ordination', one of the keywords of the post-1945 era. Another factor that made the passage of early nationalization relatively painless was the remarkably generous terms adopted in compensating private stockholders, even in such controversial cases as the coal industry. This helped to defuse much argument and keep the temperature of debate low. Not until the Transport Bill in the spring of 1947, especially over the road transport provisions for nationalizing small operators, did public ownership excite fierce dispute in the Commons and then the Lords. But, by that time, Labour's high noon of unchallengeable ascendancy had already passed.

In each case, the form of nationalization adopted was the public board model proposed by Herbert Morrison in his book, *Socialisation and Transport*, back in 1933, with the recent example of the London Passenger Transport Board in mind. It offered a prototype of efficient public management, free from political interference and from dictation from trade unions or other vested interests. The London Passenger Transport Board itself had enjoyed a high reputation for its activities in the 1930s, from its cheap, efficient services and modern rolling-stock to the patronage that Pick and Holden offered to architects and designers in underground railway stations such as Arnos Grove, the citadels of John Betjeman's 'Metroland'. The trade unions also approved of the public board idea since it would not compromise their traditional function as workers' representatives or the principles of collective bargaining. Certainly, the main unions had no wish to replace the public boards with any form of industrial democracy, let alone workers' control. The spirit of syndicalism had passed away, with only a few vestiges left in the Welsh mining valleys and the shipyards of Clydeside. G.D.H. Cole, himself immensely productive as author and communicator after 1945, had long abjured the guild socialism of his youth, while his influential wife, Margaret, was an orthodox Fabian centralizer.[7] Trade-union leaders, from Bevin and Deakin of the Transport Workers downwards, had no wish to become bosses. They were happy to replace the old private management structure with a similarly remote and potentially adversarial system in state hands. The National Union of Mineworkers, for the moment, was happy with its hard-won 'Miners' Charter', and quite agreeable to the National Coal Board as it emerged. When trade unionists like Walter Citrine or Ebby Edwards served as chairmen or board members of nationalized concerns like electricity or the National Coal Board, they resigned their trade-union posts to show there was no clash of interest between their position as workers' representatives and agents operating in the public interest. They had left the shop floor or pit-face for ever (in the case of that supreme *apparatchik*, Lord Citrine, it was a world he had never known anyway) and become public servants, non-partisan, technocratic, detached.

The idea of consensus in the public ownership measures of post-1945 can, of course, be exaggerated. There were critics on the government left, Emanuel Shinwell and Aneurin Bevan in particular, who condemned the failure of the nationalized industries to create any viable system of industrial consultation with the work-force.[8] The managerial remoteness of the public boards was much criticized by Labour back-benchers, especially the mining MPs. The very idea of outright state ownership in every case was anyway a more extreme result than that resulting from wartime consensus. The coal industry was nationalized in a far more rigorous way than that suggested by the wartime proposals of the Reid Committee, which went no further than large-scale amalgamation and price-fixing (even these proposals had been far too extreme for the Prime Minister, Churchill). The coal industry was swiftly taken over in centralized rigid form with the regional boards relatively weak.

---

[7] See A. W. Wright, *G.D.H. Cole and Socialist Democracy* (Oxford, 1979) and Betty D. Vernon, *Margaret Cole, 1893–1980* (London, 1986).

[8] *The Times*, 6 May 1948; Labour Party NEC minutes, 12 May 1948; Lord President's Committee, 29 Mar. 1946 (CAB 132/1).

Public ownership in this guise was enthusiastically celebrated in the coalfields of Britain from Kirkcaldy to Kent on 1 January 1947—'Today the mines belong to the people.'

In this particular case, the results were unfortunate. Shinwell had complained that, when he became Minister for Fuel and Power in 1945, he could find no blueprint for the mechanics of nationalizing or reorganizing the coal industry—though, as he had been chairman of Labour's relevant policy-making committee during the war, he could not escape much of the blame. An over-centralized structure was cobbled together and rushed through, with little industrial democracy and inadequate systems of line management that led to the resignation of one NCB member, Sir Charles Reid, in 1948. The industrial relations crises of the 1972–85 period were vividly foreshadowed in the public ownership arrangements put together hurriedly in the aftermath of war, when Labour were the masters. In many ways, public ownership was an ill-thought-out programme. It aroused little wider enthusiasm. Nationalization had been in large measure a middle-class idea anyway, a Utilitarian or Fabian notion rather than one emanating from the work-force. It created public figures, often patrician capitalists or even generals, as much remote pro-consular figures as were imperial representatives in Curzon's India, Lugard's Nigeria, or Cromer's Egypt. But until 1947 this pattern of nationalization met with little resistance. It was part of the planning and 'fair shares' ethos of the time. Conservatives, especially centrist figures like Macmillan, had a bad conscience over the record of private mismanagement in the 1930s. They recognized Britain's long-term inheritance of industrial decline and class conflict. They also noted that Labour's list of proposed candidates for public ownership was distinctly limited. The banks and all private manufacturing industry were to be strictly left alone. Compared with the French wave of *étatisme* in 1945–6.[9] Britain's was nationalization without tears.

---

[9] On this, see Claire Andrieu, 'La France à gauche de l'Europe', *Le Mouvement Social*, Janvier–Mars, 1986 (no. 134), 131 ff.

The welfare state, the other main governmental initiative of this period also excited only limited controversy. All parties and all commentators, it seemed, emerged from the war beneath the mightily intellectual shade of William Beveridge and the 'cradle to the grave' philosophy. That document, perhaps, was less clear-cut than it seemed since, for all its air of modernity, it included assumptions about private savings and provision, and the subordinate role of women workers, which would arouse dispute. It is also perhaps fair to comment that Beveridge and his colleagues were much fuller in their discussion of the scope of social insurance services than of the means of paying for them. They did not inquire deeply into how far state funding could be actuarially sound during coming generations when medical science was likely to increase the dependent population substantially. But the main thrust of Beveridge found immediate endorsement in 1945 in all election manifestos and from almost all commentators. Veterans like Seebohm Rowntree (who had explored poverty in York back in 1899) observed how it would provide a rational, permanent framework for avoiding the deprivation and destitution of the pre-war years. When James Griffiths introduced his National Insurance Bill in 1946, to effect the Beveridge proposals, it had almost a trouble-free passage through the House. Only a few Labour back-benchers like Sydney Silverman protested, successfully, that the scales of provision, especially for married couples, should be increased.[10] Otherwise, Griffiths found himself acclaimed as a major social reformer, with benevolent support from Churchill himself, recalling his own powerful welfare initiatives in Edwardian years. How could it be otherwise? After all, the RAF, when bombing Nazi-occupied territories in France, the Low Countries, and even Germany itself during the war, had included in their cargo not only bombs but also millions of leaflets extolling the principles of the Beveridge Report, as Britain's master contribution to a better world.

[10] See the debate of 23 May 1946, *Parl. Deb.*, 5th ser., vol. 423.

The National Health Service was far more controversial. There was no obvious consensus here. It had aroused fierce debate during the war years when schemes from Ernest Brown and Henry Willink, both of them in effect Conservatives, had foundered on the fierce opposition of the executive of the British Medical Association. The Conservative manifesto in 1945 perhaps missed an opportunity by failing to include a clear commitment to a health service, even though its existence was a prime assumption contained in the Beveridge Report.[11] British doctors were adamant in resistance to the principle of salaried employment, and also feared state interference through the regional boards of management which might imperil a medical practitioner's security of employment or rights of appeal in cases of dismissal. Worse still, the Minister of Health appointed by Attlee was the Welshman, Aneurin Bevan. He was personally a man of much charm who could, like his predecessor Lloyd George, 'charm a bird off a bough'. But he was also the most zealous and abrasive socialist in the government, with well-nourished class resentments nurtured by that crucible of socialism, the Welsh mining valleys.

The government soon produced a viable scheme. Herbert Morrison's resistance in Cabinet to the nationalization of the hospitals was resisted by a clear majority of ministers, including the veteran ex-professor of anatomy Lord Addison, now leader of the Lords. Bevan's measure thus tilted control towards central rather than municipal authorities. Otherwise, major concessions were seen to be necessary even by Bevan himself. They included the provision of 'pay beds' in hospitals and the protection of doctors' rights of private practice and the retention of the equity of their practice. Without such concessions, the goodwill of the medical profession, it was believed, could not be retained and a health service could never be launched. Bevan's bill, when it was introduced in the House, received a remarkably favourable press,

[11] Charles Webster, *The Health Services Since the War*, i. 74–5.

including from *The Times* and *The Economist*. Both of them were traditional organs of news and opinion which now subscribed to the reconstruction enthusiasm of the time.[12] But in fact, Bevan's bill soon came up against the unrelenting hostility of the British Medical Association, especially its president, Guy Dain, and its secretary Charles Hill, popularly known as the 'Radio Doctor' for his folksy medical broadcasts. By the end of 1946 there was, apparently, deadlock between the BMA, threatening a boycott of the National Health Service for its threat to the doctors' professional freedom, and an increasingly exasperated Minister of Health. Plebiscites of general practitioners showed repeatedly large majorities against participation in the NHS. As late as March 1948, a BMA-conducted poll showed only 4,735 doctors to be in favour of the Act and 40,814 against, on an 82 per cent poll.[13] It was an unattractive period in the history of British social policy.

At the same time, the achievement of a National Health Service still seemed feasible. Nor was a compromise impossible since the heads of the specialist colleges, notably Lord Moran (Churchill's private doctor) of the Royal College of Physicians and Sir Alfred Webb-Johnson of the Obstetricians, were anxious to reconcile the government with the BMA. The commitment of much of medical opinion and such journals as the *Lancet* was too powerful for the patchwork and socially maldistributed health system, as it existed, to be retained. The successful achievement of an NHS, even if one delayed until 1948 rather than 1947, was generally assumed to be inevitable even if the bad-tempered public exchanges between Bevan and Dain and Hill belied the fact.

Elsewhere, too, the movement towards a wider provision of social welfare seemed relentless. Family allowances, mostly in cash but with provision in kind as well, came into being in August 1946. Five shillings a week would be paid for every

---

[12] Also see the specialists' organ, *The Lancet*, 12 Dec. 1945.
[13] *British Medical Journal*, 6 Mar. 1948.

child other than the first, with the benevolent support of Dalton at the Treasury.[14] Housing was another long-neglected social priority. It had been given new publicity by the social surveys of PEP and other bodies in the thirties. Bevan was responsible for housing as well as health and, it seemed, was less committed to house-building than to building up a health service. He gave hostages to fortune by claiming (wrongly) that housing occupied his attention for only one morning a week. The progress made in reducing the backlog of well over three million houses that were required was slow; in addition, there was much war-damaged property and the legacies of decay over the generations. The main emphasis in building houses, as after 1918, was placed on the local authorities; more directive socialist solutions such as a National Housing Corporation were turned down.[15] Only a few thousand houses had been built by the spring of 1946 which led to a Cabinet Committee,[16] chaired by Attlee himself, being set up to eliminate bottle-necks in labour and supplies that were leading to wasteful competition between building houses, factories, schools, and much else besides. The Ministries of Health, Supply, and Works, and the Scottish Office, collided with one another. While left-wing critics attacked the absence of planning imperatives, middle-class Conservatives objected to the noose being placed around the private market, with few applications for housing to rent being granted, and curbs on the lending operations of building societies. The government seemed to be obsessed with favouring the public housing principle, and to be emphasizing housing to rent by wage-earners rather than houses for sale by salary-earners, on doctrinaire grounds. In many areas, 'prefabricated' temporary dwellings were showing signs of permanent life instead of more solid structures. Bevan,

---

[14] Hugh Dalton, *Memoirs, 1945–60: High Tide and After* (London, 1962), 64–5.

[15] See Douglas Jay to Attlee, 15 Oct. 1945 (PREM 8/228).

[16] CAB 134/220. There are doubts as to how effective this Cabinet Committee really was: see Kenneth O. Morgan. *Labour in Power, 1945–1951* (Oxford, 1984), 165.

who wanted high standards of housing for working-class occupants, privately derided the 'pre-fabs' as 'rabbit-hutches', no more than a temporary stopgap. The fact remained that by 1948 well over 100,000 had been put together and were proving to be popular, not least for their air of privacy, including a cottage garden.

Bevan's reputation was not improved by the handling of the housing shortage by his Ministry. Much unfavourable publicity resulted in demonstrations by squatters' occupying empty property, including offices in London and other cities. Some left-wing populist figures were prominent here. Even so, by the start of 1947, houses were being constructed at the rate of 200,000 a year, and many of the bottle-necks were being removed. Further, Bevan was able to insist that 'council' housing was built to high standards, including three bedrooms and an indoor bathroom and lavatory. Whatever the complaints of middle-class would-be house purchasers and the disgruntlement of owners of private property for let, whose rents were severely controlled, it was generally agreed that it was in the public market that the main initiative must lie. The scandalous state of working-class housing had long penetrated the public consciousness. The writings of Orwell and many others had given it currency in the thirties. In the 1945 election, housing was perhaps the most popular single theme for Labour candidates to emphasize. As terraced council-house estates sprang up in suburban areas, each built to Bevan's generous specifications, the principle of social provision and state subsidy was the more enshrined. It was noticeable that an older sense of community and neighbourhood could be rekindled in these newer estates, and that they remained relatively free from vandalism and threats of burglary. The soulless 'high-rise' flats of later sociological notoriety, standard targets for Prince Charles and other scourges of architects and urban planners, were products of the Tory late-1950s, not the Labour 1940s.

Education was another area where vigorous action and advance were expected and encouraged by the central government. But the limits were immediately obvious. Just as private medicine was carefully protected by vested interests during Bevan's creation of the NHS, so the private school system, elementary and secondary, increased and multiplied. The main priority for the government, it was believed, was the implementation of the Butler Act of 1944, with its tripartite division of secondary schools.[17] This was the intended objective of Labour's new Minister of Education, Ellen Wilkinson, supplemented by raising the school-leaving age to 15, which she accomplished despite resistance in the Cabinet by Herbert Morrison. The years after 1945 were a time of great expansion in state education, a considerable school-building and refurbishment programme, with a massive hierarchy at the level of local government and agencies of inspection and control within the local administration related to it. There were fierce critics on the left, notably the National Association of Labour Teachers and its spokesmen like the Welshman W. G. Cove, MP.[18] They condemned Ellen Wilkinson and her equally working-class successor as Minister, George Tomlinson, for their blank resistance to the idea of the multilateral secondary school, and their tenderness towards the social and intellectual élitism of the grammar school of which Wilkinson herself was a proud product; but to no avail. The public schools remained untouched by change. The 1944 Fleming Report which recommended that up to 25 per cent of the intake should be 'scholarship boys' (and occasional girls) from the state system had little effect, and the fees and the waiting lists of Britain's public schools increased dramatically. Educational egalitarianism was hardly on Labour's agenda. But the broad range of opinion felt confidence that, even in the post-war austerity years, the government was giving a new priority to public education. At last, criticisms of Britain's educational deficiencies by contrast to other European countries were being met. Levelling or social engineering could wait until much later.

[17]   See Rodney Barker, *Education and Politics, 1900–51* (Oxford, 1972), 81 ff.
[18]   Caroline Benn, 'Comprehensive School Reform and the 1945 Labour Government', *History Workshop*, 10 (Autumn, 1980).

The general mood, then, was one of welfare and the public ethic. This, it was believed, cohered with the spirit of egalitarianism and 'fair shares' which the war had created. Some of the usual obstacles to reform were no longer present. The civil service in most departments was anxious for change and sweeping reconstruction. The Treasury, under the benevolent gaze of Hugh Dalton, was as anxious to finance social reform as Lloyd George had been in an earlier era. It took an early decision to finance child allowances as early as September 1945. This was followed by decisions to subsidize council-house rents to high level, to pay for expanded education and health services, and to finance new towns. A high level of personal taxation, including a stiffly graduated income tax and stringent death duties, was designed precisely to meet these purposes.

Again, for all the protests of special interest groups such as the BMA, it was widely accepted that the war had confirmed the sheer supply-side inadequacy of the market mechanism in distributing social goods fairly, and of private or charitable provision for a modern system of public welfare. The welfare state was thus a long-delayed measure of social justice and, it was believed, implicitly egalitarian, whether the benefits came in cash or in kind. Above all, it would eliminate the wide regional divisions which had poisoned society in the 1930s, the 'special areas' idea which had cast its shadow even in the early war years.

There was, therefore, much popular enthusiasm for the Board of Trade's policy of the regional relocation of industry under Sir Stafford Cripps. It based itself largely on the Churchill coalition's measure, the 1945 Distribution of Industry Act. Board of Trade licences and other forms of physical controls forced new industry into the Welsh valleys, Tyneside, Cumbria, and the Clyde.[19] In part, it did so by building on pre-war initiatives such as the trading estates, or wartime developments such as ordnance or munitions factories. It took, perhaps, eighteen months for the

[19] For an excellent account see Douglas Jay, *Change and Fortune*, 112 ff.

policy to bear fruit. In the harsh winter of 1946–7, unemployment was again rising and old fears of mass depression were aroused. But by the spring of 1947, with the emphasis firmly on exports and the dampening down of domestic demand, the government's policies seemed to be producing results. Unemployment at the start of 1947 stood at 1.6 per cent. Coalfields, textile mills, shipyards, dockyards were humming with life. British manufacturers were showing signs of responding to pressure for innovation in production and design, and identifying growth points in the market. There was, for instance, the astonishing success of 'Land Rovers' and the buoyancy of the British car industry generally, at least down to the recovery of the German and French car industries after 1950.[20] By mid-1947 it was shortages of labour and the inadequacy of materials in coming through rather than the contraction of demand or failures in production that were the major problems. From the older depressed areas, the spectre of unemployment had been banished. Labour Britain was on the threshold of an export-led boom. Of course, the underlying economic base remained much as it had been before the war, and antique working practices slowed the provision of industrial retraining of labour or more up-to-date forms of scientific management. The British car industry in particular would suffer from these weaknesses in the 1950s and 1960s. But for the moment the underlying mood after the war seemed to be one of bold social and economic advance.

In external affairs, the note of progress was more uncertain. The painful evidence of national and imperial decline, especially in the colossal loss of exports, shipping, and overseas investment, led to much despondency. Nevertheless, in her approach towards her imperial and colonial heritage, post-war Britain showed a good deal of confidence. In part, this was because the new Labour government was convinced that Britain remained a great power, whose strategic and financial importance on the

[20] See William Plowden, *The Motor Car and Politics* (London, 1971).

world scene would be important for decades to come. This emerged especially in relation to the Commonwealth. Labour's rhetoric had traditionally been anti-colonialist. From Keir Hardie onwards, the tone had been hostile to imperialism, even if the actual policy of the first two Labour governments of 1924 and 1929–31 was markedly different. The anti-colonialist note was voiced in September 1945 by Attlee himself when he urged the declining importance of imperial defence bases in the Middle East and questioned a continuing east-of-Suez strategy.[21] When Ernest Bevin argued in the Council of Foreign Ministers that the British Empire should actually expand further in 1945 by taking in former Italian colonies such as Libya and Italian Somaliland under British trusteeship, Attlee quietly demurred. But he did not pursue the point with much vehemence. In any case, his own background at Haileybury School, that old cradle of Indian civil servants, at Oxford, and in the Commonwealth detachments at Gallipoli made the ties of empire important to Attlee too. Senior ministers such as Bevin, Morrison, and (in a more emotional and even racist[22] way) Dalton were committed to Britain's imperial presence, partly because of uncertainty about American intentions after the war. Indeed, around the Persian Gulf, with its alluring oilfields and important air and naval bases extending from Iraq down to Aden, a major new area for British penetration was opening up. Attlee, no more than Churchill during the wartime conferences, had not become George VI's first minister in order to liquidate the British empire.

Labour's colonial policy after 1945 was full of socialist hopes about removing the burdens of empire and promoting self-government. But it was a Fabian socialism of development and partnership that prevailed, especially in the Colonial Research

[21] Memorandum by Attlee, 'The Future of the Italian Colonies', 1 Sept. 1945 (CAB 129/1).
[22] See Dalton's comments in his diaries, 28 Feb. 1950 (London School of Economics, Dalton Papers, 1/38) when he refers to the colonies as 'pullulating, poverty-stricken, diseased nigger communities'. He also referred to Seretse Khama as 'the black man who married a white typist'.

Bureau where Rita Hinden and Arthur Creech Jones had provided much of the substances for Labour's previously bare colonial planning.[23] They took issue with the view that Labour's basic colonial policy should be an early evacuation, not least because, especially in tribal West and East Africa, the political outcome, it was believed, would be governmental anarchy and economic mismanagement. When Creech Jones went to the Colonial Office in October 1946 in succession to George Hall, he thus followed a bold and vigorous policy of colonial development, especially in East Africa. The Overseas Food Corporation and the Colonial Development Corporation, both carefully geared to the needs of Britain for cheap raw materials and a liquid sterling area, were also the most vigorous statements of interventionist state colonialism since the time of Joseph Chamberlain. The Colonial Office became a hive of activity for young development economists and planners, linking up with a succession of enterprising and vigorous governors, especially in Africa. After 1950, the activities of the development corporations aroused much scepticism and many of their projects proved to be the whitest of elephants. The notorious 'ground-nuts' scheme in Tanganyika became a byword for free-spending incompetence. But in 1945–8, there seemed little dissent from state-funded enterprises of this kind. At the same time, significant moves towards self-government were taking place in Nigeria, the Gold Coast, and the West Indies, testimony to Labour's being the legatee of traditional liberal principles.

After 1945, the Commonwealth basked in a post-Victorian glow of growth and development, in a way that frustrated imperialist critics who suspected a socialist government of doctrinaire little-Englandism. With deft use of the symbolism of the Crown and frequent Commonwealth conferences, the sun of Empire rose anew. Under such friendly heads of state as William Mackenzie King of Canada, Ben Chifley of Australia,

---

[23] P.S. Gupta, *Imperialism and the British Labour Movement 1914–1964* (London, 1975).

Peter Fraser of New Zealand, and Jan Smuts, the veteran Prime Minister of South Africa, the older White dominions worked in close contact with the mother country in defence and commercial matters. At the United Nations, the essential unity of the Commonwealth, still Britain's major export market and target for investment, was eagerly stressed. At all points, extending to the reinstitution of Rhodes scholarships at Oxford and cricket test matches, the ties of communion between mother country and old and new Commonwealth were emphasized. Even in South Africa, whose restrictive policy towards the black majority was well known, a variety of elements—the importance of the Simonstown naval base for the British navy, the crucial role of South African gold movements in the currency markets, South African uranium for a nuclear arsenal, and the old-fashioned 'Round Table' liberalism embodied in Field Marshal Smuts—all encouraged the British government to give national self-interest the priority over racial equality. Indeed, down to 1948, Smuts emerged as an honoured adviser on Commonwealth defence and other issues in the early Attlee period, no less than he had been for Lloyd George and Arthur Balfour a quarter of a century earlier.[24] When John Parker, under-secretary for the Dominions, urged a more hostile attitude towards South Africa, both for its internal racial policies and over its wish to acquire the protectorates of Bechuanaland, Basutoland, and Swaziland, Parker was promptly dismissed and never surfaced again in government office.[25]

The extent to which imperial ascendancy could be reconciled with liberal principles of self-determination rested above all on India. Here, Labour had an historic commitment to self-government, going back to the days of Keir Hardie, MacDonald, and Snowden before 1914. It was reinforced by the personal ties of men like Pandit Nehru and Krishna Menon with the British

---

[24] For example, Smuts to Attlee, 8 May 1946 (PREM 8/1388): record of Prime Ministers' meeting, 28 Apr. 1946 (FO 371/57118).
[25] Kenneth O. Morgan, *Labour in Power*, 198.

labour movement in the thirties. Attlee himself had a personal involvement with Indian self-government that went back to the Simon Commission in 1927–30. The failure of Sir Stafford Cripps's mission in 1942 made Attlee the more sensitive of the gulf between the mainly Hindu Congress and the Muslim League. But it did not deflect the Prime Minister (nor, indeed, did it deflect Cripps) from the belief that a grand historic gesture was required towards the Indian subcontinent after 1945 comparable with that of Lord Durham towards the two cultures of Canada in the 1830s. Here Attlee was pushing at an open door. At least since the 1935 Government of India Act, pressure towards a decisive push towards Indian self-government was irresistible, although the power of Jinnah's Muslim League (encouraged by Britain itself during the war) made a partitioned subcontinent on the basis of a Hindustan/Pakistan division an increasingly likely outcome. Literature from English novelists such as E. M. Forster in the 1920s, with themes later followed by by Paul Scott in his 'Raj Quartet' in the 1960s, had suggested a weakening resolve to rule, compounded by a sense of guilt, amongst the more liberal governing classes of the Raj. The passive resistance during the war which had led to the imprisonment of Gandhi, Nehru, Patel, and many other Congress leaders had impressed even upon Churchill himself the physical and military impossibility of the British army keeping down the hundreds of millions of Indians under permanent submission. The Viceroy, Wavell, told the Prime Minister in October 1944 that 'the future of India is the problem on which the British Commonwealth and the British reputation will stand or fall in the post-war period'.[26]

The main problem for Britain after 1945 was not whether to grant self-government to India but how to achieve a settlement that remained under orderly British control and which left a Commonwealth connection in being. The Cabinet mission, headed by the elderly Pethick-Lawrence, Alexander, and Cripps,

---

[26] R. J. Moore, *Escape from Empire* (Oxford, 1983), 18, citing Wavell to Churchill, 24 Oct. 1944.

that went to India in March–June 1946 was in the end unable to break the log-jam of reconciling an all-India constituent assembly with the communal divisions within India.[27] This was vividly underlined by the 'day of direct action' in Calcutta on 16 August 1946, called by the Muslim League as a protest against a national assembly. It cost 5,000 lives and a further 15,000 casualties in what Sir Frederick Burrows, the Governor of Bengal, called 'a pogrom between two rival armies'.[28] In the end, Britain had to impose its own scheme for a settlement, a scheme soon overtaken by events in India and with its timing speeded up to an inordinate extent. The Viceroy, Wavell, was condemned by Attlee for a 'scuttle' policy which proposed an early withdrawal of British troops by the end of March 1948.[29] He was brusquely dismissed in favour of Lord Mountbatten, who was given broad plenipotentiary powers to negotiate a settlement. In the end, Mountbatten's talks with the Congress and Muslim League led to an ever more frenetic process of evacuation. Mountbatten began formal negotiations with Congress and Muslim League leaders on 20 March. By the end of May, it had been agreed that the 'Balkanization' of India was inevitable, with the Sikh community scattered through the Punjab and elsewhere left to determine their own future. On 15 August 1947, the flag of the Raj was hauled down for ever from Edwin Lutyens's viceroy's residence in New Delhi, less than six months after Mountbatten began his frantic period of summit diplomacy. India and Pakistan became independent states and full members of the Commonwealth. Indian's republican status was later held to be no bar to its membership of the Commonwealth under the British Crown, after infinite legal ingenuity. Earlier, Burma had received its independence in late 1946, while Ceylon (later named Sri Lanka) also became a

[27] See A. V. Alexander's diary of the Mission (Churchill College, Cambridge, Alexander Papers, 6/2).

[28] Moore, *Escape from Empire*, 162.

[29] See Attlee's memorandum, 21 Dec. 1946 (PREM 8/541 pt. 8).

self-governing member of the Commonwealth in 1949. Britain's historic domain in south Asia had been abruptly liquidated.

The withdrawal from India might well have been regarded as a national retreat, even a humiliation, after the lengthy three-hundred-year-old presence of the British in India, going back to the days of the old East India Company, and the emotive role of the Crown as emperor in India. Kipling's stories had given the Raj new currency amongst generations of children (and adult readers) from the late-Victorian era. In fact, the British reacted to the transfer of power in an almost matter-of-fact way. There was none of the national *angst* that, for instance, the French were to show with the retreat from, first, Indo-China after Dien Bien Phu and then from Algeria and elsewhere in North Africa. Indian civil servants and judges came quietly home without any of the settler traumas produced in other empires, or for that matter in southern Africa in the British Commonwealth itself later on. Most tea planters stayed on after 1947: no one was expropriated. There was no 'India lobby' comparable with the French *colons*, or the American 'China Lobby' of expatriates, or even the British Suez rebels in 1954. The explanation can only be that the processes of withdrawal from India had been long under way, at least since the Montagu-Chelmsford reforms of 1919, and had been long anticipated. In practical terms, the advantages of the imperial connection for Britain remained, as indeed the Labour government had carefully planned. The defence ties continued, for instance enshrined in the naval base at Colombo, as well as the imperial telecommunications and security system. In financial terms, India remained a vital member of the sterling area, investing its surpluses from tea and cotton sales in the sterling–dollar pool, while the enormous 'sterling balances' accumulated in Britain by the Indian administation during the war continued to be retained in the late 1940s and 1950s, to the immense advantage of the British economy since it meant compulsory lending to Britain at low rates of interest. In constitutional, or just emotional, terms the enduring presence of the Crown helped mask the erosion of imperial power that had come about.

During the Korean War, the support of influential Indian delegates like Benegal Rau at the United Nations helped give Britain an international broker's position far more influential than the national physical reserves would have implied. At the 1949 Commonwealth Conference in London, Britain's invention of the term 'member of the Commonwealth' implied a revival of old imperialist concepts. These important forces of continuity removed most of the impetus of Churchill and that dwindling band of veteran imperialists who had urged that Britain should not withdraw precipitately. In any case, Eden and Butler had nullified Churchill's negative reaction to the transfer of power on the Conservative side.[30] Churchill was to strike up a good working relation with Nehru at Commonwealth Prime Ministers' conferences after 1951.

For the broad mass of the British public, who had never responded in excessive terms to the call of Empire since Joseph Chamberlain's tariff reform collapsed in 1906, the transition from Empire to Commonwealth in relation to India and Pakistan did not convey any obvious point of departure. Nor did it in the least have tragic overtones, despite Kiplingesque lamentations in the Beaverbrook press. Test matches went on as before; Indian tea remained the legendary staple of the British way of life; Indian and Pakistani Rhodes scholars came to Oxford; the Gurkhas continued under British command; the British army was peacefully transferred to other Far Eastern stations, notably Hong Kong and Singapore. When the Canadian economist, John Kenneth Galbraith, served as US ambassador to New Delhi in the early 1960s, he was struck by the Kiplingesque nature of the Indian scene, with its polo matches, loyal toasts, and portraits of 'our sovereign lady the Queen' in Indian officers' messes.[31] Most of all, for Britain, the momentous transfer of

---

[30] Robert Rhodes James. *Anthony Eden*, 321–2. However, Eden remained distinctly sceptical of the part Mountbatten had played in India.
[31] John Kenneth Galbraith, *Ambassador's Journey: A Personal Account of the Kennedy Years* (London, 1966), 233 (16 Oct. 1961).

power in India and Pakistan was a decision which managed to retain enormous goodwill in Asia and the third world generally. It led to horrendous communal carnage in the subcontinent, notably in the Punjab. But for Britain itself it was decolonization without trauma.

The great exception to this generally untroubled start to the withdrawal from Empire in the post-war period was Palestine. Here the Attlee government inherited a hopeless legacy, a jumble of rival commitments to both the resident Arabs and the immigrant Jewish community that went back to the 1917 Balfour Declaration of a Jewish national home. In 1945 the government faced a problem in Palestine of extraordinary complexity. The two decades of conflict between Arab and Jewish residents in Palestine was now intensified by the massive Jewish exodus from Europe, following the Nazi Holocaust, and resultant pressure markedly to increase Jewish immigration into Palestine. The Labour Party Conference in 1944 had passed a strongly pro-Zionist resolution so to increase Jewish migration as to make the Jews a majority in Palestine. In addition, there were diplomatic and strategic imperatives. Palestine was a potent source of tension between Britain and the United States, with the large Jewish population of New York and other cities putting pressure on President Truman's Democratic administration. Again, the sensitive strategic position of Palestine, close to the Suez Canal, the base for 100,000 British troops and relatively near other major imperial bases elsewhere in the Middle East, was a further complication in reaching a settlement. The Labour government in 1945, with its strong support in the British Zionist community, appeared to inherit a clear commitment to develop a much expanded and protected Jewish state in Palestine. To make the situation even more difficult, Palestine came inevitably into the domain of Ernest Bevin, an otherwise skilful and innovative Foreign Secretary. In the case of the Palestine imbroglio he was to show a consistent insensitivity and crassness that verged on anti-Semitism.

British policy in Palestine was guarded and hesitant through-out, without the decisive impulse of principle that guided policy in India. The Anglo-American Palestine Committee appointed by both governments reported in May 1946 in favour of issuing Jewish certificates of immigration up to a total of 100,000, to the acute embarrassment of Bevin himself.[32] President Truman kept up American pressure along the same lines. Yet, despite these weighty factors, it had been apparent since the very first days of the Labour government that its imperialism was far more power-ful than its Zionism. Cabinet ministers like Hugh Dalton and Herbert Morrison, famous for their close links with Jewish lead-ers and their sympathy for Jewish socialists such as David Ben Gurion and Golda Myerson, bluntly announced as early as 8 September that they supported the traditional pro-Arab views of the Foreign Office. They signed a paper for the Cabinet's Palestine Committee which declared that massive Jewish immigration into Palestine was unacceptable because of the strategic position and importance as an oil-bearing region of the Middle East.[33] This made good relations with friendly Arab states such as Iraq, Transjordan, Syria, and Saudi Arabia imperative. Iraq, with its British air bases at Habbaniyah and Shaiba, and the pro-British inclinations of its head of state, Nuri-al Said, was a particularly sensitive country. After all, it was the British who had restored the Hashemite kingdom there, following the Rashid Ali revolt in Iraq in 1941, and they regarded their client, Nuri, as an elder statesman of much wisdom and vision.[34] The broad drift of British policy in Palestine, therefore, was not in doubt. In 1946 guerrilla warfare broke out between the occupying British forces and a series of extreme Jewish terrorist groups, notably the Irgun and the Stern Gang. Atrocities such as the blowing up of the King David Hotel in Jerusalem in July 1946, with the loss of

---

[32] See Richard Crossman, *Palestine Mission* (London, 1947) and James G. McDonald. *My Mission in Israel* (London, 1951).

[33] Report of the Palestine Committee, 8 Sept. 1945 (CAB 129/2).

[34] Louis, *The British Empire in the Middle East*, 307ff.

ninety-one British, Jewish, and Arab lives, led to a British campaign of retaliation and armed suppression as had been previously unhappily attempted in Ireland during the 'troubles' of 1919–21.

The British government offered no obvious or compelling solution. It proposed variations on the theme of partition, and Arthur Creech-Jones, the Colonial Secretary from October 1946 and an old Zionist sympathizer, tried to press this policy on Bevin.[35] But the reality was that the Arabs wanted no Jewish migration at all, while the Jews sought unlimited immigration and a unitary Jewish state of Israel. The United Nations failed to produce more than declamations. Bevin's insensitive policy led to publicly disastrous episodes such as the turning back of the ship *Exodus*, with 4,500 would-be Jewish immigrants on board. By the summer of 1947 the Attlee Cabinet was placing its main emphasis on the financial drain imposed by maintaining British troops in Palestine, especially in the light of the foreign exchange crisis over convertibility in the July–August period. This factor had already led to the withdrawal from the Indian subcontinent and the earlier decision to remove the British military presence in Greece and Turkey. The only solution appeared to be a similar policy in Palestine. The great difference in this case was that no future political settlement was outlined at all. Britain's dismal record of trusteeship, lasting since the mandate was granted in 1920, ended in communal chaos. In India, new Indian and Pakistani governments could take over from the Raj. In Greece and Turkey, the Truman Declaration had ensured that the United States would replace the departing British. In Palestine, there was only anarchy and carnage. The last British troops were withdrawn by early May 1948. Thenceforward the Jews and Arabs fought out their future. To Bevin's surprise—and possibly disappointment—the Jews won and the state of Israel came into being, recognized by Britain on a *de facto* basis, in January 1949.

---

[35] Cabinet conclusions, 7, 14 Feb. 1947 (CAB 128/9).

It was impossible to see the withdrawal from Palestine as anything other than a humiliation for Britain. British lives had been lost and much money spent, with no guaranteed outcome to show for them. The issue produced a lengthy crisis of conscience for the Labour Party with its historic ties to the Jewish community through Poale Zion and other bodies. A local journal like the *Morecambe Visitor* protested that 'Britain was in the grip of the Jews', and local abbatoir workers protested at having to produce kosher meat.[36] There was some residual anti-Semitism in Britain, already evident in the membership rules of such bodies as Home Counties golf clubs. It was fanned by some cases of black-market corruption such as the Sidney Stanley affair in 1948–9 in which Jewish business figures were implicated. But all this did not amount to much. On balance, the main British response to Palestine was sheer relief that an impossible and irreconcilable political legacy had been disposed of, without sacrificing the British position in the Middle East. A new command structure was created in the area. By 1949, indeed, Britain was consolidating its Middle East role after the Palestine withdrawal with defence agreements with Egypt and Jordan. The Palestine débâcle was not allowed to cloud the feeling that, overall, Britain since the end of the war had been in control of its colonial destiny and maintained direction over the course of events.

The sense of national potential and achievement was most vividly expressed in post-war Britain in its conduct of foreign policy. The Foreign Secretary, Bevin, a vigorous patriot of imperial inclinations, reflected the abiding mood that Britain was a great and victorious power. It had participated vigorously in the defeat of Germany, Italy, and Japan, on the plains of northern Europe, in the deserts of North Africa, the jungles of the Far East, and on the high seas and in the air. Its empire stood at its maximum extent in 1945, while the presence of a powerful British and Commonwealth delegation at San Francisco in

---

[36] David Leitch, 'Explosion at the King David Hotel', in Michael Sissons and Philip French (eds.), *Age of Austerity* (Oxford, new edn., 1986), 59–60.

April 1945 testified to Britain's visible presence among the 'Big Three'. With continental Europe shattered and prostrate, the United States poised between world involvement and traditional isolationism, with the Empire intact and the sterling area afloat. Britain's capacity for world leadership seemed beyond dispute. The underlying reality, of course, was a country that had been living beyond its means, as declining great powers had been doing repeatedly since the days of the Habsburg empire in the sixteenth century. Britain had lost £7,000 million, a quarter of its entire national wealth, during the war. It endured pressures that led successively to military withdrawal in different parts of the world. Britain's image of greatness relied increasingly on the subsidy or charity of the United States, plus the temporary prostration of rival powers such as Germany and Japan. For all that, there was manifestly a power vacuum in continental Europe, the Middle East, and the Far East, and in the face of a perceived threat from a hostile Soviet Union, Britain alone seemed prepared to help fill that historic role.

British foreign policy in 1945–7 had as its priority a steady pressure upon the United States to build upon its commitment as one of the occupying powers in western Germany and create a permanent involvement in a North Atlantic alliance. At successive councils of foreign ministers, Bevin urged his American counterpart, Jimmy Byrnes, a somewhat erratic figure, that the Russian threat was such that America and Britain should stand side by side. This was not only a strategic imperative; the recovery of European manufacturing and trade depended on it also. But Bevin spoke the language of independence as well as of interdependence. The Americans, for all their potential value as allies in the alleged 'special relationship', were also wilful and unreliable. Thus, in defence matters, the logic, as seen by Attlee and Bevin, was for Britain to go it alone. The American government had refused to honour the wartime Quebec agreement to share atomic materials and information with Britain. Attlee was especially disturbed by Truman's failure to respond to requests on behalf of a joint Anglo-American policy when the British premier visited Washington in November 1945. The MacMahon Act, passed by the US Congress in the summer of 1946, was to give America's refusal to collaborate on nuclear matters permanent effect. Bevin himself, therefore, felt that a British nuclear capacity on an independent basis was vital for political, even more than for defence, reasons.

In 1946, therefore, Britain embarked secretly on its own nuclear programme.[37] It was veiled from public gaze by the pretence that it was solely intended for civil energy purposes. The decision to produce fissile material in the United Kingdom for use in a weapons development programme was taken as early as January 1946. A gas-cooled nuclear reactor at Sellafield in Cumberland, later known as Windscale, was authorized, with a plutonium separation plant to be connected with it. A full atomic research programme was now to be undertaken. Bevin swept aside protests from Dalton and Cripps that the programme was beyond Britain's capacity to pay. Severe criticism from the scientists, Henry Tizard and Patrick Blackett, that the scientific and medical implications of nuclear research were unquantified and potentially disastrous for the human race never reached the main forums of discussion at all. In any event, other eminent scientists concerned with the atomic field, including Cockcroft, Appleton, and Penney, argued against Blackett's conclusions. In January 1947 a secret Cabinet committee (GEN 163) took the firm decision that Britain should go ahead with its own atomic bomb programme. Attlee and Morrison argued for freedom from an American monopoly of the world nuclear stockpile. Bevin, in a memorably crude observation, declared that he wanted the bomb 'with a bloody Union Jack on it'.[38] On this basis, Britain's nuclear programme went ahead.

[37] The classic work on this topic is Margaret Gowing, *Independence and Deterrence: Britain and Atomic Energy. 1945–1952* (London, 1974).
[38] Peter Hennessy, 'Birth of the British Bomb', *The Independent* 5 May 1988. The GEN 163 files in the Public Record Office (CAB 130/16) are blank.

The entire development was concealed from Cabinet and Parliament. Not until an off-the-cuff remark by A. V. Alexander, the Minister of Defence, in answer to a parliamentary question in May 1948, was the mere existence of a British nuclear weapons programme revealed.[39] Even then there was no public debate or private discussion, and the £1000 m. cost involved was laundered away in the estimates. The existence of a British nuclear programme was, no doubt, a tribute to the British tradition of secret government, and produced much later controversy. However, there are scant grounds for supposing that there would have been much outcry if the nuclear programme had been revealed at the time. When Aneurin Bevan eventually heard about it, he seems to have accepted it as almost inevitable, given the active foreign policy that a socialist government in Britain ought to pursue.[40] It was commensurate with Britain's great-power status and moral influence in the world. It is improbable that anything like the Campaign for Nuclear Disarmament, founded in 1958, could have flourished in the late 1940s, with memories of past appeasement of foreign dictators and present fears of imminent attack from Communist Russia. 'Pacifists' and 'fellow-travellers' were part of the demonology of the time, with spies like Pontecorvo, Klaus Emil Fuchs, and later Burgess and Maclean, to fuel it. One of the determining features of British satisfaction with the nation's role as a major power after 1945 is that the nation was not in unilateralist mood. Left-wing tracts denouncing pre-war feebleness by Chamberlain and his colleagues as 'guilty men' had seen to that.

On a variety of fronts, under Bevin's aegis, Britain pushed into a lumbering form of international leadership after 1945. In particular, Bevin sought to give Britain primacy in western Europe in the aftermath of its occupation and economic collapse. Precisely what kind of leadership this would be, or the very geographical extent of western Europe (did it include post-Mussolini Italy, for

---

[39] On 19 May 1948.   [40] Campbell, *Nye Bevan*, 195.

instance?) remained obscure. So did the relationship of this question to Britain's position as one of the three occupying powers in the western zones of Germany. Indeed the British zone included the old industrial heartland of North-Rhine Westphalia, including the mines and steelworks of the Ruhr. In practical terms the immediate option presenting itself to the British Foreign Office seemed to be some kind of rehabilitation of the entente with France. Anglo-French relations in 1946, already soured by de Gaulle's tussles with the British and US governments during the war, were not in a happy condition. There was much tension variously over the Levant, steel production, gold prices, and especially over future economic and political organization of western Germany.[41] Somewhat unexpectedly, Britain concluded a so-called treaty with France on 1 March 1947, signed in the historic setting of Dunkirk. It was a long-term mutual defence agreement based on the postulate of possible future German aggression. Bevin and his French opposite number, George Bidault, were anxious to play down any anti-Russian implications, though joint-chief-of-staff discussions certainly pursued this point.

This treaty, combined with Bevin's other moves at this time towards British and European commercial and currency collaboration, encouraged some to believe that an historic shift in Britain's self-perception was taking place. Britain, it was thought, might emerge as the head of some form of united Europe. The Americans were enthusiastic for this idea, as much on political as on economic grounds. They saw economic recovery in Europe as vital to the national security of the United States. Within the Labour Party, at least a hundred MPs, including many on the left such as Crossman, Driberg, Foot, and Mikardo, were enthusiasts for the idea of a European 'third force', independent of Russia and the United States equally.[42] It would be based in

---

[41] Sir E. Hall-Patch to Roger Makins, 27 February 1947 (FO 371/67672).

[42] See Jonathan Schneer, *Labour's Conscience: The Labour Left, 1945–51* (London, 1988), 52ff.

part on liaison with sympathetic movements such as Léon Blum's French Socialist Party and Labour spokesmen in the Low Countries such as the Belgian Paul-Henri Spaak. It was soon evident that Bevin himself and indeed all the Labour Cabinet, had little sympathy with such a concept. A united Europe would indeed go against 'a thousand years of history', as Gaitskell was to declare in 1962. The idea of a united Europe, especially of a federation, would conflict with Britain's view of its world-wide role as leader of a multi-racial Commonwealth, and with its special relationship with the USA as well. Any surrender of British sovereignty would be unacceptable, especially to the labour movement intent on building up its own version of socialism in our time. At the time, though, even Bevin's limited, functional view implied a more vigorous policy of European intervention than the Foreign Office had previously endorsed.

When the European states began to co-ordinate their economic and commercial activities from June 1947 onwards, following General Marshall, the American Secretary of State's, speech at Harvard, it was largely British measures that gave the idea practical effect. Indeed, it was a very British academic philosopher, Oliver Franks, Provost of The Queen's College, Oxford, who chaired the committee and produced its report, one strongly favourable to the British functional viewpoint. Britain, it was clear, would not collaborate in the interests of a united Europe. But it would take the lead in promoting the more flexible concept of European union. It did so in the form of the Organization of European Economic Recovery (OEEC) and, in 1950, of the European Payments Union. It also did so in the later European defence arrangements that resulted from the Brussels pact of March 1948—'a sprat to catch a mackerel' in Bevin's view.[43] Britain was later to ensure that the new Council of Europe at Strasbourg was strictly limited in its role, reflecting the presence of autonomous national delegations rather than in any sense a

---

[43] See Alan Bullock, *Ernest Bevin, Foreign Secretary* (London, 1983), 529ff.

European parliament with legal or legislative powers. Until the new phase heralded by the French initiative of the Schuman Plan in 1950, British policy-makers could be well pleased with a form of European collaboration that protected the British national interests and the island's identity. They had wrested the initiative from the hands of the theoretical federalists. Only a few Euro-fanatics like the Australian Labour federalist, 'Kim' Mackay, and a few covert Francophiles, like Gladwyn Jebb and Oliver Harvey in the Foreign Office, could argue otherwise. Bevin sought a solution in which Britain led an expanded Western European association, which had trade and other links with North America, but which did not sacrifice Britain's wider interests as a world banker and head of the Commonwealth. Down to 1950 he seemed to be succeeding.

Britain's general post-war approach to the United States strove to reconcile a sense of dependence and financial weakness with a living partnership that preserved Britain's need for autonomy. Despite the hard-won American loan of $3.5 billion negotiated in Washington in December 1945, there was also a determination that any transatlantic relationship should ensure that Britain retained its status as a world power. In contrast to American fears of a revival of British colonialism, even under a Labour government, Bevin sought to direct the attention of Americans to a new realization of the Russian threat to their interests, including in both the Middle and the Far East. In the Middle East, he persuaded Byrnes to give backing to the British in confronting a possible Soviet push through Azerbaijan in the Caucasus into northern Persia.[44] Bevin warned Byrnes that 'it looked as if Russia were undermining the British Empire'. President Truman privately recorded that he was tired of 'babying the Soviets': Bevin was sowing on hopeful ground. By mid-1946, the United States had carved out new military obligations in the Persian Gulf which, nevertheless, still recognized British primacy in the

[44] See Gary R. Hess, 'The Iranian Crisis of 1945–46 and the Cold War', *Political Science Quarterly*, 89, no. 1 (Mar. 1974), 117ff.

region. The British withdrawal from maintaining troops in Greece and Turkey resulted in the declaration of the Truman Doctrine, as has been seen. But the assumption that the eastern Mediterranean was an area where Britain had special strategic needs survived. In Germany, Britain found itself increasingly forced to enmesh itself in American policies. Independent British initatives in the British occupied zone, including the possible nationalization of the Ruhr coal and steel industries, were vetoed. The climax came with the merger of the administration of food, transport, finance, and much else besides in the British and American zones. The merger of the British and US zones was privately agreed for July 1946[45] and on 1 January 1947 the two zones were formally joined together. A joint Anglo-American position on the prospects for German unification thus resulted. By 1948 Western Germany was clearly being included in proposed forms of European economic recovery, including Marshall Aid, and many sensed that German participation in European military integration was also possible. By the time of the Berlin blockade and airlift in June 1948 it was evident that Russia, rather than the old threat of Germany, was viewed as the potential enemy. The Cold War was well under way.

The logic of British external policy, culminating in the formation of the North Atlantic Treaty Organization in April 1949, was for the permanent involvement of the Americans in the military, economic, and political organization of western Europe. Thereafter, Bevin saw this alliance as the coping-stone of his plans for Britain and for Europe, the way of avoiding the dissipation of the strength of the democracies which had enabled dictatorship to gain the ascendancy in Europe after 1919. But it was a view of the Anglo-American relationship which was strictly finite and always geared to distinctive British interests. On issue after issue, to use Christopher Thorne's phrase, Britain and America were 'allies of a kind', their views frequently at

---

[45]   Bevin to Attlee and others, 25 May 1946 (FO 371/55589).

odds. In continental Europe, the American view that Marshall Aid and OEEC must inevitably point towards the economic union of the western European states was strenuously resisted by the British.[46] In the Middle East, where vestiges of disagreement over Palestine lingered, the British and Americans were opposed, both over conflicting pressures for oil supplies and over Britain's growing role in Persia and in the so-called 'fertile crescent' along the north side of the Persian Gulf. In the Far East, Britain and the United States diverged sharply over their response to the civil war in China, while Britain maintained its strong commercial and military/naval presence in Hong Kong and the naval base of Singapore. In wider areas of world trade and currency movements, American pressure for the liberalization of commerce and currency convertibility came up against British commitments to protection of her home industries, the valuable tariff preferences which continued to link Britain and Commonwealth countries as they had done since 1932, and Britain's preservation of sterling as a reserve currency. Thus the British deliberately proposed a Western customs union for Europe's financial arrangements, to maintain Britain's status as a world banker, and suggested an economic and defence system for western Germany which would keep Britain free from excessive dependence on the United States. To a degree that seems remarkable in the 1980s, Britain succeeded, despite its financial erosion and the manifest illusions attaching to its world role. The western world was, for a time, being remoulded according to the model proposed by the weaker member of the alliance.

Marshall Aid, OEEC, the Brussels Treaty, NATO were all plausibly viewed as British triumphs, with Bevin, the token proletarian of Carlton House Terrace, cheered on in his jousts with Molotov, the Russian Foreign Minister, by an admiring diplomatic corps. He was presented as the architect of a new grand design. Repeated signs of financial weakness, especially a long

---

[46] On this aspect, see Michael J. Hogan, *The Marshall Plan: America, Britain and the Reconstruction of Western Europe* (London, 1987), *passim.*

run of adverse balance-of-payments figures, first in early 1947 and then in mid-1949 leading to the devaluation of sterling by a third of its value, did not appear to undermine this achievement. A later generation would look admiringly to Britain's active role in world affairs in this period as the hallmark of a new internationalism. In fact, Britain's vision was more circumscribed than it appeared. It was the product rather of a preponderant mood of nostalgic nationalism, heavily anti-communist, with escapist overtones. Britain had been a major victor of the war; the allied partnership was largely invented in Britain and conceived in British terms. Recollections of 1940 and of D-Day reinforced a sense of national self-sufficiency and independence that led naturally to a British atomic bomb, and an acceptance of an expanding defence budget and a return of National Service in 1947, largely to protect the bastions of empire. In physical and financial terms, the links with continental Europe—in which the French were patronizingly regarded as politically disorganized, the Low Countries as relatively trivial, and Germany and Italy as defeated enemies who needed to be taught a lesson—were not robust. Nor did public opinion wish them to be so. Very few British people travelled 'abroad' anyhow. The famous football match at Hampden Park, Glasgow, in 1947, in which Great Britain comprehensively defeated a 'rest of Europe' side summed up much of the popular psychology. European culture was commonly presented in the newspapers in terms of simple historical stereotypes, and only of interest to a few unrepresentative intellectuals such as art or film critics. Bevin and the British did not believe there to be a coherent European political culture at all. American predominance was a recognized fact, yet the presence of thousands of American GIs and the 'coca-colanization' of British life did not make the Anglo-American partnership a closer one. There was little that resembled the enthusiasm, even infatuation, for American life-styles prevalent in western Germany after 1945. Only a small group of 'Round Table'-type cultural ambassadors, operating in such bodies as the English-speaking Union and the Rhodes Trust, tried to make the Anglo-American relationship more profound and durable. Commentators noted gloomily the widespread mood of latent anti-Americanism amongst the British public, as marked amongst suburban Conservatives as in the working-class heartlands. All the fashionable symbols of identity—the Crown, the Commonwealth, the 'mother of parliaments', the City, the ascendancy of Oxford and Cambridge—ministered to national self-esteem and self-sufficiency. If Britain emerged in the years after 1945 as 'one nation', it was a feeling rooted not only in accepted social collectivism at home but also in a spirit of complacent nationalism towards a wider world.

Many commentators on Britain in 1945-7 noted its air of unity. Posters and government documentaries urged the people to 'pull through together'. The British remained orderly and peaceful as in Victorian and Edwardian novels of years gone by. The privations of rationing, queuing, and the like were borne quietly and with good humour. There was social peace throughout the land, with only local eruptions of disorder such as the police eviction of 'squatters' in empty property in London during acute housing shortages. There were occasional troubles with Jews objecting to British policy in Palestine, or Irish republicans condemning the Protestant regime in Northern Ireland, and occasional stirrings from nationalists in Scotland. But in general the nation appeared to be in good heart. In no country did the unarmed police enjoy a more natural respect, with the folk imagery of the 'bobby on the beat', later to be given support in the film *The Blue Lamp* and later still in the highly popular television serial, 'PC 49'. The policeman was less a custodian of order, on the model of the armed French *gendarmerie*, or the New York cop, than a servant of the community who retrieved lost dogs and helped old ladies across the road. The Home Office, indeed, refused to remodel the police system in any significant respect after 1945, partly following grass-roots opposition from the Police Federation to élitism of any kind. Thus the old Hendon Police College, designed to train a superior kind of officer, was wound up after a strong recommendation by a postwar committee representative of the police service.[47] Britain after 1945 appeared the very model of social control. There was no youth movement to rise up in angry protest; easily the largest youth organization was the 'Young Conservatives', with their dances and parties making them a much more successful body than the more earnest Labour League of Youth. Britain presented to the post-war eye a spectacle of a somewhat drab society, but one where the work-force was docile and hard at work, sports crowds cheerful and peaceable, schools tranquil and orderly, family life secure. Indeed, wartime blueprints such as the Beveridge Report, had based their recommendations on the premiss that social planning would work alongside, and through, an essentially cohesive, caring, orderly society. The extended family of community and neighbourhood would supplement and underpin the cash benefits provided by the state.

The paradox was that, in reality, this placid land was divided and sectional in new and unfamiliar ways since the war. Its divisions were made all the more acute by such apparently progressive achievements as the launching of the welfare state or the public ownership of industry. The very universality of the provisions of social welfare meant, inevitably, that the middle class, as individuals, benefited disproportionately from free medical treatment, expanded educational places, family allowances, and food subsidies. Benefits in kind were especially favourable to the salaried classes, though, of course, total benefits largely aided wage-earners because there were more of them. Years after the welfare state came into being it was noted that the class profile of the country became scarcely less sharply drawn. The public ownership of industry was basically a managerial revolution, as has been noted, with no attempt to restructure the internal organization of the industries or services nationalized, let alone promoting any form of industrial democracy. On this, the shop Stewards

[47] K. A. L. Parker, 'The Police Service after the war: structure and Administration', *Public Administration*, 68, No. 4 (Winter 1990), 462 ff.

who served on Joint Production Committees protested in vain.[48] Since the rationale for public ownership was largely technocratic and practical, it had little concern with altering the class system or the distribution of economic power. Even more ardent socialists of the left were declaring, perhaps somewhat ruefully, that nationalization was 'a means rather than an end' to the socialist society. The gulf, for instance, between the villa-style housing provided for the management of nationalized coal-mines and the traditional terraces where their employees lived, remained as wide as ever.[49]

More generally, the pattern of leisure pursuits, the revival of drama and opera for the middle class contrasted with the communality of the working-class holiday camp at Skegness or Filey, the careful gradations on BBC radio between the popular entertainment of the 'Light Programme' and the culture for the literati on the new 'Third Programme', all had obvious class implications. The old vision, entertained by Sir John Reith in the early days of the BBC, for 'mixed programmes' on the air to straddle tastes and classes was explicitly abandoned.[50] The BBC confirmed its role as an instrument of middle-class hegemony with only a few echoes of the classless ethic of the war surviving, like the radio programme 'Workers' Playtime', produced in works canteens. Geographically, too, post-war Britain was markedly divided despite the apparent mobility introduced by the industrial relocation of the war years, and the post-war growth of suburbs, commuter or 'dormitory' areas, and, eventually, new towns. The gulf between town and countryside, somewhat narrowed by the protection provided for farmers by the 1947 Agriculture Act of Tom Williams and the annual price review, remained a wide one in terms of both income and amenity.

---

[48] See E. V. Batson, I. Boraston, and K. S. J. Frenkel, *Shop Stewards in Action* (Oxford, 1977).

[49] File on 'Housing for Managers', 1946 (HLG 104/5).

[50] For post-war broadcasting, see Asa Briggs, *Sound and Vision: The History of Broadcasting in the United Kingdom*, iv (Oxford, 1979).

The radio, meanwhile, fanned a new cult of rural Utopia. In urban centres, the rebuilding of inner cities, ravaged by bombing or by decades of civic decay and neglect, still preserved the class differentiation of pre-war years. The new towns, or regional house-building programmes, were anxious to avoid the impression of stereotyped uniformity. This meant providing separate accommodation, along with suitable shopping precincts, for salaried managers, skilled workers, and the semi-skilled or unskilled majority, with the minimum of social intermingling. Only the former possessed cars; the latter (along with mavericks like Oxbridge undergraduates) rode 'bikes' or used public transport.

The impression that post-war Britain, for all its collectivist rhetoric about 'fair shares', was a polarized society was fully confirmed in political identification. Of course, the Attlee government, even with such prominent left-wingers as Bevan. Shinwell, and Strachey, was anything but a doctrinaire socialist administration. Attlee's personal dedication to Haileybury public school, Dalton's to the rowing fraternity of King's College, Cambridge, alone belied the fact. In the summer of 1947, a new splinter-group of fifteen left-wing MPs formed the 'Keep Left' group in protest at the government's promotion of the mixed economy programme at home and, more especially, its hardline Cold War policies overseas.[51] Already moves were under way in Transport House, under the aegis of Morgan Phillips, Labour's General Secretary, to discipline or even purge far-left dissidents such as Konni Zilliacus, a particular thorn in the flesh of Ernest Bevin, the Foreign Secretary.'[52] Even so, for most people, the Labour and Conservative Parties represented clear ideological antitheses, in permanent conflict with one another. Public opinion surveys testified to the natural ease with which most people placed themselves in one class or another, and also to the fact that the vast majority identified themselves unambiguously as Labour or Conservative supporters. Indeed, the sharpness of the division

[51] See Schneer, *Labour's Conscience* and Mikardo, *Backbencher*, 109 ff.
[52] See file on 'Lost Sheep' in Morgan Phillips Papers. Labour Party archive.

was unusual in western Europe at that time. The rump of the centrist Liberal Party was in evident decline, with only a dozen MPs left under the cautious leadership of Clement Davies.[53] The fact that Liberalism still claimed major intellectuals like Beveridge and a popular newspaper like the *News Chronicle* (along with the London evening paper, *The Star*) counted for little. Independent MPs like Sir A. P. Herbert and Commander Stephen King-Hall were a virtual anachronism; most of them represented the surviving university constituencies. With Gilbertian precision, the children of Britain identified themselves as little Labourites or little Conservatives.

The by-elections of 1945–7 confirmed this trend. There was invariably a very high poll with both major parties polling strongly. In general, there was a slight drift back to the Conservatives. This was particularly marked in the London suburb of Bexley in a by-election in July 1946 at a time when the unpopular Bread Units ('BUs') were introduced for rationing purposes, and Labour organizers were worried at complaints about high prices, scarcities, and red tape amongst middle-class Labour sympathizers. Nevertheless, Labour held on to all its seats and in fact suffered no defeat in its six years of office, apart from a freak Glaswegian contest in Camlachie in 1948 when ILP and Communist intervention briefly let the Tory in. Even more notable was the enthusiasm that canvassers on both sides displayed and the personal popularity of Attlee and Churchill among their respective supporters. Both parties reported rising membership and growing party commitment. Labour's individual membership continued to surge ahead after the euphoria of the war years from 487,000 in 1945 to 908,000 in 1950. Later historians might see this as a time of consensus in which the fires of partisan passion dating from the thirties were dimmed. In reality, with ferocious attacks on Labour ministers like Bevan and Strachey (the Minister of Food), assaults to which Bevan replied with

[53] Material in Clement Davies Papers, National Library of Wales, Aberystwyth, J3.

particular vigour, it was partisanship rather than common identity that marked the popular mood.

The collectivist reforms of the period, after all, were imposed within a framework of sectionalism. The welfare measures of post-1945 helped perpetuate the group self-interest of the professional and other bodies involved. The prolonged guerilla war of the doctors in the British Medical Association against the National Health Service reaped its reward. In 1948 Bevan would have to climb down by confirming his opposition to a full-time salaried medical profession. As has been seen, private practice continued to flourish, especially in the suburban areas and greater London. The administration of the National Health service was dominated by the medical profession at all levels, while restructuring proposals such as the health centres urged by the Socialist Medical Association never got off the ground. In the first ten years of the NHS, less than a dozen health centres saw the light of day. The involvement of the relevant trade unions, especially within the hospital service, was meagre; little industrial democracy intruded here. The Beveridge social insurance system continued to rely heavily on the 'approved societies', which meant a vast surge forward for private industrial assurance companies. In education and in local government, the fragmentation and dispersal of the professional and technical groups involved was equally clear, as a bewildering mass of trade unions and occupational associations showed.

In no area was the lack of cohesion in post-war Britain more apparent than in financial and economic planning. From the start, Labour was aware that its brave new world was threatened by financial problems of frightening intensity. Keynes's gloomy memorandum in August 1945 spelt out the loss of overseas markets, the sale of assets, and the wartime legacy of a national debt four times the pre-war level. Britain faced, in Keynes's view, 'an economic Dunkirk'.[54] The end of American Lend Lease only

---

[54] Memorandum by Keynes on 'Our Overseas Financial Prospects', 14 Aug. 1945, CP (45) 112 (CAB 129/1).

six days after the war with Japan ended on 15 August 1945 added to the immensity of the problems facing the Labour government. With great difficulty, as has been noted, a loan of £3.75 billion was negotiated by Keynes and others with the American government in November 1945.[55] Keynes himself, an ailing man, found relations with Vinson, the US Secretary to the Treasury, singularly strained, and only with the dispatch of the head of the Treasury, Edward Bridges, was an agreement finally sewn up. The loan, however, was accompanied by stern restrictions, including a pledge towards the liberalization of trade, an unexpectedly severe rate of interest, and the agreement that the pound would become freely convertible against the dollar and other currencies, as a move towards world monetary liberalization, in July 1947, twelve months after the US Congress approved the loan.

The US loan was, therefore, a somewhat disturbing lifeline, even though the Attlee government, with some socialist dissent from Bevan and Shinwell, had no alternative but to accept it.[56] But it meant a huge effort at economic recovery, with a target of at least a 150 per cent increase in the value of exports in 1938 being now set. In fact, the British approach towards planning, even under a Labour government apparently devoted to long-term state direction and collective effort, was piecemeal and indirect. The Cabinet's chosen instrument of planning was the Lord President's Committee under Herbert Morrison.[57] He was not a specialist economist at all. His expertise lay in public administration rather than in economics, and his committee proved to be a hesitant and haphazard instrument of planning. It was unable to draw up real targets for production, investment, or consumption. Again, Hugh Dalton, the Chancellor of the Exchequer, was a man with a strong radical conscience and a celebrated academic expert in public finance. But he was no

[55] The discussions on the US loan appear in the Public Records (PREM 8/35).
[56] Cabinet conclusions, 29 Nov. 1945 (CAB 128/2).
[57] CAB 132/1–15.

planner in the Keynesian sense, and indeed was personally wary of Keynes, once his tutor at Cambridge. Dalton refused to correlate the fiscal calendar (April–March) with the Economic Plan timetable (January–December).[58] The modern currents of economic thought had largely passed him by, even though they inspired Dalton's talented protégés like Gaitskell, Jay, and Durbin. The result was that British economic planning under Labour was distinctly weak at the centre. Civil service advisers like Meade, Clarke, and Hall found themselves often frustrated by a government of the left that steadfastly refused to plan. Public ownership, as has been seen, was felt to be in a separate category of its own and removed from the overall economic design.

The result was a growing indirection in the handling of the economy, highlighted by the diminishing impact of the wartime framework of a manpower budget. By the early summer of 1947, with the onset of the convertibility of sterling and a massive run on the gold and dollar reserves, the central weakness of economic direction was plain. Belatedly, and much to Morrison's personal displeasure, a new Economic Planning Council was set up under Sir Edwin Plowden in July 1947.[59] Though concerned with short-term rather than longer-term planning considerations, it did include a revamped Economic Planning Staff along with a new statistical apparatus. In addition, there was the expanded Economic Section of the Cabinet, under Robert Hall. In September 1947, after the crisis of convertibility had been averted and the provisions laid down in the US loan suspended, the Cabinet created a new battery of committees. The Economic Committee, the Import Programme Committee, and an Overseas Committee came into being, along with a Production Committee which dealt with key matters of capital investment and the allocation of raw materials and manpower.

---

[58] See Alan Booth, '"The Keynesian Revolution" in Economic Policy-Making'. *Economic History Review*, 36, 1 (Feb. 1983).

[59] Jacques Leruez, *Economic Planning and Politics in Britain* (London, 1975), 49ff.

This impressive array, however, did not amount then, or later, to a proper system of planning. The main strategy was indirect, relying more on partnership with private business and the unions rather than on direct or more coercive intervention. The government's *Economic Surveys*, starting with one in 1947, seemed to portend a new approach to purposive planning, but important instruments such as the price mechanism were omitted. By 1950 the *Surveys* were to be little more than a consolidated offering of forecasts and guidelines. There was throughout a heavy emphasis on patriotic endeavour for the common good and freedom from governmental harassment. The 1947 *Economic Survey*, written by Cripps, drew a sharp contrast between 'totalitarian' and 'democratic' planning. Government could work only within flexible frameworks and essential needs. 'When the working pattern has thus been set, it is only by the combined effort of the whole people that the nation can move towards its objective of carrying out the first things first and so make the best use of economic resources.' A high-level economic adviser like 'Otto' Clarke was at a loss to see how so uncoordinated and vague a system could ever work.[60] The government's main instrument would be demand management through the annual budget rather than any coherent planning of resources. Such continental novelties as the French Monnet Plan excited little interest or attention in Whitehall. In particular, the economic activity of the period was conducted with relatively little re-equipment of an industrial base that was generally acknowledged to be outdated.

The public ethic of 1945–7, then, was more a matter of exhortation and an assumed public morality than of concerted planning. A heavy emphasis was placed on physical controls of raw materials, foodstuffs, and consumption. Ultimately, a disciplined consumer response would determine the success of the government's approach. The well-known controls on personal consumption of the war years were invested with an aura of

[60] See Alec Cairncross (ed.), *Anglo-American Economic Collaboration in War and Peace, 1942–1949* (Oxford, 1982) for Clarke's views.

patriotism. The ration book was a badge of good citizenship, queuing for buses or food a necessary privation. The government relied, it seemed, on promoting a kind of secular religion in dictating the public's response. The mood of collective endeavour would give impetus to the drive for economic recovery. With conventional religion in continued long-term decline, Sir Stafford Cripps, the high Anglican prophet of austerity, took over from the Archbishop of Canterbury. 'Fair shares' conveyed that reassuring creed. The year 1945 marked the high noon of Victorian values. Cases of public corruption were exposed with evangelical zeal, and 'black market' practices fervently denounced. But it was all somewhat harder to sustain. The mood rested on a preservation of the puritan singleness of purpose proclaimed during wartime. By 1947 a nation increasingly aware of its internal divisions was finding it harder to respond with the same kind of enthusiasm. A left-wing weekly like Kingsley Martin's *New Statesman and Nation* attracted a large and growing readership with its editorial calls for greater collectivism and social sacrifice. But it was surely the latter half of that famous publication, with its reviews of books, music, and opera designed for the middle-class intellectuals, rather than the clarion calls for a new morality in Martin's own columns (he was himself a product of the Congregationalist manse), that provided the essence of the *Statesman's* appeal. Perhaps without realizing it, the *New Statesman* was an advertisement for Churchill's call to 'set the people free'.

The façade of national unity began to crack in early 1947. There was unprecedentedly severe weather in late January and February, with snow and ice covering the land.[61] Some areas of Britain saw not one hour of sunshine for weeks at a time. Industry almost seemed to close down, and unemployment mounted rapidly. But what the episode did was to confirm long-held feelings that Labour's planners had failed to plan. The desperate

---

[61] An excellent discussion of the fuel crisis is Alex Robertson, *The Bleak Midwinter*, 1947 (Manchester, 1987).

crisis in coal production was not just the result of the severe winter weather. From early 1946 economic specialists such as James Meade and Douglas Jay had pointed to weakness in the running of the coal industry, the shortfall in the workforce, the absence of any policy for planning consumption or determining industrial priorities.[62] The National Union of Mineworkers had won the great prize of the Miners' Charter in 1946, including the five-day week. But productivity remained low by comparative standards, work practices antique, the labour intensity of the industry chronic. The minister who presided over the coal industry and took it into public ownership, Emanuel Shinwell, was a monument of complacency. As late as the end of October 1946, he denied the existence of a manpower shortage or any real production crisis in the coal industry. When the crisis struck in the wintry weather, he blamed the climate, the privately-run railway system, or simply 'capitalism'. His blindness to approaching disaster appalled his colleagues, and belatedly a Cabinet Fuel Committee had to take control of fuel policy away from him though he remained in his department.

The fuel crisis passed away during the spring as the weather warmed up. But public morale continued to suffer. The approach of the convertibility of sterling in July 1947 was already putting pressure on the balance of payments and the value of sterling itself. The fuel crisis meant a 25 per cent loss of exports that accelerated the sense of crisis. When convertibility of sterling came on 15 July, there was already a roaring balance-of-payments crisis with which the Treasury and Hugh Dalton were ill-equipped to deal. A halt to convertibility announced on 20 August and resultant stern cuts in public spending finally brought the crisis to an end.[63]

---

[62] See Jay, *Change and Fortune*, 143–52, and letters from Jay to Attlee in PREM 8/440.

[63] An excellent treatment of the convertibility crisis appears in Cairncross, *Years of Recovery*, chap. 6.

The combination of the fuel and convertibility crises brought a grim conclusion to the first phase of the post-war British experience. The crises in themselves were far from terminal. As will be seen, there was a distinct improvement in economic growth when Cripps went to the Treasury in place of Dalton in November 1947. The year 1948 was to set new records for production and for exports. The Labour government retained much of its popularity with its usual working-class supporters. While there were losses in local government elections, Labour successfully defended all its seats in by-elections. These included a tricky one at Gravesend in Kent in November 1947, where Sir Richard Acland, the ex-Common Wealth Labour candidate gave the defence of 'socialism' a Christian and patrician aura.[64] Trade-union loyalty to 'our government' remained remarkably solid.

But the crises of 1947 did nevertheless mark something like the end of an era. The wartime enthusiasm and self-confidence had been seriously challenged for the first time. Britain, like the Labour government itself, felt under siege. Aspects of the welfare state like the council-house building programme were sharply cut back. The financial imbalances of the planned National Health Service and the school-building programme were thrown into relief. In any event, they rested on the charitable base of American Marshall Aid. The hollowness of many of the pretensions surrounding Britain's presumed status as a world power of international significance was cruelly revealed. After all, in overseas affairs, from Greece to India, 1947 had been largely a year of withdrawal and retreat. The literature of public comment and debate marks something of a reaction against planning, controls, and austerity, and an urge for a flexible society, even if, ironically, it was really the absence of planning that had led to the fuel and financial crises of the year.

---

[64] Philip Williams (ed.), *The Diary of Hugh Gaitskell, 1945–1956* (London, 1983), 49 (4 Dec. 1947). Gaitskell wrote of Acland, 'What a bore he is!... He hardly condescended to shake hands and uttered no word of thanks afterwards.'

The summer and autumn of 1947 in many ways marked the real end of the war for the British people. They still treasured a rich inheritance with unquenched patriotism—witness the popular enthusiasm for the wedding of Princess Elizabeth, the heir to the throne, to Prince Philip Mountbatten. But the future, somehow, lacked its pristine certainty. The confident civil-service titans of 1945 now found their achievement cast into doubt. The Prime Minister, Clement Attlee, the calm pilot in the storm in the period of advance in 1945–6, proved to be all at sea during the convertibility crisis. He did not really understand its root causes, and responded only slowly and inadequately to it. There was even a move in August–September to replace Attlee as premier by Sir Stafford Cripps, but the Prime Minister had managed to deflect his adversaries by promoting Cripps to the new Ministry of Economic Affairs.[65] Hugh Dalton, the booming, confident prophet of socialist advance, was discredited by the financial hammer-blows of 1947; that November he had to resign from the Treasury. There was thus a growing sense that the socialist tide was beginning to turn. The Cabinet, after anguished and lengthy debate, agreed to press on with iron and steel nationalization as a symbol of socialist intent,[66] but it would be delayed until 1948–9 and in any case perhaps be contingent on the calling of the next general election. Democratic socialism, Britain's 'middle way', assumed a defensive air, its main work already accomplished. In divided, apprehensive mood, the British lurched into the unpleasant challenges of post-war change.

[65] See Morgan, *Labour in Power*, 350–8.
[66] Cabinet conclusions, 24, 31 July, 7 Aug. 1947 (CAB 128/10).

3. *The Collectivist Retreat*
1948–1951

AFTER the traumas of the fuel and convertibility crises of 1947, the Labour government and the nation as a whole moved into the culture of 'consolidation'. Its prophet was Herbert Morrison. He had apparently been the main political casualty of the events of 1947 since he lost his control of economic planning (while away on holiday in the Channel Islands) and was replaced, both in his official role and in the public estimation, by Sir Stafford Cripps. In political terms, the failure to get rid of Attlee was particularly Morrison's failure. However, Morrison, with all the resilience that had marked his political career since his creation of the London Labour Party in the 1920s, bounced back from heart trouble and political setbacks as his party's main political strategist and even theorist. It was he who spelt out the premisses of 'consolidation' as the government's main priority henceforth.[1] In broad terms, it meant a halt—not necessarily a permanent one—to further measures towards planning or socialism. It was a domestic version of George Kennan's philosophy of 'containment' as advocated in the US journal *Foreign Affairs*. He pressed strongly for an approach which combined 'idealism and realism'. He urged the need to pay heed to the 'floating voters' and especially to the grievances of the deserving middle class, well represented as they were in his own Lewisham constituency. He argued successfully in Labour's Policy Committee against any

---

[1] See Bernard Donoughue and G. W. Jones, *Herbert Morrison: Portrait of a Politican* (London, 1973). 442ff.

more measures of nationalization. He urged passionately the cause of the 'small man', usually illustrated in 'the shop around the corner', an important image in working-class community life.[2] Morrison, in fact, was pushing at an open door. After the convertibility scare and Cabinet deadlock over steel nationalization, hardly any major figure in Cabinet or party wanted any further 'mucking about' or experiments in socialism. Even Aneurin Bevan, who infuriated the Tories with class-war rhetoric and allegations that they were 'lower than vermin', also recognized the fact of the relative unpopularity of public ownership including amongst the work-force, the need for better public relations in presenting the case for state intervention, and the public demand for greater economic relaxation after grim years of controls. After a torrent of reformist legislation over the past three years—indeed, over the past six years since Beveridge appeared in 1942—Labour was in the mood for digging in. An increasingly self-confident Conservative opposition, backed by auxiliary middle-class pressure-groups such as the self-styled 'Housewives' League', prepared to exploit the government's defensive stance accordingly.

Consolidation was not a wholly passive creed. It did not urge any further move towards state intervention. But neither did it imply much dismantling of what had already been achieved. It was also anxious to show that British-style democratic socialism was administratively competent. The presence of hard-headed economists in the remodelled government like the Wykehamists, Hugh Gaitskell as Minister of Fuel and Power (in place of Shinwell) and Douglas Jay as Economic Secretary to the Treasury, was a portent here. Above all, the replacement of the somewhat discredited Hugh Dalton (undone by a mild budget 'leak' to a journalist) by the spartan figure of Sir Stafford Cripps as Chancellor in November 1947 gave a new impetus to the authority of the Treasury. Over the next three years, fuelled of course by

[2] Morrison's observations, Labour Party NEC Policy Committee minutes, 25 November 1947.

massive aid under the Marshall Plan programme, the economy showed a distinct mood of expansion. The year 1948 was especially thriving for exports, with employment and production at full throttle. Government publicity boosted the 'Britain can make it' campaign. Even coal production, highly suspect after the miseries of the fuel shortage in 1947, showed a great leap forward. Harold Wilson, the youthful President of the Board of Trade (only 31 at his appointment), became the monthly harbinger of glad tidings as the level of exports soared to almost 150 per cent above the value of prewar.

His master, Cripps, became the new public giant. He was a controversial figure with a far-left past, a vegetarian, a teetotaller, an earnest Christian of a pungently evangelical kind.[3] His own severe personality seemed a personal embodiment of the spirit of austerity, not least when he denounced women who adopted the 'new look' of longer skirts because of the wastage of textile supplies. But the public admired his rectitude and his commitment to duty. The record of byelections and the findings of the opinion polls did show that Labour's prospects were not destroyed by the restrictions, rationing, and controls that Cripps imposed and operated. He was clearly the great success of government in 1948–9, regarded by many as the coming Prime Minister of the future. His old Popular Front background kept him friendly with left-wingers like Aneurin Bevan, who stayed on in the government despite severe cuts in his housing programme and threats to impose charges on doctors' medical prescriptions in October 1949. At the same time, Cripps's clearly centrist, technocratic image, his wish to work closely with private industry and former business executives like Plowden made him fully acceptable to younger economists on the party right like Gaitskell and Jay. With the government gradually regaining its nerve, Cripps helped to give it hope of recovery. One useful popular

---

[3] There is no satisfactory biography of Cripps. See the portrait of him in Douglas Jay, *Change and Fortune* 170ff., and Morgan, 'Sir Stafford Cripps as Chancellor', *Labour People*, 162ff. Peter Clarke is writing a new life.

portent was the successful holding of the London Olympic games in 1948, a remarkable triumph of self-help, improvisation, and natural resilience.

In the course of 1949, Cripps's economic achievement suddenly began to falter. The balance of payments began to go seriously awry in the late spring, partly because of a downturn in the American economy which affected exports to dollar markets. The pound came under pressure in European monetary markets and Cripps himself was compelled to declare at Rome in May that devaluation was not on the government's agenda.[4] At this period, Cripps himself became seriously ill and had to retire to a sanatorium in Zurich for treatment. In his absence, the initiative was taken up by younger ministers, Gaitskell and Jay above all, who urged the case for devaluation as a positive measure to rebuild exports and avoid damaging deflationary policies at home. The Attlee Cabinet was in chaos in July 1949, with Morrison, Bevan, and others variously offering threats of resignation and Attlee himself as bemused in the face of financial complexities as he had been during the convertibility crisis in 1947. Cripps himself let it be known that he would think it immoral to break his word and pledges to allies and devalue the pound. In the end, Gaitskell took the lead in urging a decision by the Cabinet. Jay supported him. Harold Wilson, who had been himself remarkably indecisive and politically calculating during the crisis, became the messenger of a virtual ultimatum to Cripps, presented to him at his sanatorium in Switzerland.[5] Most reluctantly, the Chancellor agreed to a devaluation of one-third of the pound's value against the dollar to $2.80 from $4.03, and a programme of public expenditure cuts duly resulted. A public statement was agreed to in Washington and the fact of devaluation revealed to the world by Cripps on 18 September. The Chancellor regarded this as a serious economic retreat and perhaps a lasting blow to his moral authority as well.

[4] *The Economist*, 7 May 1949.
[5] Wilson to Attlee, 8 Aug. 1949 (PREM 8/1178, pt. 1).

In fact, devaluation gave Cripps's policies further momentum—while the Chancellor's health improved sufficiently for him to return to his post. The currency reserves began to turn the corner and to mount steadily.[6] In 1950 the economy was once again very buoyant and the balance of payments firmly entered the black. Exports soared, including remarkably to the North American markets where British 'small cars' did very well. Indeed, the energy and initiative displayed by car manufacturers and salesmen was remarkable at this time, boosted by the fact that rivalry from German Volkswagens, French Renaults, and Italian Fiats lay in the future. In June 1950, at the time of the outbreak of the Korean War, Britain's economy showed all the symptoms of steady growth without overheating. It was amongst the most thriving periods economically that the country as a whole had experienced since the late-Victorian era. Cripps himself, with a strict regime of budgetary management, and with high government taxation to make up the difference between public expenditure and the goods available for private consumption,[7] had created the basis for a new affluence.

In a more indirect, psychological way, the Cripps era meant fresh credibility for the collective ethic of the war years. Central government intervened widely in economic assessment, in determining patterns of production, the supply of skilled manpower, and the nature of consumption. Plowden's Planning Board was omnipresent even if it fought shy of 'totalitarian' controls. Like the war years, this programme was intended, too, to be collectivism with a social conscience. While the welfare programmes were cut back, and Bevan's house-building reduced below the 200,000 a year level, social spending retained a high profile. Food subsidies, trimmed back in the 1949 budget, still remained a leading Treasury priority. Nationalized industries such as coal and the railways were urged to keep the costs of fuel or fares down in the interests of price stability and the fight against

---

[6] Memoranda by Robert Hall, 19 Oct. 1949–4 Jan. 1950 (T229/230–1).
[7] Cripps's memorandum on 'Budget Policy', 15 May 1950 (PREM 8/1188).

domestic inflation. The National Health Service soared upwards in its expenditure patterns, causing Bevan to take the unpopular step of introducing supplementary estimates of £57 million in 1949. Estimates for public health spending rose from under £228 m. in 1949–50 to close on £400 m. in 1951–2.[8] Cripps made an attempt to modify the costs by proposing doctors' prescription charges in the autumn of 1949[9] and then charges on dental and ophthalmic treatment in the spring of 1950.[10] Bevan resisted both fiercely, and in fact neither set of charges was actually introduced. Instead, a Cabinet committee sought to monitor NHS expenditure monthly and to keep a ceiling on spending, scheduled for £392 m. in 1950–1. Despite it all, the NHS expanded steadily and proved increasingly popular with the medical profession after the storms which had accompanied its introduction; of the BMA critics of 1946, Dain retired to the mid-Wales coast and Hill turned to a political career with the Tories. These policies meant that the welfare state continued to progress. Marshall Aid helped build up industrial production and the economic infrastructure, but social provision was not neglected either. Consolidation, then, kept broadly faithful to the wartime ethics of 'fair shares'.

To Morrison's mind, consolidation should also be fun. In the depths of the years of austerity in the late 1940s, he outlined the prospect of a 'Festival of Britain' to echo the Great Exhibition of 1851. It should provide encouragement to the industrial designers, planners, and artists of the nation, and offer a conspicuous platform for Britain's technical and scientific achievement as well. It should exploit the genius of artists like Graham Sutherland and John Piper, and the sculptor, Henry Moore, who won the prize at the Venice Biennale in 1948, a unique feat for an

---

[8] Report by Cyril Jones on the Financial Working of the Health Service, 15 July 1950 (PREM 8/1486).
[9] Cabinet conclusions. 20 October 1949 (CAB 128/16).
[10] Ibid., 3 Apr. 1950 (CAB 128/17).

Englishman.[11] The Festival should embody state-sponsored gaiety, not only in the main site on London's South Bank, a derelict stretch of the waterfront, but also in local initiatives of popular festivity. There was much public scepticism, and indeed ridicule, in the right-wing press at this expensive frivolity while the economy languished, and much doubt as to whether the country could afford it. Nevertheless, a great army of scientists and artists met the challenge with zest, notably Hugh Casson, the designer of the main South Bank site. Gerald Barry, its director, was a prominent example of the type of progressive thirties intellectual whose conscience and zeal for public service had been kindled by the war. The Festival of Britain would appeal to the public's urge for innovation and experiment. It would also appeal to its patriotism, with much pageantry to evoke an imperial past. It would be Land of Hope and Glory in tune with the prosaic setting of Attlee's Britain. It would create colourful vistas of invention and fun for a weary, war-torn generation. And, perhaps usefully too, it might be a useful bonus for Labour when the next general election came.

The public certainly needed some sense of adventure and cheerfulness in Britain in the late 1940s. Austerity had taken hold of the public consciousness like a malignant disease. Right-wing daily newspapers such as Beaverbrook's *Daily Express* and its cartoonist, Giles, delighted in magnifying the gloom, shortages, and misery of the time. By contrast, skilled cartoonists like 'Vicky' in the *News Chronicle* and David Low in the *Evening Standard* (later in the *Daily Herald*) still appealed to wartime classless idealism and poured derision on the reactionary postures of 'Colonel Blimp'. The Food Minister, the ex-Marxist John Strachey (wrongly accused of being Jewish) became a predicable target because of the food and clothes rationing system ('points') in operation in 1948. On the radio, Tommy Handley's 'ITMA' poured derision on 'Mr Streaky'. The

---

[11] The retrospective exhibition of his work at the Royal Academy in 1988 suggested that some of his earlier socialism diminished after his success in the Biennale.

rightwing Housewives League trained its fury on its tiresome indignities, on the miseries of queuing and of restrictions on ordinary households. It was, indeed, a difficult policy for the government to sustain. The inter-war years had given birth to a new consumerism, with the rapid growth of the home market, especially in suburban areas with a private housing boom. The hire purchase or 'never-never' system encouraged long and easy credit. Domestic appliances like 'hoovers' and (increasingly) washing-machines, the car industry, leisure services like the cinema, all made massive headway. Much of this market was now deliberately suppressed, with productive effort directed into export-orientated industries. Other features were constant shortages of raw materials, the anxiety to avoid dollar purchases and develop home industries (thus attempts to build up British films under the 'Eady levy' and restrict American film imports), the omnipresent government taxation and controls. Private cars now sold only very sluggishly in Britain, while petrol rationing ensured that the pleasures of private motoring would be limited indeed. Nor did this mean an unpolluted atmosphere. On the contrary, the filthy 'smog' of London during the winter months, the product of high-carbon coal products being used for household and factory heating, was a notorious hazard with appalling results for lung disease. Foreign travel was almost impossible with only £30 currency allowable for overseas journeys, while the range of goods available on sale in the shops remained relatively basic.

The emphasis was almost wholly on public provision. People travelled to seaside holidays (especially on the fixed 'August Bank Holidays') in tightly packed and unmodernized rolling stock, or perhaps in ancient coaches. When they reached the seaside, they queued in cafés, pier-heads, or dance-halls, or perhaps went to Butlin's holiday camps which reproduced the crowded, classless solidarity of the Blitz. British weather was much as ever: 1948 was a particularly wet summer, with the test matches against Bradman's Australians interrupted. Investment in houses was still almost wholly concentrated in local authority 'council' housing, and perhaps in ventures such as Lewis Silkin's 'new towns' which began to rise from 1949 onwards, starting with Stevenage and Hemel Hempstead, to take London 'overspill' (an unlovely term of the period). Clothing shops were largely confined to 'utility' products made from stricly controlled government allocations of textiles, and usually of extreme drabness reminiscent of eastern Europe. Many women wore headscarves in a way reminiscent of Balkan peasants; not the least of them were the royal princesses, Elizabeth and Margaret Rose. As has been seen, fashion novelties such as the 'New Look' were presented as a gesture of new femininity by Christian Dior in Paris. Some of the popular songs of the period promoted a mood of escape and freedom—'Open The Door, Richard' and 'Don't Fence Me In' were among the favourites of 1948.

The take-home pay of the average worker was assured, but severely limited. In April 1948, with the help of Ernest Bevin, the Foreign Secretary, Cripps managed to get the TUC to agree to a wage-freeze policy as a part of the general restriction of domestic consumption. This meant that, strictly speaking, wage norms would show no percentage increase at all over the coming twelve months. In practice, bonuses, shift payments, and general 'wage-drift' tendencies meant a slowly rising curve of wage increases, especially for engineers and other skilled workers.[12] The 'cost push' factor began to operate. The wage-freeze continued until the autumn of 1950; only after that point did wages begin to rise significantly, releasing new inflationary pressures. It was, of course, an unpopular policy, but the TUC, headed by the implacable right-wing 'troika' of Arthur Deakin of the Transport Workers, Tom Williamson of the General and Municipal Workers, and Will Lawther, the ex-Communist president of the once-militant National Union of Mineworkers, successfully persuaded their

[12] See B.C. Roberts, *National Wages Policy in War and Peace* (London, 1958), and E. H. Phelps Brown, *The Origins of Trade Union Power* (Oxford. 1983), 144ff.

comrades that Labour was 'their' government, nationalizing key industries, advancing the welfare state, ensuring full employment, and implementing fair shares, however defined. For two years this astonishing policy of self-denial and abnegation continued. Even Arthur Horner, the old Welsh Communist who served as secretary of the NUM, argued the case for the wage-freeze as the inescapable consequence of a Labour government in power in a capitalist world. Not until 1950 did pressures for a break with a total wage-freeze start to build up, amongst railway workers, engineers, and others. Even then social solidarity kept their sectionalism in check, as enough of the wartime unity lingered on.

In any event, the workers undergoing this wage-freeze regime and facing the trials of austerity were not necessarily discontented. Britain conspicuously avoided the massive industrial unrest of, say, France and Belgium in the immediate post-war period, with moderate union leaders confronting employers almost desperate to avoid the conflicts of the inter-war years. Only 9 million working days were lost in 1945–50 compared with 178 million in 1918–23. In the labour market it was a sellers' paradise, with full employment almost guaranteed, and with a shortage of skilled labour, for instance in the building trades, the main problem facing employers. In the Cripps era, whatever its rigours, the shadow of unemployment was finally banished. Regional employment policies, often cumbersome to implement, meant that older Welsh mining valleys or Tyneside fully shared in this progress. In Belfast, a city of especial tensions, the Harland and Woolf shipyards and Shorts aircraft gave new dynamism to the economy of Ulster. Not only were older staples such as the pits of the Rhondda or the shipyards of Birkenhead, Newcastle, Barrow, or the Clyde in full operation; but newer industries, cars, chemicals, electronics, rubber, and much else besides were adding much-needed variety to the industrial base of the old 'depressed' regions. The natural tendency was still for investment and skilled labour to migrate to London and the south-east; but government action, especially from the Board of

Trade, ensured that employment and industrial activity would be distributed more evenly around the land. Rural communities, buttressed by guaranteed prices and by agencies such as the Milk and Egg Marketing Boards, thrived with the new market, and a rapid increase in farm mechanization and productivity was a notable feature of the post-war years. Blacksmiths went out of business as the horse disappeared from the farming scene of rural Wales or the Yorkshire Dales. Not all the results were fortunate; the activities of the Forestry Commission, for instance, benefi-cent in some respects, could also disfigure, or bring Stalinist uniformity to, varied mountainous countryside. But in general the growing liveliness of small rural towns, right up to the Scottish Highlands, was impressive. It was a uniformly richer community.

It was also a healthier one. The statistics produced by medical authorities, notably school medical and dental officers, showed that austerity did not mean a physical decline in the population.[13] Darwinian fears of the diminished vitality of the race were dis-pelled by the marked improvement in the physique of children in the post-war generation. Former scourges such as tuberculosis and other lung diseases, along with bone ailments such as rickets, were becoming things of the past. Thus, under the National Health Service, a combination of quality controls on milk, mass radiography, new forms of vaccination, and the wider availability of streptomycin and chemotherapy led to a dramatic attack on tuberculosis, even though progress in other countries was more rapid still. Old people may have found their pensions and heating and other resources scanty; but even here medical advance, assured retirement benefits, and the blessings of the welfare state meant a growing longevity. It is notable that cartoons and other popular art of the period after 1945 stop depicting old people as Brueghel-like peasants with twisted bodies, and show them sim-ply as ordinary people who happened to be older.

---

[13] See the material in Klim McPherson and David Coleman, 'Health', in A. H. Halsey (ed.), *British Social Trends Since* 1900 (London, 1988 edn.), 398ff.

Not only was it demonstrably a healthier society. It was in some ways a more leisured one. The post-war years were a golden era for mass sport of all kinds, especially football, cricket, and boxing, along with other largely working-class novelties such as greyhound racing. Sports stars like the Middlesex and England batsman, Denis Compton, were much sought by advertisers of 'Brylcreem' hair cream and other products. A post-war growth was speedway racing which helped promote the sales of the motor-bicycle industry. The cinema, as noted, was immensely popular too, notably amongst women now enjoying the freedom of greater employment, less onerous domestic tasks, and somewhat smaller families. The post-war period saw a considerable revival of the British film industry, with assistance from the Board of Trade, and a wide range of popular films from the light entertainment of the Ealing Studios comedies to heavier productions such as Laurence Olivier's *Henry V* and later *Hamlet*. The post-war popularity of the *palais de danse* was further evidence of this kind of consumer revival. It was the natural forum for boys to meet girls, in a relatively classless setting of transatlantic relaxation. But rules and order were maintained also—witness the observance paid to stern notices that there should on no account be any 'jitterbugging'. The dance-hall was a flourishing, but staid, amphitheatre where people danced in traditional 'palm court' vein to Henry Hall or where the more energetic got 'in the mood' with Joe Loss or Ted Heath but also where the partners retained chaste physical contact with one another at all times.

This post-war world of modest enjoyment, full employment, and overall restraint had led commentators like J. B. Priestley to believe that, since society was becoming classless, a nationalized culture would be the product of the end of the war and a Labour victory.[14] These expectations rapidly dissolved. The gulf between the classes and the masses remained wide, by comparative

---

[14] J. B. Priestley, *The Arts under Socialism* (London, 1946).

standards. No new cultural exploration or dissolution took place, as Cyril Connolly was to complain in his literary periodical *Horizon*. Working-class communities, not only those relatively unchanged by the war such as pit villages or mill towns, but also newer housing estates, remained content with the postwar achievement and the social demarcation it implied. Civic life remained much the same in such places as Newcastle, Manchester, Stoke, or Swansea, where the monolithic, if not actually corrupt, nature of Labour rule became legendary. Roy Hattersley's recollections of respectable artisan life in Sheffield under the aegis of its MP, 'Albert Victorious' Alexander, are not untypical.[15] Labour bosses like Ike Hayward on the LCC or Llew Heycock in Glamorgan or Jack Braddock in Liverpool became the tsars of a new entrenched regime. In general, their rule was respected and buttressed by repeated popular endorsement. Nor were these machine politicians mere philistines. They helped ensure that the budgets of public libraries and adult education classes rose steadily even in the lean years. Llew Heycock, an engine driver from Port Talbot, became a strong patron of the University of Wales and (though not Welsh-speaking himself) the national eisteddfod. Ike Hayward's name was appropriately commemorated in an art gallery on the South Bank.

Just as the by-elections and political rhetoric of the time testified to social polarization, so non-political pastimes retained a clear class image. The clientele of football matches or dog races were incontestably working class, with cricket and rugby league in the north of England and rugby union in Wales more ambiguous in composition. Public theatres like the old music hall were demonstrably in retreat, but the working-class club flourished as never before. Comedians like Robb Wilton, Sandy Powell, and Max Miller on the radio dealt confidently in familiar working-class stereotypes, including the nagging wife, the appalling mother-in-law, the ever-present 'mam', the blowzy barmaid,

---

[15] In Roy Hattersley, *A Yorkshire Boyhood* (London, 1983).

and other stock symbols of male folklore. The social life of the pub (as opposed, say, to the inexorably middle-class and largely Gentile golf club) showed remarkably little transformation in the post-war period, save that the growing oligopoly amongst the brewing companies somewhat diminished consumer choice. Brews such as 'Newcastle Brown' and 'Border Ales' preserved the local touch. Budgetary policy, even that conducted by the teetotaller, Cripps, ensured that the working man's brown ale remained relatively free of the tax burden borne by the Oxford don's wine or spirits. Similarly, the wage-earner's 'packet of fags' was comparatively unscathed by government taxation, let alone agitation about lung damage. The profile of class configuration after 1945 showed a remarkable sameness. Working-class bastions created by neighbourhood and community remained the very staple of Labour Britain.

Conversely, middle-class Britain, especially England, bore a sense of grievance and threat. While the Ascot 'season', London night-life and the revival of 'debutantes' who battened on royal patronage claimed their rich clientele, many middle-class people looked back nostalgically to pre-war years of domestic servants, creature comforts, and elegant and available private housing. Newer groups in the administrative, service, and professional classes deplored the failure of the military victory to create a land fit for the salariat to live in. Newspapers and periodicals were full of the lamentations of the middle-class consumer, deprived of choice, hemmed in by controls, alienated by a collectivized, proletarianized world. The suburbs expanded steadily in the post-war years, but the inadequacies of shopping and leisure facilities left a sense of frustration. Nowhere was this more evident than in housing. Not merely was the private housing market stagnant. Renovations or improvements of the home inherited from pre-war years were exceptionally difficult, with the licensing of building materials and other physical controls. Here, the wartime ethic of reform and solidarity was being displaced by growing pressure for consumer variety. It was improbable that the Labour Party would be the beneficiary.

As the years of peace unfolded, the pattern of social segregation became more and more noticeable. No institution responded more sensitively than did the BBC with its careful preference for middle-class accents, life-styles, and preferences. The Home Service was a monument to safe middle-class respectability. A genuine regional performer like Wilfred Pickles, whose popular weekly quiz programme 'Have a Go' was transferred from the Northern Region to the Light Programme in 1946—a show born of the simple folksy image of working-class club and pub life in the North—excited popular enthusiasm by its very authenticity. Even then, BBC officials complained that Pickles's 'unscripted social conscience' was nothing but 'an embarrassment'.[16] When television became more prevalent with the reopening of the Alexandra Palace transmitter for the London area from 7 June 1946 (the day before the Victory Parade), followed by Sutton Coldfield for the Midlands in December 1949 and Holme Moss for the North in October 1951, the ethos of middle-class security was further entrenched. News announcers wore dinner jackets. An overriding air of conformism, monarchism, and patriotism prevailed. The one exception in the BBC was the Third Programme on the radio. As noted, its sharp intellectualism and cultural depth marked it off at once from the populist aspiration of the postwar years.

Here and elsewhere, the middle class found consolation for their material impoverishment in culture and the arts. The classless solidarity of Myra Hess's piano recitals during the Blitz was forgotten in the revival of sponsored festivals and cultural events. Certainly, much of the literature of the immediate post-war years was undistinguished; important journals of criticism like Cyril Connolly's *Horizon* and John Lehmann's *New Writing* folded in 1950. Music, however, continued to flourish and so, increasingly, did the theatre as the industry picked up momentum after the ravages of the war. Christopher Fry's verse dramas, *The Lady's*

---

[16]   Asa Briggs, *Sound and Vision*, 111.

Not for Burning (1948) and *Venus Observed* (1950) enjoyed some temporary success. A new concert hall, the Royal Festival Hall, designed by Robert Matthew, would be the centre-piece of the Festival of Britain site on London's South Bank. But it was hardly for factory workers and their families that its glossy vestibules and bars were designed. One critic described the design of the South Bank site in general as ' all Heal broke loose'.[17] Culture, allegedly 'nationalized' in the aftermath of military victory, was now being compartmentalized and segregated as rigorously as before the war.

In the general election of February 1950, the great and growing gulf between the regions and classes of the land became more apparent. Labour went to the country, at a curious time of year in the depths of the winter, on a strictly consolidationist platform. Hardly any novelties were proposed in the party's manifesto. Nationalization was clearly in retreat. A 'shopping list' of public ownership proposals was random in the extreme—it included meat wholesaling, the water supply, the cement industry, sugar refining, and a modified kind of ownership of private industrial assurance companies, called 'mutualization'. This last had followed a rebuff for Bevan and James Griffiths in Labour's Policy Committee when they tried to introduce full-blooded public ownership of insurance firms, as a corollary to the welfare state.[18] This was resisted by Morrison on general political grounds, Cripps on financial grounds with an eye to the 'invisible' earnings from insurance abroad, and the Co-operative Society on grounds of self-interest. In the end, 'mutualization' was just threatening enough to give Labour no electoral advantage, but to transform every local insurance agent in the land into a Tory voice. Sugar refining was another proposal of little substance, while the cartoon figure of 'Mr Cube', brandishing the sword of free enterprise aloft, became a potent symbol of

---

[17] Michael Frayn, 'Festival' in French and Sissons (eds.), *Age of Austerity*, 323.
[18] Labour Party Policy Committee minutes, 30 May–14 Nov. 1949, and NEC minutes, 30 Sept., 30 Nov. 1949.

Conservative freedom on every sugar packet on every breakfast table in the country. The main Labour emphases were on welfare, 'fair shares', and especially full employment. The nation was being asked to set its seal of approval on Crippsian austerity.

This appealed strongly to working-class electors who turned out in vast numbers. Labour's total poll of 13,266,176 (46.1 per cent) was significantly higher than the Conservatives and allies' 12,492,401 (43.5 per cent), though the piling up of huge majorities by Labour in mining and other areas meant that votes were not at all proportionately transferred into totals of seats. In addition, Labour's self-destructive honesty in the redistribution of constituencies (the work of Chuter Ede, the Home Secretary) meant, in effect, a net transfer of about sixty seats to the Conservatives. The latter, led by a reinvigorated Churchill and Eden, were anxious to show that they were not class warriors. Their campaign stressed that welfare and full employment would be equally safe with them; their election manager, Woolton, strongly emphasized the fact. But the Tory slogans stressing freedom from controls and rationing, the ethic of consumer choice, home purchase, and economic opportunity—'the Tory ladder' as contrasted with the 'Labour queue'—were effective in suburban and commuter areas, where Labour suffered many losses. In the end, Labour still scraped home with a majority of just six, with Attlee still Prime Minister, the ailing Bevin and Cripps still at the Foreign Office and Treasury, and Morrison still omnipresent, an ageing team intent on grim, bunker-like survival and little else. The King's Speech for the 1950 parliament contained no novelties other than implementing the last rites of the public ownership of iron and steel, to which the Lords had reluctantly agreed just before the election. Two nations were clearly emerging in England—though the distinct cultures of Wales and Scotland made the position more complicated there. There were the massed clients of a decade of welfare and state subsidy and provision, and the salaried rebels against the servile state. Each stood their ground, with only limited contact or parley with the other side, military service for young men being a partial exception.

One continuing theme on which both sides could agree was the important role of Britain in world affairs. Labour continued to place a heavy emphasis on this, and to try to steal the initiative in foreign policy from Churchill, whose independent gestures on behalf of a united Europe or a tougher stance towards the Russians had made a considerable international impact.

Britain emerged from the economic crisis of 1947 in a clearly dependent posture upon the United States. The further retreat of the devaluation of the pound in September 1949 reinforced Britain's decline from greatness in the popular estimation (though not in that of professional economists). Nevertheless, government and opposition alike, with the warm approval of the public, continued to insist that Britain was still a major, inspirational force within the Western alliance and the Anglo-American relationship. Bevin took the lead in promoting further transatlantic co-operation in political relationships as well as in defence throughout 1948 and 1949. The creation of NATO in April 1949, with its loose structure and distinctly functional character, bore very much the stamp of British origin.[19] It ensured, in Bevin's view, Britain's continued influence within the charmed circle of the superpowers. This view was discreetly and effectively promoted by Oliver Franks, an Oxford don of rare diplomatic gifts, who went to the Washington embassy in 1948 and built up a close rapport with Dean Acheson, Averell Harriman, and other key US administration figures. The 'special relationship' might be largely an academic fiction but it was one to which the Americans paid deference and gave encouragement, notably in encouraging Britain's continuing dominance in the Middle East, in building up its defence bases in Egypt and Jordan after the retreat from Palestine. Whatever Britain's manifest economic weakness and the liabilities incurred by maintaining sterling as an international currency, her political and strategic influence, especially through the enduring presence of a world-wide

[19] See Nicholas Henderson, *The Birth of NATO* (London, 1982).

commonwealth, gave her importance beyond her physical means. The defence budget, a vast range of commitments from Hong Kong to British Honduras, with a gradual build-up of the share of the budget devoted to defence from 1948 onwards (quite apart from the secret massive expenditure on nuclear weapons) perpetuated this stance and this illusion.

Britain's pivotal role in international affairs emerged again in 1950. There were by now serious differences with the United States, notably over the British decision to recognize Communist China and have no truck with the revanchist aims of Chiang Kai Shek, based on the remnants of the Kuomintang regime in the island of Formosa. However, when the Korean War broke out on 25 June 1950, it was taken as axiomatic by the Attlee Cabinet both that Britain should support the 'United Nations' force in Korea (in effect, an American army under General Douglas MacArthur) and also that it would gain renewed prestige in Washington and elsewhere in so doing. Oliver Franks urged Attlee that, if only on political grounds, Britain ought to send a military detachment to Korea to fight alongside the Americans, to confirm its position as 'first in the queue' at Washington.[20] There was not much disagreement in Britain. Even *Tribune* agreed that the invasion of South Korea by the North was proven and that Labour should further divest itself of the pre-war reputation of craven and pusillanimous appeasement of aggressors.[21] Bevan went along with this view. The 'glorious Gloucesters' won fame in Korea thereafter. The old anti-Americanism was in retreat at this time, though it was soon to revive in full measure. The future seemed to belong to younger, pro-American technocrats like Hugh Gaitskell, whose close relationship with US economists in working out the European Payments Union in 1950 gave him a feeling of mid-Atlantic rapport with New Dealer liberals like Kennan, Harriman, and especially Dean Acheson ('a sensitive and cultured mind'), all of impeccable Ivy

[20] Franks to Attlee, 15 July 1950 (PREM 8/1045, pt. 1).
[21] *Tribune*, 30 June, 28 July 1950.

League background.[22] Britain was maintaining its international stature through the strategy of cultural osmosis of the American style.

The truth or vulnerability of this thesis emerged poignantly in the winter of 1950–1. The sudden change in the Korean War resulting from MacArthur's decision to take the initiative and advance through North Korea towards the Manchurian border, aroused fears of a widening of the conflict. These fears were emphasized when tens of thousands of Chinese 'volunteers' entered the war on behalf of North Korea. British fears were confirmed when, in some loosely phrased comments in a press conference on 30 November, President Truman appeared to consider the possible use of nuclear weapons in Korea. Attlee promptly flew to Washington where he took it upon himself to reassert the 'special relationship' as understood in Britain. Several days of discussion took place in Washington, the only British representatives being present being Attlee himself and Oliver Franks.[23] As presented in Britain, the outcome was that British calm and statesmanship managed to restrain trigger-happy, impetuous Americans. Attlee reminded Truman and Acheson of Britain's long acquaintance with the Oriental mind through its centuries-old presence in India, and of the dangers of inflaming Asian passions through a direct attack on China. He returned to London to something of a hero's reception, one that reinforced his authority in the Labour Party. The Prime Minister told Bevin of how the British 'had been lifted out of the European queue [a variation of Franks's phrase] and were treated as partners, unequal no doubt in power but equal in counsel'.[24]

The reality was somewhat different. The main balance of the Anglo-American relationship survived. Franks himself did not believe the talks in Washington constituted any kind of turning-

[22] Gaitskell's diary, 9 Nov. 1951 (Nuffield College Library).
[23] Record of conversations, 4–8 Dec. 1950 (PREM 8/1200).
[24] Attlee to Bevin, 10 Dec. 1950 (FO 800/517).

point.[25] The price of US agreement to consult its allies on the use of nuclear weapons (a pledge somewhat obscurely phrased and only grudgingly carried out) was a severe one. Britain had to accept a steeply rising defence programme—a rearmament budget of €4,700 m. over the 1951–4 period was forced on the British Cabinet, one that led to deep concern amongst ministers, not only left-wingers like Bevan but also centrists like Dalton and Ede. In addition, Britain agreed to promote the so-called 'Spofford Plan', the highly contentious cause of the rearmament of Western Germany as part of a European force. Again, no American assistance was forthcoming in modifying the rapid rise of the cost of raw materials, the consequence of US stockpiling and an appalling burden for the British balance of payments. The long-term consequences of the Washington talks were harmful both for the British economy and the internal cohesion of the Cabinet. They were followed by Britain's reluctant support for the US position in endorsing the so-called 'Brand China' resolution in the United States, which even the ailing Bevin opposed. Britain's influence in Washington slowly eroded, a process taken further when Morrison succeeded Bevin as Foreign Secretary in March 1951 and proceeded to demonstrate his own unease in the handling of foreign affairs. Nevertheless, the deceptive image of the Anglo-American special relationship continued to shine brightly and to flatter national esteem.

Elsewhere, British authority overseas seemed to be confirmed. In Europe, the Bevin concept of 'Western Union', rather than any more integrated kind of federal or other unity, seemed to govern developments. The euphoria kindled by the European Convention at The Hague in May 1948 somewhat dissipated, with the British Labour government declining to be officially represented. The Council of Europe inaugurated at Strasbourg in September 1949 followed the British model in being largely a talking-shop in which delegates were in some sense representatives of government. The fact that the British delegation to Strasbourg was

[25] Private information, Lord Franks.

headed by the notoriously prejudiced Hugh Dalton, with his bitter hostility towards Germany, seemed a guarantee that Europe would remain in fragmented condition.[26]

However, the potential of the British in exercising a permanent control over the future development of western Europe was increasingly challenged by other European powers, the French especially, as they themselves began to recover from the economic devastation of the war. The British Foreign Office strained every sinew to undervalue or frustrate European moves towards greater unity. It was argued that the centuries of Franco-German hostility dating from the time of Charlemagne, the urge of Germans for reunification with their fellow-nationals in the East, the internal divisions of Belgium over language and the monarchy, the post-fascist weakness of Italy, the comparative irrelevance of the Dutch and Luxembourgeois, would ensure that all grand designs for closer unity would founder. A rude shock came in May 1950, therefore, when Robert Schuman, the French Foreign Minister, suddenly promoted the idea of a European coal and steel community, a grouping that would include Western Germany. Bevin rebuffed it angrily, complaining that he had been given no public warning.[27] But it was clear that Schuman had framed his proposals in such a way that British non-participation was assumed anyway. Britain argued that the Commonwealth relationship, her association with the United States, the planning priorities of the nationalized British coal and steel industries all opposed participation in the Schuman plan. A party document drawn up by Denis Healey in the Party's International Department (and somewhat embarrassingly leaked to the press) argued bluntly against such a scheme. But the Schuman Plan went ahead anyway and by 1951 was clearly visualized as the basis of a broader, more ambitious European commercial and industrial

---

[26] See e.g. Dalton to Attlee, 10 Sept. 1949 (London School of Economics, Dalton Papers, 9/7/45).

[27] Record of conversation of Bevin, Acheson, and Schuman, 11 May 1950 (FO 371/85341).

grouping. Ministers in the Labour government, Gaitskell, Kenneth Younger, even Sir Stafford Cripps, wondered how Britain could stay on the sidelines away from a powerful European market from which its products were increasingly to be excluded.[28] By now, with the French and Germans going ahead with their concept of a European Army, and plans for Western European atomic collaboration as well, it was clear that European developments were outstripping Britain's capacity to control them. Morrison, in his much-derided period at the Foreign Office, March–October 1951, tried with some success to build bridges and modify a growing isolation. By the downfall of the Attlee government in October 1951 it was widely believed that the immediate post-war phase of British leadership of 'Western Union' in Europe, through the agency of OEEC, the Payments Union, and the Brussels treaty, was coming to a rapid end.

Britain's international pretensions received another rude awakening in 1951, in the Middle East. The transfer of power in India had been well received and in many ways presented as a triumph of planned statesmanship. Little of this could be argued in the Persian oil crisis of April 1951 when the Persian government, under a violent nationalist, Dr Mussadiq, nationalized the Anglo-Iranian oil company and its installations at Abadan. Britain's old client control over Persia, dating from the deposition of the old Shah in 1941, and in some respect from the entente with Tsarist Russia in 1907, was under direct threat. The British government debated the military options, with Herbert Morrison and Emanuel Shinwell, the Defence Secretary, urging, in bellicose terms, the need to send British troops to Abadan. A large military task force, code-named 'Buccaneer', was drawn up with the object of dispatching brigades of troops, backed up by warships and perhaps aircraft carriers, to the Persian Gulf.[29] However,

---

[28] See e.g. transcript of Younger interview (Nuffield College Library); material in FO 371/85842).

[29] Confidential annexes to Chiefs of Staff committee, 11, 17 July 1951 (DEFE 4/45).

important voices in the Cabinet argued against military interven-tion. Dalton, Ede, and more surprisingly the Chancellor, Gaits-kell, argued that an open-ended military attack on Abadan would be costly and would dangerously inflame Arab powers with whom Britain hoped to maintain good relations.[30] A vital factor was that the Americans were hostile to British involvement, both through a general hostility towards British colonialism and also because the USA itself had a powerful economic presence in the Middle East, through its own Arabian oil concern, 'Aramco'. Attlee himself was much impressed by this, and in the end the British withdrew from a projected invasion of Abadan, leaving Churchill to jibe at national humiliation resulting from 'Abadan, Sudan, and Bevan', and giving Mossadiq, for the moment, a notable triumph over the old imperialist powers. Basically, Brit-ain was withdrawing from the Persian oilfields because its mili-tary and naval strike power, and its diplomatic weight, were insufficient to maintain the pretensions of an imperial past. On the positive side, however, the Labour government did refrain from the kind of tactical disaster that the Eden government was to experience at Suez, five years later.

Elsewhere in the Middle East, Britain's position was harder to sustain. Against the client relationship existing with Iraq and Jor-dan, there was increasing pressure from Arab nationalism in Egypt. In October 1951, while the British general election was in full swing, the Egyptian government associated itself with violent anti-British demonstrations. These called for the immediate with-drawal of British troops from the Suez Canal Zone, and also for the annexation of neighbouring Sudan by Egypt. The future of the canal itself suddenly seemed uncertain. Once again Morrison ('bloody little fool', in Dalton's view) urged the possible use of force, Attlee demurring as he had done over Abadan.[31] Once

---

[30] Cabinet conclusion, 2 July 1951 (CAB 128/20); Gaitskell's diary, 11 May 1951.
[31] Morrison to Attlee, 12 Oct. 1951 (PREM 8/1388. pt. III); Dalton's diary, 27 Sept. 1951.

again, Britain's difficulty in maintaining its position in a region long thought of as a national preserve, containing as it did the strategic 'lifeline of Empire' in the canal, was fully demonstrated.

Elsewhere in Africa, the colonial version of 'consolidation', emphasizing colonial partnership and development rather than immediate decolonization was also under some threat. In West Africa, riots in the Gold Coast conflicted with the stately pace towards internal self-government set by the Colonial Office in London. The main area of conflict between African nationalist and Britain's post-imperial control came, however, in southern Africa. The Colonial Secretary, James Griffiths (with some hesitation) and the Commonwealth Secretary, Patrick Gordon Walker (with no reservations at all) pressed hard the case for a Central African Federation consisting of Northern Rhodesia and Nyasaland, both overwhelmingly black African in their population, and Southern Rhodesia with its powerful and influential white settler minority.[32] This was a policy originating from the postwar planning enthusiasm of Whitehall mandarins. Andrew Cohen, the so-called 'King of Africa' at the Colonial Office, strongly pressed the case for a Federation on economic and commercial grounds and also (less convincingly) on the basis that a Central African Federation would be a useful buffer against South African encroachment and pressure. Federation was indeed a popular Colonial Office panacea at this time. From the point of view of the British Labour government there were powerful arguments in favour. From the point of view of the black population of the three African territories, there were none, since it appeared likely to rivet upon all of them the ascendancy of white-run Southern Rhodesia, with its quasi-racist supremacy close to the apartheid regime now being administered by the Nationalist government of Dr Malan in South Africa. A conference at Victoria Falls in September 1951 showed the vehement resistance of blacks in Nyasaland and Northern

[32] Memorandum by Griffiths and Gordon-Walker, 25 Apr. 1951 (DO 121/36) and Robert Blake, *A History of Rhodesia* (London, 1977), 248ff.

Rhodesia to the idea of a Federation. Southern Rhodesia's blacks, significantly, were not present at all but were deemed to be represented by a (white) Minister for Native Affairs in the delegation headed by Sir Godfrey Huggins. A memorandum signed by Griffiths and Gordon Walker on 5 October still endorsed the principle of a Federation on political and economic grounds,[33] but blacks unanimously insisted it would mean a loss of land, and threats to their political and social advancement. Here again, British colonial designs were coming up against the realities of third-world opinion, and becoming infinitely harder to impose.

Yet, in spite of all these manifold challenges and occasional retreats, Britain emerged from the Attlee period apparently still a power of the front rank whose authority in the transatlantic alliance, in OEEC, or in the United Nations Security Council outran its physical and financial resources. The main fabric of Commonwealth/Empire remained in being. Indeed, in Malaya the British army was engaged in a difficult and lengthy guerrilla war against Communist insurgents. The British defence budget had been expanded since 1948, not only in response to American pressure, but also to maintain the colonial presence in a variety of sensitive areas. The Middle East remained an area of particular British authority, notably through the mediation of Nuri-al-said in Iraq, and proconsular figures like General Glubb of the Arab legion. Covertly, the British independent nuclear weapons programme was progressing towards the testing stage, despite the well-publicized defections of fellow-travelling scientists like Klaus Fuchs. Test sites in the Pacific and in northern Australia were already in preparation. With a united Europe still far off, the Commonwealth mostly intact, and the relationship with the Americans at least more tranquil after the Attlee–Truman talks, Britain's great-power status remained a tenet of policy. Whatever surrenders or sacrifices took place at home, the wider impact of

[33] Memorandum, 'Closer Association in Central Africa', 5 Oct. 1951 (DO 121/138).

'consolidationist', Labour-run Britain remained consoling to the national psyche.

Gradually, the national mood was changing as the euphoria and solidarity of wartime victory receded from memory. Despite the continuing rigours of austerity, there was a reviving protest of individualism and consumerism. The French have noted the rising tide of *anti-étatisme* from 1948 onwards, notably in the halting of further nationalization. The same phenomenon is detectable in the Netherlands, and in the split in the Italian Socialists in 1948, while the defeat of the Social Democrats in the first Federal German elections in 1949, at the hands of Dr Konrad Adenauer's CDU, confirmed this trend. So it was in Britain, too. The presence of so stern an arbiter of national affairs as Stafford Cripps, apparently the very model of planning and control, in fact implied something like the opposite. Despite his left-wing past, Cripps was now a strong advocate of the mixed economy. His creed implied partnership with private industry, through the mediation of the Economic Planning Council under Plowden, and encouraging private investment and entrepreneurial initiative. Despite evidence to the contrary, his regime meant in some ways a retreat from planning, not its consolidation. Harold Wilson at the Board of Trade became the instrument of at least a partial policy of decontrol. Thousands of licences and other physical restrictions were dismantled, to the dismay of the *New Statesman* on the left which spoke of 'rationing by price'.[34] The rise of Keynesian economists like Gaitskell and Jay in the government implied an emphasis on financial and budgetary management as much as on physical control. Wilson's famous 'bonfire' of controls in 1949 saw the Tawneyesque ethos of wartime control,[35] as well as thousands of ration books and 'points', go up in smoke. Labour was by 1950 well advanced towards what soon came to be called 'Butskellism' (a composite

[34] *New Statesman*, 19 Mar., 4 June 1949.
[35] R. H. Tawney, 'The Abolition of Economic Controls, 1918–21'. *Economic History Review* (1944).

of the supposed Butler–Gaitskell consensus), with the rationing first of clothes and then petrol done away with. Food, however, other than sweets, remained strictly controlled.

This policy of relaxation seemed to accord with general sentiment. The controls of post-war, however necessary, were irksome and unpopular. They were often believed to generate corruption through covert practices of the kind associated with Sidney Stanley in the Lynskey Tribunal into alleged ministerial corruption in 1949. In this, the ethos of decontrol, flavoured in part by anti-Semitism, came across clearly. Further, the sheer effectiveness of physical controls, especially in the practical allocation of raw materials and ending bottlenecks of supplies, was increasingly questioned. The cultural mood of the time also appeared to be challenging the legacy of wartime collectivism. This can be seen in the personality of the egregious Widmerpool, the left-wing anti-hero of Anthony Powell's novels in the *Dance to the Music of Time* sequence, beginning with *A Question of Upbringing* in 1951. Widmerpool, who moves on from fellow-travelling Labour MP in the 1940s to elderly 'trendy' in a hippy commune in the 1960s, embodies at least one personal vision of the post-war power élite. Angus Wilson was another novelist whose short stories and novels encouraged the creed of individual self-expression and contained a gentle (or not so gentle) ridicule of the Fabian religion of austerity and rectitude.[36] The mood was not so much anti-socialist as sceptical or quizzical. The certainties of post-war planning seemed harder to reconcile with a fluid, confused world while, in a climate of Crippsian Anglican severity, cheerfulness kept breaking through.

On the one hand, conservatism, both politically and in apolitical guise, was making a distinct recovery. The Conservative Party came close to electoral victory in February 1950, with 'Fred' Woolton the presiding genius. Its Research Department suggested an intellectual vitality less evident on the Labour side.

---

[36] In *Those Darting Dodos* and later in *Hemlock and After*, which deals with the loss of faith of Bernard and Isobel Sands, progressive thirties left-wingers.

The new generation of Tory MPs in 1950—Reginald Maudling, Ian Macleod, Edward Heath, Enoch Powell—embodied a buoyancy and contemporaneity, with the memories of guilt for the thirties and Munich duly purged. They campaigned against rationing and controls, but in a constructive way rather than in terms of pre-war private enterprise. No Bourbons here. On the other side, the left seemed to be losing some of its emotional and intellectual underpinning. The declining self-confidence of the literary left was a feature of the late 1940s, with the bold cultural experimentalism of the war years largely set aside. The air was full of intellectual recantation of the 'God that failed' variety; indeed, Richard Crossman, a left Labour MP, edited the symposium that bore this title. The omnipresent threat from Stalinist Russia, as it was perceived at the time, extending even to socialist Yugoslavia, fostered this mood.

No work is more indicative of the change than George Orwell's *Nineteen Eighty-Four*, following up themes already announced in *Animal Farm* and even in *Homage to Catalonia* before the war. George Orwell remained a socialist, though of a distinctly libertarian kind hard to compartmentalize. He kept his links with *Tribune* and the Hampstead intelligentsia, even from his retreat on a remote Scottish island. It could certainly be argued that *Nineteen Eighty-Four* is directed at centralization and conformism in all guises.[37] But the drift of his writing is obviously that of a crusade against the all-powerful centralizing state beloved of 1930s socialists, and the thought control and intellectual servility that went with it. Thereafter, literary socialists could only with difficulty retain the same pristine certainty in the components of their moral faith. Victor Gollancz, founder of the pre-war, effectively pro-Soviet, Left Book Club, was another apostate, who rediscovered God in the process.[38] Nor did the class appeal of the post-1945 period make the same impact

---

[37] See on this Bernard Crick. *George Orwell: A Life* (Harmondsworth, 1980), 561–71.

[38] See Victor Gollancz, *My Dear Timothy* (London, 1952) on this.

amongst Labour's old evangelists. Herbert Morrison was prominent amongst those rebuking his comrades for dated class-war
stereotypes. Labour, he urged, should appeal to 'the useful
people', a category which did not exclude businessmen, bankers,
and others drawn from Labour's demonology. T. R. Fyvel was
another left-wing literary and political commentator who
observed the decline of a 'Labourish' public mood, and linked
it in part with a diminution of insularity.[39] The wider public now
saw the uniformity and egalitarianism of earlier rhetoric as more
drab than inspiring. It was noticed that J. B. Priestley's populist-
style election broadcasts in 1950 had decidedly less impact upon
the electoral conscience than they had in 1945. Edward Hulton,
proprietor of the left-wing illustrated magazine *Picture Post*,
joined the Conservatives in 1950 and sacked the old radical
editor, Tom Hopkinson, for anti-American comments during
the Korean War.[40] The 'thin red line' of the Labourish intelligentsia, with its bastions in NW3, Great Turnstile, and Bush
House, was breaking ranks.

Population movements may have been accelerating this trend.
The older concept of national unity implied a relatively static
society cast into the set divisions of Neville Chamberlain's Britain
of the 1930s—'England, your England'. In fact, the 1951 population census, the first for twenty years, revealed what mass
observation had long suggested, that the population was distinctly on the move. The growth of a managerial/professional
class, the fragmentation of the workforce after 1945 into myriad
grades of skill and status, the uprooting of old industrial communities, above all the explosive growth of commuter suburbs
around London, Birmingham, Glasgow, and other cities encouraged a greater physical mobility. The drift from older industrial
centres in the North, Scotland, and South Wales was very
marked. The ideological postures and the political polarization

[39] See Fyvel's *Intellectuals Today* (London, 1968) and his articles in *Tribune* in
1949–50.
[40] Tom Hopkinson, *Of this our Time* (London, 1982), 272.

of 1947–51 might suggest rigidity, but the social reality was a far greater process of movement as politicians varying from Anthony Crosland on the left to Iain Macleod on the right were well aware. In particular, the distance and irrelevance of pre-war social stereotypes bred a growing reluctance to accept time-worn disciplines. In that sense, Labour's election slogan 'Ask your Dad' (significantly not 'Your Mum') may have been misconceived. An official cult of sexual and cultural puritanism conflicted with the emergent consumer culture, impatience, or plain boredom of young people with a drab welfarized society, and an urge to create a land fit for consumers to shop in. By 1950 a new social category, the 'teenager', employed and with money to spend, had been created. Britain in the late 1940s was still a land run by the elderly in a society in which the undeferential young were maturing ever more rapidly. Beyond the fluidities of working-class life, other points of division were suggested by the significant presence for the first time of non-white Commonwealth immigrants. They were heralded by the first migration of West Indian migrants, mostly from Jamaica, in 1948, followed by many thousands more from India and Pakistan. In 1950 the British Cabinet for the first time recognized the presence of a large nonwhite community as a potential flash-point as far as inner-city housing, social provision, and community relations were concerned.[41] Nothing, however, was done. New sources of friction and conflict emerged thereby.

Many of these social and cultural forces working against the cohesion of post-war Britain were latent and only of long-term impact. But in 1951 they were reinforced by overt political challenge as well. In the post-war period, the Labour movement had shown a rare unity and fraternity. Party morale was high, and individual membership rising. Annual party conferences were almost ritual occasions for acclaiming the leadership in Roman imperial style. Aneurin Bevan was a particular favourite,

[41] Cabinet conclusions, 28 Mar. 1950 (CAB 128/17).

though ironically it was he who fell foul of a conference at Margate in 1947 when he bluntly refused to accept a hostile motion passed in censure of his policy regarding tied cottages for agricultural labourers.[42] The National Executive was safely dominated by ministers like Attlee, Dalton, Morrison, and Griffiths. Underpinning it all was the close liaison between the party and the TUC which kept party conference loyal, and worked closely with Attlee and his ministers in maintaining a right-wing majority on the NEC, and in keeping support for the government even in the face of such problems as a wage freeze and devaluation of the pound. It is true that the unions' compliance owed much to the domination of the notoriously undemocratic party structure by the large unions all under right-wing leadership— the Transport Workers under Arthur Deakin, the General Workers under Tom Williamson, and the Mineworkers under Will Lawther, who cogently told a critic at party conference to 'shut your gob'. Left-inclined unions such as the Railwaymen or the Electricians were simply outvoted on the card vote system. It is true also that there was much covert dissent in the ranks of the party and the TUC which was swept under the table by the adroit manœuvring of Morgan Phillips. Labour's General Secretary. The left wing of the party could well complain of undemocratic tactics by the right, as could the right in their turn in the 1970s. Even so, when all qualifications and distortions have been accounted for, there does seem to have been a broad congruence of attitude between Labour leaders and the rank and file after 1945, a genuine respect for, and deference to, the leadership unique in Labour's troubled history. A party which prided itself on its populism and internal democracy, now proclaimed its eternal solidarity with 'Clem', 'Herbert', and their comrades.

But by 1949 there were clear signs that this mood of unwonted fraternity on the left was beginning to change. The unions were now becoming restive. Two points of conflict in particular arose,

[42] Resolutions on housing at Margate conference, 1947 (HLG 102/60).

both domestic, though Peter Weiler has argued that grass-roots resentment at Cold War foreign policies played some part also, for instance in the 1949 dock strike.[43] The first issue was the continuance of wartime restrictions on the right to strike, notably Order 1305 passed in 1940. Although in some ways popular with the unions, since it forced reluctant employers to accept arbitration awards, it was increasingly resented by rank-and-file unions who saw the erosion of differentials and continuing austerity.[44] More serious was opposition to the wage-freeze policy at a time of gently rising prices. There was a gulf between those whose wages were frozen and those able to raise earnings through 'wage drift'. By 1949 this was leading to strain. In 1948 and then in 1949 there were lengthy unofficial strikes, especially in the docks, which led the Attlee government to implement the 1920 Emergency Powers Act, proclaim a state of emergency and use troops as strike-breakers in unloading vessels in London, Liverpool, and Avonmouth.[45] Lord Ammon and the Dock Labour Board claimed to see the active hand of the Communist Party amongst the stevedores. The Cabinet's Emergency Committee was of one mind on this issue. Aneurin Bevan, the darling of the left, declared that emergency action was inevitable to prevent a socialist government being undermined at a critical moment by indiscipline and subversion.[46] Even so, it was clear that great hostility was being aroused by this strong action amongst rank-and-file dockers; here Communist shop stewards such as the young Jack Dash were active. The Attlee government continued to have recourse to Emergency Powers in 1950–1, perhaps the heyday of the anti-Communist passions of the time. In March 1951 a national railway strike was threatened, which led Bevan, now the Minister of Labour in place of the cautious right-wing

[43] Peter Weiler, *British Labour and the Cold War* (Stanford, Calif., 1988), especially 23off.

[44] Memorandum by R. M. Gould, Ministry of Labour, 4 July 1950 (LAB 10/975).

[45] Minutes of Cabinet Emergencies Committee, 21 June–22 July 1949 (CAB 134/176).

[46] Ibid. 28 June 1948 (CAB 134/175).

trade unionist, George Isaacs, to defend the NUR in breaching the national guide-lines for wages policy.[47] Even more severe was the imprisonment of ten North Thames Gas Board workers, not all of them Communists by any means, for defiantly embarking on strike action in October 1950 in the face of Order 1305. Gaitskell spoke gloomily of Communist involvement in strike activities in major power stations.[48] The government found more and more resistance. By mid-1951, the wage freeze was over, voted down by the TUC, and wage inflation, helped by the 'drift' factor, was on an upwards curve. Order 1305, a relic of wartime solidarity, was now destined for oblivion, partly because the new Attorney-General, Frank Soskice, himself doubted its validity.[49] One way and another, trade-union militancy was eroding the government's façade of unity.

Further opposition was growing over foreign policy. The very rigidity of Stalinist Russia had made the position of left-wing critics of Bevin's foreign policy very difficult in 1947–50. Aneurin Bevan himself was in hawkish mood in 1948 and urged that the Berlin airlift be backed up by the dispatch of allied tanks through the Eastern zone of Germany to relieve the Socialist administration of West Berlin. The pressure by the Soviet Union upon Tito's Yugoslavia, long a regime popular with the Labour left and syndicalist elements in the trade unions, further weakened the critics of foreign policy. So, too, did the Communist 'coup' in Czechoslovakia in 1948. When the Korean War broke out in June 1950, since a handful of left-wing dissidents, Zilliacus, Solley, Hutchinson, and Platts-Mills, had now been expelled from the party, only one or two fellow-travelling mavericks, notably the Welshmen S.O. Davies and Emrys Hughes, opposed the government's action in backing up the Americans in sending troops to defend South Korea against invasion from the North.

---

[47] Cabinet conclusions, 22 Feb. 1951 (CAB 128/19); Alfred Barnes to Attlee, 21 Feb. 1951 (LAB 10/1021) in which he criticized Bevan's attitude.
[48] Gaitskell to Attlee 24 Dec. 1949 (PREM 8/1290).
[49] Soskice memorandum for Robens, 3 July 1931 (LAB 43/157).

Nevertheless, the show of unity was hard to maintain in these grim Cold War circumstances. In the constituencies, support for men like Konni Zilliacus who attacked British Cold War postures was widespread, especially in London suburban constituencies.[50] The old 'Keep Left' group of 1947 showed signs of re-forming, and the constituency section of the NEC elections showed a shift to the left in both 1950 and 1951. The shock induced by General MacArthur's extension of the Korean War to the Chinese borders, the fear of nuclear weaponry to which it was now known Britain was a contributor, above all the immensity of the rearmament programme imposed upon Attlee and his government by American pressure from January 1951 onwards made for a growing sense of unease about the drift of British policy. In Cabinet, even such centrist or right-wing ministers as Chuter Ede, James Griffiths, and Hugh Dalton were vocal about the belligerence of British policy, apparently at American behest. A rising tide of anti-Americanism was reported, with American GIs stationed in Britain amongst the victims.

This kind of critique was formless and lacking in direction, however, until the start of 1951. No one expected the government to buckle, still less fall, in the face of the challenge of left-wing backbenchers like Hughes, Silverman, or S.O. Davies, let alone Driberg who was abroad an undue amount of the time anyway. But then there emerged the potential defection of a major figure—Aneurin Bevan, the hero of the National Health Service, the favourite of the constituency left, unquestionably a rebel of stature. Bevan had long been unhappy with the course of government policy on the home front—the cuts in the housing programme in 1949, the threat to impose prescription charges and then charges on teeth and spectacles by Cripps. However, on foreign policy he had been generally quiescent, and prepared to endorse both NATO and a growing rearmament programme. In the winter of 1950–1, however, he saw the defence budget

---

[50] Material in Morgan Phillips's General Secretary's files. Labour Party archives.

escalate to unprecedented levels at American dictation. Further-more, the Chancellor involved was the right-wing Wykehamist, Hugh Gaitskell, for whom Bevan had no particular respect and whose position as Chancellor he had coveted. Attlee himself must bear some part of the blame since he made no attempt to promote Bevan to major office. He allowed him to soldier on at the Ministry of Health until January 1951, shouldering the burden of rising NHS estimates. Bevan was turned down for the Colonial Office in 1950 because he was, apparently, thought too sympathetic to black members of the Commonwealth.[51] He was then passed over for the Treasury in October 1950 in favour of his junior, Gaitskell, and then for the Foreign Office in March 1951 in favour of another *bête noire*, Morrison. As a result, Bevan was a disaffected and dangerous man.

His growing unhappiness over both domestic and foreign pol-icy came together in dramatic fashion when Gaitskell launched his new initiatives in January–March 1951. Ironically, Gaitskell, an academic economist, was mainly moved by political consider-ations such as the need to back up the Americans. To conciliate them, he proposed a new £4,700 m. arms budget, as has been seen. To help pay the bill, he proposed small charges on dental and ophthalmic treatment, thus making inroads into Bevan's prize achievement of a free health service. Gaitskell had long favoured health-service charges on financial grounds. He made little effort to conciliate Bevan whom he regarded as a political enemy, even though he knew Bevan regarded this as a fundamen-tal issue of principle. Bevan fought the NHS charges furiously in Cabinet in March,[52] handicapped by the fact that his successor at Health, Hilary Marquand, a mild-mannered Welsh professor of economics, was not in the Cabinet. Many ministers at first sup-ported Bevan, including Wilson, Tomlinson, Ede, and Griffiths, It could also be plausibly claimed that the finances of the NHS were now under control with the new ceiling on expenditure imposed

---

[51] Dalton diaries, 27 Feb. 1950.
[52] Cabinet conclusion, 22 Mar. 1951 (CAB 128/19).

in April 1950. In any event, the money raised from health service charges was a mere £23 m. in a full year (only £13 m. in the balance of the financial year 1951–2), a trivial amount in the global budget, but enough to inflame party passions without making any real contribution to defence expenditure. Gaitskell, however, dug in, with the support of Morrison, Dalton, and, it seemed, Attlee himself. Under pressure from the ailing former Foreign Secretary, Bevin, he agreed to abandon prescription charges on 20 March on condition that dental and ophthalmic charges were increased.[53] Bevan found himself gradually isolated, Griffiths, Ede, and Tomlinson slowly melting away, and with only the unexpected support of Harold Wilson, President of the Board of Trade, as his ally. In an off-the-cuff remark to an angry audience of dockers at Bermondsey on 3 April, Bevan declared that he would resign from the government if NHS charges were introduced in the coming budget.[54]

The debate was now widened in Cabinet to take in a wider argument over the rearmament programme. Attlee, along with mainly right-wing figures like Gaitskell, Dalton, Younger, and Gordon Walker, later claimed to be astonished that Bevan had broadened the area of contention since they had previously believed that Bevan was content with the rearmament programme as part of Britain's inevitable contribution to the western alliance; he had defended it in the House as recently as mid-February. But this is disingenuous. Bevan's opposition to an expanded rearmament programme, partly on economic grounds, partly because it would raise new dangers in meeting the ideological challenge of communism, had been stated in full Cabinet as early as August 1950. He had strongly resisted the new defence budget on 25 January 1951, declaring it to be impractical as well as socially damaging.[55] It was widely known that Bevan was discontented, both with particular and with general policies,

[53] Gaitskell diary, 30 Apr. 1951.   [54] *News Chronicle*, 9 Apr. 1951.
[55] Cabinet conclusions, 1 Aug. 1950 (CAB 128/18) and 25 Jan. 1951 (ibid., 128/19).

and that he was talking to Michael Foot and other confidants of possible resignation.

At the start of April, there was a straight trial of strength between Gaitskell and Bevan. The position was made more difficult by the presence of Morrison acting as Prime Minister since Attlee himself was temporarily in St Mary's Hospital for an operation. This inflamed passions still further. In the event, Gaitskell, who had threatened resignation if his financial proposals were turned down (including a £400 m. ceiling on health expenditure),[56] received general endorsement. The only concessions he made were to agree that charges would not be introduced from the very date of the budget and that they would last for only one year in the first instance; a separate health services charges bill would be introduced alongside the Finance Bill. Bevan was beside himself with rage, denouncing Gaitskell for his reckless assault on 'my Health Service', and refused all compromise. A last-minute attempt at mediation by the dying Ernest Bevin failed. On 20 April Bevan resigned from the Cabinet, followed by Harold Wilson, and also by John Freeman, a junior minister at the Ministry of Supply. There was a furious row in the parliamentary Labour Party, while Bevan's inflammatory statement in the House of Commons was generally considered a failure because of its personal attacks on Gaitskell. Dalton murmured comparisons with the fascist, Mosley.[57] The weekly *Tribune* included a passionate denunciation of Gaitskell by Michael Foot, who compared the Chancellor with the traitor, Philip Snowden, who had left the party in 1931.[58] Gaitskell's programme caused widespread unhappiness in Labour ranks. A fortnight later, a group of fifteen left-wing MPs, including Bevan, formed a new parliamentary grouping. In effect, the 'Bevanites' had come into being, and a long-term civil war within the labour movement was duly launched.

[56] Gaitskell's diary, 30 Apr. 1951.   [57] Dalton's diary, 24 Apr. 1951.
[58] *Tribune*, 20 Apr. 1951.

The resignation of Aneurin Bevan, and the resultant divisions in the party, marked a notable divide in post-war politics. It left its impact in some respects down to the 1980s. In place of two relatively monolithic mass parties, each secure in their nationwide support, the Conservatives were now to be confronted by a Labour Party increasingly prey to internal divisions, especially over foreign and defence policies. The pamphlet, *One Way Only* in July 1951, in itself a constructive and non-personalized document, was taken to be a manifesto by Bevan and the disaffected left, while pro-Bevan journalists such as Foot and Driberg now became crusaders for maintaining the purity of the socialist faith against opportunists and calculating machines, whether desiccated or not. Labour Party circles in NW3 and elsewhere (Gaitskell, Jay, Anthony Greenwood, and Foot all lived in Hampstead) were rent by suburban controversy. It became more difficult to formulate a coherent Labour platform to challenge the Conservatives. Certainly, the party's morale was at a low ebb, following Bevan's and Wilson's resignation and retreats over Persia and Egypt. A balance-of-payments crisis in September 1951, the product of US stockpiling of raw materials and made worse by Gaitskell's over-ambitious defence budget which had overheated the economy, added to the government's difficulties.[59] The October 1951 party conference was marked by Bevanite gains in the constituency party section of the elections to the National Executive, and a general air of bitterness and gloom. A compromise manifesto was cobbled together by left and right, by a committee that included Bevan and Dalton; but it was an uninspiring affair, notable for its lack of precision. The main emphasis was on the achievements of the past. No new initiatives were proposed, or even perhaps desired. When Attlee unexpectedly dissolved parliament in late September, informing a small Cabinet of his intention quite suddenly (at a time when Morrison and Gaitskell

[59] See minutes of Cabinet Economic Committee. June–Sept. 1951 (CAB 134/228).

were out of the country and unable to voice their disapproval),[60] Labour's expectations were low indeed.

These events suggested strongly a change in British political culture. The confident march of democratic socialism, heralded in wartime blueprints and the ascendancy of the reforming professional intelligentsia, had been halted, almost brutally. Labour suddenly looked like an ageing party. Not only were leaders like Attlee, Morrison, Dalton, and Shinwell advanced in years and lacking in physical energy after almost eleven years in office in war and peace. The very stance of the party was backward-looking. No new horizons were visualized. Apart from possible advance in secondary education towards multilateral schools, Labour had no novelties to offer on any front. Nationalization would in future be confined to (unspecified) industries that were 'failing the nation'. The manifesto was liberally sprinkled with phrases like 'where necessary'. The government of people had been followed, in the culture of 'consolidation', by the administration of things—and none too happily so. In some ways, the left-wing pressures against the government were less extreme than contemporary comment suggested. As noted, *One Way Only* was (in Michael Foot's words) 'an essay in qualified judgements'.[61] Bevan himself was something of a maverick figure, not really the spokesman of a clear socialist alternative. His book, *In Place of Fear*, a marvellously written work in places, published in early 1952, was also a rough assemblage of individual short discussions rather than a systematic analysis of a socialist position. Bevan himself, it became clear, was hardly a Bevanite. The trade unions were far less anarchic than the rash of 'unofficial' strikes suggested, and Communist leadership in these eruptions was much exaggerated.

The root trouble was really the wider disaffection of middle opinion (not necessarily middle-class opinion) against a programme of 'consolidation' which at best was drab and

---

[60] Cabinet conclusions, 19 Sept. 1951 (CAB 128/20).
[61] Michael Foot. *Aneurin Bevan*, ii (London, 1973). 342.

puritanical, and at worst illiberal and restrictive of individual choice. Centralization, 'red tape', and the image of civil servants drinking their tea became popular targets, in place of the admiration of the mandarin titans of Whitehall in the Beveridge era. Even if the Conservatives aroused only limited enthusiasm, and Churchill himself remained widely distrusted in working-class communities as a class warrior and a 'warmonger', the community spirit of the post-war years was eroding fast. Such British tourists as ventured to continental countries saw a France recapturing its sparkle and animation after years of defeat and occupation, cities like Paris and Amsterdam (admittedly having escaped enemy bombing) cheerful and relaxed, and even the defeated Germans rising fast from the ashes until by the end of 1951 their economic growth and industrial manufacturing had outstripped that of the victorious British. In a world showing distinct signs of recovery Britain offered a siege economy and a traditional culture. Like patriotism, it was not enough.

It is not remarkable that Labour duly lost the October 1951 general election. What is surprising is that the defeat was so very narrow. Despite the unhappy background to the campaign, Labour recovered rapidly in the polls, and the eventual Conservative majority was only fifteen seats, a result greeted with much joy on the left where a massacre had been expected.[62] What happened was that the sectionalism in society noted previously reasserted itself. In Labour's industrial and urban strongholds, the enthusiasm for 'our government' was very pronounced, the campaign vigorous, and the turn-out often well over 80 per cent of voters. The solidarity of large-scale mass industry and working-class community life remained emphatic. In Scotland and Wales, Labour's dominance continued, even extending to rural constituencies such as the Western Isles, Anglesey, and Merioneth. The Communist Party put up only a handful of candidates and made no impact. The Liberals reached their

[62] Dalton's diaries, 'end of October, 1951'—'the election results are wonderful'.

lowest ebb with only 109 candidates and a tally of just six seats. Conversely, the suburban middle-class constituencies of the Midlands and south-east England saw Labour's gains of 1945 dissipated. Eleven of the twenty-one Conservative gains from Labour were in Greater London, Bedfordshire, Buckinghamshire, and Berkshire. The years of austerity and *anti-étatisme* took their toll, if only marginally. Labour still polled more votes than the Conservatives and, with almost 14 million, more votes than any other party before or since. The twenty-odd gains the Conservatives made were sufficient to tip the scale and put Churchill back into Downing Street. But Labour's performance, at least in the campaign, was sufficiently effective for the party to look to the years of opposition that lay ahead with renewed confidence.

Attlee's Britain, and the consensus it supposedly embodied, later acquired an almost legendary status amongst historians and commentators. Conservatives could look back amiably at a government whose achievements the next thirteen years of Tory rule were in large measure to re-enact. Centrists and Labour right wingers, such as Shirley Williams and other pillars of the Social Democratic Party in 1981, saw Attlee's regime as symbolic of a broad-church, moderate, 'sensible socialism' in contrast to the excesses of Bevanism or Bennery. For Labour supporters, from Morrison on the right to Bevan on the left, the six years of Labour government were a period in which they took legitimate pride as a time of social partnership, purposive planning, and creative government. Here truly was Britain's 'middle way' of democratic socialism, the inspiration for third-world leaders in Africa and Asia and progressives around the world. Later generations looked back, not only to the full employment and social welfare of the 1940s, but also to the integrative disciplines of that society. Its popular emblems acquired immense public esteem and affection, from Stanley Matthews and the still-victorious English football team, through the Ealing Studios comedies, to the post-war holiday camp popularized in the television series of the 1980s, 'Hi de Hi'. Even the austerity, drab clothing, and poor food of that era were recalled with affection to show that Britain

could take it as well as make it, while social statisticians produced figures for health, child mortality, diseases affecting
mothers and the old to show the genuine benefits that Attlee's
Britain brought to the less fortunate and privileged of its citizens.
Sociologists' academic studies of 'British social trends' were, in
varying degrees, a hymn of praise to the social consensus of the
'centralized democratic polity' that Attlee and his men (with a
few women) embodied.[63]

It is clear, though, that this progress was achieved in spite of
(perhaps because of) the fact that basic questions about modernization of an ancient culture were not posed. Full employment
thrived in an economy in which the old staples, based on large
units of production, were the mainspring of life as they had been
prior to 1914. The export drive of 1947–50 glided over the re-
equipment and restructuring of the industrial base. The settled
structure of the nuclear family was the accepted base for social
provision, with women, although increasingly in permanent
employment, still regarded as social adjuncts of their menfolk. It
is difficult to see any real changes in social mores in this period, at
least as officially recognized. Women made no advances in their
social status, with equal pay in the teaching and other professions
still far from a reality. The admission of a (Jewish) woman
lawyer, Rose Heilbron, as a QC in 1949 and later to the judicial
bench caused widespread comment, if not astonishment. Black
citizens found the organization for dealing with their housing,
employment, and social integration to be minimal, with the
awareness of Britain as a multi-racial society very indistinct.
Young people conducted their private lives, with much social
and sexual experiment, in a disapproving, elderly world in
which the Victorian ethos still prevailed (witness the popular,
and highly sexist, children's books by such writers as Enid Blyton
in this period). Love and marriage were officially inseparable
concepts. Divorce bore a considerable social stigma, with much

---

[63] A. H. Halsey (ed.), *British Social Trends*, 18.

legal ingenuity found in unearthing 'co-respondents'; illegitimacy (at least in England and Scotland, though perhaps less so in rural Wales) remained a badge of dishonour which accounted for less than five per cent of births,[64] while the reform of the penal system was a deferred commitment, the 1948 Criminal Justice Act notwithstanding.

The Labour government of 1945–51, whatever its reformist aspirations, was never really a group of social radicals. They adhered to the empire; many of them believed in white supremacy; they, or most of them, upheld the extreme penalty of the rope; they refused to upset the miners by abolishing fox-hunting (popular in some mining areas at this time) or other traditional rural pursuits such as hare-coursing. Oddly enough, the great enemies, Bevan and Gaitskell, were two rare voices for libertarianism and permissiveness. Attlee himself, a devoted son of Haileybury and Oxford, an enthusiast for cricket and *The Times* crossword, whose wife, Vi, pottered in the flower beds while her husband dealt with high affairs of state, was a token of the continuities of this period of supposed socialist revolution. Nor was there any significant institutional reform. Repeated attempts to remodel the system of local government, a relic of Lord Salisbury's rule in the 1880s, foundered, not least because the Labour Party itself was so enmeshed in its operations from the London County Council downwards. Industrial relations were encased in the voluntarist mould, with unions and management locked into a traditional adversarial system, at variance with the norm as it emerged in post-war western Europe. For all the radicalism of several of its key figures, the civil service underwent no significant restructuring at all, nor did any proper inquiry into its operations take place until the Fulton Committee in 1966. Efforts to reform the House of Lords foundered in part because of the reluctance of Herbert Morrison to embark on a basic change by tampering with a revered English institution. 'We

[64] Ibid. 62ff.

should not set up something new and different from the past', Morrison told the Liberal leader, Clement Davies,[65] in words that might have puzzled old Liberals like Lloyd George or even Gladstone. The public schools returned to their pre-war glory, with crowds flocking to Eton and Harrow cricket matches at Lords in July, as they had done for decades past. At that same sporting stadium, the 'Gentlemen v. Players' fixture kept up the barrier between amateur and professional cricketers; the former lost the designation 'Mr' but still had their initials printed before their surname on score cards to distinguish them from their journeymen colleagues such as Hutton or Compton. The monarchy was, of course, inviolate, the modest, inarticulate figure of George VI and his popular wife, Queen Elizabeth, striking new roots with the populace by their very ordinariness, while still observing the time-worn ritual and ceremonial beloved of tourists.

It was, then, a comparatively conservative nation in which rapid legislative change and innovations in welfare were superimposed on a class and institutional structure which closely resembled pre-war years. Yet it was also, so it seemed, a generally content society, despite the austerity, deeply patriotic, certain of British greatness, and observing Empire Day in state schools every May with the same intensity as under the Raj. Opinion polls testified both to the acute dissatisfaction of the British at the trials of their daily lives, and to their more fundamental pride at being British. Few other nations showed less capacity for self-criticism or less certainty about national standards and values. Even if physical weakness was displayed in the rapid retreat from India and Palestine, even if the economy staggered through repeated balance-of-payments and sterling crises, the moral, political, and cultural capital of Britain, it was believed, stayed secure, the wonder of the world and the inspiration of allies. In the Anglo-American partnership, the British believed, the United

[65] Morrison to Davies, recorded in Davies's memorandum, 1947 (National Library of Wales. Davies Papers, C/1/35).

Kingdom almost effortlessly, with its reviving theatre, its profusion of literary and other journals, its public school élite, its links through the Rhodes scholarships and the English Speaking Union, played a confident Greece to the American Rome.

Less in the public gaze, British vitality in one area was particularly notable. Stemming from wartime research and development, the post-war years proved to be a flourishing period for British science in many fields. In medicine, Ernst Chain and Howard Florey developed the penicillin culture, an extraordinary breakthrough, while in radio-astronomy, Bernard Lovell pioneered the new satellite at Jodrell Bank, the pivot of a new type of global communication. In nuclear physics, the leading role of British scientists was well known. Cockcroft and Walton gained a Nobel prize for this in 1951. In a quite different area, that of genetics, Cambridge scientists were also world leaders. In 1953 the English scientist Crick, along with the American Watson, were to discover the 'double helix' structure of DNA, the basis for genetic inheritance.[66] They symbolized jointly the typically British combination of intellectual rigour and romantic amateurism that characterized much of British science in the postwar period. The Royal Society assumed major new responsibilities. War-torn Britain could thus contemplate with some pride individual teams of scientists who brought a clutch of Nobel prizes and other distinctions to their country, even if they operated as single enterprises rather than as state-sponsored battalions. The remarkable achievements of British science in the 1940s make it the more remarkable that so little public encouragement was given to promoting and developing it in the following decade. Gloomy diagnoses of Britain's 'two cultures', however, were as yet far off.

The Attlee legend was, in general, a warm, reassuring one. But it was also somewhat deceptive. To some degree it rested on purely fortuitous and temporary factors such as the defeat and

[66] On this, see J.D. Watson, *The Double Helix* (London, 1970).

prostration of potential European rivals (including the mass migration of Jewish scientists of much distinction from Nazi Germany to Britain). British exports flourished and British capital financed world trade and investment in something of a vacuum, and on the basis of an institutional and economic structure at home which the war years had not radically transformed.

The ambiguities of the nation at this time came out fully in the last hurrah of Attlee's government, the 1951 Festival of Britain. The omens were not good, since the Festival opened in April amidst a mood of political and economic crisis. Strikes by building workers and heavy rain had made the preparations exceptionally difficult. Yet, in spite of all, it opened on time and was a triumphant success. Tens of thousands of adults, and more especially schoolchildren, flocked to the South Bank site, to wander around the Dome of Discovery, gaze at the Skylon, and generally enjoy a festival of national celebration. Up and down the land, lesser festivals enlisted much civic and voluntary enthusiasm. A people curbed by years of total war and half-crushed by austerity and gloom, showed that it had not lost the capacity for enjoying itself. Particular joy came from the Battersea Funfair, designed with help from Osbert Lancaster, John Piper, and others. With its theatre, grotto, and beer-gardens, along with a tree-walk and the famous Emmett railway of *Punch* fame, it was a huge success, a revival of the old entertainments of Vauxhall and Ranelagh along the river in years gone by. Above all, the Festival made a spectacular setting as a showpiece for the inventiveness and genius of British scientists and technologists.

There was much that was good and encouraging about the Festival of Britain. But its impact was neither deep nor longlasting. In 1952 the Churchill government dismantled the South Bank site, and sold its lease on the Battersea Funfair in 1954, amidst little public protest. Only the Festival Hall lives on for a later generation to enjoy. In practice, the Festival appears to have had only a transient impact on British technical or design skills. Nor was its impact on British exports more than cosmetic. The contrast with the self-assured certainty of Queen Victoria's exhibition at the Crystal Palace a hundred years earlier was all too clear. The main impression left by the Festival was not its innovation but its insularity. As in the 'Lion and Unicorn Pavilion', it served to celebrate past glories, age-old institutions, and hallowed and cherished folkways. The British monarchy, British sports, British pub life, London's red buses, and the village 'bobby' were on display, almost preserved in aspic. There was all too little that was dynamic or suggestive of the stimulus of other cultures. The point of reference was the Victorian or Edwardian past. Britain in 1951 was on display as the somewhat geriatric heir of those earlier societies, not the enterprising youthful harbinger of the new. The Festival pointed back in time, to the way in which continuities had been preserved and adapted to later circumstances. In this, the entire event mirrored Attlee's Britain, a resilient war victim, presided over by brave, honourable, but somewhat conservative men, and a premier whose instinct for change was still governed by the Stepney boys' clubs he had witnessed as a young Edwardian bourgeois nearly half a century earlier.

Britain, indeed, at this pivotal period, emerging reluctantly from the mood of solidarity of the war, was in many ways the haven of the elderly. Its key figures in public life were themselves surviving Edwardians, representing the enduring impact of pre-1914 new Liberalism—Attlee and Churchill in politics, Beveridge in social policy, Edward Bridges (the son of a former Poet Laureate) in administration, John Reith in mass communication, Bertrand Russell and G.M. Trevelyan, two famous dynastic names, in the humanities. The greatest veteran of them all, George Bernard Shaw, born in 1856, lived on at Shaw's Corner in Hertfordshire until 1950. A great literary success of the post-war period was George Macaulay Trevelyan's *English Social History* (1942), celebrating as it did the uniqueness and greatness of England with the same intensity as did his great-uncle, Thomas Babington Macaulay, in the mid-nineteenth century. Macaulay had linked the 1840s with the Whig triumph of 1688, a 'preserving revolution' which formed the basis of

Britain's progress and prosperity a century-and-a-half later. In the same spirit, Britain after 1945 celebrated its own preserving revolution. Trevelyan was still there, as head of a Cambridge college, to interpret the convulsive events of the twentieth century as another exercise in liberal self-preservation. The last years of Attlee's democratic socialist regime were also the final endorsement of the enduring triumph of the Whigs.

4. *The Conservative Compromise*
1951–1956

To many, the advent of the Conservatives under Winston Churchill marked a sharp transition, a turning-point in the national mood. Nicholas Davenport, a wry, leftish observer of economic mismanagement, saw in the return of Churchill's team in place of the era of Attlee and Cripps, a restoration of the cavaliers after the austere regime of the puritanical roundheads.[1] Churchill himself, still in reasonable mental fettle at the age of 77, suggested an Elgar-like reversion to imperial greatness and great-power status, a man who could talk to his wartime comrade President Eisenhower as an equal, perhaps as master. Anthony Eden, the Foreign Secretary, embodied the attractive *jeune premier* vigour of the youthful Conservative rebel of the thirties, while Macmillan and Sandys elsewhere in the administration conveyed the same appeal.

It is clear, in fact, that these beliefs were totally misplaced. Churchill's administration took office in a raging balance-of-payments crisis which continued to darken the scene until the winter of 1952–3, and in a long-term mood of social caution. Their policy from the outset was one of survival, aware as they were of the fragility of their position. Labour still stood strong in the opinion polls; until mid-1954 the expectation was for a return of a Labour government. Churchill himself was

---

[1] Nicholas Davenport, *Memoirs of a City Radical* (London, 1974), 8off.

profoundly aware of the distrust he still aroused in the trade-union movement—reports of his alleged ordering of troops to the Welsh mining valleys during the Tonypandy troubles had been hurled at him during the 1950 election campaign.[2] He was above all anxious to demonstrate his capacity for ordered, peaceful statesmanship, carrying the working class with him in patriotic endeavour, and to refute early accusations that he was an unreconciled class warrior. More important still, he was primarily anxious to achieve a settlement in international affairs in which Britain would play a key role at the summit of power. To this end, social peace in Britain was essential.

This outlook was mirrored by all his key Cabinet figures. Anthony Eden, the Foreign Secretary, was a 'one-nation Tory' in the Disraelian mould, anxious for social cohesion and with a livelier concern for domestic issues than is often credited. R. A. Butler, Chancellor of the Exchequer, and the key figure on the home front, was the leading Tory reformer of the day, architect of the 1944 Education Act and author of the main lines of the Industrial Charter. Lord Woolton, a paternalistic employer of Fabian inclinations, was even more anxious to pacify the populace on issues such as food subsidies and social welfare. Harold Macmillan, Minister of Housing, had been an ardent social reformer before the war and organizer of the 'Next Five Years' group. His outlook mirrored that of men like Lloyd George who had greatly influenced him in the 1930s. This kind of approach was general throughout the government. Superficially, they looked a very traditional group, with many peers appointed to key government positions as 'Overlords' and dynastic figures such as Lord Salisbury present in major office. In reality, this was a paternalistic, cautious, undoctrinaire body of men interpreting their role as maintaining the general lines of Labour's policy, save for a few details such as road-haulage and steel nationalization, and relying

[2] Memorandum from Conservative Political Centre to Conservative candidates and agents, 25 January 1950 (Bodleian, Conservative Party archives, CCO2/2/16).

on the market to do the rest. There is every indication that this is what the popular mood demanded and expected.

The Conservatives' domestic policy under Churchill faithfully mirrored this caution. From all parts of the party machine and hierarchy there were calls for a tranquil stance. The Conservative Research Department urged the party to retain the essence of the post-war consensus and to show its social conscience. Senior backbenchers like Sir David Gammans expressed grave alarm at local election losses in May 1952, and fears that the electors no longer felt that the Tories 'had the green fingers of Government'.[3] Lord Woolton, the architect of victory in 1951, warned Churchill about Tory abstentions in the polls because people 'are not very pleased with us at the moment' (9 May 1952),[4] while Lord Swinton, a senior grandee whose governmental experience went back to the Lloyd George government in 1916, urged the need to cut back on the defence programme in order to give priority to exports and to promote full employment.[5] Throughout, there was fear of a possible reaction by the TUC and working-class people generally at a reversion to pre-war Toryism, defined as a dedication to decontrol and the regime of the market. If the party and the press demanded caution, within the administrative machine key officials urged continuity. Major civil service figures remained from the Labour era, notably Sir Robert Hall in the Economic Section of the Treasury, and others, like 'Otto' Clarke in the Treasury, of broadly progressive reconstructionist views. In ministry after ministry, Labour, Health, Education, Transport, the Colonial Office, permanent secretaries and under-secretaries threw their influence in the direction of retaining the broad framework of postwar policies.

The effects on governmental policy were very plain. Towards the unions, the approach was one of conciliation. Talk that had

---

[3] Sir David Gammans to Walter Monckton, 30 May 1952 (Bodleian, Monckton Papers, 2).

[4] Woolton to Churchill, 9 May 1952 (Bodleian, Woolton Papers, 22).

[5] Swinton to Monckton, 7 July 1952 (Monckton Papers, 2).

emerged during the 1950 and 1951 election campaigns of clipping the powers of over-mighty unions—modifying the laws on picketing; instituting secret ballots for election of union officials or for possible industrial action; reverting to the 'contracting in' system for political funding; even repealing the 1906 Trades Disputes Act which gave the unions unique legal privileges in civil actions—all these were firmly set aside. The Minister of Labour was Sir Walter Monckton, an almost apolitical go-between with many friends on the Labour side. His previous claims to fame included a mediating role in Indian politics and a position as legal adviser to Edward VIII at the time of the abdication in 1936. Monckton was a diplomat, even a fixer. His essential role was to maintain close relations with the TUC and to defuse possible strike action.[6] The usual method here was to set up courts of inquiry and to investigate wage and other grievances. The composition and general approach of these courts was such as to encourage a generally sympathetic attitude to union demands. Not one finding was significantly resisted by the unions in the 1951–5 period, and the curve of wage inflation went gently upwards. Possible strikes by engineers and shipbuilders were settled in 1954. The most dangerous area was always the railways, which saw frequent possible crises. The most serious came at Christmas-time in 1954, and even Monckton talked briefly of tough action.[7] In fact, however, the usual solution was again adopted, with a hand-picked Commission of Inquiry reporting sympathetically on the railwaymen's claims. Butler, the Chancellor but also mindful of the approach of a general election, suggested that British Railways might be persuaded to write off some of their debt or at least increase their deficit on current operations.[8] There was much talk of

---

[6] See Monckton Papers, and Lord Birkenhead, *Walter Monckton* (London, 1969).

[7] Cabinet conclusions, 13 Dec. 1954 (CAB 128/27); see paper by Monckton, 'Industrial Disputes', 29 Dec. 1953, CP (53) 363 (CAB 129/64).

[8] Ibid. 4 Jan. 1955 (CAB 128/28).

widespread public sympathy with the low pay of lesser grades of railway workers. Guided by such precepts, the Conservatives managed to maintain a strike-free period of industrial peace, in which the unions retained their entrenched position with little difficulty. Union membership rose each year, to approach the 10 million mark.

Nor were the unions, or the opposition generally, inflamed by a policy of privatization. It was clear that Eden, Butler, Macmillan, and other leading Tories accepted the fact of massive public ownership; Churchill himself was on record as endorsing the nationalization of the railways as long ago as 1918. The outcome was that only two measures of denationalization were carried through, and both of those with much caution. Iron and steel, so recently taken into public ownership, were restored to private hands in 1953 but with the minimum disruption in the structure of the industry, while some pockets of state-owned industry remained, such as Richard Thomas and Baldwins in South Wales. The other candidate was road-haulage, and even here there was much hesitancy in dismantling British Road Services. What resulted was certainly not a reversion to pre-war private enterprise. Otherwise, the government's approach to industry was corporate and centralist. The industries and services taken into public hands were subject to massive investment programmes, notably civil aviation, gas, and electricity, and no serious governmental interference with their productivity or wages policies. In at least one case the government actually extended the principle of the public board, Morrison-style, with the creation in 1954 of the United Kingdom Atomic Energy Authority, under that centrist bureaucrat Sir Edwin Plowden, to administer the civil policy for nuclear energy and develop atomic research. These Tories remained collectivist and adherents of the mixed economy.

On the welfare side, the Conservatives were particularly anxious to underline their Disraelian, 'one-nation' credentials. Indeed, the balance of public spending swung, especially from 1953, towards an increase in the social budget. The National Health Service, however tortured its origin, now became a favoured target for Conservative munificence. The principle of private health charges, already started with Gaitskell's budget in 1951, was continued, with charges for medical prescriptions and for dental and eye treatment introduced and extended. But the charges remained at a low level, and the broad principle of free health treatment at the point of need remained. The Minister of Health from May 1952 was an interesting paternalistic Tory of Scottish ancestry, Iain Macleod.[9] He had been in charge of social policy in the Conservative Research Department under Butler down to 1950. He made his name with a ferocious debating attack on Aneurin Bevan in a Commons debate on the Ministry of Health. But, this polemic aside, he soon proved himself a formidable partisan of the Health Service, and indeed set the tone for the Tory social outlook for the remainder of the fifties. Under his tenure at the Ministry of Health, the budget for the NHS rose steadily. There continued to be grumbling in the press at Arab sheikhs and other exotic figures coming to our shores to exploit Britain's free health services for their appendix or hernia operations. There was also much talk of 'waste'. It was to some Labour alarm that Macleod appointed a committee under Claude Guillebaud to investigate the efficiency of the health service. But, in fact, when it reported in 1956, it unambiguously pronounced in favour of the cost-effectiveness and overall administrative efficiency of the National Health Service. Earlier spending excesses had been brought under control and there was no longer a crisis. The Guillebaud Committee actually advocated a large increase in capital expenditure; this was the basis for Enoch Powell's expensive hospital-building programme in 1960–2. The Guillebaud report, in fact, was much influenced by the views of two strongly pro-Labour social scientists, both typical products of the wartime intelligentsia, Richard Titmuss and Brian Abel-Smith.[10] They reported in somewhat uncritical

[9] See Nigel Fisher, *Iain Macleod* (London, 1973) and John Vaizey, *Breach of Promise* (London, 1983), 34ff., a more critical account.

[10] Charles Webster, *The Health Services Since the War*, 206–10.

terms about the financial strength of the Health Service, setting aside long-term problems of an ageing population with rising expectations. The government accepted Guillebaud *en bloc*. It was, in any case, what they wanted to believe.

What was true of the Health Service was equally the case with pensions, social insurance, and education. There was some injection of funds into the state education system from 1954 when the economy showed signs of recovery after the Korean War ended. There was little conflict between the Ministry of Education and the various teachers' unions, nor with largely Labour-run local education authorities. Progress towards comprehensive education was slow. Starting with one in rural Anglesey in North Wales, only thirteen out of over 5,000 state secondary schools had gone comprehensive by mid-1954.

The most characteristic area of Conservative social policy came in housing, where the minister in charge was that old social Tory, Harold Macmillan. The Conservatives inherited a pledge, wished on the party leadership and Lord Woolton at the 1950 conference, to build 300,000 houses. Certainly the restrictions of the housing market, however inevitable with the restrictions of raw materials, were a particularly unpopular feature of the Labour years. Macmillan thus rapidly built up his housing programme from 260,000 in 1952 to 318,750, well over the target of 300,000, in 1953, assisted by an aggressive junior housing minister, Ernest Marples.[11] Restrictions were partly removed from private house building and many kinds of licences on smaller houses abolished. Macmillan's personal prestige was much enhanced as a result. The Conservatives proudly claimed that they were well advanced towards the objective of a property-owning democracy. And yet, *The Economist* shrewdly observed that Macmillan's housing programme 'was of the kind that might typically be expected from a Coalition government'.[12]

---

[11] Cabinet conclusions, 18 Jan. 1954 (CAB 128/27). The total for 1953 was 318,779.
[12] *The Economist*, 7 Nov. 1953.

Of the total of 300,000, four-fifths were in fact built in the public sector by the local authorities, with expenditure permitted also on a large slum-clearance programme and much renovation and repair—'Operation Rescue'. The expansion of the private housing market was a gradual affair, with only modest amendment of the Rent Restriction Act to enable controlled houses to have their rents increased by their landlords by up to £16 a year. Only limited changes were made in tax allowances for private housing and in the interests of mortgage holders. Certainly, Macmillan's policy did not mean a total reversion to the private market mechanism, while wartime controls on land use remained stringent. When they appeared to be abused in the case of agricultural land in Crichel Down in Dorset, the Minister of Agriculture, Sir Thomas Dugdale, although only very marginally to blame, resigned on moral grounds. The Conservatives' housing programme, based on 'the tactic of minimum offence', was enormously effective.[13] Labour critics might reasonably complain that the new houses were built in part by relaxing standards of quality in building, the size of rooms, and inside amenities. Economists could argue that excessive resources were devoted to this end rather than to modernization or investment. But it was also clear that the policy was popular not simply because a vast housing need was beginning to be met but because a fair social balance could be claimed to be struck between private and public needs.

This policy was parodied by *The Economist* in February 1954 as that of 'Butskellism'.[14] This was implying, of course, a congruence between the Conservatives and their Labour predecessors. But the very concept of Butskellism needs considerable revision. On social and industrial policy, a gulf existed even between the Labour right such as Gaitskell and Morrison and the Tory leadership. On fiscal policy there was a clear distinction in approach. Gaitskell's emphasis still lay on physical planning

[13] *The Economist*, 7 Nov. 1953.   [14] Ibid. 13 Feb. 1954.

and heavy state involvement, including high direct taxation. Butler, much the less competent economist of the two, favoured financial levers, especially the use of credit restrictions such as the raising of bank rate. The balance-of-payments crisis in the winter of 1951–2 saw bank rate pushed up sharply from $2\frac{1}{2}$ per cent to 4 per cent, with a consequent slump in the Stock Exchange to greet the incoming Tory administration. The 1953 budget was marked by a £160 m. cut in food subsidies, but credit restrictions remained severe. In the 1953 budget, with the cost of imports now beginning to fall as the international economy recovered, Butler decided to give away £170 m., including reductions of *6d.* in the £ in all rates of income tax.[15] Butler's emphasis was on the relief of private consumption rather than public investment; he was to be severely criticized for this approach. In 1955 his policy was to result in a considerable crisis for the balance of payments and renewed talk that the pound might have to be devalued. As a financial strategy, 'Butskellism' did not really exist.

But as a state of mind, it probably did. It implied a coherent attempt to maintain a social consensus and to try to 'set the people free' through greater liberalization, lower taxation, and decontrol, without dismantling the popular welfare and industrial fabric of the Attlee years. It was enormously assisted by the wholly fortuitous economic circumstances in 1953 which saw a large fall in the cost of imports and Britain's balance of payments go decisively into the black in 1953 and 1954. *The Economist* could even ask in mid-1954 'No More Crises?'.[16] 'Butskellism' was the product of highly fortuitous, unplanned developments; but it was sufficiently contemporary to make it acceptable to a rapidly changing society. In particular, Conservatives could boast by 1955 that full employment, the prized possession of the war years, was fully sustained. Over $22\frac{1}{2}$ million British people were at work in an economy working to something near full capacity, and the rate of unemployment was barely 1 per cent, even at a

[15] Ibid. 18 Apr. 1953.   [16] Ibid. 14 Aug. 1954.

time when rival economies in Germany, France, and Japan were now making rapid inroads into world markets. The share of British exports might have been falling but their value, as measured in world prices, continued to rise. This newly conceived social contract, therefore, appeared secure in Conservative hands.

The dominant mood was confirmed by the steadfast refusal of Churchill and his colleagues, and indeed Anthony Eden when he succeeded to the premiership in 1955, to divert the course of policy away from this path of studied moderation. Monetarist or other strategies which might have restored fiscal rigour at the cost of social harm like rising unemployment were rejected on all fronts. The main test came with the so-called 'Robot' controversy early in 1952, the one occasion when the Conservatives seriously considered adopting a policy that could have conflicted sharply with the post-war mood of social harmony. The name 'Robot' was made up from its three main civil-service advocates—ROwan, Bolton, and OTto Clark. Butler, the new Chancellor of the Exchequer, had reacted with much alarm to the deteriorating financial situation in his first few months. He told the Cabinet on 22 January 1952 that the reserves would soon be down to £500 m., below the level they had reached when the pound was devalued by Cripps in September 1949. He thus made proposals for stringent measures, including a severe cut in food imports which aroused Cabinet anxiety at the proposed standard of nutrition.[17] But the nub of his proposals, offered while Eden, the Foreign Secretary, was away in Washington, was a complex scheme for floating the pound. To avoid a disastrous drain on the reserves, he proposed to allow the exchange rate to float and the pound to find its own level; to block all sterling balances held by non-members outside the dollar area; and to use, for British purposes, 90 per cent of the sterling balances held by independent sterling-area countries and central banks. It would, Butler

---

[17] Cabinet conclusions, 22 Jan. 1952 (CAB 128/26 pt. 1); 'Food Subsidies' (T 171/409); Churchill to Butler, 16 Mar. 1952 (T 225/201).

acknowledged, reverse the financial policies of the past twelve years; among other things it would blitz the European Payments Union, while the United States might look on it with disfavour. But the important thing was that the 'strain' would henceforth be taken by the exchange rate and not by the gold reserves. Britain henceforth would be able to control its own destiny. Supported by Oliver Lyttelton and with little apparent dissent among his Cabinet colleagues, Butler boldly advanced this new scenario.[18]

It soon became clear that 'setting the pound free', whatever the technical financial arguments in its favour, came up sharply against the abiding social philosophy of the period. Butler himself freely acknowledged that floating the pound would mean rising prices of food and raw materials, and probably higher unemployment. Churchill, whose own understanding of these matters was scanty, was uneasy on this point, and also worried by possible American reaction. The strongest assault on Butler, indeed, came from one of Churchill's private advisers, the ex-scientist Lord Cherwell. Cherwell starkly spelt out the consequences as he saw them—a sharp rise in unemployment, an increase in the price of food including perhaps a 2s. loaf, a 6 per cent bank rate, and perhaps one million unemployed. Pre-war faith in the pound could not be sustained anyway now that it had lost two-thirds of its gold value in twenty years. 'Imports are cut to the bone. The people will not accept mass unemployment.' Churchill sent this on to Butler with the comment: 'This is a formidable statement.'[19] Elsewhere, Cherwell denounced this policy as

a reckless leap in the dark involving appalling political as well as economic sacrifices at home and abroad in the blind hope that the speculation will see us through. Unemployment and rising prices would not necessarily be accompanied by balanced trade account, and galloping inflation might well follow. In a hard-pressed community like

[18] Butler's memorandum on 'External Action', 21 Feb. 1952 (PREM 11/140): Lyttelton to Churchill, 28 Feb. 1952 (ibid.).
[19] Cherwell to Churchill, 18 Mar. 1952 (PREM 11/137).

ours, this form of rationing imports by the purse can surely scarcely be promulgated as Conservative policy.

The Treasury's proposals were ill thought out: 'It will have appalling effects on the Commonwealth and the sterling area. We shall be pilloried, and justly throughout the world.'[20] Cherwell's approach was broadly endorsed by such emollient figures as Woolton and Monckton. Even a right-wing figure such as Lord Salisbury worried about Commonwealth reactions at such a unilateral *démarche*. Finally, Anthony Eden, furious at such a new development being suggested while he was abroad, attacked it vehemently on broad social grounds. Any other policy— including a sharp cut in rearmament—should be preferred. It would have the most serious effect on unemployment figures.[21] By the end of March Butler had admitted defeat on his 'External Sterling Plan' and was turning to a 'strong and severe budget' instead, including raising bank rate. Economic advisers, in the formidable persons of Robert Hall and Edwin Plowden, were vehemently arguing against it: indeed, the Economic Section strongly resisted the Treasury team of Rowan, Bolton and Clarke. 'Robot' continued to be bandied about in governmental circles as a possible solution until the end of May.[22] By that time, Butler alone was in favour and, with the reserves now looking less frail, the momentum behind a policy of convertibility and freeing the exchange rate had passed. A policy which Sir Alec Cairncross later commented would have been 'disastrous, politically and economically'[23] was finally abandoned, and the Chancellor strove to recoup his lost prestige.

It was an historic moment in post-war Conservative history. A party devoted to decontrol and encouraging the private market, decided firmly in favour of control and management. It did so for a variety of reasons, including technical arguments from

---

[20] Cherwell to Churchill, 26 Feb. 1952 (PREM 11/140).

[21] Cabinet minutes in T 236/3242.

[22] Cabinet conclusions, 29 May 1952 (CAB 128/25).

[23] Cairncross, *Years of Recovery*, 270.

Hall and other key advisers. But the background for dissent was social and ideological. Faced with the prospect of being stigmatized again as being the party of dear food and rising unemployment, the Conservatives prudently withdrew. No such policy was significantly advanced again for several more years. A Disraelian cohesion, fortified by favourable economic circumstances, dominated the public mood.

This meant an expansionist programme, as soon as world trade permitted, and it was on the basis of this that the culture of affluence, with which all Conservatives down to Macmillan in the later fifties were associated, took firm hold. It is extremely debatable whether the undoubted prosperity of the fifties owed much to Conservative economic management. Indeed, Butler himself was an erratic figure at the Treasury, for all the apparent success of Tory policies. He veered between policies of monetary restraint and the expansionist encouragement of investment. His strategy reached its nadir in his budget of April 1955. influenced heavily by the consideration that a general election was now imminent. The background to it was a 'supply side' argument which placed the encouragement of consumption foremost, and which, to Butler's mind, meant tax cuts. Faced with a budgetary surplus of £242 m., he decided to give away £134 m. in the standard rate of income tax.[24] After a brief mood of political and stock-exchange euphoria (which spanned the Tories' election victory that May), this led by the summer of 1955 to acute inflationary pressures and a calamitous slump in the British balance of payments.

By 5 September Butler, the advocate of tax cuts, was talking of the urgent need to restrict credit and reduce consumption.[25] Reductions in both defence and domestic expenditure were urgently needed, and the abolition of the bread subsidy was

---

[24] *Financial Times*, 21 Apr. 1955. Astonishingly, in its leading article, this newspaper commented that the budget 'in its broad effects seems to be a good one'.

[25] Cabinet conclusions, 5 Sept. 1955 (CAB 128/29).

proposed. Butler had to deny publicly at the International Monetary Fund meeting at Istanbul that Britain proposed to introduce convertibility, let alone devalue the pound. Leslie Rowan, second secretary in the Treasury, somewhat sycophantically claimed that Butler's prestige at Istanbul was immensely high when he admitted that United Kingdom policy was too inflationary, and that he was 'going to put it right by classical measures of internal policy'.[26] Butler, however, faced trouble at home, especially from his Prime Minister, Eden, who strongly objected to the decision to abolish the bread subsidy on grounds of social fairness. Monckton, Minister of Labour, argued that the unions would have to press for higher wages. Osbert Peake, Minister of Pensions, added that an increase in National Assistance payments would be inevitable. To the alarm of Bridges, the introduction of a tough budget was delayed by some weeks despite the deterioration in the reserves.[27] Butler, in the end, had to introduce a compromise budget to satisfy the Prime Minister, which, despite many cuts, left the bread subsidy intact. Bridges was confronted by Leslie Rowan with observations to the effect that costs were rising, the reserves had fallen, sterling was losing ground, and all largely because of the inflationary policy which Butler's consumer-led approach had promoted.[28] Butler left the Treasury in favour of Macmillan in December, tarred with the reputation of having imperilled the finances in his budget for purely electioneering purposes. He moved to the non-departmental post of Lord President, with Macmillan having deftly ensured that Butler would not be recognized as 'deputy Prime Minister'.[29] For the opposition, Gaitskell led a ferocious attack—'he has behaved in manner unworthy of his high office. He began in folly, he continued in

---

[26] Rowan to Bridges, 18 Sept. 1955 (T 171/468).

[27] R. W. B. ['Otto'] Clarke to Bridges, 15 Sept. 1955; Bridges to Butler, 21 Sept. 1955 (ibid.).

[28] Rowan to Bridges, 11 Oct. 1955 (ibid.).

[29] Anthony Howard, *RAB: The Life of R. A. Butler* (London, 1987), 220.

deceit, and he has ended in reaction.'[30] So much for 'Butskellism'. Within a few months or even weeks, Butler's star had waned with remarkable speed.

Whether Butler really was the author of sustained affluence, therefore, is exceedingly doubtful. But the fact of affluence was by 1955 incontestable. Butler himself encouraged belief in it in 1954 by asking rhetorically whether individual British people could not double their standard of living in the next twenty-five years. He was addressing a society in which the weekly earnings of adult males was rising from £8.30 (£8. 6s.) in 1951 to £15.35 (£15. 7s.) ten years later.[31] Despite slowly rising inflation, excessive subsidies to farmers, and considerable social inequality of outcome, living standards were rising sharply. Private savings, in particular, were racing ahead to a level of £1,000 m. per year. Private home ownership, boosted by cheap mortgages promoted by expanding building societies, increased rapidly, especially from 1954, while growing private affluence was equally confirmed in the domestic sales of consumer goods. Sales of televisions and refrigerators mounted very rapidly, as did those of washing machines, with alarming consequences for rivers and sewers clogged by detergent foam. It was truly a sellers' market in the mid-1950s, with a huge boom in private car sales and every manifestation of consumer contentment. Urban planners took account of the fact that this was becoming a car-owners' democracy, with the demand for rail transport and rural bus services beginning to drop sharply.

One index of growth was the rapid expansion of all the 'new towns' scheduled in the late 1940s—Harlow, Basildon, Stevenage, Hemel Hempstead, Welwyn, Hatfield, Crawley, and Bracknell around the perimeter of London; Corby in Northants; Newton Aycliffe and Peterlee in the North East; Glenrothes and East Kilbride in Scotland; Cwmbran in South Wales. In each of them, especially those in the London area, thriving shopping centres testified to consumer buoyancy, while somewhat hesitant

---

[30] *Parl. Deb.*, 5th ser., vol. 545, 390 ff. (27 Oct. 1955).
[31] Arthur Marwick, *British Society since 1945* (Harmondsworth, 1982), 118.

steps were taken to protect environmental aspects as well. Cwm-bran boasted both new pubs and new chapels, those rival poles of Welsh life, while targets for population growth were raised from 35,000 to 55,000.[32] By the end of 1954, food rationing had finally been abolished, with the destruction of ration books marking the finale of post-war austerity. Women especially bene-fited from less constrained domestic circumstances and greater leisure opportunities, with much household drudgery associated with 'wash day' or 'spring cleaning' removed. The prospect of cheap package foreign travel first became a reality for working-class people in the early 1950s too, with the Spanish coast becoming a favourite area, for all the left-wing memories of the Spanish Civil War and opposition to the Franco regime.

At home, the theatre showed every sign of recovery after its near-closure during the war, and literary and artistic life seemed altogether much livelier than in the immediate post-war years. 'The Movement' of new fifties poets, including Wain, Amis, and Davie, attracted attention. For the masses, popular sport reached new heights of popularity, even if there were varying fortunes for British participants. The success of the England cricket team in defeating the Australians and recapturing the mythical 'ashes' in 1953 was countered by a 6–3 home defeat for the English foot-ballers at the hands of the Hungarians at Wembley the same year. In domestic life, television became the increasingly domin-ant arbiter of popular taste and interest, with sport, panel games, but also good drama and current-affairs programmes well to the fore. The advent of commercial television in 1954 caused much anguish about a threat to standards, but in fact the market emphasis on ITV differed in degree rather than in kind from the productions of the BBC. Skilfully, the government chose Sir Kenneth Clark, a distinguished man of the arts, former Director of the National Gallery and Chairman of the Arts Council, as Chairman of the new Independent Broadcasting Authority.

[32] See Philip Riden, *Rebuilding a Valley* (Cwmbran, 1988), 115–20.

When commercial television first transmitted its programmes in September 1955, despite the advertising, the general impact was one of respectability, almost solemnity.[33] With early offerings on ITV from Oscar Wilde, 'Saki', and Noel Coward, the new service was hardly promoting cultural revolt.

In this climate, then, Churchill's house seemed secure. Within the closed circles of government, indeed, there was much tension. The Prime Minister's relations with Eden, his Foreign Secretary and presumed heir-apparent, were difficult, and soured throughout 1954 by the premier's refusal to resign, despite approaching his eightieth year. Butler and Macmillan were two other key ministers distinctly wary of one another. Woolton, the key election manager of 1951, found himself increasingly at odds with Churchill and was virtually side-tracked from 1953 onwards along with most of the other former 'overlords'.[34] Churchill did not appreciate his advice that 'the government is trying to do too much' and that devaluation might result, which would be 'the end of the Conservative government'. Churchill himself, a veteran who suffered major heart-attacks on two occasions (which for a time incapacitated him as a head of government) inspired fear as much as affection from his colleagues. He finally resigned in April 1955. His successor, Eden, called an immediate general election and, fighting a low-key campaign, won an overall majority of 70, with 345 Conservatives being returned to Labour's 277 and the Liberals' 6. But tensions at the top, Butler's failing reputation as Chancellor, and other difficulties were as little contrasted with the popular mood of contentment. Following the accession of Elizabeth II in February 1952 and a spectacular coronation the following year, there was much talk in the press of a 'new Elizabethan age'.

---

[33] Asa Briggs, *Sound and Vision*, 1003.

[34] See e.g. Woolton to Churchill, 1 Sept. 1954, in which Woolton vainly pressed the case for an election in autumn, 1955, and Macmillan to Woolton, 12 Apr. 1953. 'secret and confidential', in which he observes, 'Churchill is a very queer man' (Woolton Papers, 22). Also Woolton to Churchill, 21 July 1952 and Churchill to Woolton. 2 Sept. 1953 (ibid. 25).

The relaxation that characterized much of the early 1950s was sustained by the relative moderation in Britain's overseas policy. Eden, the Foreign Secretary, was always a conciliator rather than an innovator in foreign affairs. Churchill himself was anxious to restore the wartime mood of the 'Big Three' which had operated during his first premiership. From early 1953 he exerted as much pressure as was feasible on President Eisenhower, the new US president, for a summit conference with the Russians. With the new situation created by the death of Stalin, Britain saw itself as the experienced honest broker, its own adventurism severely curtailed. One sign of the times was that the new Conservative government briskly cut back Gaitskell's huge rearmament budget of 1951. Ian Bancroft and other Treasury figures ridiculed its maladroit costing, facile optimism, and wilful ignorance of 'the world as it is'.[35] Faced with a growing balance-of-payments deficit and the urgent need for at least £40 m. of savings on defence expenditure, the Cabinet promptly decided to phase the programme over four years rather than three. On 7 November 1952, Field-Marshal Lord Alexander, the Minister of Defence at the time, found little sympathy even with sharp reductions in defence spending that he proposed. His suggestion to reduce the first year's spending from £ 1,719 m. to £1,645 m. was clipped, after protests by Butler and Peter Thorneycroft (President of the Board of Trade), to a mere £1,610 m. Butler commented that 'the financial position of the country and the fall in the productivity rate made it impossible to contemplate a rising curve of defence'.[36] Churchill himself (somewhat ingenuously) adopted in the House the posture more commonly associated with his old adversary on the left, Aneurin Bevan.[37] For several years, Britain's defence posture was one of containment and gradual withdrawal. The new emphasis on 'massive retaliation' through the hydrogen bomb, underlined in the 1954 Defence White Paper,

[35] Bancroft to Humphrey Davies, 3 Nov. 1951 (T 225/124).
[36] Cabinet conclusions, 7 Nov. 1952 (CAB 128/25).
[37] *Parl. Deb.*, 5th ser., vol. 494, 2601–2 (6 Dec. 1951).

made sharp reductions in conventional forces possible, and the confining of defence spending within a budgetary ceiling. It was the external accompaniment of a more tranquil life at home.

This moderation was not always so obvious to the contemporary eye. Britain still spent heavily on defence hardware by comparative international standards, with national service (for two years) ensuring a military presence of over 300,000 troops in foreign and Commonwealth outposts across the world. The British nuclear programme was now publicly admitted, and finally unveiled with the testing of atomic rockets at Woomera in northern Australia in 1952. Churchill then pressed on with a hydrogen bomb programme. There was anxious debate on this in the Cabinet in July 1954, with many ministers querying the huge cost of £10 million, and urging the need to restrain Germany from making thermonuclear weapons, along with the moral dilemma confronted by the manufacturer of such horrendous forces of mass destruction. Churchill, however, was clear and traditional on the point. 'The Prime Minister said that we could not expect to maintain our influence as a world power unless we possess the most up-to-date weapons.' This political emphasis, setting aside financial, scientific and moral considerations, carried the day.[38] Britain's first hydrogen bomb was to be tested at Christmas Island in the Pacific in May 1957.

In several parts of the world, Britain's colonial heritage led to damaging and costly military operations. In South America, a Marxist-led nationalist government under Dr Cheddi Jagan in British Guiana (Guyana) led to the constitution being suspended and a British cruiser and military forces being sent there in 1953. More serious was the Mau Mau outbreak amongst the Kikuyu tribe in Kenya in 1952, which led to severe guerrilla warfare and the eventual loss of 10,000 African and European lives. The Colonial Secretary, Alan Lennox-Boyd (who succeeded Oliver Lyttelton in 1954), responded to a state of emergency declared

[38] Cabinet conclusions, 8 July 1954 (CAB 128/27).

by the Governor of Kenya by dispatching a substantial detachment of British troops. Heavy fighting dragged on for some
years, with the Kikuyu leader, Jomo Kenyatta, being imprisoned.
Years later, he was to become President of Kenya and a respected,
even revered, elder statesman of the Commonwealth. The war in
Malaya continued to rage fiercely also, with Sir Gerald Templer a
stern commander of the British forces. Not until later 1955 was it
felt that enough progress had been made for military operations to
be scaled down, though political proposals for a federation between
the old Malay states and Singapore (possibly including North
Borneo, Sarawak, and Brunei as well) led to further tension, especially in the Chinese population of Singapore.

An even more alarming crisis then loomed up in Cyprus, with
its old tensions between the majority Greek and the minority
Turkish communities. Here again the emphasis seemed to be on
military suppression as much as on a political settlement. The
Greek majority declared in favour of 'Enosis', union with Greece.
As in India, the British administration stood accused of encouraging conflict between the rival communities on the 'divide and
rule' basis, In 1955 open warfare broke out between the British
forces in Cyprus and a Greek underground organization EOKA,
under its resourceful leader, Colonel Grivas. The flames had been
fanned by an unguarded statement by a short-lived and politically inexperienced Minister of State, Henry Hopkinson, in 1954
that Cyprus would 'never' receive independence,[39] an astonishingly foolish statement in the light of the recent transfer of power
to India, Pakistan, Burma, and Sri Lanka. Another determining
factor for the British government was the growing importance of
Cyprus as a British military and air base, following the withdrawal from the Suez Canal in 1954. Violent and bloody fighting
continued in Cyprus for several years, with much loss of life
amongst British soldiers, including many young national servicemen. The government's eventual decision to imprison the Greek

---

[39] Anthony Seldon, *Churchill's Indian Summer* (London, 1981), 350.

Cypriot leader, Archbishop Makarios, in the distant Seychelles Islands made a solution all the more improbable.

With Guyana, Malaya, Kenya, and Cyprus all explosive, the British government's colonial policy hardly seemed a testament of peace. And yet the overriding tendency, even under a relatively hard-line Colonial Secretary like Lennox-Boyd from July 1954 onwards, was towards colonial liberation. Independence was granted to Ghana (the Gold Coast) and Nigeria in West Africa, and finally to Malaya where the first federal legislative council was elected in May 1955. In southern Africa, the manifest hostility of black leaders in Northern Rhodesia and Nyasaland to the new Central African Federation made the government proceed cautiously. The Federation did indeed come into being in late 1953, but Southern Rhodesia's Prime Minister, Garfield Todd, an avowedly liberal figure, felt that a federation in territories where blacks outnumbered whites 66 to 1 could never be feasible.[40] Whatever the alleged economic advantages or the desirability of having a buffer state against the Union of South Africa, Britain could hardly contemplate a limitless war against resourceful African guerrillas in southern Africa. In Commonwealth economic and trading policy, the Conservatives tended to reverse Labour's policy of the bulk purchase of colonial foodstuffs and encourage private enterprise. But the broad emphasis remained on development and consensus, a kind of colonial Butskellism.

Britain in the fifties, indeed, was an ancient land coming to terms with a less flamboyant, more restrained role in the world. For all Churchill's personal reluctance to see the old Empire diminish, the process of slow retreat continued. Nowhere was this more evident than in the Middle East, the key area of British concern since the war. Churchill had taken office with loud condemnation of the Attlee government's policy of 'scuttle' and surrender, in the face of Dr Mussadiq of Iran and the Wafd party in Egypt. In fact, caution prevailed in handling both countries.

[40] Blake, *Rhodesia*, 287–8. Todd believed his role as premier was 'to work myself out of a job'. The Federation's first premier was Sir Godfrey Huggins.

No effort was made to revive the military plan 'Buccaneer' for the invasion of Abadan. In 1953 subversion by the American CIA achieved the fortunate deposition of Mussadiq as Prime Minister of Persia. Allen Dulles's Operation 'Ajax' achieved the return of the Shah and the arrest of Mussadiq by the end of August. Elsewhere in the Middle East, Britain continued to place heavy reliance on its client regimes, Nuri in Iraq and the young King Hussein in Jordan. When Iraq and Turkey formed the so-called Baghdad Pact in February 1955, Britain joined it as well, and tried to get the Americans to do the same.

In Egypt, the supreme test, the Churchill government, for all the Prime Minister's fire-eating remarks during the 1951 election, in fact pursued a conciliatory policy. This was despite the apparent volatility posed by the overthrow of the corrupt King Farouk and the emergence of a new regime under General Neguib (at least nominally) in December 1952. By mid-1953 Eden was clearly well on course with a policy of accommodating Egyptian opinion by the withdrawal of British troops from the Canal Zone; in the face of militant Arab nationalism, he believed the British presence there was insupportable. The main outstanding difference with Egypt, policy towards neighbouring Sudan, was settled on the basis of Sudan achieving independence in 1954. Churchill tried to sabotage this policy and at one stage proposed redeployment of two battalions of British troops and four RAF squadrons in Khartoum 'to restore order', following pro-Egyptian demonstrations there. According to Evelyn Shuckburgh at the Middle East desk of the Foreign Office, Churchill wanted to invent a reason for sending troops to Sudan in order to mask the 'disgrace' of withdrawing them from Egypt: there was brief talk of Eden resigning in December 1953.[41] But the Foreign Secretary, with the backing of his colleagues, managed to get British forces redeployed in Cyprus, Libya, Jordan, and the Persian Gulf instead. 'The Treaty still seems to be the only course', Eden told

[41] Evelyn Shuckburgh, *Descent to Suez: Diaries, 1951–56* (London, 1986), 118 (entry for 12 Dec. 1953).

Churchill firmly.[42] He also successfully concluded a treaty with the Egyptian government, now led by the younger and more aggressively nationalist figure of Colonel Nasser. On 29 July 1954, Eden announced in the Commons that the 38,000 British troops in the Canal Zone would be progressively withdrawn over the next twenty months, the agreement to come into total effect on 25 June 1956. Only a small number of civilian contractors would stay on to maintain and repair stores, workshops, and equipment, together with British pilots engaged in the navigation of ships through the Canal, still a free international waterway as guaranteed in a convention in 1888. Many ministers were apprehensive about possible Egyptian designs on the Canal itself. Lord Leathers wrote to Churchill on 14 May 1953 that 'we have to be on guard against an attempt to gain complete control even before the Company's concession terminates in 1968 when as things stand Egypt succeeds to the profit and control of the Canal'.[43] But, pending a crisis in the Canal's own operations or ownership, Britain's military presence in Egypt was over.

The withdrawal from Egypt, after eighty years of occupation since the original expedition under Sir Garnet Wolseley in 1882, was a momentous landmark in the contraction of Empire. In the event, the sheer physical and financial impracticability of maintaining a military encampment in the face of local Arab resentment proved insuperable. Britain remained a major force elsewhere in the Middle East, as has been seen, with a growing presence in the Persian Gulf, and its forces remained widely distributed 'east of Suez' from Jordan to the Seychelles. But the main military base in the Canal Zone, a pivot of imperial defence strategy since the late nineteenth century, was being voluntarily abandoned. The British presence in Egypt had, in fact, been slowly diminishing since 1919 when Churchill himself had been Colonial Secretary under Lloyd George. Only a small group

---

[42] Churchill to Eden, 11 Dec. 1953: Eden to Churchill, 12 Dec. 1953 (PREM 11/700).

[43] Leathers to Churchill, 14 May 1953 (PREM 11/703).

of right-wing protesters—the 'Suez Rebels' led by Lord Hinchingbrooke and Captain Waterhouse—objected with any degree of seriousness. Churchill and Eden placated them. In any event, the Anglo-Egyptian community was a far less important element, politically and socially, than the Anglo-Indian. The great days of the white ascendancy based on élite institutions such as Cairo's Shepheard's Hotel, were long over. Relations with Egypt seemed, for the moment, more tranquil, assisted by the decision of Butler, against Churchill's wishes, to release £5 m. of blocked sterling balances for the Egyptian government in January 1954. Churchill himself had to admit that the Egyptian base was much less important now, with more mobile conditions of modern warfare and a strong American presence in the Middle East as well. He told the Cabinet on 7 July 1954:

In spite of his earlier doubts he was now satisfied that the withdrawal of British troops from Egypt could be fully justified on military grounds. Our requirements in the Canal Zone had been radically changed by the admission of Turkey to the North Atlantic Treaty Organization and the extension of a defensive Middle Eastern front as far east as Pakistan. Furthermore, the advent of thermonuclear weapons had greatly increased the vulnerability of a concentrated base area and it would not be right to retain in Egypt 80,000 troops who would be better placed elsewhere.[44]

Eden's agreement with the Egyptians provoked only twenty-six dissentients in the Commons. Shuckburgh walked back to Albany from Westminster on a sunny afternoon on 29 July 1954 'feeling altogether rather pleased with myself'.[45]

The British, therefore, were in a mood to make strategic retreats from their own imperial possessions. This was much their view in the disposal of other people's empires also. In South East Asia, the Dutch East Indies had already become the independent republic of Indonesia with British encouragement.

[44] Cabinet conclusions, 7 July 1954 (CAB 128/28).
[45] Shuckburgh, *Descent to Suez*, 235.

More important was the situation in French Indo-China where the disastrous French defeat at Dien Bien Phu revealed the impossibility of the French army holding on henceforth against a powerful Vietnamese nationalist guerrilla movement. The American Secretary of State, John Foster Dulles, allegedly a man with a powerful aversion to European colonialism, actually contemplated sending in US troops to Indo-China as had been done in Korea a few years earlier. Eden and the new radical French government of Mendès-France resisted this. Eden himself achieved a notable diplomatic coup at the Geneva Convention (May–June 1954), perhaps the highlight of his post-war career, when he got Dulles and Molotov to accept a new settlement for South East Asia on the basis of new states of North and South Vietnam, Laos, and Cambodia.[46] No one imagined that these precarious new constructions would remain secure for ever; but at least Eden had averted Indo-China's being made the cockpit for a wider conflagration between the great powers, in which China would certainly be drawn in at an early stage. Indeed, the Geneva Conference, along with the Egyptian settlement and his negotiation of a new European Defence Force to circumvent difficulties between the French and Germans, made this a period of remarkable diplomatic achievement by Eden himself.

Britain visualized itself clearly as a great power still, but as the world's broker rather than the world's policeman. Churchill himself broadly subscribed to this posture, for all his hankerings for past imperial glory. He spent much of his time in 1953 and 1954 trying to bring President Eisenhower to the negotiating table with the Russians on the same basis as in wartime. He made little headway; indeed, he was rebuked by Eisenhower in 1953 for the 'astonishing' suggestion that the venue for a summit conference should be Moscow.[47] Yet much of Churchill's waning energy, and his apparently stubborn refusal to retire, arose from

[46] Rhodes James, *Anthony Eden*, 377–9.
[47] Churchill to Eisenhower, 21 Apr. 1953; Eisenhower to Churchill, 5 May 1953 (PREM 11/421).

his endeavours to create some kind of international settlement in the new situation created by the death of Stalin and the apparently less intransigent new regime of Malenkov. The premiss, of course, was Churchill's set belief that Britain was America's closest partner and confidant still. It was a view that the Americans themselves sedulously fostered on occasion. Eisenhower told Eden during discussions on the possible use of nuclear weapons and also over Egypt in March 1953 that 'he regarded Britain as his principal ally and that Canada ranked next'.[48] The reality was rather different. Indeed the period of Conservative rule down to 1956 saw Anglo-American viewpoints in conflict over Europe, Iran, Indo-China, and policy towards Communist China and the Chiang Kai Shek regime. Eden and John Foster Dulles, the US Secretary of State, were constantly at odds, and had a generally difficult personal relationship. In trying to foster the notion of some kind of revived international summitry, Britain was drawing on diminishing moral capital, while in event the Americans were displeased by Britain's continuous whittling down of its military commitments and defence expenditure.

The rhetoric of the period favoured declarations of national greatness. They were encouraged by the abiding presence of Churchill, that living embodiment of many of the Victorian values, at the head of government. The coronation of Queen Elizabeth II in 1953 gave this sentiment an emotional propulsion. In fact, Britain was now not only a weakened giant, but also an indecisive one. With the world in flux in the Middle and the Far East, the way in which British power and influence could best be deployed was uncertain. The Anglo-American relationship was under constant challenge; the Commonwealth was diminishing year by year, as a significant defence and trading unit. Some argued that the logic could only be that Britain should resume its position of 1947–8 as a leading power in Western Europe. But in fact the years of Conservative government saw a deliberate

[48] Eden to Churchill, record of conversation with Eisenhower, 9 Mar. 1953 (PREM 11/666).

policy both of isolationism towards European collaboration and of wilful disinformation towards the real evidence of the continental powers themselves coming together in greater unity. Macmillan in early 1952 tried to ensure both that Britain would retain its full membership of the Council of Europe, and also ponder the creation of links with the Schuman Plan and the European Defence Force. But he was sternly rebuked by that old imperialist, Lord Salisbury.

He himself did not believe that the United Kingdom should ever commit itself to full membership of a continental *bloc*: and he felt sure that in this view he would have the support of a substantial body of opinion in this country. We were not a continental nation, but an island power with a Colonial Empire and unique relations with the independent members of the Commonwealth. Though we might maintain a close association with the continental nations of Europe, we could never merge our interests wholly with theirs. We must be with, but not in any combination of European powers.[49]

This view was still the prevailing one. Churchill himself treated his earlier pronouncements on European unity while he was leader of the opposition with the utmost casualness. Eden emphasized the links with the United States. Others pointed to the threats to British sovereignty and perhaps defence security if there was any further involvement with continental Europe.

The consequence was that Britain drifted along in the early fifties quite detached from the Coal and Steel community and other clear manifestations of a growing European presence on a concerted basis. The Conservative election manifesto, on which Eden won the 1955 election, stated that the British pledge to keep its forces on the continent under the terms of the new European army 'has restored the basis of European unity'. Eden's covering letter urged the need 'to invest in the future—at home and in the

[49] Cabinet conclusions, 13 Mar. 1952 (CAB 128/24).

Commonwealth and Empire'. Beyond this, the Conservative position seemed unprepared to go.[50]

The problem was that, whatever the geopolitical, legal, or economic arguments against entering such arrangements as the Schuman Plan, the world position was anything but static. Events were moving beyond the capacity of the British government to control. In the summer of 1955 the six powers of the Schuman Plan, France, Western Germany, Italy, and the three Benelux countries moved rapidly to promote a broader economic unity. This provoked intense dismay in Britain, from the Foreign Office to Eden himself. Partly the move was objected to on economic grounds. D.J.C. Crawley of the Commonwealth Relations Office explained that a European Common Market would be an exclusive group and would aggravate protectionism and regional tendencies throughout the world, as well as weakening OEEC with its US and Canadian involvement. Commonwealth sentiment loomed large also, with Lord Home urging the case of the Commonwealth preferences for produce such as Australian wheat, wine, and fruit. Harry Crookshank, Leader of the House, argued that membership of any form of European Customs Union would gravely harm the Commonwealth, and he hoped for 'an early unexpected opportunity to disengage ourselves'. Political factors were adduced by C. H. Johnston of the Foreign Office who feared that an inward-looking pro-Europe sentiment would be encouraged in Western Germany instead of a more outward-looking transatlantic approach. More broadly, Eden and others urged Britain's special relationship with the United States and the generally world-wide stance adopted by British foreign policy over the centuries. Instead, the Foreign Office tried to build up the vision of a wider, more flexible OEEC in place of the supra-national authority of the proposed customs union. At the same time, the British government made clear its refusal to participate in the Euratom scheme since it was argued that the sharing of

---

[50] Rhodes James, *Anthony Eden*, 407.

atomic information would imperil British national security. Thorneycroft accused the Americans of 'living in a fools' paradise about Messina'.[51]

The European powers went ahead anyhow, with a conference at Messina in Sicily in November 1955. The British government made every attempt to undermine, or even ridicule, its importance.[52] Heavy emphasis was laid on the long history of Franco-German rivalry. The impression is left that the Foreign Office seemed to feel the real impetus for European unity came only from the mini-state of Luxemburg. An astonishing, concerted attempt at disinformation was mounted. In fact, the Messina Conference was a great success and proposed a move towards a common market; it was a move which, the British government observed, could lead to 'the nucleus of a "Third Force" which might even merge into neutralism'. In vain did Beyen, the Dutch Foreign Minister, and M. Spaak, the Belgian leader of the new European grouping, try to get the British to consider joining or at least being indirectly involved with, the new formation. It was, after all, Spaak cheerfully explained, a '*boutique*' which he hoped could be accommodated with some form of trading association with the Commonwealth nations.[53] But it was all in vain. The Treaty of Rome was concluded in 1956 with the British resistant and, indeed, actually trying to undermine it by creating some form of rival trading grouping. Anthony Nutting, a Foreign office minister, urged the Chancellor, Macmillan, the only leading minister sympathetic to the European idea, to try to urge Britain to be less lukewarm about the Atomic Energy Pool and to

[51] Draft letter from Crawley to UK High Commissioner in Ottawa, 21 Nov. 1955 (FO 371/116035 A); Crookshank to Butler 21 Sept. 1955 and Macmillan to Butler, 23 Sept. 1955 (FO 371/116049); draft policy brief, 30 Dec. 1955 and Thorneycroft to Eden, 20 Jan 1956 (FO 371/122022).

[52] See e.g. record of conversation of Sir Roger Makins with Livingstone Merchant and Burke Ellrick of US State Department. 21–2 Dec. 1955 (FO 371/115999) M 1017/14.

[53] Record of conversation of Edward Boyle with Spaak, 21 Nov. 1955 (FO 371/116035 A) M 6011/111.

try to launch a European initiative. 'I am worried about Europe', Nutting wrote.[54] But to no effect. The whole episode was a remarkable exercise in passivity and disinformation, with Britain resolutely declining to join in shaping a new European formation at the outset. By late 1956 it was clear that, nevertheless, Britain had to respond in some fashion since a European Customs Union would have inescapable consequences for British agriculture and manufactured goods, and for Commonwealth exports as well. Yet even Anglophiles like Spaak had to conclude that Britain was 'unfavourable, even hostile' to the European idea.[55] Whatever Britain's world posture was seen as being in the mid-1950s, it was heavily coloured with historic imperial overtones, and a refusal to accept that Britain was in any significant sense a European power. Even if economic and legal requirements could be reconciled, there were always 'a thousand years of history' dividing Britain from the French and other continentals. This viewpoint was evidently one that the vast majority of the British shared. Until the sixties, as opinion polls showed, the concept of any kind of merger into a Common Market was resisted by the overwhelming mass of the British people.

The mood of the nation in the mid-fifties was an uneasy combination of complacency and insularity. The moral passion of the thirties, the social idealism of the war years was evaporating in favour of a passive, uncomplaining, reformism. There were many complaints of apathy, the result many believed of the ethic of consumer materialism. Britain suddenly seemed remarkably tranquil, marooned in what the Americans once called 'the politics of dead centre', all passion spent. Developments like the influence of Sir Lewis Namier's methodology in history, more econometric forms of post-Keynesianism in economics, Leavisite approaches to literary criticism and linguistics, logical positivism in the Oxford school in philosophy, seemed to be 'taking the mind out of' the arts and social sciences. At the end of the decade,

---

[54] Nutting to Macmillan, 10 Jan. 1956 (FO 371 /122023) M611/20.
[55] Hugh Ellis-Rees to W. Strath. 3 Oct. 1955 (FO 371/116049) M606/257.

the American sociologist, Daniel Bell, a former Marxist, was to write of *The End of Ideology*. Yet there were important movements of protest in this period. Politically, most of them were on the left. Right-wing protest was relatively ineffective, with the Suez rebels and other imperialist critics, as has been seen, voiceless at the highest levels. The rhetorical jingoism of Lord Beaverbrook's *Daily Express* was conveying less and less to its readers, oblivious of what his early Empire Free Trade crusade might have been like. Its whimsical veteran proprietor increasingly turned his energies to his youthful days, to writing up the history of the premiership of an old hero, David Lloyd George.

On the left, the main dissent took place, inevitably, within the Labour Party. The resignation of Aneurin Bevan and Harold Wilson left a bitter legacy and from 1952 onwards bipartisanship in foreign policy was challenged by a series of major disputes over foreign policy. The rearmament of Western Germany was one source of dissension, with Bevan and up to 100 parliamentary supporters, along with several trade unions, resolutely opposed. Only by the most blatant manipulation of the still mainly right-wing block vote did party conference endorse German rearmament in 1954, by 3,270,000 to 3,022,000. The political scientist, Robert McKenzie, used this episode to argue that Attlee and his colleagues were deeply confused over party democracy, and that in reality the Labour Party was as authoritarian as the Tories towards the rank and file.[56] American foreign policy in the Far East, with Britain having to give indirect backing to Chiang Kai Shek, defend the regime in Formosa, and risk being dragged into nuclear war in South-East Asia, led to further fierce disputes. In March 1955, Bevan was, for the third time in his life, removed from the party whip for attacking Attlee and his colleagues over accession to the South-East Asia Treaty Organization (SEATO). A growing current of opinion was welling

[56] Robert McKenzie, *British Political Parties* (London, new edn., 1963). 598.

up to urge that Britain should not involve itself with nuclear weapons at all.

All these incidents, however, were caught up in internal personal and factional disputes in the party, especially the intense hostility between the Gaitskellite right and the Bevanite left. Much fury erupted when Gaitskell, in a vehement speech at Stalybridge in 1952, seemed to link the Bevanites with the Communists and depicted *Tribune* as 'an attempt at mob rule by a group of frustrated journalists' which must be stopped.[57] Incidents such as the defection of Harold Wilson from the Bevanite camp back to the party mainstream by rejoining the shadow Cabinet in 1954 when Bevan left it, underlined the byzantine quality of these Labour manœuvres. Bevan himself was saved from outright expulsion from the party in March 1955 by the intervention of the ageing Attlee himself, and the conscience of James Haworth, a trade-union member of the National Executive who was a Moral Rearmer.[58] But the prevalence of widespread alarm with the course of foreign policy, laced with growing anti-Americanism, was widespread on the left. It was, in any case, not necessary to be a left-wing socialist to see that the world was already more fluid than in Stalin's era, with such developments as a new regime of change in Russia, the possibilities of tension between the Soviet Union and Communist China, and the growth of non-aligned third-world powers in Africa and Asia. There was more talk of 'third force' movements and nuclear-free zones in Europe as a prelude to German rearmament. The stereotypes of the Cold War were harder to defend by the time Eden became premier in April 1955. Indeed, he himself had been a major factor in urging that they be looked at afresh.

Dissent on international matters was accompanied by rising tides of grievances at home. The Bevanites were notably active in enlisting support among the trade unions, the railwaymen and engineers for instance, as well as amongst middle-class

[57] Philip Williams, *Gaitskell*, 304–8.   [58] Ibid. 344.

constituency party activists. Much the same was true of another left-wing body, the Movement for Colonial Freedom, headed by old leftists like Fenner Brockway and Sydney Silverman, but also drawing in a much younger figure like Anthony Wedgwood Benn.[59] Trade-union disaffection with the leadership of Attlee and Morrison, two inert personalities now, encouraged a growing left-wing tendency in the Labour grass roots, as shown in the entrenched position of the Bevanites on the NEC from the bad-tempered conference at Morecambe in 1952 onwards. By 1955 James Griffiths was the only non-Bevanite on the seven-member constituency section of the NEC, while Michael Foot's editorship made *Tribune* highly influential within radical opinion, perhaps the more so after he lost his Plymouth seat in 1955. The old right-wing domination of the main unions was harder to defend, while a growing rash of strikes among engineering, shipyard, and railway workers showed the pattern of dissent. A major new development came with the new leadership of the giant Transport and General Workers. Arthur Deakin, the stern anti-Communist who had followed Bevin's policy, died in 1955, and his successor, Jock Tiffin, had a very brief tenure of office. He was followed in 1956 by Frank Cousins, a left-wing opponent of any form of wage restraint, and also a man with strong, if confused, views on foreign affairs including moral objection to any kind of nuclear defence policy. By mid-1956, the old consensus in the Labour Party was weaker. Gaitskell's election as leader in place of Attlee in December 1955 did not help, even if it was modified by Bevan's return to the fold and his appointment as shadow Colonial Secretary in 1956. A new mood of political protest was in the making.

Further to the left, socialist critiques took another form in 1956, following Nikita Khrushchev's denunciation of Stalinism and the 'cult of personality' prior to 1953, at the Twentieth Party Congress. This was followed in October, as will be seen, by the

[59] Partha S. Gupta, *Imperialism and the British Labour Movement*, 360ff.

Russian invasion of Hungary. These events caused a great crisis of conscience on the far left, and several important intellectuals left the Communist Party, including historians like E. P. Thompson and John Saville, and philosophers like Alasdair MacIntyre and Charles Taylor. They founded a new journal, shortly to be named *New Left Review*, an important attempt to fuse Marxist diagnoses of the class structure with libertarian republicanism derived from the Renaissance, and to reconcile both with national identity.[60] With their ability to influence many on the Labour left, the New Left group suggested another important deviation from the political quiescence and apathy of the period.

The major protest movement of the time, however, was less political than cultural. To some extent it focused on the educated young, short of idealism but feeling discontented with the drab and uninspiring nature of their welfarized society. One factor that, unexpectedly, boosted youthful discontent was the existence of National Service. Far from serving as a crucible of patriotism, the forced drafting of hundreds of thousands of young men to serve in disagreeable and frequently time-wasting activities at huge public expense, gave many of them their first sense of protest at authority, a taste of forbidden fruit. A new radicalism was in the making.

In the literary and theatrical field, the mood of dissent welled up. It was not directly political on the model, say, of the war poets of 1914–18 or the poets of the thirties with their concern for Republican Spain. It often took the form of a bored bloody-mindedness, resentful at authority in general, but also caustic over stereotypes of Empire and class rule which still inhabited the land. There was no great indication of this kind of mood emerging in the years after 1951. The theatre was still genteel; its more serious productions were illustrated by Enid Bagnold's *The Chalk Garden*, a hymn of praise to middle-aged, middle-class tastes. The Haymarket Theatre seemed to turn into a permanent

[60] Geoffrey Foote. *The Labour Party's Political Thought: A History* (London, 1985). 287ff. The *NLR* came into being under that name in 1960.

home for distressed gentlewomen. The rising novelists of the period, notably Anthony Powell and Iris Murdoch, were not free with wider social comment, and certainly not expressive of a generalized discontent with their times. Commentators wrote of 'curious placidity, the half-living' of Britain at this period.[61] Literary editors complained of the lack of challenge to the older pre-war literary orthodoxies, even if English writing picked up a good deal after the nadir of the forties. Kingsley Amis's novel, *Lucky Jim*, published in 1954, was later claimed to mark a new kind of social comment and categorization. Certainly, Jim Dixon, the rootless, disenchanted university lecturer hero (or anti-hero) of Amis's book, was a highly distinctive post-war creation. But the book as a whole was a satirical treatment of a personal predicament and a private set of human relationships rather than a diagnosis of underlying social forces. Amis himself, in the bluntest language, denied that his book was in any way concerned with class consciousness or social analysis.[62] The most that could be said was that Amis, a lecturer at Swansea, was offering a study in a kind of provincialism. Something similar could be said of John Wain's *Hurry On Down*.

The new cultural genre burst upon British, or rather London, sensibilities in May 1956 with the appearance of John Osborne's play at the Royal Court Theatre, Sloane Square, *Look Back in Anger*. Almost immediately afterwards there appeared Colin Wilson's philosophical/mystical work, *The Outsider* which, astonishingly, was for a time linked with Osborne's play. Followed by the northern abrasiveness of Joe Lampton in John Braine's *Room at the Top*, these works promoted the famous cult of the 'Angry Young Man' which, quite unexpectedly, became one of the important stereotypes of the fifties. Of all

---

[61] Kenneth Allsop, *The Angry Decade: A Survey of the Cultural Revolt of the Nineteen-Fifties* (London, 1958), 182.

[62] Harry Ritchie, *Success Stories: Literature and the Media in England, 1950–1959* (London, 1988), 86–8. Amis points out that Dixon's dislike for Professor ('History Speaking') Welch is based on personal, not class, factors.

these, it was clearly Osborne's play which was the most important cultural symbol. Colin Wilson's book, ecstatically hailed by
critics like Cyril Connolly and Philip Toynbee in the serious
Sunday newspapers, was intensely personal, an almost nihilist
mélange of Sartre, Camus, Beckett, Hesse, and many others. It
was, said Wilson, the work of 'a man who has awakened to
chaos'.[63] Wilson himself, living rough in a slum flat, eating junk
food, bespectacled, longhaired, wearing turtle-neck sweaters
and dirty sandals, was a perfect image of the new Bohemian,
and for perhaps a year he enjoyed a huge celebrity. *The
Outsider*, within its first two months, went through nine
printings and sold over 20,000 copies. Its title was widely
applied, and misapplied, to a variety of personalities from
Lloyd George to the film actor, James Dean. But the bubble
soon burst. Wilson's second book, *Religion and the Rebel*,
received so savage a reception that his fame rapidly evaporated. So far as it had any philosophical weight, which is
doubtful, it verged towards a private form of fascism. John
Braine's work, like that of Alan Sillitoe at the end of the fifties,
far from celebrating egalitarianism or rediscovering working-
class life, was a saga of a man who embraced capitalist values
in their rawest form, in order to escape from the proletarian
drabness of provincial Bradford.

John Osborne, however, was much more important. The
Royal Court, under the direction of George Devine, became the
citadel of a new, outspoken form of cultural criticism. It was
joined by Joan Littlewood's Theatre Workshop, based in Strat-
ford-atte-Bowe in London's East End, a much more avowedly
socialist enterprise. This new theatrical radicalism at first
expressed itself in the staging of plays by eminent foreigners
like Bertold Brecht and Brendan Behan. Brecht, in particular,
proved to be an immense influence in encouraging playwrights
and drama producers to turn to political and social themes. Not

[63] Ritchie, op. cit., 141 ff.

until Shelagh Delaney's *A Taste of Honey* (1959), set in the slums of Salford, did an authentic new British talent begin to emerge. Osborne, however, stood on his own.

The element of 'anger' in his plays was unfocused. Much of it was based on its content and raw language, rather than its form or message. In part, Jimmy Porter was angry because there was nothing obvious to be angry about—there were 'no great causes left' like the Jarrow March or the Spanish Civil War. Its passion was sprayed around indiscriminately, as from a Sten gun, but was no less effective for that. The play denounced Tory bourgeois values on the hoof, including bishops who blessed the hydrogen bomb. 'I want to hear a warm, thrilling voice cry out Hallelujah', Porter exclaims. But the play was equally contemptuous of Attlee-type conventionality, the unquestioning conformism and pedestrian quality of welfare democracy, British-style. Britain, as presented by Osborne in *Look Back in Anger* and later in *The Entertainer*, a study of a seedy music-hall comedian in his declining years (played on the stage by Laurence Olivier), was a dreary, ramshackle kind of museum. It was obsessed by class distinctions and dead history, a mausoleum of repressed emotion and unarticulated guilt. The social and political drift of it all was hard to follow. Osborne's rage against Tory England ('Tory is the rudest four-letter word I know') was paralleled by attacks on the Labour leadership too—'I hate you, Gaitskell.'[64] Osborne's fire in time became so ill-directed and perhaps so modish—the Church, the bomb, women in general, gardening, and home improvement were all grist to his whirling mill—as to be ineffective or even boring. In the fullness of time, like Amis and Braine, his political sympathies became increasingly conservative, perhaps patriotic, while as a social philosopher he scarcely existed. But the intellectual impact of *Look Back in Anger* and the youth revolt it was held to represent was important for the

---

[64] Robert Hewison, *Too Much: Art and Society in the Sixties, 1960–75* (London, 1988 edn.), 1 ff. referring to Tom Maschler (ed.) *Declaration* (London, 1957).

period. It began an iconoclastic impatience with convention that found expression, much later, in the satirical productions of the early 1960s, and later still in the student revolt of that decade. In a placid, conventional society, blunt questions had been asked, in a way that made the given structure of post-war Britain seem unstable, perhaps undesirable. The ultimate target was not the capitalist order but 'the establishment', a popular term at the time, a *mélange* of entrenched attitudes, dynastic order, and social clichés. In its modest way, it was less of a revolt, more a revolution.

At a more popular level, there were signs that young people were losing patience with the schmaltz offered by ballad singers like Vera Lynn, Anne Shelton, and Donald Peers. Pop music which spoke much more directly of sexual experiment, liberation, and the problems of adolescence became increasingly popular. An astonishing cultural landmark was the impact of the American film, *Rock Around the Clock* (1955), which brought teenage hysteria to hosts of cinemas and, through the impact of Bill Haley and the Comets, the liberating influence of 'rock and roll' to dance halls all over the country. There was much violence and much conventional head-shaking at the forms the youth cult now took, like the mod-ishly dressed but potentially aggressive Teddy Boys[65] and clashes between rival gangs of youths in seaside resorts. The wider social import was hard to analyse. But, with its growing emphasis on emotional emancipation, bisexualism, and physical interaction or conflict, 'rock and roll' was another sword pointed at the heart of Anthony Eden's England.

Less heeded at the time was another critique which was to prove important. The inability of the British to sustain or even acknowledge the role of the distinguished scientists working within their society led to much dismay. Britain in the 1950s was still the humane, ordered, static world that Matthew Arnold had prescribed. Issue was taken with all this in the works of C. P. Snow, a Cambridge physicist by origin who was embarked on a

[65] See Kenneth Leech, *Youthquake: The Growth of a Counter-Culture through Two Decades* (London, 1975) on this.

notable series of novels dealing with the issues raised by life in a Cambridge college. The 'Strangers and Brothers' sequence began with the introverted events of the election of a college head, *The Masters* (1951), but Snow was also fascinated by the way education interlocked with human ambition, with science, technology, and the processes of government. He wrote sombrely of the 'corridors of power' which his characters stealthily trod—and in which they often lost their way. In 'The Two Cultures' in 1956, an article in the *New Statesman*, a controversial but undeniably influential work, he drew attention to the disparity in Britain whereby a declining, literary culture retained all its traditional power and prestige, while the new, assertive, expansive culture of the scientists sought in vain to capture the universe.[66] Whether these two cultures existed at all, let alone in the stark polarization that Snow described, was much disputed. F. R. Leavis and other literary critics were to pummel Snow for his philistinism.[67] But he touched an important chord—that what was wrong with fifties Britain was not that it was class-ridden or even cruel, but rather that it was pathetically backward and inefficient, lagging far behind others in modernizing, re-equipping, or redefining its structure and values.

Snow was not averse from more direct political exploration. His novel *The New Men* (1954), examined the crisis of conscience posed for the scientist engaged on atomic research which would obliterate humanity. But his 'Two Cultures' probed a wider theme, a failure of national will, the incapacity of an ageing society to adapt itself to the challenge of the new. It was shown in the inadequacies of the educational system, in the differing prestige accorded to men of letters and to scientists (affectionately derided as 'boffins'), in the unwillingness to invest in or sponsor technical change. Every year, the somewhat

---

[66] *New Statesman*, 6 Oct. 1956. Snow developed his views in the Rede Lectures in Cambridge in 1959.

[67] For a good discussion, see Robert Hewison, *In Anger: Culture in the Cold War, 1945–60* (London, 1981), 45ff.

enfeebled Advisory Council on Scientific Policy, chaired by Sir
Alexander Todd, with Zuckerman, Cockcroft, and Waddington
among its other luminaries, complained of how government,
education, and industry were being starved of scientific talent.
Cherwell ensured that his prickly but undeniably innovative
rival, Tizard, was sidetracked for the chairmanship.[68] This kind
of critique had been steadily repeated in Britain since the obsession with the German technical challenge in the 1880s and
1890s. This time, though, it had a new urgency and, perhaps
for the first time, some genuine popular appeal.

This varied current of political, social, and cultural dissent
enriched public debate. But the general tendency of the times
still appeared grooved in consensus and complacency. Such contemporary themes as the abolition of capital punishment or the
reform of the legal approach towards homosexuality aroused
more passion than did political or social controversy. The phenomenon of the Angry Young Man, with Osborne and Wilson as
its sandalled, nonconformist symbols, burst upon a society which
had changed remarkably little since the war, and in which the
note of protest or conflict was muted. The upper-class whimsy of
Julian Slade's *Salad Days* or Sandy Wilson's *The Girl Friend*
captured for many the mood of the hour, especially perhaps in
the 'shoddy-chic jungle between Belgravia and Cheyne Walk
where the young men in bowlers chatter with debs training as
Constance Spry flower arrangers'.[69] Two months later it was all
totally different. Anthony Eden's invasion of Suez divided opinion with a passion and a savagery unknown since Munich.

Eden's premiership had begun in placid enough vein, with the
comfortable election victory of May 1955 and the Labour opposition paralysed by the conflict between Gaitskellites and Bevanites. Attlee's decision to delay his resignation as leader until
December 1955, to frustrate the ambitions of Morrison, made

---

[68] Solly Zuckerman, *Men, Monkeys and Missiles* (London, 1988), 104. Todd
was an OM and Professor of Chemistry at Cambridge.
[69] Allsop, *Angry Decade*, 86.

the uncomradely conflict distinctly worse. Eden's position as premier was not wholly stable in personal terms. Complaints of his neurotic, interventionist style as Prime Minister led to public statements in January 1956 that he had no intention of resigning,[70] a somewhat discouraging start. Churchill's doubts about his capacity to lead seemed justified. Butler was misquoted as describing Eden as 'the best Prime Minister we've got'. Ambitious subordinates like Macmillan, Chancellor of the Exchequer from December 1955, were plotting against him. Butler's mishandling of the economy which encouraged the sterling crisis of the autumn of 1955 also created problems, even while *The Economist* boasted that 'the financial leadership of the United Kingdom was undisputed'.[71] However, by the spring of 1956 the economy seemed again secure. There were 400,000 unfilled job vacancies, and only 216,000 registered unemployed. Social peace remained the watchword. Macleod and other ministers argued successfully against Macmillan's plan to abolish the bread subsidy—'The more responsible elements in the Trade Union movement would fail to comprehend the action of the Government in deliberately raising the cost of living at this stage, and the leaders would be unable to sustain a policy of moderation if the Government took this step.'[72] Monckton was another, predictable supporter of the *status quo*, as was the Prime Minister himself.

In the event, Macmillan's first (and only) budget in 1956 was generally acclaimed save for protests from churchmen about the introduction of premium bonds to encourage saving, which in their view reinforced the moral dangers of gambling. For Labour, Wilson denounced the scheme as 'a squalid raffle'. By the start of June, record British exports of £238.3 m. were being recorded, including a sharp rise to North America. Britain's eminence in international affairs seemed confirmed by Eden's presence in Number 10 and by the visit of the Soviet leaders, Bulganin and

---

[70] Rhodes James, *Anthony Eden*, 425–6.
[71] *The Economist*, 24 Sept. 1955.
[72] Cabinet conclusions, 10 Feb. 1956 (CAB 128/30 pt. 1).

Khrushchev, to Britain in April 1956. Their observations on Oxford college customs and the feudal remnants of society which their hosts chose to show them made rich copy for journalists: when Khrushchev had the custom of choral singing on Magdalen Tower on May morning explained to him, he memorably (perhaps unanswerably) asked 'Why?' To Epstein's sculpture of Lazarus in New College Chapel, he applied the description 'decadent rubbish'. The visit was generally successful, marred only by a row with Labour leaders, including Bevan as well as right-wingers like George Brown, on the state of civil liberties and the plight of dissidents in the Soviet Union. 'May God forgive you', exclaimed Brown to Khruschev. The latter responded that 'if these are your socialists, I am for the Conservatives'.

Then came the dramatic impact of Suez. A crisis had long been foreseen by the British government. Eden himself reacted in sharply personal terms to the failure to get relationships with the Egyptian government on a new basis after the treaty to withdraw British troops. There was a disastrous meeting with President Nasser in Cairo in early 1955, at which the dinner-jacketed Eden's recollections of having read Oriental Languages at Christ Church and choice of Arab proverbs as conversational gambits did not go down well with his hosts.[73] Eden now became obsessed with Nasser as a Napoleonic or (alternatively) Hitler-like figure bent on establishing a pan-Arab dominion from the Persian Gulf to Morocco on the Atlantic seaboard. He also saw Nasser as a man flirting with communism. He was to tell Eisenhower how Nasser was a 'Moslem Mussolini' with broad expansionist ambitions, who must be dealt with as the dictators in the thirties should have been. He added, 'I have no doubt that the Bear is using Nasser, with or without his knowledge, to further his immediate aims. These are, I think, first to dislodge the West from the Middle East, and second to get a foothold in Africa so as to dominate that continent in turn.' When the Mussolini metaphor

[73] Mohamed H. Heikal, *Cutting the Lion's Tail: Suez through Egyptian Eyes* (London, 1986), 61 ff.

lost its savour, he added that Nasser was bent on becoming 'the Napoleon of the Arabs'. 'We have many times led Europe in the fight for freedom. It would be an ignoble end to our long history if we tamely accepted to perish by degrees.'[74] Thus a combination of bad temper and bad history led Eden into fatal directions.

Nasser's involvement with the Russians dominated Eden's mind. He told the ambassador in Cairo, Sir Humphrey Trevelyan, that 'Russia has put us on notice that she intends to open a third front in the Cold War, this time in the Middle East.'[75] Sir Ivone Kirkpatrick of the Foreign Office observed that 'Nasser was a man who did not seem to realize the dangers of putting his head into the Russian jaws'.[76] By the start of 1956, it was official British policy to destabilize the Nasser regime: according to one controversial account,[77] there were MI5 security schemes to assassinate the Egyptian President through the use of canisters of nerve gas. Eden, intent on building up the Baghdad Pact with friendly Arab powers, became convinced that Nasser was a demonic, unstable force and a threat to the west. Friendly relations with Egypt, he told the Cabinet, were no longer possible. His hatred of Nasser reached a new pitch in February 1956 with the dismissal of General Sir John Glubb, the legendary British commander of the Arab Legion, by the formerly friendly King Hussein. Eden was convinced that the hand of Nasser could be detected here. He urged Anglo-US moves against the Egyptian government, including blocking the sterling balances and withdrawal of financial aid for the planned Aswan Dam.[78] On 19 July, the American Secretary of State, John Foster Dulles, did indeed stop aid for the Dam project. Even though anticipated, this was a mighty blow to Egyptian pride which made Nasser more dependent on Russian and Czech assistance than

---

[74] Eden to Eisenhower, 5 Nov. 1956 (FO 800/721).
[75] Eden to Trevelyan, 27 Oct. 1955 (PREM 11/859).
[76] Kirkpatrick memorandum, 29 Nov. 1955 (FO 371/113786).
[77] See Peter Wright, *Spycatcher* (New York, 1987), 160–1.
[78] Cabinet conclusions, 21 Mar. 1956 (CAB 128/30 pt. I).

previously. The irony was that the cast of British policy in the region was still broadly pro-Arab and unsympathetic to Israel. If Israel attacked Syria or Jordan, Britain was committed under the 1950 Tripartite Declaration to dispatch forces to fight the Israelis. But the prevailing factor was the growing rift between Britain and Egypt which, in the face of American warnings and clear coolness from the Commonwealth, was coming to dominate British external planning.

The crisis broke on 25 July when the Egyptian government proclaimed that it had nationalized the Suez Canal. The British reaction was furious.[79] The British admitted that it was hard to argue that the Egyptian move was illegal under international law; indeed, the Attorney-General, Manningham-Buller, was studiously kept at arm's length from government policy towards Egypt. Rather was it argued that an international asset was in grave peril, and that incompetent Egyptian administration should not take over the running of this mighty waterway and hold the world to ransom. Eden, Selwyn Lloyd (the Foreign Secretary), and Macmillan were hawkish from the outset. Macmillan urged a landing west of Alexandria 'to seek out and destroy Nasser's armies and destroy his government'.[80] From 27 July, the Chiefs of Staff were urged to prepare a timetable for military action against Egypt with perhaps three divisions being sent to the Canal Zone to protect it.[81] The Cabinet's Egypt Committee, which met almost daily, was unambiguous on its role.[82] While an international conference would be called, to which Egypt would be invited, the emphasis was on military force. The aircraft carrier, *Bulwark*, parachute and other troops, Valiant bombers from Malta, Libya, Aden, and Bahrein would all be put on a war footing. 'While our ultimate purpose was to

---

[79]   Ibid. 27 July 1956 (CAB 128/30 pt. II).

[80]   Lord Ramsden, brief for Macmillan, 21 Jan. 1957 (PREM 11/1789): note by Macmillan, 7 Aug. 1956 (PREM 11/1098).

[81]   Material in DEFE 4/93.

[82]   Material in PREM 11/1098–1105.

place the Canal under international control, our immediate objective was to bring about the downfall of the present Egyptian government.'[83] Selwyn Lloyd told the US envoy, Murphy, and Pineau, the French Foreign Minister, on 29 July that Britain was already preparing possible military action.[84] In a debate in the Commons, Eden's fury at Nasser was compounded by the Labour leader, Gaitskell, who compared Nasser with Hitler and referred to the failure of the appeasement of dictators before 1939.[85]

Throughout August, while a conference of Canal Users was convened in London by Eden and Dulles, the military preparations went on. It was assumed that collaboration with the French would be essential, even though France was exceptionally unpopular in the Arab world at that time owing to its repressive policy in the war in Algeria (and even though the French Prime Minister, Guy Mollet, was a socialist). A military plan was drawn up, to be implemented no later than 15 September, on present intentions. But already, despite Eden's commitment, dissent was building up. Within the Cabinet ministers like Walter Monckton and Lord Salisbury were urging caution. Monckton argued that the Egyptians should not be underrated as a fighting force, while Salisbury, with his sensitivity for Commonwealth opinion, urged action through the UN rather than a unilateral military attack by Britain and France.[86] The American government, under Dulles (who had a strong aversion to British colonialism though he was quite content with US policy of a similar kind in South-East Asia and Central America) urged against military intervention, as did President Eisenhower, who became increasingly assertive on the point. After Gaitskell's early somewhat inflammatory remarks, the Labour Party, Lord Salisbury observed on 9 August, was 'steadily sliding away',[87] with centre-right figures like Healey

---

[83] Minutes of Cabinet Egypt Committee, 30 July 1956 (PREM 11/1098).
[84] Record of meeting of Lloyd. Pineau, and Murphy, 29 July 1956 (ibid.).
[85] Parl. Deb., 5th ser., vol. 557, 1609ff (2 Aug. 1956).
[86] Cabinet conclusions, 28 Aug. 1956 (CAB 128/30 pt. II).
[87] Salisbury to Eden, 9 Aug. 1956 (PREM 11/1099).

and Jay urging caution on Gaitskell, and the Bevanite left reacting strongly to imperialist assaults on Egypt. The Labour Party declared in favour of joint diplomatic action through the United Nations, and it became clear that British opinion was increasingly divided on how to respond to the nationalization of the Canal. There was also dissent between Eden and Keightley, the general in charge of the military operations, which were now postponed to at least 6 October. It became clear that launching a military operation from three hundred miles' distance, using the Cyprus base, was a difficult prospect, while Egyptian defences might well be hard to breach. Keightley urged that it was vital that 'the invasion of Egypt is launched with our moral case unanswerable'. Eden's scribbled comment was: 'Yet he won't delay to strengthen it.'[88]

By mid-September Eden, Macmillan and the Cabinet hawks were in a dilemma. The Suez Canal Users Conference led to the formation of a Users' Association but with no guarantees that it would be able to impose its authority on the Egyptian government. A mission to Cairo by Robert Menzies, the Australian Prime Minister, a somewhat surprising emissary, led nowhere. The United States, with a presidential election looming, was more and more uneasy at a possible Anglo-French assault on Egypt before the processes of diplomacy had been used up. The Conservative Party Conference at Llandudno at the start of October included a surprisingly moderate statement on the desirability of a settlement, given by Anthony Nutting the Foreign Office minister with responsibility for the Middle East.[89]

But, behind the scenes, a new departure was under way. The government of Israel, in theory still the target for British military plans through its threat to Jordan, now became a secret ally. The idea first emerged at a meeting at Chequers on 14 October between Eden and General Maurice Challe. At two private

---

[88] Memorandum on 'Operation Musketeer. Implication of Postponement', 6 Sept. 1956 (PREM 11/1104).
[89] *The Times*, 12 Oct. 1956.

meetings in Paris on 16 October, with Mollet and Pineau, Eden and Lloyd urged the Israeli premier, Ben Gurion, to direct his attack on Egypt, not Jordan. If that happened, Eden guaranteed that Britain 'would not come to the assistance of Egypt because Egypt was in breach of a Security Council resolution and repudiated Western aid under the Tripartite Declaration'. At a further secret meeting at Sèvres on 22–3 October, the plan was drawn up by Lloyd and Pineau that Israel should attack Egypt, that Britain and France should then urge both sides to stop hostilities and withdraw ten miles from the Canal, and that, in the certain event of Egypt not accepting this ultimatum, the Anglo-French forces would then attack and occupy the Canal Zone. On the 24th, Patrick Dean of the Foreign Office signed a record of the agreement in Paris: the Prime Minister then had the document destroyed. Eden told the Cabinet on 25 October, 'We must face the risk that we should be accused of collusion with Israel. But this charge was liable to be brought against us in any case...'[90] There were still dissenting voices in the Cabinet, including Butler according to some accounts: but one critic was downgraded when Monckton was moved from the Defence Ministry and replaced by the hawkish Anthony Head. On 30 October the Israelis duly attacked.

According to the timetable, the Anglo-French ultimatum then followed. The Egyptians predictably refused to withdraw from the Canal and air bombardment ensued of Cairo and Port Said. A tense few days followed, with signs of acute ministerial dissension. At a Cabinet meeting on the evening of 4 November, Eden for the first time faced open opposition from Butler who proposed a deferment of military action since fighting in the Canal Zone had already stopped. At this point, Eden, according to Butler's and other accounts, threatened resignation, or at least came close to doing so. In the end, a Cabinet vote was taken that evening, and the vote in favour of an immediate airborne landing

[90] Cabinet conclusions, 18, 25 Oct. 1956 (CAB 128/30 pt. II).

was 12 to 6 (Butler, Kilmuir, Salisbury, Monckton, Heathcoat-Amory, and Buchan-Hepburn). No one, however, resigned, not even Monckton, and Eden could claim that the majority in favour of armed intervention was overwhelming. The following day, British forces landed and soon occupied Port Fuad and part of the Canal area. There was also some bombing of the suburbs of Cairo itself on 5–6 November, inflicting considerable military and civilian casualties, perhaps 1,000 in all. Unilateral British military action had occurred.

The next few days shook the world. There was a huge rift in Anglo-American relations. Dulles urged that the attack on Suez was 'a pretty brutal affair', while Eisenhower angrily ordered Eden to withdraw British troops and obey the edict of the UN.[91] Eden himself tried to obscure the facts of British collusion with Israel by telling Eisenhower on 5 November how relieved he was that the Israelis had turned their attack on to Egypt rather than Jordan. He denied that Britain wanted to occupy Egyptian territory on a permanent basis. 'We could not afford it and that is one of many other reasons why we got out of Suez two years ago.' Eisenhower was not deceived, and emphasized again the effect of Britain's military action on Arab and third-world opinion, and the need to find alternative forms of action through the United Nations.[92] It became obvious that the American government, to intensify the pressure, was encouraging a run on the pound and on the reserves, which could lead to a huge sterling crisis, worse than 1947. In the UN General Assembly, Britain was condemned by 64 votes to 5, and denounced as an international aggressor. There was loud complaint that the outrage expressed by the west at the Russian invasion of Hungary had been nullified. Sir Pierson Dixon, the unfortunate British representative at the UN, complained to Eden that he and his French colleague were

---

[91] Winthrop Aldrich to Eden, 30 Oct. 1936; Washington Embassy to Lloyd, tel. 2206, 31 Oct. 1956 (PREM 11/11055).

[92] Sir Pierson Dixon telegram to Foreign Office, 31 Oct. 1956, tel. 1035 (ibid.).

friendless in the world unless they announced an immediate end to hostilities.[93]

In Britain there was a huge outcry. Individuals like Hugh Thomas resigned from the Foreign Office. Two ministers, Anthony Nutting, a Foreign Office minister, and Edward Boyle, resigned from the government, while William Clark, Eden's press spokesman, also resigned. Middle-opinion newspapers like the *Observer* spoke of 'gangsterism'[94] while Alastair Hetherington's leaders in the *Guardian* took the same line. The Labour Party, backed by the Liberals, some dissident Tories like John Grigg, and the United Nations Association in a kind of revived Popular Front, led a huge public outcry in a 'Law not War' campaign. Gaitskell now became a passionate critic of the government, more so than Bevan himself, whose Zionism made him temperamentally hostile to Nasser. A public meeting at Trafalgar Square on 4 November, addressed by Bevan and others, led to violence between mounted police and angry student protesters in Whitehall. On television, Gaitskell, the Labour leader, condemned Eden with cold passion and urged the Prime Minister to resign. In the end, less because of this political campaign than because of financial pressure from the United States, the British government declared a cease-fire in Port Said and elsewhere in the Canal area on 8 November. The worst of the crisis was over.

Over the next four weeks, a shabby and humiliating retreat took place. The American government, through representatives such as Dulles and Henry Cabot Lodge, directed the full flow of its fury on the British UN delegates and ministers. Under US pressure, Britain had to concede the principle of withdrawal in favour of a United Nations force of Scandinavians, Canadians, Irish, and others, even though no guarantees of a clearance of the

---

[93] Ibid., and Dixon to Foreign Office, 4 Nov. 1956 (ibid.).

[94] *Observer*, 4 Nov. 1956: David Astor (editor of the *Observer*) to Iain Macleod, 14 Nov. 1956 (PREM 11/1127); William Clark, *From Three Worlds* (London, 1986).

Canal had been secured. It was, recorded Dixon, 'a disaster'.[95] The Canal itself, whose freedom of navigation was the ostensible purpose of the Anglo-French-Israeli collusion, was now totally blocked, with Egyptian-sunk blockships obstructing shipping of any kind. By 5 December there would be 4,000 UN troops in the Zone.[96] Lloyd complained to Butler:

I think we may have to tell certain selected individuals that the Americans have no intention of lifting a finger to help to preserve us from financial disaster until they are certain that we are removing ourselves from Port Said quickly. Although they may help Europe over oil (and possibly us at the same time) on broader economic issues they are just non-negotiable until we have taken this step.

Lloyd complained that the Americans were 'completely irrational' but he had no real choice.[97] Macmillan, formerly extremely hawkish, had to tell his colleagues of an outflow of perhaps $ 300 m. of gold and dollar reserves in November with a huge shock effect on international confidence in sterling. On 28 November Macmillan reversed his position completely. 'He therefore favoured a prompt announcement of our intention to withdraw this force, justifying this action on the ground that we had now achieved the purpose for which we had originally launched the Anglo-French military operation in Egypt.' Bridges had in fact warned Macmillan as early as 13 August that the economy was in a poor condition to withstand further strains on resources, but to no effect.[98]

The British leadership, individually and collectively, cut a sorry figure. Monckton, a rare voice of moderation, was sent to the Canal Zone to produce for cosmetic purposes an account of the small number of Egyptian war casualties there had actually been, and detail the fastidious care taken by British bombers in

---

[95] Dixon to Foreign Office, 10 Nov. 1956, no. 1163 (PREM 11/1106).
[96] Dixon to Foreign Office. 26 Nov. 1956, no. 1406 (ibid.).
[97] Lloyd to Butler, 28 Nov. 1956, no. 1431 (ibid.).
[98] Cabinet conclusions, 28 Nov. (CAB 128/30 pt. II). For the effect of the Suez operation on sterling, see materials in T 236/4188–4190.

avoiding civilian targets.[99] Monckton had been previously an embarassed critic of the Anglo-French action who had failed to resign. Ministers like Butler, Macleod, and Heathcoat-Amory had been ambiguous in the crisis, too. Butler, to adapt Bevan's observation on Lloyd, found himself forced in the Commons to sound the bugle of advance to cover his retreat. The hawks in the Cabinet, like Lloyd, Head, and Lennox-Boyd, all lost stature. The worst casualty of all was the Prime Minister. Eden, the stylish prince of international diplomacy, with a rare hold on the public affections since he resigned as Foreign Secretary not long before Munich, was now stamped as an intemperate, almost hysterical, man of war. On 23 November he told his colleagues that, on medical advice, he had to take an immediate vacation, and he departed for the West Indies to recuperate. While he was away, the last rites of the Suez operation were conducted, with much bitter vituperation between the British and French erstwhile allies, and between both and the Israelis. On 22 December, six weeks after their dispatch, the last British troops were withdrawn from the Suez area. It was almost the last British independent military venture in the twentieth century, and amongst the most humiliating. It tore apart the Anglo-American relationship and damaged the unity of the Commonwealth. It made Britain a pariah at the United Nations and brought its economic stability into grave question. Even as a military operation, it was a doubtful success. Malta was too distant, while the Libyan bases could not be used. The launch of the British airborne force from Cyprus had been erratic and cumbersome, with the element of surprise lost. The bombing raids on the Suez area anticipated the drop of British paratroops by six days. The tank-loading ships were too few in number, and the tanks used far too big.[100] Worst of all, the British stood branded as offenders

[99] Monckton's record of a visit to Port Said, 24–5 Nov. 1956 (Monckton Papers, Dep. 8, 231 ff.); Monckton to Head, 17 Dec. 1956 (ibid).
[100] Liddell Hart in the *Observer*, 24 Feb. 1957; material in Conservative Research Department archive (CRD/2/34/19).

against international law, if not plain liars. Eden returned almost in disgrace, and still in indifferent health, early in the new year. On 9 January 1957 he resigned, his reputation in tatters. Harold Macmillan, the hawk turned dove who had been manœuvring for the succession throughout Eden's absence, beat off the challenge of Butler and succeeded Eden as premier.

The entire Suez affair had been extraordinarily bitter. British life was rent with a passion almost incomprehensible to those who had visited the placid, dormant land basking in the cricket victories over the Australians in the summer of 1956. Friendships were severed, as at the time of Munich. Middle opinion seems to have reacted particularly strongly—readers of the *Observer* or *The Economist*, or veteran Liberals like Lady Violet Bonham-Carter who wrote as follows to Monckton: 'I had almost persuaded myself during the 51–56 Govt. Toryism was shading into Liberalism (partly perhaps because of my close touch with Winston—who has never been a Tory). Now I feel there is a reversion to type.'[101] Some observers have claimed to detect a long-term defection of middle-class liberal opinion away from the Conservatives which finally resulted in the Labour election victory of 1964. Conservative Central Office was told how 'intellectual and academic opinion' was hostile 'on the moral and legal aspect'.[102] There may be some truth in this, though it must be said that it was hardly detectable during the intervening 1959 general election which the Tories won by over 100. In Labour ranks, the Suez issue and the 'Law not War' campaign served as a powerful instrument for welding the party together in clear opposition to Tory jingoism. Gaitskell's own position was much strengthened as leader, and indeed he and Atlanticist colleagues like Denis Healey were more vehemently anti-government

[101] Violet Bonham-Carter to Monckton, 24 Oct. 1956 (Monckton Papers, Dept. 67).
[102] Memorandum by Douglas on 'Opinion on Suez', 6 Nov. 1956 (Conservative Research Department, CRD/2/34/20). This paper added that 'many people still do not understand why, if the object was to prevent a war, we moved into the Suez Canal instead of separating the combatants'.

than were left-wingers of Zionist background, while Bevan seemed almost a patriot with a Beaver-brook-type regard for Empire. For about three weeks, the country was rent with passion, marches, demonstrations, and street battles reminiscent of the thirties. Anger had returned to post-war Britain.

But it lasted only for three weeks. The temperature rose sharply after the ultimatum to the Egyptian government on 30 October. With the announcement of a cease-fire on 8 November, it fell equally abruptly. The relief was almost audible. Opinion polls showed that most working-class people appeared to support the dispatch of British forces, on general patriotic grounds. Eden's personal standing rose in the Gallup poll findings after an initial setback. From 40 per cent on 2 November it reached 53 per cent on 15 November.[103] After the end of the Suez affair, Labour election activists in Warwick and Leamington (Eden's former seat) and North Lewisham were instructed not to emphasize the Suez issue, where the government had much support, and to focus instead on domestic issues like the Rent Act. Most people probably did not feel passionately either way as long as Britain's honour retained some kind of credibility and the outcome led neither to a prolonged foreign war nor to bankruptcy. While some 'Suez rebels' complained that the goverment should have sent their troops 'right through' to occupy the whole of the Canal Zone, and condemned craven withdrawal at the hands of miscellaneous foreigners in the UN, they were not typical. The dominant reaction to Nasser's action and the subsequent Anglo-French withdrawal was 'goodbye to all that'.

Even the trauma of Suez, therefore, commonly seen later as a major step in the retreat from Empire, did not radically disturb the tranquillity of Britain in this period. In general, the years of Tory rule after 1951 were a time of social balance, with a recovery of morale after the war and post-war austerity. No major divergence, other than the apolitical cynicism and satire of

---

[103] Memorandum from Conservative Research Department, 15 Nov. 1956 (CRD 2/34/21).

authors like Amis or Osborne, arose from the climate of the times. The most trenchant work of the period was *The Future of Socialism* (1956), by a Labour economist of distinction, Anthony Crosland. It was intellectually powerful, the most important work of Labour rethinking since the thirties. Crosland showed that there was still a gulf between left and right in Britain over taxation, workers' democracy, and especially education and the broad issues of social equality. He still believed in the validity of socialism. Yet the drift of much of his argument was also to confirm many of the premisses of the time. He accepted that the main problems of economic policy were over, that all major parties endorsed the Keynesian model of budgetary stimulation and demand management, that affluence was guaranteed and mass unemployment probably over for good. 'We stand on the threshold of mass abundance', Crosland wrote in Rooseveltian terms.[104] Instead, Labour should focus on the quality of life and on those minorities who were still denied the comforts of the affluent many. He also turned in places away from the austerity and puritanism of the Fabian-type socialism, through which Sidney and Beatrice Webb had spent their honeymoon investigating trade unions in Dublin. He called for more creative leisure, more gaiety, more fun. Crosland's work was, for all its great originality, a product of its time. It showed that, despite the enormous San Andreas fault of Suez, there remained a broad continuity in British post-war history, for all its divisions. An aura of comfort and contentent, of rising expectations and diminishing concern prevailed. People could now turn to 'the arts of life'[105] rather than the strategy of survival.

---

[104] Crosland, *The Future of Socialism* (London, 1956), 515.
[105] Ibid. 528–9.

5. The Zenith of
One-Nation Toryism
1957–1961

On 3 January 1957, the Chancellor of the Exchequer, Harold Macmillan, addressed his Cabinet colleagues on the lessons of Suez.[1] He argued that the crisis had shown up the 'weakness of our post-war economy'. There was a prospective deficit of £564 m. for 1957–8 following the run on the reserves and the loss of exports. 'The Suez operation', he declared, 'has been a tactical defeat. It is our task to ensure that, like the retreats from Mons and Dunkirk, it should prove the prelude to a strategic victory.' There was a ringing note to Macmillan's paper, clearly a bid for power. It surely helped his campaign to overtake the diffident and enigmatic Butler in the contest for the premiership a few days later. But the overall comment, nevertheless, was one that implied structural weakness. In somewhat similar vein on 8 January, the very eve of Eden's resignation, Selwyn Lloyd introduced the previously unpopular theme of a closer association between Britain and western Europe.[2] After the rift with the United States, shown up during the Suez affair, Lloyd suggested the prospect of pooling resources with the Europeans to become a 'third nuclear force'. Again, it was in its way a commentary on perceived weakness by a nation that could no longer stand alone,

---

[1] Memorandum by Macmillan, 3 Jan. 1957, CP (57) 4 (CAB 129/84); Cabinet conclusions, 8 Jan. 1957 (CAB 128/30 pt. II).

[2] Ibid. 8 Jan. 1957, meeting at 3.45 p.m. (ibid.)

and whose wartime 'special relationship' with the Americans had been cast in question. The British suddenly saw the reality of second-rate-power status. For the ordinary citizen this showed itself in unwelcome currency restrictions, cuts in social spending, and petrol rationing for the next six months as a result of the curtailing of oil supplies. Car mileage was limited to 200 miles a month: one beneficial result was that Alec Issigonis, a leading engineer at the British Motor Corporation in Birmingham, was to invent the immensely successful 'Mini' small car for BMC to economize on petrol consumption. Despite the sense of defeat, however, Macmillan's insistence that a 'strategic victory' should be achieved remained the objective. The next few years, in fact, far from being a tense period of national decline, were in many ways euphoric as the nation recovered its morale and sought to play something of the same role in straitened circumstances.

Certainly, the aftermath of Suez meant a cut-back in Britain's overseas obligations. This accelerated a trend already well under way. The military budget was steadily cut. The Joint Planning Staff spelt out the need for Britain to reduce her world-wide commitments in 1957.[3] The army's contribution to NATO would be cut by one-third. Land forces in the Mediterranean would be reduced to one brigade in Cyprus 'for garrison purposes', along with support of the Baghdad Pact in the oil-producing regions of Iraq and Iran. There would also be other forces stationed in Libya, Malta, and Gibraltar, plus a reserve of one brigade stationed in Kenya. The main air-force deployment henceforth would be in the United Kingdom itself, though with a force of four light-bomber squadrons, capable of dropping nuclear weapons, in the Middle East. Even under Anthony Head, one of the Suez hawks, the intake of national servicemen was reduced to only 70,000 in 1957, and the total of men in the services was steadily run down from 760,000 to less than 300,000. Prior to the 1959 general election, the popular decision

---

[3] 'Long-Term Defence Policy', attached to Chiefs of Staff Committee conclusions, 4 Feb. 1957 (DEFE 4/95).

was taken to abolish National Service altogether. Few lamented this wasteful dispersal of the nation's youth. There were right-wing commentators who deplored the end of what some saw as a form of social discipline for potentially rampant teenagers such as the Teddy Boys, but no real case for military service, as opposed to some kind of civilian community activity, was really made out. It was, in large measure, the need for economy which underlay Duncan Sandys's important Defence White Paper of April 1957.[4] This argued that for defence to take 10 per cent of British gross national income was excessive. Instead, it emphasized the use of intercontinental missiles as instruments of air power, and the concept of 'massive retaliation' by nuclear force in place of conventional striking power. This White Paper, as will be seen, generated lively debate over Britain's nuclear arsenal, but in the short term it led to large cuts in RAF Fighter Command, the British Army on the Rhine (BAOR), and ground forces generally in 1957–8.

There was, in any case, less military activity for the forces actually to undertake. The two main engagements of the period, Kenya and Cyprus, were gradually wound up. The campaign against the Mau Mau in Kenya reached a successful conclusion in 1957 and moves towards a multi-racial self-governing colony rapidly followed, Iain Macleod, Colonial Secretary from October 1959, ended the state of emergency, a new constitution followed, and in 1963 Kenya was to become an independent member of the Commonwealth. Its first President would be the charismatic figure of Jomo Kenyatta who had been imprisoned during the Mau Mau troubles among the Kikuyu, and who was now to preside serenely over Kenya's White Highlands. Cyprus was also removed from the category of essentially military problems and dealt with on a political basis. Even the Chief of the Imperial General Staff, General Templer, suggested that, after the Cyprus troubles, 'the only stable influences acting in our favour in the Near East were Turkey and Iraq'.[5] In 1957 the Macmillan

---

[4] See Sandys's revised draft of the White Paper, 26 Mar. 1957 (CAB 129/86).
[5] Templer in Chiefs of Staff Committee, 8 Feb. 1957 (DEFE 4/95).

government decided to release Archbishop Makarios from imprisonment on the island of Seychelles, and to advance proposals for a form of partition between the Greek and Turkish Cypriots, with Britain retaining bases such as the airfield of Limassol. Lord Salisbury resigned in protest but he was ignored. Under the aegis of an undeniably pacific governor, Sir Hugh Foot, the brother of two prominent Labour MPs, Michael and Dingle, a peaceful settlement was gradually carved out and in 1960 Cyprus was given its independence on a partitioned basis. As in Kenya, the new President of the Greek majority was a former denizen of a British jail, Archbishop Makarios.

The most difficult area, potentially, was southern Africa. Progress under the Central African Federation was slow, with undeniable black African hostility. A major blow came in early 1958 with the fall of the liberal premier of Southern Rhodesia, Garfield Todd, whose attempts to build bridges between white Liberalism and African nationalist leaders such as Joshua Nkomo, were resented within his United Party. He was succeeded by the more inflexible figure of Sir Edgar Whitehead. The Federation now rapidly lost any claim to legitimacy, with much disorder in Nyasaland resulting. After widespread rioting, a state of emergency was declared in 1959 with black African leaders like Dr Hastings Banda in Nyasaland and Kenneth Kaunda (two future presidents of their countries) being gaoled. A report by a commission, headed by the judge Sir Patrick Devlin, declared bluntly in 1959 that Nyasaland was 'no doubt temporarily, a police state'. At the same time, the scandal of Hola Camp in Kenya, where eleven Mau Mau prisoners were battered to death by guards, made African nationalist opinion as a whole highly inflamed. Macmillan appointed a wider committee of inquiry into the Central African Federation in late 1959, under the ever-emollient Lord Monckton. It duly reported in October 1960 in terms that confirmed the almost unanimous opposition of all Africans to the idea of federation. It also enraged white Southern Rhodesians by suggesting that some territories might be able to secede from the Federation. Roy Welensky, now the

Federation's prime minister, declared that 'the death knell of the Federation had been sounded'. With Iain Macleod, the new Colonial Secretary, making clear his sympathy for inexorable pressures towards decolonization at an early stage, the unhappy Central African Federation was already close to the end of its shadowy life.

Elsewhere in the continent, by 1960, Ghana (1957), Nigeria (1960), Sierra Leone (1961), and Gambia (1963) in West Africa had achieved, or were all well advanced towards, self-government, with major territories such as Kenya and Tanganyika likely to follow in East Africa. Harold Macmillan's outspoken pronouncement on the 'wind of change' blowing through Africa before the South African parliament in Cape Town in February 1960, and the resignation of South Africa from the Commonwealth after it declared itself a republic in 1961, confirmed the ways in which the sympathies of 'one-nation' Tories like Macmillan and Macleod were tending. The old Rhodes vision of British hegemony in Africa from Suez to the Cape was dissolving fast, with few regrets outside Rhodesia. At least, though, the British could feel that, by comparison with the chaos left by the Belgians in the Congo, which led to the serious crisis over Katanga in 1960, and the years of bloodshed under the French regime in Algeria, Britain's retreat from colonial domination was relatively tranquil and civilized. Macmillan himself presented it as a long-conceived policy of colonial development and maturity, on the lines of the withdrawal from India and Egypt previously. The adhesion of country after country to the Commonwealth, with the royal family ever present to preside over the independence celebrations, gave a sense of continuity and achievement rather than of surrender.

With its Empire contracting fast, the British presence across the globe became less dominant. In the Middle East, the advent of the more flexible Macmillan, even with Selwyn Lloyd of Suez fame remaining as his Foreign Secretary until mid-1960, meant a slow move towards the normalization of relations with Egypt. The British wisely decided not to press their case against

Egyptian nationalization of the Canal in the World Court, for the good reason that it was apparent that Britain would lose. In any event, the Attorney-General, Sir Reginald Manningham-Buller, advised his Cabinet colleagues that Britain had no legal standing because 'the military action which we had taken against Egypt in October was inconsistent with the provisions of the Agreement [of 1888]'.[6] Despite British warnings, the efficiency of the pilots of the Canal under Egyptian management was beyond question. In due course, British oil tankers passed through the canal, paying dues to the new Egyptian authority, just as before. The British presence elsewhere in the Middle East remained substantial. British military and air bases in Libya, Aden, and along the Persian Gulf remained powerful. The 1950 Defence Treaty with Jordan still stood. But even in this client kingdom British influence was not what it had been since the dismissal of General Glubb of Arab Legion fame by King Hussein in February 1956. Jordan had declared against Britain's Israeli allies in the Suez crisis. On the other hand, it was still in Jordan, along with Aden and Kuwait, that Britain's imperial presence in the Middle East remained most visible.

The nature of Britain's enduring role in the Middle East, along with its limits, came out vividly in July 1958. Following the federation of Egypt and Syria into a United Arab Republic, it was believed that the internal stability of both the Lebanon and Jordan were threatened. In the Lebanon, as will be seen, the Americans promptly dispatched troops to Beirut with the minimum of formal consultation with its British allies. In the case of Jordan, however, the British government had to be more circumspect. Macmillan was anxious to land British troops in Jordan to assist King Hussein, since Jordan 'was faced with an imminent attempt by the United Arab Republic to create internal disorders and to overthrow the present Jordan regime', while 'the territorial integrity of Jordan was threatened by movement of Syrian

---

[6] Cabinet conclusions, 29 Jan. 1957 (CAB 128/31 pt.I); memorandum by the Attorney-General, 5 Mar. 1957 (CAB 129/86).

forces towards her northern frontier and by infiltration of arms across it'.[7] The American government, however, was distinctly cooler towards Jordan. The Secretary of State, John Foster Dulles, declared that 'Jordan was an artificial creation, not viable as a State, without natural resources, dependent for its livelihood on external subsidies and with an unstable element in its large refugee population'.[8] To the Americans, the Lebanon and especially Iraq were of far more crucial importance. The British Cabinet found the American response 'disappointing': Macmillan gloomily noted that 'the Americans assume that Jordan cannot be held, and that we must make the best terms we can with the consequences of Jordan's collapse'.[9] He had to persuade the American government not to compel King Hussein to abdicate.

The impression from these exchanges is that Britain was anxious to intervene to some degree, not so much because of imminent danger to the stability of Jordan (which was never demonstrated) but rather to show the world that it still retained great-power status in its old Middle Eastern domain. Reluctantly, the American government agreed that Britain could legitimately intervene under the Anglo-Jordan Defence Treaty, and from 16 July onwards 2,000 British paratroopers were dropped in Amman airport, having obtained reluctant agreement from the government of Israel that they should fly through Israeli airspace *en route* from Cyprus to Amman. The precise terms of King Hussein's request for assistance were actually drawn up by the Attorney-General Manningham-Buller, for the King to sign: the Cabinet was well aware of the doubtful legal propriety of the British action and anxious not to infringe international law

[7] Foreign Office to Amman embassy, 17 July 1958, no. 1954 (FO 371/134038); statement by C. H. Johnston (ambassador to Jordan) to Chiefs of Staff Committee, 15 July 1958 (DEFE 4/109).

[8] Sir Pierson Dixon to Foreign Office, 14 Aug. 1958, no. 847 (PREM 11/2381).

[9] Cabinet conclusions, 15 July 1958 (CAB 128/32, pt. II): Lord Hood to Foreign Office, 16 July 1958 (PREM 11/2380); Macmillan note, 5 Aug. 1958 (PREM 11/2381).

so blatantly as at the time of Suez.[10] In the event, British paratroops remained in Jordan until the end of October, without
firing a shot, by which time the threat to Jordan's 'independence
and integrity' was deemed to be over. All the same, it was a fairly
hesitant assertion of post-imperial power. The British force was a
token one only, since the Americans refused British appeals to
dispatch ground forces to Jordan as well.[11] It was fortunate for
the paratroopers that no large-scale assault was mounted against
them, either from Syria or even by disaffected Jordanian soldiers:
Macmillan himself admitted to his Cabinet that the Jordan airlift to a
landlocked region was 'a quixotic undertaking'.[12] On balance, the
crisis of the summer did not redeem Britain's Middle Eastern position. The Jordanians, still full of virulent hatred of Israel, were glad
enough to see the British troops leave. In Iraq, meanwhile, Britain's
influence had seriously deteriorated with the coup there on 14 July, in
which the Crown Prince, the King, and the aged, pro-Western premier, Nuri-al Said, were all assassinated. President Nasser's influence
seemed to have reached its zenith, although events soon showed that
the pro-Egyptian inclinations of the new Iraqi government were
much exaggerated: on 1 August, Britain formally recognized the
new regime in Iraq as the United States and the other members of
the Baghdad Pact had already done.[13] Britain's role in the Middle
East, so immense in the post-1945 period, was becoming more
peripheral. It was only in the Persian Gulf, notably in Kuwait, and
in Aden and South Arabia generally that the British military presence
was a key component of the western commitment.

[10]   Cabinet conclusions, 14, 15, 16 July 1958 (CAB 128/32, pt. 11); Foreign Office
to Amman embassy, 19 July 1958, no. 2043 (F 371/134038), for Foreign Office
pressure on the Jordan Prime Minister to rewrite his request for British assistance
because, among other things, of the potential anti-Israeli bias of his first draft.

[11]   Eisenhower to Macmillan, 24 July 1958, no. 2034 (FO 371/13409). The
Americans, however, did send Globemaster planes to help transport British
equipment and supplies from Cyprus to Jordan, and gave assistance in establishing a land route from the Gulf of Aqaba to Amman which would not infringe
Israeli territory.

[12]   Cabinet conclusions, 16 July 1958 (CAB 128/32, pt. II).

[13]   Ibid 31 July 1958.

When unilateral military action was called for in the area, it was usually the Americans who now supplied it. In October 1957 President Eisenhower proclaimed the so-called 'Eisenhower Doctrine', on the lines of the 1947 Truman doctrine, to justify possible military involvement in the Middle East. The key aspects of Eisenhower's 'doctrine' were the granting of up to $300 m. in economic and military aid to Middle East countries 'in order to maintain their national independence', and the use of armed force to defend nations in the Middle East against aggression 'from any country controlled by international communism, provided such nations requested US assistance'.[14] On this basis, the US Seventh Fleet was dispatched to Beirut in July 1958, just before the British airlift to Jordan, despite protests in the United Nations. It was a clear statement that the United States now considered stability in the Middle East, unilaterally defined, as vital to assistance to President Chamoun of the Lebanon justified the British intervention in Suez in 1956, but this was academic. The decisive point was that the balance of power in the region had drastically changed, with US forces in the Lebanon for an indeterminate period, America joining the Baghdad Pact, and long-term US military assistance to Israel. The comfortable British ascendancy in the Middle East, as assumed by Foreign Secretaries from Curzon in 1920 to Eden in 1955, was now largely eroded. Yet even in the post-Suez twilight, Britain played a vigorous subordinate role in southern Arabia while Nasser's influence in Yemen was suspected or alleged. This especially applied to Aden where the British military presence cost £3 $\frac{1}{4}$ m. a year.[15] Thus, in the course of 1958, British planes based in Aden launched air attacks on neighbouring Yemeni villages, while two Special Air Service squadrons were sent from the Malayan jungle to protect the despotic Sultan of Oman against

---

[14] Foreign Office note on 'The Eisenhower Doctrine'. 1 Oct. 1957 (PREM 11/2192).
[15] Cabinet conclusions, 26 June 1958 (CAB 128/32, pt. II): contributions by Lennox-Boyd and Heathcoat-Amory.

his rebellious subjects. In return for a 99-year lease of the airbase there, the Sultan received an annual subsidy from Britain of £371,000, along with British officers for his army and the services of Julian Amery, a right-wing Conservative MP with experience of MI6 espionage during the war, to assist with aspects of 'psychological warfare'.

Britain's new international standing emerged with much clarity in a conference held at Bermuda between President Eisenhower and Prime Minister Harold Macmillan in March 1957.[16] It was intended, broadly, to heal the rift between Britain and the United States so painfully opened up by the Suez crisis. Indeed, Suez had only confirmed long-held antagonism between the two countries over most theatres of policy since the Korean War, symbolized in the tense relationship between Eden and Dulles. Sir Roger Makins, ambassador to Washington in the early stages of the Suez affair, had written a valedictory message on his departure in October 1956, to the effect that it was 'the end of an era' in Anglo-US affairs and that the old intimacy had now gone. In general terms, Makins's appraisal was confirmed by his successor, Sir Harold Caccia, on 1 January 1957. He agreed that a sentimental attachment towards Britain in the US administration, created by wartime bonds, was over. There had been lost, too, an innate trust in British experience and judgement in international affairs, and a reputation for reliability. Gone, too, was the largely unquestioned British right to a 'special relationship' based on ties of kinship and culture. Instead, Caccia urged, there was now a more businesslike connection based on practicalities, which would need patience and understanding in their working out.[17] Clearly, it was felt that the old English-Speaking Union, embodied in Oliver Franks's historic period at Washington in 1948–52, the era of Marshall Aid, NATO, collaboration over Korea and the bomb, was over. A more wary period was under

---

[16]   Materials in PREM 11/1837–8.

[17]   Makins memorandum, 21 Nov. 1956 (PREM 11/2189); Sir Harold Caccia to Selwyn Lloyd, 1 Jan. 1957 (PREM 11/2189).

way in which Britain's perceived dependence was visible at every turn.

The Bermuda Conference, to which Macmillan personally attached great importance, largely confirmed this dependence, concealed to some degree by the friendly relationship of Eisenhower and Macmillan born of wartime partnership in North Africa. Britain's sense of its international stature or the widespread popular belief that it stood first among equals as far as the European powers were concerned, did not disappear. An adroit compromise was struck between abject dependence and the illusion of parity, despite many ambiguities especially over British reliance on US assistance for its nuclear weaponry, which led to much transatlantic tension over the next seven years.

Not much time was spent at Bermuda in raking over past differences over Suez, though Dulles urged on the British that the Egyptians were not necessarily wholly negative on paying Canal dues. There was much emphasis on restoring the western position in the Middle East, perhaps by building up King Saud of Saudi Arabia as a counterweight to President Nasser, certainly by reinforcing the British position in Kuwait. The preservation of the Kuwaiti oil reserves indeed was vital if there were problems with Saudi Arabia and Iraq. The general mood was cordial and Macmillan made much of its effect with some bravura, including having to assure the French that a renewed exclusive Anglo-American partnership was not intended.[18] He could point to the achievement of getting the United States to join the Baghdad Pact, that British creation which the US Congress had now agreed to accept. Anglo-US nuclear co-operation was restored, too. Even so, the general drift of the Bermuda talks was one of a discussion between master and servant. Dulles spent some time in urging the British to take a less expansive view of their Middle East role, notably in connection with Buraimi, and especially Aden where the British government had endorsed General

[18] Sir Gladwyn Jebb to Macmillan, 18 Feb. 1957 and agenda for Macmillan–Mollett talks of 9 Mar. 1957 (PREM 11/1831A).

Templer's view that troops could be used there 'against dissident tribesmen'.[19] Most crucially, it was evident that the British 'independent' nuclear strike force, operated through the V bombers, was, in fact, highly dependent. It would operate through US-made Thor intermediate missiles, but the atomic warheads would remain in US custody and be operational only with US sanction. The hardware would be on display in Britain and have British crews, but the levers determining its use would be located elsewhere. The corollary came with Duncan Sandys's Defence White Paper in April, which placed the emphasis of British resources heavily on the use of missiles and the continuance of a British nuclear force. It was a strategy widely questioned, including by Cabinet ministers like Peter Thorneycroft, the Chancellor of the Exchequer, and was to play a major part in stimulating the rise of the Campaign for Nuclear Disarmament. But in the post-Bermuda context, it had its own logic.

Thereafter, Anglo-American defence arrangements continued to veer between a revival of the former intimacy and a background of mutual mistrust. An agreement to station sixty US Thor missiles in Britain in 1957–8, was followed in 1960 by Macmillan's agreement to allow the United States to use the Holy Loch base in Scotland for American submarines carrying Polaris nuclear missiles, to the fury of anti-nuclear campaigners, Scottish nationalists, environmentalists, and others. Secretly, Macmillan agreed that the Americans might instal yet more Thor missiles in Britain, with US crews this time. But the post-Suez Anglo-American relationship was now manifestly shaped by the culture of dependency. This was vividly underlined in April 1960 when Harold Watkinson, the latest in a long line of Ministers of Defence, had to announce the abandonment of Britain's only long-range ballistic missile, Blue Streak, which had cost so far £65 million.[20] This marked the effective end of Britain's claim to be an independent nuclear power. Its future in

---

[19] Chiefs of Staff Committee minute, 1 Mar. 1957 (DEFE 4/95).
[20] *The Times* and *Financial Times*, 14 Apr. 1960.

this field depended on the possible purchase of US Skybolt air-launched missiles, but it was probable that they would not be ready until 1964. Britain's client status was thus confirmed. It had poured out scarce resources on unused (perhaps unusable) missiles, while the US Thors were likely to become out-of-date soon enough. With no certainty that Skybolt missiles would eventually reach Britain anyway, national security remained peculiarly uncertain and national pride was further deflated.

Elsewhere, the role of the British government was more wary and detached. Towards the new European Common Market, the approach of Macmillan and his colleagues remained unenthusiastic. Since the EEC now existed, all prophecies to the contrary notwithstanding, Britain had to take some view of it. Much diplomatic effort was now expended in trying to form a customs union which would link the Six of the EEC with perhaps six other nations in a European trading bloc, Norway, Sweden, and Denmark, Portugal, Austria, and Switzerland. This, however, came to little, with the British insisting on the need for special protection for British agricultural produce, as well as for Commonwealth foodstuffs.[21] The British stance towards European unity was as hesitant as ever. Selwyn Lloyd, the Foreign Secretary, was wary about both economic links and political contacts with Europe. 'The most useful ground for advance', he considered, 'is in the military field at the moment.'[22] He thus revived his idea for making western Europe a third nuclear force. The trade negotiations were, it was hoped, given new momentum with the appointment of Reginald Maudling as Minister in charge of European negotiations in August 1957—'a difficult and exacting task', Macmillan told him, bleakly.[23] Maudling was preferred to Edward Boyle as negotiator because he was politically more

---

[21] See Interim Report on 'United Kingdom initiative in Europe', 23 July 1956 (FO 371/122032) M611/156; policy brief on 'European Integration', 30 Dec. 1955 (FO 371/122022) M/611.

[22] Lloyd to Macmillan, 28 May 1957 (PREM 11/1841).

[23] Macmillan to Maudling, 5 Aug. 1957 (PREM 11/2132).

acceptable to the party. 'We already have the Suez rebels; we shall soon have the nationalised industries rebels, followed by the anti-inflation rebels, and I do not think we can stand for it.'[24] However, time was to show that Maudling, amiable and intelligent though he was, failed to build significant bridges with the EEC and the outcome was the formation of a much looser European Free Trade Area in January 1960, with only the most indirect links with the EEC. The European nations were thus fundamentally divided into rival blocs, while Britain's European credentials were hardly more plausible than before. Furthermore, the emergence of General de Gaulle as President of France in 1958 meant that the political leadership of Europe now lay elsewhere, and that Britain could no longer hope to shape events.

At the end of 1960, Britain's demise as a world power would often be exaggerated. The lack of weight in Europe was to some degree countered by its role in the Middle East, where British attacks on rebels in Oman and South Yemen drew strong Russian criticism.[25] The Kremlin still considered Britain to be a significant international force. President Bulganin wrote that 'We do not tend to belittle, as it became recently fashionable [*sic*], in some places, the role which Great Britain continues to play in the international field as a great industrial, trade and sea power'.[26] In confirmation of this, Macmillan paid a heavily-publicized (and pre-election) visit to Moscow early in 1959, to press the cause of international arms control and a world summit conference. This was far from being a complete success, with mutual threats over West Berlin, and Khrushchev breaking one engagement with the British premier on the grounds that he had toothache. On the other hand, Macmillan's address on Soviet television, in which he referred to British scientific achievements, was a useful propaganda coup. Britain could take some credit for the later meeting of American and Russian leaders, and the progress towards a

---

[24] Macmillan to Thorneycroft, 22 July 1957 (ibid.) M 350/57.
[25] Russian government response to Macmillan, 4 Sept. 1957 (PREM 11/2101).
[26] Bulganin to Macmillan, 20 Apr. 1957 (ibid.).

test-ban treaty. Macmillan's personal stature was also reinforced by his remarkable and powerful speech to the South African parliament at Cape Town in February 1960, at which he urged the need for his hosts to pay heed to the 'wind of change' in Africa. This, together with renewed British pressure on the South African government after the massacre of black South Africans at Sharpeville, gave Macmillan new significance as the voice of an enlightened western approach towards relations with the third world. Commonwealth relationships with South Africa were to be a critical issue for the next thirty years.

The Prime Minister also remained a figure of substance at the United Nations, and gained much cachet with east-coast American opinion by an urbane response to interruptions by Khrushchev during a speech to the UN General Assembly. The episode was presented, at least in the Anglo-American world, as a magnificent demonstration of Prime Minister's question time at work. Even so, with Britain's influence within the Anglo-American relationship erratic at best, and no clear avenue of advance elsewhere, the precise way in which British influence could most usefully be deployed was far from clear. The continuing presence of Selwyn Lloyd at the Foreign Office until July 1960 (when he was succeeded by the aristocratic figure of Lord Home, the first Foreign Secretary to sit in the Lords since Halifax in 1940) suggested that international initiative was hardly the prime concern of the British policy-makers. At the same time, enough remained of the old imperial posture (popularized in current films such as *Zulu* and *Lawrence of Arabia*) for some credence still to be given at home to the legend of Britain's international credibility.

The main test of British achievement, though, would clearly lie not in diplomatic or defence manœuvrings, but on the home front, in trying to rebuild the economy and restore confidence after Suez. Macmillan's own approach aroused some uncertainty, not least because the new Prime Minister's casual, relaxed style was in such contract to the tetchy, temperamental methods of Eden. The Prime Minister, wrote *The Economist*, was the 'mystery man' of the government,[27] who might turn out to be a stern realist, as in the decision to evacuate Suez, or else a political dilettante who fiddled (or perhaps read Trollope) while Rome burned. The omens were grim when he took office. His new Chancellor, Peter Thorneycroft, emphasized the precarious position of sterling and the need for retrenchment in defence, in public expenditure on welfare and the nationalized industries, and in curbing wage settlements. However, by the time of the April 1957 budget, the situation appeared distinctly more cheerful. United Kingdom exports had reached a record level of £296.9 m. in March, with car exports well up and a major increase in orders for shipyards. Thorneycroft spoke the language of optimism and renewed expansion, while his main measure was the pump-priming one of a £100 m. remission in taxation, including both standard income tax and surtax.[28] Ministers like Vosper (Health) and Hailsham (Education) expressed gratification that spending on their departments had not been cut back, while there was also general satisfaction at the decision not to impose undue burdens on that hard-pressed and deserving section of the community, the middle class.[29]

In the summer of 1957, however, quite unexpectedly, a major financial crisis blew up. Thorneycroft had to tell the Cabinet on 10 September that there had been a fall of more than $200 m. in the gold and dollar reserves in August, with a similar decline expected in September. There was much speculation against the pound and fears that Thorneycroft would have to announce to the IMF in Washington that Britain would have to devalue the pound from its present level of $2.80 against the dollar.[30] The debate that then ensued went to the heart of Tory social and economic policy in this phase, indeed in the entire period down to the regime of Margaret Thatcher in 1979.

---

[27] *The Economist*, 20 Apr. 1957.
[28] *Financial Times*, 10, 11, 13 Apr. 1957.
[29] Cabinet conclusions, 15 Feb. 1957 (CAB 128/31 pt. I).
[30] Ibid. 10 Sept. 1957 (CAB 128/31 pt. II).

Peter Thorneycroft had from the outset been, in modified form at least, a monetarist (as was his strong-minded junior minister, Enoch Powell). He had since March spoken the language of cash limits (for instance in the determining of wage demands) and of strict curbs on the money supply. On 30 April he had pointed out the dangers of a rise in wage costs, whereby incomes had risen by 75 per cent between 1948 and 1956, whereas output had risen by only 28 per cent in that time. He proposed that the government should announce a monetary limit to the amount the country could afford in wage increases. However, the majority in the Cabinet felt that so rigid a policy would be politically unwise, especially committing themselves to a specific figure for increases in productivity as the criterion for wage advances.[31] On 19 July, with inflation now rising fast and a threat to the pound looming up, Thorneycroft tried a broader approach including restrictions on credit and a limit to wage increases in cash terms.

Indeed no other source was open to them unless they were prepared to adopt a wholly different approach to the problem of inflation and to have recourse to such measures as direct control over the monetary system. Control over the supply of money at its source had hitherto been regarded as inconsistent with their political principles. The extent to which such measures would have to be pressed in order to achieve the desired result was often underestimated.[32]

By September the sterling crisis was raging almost uncontrollably and Macmillan himself was now contemplating a policy for inflation that radically reduced demand by reducing the total volume of money that came into the system, for instance by restricting bank advances and credit generally.[33] Thorneycroft's proposals were for direct government initiative for pegging public investment by limiting the money supply. This was, he

[31] Cabinet conclusions, 30 Apr. 1957 (CAB 128/31 pt. I).
[32] Ibid. 19 July 1957 (CAB 128/31 pt. II).
[33] Macmillan memorandum on 'Inflation'. 1 Sept. 1937 (PREM 11/1824); Macmillan 'Brief for Ministers' on inflation, 9 Oct. 1957 (PREM 11/1823).

declared, 'the key to the problem', and he reiterated his argument two days later with proposals for curtailing the supply of finance to the public sector. On 17 September he urged, it was 'essential that the supply of money should be restricted if the inflationary pressure was to be contained'.[34] To this end, he proposed that bank advances be restricted to their present level in the private sector, and that public investment be frozen at its existing value for the next two years.

This *démarche* by the Chancellor of the Exchequer raised basic questions about the government's policy and priorities. There was certainly support for Thorneycroft, notably from Heath-coat-Amory who in time was to succeed him at the Treasury.[35] But prudential social and political considerations from the start began to obtrude. Henry Brooke, Minister of Housing, raised anxieties about the serious effects on housing and slum-clearance programmes. Pensions and education raised similar worries. Macleod, Minister of Labour, attacked a policy that might mean unemployment rising to 3 per cent, with 700,000 being thrown out of work, and the unions inflamed. There was also a strong demurral from Butler, the deputy Prime Minister, while Roger Makins, permanent Under-Secretary at the Treasury, was another opponent. On 17 September it was recorded that a number of ministers commented that public opinion would inter-pret these proposals as meaning that the government were departing from the objectives on the 1944 White Paper on Employment (wrongly termed the White Paper on Full Employ-ment, significantly enough). 'They constituted an implicit admis-sion that the Government had failed in their attempt to manage the economy on a basis of voluntary agreement and that they were unable to maintain for more than a brief period the state of balanced prosperity which they had achieved during 1953.' It was also argued that, in any case, sterling could not be defended

---

[34] Thorneycroft memorandum on 'The Pound Sterling', 3 Sept. 1957 (PREM 11/1824); Cabinet conclusions, 12, 17 Sept. 1957 (CAB 128/31 pt. II).
[35] Heathcoat-Amory to Macmillan, 6 Sept. 1957 (PREM 11/1824).

by such measures as Thorneycroft proposed. Macmillan himself, typically, laid much emphasis on the issue of presentation of policy. 'The Government's decision to restrict the supply of money should not be taken as a challenge to organized labour.' On the other hand, the stability of sterling was a precondition to full employment, the Prime Minister commented.[36]

Strong measures were indeed taken on 19 September, with bank rate being raised from 5 to 7 per cent, and the clearing banks being told to restrict advances to the level of the previous year. The threat to sterling seemed to have receded. Thorneycroft, however, kept up his campaign. Shortly before Christmas, he told Macmillan of how Britain was living beyond its resources. 'With relatively few assets and large debts, we continue to live upon the scale of a great power. We have the most expensive defence forces in Europe. We have joined the nuclear "club". We claim at the same time a very high standard of life. We seek to lead the world in the social services we provide.'[37] At a crucial Cabinet meeting on 3 January 1958 he demanded that public expenditure for 1958–9, instead of increasing by £153 m. as government policy decreed, should be frozen to the 1957–8 level. He proposed various drastic economies, including deferring an increase in servicemen's pay (intended to ease the way to abolishing National Service) and various possible cuts in the social services, including abolishing the family allowance for the second child, charging a board fee for hospital treatment, raising the charge for school milk, ending a supplementary ophthalmic service, or increasing the National Health Service contribution. But to Macmillan and his colleagues only the last was acceptable, and only £100 m. of the intended £153 m. economies that Thorneycroft sought were offered. Duncan Sandys, Minister for War, argued strongly against deferring a rise in service pay and allowances. Macleod, Minister of Labour, attacked ending the family allowance for the second child—'it would imply the

---

[36] Cabinet conclusions, 17 Sept. 7 Oct. 1957 (CAB 128/31 pt. II).
[37] Thorneycroft to Macmillan, 19 Dec. 1957 (PREM 11/2306).

withdrawal of more than half of the only post-war social service which a Conservative Government could claim to have created.'[38] Further Cabinet meetings on 3 and 5 January (a Sunday) failed to resolve the deadlock. At the last, Macmillan summed up strongly against Thorneycroft on largely political grounds. 'Disinflation, if enforced to the point at which it created a stagnant economy or provoked a new outbreak of industrial unrest, would defeat its own ends.' Abolishing the family allowance for the second child 'was neither politically nor socially desirable. It would be contrary to the traditions of the Conservative Party.' Other cuts in welfare services would create disaffection and provoke a concrete basis for fresh wage claims.[39] On 6 January, to the bewilderment of the Press which had thought the Sunday Cabinet meeting was called to resolve disputes over the handling of the Cyprus issue,[40] Thorneycroft resigned from the government, along with his junior Treasury ministers, Enoch Powell and Nigel Birch.

A later generation of Thatcherites, therefore, made Thorneycroft an early martyr for monetarism. So, to some extent, he was. But Macmillan managed to cover the entire episode up with rare political flair. His published letter made it appear that Thorneycroft had really resigned on a very narrow point, of just £50 m. additional economies or 1 per cent of national expenditure, with no wider implications.[41] A concerted assault by Butler, Hailsham, Lloyd, and other Cabinet ministers made Thorneycroft appear unrealistic and inconsistent, somewhat as Bevan had been when he resigned over NHS charges in 1951. The Prime Minister observed that, 'I have watched with some alarm this rigidity of thought descending upon [Thorneycroft] over the past few weeks and even months.'[42] He breezed off to a

[38] Cabinet conclusions. 3 Jan. 1958 (CAB 128/32, pt. I): Thorneycroft's Cabinet paper 'Government Expenditure for 1958-9', C(58)2 (CAB 129/91).
[39] Cabinet conclusions, 3, 5, 6 Jan. 1958 (CAB 128/32, pt. 1).
[40] *The Times*, 6 Jan. 1938.
[41] Macmillan to Thorneycroft, 6 Jan. 1958 (PREM 11/2306).
[42] Macmillan to David Eccles, 6 Jan. 1958 (ibid.).

Commonwealth Conference in India with the observation that it was merely 'a little local difficulty'. Heathcoat-Amory, the former Minister of Agriculture, was appointed Chancellor instead: soon Macmillan was badgering him for income-tax cuts or other concessions to the 'middle and salaried classes'.[43] Thorneycroft's speech to his Monmouth constituents made it clear that he had no intention of leading a putative revolt against the government.[44] Indeed, he was to reenter the Cabinet himself in 1960, along with Enoch Powell. The entire affair was passed off as a magnificent exercise in *sang-froid*.

In fact, the episode meant that social priorities had taken precedence over the curbing of inflation. The battle fought out over 'Robot' in 1952 was again won by the consensus, one-nation party, with the significant difference that Butler was now chief amongst the doves. The economy, it appeared, continued to expand.[45] Heathcoat-Amory's first budget in 1958 included some modest tax reliefs. Thereafter the bank rate was steadily reduced from 7 per cent to $4\frac{1}{2}$ per cent, while the stock market moved steadily upwards. Sterling continued to recover strongly in the exchanges, and the pressure now turned against the American dollar, at least for the moment. Britain ended the year with a balance-of-payments surplus of over £500 m. In somewhat euphoric mood, Heathcoat-Amory's budget of April 1959 gave away £370 m. in tax relief, more than any previous Chancellor in British history had felt able to do. He took 9*d.* off the standard rate of income tax, cut purchase tax, and offered investment and initial allowances for industry.[46] With the economy buoyant, the Conservatives cruised to a comfortable victory in the October 1959 general election with a majority of over 100 seats, mainly on the basis of the mood of affluence and social balance. Fears for the economy returned in early 1960 with the bank rate raised to 5

---

[43] Macmillan to Heathcoat-Amory. 5 Mar., 5 Apr. 1958 (PREM 11/2305).
[44] *The Times*, 16 Jan. 1958.
[45] *The Economist*, 11 Jan. 1958 took this view.
[46] Ibid., 11 Apr. 1959.

per cent in April and 6 per cent in July. Heathcoat-Amory's budget of 1960 was a more restrained affair, and criticism now came to be heard that the Chancellor was unduly passive.[47] There was now talk that Heathcoat-Amory wished to leave the Treasury and in July he was replaced by Selwyn Lloyd, the former Foreign Secretary, in a reshuffle which saw Lord Home move to the Foreign Office instead. A new policy of credit restriction and squeeze was heralded as balance-of-payments difficulties mounted.

Nevertheless, the main thrust of Conservative financial management was a confident, consensus approach, one which preserved the main lines of a mixed economy. Keynesian demand management, and counter-cyclical intervention as in Labour's later period from 1947. It was a time of considerable expansion both in demand and supply, following the check at the time of Suez. Output went up, exports rose and the reserves recovered. The Radcliffe Committee in 1958 helped restore confidence in the banking and monetary system. Much rested on the cost of imports remaining low which in itself helped Britain's trade balance into the black. By the end of 1960, though, there were signs of rising inflation everywhere, being met with a growing pressure to restrict credit and curb production. After six thriving years, the British economy was ceasing to expand. However, with continued near-full employment, a vigorous factory programme in the regions from the Board of Trade, and the fabric of social and industrial consensus maintained, the Conservatives remained well satisfied throughout much of this period. Their success in winning the general election of October 1959, their third victory in succession, reinforced their confidence. In all, they won 44.3 per cent of the votes, with 365 seats to Labour's 258. As Macmillan was popularly supposed to have told a Bedford heckler in 1957 (when, in fact, he was giving a warning about possible inflation): 'You've never had it so good.'

---

[47] *The Economist*, 9 Apr. 1960; *Financial Times*, 5 Apr. 1960.

It was apparently hard to goad public opinion to any great movement of protest at this period. John Osborne and his literary colleagues might call for anger, but the general mood of the times was tranquil, even urbane. The volume *Declaration*, a symposium by a variety of writers in 1957, was a highly miscellaneous work with no common theme.[48] The authors tended to agree that some kind of cultural collapse had occurred in Britain since the war, but how and where it could be detected, still less what could be done about it, met with varied and often confused diagnoses from John Osborne, Colin Wilson, John Wain, Doris Lessing, and the other contributors. The theatre critic, Kenneth Tynan, pinned some hopes on socialism, with nostalgia for the Attlee years, but was inclined to believe that affluence, advertising, and the consumer culture would swamp the voice of protest and conscience. The sheer violence of John Osborne's assault on his society (the Royal Family was 'the gold filling in a mouth of decay') suggested that he himself felt that Britain was not in revolutionary mood. In public affairs, the major debates took place on cross-party moral issues like the abolition of capital punishment, or the reform of the laws on the treatment of homosexuals. The latter was given much momentum by the publication of the Wolfenden Report in 1957 and several unsavoury cases which involved the persecution of homosexual politicians and others. But only a compassionate minority of the middle class were roused to action by such a theme.

The main threat to Macmillan-style Conservatism still came from conventional political sources. In 1958, the Liberals, long a peripheral factor in British politics, suddenly showed a new capacity to appeal to anti-Conservative dissenters. In place of the elderly Welshman, Clement Davies, the Liberals had had since 1956, an attractive younger leader. This was Jo Grimond, a thoughtful, intellectual figure, with a marriage relationship to the Asquith family and a powerful line in rhetoric. He urged that

[48] Tom Maschler (ed.), *Declaration* (London, 1957).

his party should remain 'left-of-centre' and maintain a more distinctly anti-Tory stance than had been evident under Davies. It should 'march towards the sound of gunfire'. The fruits came in 1958. In February, the party came in a strong second to Labour in the Rochdale by-election, where they put forward a charismatic broadcaster, Ludovic Kennedy, as their candidate. The next month, they actually won the Devon seat of Torrington, with Mark Bonham-Carter, the grandson of Asquith: it was the first Liberal by-election victory since the Lloyd George period in 1928. But, as a general election approached in 1959, the Liberals suffered the usual 'squeeze' effect from the two major parties. In the general election in October, the Liberals lost Torrington and ended up with six seats, a rash of lost deposits, and only 5.9 per cent of the total votes cast.

Labour was still the main threat as the only plausible alternative government. In 1957–8 it had shown its ability to win urban seats like Ipswich and Rochdale, with a rare rural seat in south-west Norfolk in early 1959. Gaitskell's position had been strengthened by the Suez crisis, while old Bevanites were beginning to return to the fold. Harold Wilson, one of the resigning Cabinet ministers in 1951, voted for Gaitskell in the 1955 leadership election and was now shadow Chancellor; he showed his mettle with several lively parliamentary performances. Richard Crossman, another ex-Bevanite, was also in the shadow Cabinet now. Above all, Bevan himself accepted the limited value of revolt, and from December 1956 he had served as shadow spokesman on foreign affairs. He did not always cut the most commanding of figures here, but at least his presence made Labour appear much more united and a plausible alternative government. Gaitskell now seemed much more confident as leader. The party was generally thought to have fought a vigorous, centrist type of campaign in the 1959 election, assisted by lively television programmes fronted by the youthful Anthony Wedgwood Benn. The heavy defeat by Macmillan was a surprise, usually explained by Gaitskell's perhaps unwise pledge that Labour would not raise the basic rate of income tax—'a fatal stumble' in Crossman's view.[49] But in general the party ended the campaign in apparently good heart.

The main challenge to the conventional wisdom, however, came from outside the usual political circles, from the social/cultural critique posed by the Campaign for Nuclear Disarmament. From the aftermath of Suez and the Soviet invasion of Hungary, a new left-wing ideological position had been evolving. It focused mainly on ex-Communists who had defected from their old party after Hungary and on the neo-Marxist *Universities and Left Review*, to be rechristened in 1960 the *New Left Review*. This was an interesting blend of post-Marxism. It was allied to sociological critiques derived from the American C. Wright Mills in analysing the concentration of power in capitalist societies, and to the current attack by the Canadian liberal economist, J.K. Galbraith in *The Affluent Society* (1958). Galbraith's memorable phrase about 'private affluence and public squalor' made a considerable impact on leftist thought at this time, notably on the writings of the Marxist sociologist/literary critic, the West Indian Stuart Hall, a powerful intellectual force in the far left. The collective volume *Out of Apathy*, edited by E. P. Thompson (1960), was an impressive symposium of many of the new ideas.[50] But these movements were largely theoretical and culturally isolated. As always, Marxism or neo-Marxism lacked a mass following and an effective political instrument.

Elsewhere, the trade unions were in increasingly rebellious mood. The old solidarity which had sustained the Attlee government and brought industrial peace under Walter Monckton's cosy regime, seemed harder to sustain. Full employment was giving the unions a new power in dictating the ebb and flow of the labour market, while the 'hinge' effect (a sharp vertical pressure on earnings) was forcing wages ever upwards. In 1956 a key change had occurred with the election of Frank Cousins as

---

[49] Janet Morgan (ed.), *The Backbench Diaries of Richard Crossman* (London, 1981), 787 (entry of 9 Oct. 1959).
[50] E. P. Thompson (ed.), *Out of Apathy* (London, 1960).

General Secretary of the Transport and General Workers. After decades of right-wing leadership under Bevin and Deakin, the biggest union in the country had now a marked left-wing impetus. Cousins was in many ways a traditional union figure; for instance, he showed little interest in internal democratization of industry, let alone workers' control. But he took the lead in rebuffing wage restraint in any form. In May–July 1958 he led the transport workers in a major challenge to the Macmillan government, a strike by the London busmen, which coincided with a threatened national strike by the National Union of Railwaymen. Cousins rejected an industrial tribunal's findings that there should be an 8s. 6d. increase per week for the busmen, and a strike duly followed.[51] But in fact Cousins's strategy proved to be unwise. The TUC lent no support. The prevalence of private cars and the continuance of other forms of public transport meant that the busmen had little change of winning their dispute, and the result was a union defeat of major magnitude. The Conservatives' standing in the polls duly rose, while Iain Macleod, the Minister of Labour, like his successors Edward Heath and John Hare, found it easy to argue that the unions, however aggressive, could be contained without recourse to inflammatory actions such as legislation to curb the right to strike or to amend the Act of 1906. In fact, though, union discontent continued, especially among the growing white-collar employees in service employment, though in more muffled form.

It was, however, middle-class rather than working-class radicalism which posed the biggest threat to the one-nation *status quo*. The agitation against Britain's possession of nuclear weapons had been mounting with the atomic tests conducted from 1952 onwards. The British hydrogen-bomb tests in 1957 gave them new force. Gaitskell attempted to placate his followers with proposals for a nuclear-free zone in central Europe and a cessation of nuclear testing, but protests in Labour's ranks continued.

---

[51] Cabinet conclusions, 22 May 1958 (CAB 128/32, pt. I).

The 'massive retaliation' doctrine contained in Duncan Sandys's White Paper in 1957 caused widespread concern. The hazards of nuclear power were also underlined by a major accident at the plutonium plant at Windscale (10 October 1957), where many technical shortcomings had been discovered and a major leakage of radiation had occurred. Macmillan blandly told the Cabinet that it would be imprudent to publish Sir William Penney's somewhat alarming report on the Windscale mishap, potentially a disaster of Chernobyl proportions. 'It would be explained why it was improbable that such an accident could happen at Calder Hall or any reactors to be erected under the programme for the production of nuclear energy.'[52] The Prime Minister himself ensured that news of an earlier escape of Strontium 90 from Windscale in the spring of 1957 was hushed up, while John Hare, Minister of Agriculture, took part in a concealment of the full facts of the contamination of milk supplies from farms in Cumberland in October–November 1958. 'The figures cannot indefinitely be withheld', commented the minister, though he was responsible for a blurring of the medical and other issues.[53] As always with developments in nuclear policy, civilian or military, secrecy and subterfuge prevailed.

The rise of the Campaign for Nuclear Disarmament (CND) in early 1958 went far beyond Labour's natural constituency, even though it did bring in union leaders such as Frank Cousins.[54] It was most notable for its wide range of middle-class activists. Many of them were not previously involved in political movements at all but found CND an appropriate vehicle for wider cultural discontent with the supposed materialism and cynicism of Macmillan's Britain. CND members tended to come from suburban Golders Green and Hampstead rather than from London's East End. The presence of nonpolitical academic, literary, or religious figures such as the veteran philosopher Bertrand

---

[52] Cabinet conclusions, 6 Nov. 1957 (CAB 128/31, pt. II).

[53] John Hare to Macmillan, 12 Sept. 24 Oct., 14 Nov. 1958 (PREM 11/2540).

[54] For CND, see Frank Parkin, *Middle Class Radicalism* (Manchester, 1968).

Russell, the historian A.J.P. Taylor, the author J.B. Priestley, the theatre producer Joan Littlewood, Christian spokesmen like Canon John Collins, Father Trevor Huddleston, and the Revd Donald Soper, with senior political dissenters like Fenner Brockway and Richard Acland along with Michael Foot, Tom Driberg, Ian Mikardo, and almost all the Bevanites, gave it a wide impact. After an initial meeting at Amen Court, London, near St Paul's, chaired by John Collins, a canon of the cathedral, a launch meeting was held at the Conway Hall in February 1958. It proved immensely successful. The first Aldermaston march took place on Easter Day, when several thousand people marched the fifty miles from Trafalgar Square to the weapons-research establishment in Berkshire. Eight thousand finally assembled outside Aldermaston on Easter Monday. Despite the alarmist predictions of Sir Edwin Plowden of the Atomic Energy Authority, the demonstration was wholly peaceful.[55] It drew in many more thousands inspired by a moral gesture of this kind to a degree unthinkable in conventional politics.

CND became easily the most celebrated pressure group of the day. It was conceived of in the grand tradition of Fox, Cobden and Bright, and the UDC in the past. Indeed, A.J.P. Taylor's remarkable Ford Lectures on foreign-policy dissenters given at Oxford in 1956, printed under the title *The Troublemakers* in 1957, became a powerful (and best-selling) historical text. Members of CND genuinely believed in Britain's international moral authority, and felt that a moral gesture like the unilateral renunciation of nuclear weapons by Britain would find an immediate response in other countries. Others, not necessarily convinced by this view, accepted that the likely spread of nuclear weapons, for instance to both Jewish and Arab powers in the Middle East, was a major cause of alarm. CND continued to mobilize its forces in 1959, with the second Aldermaston March even more strongly attended than the first. It could attract religious pacifists,

[55] Materials in PREM 11/2542.

environmentalists concerned with the hazards of nuclear testing, many women previously apolitical (indeed its women leaders such as Pat Arrowsmith and Peggy Duff were a notable feature of the movement), Welsh and Scottish nationalists who objected to a London government's imposed policy, and a wide swathe of progressive opinion. A kind of simple naturalism was conveyed by its message: folk singers and home-made 'skiffle' groups were a feature of entertainment provided by the marches. Each year, marches and meetings grew in passion and in size.

Inevitably, CND spilled into the internal politics of the Labour Party, for all its wider appeal. Left-wing critics of Gaitskell's revisionist leadership and the drift to the right that they sensed found a launchpad for their views. The Victory for Socialism group of left Labour MPs, headed by Sydney Silverman and Frank Allaun, along with at least fifty Labour members in all, endorsed unilateralism. There had been mounting dissatisfaction with Labour's support of NATO and then SEATO, and cleaving to the broad lines of American policy in the fifties. In home affairs, the mixed-economy line of the party document *Industry and Society* (1957), in which old-style nationalization was to be set aside in favour of other methods such as buying equity shares in industrial firms, was in itself alarming. That Bevan himself appeared to endorse it made the document the more ominous. CND gave these concerns a new cutting edge. It was much wider than the old Bevanite split. Indeed, Bevan himself had sharply rebuked the CND approach in a speech at party conference in October 1957 in which he attacked unilateralist arguments as 'an emotional spasm' and claimed that for Britain on her own to renounce nuclear weapons would send her 'naked into the conference chamber' and thus unable to exercise any major influence on behalf of peace and disarmament.[56] The CND protest, therefore, backed up by *Tribune* and the *New Statesman*, both of which had rising circulations at this time, aligned critics of all

[56] *Labour Party Annual Conference Report, 1957*, 179–83.

shades against the Labour leadership. It was a major retrospective rebuke for Attlee's consensus.

After the 1959 general election, CND's capacity to generate
outrage, and to fuse this with criticism of the Labour Party's
policy and structure, reached a new pitch. In the October 1959
party conference, left-wing suspicions of Gaitskell were intensified when he unwisely tried to abolish the commitment to nationalization in Clause Four in the party constitution. He pointed to
the German Socialists' decision to renounce their old Marxist
heritage in the party conference at Bad Godesberg earlier that
year. On this point of fundamentalist philosophy, Gaitskell was
opposed by wide ranges of party opinion, including many in the
unions, and he had to back down. But doubts remained about his
style of leadership and the Hampstead chic supposedly associated with it. Alarm had already been created on the left when
Douglas Jay, one of Gaitskell's close friends, actually proposed,
in the journal *Forward*, changing the historic name of 'Labour
Party'.[57] The general trend appeared to be a drift away from
anything that could reasonably be called socialism. CND was the
ideal platform for reinforcing these fears, both about the party in
general and Gaitskell in particular. The use of the Holy Loch for
US Polaris submarines intensified these fears, and infuriated the
Scottish nationalists, just as the later use of land in Pembrokeshire to train German *panzer* units infuriated the Welsh.

In the October 1960 Labour Party Conference at Scarborough
a furious row broke out, reminiscent of 1931. The conference,
with major unions such as the Transport Workers and the Railwaymen, declared in favour of a unilateralist defence policy by
just under 300,000 votes. During the debate, Gaitskell had
hurled a ferocious condemnation at CND as 'pacifists, unilateralists, and fellow travellers'. He declared his determination to 'fight
and fight and fight again to save the party we love'. There was
an explosive atmosphere of rancour between right and left over

[57] See Jay, *Change and Fortune*, 273–5.

the bomb issue, with men like Harold Wilson and Anthony Greenwood trying to find a verbal formula that would unite the rival positions. Labour was manifestly torn and in appalling disarray. And yet, how far schism over CND and the bomb implied a wider mood of public disaffection is open to much doubt. Gaitskell's crusade to 'fight back' in the cause of British nuclear weaponry and membership of NATO aroused wide support. He mobilized his 'Praetorian Guard' in the Campaign for Multilateral Disarmament, while a right-wing caucus, the Campaign for Democratic Socialism, organized by William Rodgers, the Nuffield College don Philip Williams, and others, began the fight back in the constituencies.'[58] On the left, figures like Michael Foot and Barbara Castle urged that the party should not be totally destroyed or made incapable of removing the Tories from office. CND itself by the end of 1961 was showing signs of schism. In part, this resulted from the fact that such a high proportion of its active membership consisted of the apolitical middle class anxious for a great cause. The Campaign began to divide, in the end fatally, between supporters of Bertrand Russell and the Committee of 100 who advocated wholesale disobedience to parliament, and the constitutionally minded majority. The Committee of 100 met with the support of theatrical personalities such as Osborne, Wesker, Braine, and Vanessa Redgrave, but Michael Foot, Barbara Castle and almost all the politicians opposed it. Mervyn Jones, CND's press officer, resigned in protest at the intemperate statements of Russell and his American aide, Ralph Schoenman.[59] By the end of 1961, the crusading edge of CND was blunted, its key figures lapsing into internal acrimony.

In a wider sense, the end of the fifties did not appear to be a time for effective campaigning or protest. The decade ended with notable writing on popular or working-class themes by such authors as Alan Sillitoe, Shelagh Delaney, Arnold Wesker, and

[58] Williams, *Gaitskell*, 631–2.
[59] Mervyn Jones, *Chances* (London, 1987), 171–5.

Keith Waterhouse, amongst others, while more established figures like Osborne and Amis continued in full flow. Yet the general drift of their writing did not diverge from a broad social consensus. An attempt by Arnold Wesker to fuse TUC industrial protest with support for the arts in the 'Centre Forty-Two' movement did not get very far. Many of these talented writers were writing about a working class that was already becoming in many parts of Britain something of a museum exhibit, as in Shelagh Delaney's study of classic Lancashire working-class life, *A Taste of Honey*, or Arnold Wesker's portrayal of the *mores* of the old Jewish communities of the East End of London, in the trilogy *Roots, Chicken Soup with Barley*, and *I'm talking about Jerusalem*. In examining a popular culture and what its components might be, they all wrote in familiar, anti-Modernist terms which adopted traditional modes of expression and style. The British cinema tried to recapture audiences lost to television; thus, epics such as *The Battle of the River Plate* (1956) and *The Bridge over the River Kwai* (1957) appealed successfully to wartime memories of comrades in arms. There was also a new wave of socially realist British film-making at the end of the decade, with *Room at the Top, A Taste of Honey*, and especially *Saturday Night and Sunday Morning* (1959), based on Allan Sillitoe's stories of proletarian Nottingham, with Albert Finney admirably cast as the anti-hero. But, while these brought much-needed life to a flagging film industry, there is no suggestion that it encouraged an alienation from British fifties society and culture, as happened with French film-writers and Communist intellectuals at this time. The media, especially television, both BBC and ITV, paraded reassuring and complacent images, symbolized by Richard Dimbleby's awestruck commentaries on royal occasions. On balance, stereotypes of the 1950s as an 'angry decade', or one caught up in a whirl of popular protest, seem misplaced indeed.

On the other hand, British artistic life, if not angry, was nevertheless creative and often distinguished. Major landmarks like Covent Garden opera and Sadler's Wells theatre and ballet were financially out of danger now. New theatres were being built in a variety of provincial towns, resting on cheap money and easy loans, with the Belgrade Theatre in Coventry arousing especially warm comment. Many new theatres opened up in London itself, such as Bernard Miles's experimental theatre, The Mermaid, at Puddle Dock Wharf, in May 1959. Along the Festival Hall site were rising up (around a depressing wasteland of car parks) a smaller concert hall, the Queen Elizabeth Hall, and the Purcell Room for chamber concerts. A National Film Theatre had also been created on the South Bank, featuring socially realistic work by Tony Richardson and others, while endless talk concentrated on a National Theatre to consolidate, or perhaps, replace the wavering Old Vic.

There were still many obstacles to the fine arts in Britain. Public funding remained ungenerous by comparative standards. There was also a gloomy Sabbatarianism, especially acute in Scotland and Wales, which imposed great burdens on Sunday performance; a reluctance by private business to be involved in sponsorship of the arts; and the impact of television which made families less enthusiastic about venturing out of doors to see films or five theatre. Simultaneously, the old music hall rapidly declined, save as an historic exhibit in the television series 'The Good Old Days', set in late-Victorian England. A particular hazard was the work of the censor, whether exercised by the ever-vigilant Lord Chamberlain or by challenge in the courts. The Lord Chamberlain in the fifties, the Earl of Scarborough, a former Governor of Bombay and a leading freemason, was especially active in this post-imperial role. A case which aroused intense public interest, and added much to public entertainment, was that of D. H. Lawrence's novel *Lady Chatterky's Lover*, of which Penguin Books had distributed 200,000 unexpurgated paperback copies on sale at 3s. 6d. each. The case brought by the Crown came up at the Old Bailey in October 1960. The presiding judge, Mr Justice Byrne, showed apparent bias against the publication of the book. On the other hand, a series of churchmen, literary critics, psychologists, and other witnesses declared in favour of the essentially non-pornographic character of Lawrence's work. The prosecuting counsel, Griffith-Jones, brought much derision on himself by asking the jury: 'Is it a book you would wish your wife or servants to read?' The jury took a mere three hours to decide in favour of Penguin Books. It was followed by the publication of far more sexually explicit books like the American novelist, Hubert Selby jr.'s *Last Exit to Brooklyn*. Even if the Lady Chatterley case had been lost, the seriousness of the defence of Lawrence and of free expression in art, even if in forms previously held to be pornographic or erotic in effect (if not in intent), would have had its impact. Censorship continued, and the impact of the case was not immediately dramatic. Nor did churchmen necessarily follow the bishop during the trial who described sexual intercourse as 'an act of holy communion'.[60] But the general long-term effect was to promote a slow revolution in which the unrestricted use of native English became easier, the accurate revealing of sexual or other experiences became more natural, and in which the very ingenuity with which the Lord Chamberlain and other censors were challenged or evaded became in itself a force for free expression. The centuries-old campaign against the puritan ethic was nearer to victory.

The more permissive, affluent age was felt to be the creation of the paternalistic Tories who governed the land in the later 1950s. Macmillan's grouse-moor air of dilettantism conflicted with a shrewd, even ruthless, sense of what was politically possible and socially feasible. Both aspects had been fully on display in the Byzantine manœuvres which saw Macmillan outflank Butler to become Prime Minister, and again when he transcended the Thorneycroft resignation in January 1958 as a 'little local difficulty'. The Prime Minister presented a hooded mask to the world, covering up private domestic unhappiness and political vulnerability; in the argot of the time, it was a façade of 'unflappability'. The left-wing cartoonist, 'Vicky', depicted him as a

---

[60] This was John Robinson, Bishop of Woolwich.

surrealistic Batman figure, 'Supermac'. All the dominant figures of the goverment presented a studied air of continuity and consensus. Macmillan himself drew heavily on his memories of Stockton in the depressed thirties. He stressed that his Conservatism was compassionate and reflected social balance. Thus the boost to private housing and the surge in the lending operations of the building societies in that decade went alongside a continued programme of local-authority 'council' housing. The 1957 Rent Act, which decontrolled rents in some private housing, remained limited in its scope. Below a certain rateable value, rents would rise only very modestly, and Opposition uproar soon died down. The Conservatives were anxious to show that they were not the landlords' party.

Nor would abrasive initiatives be expected from R. A. Butler, Chancellor until December 1955, Lord Privy Seal thereafter, and Home Secretary from January 1957. Butler was a centrist figure who had been the inspiration of the Conservative Research Department after 1945. As Home Secretary he proved to be a liberal exponent of penal reform, though capital punishment remained, with Butler sanctioning a number of executions down to that of James Hanratty for the 'A6 Murder' in 1962. The new impetus in the party, though, came from younger figures. The new intake of MPs elected in 1950 produced some extremely competent ministers such as Edward Heath, Reginald Maudling, and Enoch Powell (who resigned with Thorneycroft in January 1958 but later returned to Cabinet). The philosophical inspiration came from one of their colleagues, Ian Macleod. His influence over public life in the fifties was immense. As Minister of Health in 1952–5, he proved to be an ardent supporter of the National Health Service. As shown in the previous chapter, the 1956 Guillebaud Committee praised the service as cost-effective, and in effect loosened Treasury control over NHS capital expenditure. A mighty programme of hospital building all over the country was Macleod's major legacy here. In 1955–9 he was Minister of Labour, a voice of moderation towards the unions as Monckton had been before him. Dispute after dispute was settled through conciliation procedures or else by arbitrators such as Lord Evershed or later Professor D. T. Jack, both of whom went far to satisfy union demands. The one apparent exception, Macleod's successful standing up to Frank Cousins and the London busmen in 1958 was largely accidental, and in any case gave Macleod a reputation for toughness hardly merited elsewhere. On unofficial strikes, Macleod was to write in 1963 that he was 'frankly schizophrenic'.[61] Something had to be done about a rash of unauthorized wild-cat disruptions; but on the other hand the Conservatives would never get elected without the votes of one-and-a-half million trades unionists and their wives. Strike ballots, he felt, would be unlikely to be effective. In practice, Macleod, after mature consideration of the whole field of industrial relations, elaborately gave his vote in favour of doing nothing. The boat need not be rocked.

In 1959–61, Macleod went on to the Colonial Office. Here he was a mysterious and complex figure. Roy Welensky, who distrusted him totally, found him 'subtle and secretive';[62] Lord Salisbury was to denounce him as 'too clever by half', a notable criticism in Tory ranks. But the effect of Macleod's regime was markedly to speed up colonial independence. He was the key figure in the post-war retreat from Empire. In a bewildering succession of moves and conferences, he speeded up the independence of Kenya, Uganda, and Tanganyika in east Africa, and Nigeria and Sierra Leone in the west. He went far on the path to breaking up the Central African Federation. It was profoundly unpopular with black Africans, and Macmillan stoutly defended Macleod from his critics. He took the Conservatives far along the centrist road, close to that of the Gaitskellite Labour right. John Vaizey remarked of him (and a compliment was not intended), 'Had he been a Wykhamist, he might have been Gaitskell's double.'[63]

[61] Minutes of Advisory Committee on Policy, 6 Feb. 1963 (Conservative Party archives, ACP/63/103).

[62] Blake, *Rhodesia*, 327–8.   [63] Vaizey, *In Breach of Promise*, 55.

A younger man still, also symptomatic of the Tory mood, was Sir Edward Boyle. Born in 1923, Boyle was a youthful aristocrat and an intelligent product of the Oxford History school after the war. He became the very embodiment of the Butskellite spirit, and committed the government to new spending policies. He believed in the rational management of demand, in the beneficent results of full employment , and in public spending as a multiplier of economic activity. Like Macleod, he was also an early enthusiast for Britain's joining the European Common Market. His career suffered a setback when he resigned on grounds of conscience over the Suez affair in November 1956. But he was too able to be kept adrift for long, and also too close to Macmillan and his thinking. He became junior minister to David Eccles, the Minister for Education, in 1957. It was the period of the 'baby-boom', when children born in 1946–8 took the 11-plus examination,and he took part enthusiastically in the large expansion of the state education programme, including the provision of more school teachers. Colleges of Education greatly expanded under his aegis. He was later to become a powerful and progressive Minister of Education himself.[64] In 1959 he became junior minister at the Treasury, when Keynesian influence was at its height. A cultured, intellectual figure, with a profound love of music, later on a university vice-chancellor, Boyle embodied the kind of civilized, moderate Toryism, closer in spirit to Peel than to Disraeli perhaps, which exercised public ascendancy at that time. Working with him were key economists within the civil service like Robert Hall and Donald MacDougall, themselves representatives of the semi-Fabian welfare democracy then prevalent.

The usual adjective applied to Tory Britain at this time, sometimes pejoratively, was 'affluent'. As in the thirties, the Tories were proving their competence in office. Cultural critics like Wesker and Osborne complained of the deadening effects of

---

[64] For Boyle's views, see *The Politics of Education: Edward Boyle and Anthony Crosland in Conversation with Maurice Kogan* (Harmondsworth, 1971), 65–143.

prosperity rather than of the numbing effects of poverty. They found there were 'no great causes left'. Nor did CND basically challenge the prevailing social ethos. After all, it found its key cause in an external theme, not in domestic division; its members still believed in Britain as a beacon of hope for a tormented world. *The Economist*, in January 1960, in bidding farewell to the fifties, noted that 'recovery was turning into a boom'.[65] Regional policies meant that a temporary downturn in the economies of the old depressed areas in 1959–60 was countered with new initiatives. The 1960 Local Employment Act gave incentives to private industrialists and brought in car-component works among other new enterprises. Critics in those regions, such as Welsh nationalists who complained of the drowning of Tryweryn valley in Merioneth to construct a reservoir for Liverpool, and who denounced the policies of Henry Brooke as Minister for Welsh Affairs, could be plausibly depicted as opponents of modernity. Industrial production was higher even than in the boom year of 1958. There was a great surge in the production of motor vehicles, chemicals, engineering products, textiles and clothing, and all ranges of household goods, benefiting from the rapid rise in home ownership.

The steel industry was especially buoyant, benefiting from the growth in car production, house-building, and much else. Old arguments about nationalization and privatization were set aside as crude-steel output soared to the record total of 474,300 ingots in December 1959, an output of 20 million tons a year.[66] The steelworks of the land, from Consett in Durham to Corby in Northampton, were working at near full capacity. The giant Steel Company of Wales spread its mighty operations across the sand dunes of Port Talbot, employing over 20,000 men, while another giant works was scheduled for location in east South Wales, the Spencer works at Llanwern on the mud flats to the east of Newport. Coal, though, was something of an exception. The

---

[65] *The Economist*, 2 Jan. 1960.   [66] *The Economist*, 2 Jan. 1960.

part played by coal in the national energy supplies fell from over 90 per cent to just over 70 per cent in this period. Oil was increasingly the cheaper and more acceptable form of energy for factories and domestic heating, especially from the Middle East. In South Wales again, mighty oil terminals around Milford Haven in Pembrokeshire transformed the industrial pattern. In nuclear power, the Calder Hall reactor began operations in 1957, and was followed by three more civil Magnox power stations at Berkeley, Bradwell, and Hunterston, with five more due at Dungeness, Sizewell, Trawsfynydd, Oldbury, and Hinkley Point. Nuclear power stations were working now in the very extremities of the land, at Wylfa in Anglesey and at Dounreay in the far north of Scotland in Caithness. There were also hydro-electric schemes in the Scottish Highlands. As a result, coalpits were closed in their scores by Lord Robens, an ex-Labour Cabinet minister, now the chairman of the National Coal Board. The work-force fell from 712,000 in 1949 to 517,000 in 1964.[67] Yet, the contraction of the historic Victorian coal industry did not unduly disturb the general pattern of growth. Those pits that remained were more productive, with their colliers better paid, well housed, and entertained in their leisure time as never before. The NUM accepted the closures with relatively little demur, even though its General Secretary was Will Paynter, a tough lifelong Communist who had fought in Spain in the thirties. In any event, a buoyant regional policy which saw new advanced factories brought to Scotland, Tyneside, Cumbria, and South Wales, meant that the general level of unemployment showed little upwards movement. Ex-miners could find in car plants better-paid and much more safe and assured employment. The old militancy of the pits seemed to have evaporated, with miners taking their sunny holidays on package tours in Franco Spain; memories of the Spanish Civil War and the International Brigade

---

[67] A superb account of the industry is William Ashworth, *The History of the British Coal Industry, vol. 5, 1946–1982* (Oxford, 1986); see the statistical appendix, 671ff.

were largely forgotten, save by labour historians at the universities.

On all sides, the media spoke the excited rhetoric of consumer demand. Young people could buy cheap Vespa or Lambretta scooters, or invest in cheap foreign cars like the Volkswagen 'Beetle'. There were only just over 2 million cars in Britain in 1950; by 1964 there were over 8 million. Television advertisements touted the merits of consumer goods of all kinds. Building societies constructed their glossy offices in town centres, often replacing old grocers', hairdressers', or clothing-shops in the process to create a kind of dead urban heartland. The fourteen new towns all seemed to be thriving. Whatever conclusions might be reached about Galbraith's public squalor, the facts of private affluence seemed indisputable.

The challenge of affluence was evaded rather than accepted by many social critics. It was, in any case, difficult for middle-class progressives to denounce on high-minded grounds the possession of cars, televisions, or washing-machines by working-class families enjoying for the first time the benefits of comfort and prosperity. On the Labour side, there was much anxious discussion of the challenge posed to the socialist vision by the spread of affluence. As has been seen, Anthony Crosland's diagnosis in 1956 had accepted the extension of private wealth as inevitable and cumulative. So, too, did Richard Crossman's Fabian Society pamphlet, *Labour and the Affluent Society* (1960), though it still upheld the case for nationalization against the kind of centrist revisionism associated with the Gaitskellite wing, of which Jenkins, Jay, and Crosland were in different ways impressive and articulate spokesmen. Conservatives admitted that 'it did address itself to the very real problem of economic growth'.[68] On the Bevanite left, too, there was some awareness that Marxism was now discredited, and that the old Labour watchwords of

---

[68] Published in June 1960. The Conservative comment on Crossman's pamphlet appears in minutes of Advisory Policy Committee, 6 July 1960 (Conservative Party archive, ACP/1/11).

nationalization, higher taxation, and a thrust towards collectivism needed redefinition at the very least. Richard Crossman in 'Planning for Freedom' (1959) wrote that the crudity and waste of capitalism, rather than its inherent inefficiency, were the appropriate targets for modern-minded socialists. He also argued, in somewhat drastic terms, that Labour might serve as a permanent vehicle for nonconformist critics of the Establishment, even if this meant permanent opposition.[69]

Labour's General Secretary, Morgan Phillips, a former Welsh miner and certainly not a friend of Gaitskell, whom he thought patronizing, also tried his hand at policy-making. He did so in a document, *Labour in the Sixties* (July 1960), a controversial work which was disavowed by the Labour Policy Committee and, unusually, bore Phillips's signature alone. In the language of revisionism and 'realism' it urged that Labour should turn to find new support amongst technicians, architects, managers, skilled craftsmen, even small businessmen, and generally acknowledge the changes brought by affluence which had dissolved the old class system to which Labour had appealed. Labour had to stand for something distinct. It was difficult now to argue that, since capitalism was proving technically competent, statist planning was the remedy. Labour should rather try to improve the quality of life through social egalitarianism and levelling up. At the same time, Phillips still proudly affirmed the socialist faith, including such themes as industrial democracy, which made his text appealing to an old Bevanite like Ian Mikardo, himself an industrial consultant by profession. There was also much talk of fostering personal freedom (not recently a strong Labour theme) and of sponsoring the arts in place of a 'candy-floss' society which was philistine and value-free.

One particularly interesting work of the time was *The Rise of the Meritocracy* by Michael Young (1958), the work of a Labour sympathizer who, while in Transport House, had actually drawn

---

[69] Richard Crossman, 'Planning for Freedom' (1959) in his *Planning for Freedom* (London, 1965).

up the 1945 election manifesto which won the party its landslide victory. Young argued that the growth of a modernized educational system, including comprehensive schools which were now beginning to spread, was in fact producing a different kind of unequal society, in which merit in the professions would lead to more sharply defined strata than the old social barriers based on birth and/or class. Even Young, though, assumed the onward march of Keynes, Beveridge, and the rationalist heirs of 1945. What he sought to do was to instil the socialist spirit of Tawney, or perhaps William Morris, as a leaven. He based his argument on the postulates of continuing technical advance, organizational size, more public spending, and increasing rewards for the able and energetic meritocrats. Even a social critic like Young took as granted the premise of everlasting affluence. One consequence he saw was 'the decline of the Labour movement' as new priorities took hold and, as he put it, 'parents harboured ambitions for their children rather than for their class'.[70]

Britain entered the sixties still in confident mood, despite the legacy of divisions and tensions inherited from pre-war years. The sense of national decline, even humiliation, at the time of Suez drifted away. Externally and internally, the land appeared to be thriving and self-confident, with Macmillan's curious ability to bridge old and new values highly appropriate and symbolic. Yet much of it was based on illusion and evasion. Underlying the surface of growth was a pattern whereby Britain had steadily lagged behind other western nations rising from the ashes of defeat. The upward curve of public spending masked serious discussion of the productive base whereby it could all be financed. An expanding economy sucked in imports, to an extent that the balance of payments could no longer sustain. By the end of 1960, the economic omens were distinctly less cheerful, after a year which had seen tremors in the economy,

[70] Michael Young, *The Rise of the Meritocracy* (Harmondsworth, 1958), 140.

Heathcoat-Amory leave the Treasury in something less than a triumphalist glow, and a sticky mood on the stock exchange. Perhaps, after all, the Tory success in the late fifties owed more to good fortune, the fall in the cost of imports, accidents that prevented wage inflation from getting out of hand. The omens for 1961, some thought, were a downturn in the economy that might prove to be the worst since the war.[71] Overseas, Britain's standing as a world banker and sterling's role as an international currency were cast into doubt. Beyond the surface affluence, living conditions in terms of housing in inner-city areas, the circumstances of old people whose pensions lagged behind inflation, for many women and the socially disadvantaged such as the disabled or mentally handicapped, had shown scant improvement in either absolute or comparative terms under the post-1945 welfare state. Urban development was falling into the hand of property tycoons, like Jack Cotton and Charles Clore who decided to join forces in 1960. In social terms, the start of ripping out old working-class communities which began at the end of the fifties, in favour of impersonal tower blocks, often badly designed ghettos of violence and fear, had impoverished community life in a dangerous way.

But the general perception of these enduring problems was limited indeed. The general sense of Britain at this pivotal period was of a land that had clambered out of post-war austerity, without dismantling the welfare apparatus and communal underpinnings that Labour rule had brought. Conservative efficiency in management had reinforced the social conscience. The general tone was one of buoyancy. Conservative propagandists struck the right note, urging the need for the public presentation of government policy to conform to the generally cheerful reality. Millions of people, it was claimed, were emerging from the 'cloying cocoon' of socialist restrictions. 'The lights in Acacia

---

[71] *The Economist*, 31 Dec. 1960.

Avenue are brighter than the lamps in Mill Lane. They're not little capitalists yet but they're on their way.' The 'New Conservatism' was uniquely appropriate for a 'new Age'.[72] The only remaining priority was to sell the product and to target the consumers aright.

[72] Horniblow report on 'The Conservative Party at the next Election', May 1961 (Conservative Party archives, Minutes of Policy Advisory Committee, ACP/1/12).

II

The Years of Retreat
1961–1979

6. The Stagnant Society
1961–1964

In the 1950s, Britain had offered the world, many felt, a spectacle of hedonism and insular complacency. Evident defeats like Suez, economic setbacks like the threat to sterling in mid-1957, the crisis of defence policy with the end of Blue Streak in 1960, were publicly presented as 'little local difficulties'. But from 1961 this form of genteel evasion was no longer possible or credible. Britain embarked on a traumatic process of self-examination, self-doubt, and declining morale, a perception of external weakness and internal decay from which it had yet fully to recover in the late 1980s. Changes in the popular mood are hard to define and often provoke flaccid generalizations in almost Gibbonian terms about 'the spirit of the times'. It is possible, however, to diagnose this change with somewhat more precision. It began with sociologists and social observers pointing to deep structural obstacles rooted in British history which prevented dynamism or innovation. Indeed, sociology as a discipline acquired a growing stature at this time, as evidenced by the impact of Peter Townsend's investigations of the elderly or W. L. Gutsman's *The British Political Elite* (1963) which dissected the so-called 'Establishment'. A new weekly journal launched in 1962, *New Society*, edited by a future Conservative MP, Timothy Raison, was symptomatic. In part the critique was a more empirical and scholarly diagnosis of the kind of malaise variously expressed by some of the novelists and dramatists of the mid-1950s, and take further by the apolitical crusaders for CND. But this time it was buttressed by hard statistical data, much of it coming from governmental material through agencies such as the National Economic Development Council (NEDC), or from international bodies such as the OEEC, a pessimistic witness of the British economy at this time. This material gave the critique a solidity and a base of reliable international comparison which made it impossible to brush aside. From 1961, therefore, paternalist one-nation Tory Britain began to sink into various forms of disarray. The social balance of the 1950s began to break up with much cultural and psychological upheaval in its train.

In large measure, the rising discontent came from books. The British were still a highly literate people with a matchless array of literary and political weeklies and quarterlies. Many new publishing houses had sprung up in the fifties with the removal of the restrictions on printing. Bloomsbury was still alive and well, with Bedford Square its epicentre. The left-wing *New Statesman*, passing from the hands of Kingsley Martin to those of the ex-Bevanite John Freeman in 1960 (with a flame-haired, left-wing militant Paul Johnson as assistant editor), commanded respect not so much for the utopian socialism in its front half but rather for the searching literary and art reviews in its latter section. This was edited by V. S. Pritchett, himself a latter-day instance of the polymath man of letters powerful in Victorian days. It was books in particular that generated the new mood of unease, though perhaps the 'new wave' cinema and satirical productions on television gave it more popular currency. Suddenly it was fashionable, not to be conventionally 'angry', but to be satirical and mordant in puncturing national self-esteem. Many casualties followed, though most of the *bêtes noires* were to survive. The supreme casualty was to be the Prime Minister, Harold Macmillan himself. He changed, almost dramatically, from the dominant, unflappable Supermac of Vicky's half-admiring cartoons to the fading Edwardian caricature of the Profumo scandal, an antiquated poseur, the ready butt for university satirists, the grouse-moor image come to life. When in October 1963 he was succeeded by a fourteenth earl who confessed that he worked out economic problems by the use of matchsticks, derision knew no bounds. The British laughed at their leaders as they had done in the days of Gillray and Rowlandson. The trouble was that, this time, much of the rest of the world joined in.

A particularly influential work was that by Michael Shanks, the industrial editor of the *Financial Times*. His Penguin paperback, *The Stagnant Society*, made an immense impression on the public mind and rapidly sold over 60,000 copies. Shanks was an applied economist of centrist, Keynesian disposition, with links with the Fabian Society. He saw Britain as tired, flaccid, and falling hopelessly behind its foreign competitors. Yet, though he was an economist, the nub of his criticism was less economic than sociological in his treatment of Britain's social structure and industrial relations. Shanks linked Britain's sagging industrial performance with backwards-looking, semi-Luddite trade unions, an inefficient and ignorant management based on 'old-boy' networks of terrifying complacency, and a timeworn adversarial stance in industry which made Britain incapable of modernizing or competing in the modern world. He called his diagnosis 'a mission for moderates'. But it was hardly surprising that his scathing commentary on Britain's trading performance, falling productivity, record of industrial disputes, and unconcern with new technology or re-equipment provoked remarkably immoderate comments elsewhere on Britain's position as a kind of antediluvian refugee from some past age. Indeed, Shanks himself began his book with a remarkably favourable account of the sense of purpose and national effort visible in, of all countries, Bulgaria.[1]

He helped trigger off a wide variety of diagnoses on the 'What is Wrong with Britain' theme. Penguin Books launched a series of books with this title, with almost as potent an effect on the national psyche as the works of the Left Book Club in the thirties. They focused on key institutions such as the trade unions, management in industry, or the educational system. There was a

[1] Michael Shanks, *The Stagnant Society* (Harmondsworth, 1963), 13–17.

growing obsession with Britain as a kind of museum piece of insular decay. Anthony Sampson's *Anatomy of Britain* (1962) was a highly effective piece of journalist's observation which examined in turn the monarchy, civil service, the parliamentary and legal system, the public schools, the churches, and much else. He noted the existence of two hundred or so 'top people', representative in most cases of institutions riddled with dry rot or decay. Sampson saw some signs of social change, not all of it welcome since it was associated with commercial American intrusions such as tower blocks, pre-packed food, and Wimpy bars. But what all his targets had in common was that they were interlinked with each other, usually with a common background in the public schools, Oxford and Cambridge, and the convivial umbilical cord of London's clubland. Indeed, such institutions as the Athenaeum, the Reform, the Saville, Brooks, and other baroque, male-run monuments along Pall Mall or in the heart of Mayfair, figured prominently in the demonology of the period. Anthony Hartley's *A State of England* (1963) voiced the intellectual's frustration with the stagnant condition of his country—though his solution was the political one of joining the European Common Market.

These commentaries were frequently descriptive and reasonably value-free in their approach. But they tended to merge with an older, semi-puritanical kind of tradition which sought refuge in attacks on a consumerist, 'candy-floss' society, especially in the way in which commercial nexuses and suburban sprawl tended to replace genuine, living communities. As one of Arnold Wesker's Jewish characters exclaimed, 'Do you want me to live in Hendon and forget who I am?' The implicit contrasts of the values of the honest life in the classless Yiddish strongholds of London's East End, as opposed to the gentrified Jewry of NW3, were plain to see. Richard Hoggart's *Uses of Literacy* (1957), the work of a university lecturer in English, had mounted a furious attack on the styles, values, and particularly the language of commercialism, consumerism, and sex. In the process he drew a perhaps over-sentimental contrast with the former back-to-back warmth and intimacy of working-class life in downtown Leeds. A distinguished Marxist literary critic, the Cambridge don Raymond Williams, in *Culture and Society* (1958) and *The Long Revolution* (1961), sought to recapture, or at least identify the sense of working-class community, as exemplified by his own boyhood in Abergavenny on the Welsh border.

Indeed, one of the popular ways of attacking middle-class Tory capitalism was in the rediscovery of the working class, very evident in the socially realist films by Tony Richardson and others in the early sixties. Perhaps a work like *A Taste of Honey* went beyond Richard Hoggart to suggest the despair and danger of working-class society as well as its potential in developing and defining human relationships. In popular form, the appearance of the weekly serial 'Coronation Street' in 1962, a folksy view of working-class life in Lancashire, focusing on the archetypal Edwardian image of the proletarian pub 'The Rover's Return', with flat-capped citizens and aged crones being served endless pints by blowzy barmaids, was a landmark. It was a cultural symbol of change, just as BBC Radio's long-running serial 'The Archers' suggested the quest for rural Utopia in Ambridge in the austerity of the early 1950s, and 'Mrs Dale's Diary', a long-running radio serial of the life of a doctor's wife, was an odyssey of suburban middle-class respectability and family cohesion in a dissolving world. It was generally agreed that Britain was a markedly unequal society whose class divisions had survived, and indeed been reinforced, by post-war welfare democracy. The sociologist, Brian Jackson, showed the permanence of an enclosed working-class life and attitudes in Huddersfield, based on work, neighbourhood, and the extended family. He linked variation in educational opportunity directly to social class.[2]

Thus it was that the cherishing of an older working class, often little known to the middle-class critics who proclaimed its

[2] Brian Jackson, *Working Class Community* (London, 1968), 157ff.

undying, earthy values from the safety of the suburbs, merged with an attack on economic and commercial society for being inefficient and out-of-date. The links between the two were usually explained in terms of Britain's evident decline in economic growth and productivity being rooted in social division and a basic inequality unaffected by the changes of the war or the Attlee government. Without doubt, it was agreed, there was something basically wrong with Britain, with its pathetic rituals, its obsession with class and accent, its introspection and inability to find a world role. There was talk of 'the British sickness' and of the 'British disease', variously linked with targets as diverse as public-school homosexuality or compulsory Latin. In 1963, Arthur Koestler, a somewhat flailing critic, who was much concerned with the obsession with retribution and cruelty which made the British unwilling to abandon their Victorian commitment to hanging by the neck, wrote of *Suicide of a Nation?* He compared its *mores* satirically with countries such as de Gaulle's France, now rising up proudly after the anarchy of 1958, Adenauer's 'miraculous' Germany, the Swedish social planners, or even such traditionally comic and ineffective people as the Italians and the Spaniards.

More sinister than inefficiency or social conservatism, it was believed, were the elements of plain criminality which festered in the Tory pursuit of consumerism and the free market. There was much public attention to the operations of property developers, and especially to the notorious activities of Peter Rachman, a commercial speculator who cashed in on the development of London terrace property, often using open methods of Mafia-type terror to coerce elderly tenants who got in his way. Rachman's association with a seedy underworld of call-girls and Soho vice rings added to the impact. So, too, did the mysterious activities and contacts of a fashionable osteopath, Stephen Ward.[3] A huge mail-train robbery in 1963, the largest haul in

---

[3] See Ludovic Kennedy, *The Trial of Stephen Ward* (London, 1964).

the history of British burglary, seemed another tract for the times. A series of city or business scandals aroused press comment, sometimes with anti-Semitic overtones. Particular attention was paid to the bizarre affairs of the washing-machine entrepreneur John Bloom, whose Rolls empire came crashing down, and a series of stock exchange scandals culminating in the Jasper affair in 1964. Public opinion polls confirmed that public expectations of honour and decency in high places had fallen markedly since the rectitude of the Cripps years. Corruption was rife, but now it was conducted by multi-million-pound speculative enterprises trading on the margin of legality, rather than through the individual petty graft of spoilsmen like the 'spivs' of the post-1945 period. Crime had become collectivized and cartelized; social diagnoses increasingly tended to link this, too, with the economic and ethical failures of late-imperial Tory rule. There was fanciful reference to a disintegrating 'bastard capitalism' at work, parallel to the 'bastard feudalism' of the fifteenth century currently dissected by the Oxford medieval historian, K. B. Macfarlane.

There was thus a growing sense of a culture in dissolution, where social criticism, by its very generality, was hurtful and self-generating in that it helped destroy national self-confidence without necessarily discovering an alternative panacea. In part, this was simply because old problems, long swept under the table, emerged with new force in the light of social investigation and political pressure. One of these was the phenomenon of race. Britain in the 1950s had seen a notable increase of Commonwealth immigrants, especially from the West Indies, but to a lesser extent from India and Pakistan, with some from West Africa also. Lord Hailsham told the Cabinet in June 1958 that the coloured population of Britain was believed to be 180,000, an increase of 40,000 over the previous year. West Indian immigrants totalled 27,551 in 1955, 29,812 in 1956, and 23,016 in 1957, with a further 3,208 in March 1958 alone.[4] Unemployment

---

[4] 'Commonwealth Immigrants': memorandum by Lord Hailsham, 20 June 1958, CP (58) 129 (CAB 129/93).

among coloured immigrants was not high—perhaps 8 per cent compared with a national average of 2 per cent; it was, indeed, Indians and Pakistanis who were harder to place in jobs than were West Indians, since their range of skills was likely to be lower. Immigration continued to rise, reaching a crescendo in 1961, with 113,000 in the first ten months alone. For years, successive British governments acted with extraordinary complacency. Gwilym Lloyd-George, Home Secretary in 1954–7, had raised the issue before his Cabinet colleagues, and an interdepartmental committee reported on it in August 1955, examining 'the influx into the United Kingdom of Coloured Workers from other Commonwealth countries'.[5] But it concluded that the vast majority of them made few demands on national assistance and had little difficulty in finding jobs. Inevitably, they would do the less salubrious work, as the Irish had done over the generations, in public transport like the London Underground, street-cleaning, and other public services, and also manual or menial positions in the National Health Service. The Cabinet reached a similar view in 1958. However, there was agreed to be a clear problem of discrimination in finding housing, with black and brown Commonwealth citizens tending to merge in ghetto areas such as Brixton in London, the St Paul's area of Bristol, and particular inner-city regions in Bradford, Leeds, or Manchester. The police were usually uncomprehending, and sometimes aggressive, as befitted an almost wholly white force. There were alarming race disturbances in Notting Hill in London in the summer of 1958, along with clashes between young whites and blacks in the St Ann's district of Nottingham. One result was the rise of the hitherto dormant and openly racialist National Front. Sir Oswald Mosley, the fascist anti-hero of the 1930s, re-emerged from exile abroad to fight North Kensington in the 1959 general election on behalf of the 'British Movement'. Blacks now replaced Jews as the threat to the Aryan master race. However, the vast bulk

---

[5] Report of Interdepartmental Committee on the social and economic problems arising from the growing influx into the United Kingdom of Coloured Workers from the Commonwealth, 22 Aug. 1955, CP (55) 102 (CAB 129/77).

of British people remained unexcited by Mosley's racist appeal. He finished bottom of the poll at North Kensington, with 8 per cent of the vote and a lost deposit.

For many years, governments were most reluctant to take measures to restrict immigrants, other than seek powers to deport individuals who were hazards to public health or personally undesirable, such as prostitutes. At the time of the Notting Hill riots in 1958, the Home Secretary, Butler, along with Hailsham and other ministers, spoke of the need for controlling immigration from the Caribbean especially. The West Indies Federation government was approached with a view to their exercising administrative controls on prospective immigrants. But the flow of immigrants continued apace, with notable benefits for family and friends in their country of origin through the remittances sent home from Britain.

By 1962, however, the Macmillan government felt compelled to take action, even if the racial problems of Britain were minute compared, say, with the American South at this time. The 1962 Commonwealth Immigrant Act, therefore, set up a voucher system for immigrants, the Irish being excluded, with priority given to those with skills or guaranteed jobs.[6] The effect was immense for would-be immigrants from the West Indies and the Indian subcontinent. It was also harmful for the family cohesion of blacks already in Britain and it created many anomalies, for instance between Afro-Caribbeans and East African Asians who held British passports. The Labour Party condemned the government as discriminatory and racist. But the great mass of British opinion, including trade unionists, alarmed by the flood of black immigrants on cultural, social, or psychological grounds, and having long absorbed stereotypes of black inferiority carefully tried and tested in the imperial heyday long ago, approved of the fact that the government was acting. British social change and self-analysis in the sixties thus took place

---

[6] Cabinet conclusions, 8 Sept. 1958 (CAB 128/32, pt. II); also see Paul B. Rich, *Race and Empire in British Politics* (Cambridge, 1986), 189–90.

against a growing awareness of the problems resulting from (or said to result from) Britain's being a polyethnic society. The active role of the Institute of Race Relations helped promote a more interventionist government role in improving community relations, at the same time.

Another major segment of society whose grievances began to be ventilated anew at this period were the Welsh and the Scots. The fifties had been an era of British unionism, with the nationalist parties of Wales and Scotland regularly losing deposits in elections. Such excitements as the theft of the 'Stone of Scone' from Westminster Abbey in 1950 by a group of Scottish nationalists were safely forgotten. The Welsh began to develop new nationalistic agendas which many English people found tiresome.[7] There was an abortive Parliament for Wales Campaign, supported by Welsh-speaking Labour and Liberal MPs in the early 1950s, but it was disavowed by Aneurin Bevan and other front-bench Labour spokesmen. The Conservatives had set up a Minister of Welsh Affairs linked with the Ministry of Local Government from 1951, initially the Scotsman David Maxwell-Fyfe ('Dai bananas'), then the Welshman Gwilym Lloyd-George. The regime of Henry Brooke, an Englishman who acted as Minister for Welsh Affairs from 1957–61 was marked by much economic advance in Wales, but also local discontent at his failure to respond to Welsh political and constitutional demands. He gave little authority to the advisory Council for Wales. Its chairman, the trades unionist Huw T. Edwards, resigned in 1959 and was later to join Plaid Cymru. A furious controversy emerged in 1957–8 with the drowning of a small Welsh village, Tryweryn, in north Merioneth, to allow for a reservoir to be constructed to provide water for the English metropolis of Liverpool. The angry Welsh-speaking Welsh protested vehemently at 'Welsh water' being given, virtually free of charge, to distant, wealthy Englishmen. But this kind of protest could be brushed

[7] On this, see Kenneth O. Morgan, *Rebirth of a Nation*, 381ff.

aside with ease by the government as a backwoods revolt by Celtic peasants against the onwards march of technology and the twentieth century. In the 1959 general election, Plaid Cymru put up only 20 candidates, all of whom lost their deposits, and gained only 5.2 per cent of the Welsh vote.

But Welsh nationalism reached a new pitch of excitement in the early sixties. The veteran man of letters, Saunders Lewis, imprisoned in 1937 for arson on an RAF base in Caernarfonshire, emerged from seclusion to broadcast a powerful radio talk, *Tynged yr Iaith* (The Fate of the Language) in which he called for a new public campaign on behalf of the ancient Welsh language brushed aside so contemptuously by English governments and agencies. Only recently a non-Welsh-speaking woman had been appointed chairman of the Welsh BBC. Lewis's talk launched, quite unexpectedly, a vigorous campaign of civil disobedience, especially among students and other young Welsh-speaking people. They defaced road signs, daubed slogans on government buildings, climbed up the television masts which sent out English-language programmes, and later inflicted some damage on 'second homes' owned by English residents in the Welsh countryside. By 1964 Welsh linguistic nationalism was in some ferment. Even the Labour Party, traditionally centralist and unionist as laid down by Bevan and others, had to insert a commitment to a Welsh Secretaryship of State in its election manifestos in 1959 and 1964. The veteran Welsh-speaking ex-miner, James Griffiths, deputy-leader of the party down to 1959, was a key influence here. The Scots were also becoming more belligerent, fighting, among other causes, rising unemployment in parts of Scotland and the alien presence of US Polaris submarines in the peaceful waters of Holy Loch. The President of the Scottish National Party, Willie Wolfe, a much-respected figure somewhat resembling Gwynfor Evans, the President of Plaid Cymru, in his appeal and style, came in a good second in a by-election in West Lothian in 1962. Celtic nationalism was manifestly another potentially explosive factor with which a bemused British government had to deal.

Nor could Northern Ireland, frozen in the Protestant ascendancy under the 1920 Government of Ireland Act, escape the processes of change. The presence of Sinn Fein, occasionally surfacing in the theft of weapons from British army bases such as the Royal Engineers' depot at Arborfield, Berkshire, was always there, although occasions of outright public violence were very few. Northern Ireland remained a smouldering powder-keg, with gerrymandered politics and an acknowledged structure of public appointment, housing, education, apprenticeships, and the rest which kept the one-third Catholic population in permanent subjection. A potential source of transformation was the election as premier of the Stormont government in 1963 of Captain Terence O'Neill, a Unionist leader of traditional, public-school landed background, but a man committed to some internal change and a better relationship with the Dublin government. However, there was little public discussion of Irish affairs at that time, potentially the most alarming Celtic problem of all. The island remained partitioned, with the Republican government of Sean Lamass anxious to maintain reasonable relations with London on which it depended for the free entry of its unemployed young people. The religious and ethnic feuds of Northern Ireland continued to smoulder on.

The liberation of women, a theme to arouse much comment and controversy later in the decade, was, by contrast, low on the public agenda at this time. The presence of employed women in immense numbers, freer from household drudgery and with ampler leisure opportunities, was much commented upon. The 1961 population census showed that women numbered 32.4 per cent of the employed work-force, including 65.9 per cent of the clerical grades, notably secretaries and other office employees. But the wider presence of women in public life, in politics, the law, the universities, or the civil service was a limited one. Only 9.7 per cent of 'higher professionals' in 1961 were women.[8]

---

[8] Halsey (ed.), *British Social Trends since 1900*, 165ff.

A dominant administrative figure like Evelyn Sharp in the Housing Department was a relative rarity, as was a woman like Grace Wyndham Goldie in the BBC or the historian, Dame Lucy Sutherland, and the scientist, Dorothy Hodgkin OM, at Oxford University. The Britain 'anatomized' by Anthony Sampson was overwhelmingly a male one, and he himself appeared not greatly interested in gender distribution and discrimination. The official view of the Inland Revenue that the woman, whether as wife or daughter, was the dependant of the male bread-winner, was the dominant stereotype. 'Women's rights' only emerged on the public agenda in the later 1960s, mainly through American stimulus. Divorce for a married woman could be a financial as well as a human tragedy. Some public stigma still survived, as had been noticed in the refusal to allow Princess Margaret, the Queen's younger sister, to marry a divorced man, Group-Captain Peter Townsend, in the fifties. Even so, the number of divorce petitions filed increased slowly, from 27,000 per year in 1956–60 to 37,000 per year in 1961–5. For politicians, 'women's issues' were thought to concern the shopping-basket and the kitchen sink, with some reference to family allowances since they were paid directly to the mother. Equal pay and equal opportunity legislation took a lower place. The other fissures of early 1960s Britain transcended these potentially more disturbing strains and stresses.

Britain was clearly in a volatile mood at this time. Old symbols were not revered as in the past. The young, with men wearing longer hair and women much shorter skirts, were developing an irreverent, anti-establishment culture all their own. A more definable, more permissive youth culture was beginning to emerge. It reached a new stage of pop musical art in 1963 with the appearance of the Beatles, four Liverpudlian youths whose simple tunes have been well described by Robert Hewison as 'a mixture of sexual invitation and adolescent pathos'. Eight of the 'top twenty' pop tunes in December 1963 were Lennon-McCartney songs popularized by the Beatles. 'I Want to Hold your Hand' stayed at the top of the 'hit parade' for two months, November

1963–January 1964.[9] There was much conventional middle-class head-shaking at the new youth culture, with its overtones of psychedelic drugs like LSD and, conversely outbreaks of violence between the highly physical Rockers and the almost bisexual Mods at Brighton and other seaside resorts in 1962–4. The monarchy, the supreme object of popular veneration since Queen Victoria's Golden Jubilee, seventy years earlier, was also less removed from popular criticism or satire. John Grigg and other critics had complained of the Queen's air of anti-intellectualism, obsession with horses, and reverence for time-worn protocol and ceremonial. There was some gradual response, for instance, in the ending of debutantes' 'coming out' appearances at the Palace, and a more contemporary and even critical air to the Queen's Christmas broadcasts on television.

The Church was also under fire. The Bishop of Woolwich, John Robinson, created a sensation with his *Honest to God* (1962), in which the very fundamentals of the Christian religion were subjected to critical scrutiny and perhaps even rejected. There was frequent talk of a religious revival in the universities and elsewhere, and the American revivalist Billy Graham paid a number of spectacular missionary visits to Britain which won many converts. But the reality was a picture of falling church membership with perhaps 10 per cent of the population going to church or chapel once a month and a further 7 per cent going occasionally, such as at Easter or Christmas.[10] There was also a rising problem of church indebtedness, an uneasy Anglican straddling of official sanction of the state and liberal criticism, and a public which treated the churches with more and more indifference. Religious bodies suffered frequent defeats in local decisions or polls over the Sunday opening of cinemas or (in Wales) public houses under the 1961 Licensing Act. The more general opening of public houses on Sundays was symptomatic. A nonconformist

---

[9] Robert Hewison, *Too Much*, 66; Michael Brown, *The Beatles' Progress* (London, 1974).

[10] Chapter by Peter Brierley in Halsey (ed.) *British Social Trends*, 518ff.

minister in 1961 complained of how 'Swansea has bowed the knee to Bacchus'. Only the Roman Catholic churches, with their strongly Irish clientèle, showed signs of rising membership.

The pattern in this less deferential age was, therefore, towards satire, a cynical or even trivial commentary on the times, often in place of hard-headed analysis. A great stir was created by *Beyond the Fringe*, a revue by four highly talented and intellectual Oxford and Cambridge graduates which opened in London in May 1960. Its irreverent treatment of public attitudes and figures such as Macmillan, bishops, scout leaders, or other symbols of middle-class rectitude, brought immense acclaim, first in the West End, later on Broadway. At the same time, the television weekly, 'That Was the Week that Was', started up in a series from November 1962 to April 1963. It showed dramatically how the BBC had moved beyond the conventional images of the fifties under a more radical and relaxed Director-General, Hugh Carleton Greene. In the argot of the time, he and it were 'trendy'.

Another production from this period, destined to survive into an apparently limitless future, was the satirical periodical *Private Eye*, edited by Richard Ingrams and Christopher Booker. This combined *Beyond the Fringe* type humour with investigative journalism which came in especially useful during the Profumo affair. How wounding or damaging these attacks on authority were may be doubted. 'That Was the Week that Was' (or 'TW3') was assailed by Mrs Mary Whitehouse, a self-designated moral reformer, for being anti-patriotic, anti-religious, and frequently obscene. Yet to be satirized may have been one way of shoring up a sagging regime, a sign almost of affection, at least in such a free society as Britain. The lack of inhibition, and freedom of expression of 'TW3' and its successors, though, seemed to go notably beyond any previously accepted forms or limits of ridicule. It was possible for four-letter vernacular words to be used without causing a public crisis, and to assail revered targets in church and state without censorship. In any event, with events like the Profumo affair and associated scandals, 'TW3', *Private Eye*, and others did not need to try very hard to find themes for public cynicism or entertainment. They reinforced at least a mood in which the conventional interpretation of Britain as a land sunk in a deep sleep of complacency was replaced by one of a nation discovering itself, seeing itself anew, and proclaiming itself dissatisfied or even disgusted with what it beheld.

A backcloth to the period was a growing sense of economic indirection. As has been seen, the satisfaction of the late fifties, perhaps reaching its climax with Heathcoat-Amory's pre-election budget in April 1959, was rapidly to be dissolved. The press and politics were full of comment on how Britain was being cast into economic decline. Its annual rate of growth, at 2.6 per year, was less than any other developed country in the western world save for Ireland. Its investment and the return on it was falling steadily. Its share of world exports fell from 26.2 per cent in 1953 to 20.6 per cent in 1961, and its share of manufacturing exports from the eleven major manufacturing countries fell from 20 per cent of the total in 1954 to well under 14 per cent in 1964. Nor were these figures viewed in isolation. The British noted that they were cast into a series of balance-of-payments crises between 1961 and 1964 at a time when other countries such as Germany, France, or Japan were shooting ahead. British visitors overseas noted that abroad the streets were unexpectedly clean, the people better dressed, the food richer and more interesting, and life in general more hopeful and buoyant.

Government economic policy was still advised by largely Keynesian figures, with Sir Robert Hall giving way to Sir Alec Cairncross as chief economic adviser to the Treasury in 1961. It reflected this growing concern and loss of confidence to the full. Selwyn Lloyd's first budget in April 1961 was generally disinflationary, with new profits taxes among other features. Its most remarkable novelty was the invention of two new so-called 'regulators' which gave the Chancellor power to vary the main revenue duties within a maximum range of 20 per cent, and a variable payroll tax on employers of up to a maximum 4s. gross per week per employee.[11] It manifestly gave the Chancellor considerable powers over consumption and investment. But it also encouraged the fear that there was an episodic, or 'stop–go', aspect to the government's economic conduct of affairs. It certainly did not reverse the continuing fall in the reserves throughout the first half of 1961 or the need for restraining the consumer boom with attendant fears of rising inflation. The *Financial Times* spoke openly of a sterling crisis. In July 1961 Selwyn Lloyd, therefore, introduced another novelty, the so-called 'pay pause', which abruptly stopped pay increases for broad categories of publicly paid employees. At the same time, he raised the bank rate to 7 per cent, imposed a squeeze on credits through bank deposits, and advocated the raising of indirect taxes by a further ten per cent. These measures, commented *The Economist*, added up to 'the biggest immediate cut in demand that has been deliberately imposed by a British government on any single afternoon in peacetime history'.[12] The measures immediately began to have some effect in dampening demand and curbing inflation.

Even so, the 'pay pause' was a damaging landmark in the Tory party's reign: Labour promptly raced to a five per cent lead in the Gallup polls. Indeed, the long-term demise of Tory rule may well have been anticipated in the 'pay pause'. In the first place, it was erratic and unfair since it imposed a clear barrier between those fortunate enough to get their advances just before the deadline and the rest whose rises were totally frozen. Secondly, it created a huge sense of distinction between publicly and privately employed people, the latter of whom continued to surge ahead in rising wage and salary bills. Perhaps worst of all, the pay pause, unlike attacks on the working class or the mass unions, aroused highly articulate groups of middle-class critics—civil servants, schoolteachers, university lecturers, hospital consultants, and other medical people. All were apparently valued by

[11] *The Economist*, 22 Apr. 1961.
[12] Ibid. 29 July 1961; *Financial Times*, 26 July 1961.

society and in need of public endorsement of their status and skills, but were now frustrated. The white-collar trade unions grew rapidly at this period and led a mounting public campaign against what was seen as a one-sided policy. Public arbitration awards on behalf of public servants were set aside. The Burnham Committee on teachers' pay was asked to defer a proposed pay increase. Doctors' and lecturers' pay increases were sidetracked. A whole series of well-armed, well-publicized critics were antagonized and inflamed.

Selwyn Lloyd sought to combine wage and credit restraint with a growing public control. The Treasury was also perhaps responding belatedly to concern at the success of other countries with indicative planning, as in the French Monnet Plan. Following up a suggestion from the Federation of British Industries, he set up the National Economic Development Council (popularly termed 'Neddy') in early 1962, with Sir Robert Shone as director-general and Sir Donald MacDougall as economic director. This laid out the broad principles of government's setting targets for increases in production each year, alongside factual information on which arbitrators and wage bargainers should make their assessments on pay increases. The government quite suddenly appeared to be moving towards a 'hands-on' type of economic management, more interventionist than since 1951.[13] It was also an attempt to meet criticisms that the Treasury was unduly precoccupied with traditional financial accounting, and inadequately prepared to address itself to longer-term issues of the growth and modernization of the economy. He also introduced a National Incomes Commission ('Nicky') to relate wages to planning considerations as well. For once in his ministerial career, Lloyd seemed to be a modernizer. However, in practice, both the FBI and TUC were unable to do more than merely advise their member organizations to pay heed to these new bodies. This was planning without teeth, let alone penal or legal sanction. The

[13] *The Economist*, 10 Feb. 1962.

trade unions, in any event, opposed the creation of the NIC and refused to co-operate with it.

For this and wider reasons, Lloyd's endeavours were accompanied by persistent failure in securing an upturn in the economy. The run on sterling was checked, and inflationary pressures somewhat subsided. But the holding back of domestic demand failed to have the regenerating effect on exports that Lloyd intended. Exports as a whole rose by only 4 per cent in 1961, with a drop of 8 per cent registered in North America. Production continued to slow down, assisted by strikes in key industrial sectors such as Rootes Group car production, with engineering exports especially disappointing. Lloyd's budget of April 1962 was widely condemned as failing to address itself to the problems of exports and as being almost wholly negative. No scenario of expansion was offered for 1962–3, with only the political sop of the abolition of Schedule A on house owners after the revolt of thousands of middle-class Conservative electors who voted Liberal in the Orpington by-election.[14] Stagnation in production and exports continued to predominate, and it was no surprise when Lloyd was removed from the Treasury in July 1962 though, as will be seen, the wide-reaching implications of Macmillan's 'night of the long knives' caused wider Tory disarray.

Selwyn Lloyd's successor as Chancellor was the emollient and rotund figure of Reginald Maudling. He had been much involved in European trade negotiation in the late 1950s. He neither looked or sounded like a restrictionist, nor an advocate of austerity.[15] In general, he was expected to be an instrument of reflating the economy, and so it proved. In early October he relaxed public taxation to the tune of £112 m. followed by a cut of £55–60 on car purchase tax and a speedier write-off for new industrial investment. Just as Lloyd had introduced new levels of squeeze and restriction on the economy in 1960–2, Maudling's measures amounted to the biggest level of tax relief

---

[14] *The Economist*, 14 Apr. 1962.
[15] See his *Memoirs* (London, 1978), 110ff.

since Hugh Dalton in Labour's high noon after 1945.[16] There were fears of the knock-on effects on wage and other costs, but the general thrust was towards massive expansion. Maudling proposed an expansion of public investment, especially in areas of Northern England, Scotland, and Wales where unemployment was rising, to rise by $7\frac{3}{4}$ per cent in 1962–3 and 10 per cent in 1963–4. Allowances were raised for plant and industrial buildings, and annual depreciation rates were revised downwards in the general cause of economic growth.

Maudling created a good impression as an economically literate Chancellor, more so than Lloyd. He was also, at 45, comparatively youthful. He remained at the Treasury throughout the last phase of Macmillan's period of office and through the Douglas-Home government, from July 1962 to October 1964. Yet the contrast between Maudling and Lloyd, like that between Dalton and Cripps in 1947, can be overdone. Samuel Brittan has argued that Maudling may have been appointed 'several years too late', unable to repudiate his predecessors' heritage.[17] Maudling was actually too slow, in the view of many critics, in pursuing some initatives, in particular in making effective use of Lloyd's 'regulator' in the difficult (and extremely cold) winter of 1962–3. In fact, the dominant force in the Treasury was Sir William Armstrong, the new Joint Permanent Secretary in place of Sir Frank Lee; he was due, in time, to become head of the civil service as a whole. He proved to be a vigorous centralizer, notable for his reorganization of the Treasury in 1963, and a strong ally of Maudling's eventual expansion. Throughout 1963 the economy continued to expand, by almost 4 per cent, with NEDC looking to a possible 5 per cent expansion in 1964. At the end of the year there could be reported a 7 per cent increase in exports, a fall in unemployment of 2.4 per cent, and rising productivity. Maudling was suddenly considered a likely future Prime Minister. But the evidence of growth, full employment, and rising output was nullified by repeated pressure on the balance of payments in 1964. Maudling found himself compelled to introduce at least the basis of a kind of incomes policy at home. He followed NEDC's prescription for 4 per cent target in the growth of national production, meaning a 'guiding light' of 3 to $3\frac{1}{2}$ per cent for incomes.[18] Selwyn Lloyd's 'pay pause' was only hesitantly discarded, as a result.

Maudling's room for manœuvre was now much restricted at home. This accounted for the pedestrian nature of the 1964 budget, widely condemned as dull and unimaginative. Harold Wilson, the new Labour leader, poured derision on 'a lame duck government', and Conservative electoral fortunes continued to sag. As Maudling 'went for growth', the economy continued to boom, unemployment in June 1964 falling to only 1.4 per cent. But the balance of payments grew steadily worse, in inevitable reaction. There was a projected deficit of £500 m. in the summer. By the time of the October 1964 general election it was nearer £800 m. if not higher. James Callaghan describes his final pre-election meeting with Maudling on 18 June 1964. The Chancellor was 'his usual, unruffled, amiable self, reflectively sipping a large whisky and soda'.[19] Maudling believed that expanding production would meet the need both of home demand and of more exports and that the economy did not show signs of overheating. Yet all around him was the evidence of an overheated economy living off a rising volume of expensive imports rather than on its own capacity for productive improvements or innovation. The restrictive policy of Lloyd had been lifted at very grave cost, with an unprecedented adverse trade balance, runs on the reserves, and already talk of possible devaluation even though Maudling himself discounted it. For years afterwards, Britain struggled against a deteriorating balance-of-payments problem. It was rooted in deep-seated phenomena, which could be traced

[18] *The Economist*, 14 Dec. 1963.
[19] James Callaghan, *Time and Chance* (London, 1987), 154.

even to the years before 1914—a lack of competitiveness in exports; a propensity to raise imports faster than domestic output; the loss of income on overseas assets in 1939–45; and a pegged exchange rate which could lead to devaluation since it encouraged speculation against sterling at little cost to the speculator. But these factors were not helped by the blithe indirection of Maudling's expansionist boom in 1962–4. Just as Selwyn Lloyd had apparently jettisoned the Tories' reputation for social balance and a preference for avoiding confrontation, so Maudling weakened their image of financial competence and rectitude. The gamble failed. While production and productivity went on rising, the balance-of-payments calamities meant that by 1964 expectations for growth on a sound basis had deteriorated to an alarming extent. Lamentations of future disaster were heard on all sides, as they had not been at the end of the fifties. In a wider context, the competence of the economic managers, and the Keynesian premisses which had governed recent experiments in pump-priming, were being cast into some doubt, not by specialist financial commentators alone. A major component of the ideological legacy of the Second World War was thus losing its sheen.

The lack of direction in economic management was paralleled by a somewhat empty phase of foreign policy as well. If one image of Britain in the early sixties was of economic stagnation and maladroit financial conduct, the other was of declining overseas stature, masked by a still inflated military commitment across the globe. Britain's international role largely hinged on what had been salvaged of the Anglo-American relationship after Suez and the Bermuda Conference. But this partnership was becoming harder and harder to sustain, especially when John Kennedy, a youthful, energetic figure, was elected US President in November 1960. Anglo-American relations, still cordial in the old wartime partnership of Eisenhower and Macmillan, now became more difficult. The contrast between Kennedy's vitality and the fading Edwardian grandeur of Macmillan's publicly contrived persona, became more and more marked, with Britain feeling that its client status led to increasing humiliation. In the field of nuclear weaponry, Britain totally depended on the provision of the US Skybolt missile which Eisenhower had promised Macmillan in a secret agreement in March 1960, with a provision that the USA would offer Polaris missiles instead if Skybolt proved unsatisfactory. A huge crisis was, therefore, caused when the US Defense Secretary, Robert McNamara, suddenly announced at a NATO meeting in Paris in early December 1962 that the US was now cancelling the Skybolt missile on grounds of its cost-effectiveness. It had already cost $500 m. while its technical feasibility was said to be in doubt.[20] Britain would indeed be given the Polaris instead, but it would be specifically assigned to the Atlantic Multilateral Force. Britain's posture of nuclear independence was suddenly threatened, and British press and politicians launched a violent reaction. Skybolt was indeed desperately expensive, but Britain, and especially Peter Thorneycroft, now Minister of Defence under Macmillan, felt deeply let down. Kennedy himself was sufficiently concerned to ask the Columbia University political scientist, Richard Neustadt, to examine how this crisis in Anglo-American relations had occurred. At the Nassau Conference in the Bahamas on 18–21 December 1962, therefore, Macmillan tried to find a solution, if only as a solace to national self-esteem. The fact that the French had been cheerful witnesses of the British humiliation in Paris made the wound more painful.

The negotiations between Macmillan and Kennedy at Nassau were the most tense and least intimate to take place between British and US leaders since the wartime conferences. Never before had Britain's subservience been so explicit. British pride was hurt by claims by McNamara and McGeorge Bundy that there was in reality no obligation for the US to provide Britain with Skybolt anyway. In the immediate background, there was Dean Acheson's speech at West Point on 5 December in which he condemned British 'delusions' about both the Commonwealth

---

[20] *The Times*, 12 Dec. 1962.

and the Anglo-American relationship. Britain, he proclaimed, 'has lost an empire and not yet found a role'.[21] In very difficult negotiations at Nassau, Macmillan insisted on Polaris being substituted for Skybolt; Kennedy was reluctant to agree for fear of upsetting President de Gaulle. Macmillan regarded Kennedy's counter-offer of a multilateral nuclear force as no substitute, since the loss of Britain's great-power status would be impossible to sell to the British electorate at a time when the Tories' by-election record was calamitous.

In the end, Macmillan's persistence, and astute reference to Eisenhower's pledge, did bring very grudging agreement from the Americans that Britain should indeed have Polaris missiles without warheads, to be employed on British submarines. Britain had thus to switch from an airborne nuclear force to a seaborne force, but could claim to have preserved the elements of its nuclear independence nevertheless, and at relatively low cost. It was agreed that the British nuclear fleet would be assigned to NATO except when (undefined) 'vital national interests' were at stake. British honour may have been satisfied, but the Anglo-American alliance remained in some disarray. While papers such as *The Guardian* condemned the continuing illusion of British nuclear independence, the right-wing *Daily Telegraph* complained that the supply of Polaris missiles would continue to be totally dependent on the whim of the US government. 'It is very hard to conclude other than that Britain has had very much the worst of the bargain at Nassau.'[22] There were strong suspicions that statements by McNamara and others that missile tests had thrown doubt on the technical feasibility of Skybolt were in any case untrue. For their part, the Americans were angry at what they considered a British lack of recognition of US generosity. They also disliked having to give pledges that Britain would have 'an absolute right' to use Polaris independently if there were some supreme national emergency. The view of the Kennedy

---

[21] *The Times*, 6 Dec. 1962.
[22] *Guardian*, 22 Dec. 1962; *Daily Telegraph*. 22 Dec. 1962.

administration now was that the Nassau arrangements should be seen as part of a wider design, to take in continental Europe as well as Britain, under which there would be a NATO multi-national nuclear force under the command of a Supreme Allied Commander.[23] Skybolt would be part of this scenario. On the other hand, a very different result from Nassau was that President de Gaulle was able to present the agreement as a kind of Anglo-American conspiracy which afforded an excuse to keep Britain out of the Common Market. Britain, it seemed, had had the worst of both worlds, Atlantic and European.

British defence, meanwhile, was being far from cost-effective still. On the contrary, 55,000 British troops remained in West Germany at the start of 1962 at an annual cost of over £70 m., while the wages bill for the 44,000 West Germans employed by the British Army amounted to a further £30 m. British troop deployments east of Suez were being somewhat thinned out, but there remained heavy commitments to bases in Hong Kong and Kenya, with Aden and Singapore also being built up. As recently as June 1961, Britain had sent 6,000 troops, with two squadrons of Hunter aircraft, to aid Kuwait against an apparent threat from Iraq. Aden, which was merged with the federation of South Arabia in 1963, also proved to be a difficult and expensive commitment, after Egyptian troops were intruded into South Yemen by President Nasser. In early 1963, Britain found itself engaged in virtually a small-scale war in Southern Arabia, as pro- and anti-Egyptian forces fought it out in Yemen. Kennedy, having recently escaped from the ordeal of the Cuban crisis, viewed continuing British involvement in the Middle East with something less than enthusiasm: he told Macmillan at Nassau, 'I don't even know where Yemen is'.[24] The drain on British defence resources, however, continued. One by-product of these events was that expenditure on the navy became increasingly severe as

---

[23] *The Times*, 24, 27 Dec. 1962.
[24] Harold Macmillan, *Memoirs*, vol. vi, *At the End of the Day, 1961–1973* (London, 1973), 271.

Britain felt it necessary to maintain a large amphibious force east of Suez. By 1964 the navy had become the most expensive of the three services—but not to protect home waters and the Atlantic seaways as in the historic past, but to pursue a quasi-imperial role in the Middle East long after the retreat from Empire had begun.

Overall, defence expenditure in 1963 was running at £1,721 m. a year, almost a tenth of the gross national product. It was higher than for any other Western European power, for all Britain's economic difficulties. Yet another expensive commitment had been announced by Thorneycroft in August 1962 with an expansion of procurement for the RAF which would mean six more VC 10 long-range jets, while other aircraft and missile programmes such as the TSR 2 (tactical strike and reconnaissance aircraft), Blue Steel, Thunderbird 2, and Sea Slug 2 would continue as planned.[25] There was clearly no sign of defence economy here, five years after the Sandys white paper had outlined its new schemes for retrenchment. Defence programming, indeed, seldom appeared to be planned or fully thought out. The fact that the thirteen years of Tory government saw no fewer than nine Ministers of Defence—Churchill, Alexander, Macmillan, Lloyd, Monckton, Head, Sandys, Watkinson, and Thorneycroft—suggested an unsettled, almost transient, place for defence planning in Tory priorities. Meanwhile the American response to the Cuban missile crisis in November 1962 showed how little the US notion of national security rested on the co-ordinating of policy with Britain; it confirmed Britain's diminishing status in the alliance and NATO generally. Britain did finally appear as one of the signatories of the nuclear test-ban treaty at Moscow in July 1963—in the unlikely person of Lord Hailsham, then Minister of Science in a somewhat kaleidoscopic ministerial career. But no one had any illusion

---

[25] Good discussions are C.J. Bartlett. *The Long Retreat* (London, 1972) and R.S. Rosecrance, *Defense of the Realm: British Strategy in the Nuclear Age* (New York, 1968).

that Britain, despite the Nassau agreement, was the key element in a treaty in which Kennedy and Khrushchev were obviously the main *dramatis personae*.

There remained one great prospect for developing British external influence in these years—that Britain should play its full part in Europe. After 1960, it was widely believed that the European Free Trade Area (EFTA) was at best a loose trading group, and that British links with the expanding Common Market should be expanded, for political reasons as much as economic. Business opinion in Britain was moving towards entry into Europe, while the political implications of the Skybolt affair confirmed the futility of pronouncing platitudes about a 'special relationship' with the Americans. In August 1961 Macmillan, therefore, announced that Britain had decided to apply for membership of the Six. There were some protests in Tory ranks, mainly from pro-Commonwealth MPs, but a general disposition on the Conservative side to see that Britain, with its economic weakness and political indirection, desperately needed a new forum in which to perform. This departure, inevitably, caused much alarm in the Commonwealth where New Zealand and Australia, and to a lesser extent Canada, leaned heavily on preferential treatment in the British market. Black African countries like Nigeria and Ghana, also much dependent on British bulk purchasing, rejected associate status with the Common Market on the same lines as some of the French dependencies. The entire episode was seen to be severely disruptive of Commonwealth unity and morale. Some new nations such as Tanzania and Trinidad seemed rather less close to the history and spirit of the Commonwealth than older nations such as India or Sri Lanka.

In Britain itself, the Labour Opposition went through some disarray in 1962, but finally decided emphatically against Britain's joining the Common Market. Gaitskell's own position was uncertain. But a meeting with Jean Monnet, whose mysticism about the European spirit offended Gaitskell's rationalist mind, turned him decisively against. He had a bitter public clash with the Belgian, Spaak, at the Socialist International at Brussels that July. Gaitskell, in any case, had a strong feeling for the Commonwealth, black and white, and had also no desire to open up a huge fissure in his party after recent divisions over nationalization and nuclear weapons. He had defeated the unilateralist challenge decisively at the 1961 party conference. In unwontedly emotional terms, he appealed to 'a thousand years of history' as a basis for rejecting membership of the Common Market outright.[26] Since almost all the Labour left and centre were hostile to the EEC, which they regarded as an introspective capitalist club, and significant figures on the right such as Douglas Jay were opposed to changing an age-old policy of cheap food and to undermining British national sovereignty,[27] Britain's Opposition was clear in its rejection of participation in Europe. Public opinion in general took much the same line. It remained insular and unconvinced of the virtues of getting closer to unreliable European foreigners.

For Macmillan and his colleagues, membership of the Common Market would fill a huge vacuum in British foreign policy. It would give Britain a different kind of regional association, one highly acceptable to the Americans. It would also give Britain a guaranteed and growing market on the continent as well. But the British negotiators, headed by the up-and-coming figure of Edward Heath, had also to urge the need for special treatment of British Commonwealth imports of food and other raw materials. Heath also stressed the need to have regard for British agriculture. Yet the outcome was that President de Gaulle of France, always unhappy that Britain's entering the EEC would dislodge French leadership and introduce an alien 'Anglo-Saxon' theme into the affairs of the Market, applied a total veto in a press conference at the Elysée on 14 January 1963. He compelled the other five members of the Six to agree, citing agricultural

---

[26] Williams, *Gaitskell*, 702ff.; Jay. *Change and Fortune*, 281ff.

[27] Jay, op cit., 281, and also his book, *After the Common Market* (Ilarmondsworth, 1968).

policy, tariffs, Commonwealth preferences, and the Nassau agreements as various reasons for rebuffing the British application. Britain's bid for a new direction in foreign affairs had ended with brutal suddenness. Other alternatives had, therefore, to be explored such as the possible enlargment of EFTA or further tariff reductions under the GATT agreements, but none had the impact of membership of the Market. British opinion appeared sanguine, almost relieved. The *Guardian*, more sympathetic to 'Europe' than most newspapers, commented almost blithely that: 'In the last resort, Britain is an Atlantic Power before she is a European one.'[28] For Macmillan, however, it was a colossal blow. R. A. Butler, whose approach to the Market had been typically enigmatic, not least because he represented a parliamentary constituency in Essex where the dissident farmers were vocal, regarded it as destroying the government's entire strategy. He told Labour's Anthony Wedgwood Benn in February 1963, 'You know, the Common Market breakdown was a bigger shock for us than you chaps realized.'[29] Henceforth policy was to drift. Acheson's blunt declaration that Britain had failed to find a post-Imperial role was over-simple. But it was also the conventional wisdom of the time.

The worst feature of de Gaulle's rebuff over the Common Market was that it was obviously not the end of the affair. With the EEC continuing to thrive and vastly outstrip Britain in exports and productivity, it was probable that Britain would again have to apply, under a Tory or a Labour government. Next time it would be a suppliant with reduced bargaining capacity. There were hopes in diplomatic circles that Franco-German solidarity might wane as the CDU domination in Germany began to weaken, and that the clear sympathy of the Benelux countries and Italy for British participation would have some effect. Anyhow, de Gaulle would not live for ever.

[28] *The Times*, 15 Jan. 1963; *Guardian*, 15 Jan. 1963.
[29] Howard, *RAB*, 297n.; Tony Benn, *Out of the Wilderness: Diaries 1963–67* (London, 1987), 6–7 (entry of 20 Feb. 1963).

Major politicians in Britain were committed to joining Europe, including almost all the younger Tories like Macleod, Boyle, Rippon, and especially Heath, whose technocratic instincts and belief in modernization allied with memories of the thirties made him an instinctive European. Relations between Britain and Europe remained unfinished business in a way that would only produce uncertainty.

By 1964 the course of British foreign policy was decidely obscure. The Commonwealth seemed to be losing cohesion as it expanded. It had been much shaken by the Common Market negotiations and a belief that Heath as a negotiator was not responsive to Commonwealth interests. There was a total impasse in Europe. In the transatlantic alliance, the assassination of President Kennedy in November 1963 and the succession of Lyndon Johnson, whose knowledge of Europe was minimal, made relations less intimate. When Douglas-Home became Prime Minister in October 1963, his Foreign Secretary was to be the veteran 'Rab' Butler, whose last unhappy association with foreign affairs had been with Chamberlain at the time of Munich. He had then been a supreme appeaser, perhaps more than Chamberlain himself. Many felt that Butler treated his time at the Foreign Office as 'a self-imposed exile',[30] and he took no new initiatives. Nor indeed did he travel much. His one major foray was a visit to Washington in April 1964 when he had to withstand a harangue by Lyndon Johnson on the sale of British buses to Castro's Cuba. Butler's later visit to Moscow, where he became the last western statesman to have an interview with Khrushchev prior to his downfall, was equally unproductive. His very presence suggested a dying government that, in defining or determining British overseas influence and power, had lost purpose and hope.

Butler's one great policy success had really come much earlier in 1962, when, with much deftness and artistry, he effectively

[30] Howard, *RAB*, 328.

wound up the Central African Federation. This was a time, as has been seen, of very rapid decolonization in Africa especially, with independence being granted successively to Kenya, Uganda, and Tanzania, and the old crises of imperial rule in Kenya and Cyprus largely wound up. Maudling, at the Colonial Office in 1961–2, followed similar policies to those of his predecessor, Macleod. But the Central African Federation was the great remaining problem, perhaps the more so after the recent chaos in the Congo following the secession of Katanga. The Monckton Commission in 1960 had provided for the black African states of Northern Rhodesia and Nyasaland to secede. In 1962 this was formally conceded to Nyasaland (shortly to become the independent state of Malawi under Dr Hastings Banda) and it was clear that Northern Rhodesia would follow shortly under the lead of Kenneth Kaunda. Butler, whom Macmillan appointed to take charge of Central African affairs in March 1962, faced a situation in which the pledges on federation, dating from 1953, were no longer operative, and the entire structure was falling apart.[31] The white minority regime in Southern Rhodesia, the last remaining prop of the Federation, was proving itself divided, with the leadership of Edgar Whitehead being overthrown by the more intransigent extrades-unionist Roy Welensky. Whitehead had been too slow to react; Welensky was far too much of an irreconcilable in the eyes of all Africans. Most white Southern Rhodesian opinion now turned to the populist Rhodesia Front party, with the object of securing territorial independence as soon as the Federation came to an end.

In a conference at Victoria Falls in June–July 1963, the inevitable was recognized, and Butler briskly negotiated the Federation out of existence. Formally, its unhappy history ended on 31 December 1963 when it was finally dissolved. The new independence granted to Malawi and Northern Rhodesia (Zambia) won over much black African opinion and no doubt prevented a

---

[31] See Blake, *Rhodesia*, 345ff., for an excellent account.

blood-bath. But the enduring problem of the position in Southern Rhodesia, now ruled by the Rhodesia Front under Winston Field and the up-and-coming figure of Ian Smith, remained. Butler had wound up a supremely embarrassing old legacy, but the way forward was anything but clear. Pressure from Southern Rhodesian whites for independence continued, especially when Ian Smith overthrew Field as Prime Minister in April 1964. At the time of the fall of the Conservative government that October, the crisis in southern Africa had far from been resolved.

Along with these economic and external failures, there was an even more obvious loss of political impetus. Macmillan suddenly became the main target. He had traded on his reputation as a master tactician, effortlessly in control of party, Parliament, and public. In 1961 this reputation lingered on. But by 1962 it was no longer credible. Tory radicals were disappointed at the slackening of the pace after the conclusive electoral victory of 1959. David Price, a younger MP, wrote in May 1962, of how 'Progressive Conservatives are disappointed that the momentum for reform has died down and feel that the Party has lost its momentum. The younger and more radical members quietly move away from us.'[32] A popular target for these critics was Selwyn Lloyd. A controversial Foreign Secretary, he was now a discredited Chancellor of the Exchequer with, in addition, an alarming inability to communicate his intentions or policies effectively. Macmillan was repeatedly urged to remove him, especially after a lack-lustre budget in April 1962.

On Friday, 13 July 1962 (a day of ill omen) he did so, but with an all-encompassing violence that many later saw as the origin of the Tories' downfall. No longer could Lord Kilmuir's dictum about 'loyalty being the Tories' secret weapon' be seriously entertained. Indeed Kilmuir was to be one of those stabbed in the back. On this 'night of the long knives', no less than a third of the

---

[32] David Price to 'Report on Current Issues in Eastleigh', 24 May 1962 (Conservative Party Archive, ACP 1/13).

Cabinet, seven ministers in all, were removed from office.[33] Maudling replaced Lloyd at the Treasury; Boyle replaced David Eccles at Education; Thorneycroft, now back in favour, replaced Watkinson at Defence; Keith Joseph replaced Charles Hill at Housing and Local Government (along with Welsh Affairs); Dilhorne, formerly Manningham-Buller the Attorney-General, replaced Kilmuir on the woolsack, and Maclay and Mills were other ministers to disappear. Duncan Sandys went to the Colonial Office, with Henry Brooke replacing Butler at the Home Office to allow the latter to become First Secretary of State with special responsibility for Central Africa. Butler was unhappy at losing a major portfolio—'I shall be out on an African limb', he told Macmillan.[34] The following few days saw nine other ministers removed—Renton, Waldegrave, Vane, Taylor, K. Thompson, R. Thompson, Hope, Bathurst, and Edith Pitt. Some attractive new blood was brought in to replace the fallen. The Cabinet now included Boyle, who was 38, and Joseph who was 44. Elsewhere, the 38-year-old Geoffrey Rippon and the 38-year-old Edward du Cann were new recruits. Edward Heath and Reginald Maudling, both in their forties, appeared clear beneficiaries of the holocaust. But the entire affair gave an impression of savagery and even panic, with the touchpaper lit, it was said, by a newspaper leading article in the *Daily Mail*. There was a torrent of ministerial leaks. Macmillan's position was undeniably weakened by the entire affair. He admitted in his memoirs that masking the removal of Lloyd in a general reconstruction of the government was 'a serious error'.[35]

The government now seemed on the run. Its by-election record in 1962 was unhappy, with a shock defeat by the Liberals in the Orpington by-election, and other bad results including Labour's victory in Middlesbrough West, the party's first gain since 1959. There then followed a series of quite fortuitous events which all

[33] *The Times,* 14 July 1962.
[34] Howard, *RAB,* 292, quoting Butler to Macmillan.? 1962.
[35] Macmillan, *At the End of the Day,* 92.

showed some mishandling. In the Vassall affair, involving security and homosexuality, in which junior ministers were supposedly implicated (one of them, Galbraith, resigned), the government appeared under pressure. There was repeated talk of security leaks and governmental scandal. The old affairs of Burgess and Maclean, defectors to the Russians in 1951, continued to haunt Whitehall. In 1963 it was announced that Kim Philby, a former Middle East expert in the Foreign Office, had also fled to Russia and was indeed the man who had 'tipped off' Burgess and Maclean. Rumours flourished about other defectors or deviants in high places. The Duchess of Argyll divorce case, with its tales of ministerial involvement, was especially intriguing.

The dénouement came with the Profumo scandal in June 1963.[36] In this episode, John Profumo, the Secretary of State for War, was forced to resign. He had to admit to an affair with a call-girl, Christine Keeler (the ex-mistress of the property racketeer, Peter Rachman), who was simultaneously involved with a Russian diplomat, Captain Ivanov. In the background there was the allegedly sinister, bisexual figure of Stephen Ward, a rich osteopath with medical and personal connections with the Tory Party. He was to commit suicide after being found guilty of living on the earnings of prostitution. In itself, the Profumo case, reaching its aristocratic climax at the swimming pool of Cliveden House, the country mansion of the Astor family, was almost farcical. Lord Hailsham exploded with wrath in the presence of his television interviewer, Robert McKenzie, in deploring such credence in the affairs of a proven liar and a tart. Macmillan's statement to the House (following persistent questioning by George Wigg) emphasized that Profumo was being dismissed for lying to the Commons. In the permissive state of opinion, it

---

[36] For the Profumo affair, see Wayland Young, *The Profumo Affair: Aspects of Conservatism* (London, 1963); Clive Irving. Ron Hall, and Jeremy Wallington, *Scandal '63: a Study of the Profumo Affair* (London, 1963); Mandy Rice-Davies's memoirs. *The Mandy Report* (London, 1964).

is doubtful whether the association of a minister with a prostitute caused much public surprise, let alone dismay. But the general effect was to show Macmillan as out of touch with the course of events, naïve, slow-moving, relying on public-school *bonhomie* to cover up a crisis. In the debate on Profumo's resignation, Nigel Birch (one of the Treasury ministers who had resigned in 1958) quoted with devastating effect from Robert Browning's 'The Lost Leader'—'Never glad, confident morning again.'[37] Butler's absence from the country during the handling of central African problems, added to Macmillan's difficulties and seemed to confirm the master politician's loss of political touch. The Profumo scandal added enormously to the grist in the mill of popular satirists and humourists across the globe, as well as providing fascinating copy for journalists and photographers. Such varied personalities as the upper-class Profumo, his unfortunate actress wife, Lord Astor, Stephen Ward, Peter Rachman, 'Lucky' Gordon, Christine Keeler, and her Welsh associate, the blonde Mandy Rice-Davies, were the answer to any journalist's prayer. But it also weakened Macmillan's credibility decisively at a key moment in a turning-point in his party's and his nation's history. Speculation was now rife about the Prime Minister's resignation. The present writer, absent in the United States between August 1962 and September 1963, returned to find a strange country awash with scandal and rumour, almost an international joke. Commentators drew inflated parallels with the moral decay that accompanied the later Roman empire, orgies and all, with extensive and inflated Gibbonian comparisons.

The situation was partly resolved by a crisis even more damaging to Tory morale.[38] The Conservative Party Conference in October 1963 followed a Labour conference of unparalleled unity, in which the leadership of Harold Wilson, the new leader, seemed unassailable. By contrast, the Tories were engulfed in intrigue. The Chief Whip, Martin Redmayne, seemed out of his depth. At its height, it was announced that Macmillan would resign owing to extreme ill-health. In fact, he had an inflamed prostate gland, not normally a fatal matter: it might be noted that, in the event, he was to live on a further twenty-five years to reach the ripe age of 90. Various candidates for the premiership were now bandied about—Maudling, who made a boring conference speech; Hailsham who tried to cheer delegates up with a rousing knockabout performance; perhaps Butler, whose own performance also proved to be disappointing on the day. The almost unregarded figure of the Fourteenth Earl of Home, the Foreign Secretary, who then announced he would renounce his title to stand for a Commons seat, unexpectedly emerged as the new Prime Minister. Even on his sick-bed, Macmillan was able to out-manœuvre Butler and insert Home, almost invisibly, into 10 Downing Street. But important elements in the Conservative Party were deeply shocked by the role played by the 'magic circle' of key advisers around Macmillan's sick bed, and Ian Macleod and Enoch Powell refused to serve in Home's Cabinet. In a famous *Spectator* article designed to rebut an anti-Butler account by Randolph Churchill, Macleod acidly noted that eight of the nine key figures in the crisis, including Lords Dilhorne, St Aldwyn, and Poole, had been at Eton.[39] With reluctance, Butler was persuaded to continue in the Cabinet, having been rejected by the party in 1963 as in 1957. His own refusal to cabal, allied to a sense of diffidence amounting almost to fatalism, left him on the sidelines yet again. The carnival effect, with an amateurish peer emerging at the head of the pack, added acutely to Conservative disarray. The long-term effect was to impel Tory MPs towards Labour's way of electing a leader by secret ballot.

The elevation of Sir Alec Douglas-Home, as he renamed himself, to the premiership is normally thought of as having been disastrous for his party. He had to find a constituency in Kinross

---

[39] Iain Macleod, *The Spectator*, 17 Jan. 1964.

and West Perthshire, in his native Scotland. Harold Wilson, for Labour, poured scorn on 'the fourteenth earl', while the Prime Minister's lack of acquaintance with even the most elementary wisdom on economics, and his diffidence as a public speaker augured badly for his party. In addition, he did not look well under the glare of television lights. For all that, the Conservatives' decline under Home has probably been exaggerated and Home himself unfairly treated. Despite the loss of able men like Macleod and Powell, and a controversial account from Randolph Churchill on the way in which the premier was selected,[40] the new government did not lack credibility. Its omnipresent figure was Edward Heath, the Chief Whip at the time of Suez, now in the Cabinet as Secretary for Industry, Trade, and Development as well as President of the Board of Trade, with a wide-ranging economic brief and a commitment to structural modernization. But 'Modernization' was not necessarily the most promising of themes, especially for Conservatives, at a time when the Beeching Report on the railway system was axing a third of the nation's railway lines to immense local uproar. Heath's modernizing bent also caused much internal displeasure when his bill to abolish resale price maintenance drew on him the wrath of defenders of small shopkeepers all across the country. *Private Eye* satirically called him 'Grocer Heath' from that time onwards. But he was certainly well in the public limelight at this time. A disappointed candidate for the leadership, the Chancellor, Reginald Maudling, was conducting an expansionist, if unsafe, financial policy in 1964 as has been noted. New ministers such as Joseph Godber, Anthony Barber, Edward du Cann and Maurice Macmillan, son of the former Prime Minister, suggested some new blood. An able young financial journalist, Nigel Lawson, a recent critic of Tory economic policy in the *Spectator*, was brought in as Home's special policy adviser.

[40] Randolph S. Churchill, *The Fight for the Tory Leadership* (London, 1964).

The general impression, in at least early 1964, was of a ministry hanging on and no more. Lords Poole and Blakenham were brought in to modernize a Conservative Party machine which was distinctly run down after all the recent traumas. The mood in party ranks was still jumpy. Heath's attack on resale price maintenance seemed to threaten the cherished 'corner shop' of which Herbert Morrison had once spoken so affectingly (see above, p. 71). There appeared to be little forward planning of policy initiatives in Conservative ranks. In the words of Butler and King: 'In behaving like a government, they showed signs of ceasing to behave like a political party.'[41] Nevertheless, goverments under siege could weather the storm and press on to victory, as in the Waterloo legend. By the summer of 1964 Home looked a more plausible figure as premier, with especial authority on foreign and defence policy. His very honesty and simplicity helped clear the foetid atmosphere. Party morale was raised by an improvement in the polls, and by success in beating off the Liberal challenge in Devizes in Wiltshire, near the Liberal West Country heartland. The years since 1960 had been a time of disaffection and disarray in Tory ranks unparalleled since the backbench revolt against the Lloyd George coalition in 1920–2, but they might yet leave the Conservatives with a foothold, or toehold, on power.

For much of the time, the Tories had benefited from the absence of a clear alternative. In 1959 Labour had lost its third election in a row. Thereafter, it plunged into the ferocious battles over the bomb in 1960–1. It was seen by the voters as a deeply divided party. The Liberals, after a disappointing election in 1959, continued to pose a lively challenge; but they only really emerged in the public's estimate after a dramatic victory they gained in the suburban Kent seat of Orpington in March 1962. Here their share of the poll leapt by 31.7 per cent and Eric

---

[41] David Butler and Anthony King, *The British General Election of 1964* (London, 1965), 87.

Lubbock captured an impregnable Tory seat by over 7,000 votes, with Labour losing their deposit. The Liberals, it seemed, could now find a new social base for their party. There was talk of 'Orpington Man' (and woman) in the suburbs and the middle-class housing estates, worrying about commuter train services threatened by Beeching, the price of season tickets, neighbourhood schools, and the rising cost of mortgages. But the much-touted middle-class commuter proved to be an elusive quarry. The Liberal challenge did not retain its fervour of Orpington days. In 1963, three promising constituencies—West Derbyshire, Chippenham, and Colne Valley—were not, in fact, won. The Liberal vote began to decline in local elections and by-elections alike as Labour improved. Their main asset was Jo Grimond, a lively and attractive personality, who genuinely supplied a kind of radical passion in the search for the middle ground. But, apart from him, they still seemed an uncoordinated and somewhat elderly party.

More unlikely than a Liberal revival, but in fact the eventual outcome, was a recovery of the Labour Party. There was a steady process of recuperation after Gaitskell and his supporters captured the inititiative by winning the day over the H-bomb in 1961. A major factor was successful penetration of the constituency parties by the Campaign for Democratic Socialism. The right were very much in command now, with left-wing rebels like Zilliacus and Michael Foot removed from the party whip, and the left-wing challenge to Gaitskell in the person of Anthony Greenwood in late 1961 a forlorn hope. Gaitskell steadily improved his command and public standing in 1962, capped with notable speeches on international affairs. His decision to declare against the Common Market was another bonus to him in gaining command of the party's loyalties. By the autumn of 1962 he was truly beginning to behave like a prospective Prime Minister, discussing with friendly journalists how a new Labour government would possibly drop paratroops in Southern Rhodesia to speed up the process of majority black African control. But in January 1963 Gaitskell fell ill and died, quite unexpectedly, from a virus—the result of KGB poisoning in one excited later account. He left affectionate legends of a talented would-be Prime Minister,[42] a lost leader. His successor proved to be not the excitable right-wing trade unionist, George Brown, but the broadly leftist Harold Wilson. He owed much to the decision of James Callaghan to stand also, backed by Anthony Crosland amongst others. This split the Brown vote and in the event almost all the Callaghanites voted for Wilson. It was Wilson who triumphed by 144 votes to 103, accompanied by a lead for Labour in the opinion polls of $15\frac{1}{2}$. It was to mark, against all the odds, a new era for Labour, a second wind for the flagging forces of British socialism.

Harold Wilson was indeed an unlikely figure to offer a new departure in British public life. Although only 46 at the time of his election as Labour leader, he was already a distinctly shop-soiled, enigmatic politician. A young Liberal, he had begun his political involvement during the war as a centrist-minded statistician working for Beveridge and Dalton on aspects of wartime planning. He seemed more of a corporate technocrat than a reformer at this stage. He made a reputation for himself as a competent, pragmatic President of the Board of Trade in 1947 at the remarkably early age of 31, but in no sense was he radical in outlook. Unexpectedly, he resigned along with Bevan from the Attlee government in April 1951 in protest partly at the charges to be imposed on the NHS, but more because in his economist's judgement the defence budget embarked upon by Gaitskell was over-ambitious and damaging. It is worth noting that Wilson was a disappointed political rival, overtaken by Gaitskell in the race to be Chancellor in succession to Cripps in October 1950. From then on, Wilson acquired the reputation of being a Bevanite and man of the left. Yet in the internecine turmoil of the Labour Party in the 1950s he played a highly flexible role. He took Bevan's

[42] See Stephen Haseler, *The Gaitskellites* (London, 1969). Peter Wright, *Spy-catcher*, spreads the story of Gaitskell's murder by the KGB, but there is no evidence.

place on the shadow Cabinet to the fury of his Bevanite associates. After voting for Gaitskell in the leadership contest in December 1955, he became shadow Chancellor, where he emerged as a sharp and humorous Parliamentary performer. Less happily, he appeared as shadow foreign affairs spokesman from 1961 onwards. He was not deeply involved in the policy planning of the fifties, and stamped himself mainly on the party's mind as a reformer of the party organization, which he described memorably as 'a penny farthing in the jet age'—this remark earning him the undying hatred of Morgan Phillips, the General Secretary. By all tests, Wilson was in the pragmatic centre of the party. Yet he still retained his old Bevanite associations, ran against Gaitskell in the 1960 leadership contest as the left's candidate, and tried to produce a verbal formula to reconcile factional differences over the bomb. Certainly in the contest with George Brown after Gaitskell's death, Wilson was the left's man, with old Bevanites like Crossman, Mikardo, and Foot working zealously on his behalf. When he was elected, Wilson took his bemused colleagues along to toast a portrait of the dead hero, Nye. To Michael Foot, it seemed like a dream realized.[43] The old left had won at last, twelve years on.

As party leader, Wilson continued to make leftish noises about public ownership, South Africa and the bomb. Michael Foot wrote his campaign biography. Wilson emphasized his socialist credentials and his ability to speak Russian. Somewhat ludicrously, he told Crossman he was conducting a Bolshevik revolution with a Tsarist shadow Cabinet.[44] Yet, in fact, Wilson was carving out a new niche all his own. Apart from repairing party morale with a more open style of leadership than Gaitskell had managed, he tried to renew Labour's standing and image by his ideological approach. He bypassed what he called 'the theology' of arguments about Clause Four and the like. For years,

[43] Janet Morgan (ed.), *The Backbench Diaries of Richard Crossman*, 973 (entry of 8 Feb. 1963).
[44] Ibid. 987 (entry of 12 Mar. 1963).

psephologists had argued that Labour's natural vote was eroding as the old working class became bour-geoisifled. Drawing on his wartime memories of the application of science to government, Wilson sought to reconcile Labour's old appeal with a much-changed society by harnessing the magic name of science. The white-coated workers, the scientists, the technicians, the managers, professional and skilled people repelled by Labour's dated dogmatism, would be won over by claims that socialism was 'about science', and that the party stood for modernization in a way more fundamental than the proposals of the Tories. With Wilson, a folksy northerner full of reminiscences of Herbert Chapman's Huddersfield Town in the 1920s, ranged against the aristocratic languor of Douglas-Home, the contrast between a down-to-earth modernizing Labour Party and a grouse-moor Tory Party of the old school was set out in personal terms. Wilson pointed out his own membership of the Society of Statisticians. A policy document written by Peter Shore, 'Labour and the Scientific Revolution', called for a further £100 m. to be spent on scientific research.

Wilson's challenge was mounted with particular effect at the October 1963 Party Conference at Scarborough. In a speech rewritten at the very last moment during the small hours, he called for Labour to embrace the cult of the new, to harness 'the white heat of a second industrial revolution', to modernize and re-equip their society. Many more scientists should enter Whitehall. There should be a Ministry of Technology set up, and far more investment in scientific research.[45] For the twelve months prior to the October 1964 general election, Wilson's appeal carried all before it. One passionate young believer was Anthony Wedgwood Benn, a technocrat by instinct who felt that Wilson (whose speech-writer he became) had forged a creed and

---

[45] 'Labour and the Scientific Revolution' (LRD 518), August 1963, accepted by Labour Home Policy Committee, 11 November 1963 (Labour Party archives, NEC documents); *The Times*, 2 Oct. 1963 for Wilson's speech.

an imaginative appeal that Labour had lacked since 1945.[46] There was, Wilson proclaimed, no room for Luddites in the labour movement, no place for trade unionists defending antique work-practices, or managers protecting methods which depended on social contacts rather than technical ability. It should appeal directly to the professional, wealth-creating classes won over in 1945 but lost to the Tories in the soft, 'affluent' years since. Wilson sounded a note unknown since the techno-cratic/administrative appeal of the Fabians before 1914, or the scientific gospel of the young H. G. Wells. For some of 1964 this exciting, apparently novel, message swept the board.

It was a particularly artful appeal in political terms. It enabled Wilson to circumvent old arguments about more or less nation-alization, lower or higher taxation, flat-rate or earnings-related social benefits, universality or selectivity, joining or ignoring the Common Market. Science and economic growth would provide the basis for a fuller, more equal, but also more productive society, a plain hardworking society with room at the top and Huddersfield's Harold Wilson as Bradford's Joe Lampton born again. It evaded deeper issues, including the sense, if any, with which socialism could realistically be equated with science. It also failed to relate Wilson's technocratic dream to the Labour Party as it actually existed, dominated as it was by unions which were not only Victorian relics but almost wilful in their defence of job demarcations and the proliferation of employment, whether productive or not. Wilson's call, however, carried con-viction because it chimed in with the national mood. There was much comparison with President Kennedy's New Frontier.

In a more general way, these years had seen the attempt to reestablish the credentials of science and technology within a national culture. For years, British scientists, eminent in medi-cine, biochemistry, nuclear physics, radio-astrology, and much else besides, with clutches of Nobel prizes to their credit, had felt

---

[46] See Tony Benn, *Out of the Wilderness*.

excluded in a humanist world. Leading civil servants, university chiefs, and business executives were seldom trained scientists. C. P. Snow's diagnosis of the 'two cultures' in his 1959 Rede lectures, though fiercely attacked by F. R. Leavis and other defenders of the old humane disciplines, had touched a real chord. Popularizers like Dr Bronowski and Dr Julian Huxley, both pillars of the BBC 'Brains Trust', and the journalist Ritchie Calder, tried to promote the cause of science in down-to-earth terms. In Anthony Eden's time as premier, he had tried to sponsor technical instruction and government patronage of the sciences, pure and applied, and with some effect. In January 1956, a report by Sir David Eccles proposed expenditure to the tune of £70 m. on technical projects over the next five years.[47] The outcome was the Colleges of Advanced Technology which later became universities in the sixties.

The Macmillan government in its later phase began to pay belated heed to this issue, as the facts of greater scientific sponsorship by Britain's industrial rivals began to sink in. Lord Hailsham, somewhat improbably for a barrister classicist who was a fellow of All Souls, became Minister of Science. He brought energy to the task, though the effect was somewhat spoilt by his departmental responsibilities including education, the North-East, and even sport! Hailsham's opposite number was another former Oxford arts don, R. H. S. Crossman. He and Gaitskell had been associated in the fifties with scientists anxious to evolve a new governmental approach to science and technology: they included Snow, Howard Florey (the Nobel prize-winner who had developed penicillin), C. F. Carter, Bronowski, and Ritchie Calder. The most prominent of all was Professor Patrick Blackett, who had been somewhat in the shadows since his opposition to British development of the atomic bomb in 1947 and a series of caustic attacks on Anglo-American nuclear policy since.[48]

---

[47] Cabinet conclusions, 4 Jan. 1956 (CAB 128/30); Eccles's white paper is in CAB 129/77.

[48] Sir Bernard Lovell, 'Patrick Maynard Stuart Blackett', in *Biographical Memoirs of Fellows of the Royal Society*, xxi (London, 1975).

He had many meetings with Crossman, the shadow Minister of Higher Education, from early 1963 and pressed the cause of a Ministry of Industry and Technology. Blackett's influence was very apparent in Wilson's Scarborough speech at Party Conference in October. Indeed, Blackett attended this conference. In September 1964 he sent a paper to Wilson, outlining the case for a powerful Ministry of Technology. This was developed in an article in the *New Statesman* and the new ministry came into being in October.[49]

Perhaps the most important offshoot of this campaign for science and technology was the publication of the report of the Robbins committee on Higher Education in October 1963.[50] It strongly urged the need to promote scientific studies in British universities, by much enlarging the places for scientific subjects, and indeed expanding higher education in general. The twelve Colleges of Advanced Technology should be elevated to university status. The total of students at universities should rise from 216,000 to 560,000 in 1980. The expansion of British higher education called for by Robbins was welcomed at the time. Some critics like Kingsley Amis, however, complained that 'more means worse'. Whatever the truth of this, the irony was that the main impetus of Robbins, in fact, went to encouraging arts and social science subjects already flourishing—history, languages (where girls enlisted in large numbers), politics, economics, and the newish subject of sociology. Expensive new engineering or metallurgical laboratories languished for lack of suitable applicants, much of their space unused. Only two of the prestigious institutes of science and technology proposed in Robbins came to fruition. Putative scientists often preferred to go directly into industry. Nor was industry itself necessarily content with the kind of non-vocational training the universities offered. But in the 1963–4 period, Robbins chimed in with the general

---

[49] *New Statesman*, 11 Sept. 1964.
[50] *Higher Education: Report* (Cmnd. 2154). HMSO, 1963. See also E. H. Phelps Brown's memoir, 'Lionel Charles Robbins, 1898–1984', *Proceedings of the British Academy*, 73 (1987), 621–3.

urge to legitimize the man in the white coat, to restore parity of esteem to science in Britain, and indeed to avert a 'brain drain' to American universities. In this last connection, the Royal Society's paper on 'The Emigration of Scientists from the United Kingdom' (February 1963) had caused a great stir. Whatever the intellectual thrust of the cry for the support of science, it did not so easily consort with the humane, somewhat amateurish style of one-nation Toryism in its final, rather desperate phase.

Along with the satire, therefore, there was also a serious sense that a major cultural shift could be in the making, to reverse certain deep-seated tendencies in British intellectual life as they had unfolded since the Victorian period. Wilson's campaign, Robbins, the public approval of the 'two cultures' argument, coincided with, and fostered, a current of opinion that British skill at invention and scientific pioneering had not been followed up by effective application, especially to manufacturing industry. Britain since 1945 had pioneered atomic energy and produced the world's first nuclear power stations. It had developed jet aircraft and maritime propulsion; it had led the way in the development of computers. But it was now being overtaken by others. In 1963, for instance, there were 750 computers in operation in Britain (mostly from IBM), compared with 12,000 in the computerized, transistorized United States.[51] The gap, not only with America, but with Western Germany, France, or Sweden, grew ever wider. Industrialists were vocal on the need for wider investment in science, in place of the few 'big science' projects of the fifties. The wider projection of science through the media and in the schools was actively proposed. Studies such as those by Michael Kaser implied that there was a direct correlation between investment in science and higher education generally and sustained economic growth.[52] The case was often presented

[51] A valuable source is *Report of a Joint Working Group on Computers for Research* (Cmnd. 2993), Parl, papers, 1965–6, V.

[52] Michael Sanderson, *The Universities and British Industry, 1850–1970* (London, 1972), 363. Kaser was an Oxford expert on the Soviet economy.

in over-simple or over-stark terms. Snow's 'two cultures' argument was in some ways unhelpful or misleading. But at the time the very debate suggested an intellectual upheaval which could have wider political and social implications.

This provided the backdrop to the October 1964 general election, popularly presented as the 'two cultures' in polarized party form. The election was delayed to the last possible moment, which gave the Douglas-Home government no room for manœuvre. Nothing much seemed to be going right, with mounting financial difficulties and sullen back-benchers low on morale. Another problem was the rising tide of unofficial strikes. In the past, these had usually redounded to the discredit of the Labour Party. Harold Wilson reflected this during the campaign when he suggested that a strike in Hardy Spicers in Birmingham had, in some unspecified way, been stirred up by the Tory Party—which raised the odd spectre of Conservative shop stewards on the rampage. But now the strikes that took place were not necessarily bad news for Labour. They included a strike by postmen, one of the most popular and much-loved groups of workers in the land. The Postmaster-General, J. R. Bevins, was later to reflect with some bitterness how he, a rare working-class Tory Cabinet minister, had been left in the lurch by aristocratic colleagues, who refused to endorse a $5\frac{1}{2}$ per cent pay award that would have averted industrial action, whereas in the end 6 per cent was agreed after a politically damaging dispute.[53] Wilson toured the country propounding his thesis of state-sponsored science, an overhaul of education, and general modernization. George Brown, shadow Minister of Economic Affairs, and James Callaghan, shadow Chancellor, both campaigned in lively fashion, and Labour as a whole showed an unwonted unity and sense of direction with a real prospect of office after the so-called 'thirteen wasted years' of Tory rule. Home tried to deflect attention to defence policy, where Labour campaigned against the 'independent'

[53] J. R. Bevins, *The Greasy Pole* (London, 1965), 128ff.

British nuclear deterrent, and argued for a renegotiation of the Nassau agreement.

At the same time, it was clear that Labour would have to work hard to win any majority at all. The troika at the top were hardly a band of brothers. Wilson himself was an elusive figure with few close friends. The erratic and irascible George Brown was angry at being denied the Foreign Office portfolio, while James Callaghan made clear his public disagreement with Wilson's plan to set up a Ministry of Economic Planning, distinct from the Treasury. Callaghan argued that planning should be linked with fiscal and monetary policy, while in any case his personal prestige would be undermined by such an arrangement.[54] The dispute was not really resolved on the eve of the election. Again the years of Tory affluence were hard to gainsay. At the end of September there was even a Tory lead in the polls, with the NOP actually recording a lead of 2.9 per cent. The effect of this was somewhat nullified by bleak economic figures on the balance of payments and by characteristically enigmatic comments on a likely Tory defeat by Butler.[55]

In the event, there was an average swing from Conservatives to Labour of 3.5 per cent in Britain as a whole, with Labour doing particularly well in Wales, Scotland, and much of northern England. Racial issues somewhat frustrated Labour's advance in the Midlands as will be seen in the next chapter. But this all carried Labour into office, and Wilson into Downing Street, by the barest of majorities. Labour ended up with 317 seats, the Conservatives with 304, and the Liberals with nine, an overall Labour majority of four. Labour's reward was the certainty of having to make another appeal to the people within the next two years. On balance, while Wilson gave an impression of energy and earthy practicality in his period as party leader from February 1963, it was hardly enthusiasm for Labour, let alone for

[54] *The Times*, 2 Oct. 1963.
[55] Butler and King, *The British General Election of 1964*, 118. Butler spoke of 'a strong undercurrent of Labour' (*sic*).

anything resembling socialism, that led to the Conservatives' downfall. Labour's campaign concentrated less on questioning the reality of Tory affluence, and more on charges that it would manage it more efficiently and also improve the quality of life.

There are those who have seen the 1964 election as a watershed, a long-term consequence of the disaffection of middle opinion and the intelligentsia, first detectable at the time of Suez, and continuing with the 'pay pause' and 'night of the long knives'. Some nostalgically thought of it as another 1945, a view encouraged by the octogenarian Earl Attlee taking an active part in the campaign.[56] It is doubtful if the record confirms this view. The early sixties were a time of an urge towards modernization in various directions, as in the Robbins Report on higher education, the Buchanan Report on road traffic and the Trend Inquiry into the organization of civil science—along with the much less popular Beeching Report on the railways. But these were superimposed on a society that was losing some of its wartime apparent cohesion and sense of shared values. Snow had written of two cultures, distinguishing sharply between the two. Many commentators wondered whether there was even one, any enduring base to shore up the national morale at a time of unease and growing pessimism. At least, though, the advent of a new leader and new initiative afforded some grounds for a renewal of hope.

[56] Kenneth Harris, *Attlee* (London, 1982), 559–60. Attlee spoke twice each night during the campaign as well as appearing on television.

7. *Labour Blown Off Course*

1964–1967

DESPITE its narrow majority, Harold Wiilson's Labour government took office in October 1964 amidst a mood of some optimism. After the sense of national erosion in the late, stale years of the outgoing Tory government, there was hope of a fresh start. A good deal of it was embodied in the new image carved out for himself by the new Prime Minister. He offered a no-nonsense, classless style associated with modernization and the therapeutic qualities of the application of science to government. He frequently evoked the spirit of John F. Kennedy, if not indeed of Franklin D. Roosevelt, with talk of a 'new frontier' and his 'first hundred days' of purposive action. His Gannex raincoat, his Yorkshire accent, his skill in television interviews, where well-timed puffs from his pipe were interspersed with shrewd political comment, gave him, for a time, a dominant political appeal unmatched since Macmillan's in the days of 'Supermac' fame.

There was a good deal to support this new optimism in the early months of the Wilson administration, to an extent that was later too easily forgotten. The new attention to science and technology was confirmed in the structure of the government. C. P. Snow, the guru of the 'two cultures', received both a peerage and appointment as Minister of State for the Support and Encouragement of Science. Sir Solly Zuckerman, a far more eminent scientist (who turned down an offer of government office) was given a wider role as

Chief Scientific Adviser to the government, and to the Ministry of Defence in particular.[1] A new Ministry of Technology was created, too. This was, surprisingly, placed in the charge of Frank Cousins, the Transport Workers' General Secretary, now given a forward-looking role as an industrial modernizer instead of serving solely as the voice of protest on behalf of unilateralism and fundamentalist socialism. Professor Blackett became his scientific adviser. Blackett was soon to become disillusioned, both with Cousins personally and with the new Ministry, which became bogged down in problems of labour relations. But at the time it seemed a hopeful portent of the new 'white heat' enthusiasm.

The arts, no less than the sciences, appeared to be injected with new life. In one of Wilson's most inspired appointments, Jennie Lee, the widow of Aneurin Bevan, was made Minister for the Arts. She proved to be a vigorous patron of theatres, art galleries, libraries, the British Film Institute, and much else besides. Her White Paper in February 1965 set the agenda for public debate on the arts for years to come. 'High points of excellence' were to be created throughout the land.[2] The Arts Council, soon to be chaired by Arnold, Lord Goodman, Wilson's friend and much-used solicitor, was given considerable new funding, from £3,200,000 in 1964–5 to £9,300,000 in 1971. Its responsibilities were transferred from the Treasury to the more welcoming supervision of the Department of Education and Science.[3] There was new buoyancy in the world of theatre especially, with Peter Brook as director of the Royal Shakespeare Company and Kenneth Tynan as literary adviser of Olivier's National Theatre Company. Music was also remarkably lively. London boasted five orchestras and could claim to be the musical capital of Europe, perhaps the world. Elsewhere in Britain, the Royal Liverpool Philharmonic, Manchester's Hallé Orchestra, the

---

[1] Zuckerman, *Men, Monkeys, and Missiles*, 369ff.

[2] *A Policy for the Arts: the First Step* (Cmnd. 2601), P. P., 1964–5, xxix.

[3] Sec *Annual Reports of the Arts Council*, 1964–70, and also *Twenty-sixth Annual Report*, 1971–2, in which Lord Goodman surveys the past fifteen years.

City of Birmingham, and the Bournemouth symphony orchestras maintained distinguished programmes through the year, while the Welsh National Opera was building up a glowing reputation. Apart from being life-enhancing in themselves, these were all highly beneficial for the balance of payments and in sustaining Britain's booming tourist industry.

Education was also thriving, particularly through the impetus given to higher education after the Robbins Report. By 1966 seven new universities were in being (Sussex, East Anglia, York, Kent, Warwick, Lancaster, and Essex) and the older civic universities were much expanded, while the ten Colleges of Advanced Technology, founded since the Eccles Report in 1956, were also given enlarged funding and new status as university institutions. A particularly valuable innovation was the Open University, which Jennie Lee promoted and in which Wilson himself took a close interest. Finally beginning teaching operations in 1971, it was designed to advance educational opportunities for mature students, working people, housewives, and others. Even if the eventual recruitment for the Open University proved to be distinctly more middle-class than anticipated, with schoolteachers in particular taking advantage of the opportunities of gaining a university degree and thereby acquiring professional advancement, the Open University proved to be a pioneering and socially valuable instrument of mobility and cultural inspiration. It also proved to be remarkably innovative in distance-learning instructional techniques, including the use of television and in developing American-style, credit-based modular courses. Again, welfare policy was revamped, with Labour drawing on the talents of Richard Titmuss, Brian Abel-Smith and Peter Townsend. Pensions and family allowances were to be increased, and new benefits for poorer people such as rent rebates to be introduced. In the Celtic nations, patriotic Welsh men and women took heart from the presence of James Griffiths as the first Secretary of State for Wales, while in Scotland the expanded responsibilities and funding of the Scottish Office, and the creation of the Highlands and Islands Development Board in 1965, were generally acclaimed. The creation of a Parliamentary

Commissioner ('Ombudsman') confirmed that a Labour government could show concern for individual rights.

These were changes directly attributable to government action. But the Wilson government also seemed to encourage a wider mood sympathetic to reform. In part, it was stimulated by the wide array of university teachers, and others of the 128 professional people returned in 1964 as part of the Labour majority, and by the scientists, economists, and others who entered the government service on a temporary basis. By 1966 there were eighty economists in various branches of central government. A year later, there were 120, at a time when the prestige of experts at universities had never stood higher.[4] Penal reform was also a beneficiary of the new mood, with the benevolent patronage of the Home Office, especially under the regime of Roy Jenkins from 1965 onwards. In due course, the long campaign of the veteran left-winger, Sydney Silverman, for the abolition of capital punishment resulted in his motion being carried through the Commons by a comfortable majority in 1965, and eventually getting over the hurdle of the House of Lords as well. After 1966 the British no longer hanged, and, save in parts of Scotland, seldom flogged. Homosexuals and other minority groups were also made to feel that the climate of opinion was less oppressive and discriminatory, not least because the diminution of the powers of the censor over books and plays allowed the more open discussion of their situation. There was also the promise of a less restrictive approach towards race relations. It was encouraged by the Prime Minister's onslaught on Peter Griffiths, a Tory MP who had defeated Patrick Gordon Walker at Smethwick in the general election on an overtly racialist campaign. Griffiths, Wilson declared, would henceforth be 'a parliamentary leper'.[5] There followed the 1965 Race Relations

---

[4] See D. N. Chester. 'The role of economic advisers in government', in A. P. Thirlwall (ed.), *Keynes as a Policy Adviser* (London, 1982).

[5] Harold Wilson, *The Labour Government, 1964–70* (Harmondsworth, 1971), 55.

Act to set up the Race Relations Board, and later the Community Relations Commission. Able Indians, Pakistanis, and West Indians were gradually brought into the government service, the police, and a wider range of the professions. In these and many other ways, Britain seemed to be mellowing in its post-imperial phase and becoming a more open and civilized society where social, racial, and sexual equality underwrote the public culture and the idea of citizenship.

But these attractive and humane developments rested on Labour's wider claim to create a sustained, expanding economy, based on planning and growth, an end to the negativism of 'stop-go' and the credit squeeze which had marked the last six years of Tory rule. It was widely believed that much care had been taken in preparing planning mechanisms that would achieve a balanced expansion. It would increase the gross national product without being interrupted by incessant balance-of-payments crises through a surge of imports, or threats to the value of sterling. Especial hope was vested in the new Department of Economic Affairs, with the aid of two energetic civil servants, Sir Donald MacDougall (formerly of NEDC) and Sir Eric Roll. The origins of this new department were curious indeed. It emerged in a somewhat indirect fashion during the discussion between Wilson and his colleagues about the machinery of government under a future Labour administration. Brown later alleged that the idea for a new ministry had been drawn up in the back of a taxi by Wilson and himself late one night, though Wilson and Callaghan denied this.[6] It was hard to avoid the feeling that the motivation was less economic than political, namely the need to satisfy the ambitions of both Brown and Callaghan, the new Chancellor, Wilson's two rivals for the party leadership in February 1963. Wilson felt that Brown would not be sufficiently diplomatic or stable to go to the Foreign Office (which did not prevent his going there, for similar political reasons, in 1966). Callaghan, for his

[6]   George Brown, *In my Way* (Harmondsworth, 1971), 89; but cf. Wilson, op. cit., 24 and Callaghan, *Time and Chance*, 153.

part, made it plain that he disapproved of a new ministry being created to trim his own powers at the Treasury. The entire relationship between the established Treasury apparatus and the new Ministry of Economic Affairs, and the alleged distinction between short-term and long-term planning, were wreathed in uncertainty. To some degree it damaged Labour's brave new experiment from the very start.

Labour took office, in fact, not in a mood of optimistic progress but in the midst of a huge balance-of-payments crisis. There was an £800 m. deficit bequeathed by the boom stimulated by the outgoing Conservative Chancellor, Reginald Maudling. For a time at least, Callaghan the new Chancellor would have to undertake a traditional job of major repair. The government, however, decided on a strategy that would not mean its surrendering the initiative at the outset. Wilson thus made it clear that the Labour government would not devalue the pound—partly because of fear of competitive currency devaluation, but also because Labour had been linked in the public mind with devaluation since Cripps's time in 1949.[7] In its place, Callaghan introduced a package of measures headed by a 15 per cent import surcharge on manufactured goods, along with export rebates and negotiations for a loan from the International Monetary Fund. This was Labour's answer to deflation and massive public expenditure cuts. In early November, Callaghan added an emergency budget which included major tax increases of an extra 6d. on the standard rate of income tax, an extra 6d. on petrol, and a forthcoming capital gains and corporations tax which, oddly enough, it was announced would form part of the usual budget five months later. These taxes, however, were in part designed to pay for increases in pensions and in health and social insurance benefits to the tune of £300 m. a year.[8]

[7] Alec Cairncross and Barry Eichengreen, *Sterling in Decline* (Oxford, 1983), 166ff.

[8] *The Economist*, 14, 21, 28 Nov. 1964.

The world reaction to these measures was unfavourable. The Labour government, said *The Economist*, had 'gone to Canossa'. A heavy run on the pound followed, reaching a crescendo on 21 November. In a mood of desperation, bank rate was belatedly put up to 7 per cent, a rise of two points, and a colossal loan of up to $3,000 m. in credits arranged with the central banks of the United States, Germany, and nine other countries. This was in addition to credits obtained under the Basle Agreement and from the IMF. Only then did some confidence return and the pressure against sterling ease. The immediate crisis seemed to be over. Even so, the traumatic first month of the Wilson government, far from heralding a fearless Roosevelt-style 'hundred days', set a pattern which was long to continue, with a series of short-term financial arrangements mixed up with party-political considerations. The impression was of an economy almost out of control and a government close to being on the run. The City, quite apart from political prejudices, was distinctly unimpressed by Labour's first attempts to control the run on the reserves, not least because increased pensions and an abolition of NHS medicine prescription charges came simultaneously with new taxes and attempts to curb public spending. The moment for public welfare largess hardly seemed to have arrived. There was a public row between Harold Wilson and the Governor of the Bank of England, Lord Cromer, who urged massive public-expenditure cuts and seemed to hint that he might find it difficult to arrange international support for the pound on the present basis. Wilson in return threatened him with a dissolution of parliament and an immediate election, which (the Prime Minister claimed) Labour would win by a landslide, a kind of reversal of the 'bankers' ramp' débâcle of 1931.[9] But Labour's belief that it had a panacea in the form of co-ordinated planning seemed hard to sustain. George Brown's attempts to expand the economy through the new DEA already seemed redundant.

[9] Wilson, *The Labour Government*, 61–6.

Nevertheless, throughout much of 1965, attempts were made to breathe life into Labour's alleged schemes for planning. Brown, backed up by a huge legion of Oxford and Cambridge economists and statisticians, Keynesians to a man (and occasional woman), began to draft a National Plan for the planned growth of production and exports. Crucial to it would be an incomes policy to restrict the growth of wages and salaries. To those who pointed out that the TUC had always resisted such a policy, it was replied that back in 1963 Frank Cousins, now a member of the Cabinet, had urged the need for 'planned growth of wages', though in terms of Delphic obscurity. Brown's crusade for a National Economic Plan was accompanied by the maximum of bustle and public-relations bravado. But it was noticeable that the machinery employed was largely that of the discredited Tory regime of the past, especially Selwyn Lloyd's NIC and NEDC. It was the National Incomes Commission, now enjoying a new lease of life under a former Tory Cabinet minister, Aubrey Jones, which was supposed to produce the incomes policy that the unions would observe. Otherwise, Brown relied on putting together an agreement with the suspicious Tory-dominated CBI, and with the TUC whose General Secretary, George Woodcock, was notoriously cautious, even unimaginative. In September 1965, Brown proclaimed his National Plan to the world. It would embody a 25 per cent increase in national output over the period 1964–70. There would thus be an annual growth rate of 4 per cent.[10] Yet despite Brown's euphoria, the impact on public opinion was limited. It was clear that the Plan, for all its psychological impact, had no real teeth or mechanism for raising production or exports. Although it followed a visit to Paris by a Treasury team headed by Edward Boyle and 'Otto' Clarke in 1963, in no sense could it be compared with the Monnet Plan in France, or the indicative planning of the Scandinavian countries. Long before the end of 1965 the National Plan was seen to be

[10] For a good discussion, see Michael Stewart, *The Jekyll and Hyde Years: Politics and Economic Policy since 1964* (London, 1977), 37ff.

stillborn. It was finally wound up quietly on 20 July 1966, and
the Department of Economic Affairs itself petered out in the
latter part of 1966. Nothing like it was ever visualized again.
The entire notion of a DEA was ill-thought-out and ill-prepared.
As in 1954–51, Labour's planners proved unable, even unwilling, to plan. Wilson's brave new world of planned expansion
ended almost before it began.

In its stead was the traditional Treasury policy of trying to
recover from the latest batterings over the balance of payments
and the parity of the pound. Callaghan achieved a good deal of
success in eliminating the deficit on the capital account during
1965 with a generally deflationary policy, and also proved very
innovatory as a tax reformer. The April 1965 budget was suit-
ably prudent, with cuts of £500 m. forecast in home demand for
1965–6.[11] Exports revived, with a vigorous policy pursued by
Douglas Jay at the Board of Trade, himself the architect of the
distribution-of-industry strategy conceived during the war. There
was also a mending of fences with Britain's EFTA partners, who
had been much incensed at Callaghan's import surcharge the
previous October, landed on them without warning. Even so,
the economic omens in 1965 were still generally gloomy. Following more speculation against the pound, an emergency budget
was introduced in July 1965, including tighter exchange controls
and a cut in import finance. One disturbing consequence of this
was a growing dependence on, almost a subservience towards,
the United States in return for help in bailing out the British
economy. Fowler, the US Secretary of the Treasury, insisted on
stringent terms in talks with Callaghan in Washington in August
1965 to ascertain whether the US government would aid the
ailing pound. An agreement reached on 8–9 September between
Harold Wilson and George Ball of the US State Department laid
down that, in return for massive American assistance in propping

---

[11] *The Economist*, 17 Apr. 1965, described it as 'orthodox-Treasury-deflation-
ary' rather than 'heretical-Labour-expansionary'. It took the budget as proof that
the Treasury had won its battle with the DEA.

up the pound on the foreign exchange markets, Britain would agree neither to devalue nor to withdraw from the Singapore base or cut its other defence commitments east of Suez.[12] Even so, the balance of payments showed another huge gap (£236 m.) for the third quarter of 1965 and pressure on sterling continued. Despite disavowals by Wilson, Callaghan, and Lord Cromer, the belief persisted that a devaluation of the pound would only be a matter of time. Worst of all, the economy was static, showing hardly any growth at all. The promise of expansion had so far not been fulfilled. So despite good news in relation to welfare, penal reform, race relations, and the arts, the basic weakness of the economic structure seemed to show little improvement under Labour's new deal.

If the first dominant theme of the Wilson period was economic disarray, the other was political indirection, with a background of paranoia. The Prime Minister firmly believed that his administration was being hamstrung by hostility and speculative sabotage from the City and international speculators. He spent much time in denouncing the 'sell Britain short Brigade' and other sinister, unnamed conspirators against a Labour government. His attacks carried the more credence because he himself had operated with similar methods during the years of Tory government. Wilson's technique in part was to work through friendly press lords and journalists, such as Cecil King of the *Daily Mirror*. His administration was consistently tormented by a series of quarrels with the media, especially with Lord Hill and the BBC: Wilson believed the Corporation to be operating against the Labour government.[13] Here George Wigg, notionally the Paymaster-General, operated on the margin between politics and presentation in a quasi-conspiratorial way. It was Wigg, after all, who had unmasked the personal and security implications of the behaviour of John Profumo in 1963; no one better

---

[12] Ibid. 31 July 1965. Documents on the Anglo-US agreement appear in Clive Ponting, *Breach of Promise* (London, 1989), 53–4.

[13] See Lord Hill, *Behind the Scenes* (London, 1974), 98ff.

understood the *demi-monde* of rumour, scandal, unattributable leaks, and disinformation. Wilson also brought in something like a kitchen Cabinet of personal advisers, reminiscent in some ways of the latter phase of the rule of Lloyd George, though without the intellectual distinction of men like Kerr, Grigg, and W. G. S. Adams in that earlier period. His personal secretary, Mrs Marcia Williams, played an unusually dominant part in protecting the Prime Minister against rebuffs and deflecting pressures and pin-pricks. Her role aroused much public suspicion.[14] The atmos-phere from the start was frenetic, and a disappointment to those who had linked Wilson with a more open and positive style of leadership after the regime of Gaitskell and the so-called 'Hamp-stead set'. Tony Benn, Postmaster-General, was one former admirer of Wilson's disturbed by his conspiratorial approach.[15]

Of course, some features of the political structure of the new government were sound, even impressive. Roy Jenkins cut a powerful figure at the Aviation Ministry; he was rapidly to ascend to the Home Office and then the Treasury. He was a biographer of the old Liberal premier, Asquith, and there were many who felt that a similar progress awaited Jenkins also. Anthony Crosland, the author of the influential book, *The Future of Socialism*, also proved himself a powerful and charismatic administrator. Soon he was to move to the Department of Edu-cation, where he both gave a stimulus to the Robbins findings (though creating a 'binary' system of university and other higher education), and carried on a radical programme of the compre-hensivization of secondary schools. He promised his wife: 'If it's the last thing I do, I'm going to destroy every fucking grammar school in England and Wales and Northern Ireland.'[16] Following his circular 10/65 for 1965, the proportion of secondary-school

---

[14] See Marcia Williams (Falkender), *Inside Number Ten* (London, 1972) and Joe Haines, *The Politics of Power* (London, 1972).

[15] See Tony Benn, *Out of the Wilderness*, e.g. 466 where he refers to 'the atmosphere of intrigue' at Number Ten (entry of 6 Aug. 1966).

[16] Susan Crosland, *Tony Crosland* (London, 1982), 148.

pupils in comprehensive systems rose rapidly, to reach 32 per cent by 1970. Richard Crossman, Minister of Housing and Local Government, was another commanding figure, rising up within the administration, keeping his diary when he returned home in the small hours, even if his prolonged departmental wrangles with the formidable Dame Evelyn Sharp had their hilarious side apart from their serious constitutional impact.[17] These ministers made a powerful impression, more so indeed than Callaghan, Brown, and Michael Stewart (who succeeded Gordon Walker as Foreign Secretary in January 1965), in the more senior posts.

Perhaps the most impressive of all the new ministers was Denis Healey, Minister of Defence and thus in a department where Labour had traditionally cut an ambiguous and hesitant figure.[18] Healey had served for some years in the International Department of Transport House and had a sophisticated intellectual grasp of foreign affairs. He was also unusually versed in the latest technology regarding weapons systems, and personally on close terms with Robert McNamara, the US Secretary of Defense. At his new ministry, Healey tried for the first time to restore sense and science to Britain's defence commitments. He was a tough-minded, no-nonsense supporter of NATO and the philosophy of nuclear deterrence. At the same time, the cost of Britain's defence effort extended far beyond her real resources. Indeed in 1964 military engagements were claiming the attention of the British forces in places as far removed as North Borneo and Aden. Healey's Defence White Paper of January 1965, based on up-to-date techniques of cost-benefit assessments and new management and budgetary methods, cut defence expenditure by £56 m., the first real cut since the early 1950s.[19] The main spending would focus on US-built Phantom and British Buccaneer fighter aircraft.

---

[17] See Janet Morgan's editions of Crossman's diaries in three volumes for 1964–70 (London, 1975, 1976, 1977), especially the volume for 1964–6.

[18] B. Reed and G. Williams, *Denis Healey and the Politics of Power* (London, 1971).

[19] 'Statement on the Defence Estimates', Feb. 1965 (Cmnd. 2592), P.P., 1964–5, XXV.

The British-built TSR 2, designed to carry airborne nuclear weapons, was to be scrapped. One after another, the sacred cows of Britain's past in imperial defence were killed off. Despite American protests, from 1967 British detachments were steadily brought home from east of Suez. No further aircraft carriers would be built (which resulted in the resignation of Christopher Mayhew, Minister for the Navy). The famous Territorial Army, a legacy of Haldane's days before the First World War, would disappear. The mild-mannered Attorney-General, Frank Soskice, tried to object but Healey battered him down in Cabinet. Soskice, recorded Crossman, was 'no match for this rough, rather ruthless, young man'.[20] Significantly, though, the British nuclear strike deterrent still remained, in breach of Labour's election pledges.

Healey and his younger colleagues showed the range of administrative competence and physical vigour within the Wilson administration. But it was not universal. There was some dead wood in what was a generally senior government. Much ingenuity had been devoted by Wilson to balancing out the old right and left. Thus former Gaitskellites such as Jay, Jenkins, and Crosland were countered by promoting ex-Bevanite figures like Crossman and Barbara Castle. Michael Foot, though not in the government, was now a loyal and influential back-bencher, while Ian Mikardo, another old Bevanite, was from 1966 kept busy on the Select Committee on Nationalized Industries. Balance and resource dictated much of the government's policy. Thus the government went on with renationalizing the iron and steel industry, even though the only real purpose was to reassure Labour's faithful that socialism was not being totally discarded despite appearances to the contrary. This gave the opportunity for Wilson to lambast Woodrow Wyatt and Desmond Donnelly, two right-wing Labour MPs who opposed steel renationalization, and thereby deflect the wrath of left-wingers who disliked

---

[20] *Diaries of a Cabinet Minister*, i. 414–15 (entry of 16 Dec. 1965).

the government's policy on the economy, Vietnam, and race relations.

Politically, the government was in constant ferment. A crisis came when the Foreign Secretary, Patrick Gordon Walker, already out of parliament after election defeat at Smethwick, was defeated again in the Leyton by-election in January 1965. Since race considerations did not loom very large in Leyton, it might have been concluded that one problem was that Gordon Walker was not a very clubbable candidate. He was replaced as Foreign Secretary by Michael Stewart. The borough elections in May showed a 7 per cent swing against Labour compared with the general election the previous October. Gradually, by the end of the year, Labour's standing began to improve. The Conservatives had now had their own internal crisis, with Home resigning as leader. After the shambles of 1963, they had adopted Labour's method of election by MPs. In the ensuing ballot, Edward Heath (a grammar-school product, like Wilson) narrowly beat Reginald Maudling for the leadership. William Whitelaw proved a big improvement on Martin Redmayne as chief whip. But the Conservatives' standing did not benefit overall.

On balance, perhaps, Wilson's skills were mainly suitable for the politics of survival. He remained master of his party both in parliament and in the country. He was still personally popular. In a situation where Labour had a majority of two, his ability was seen at its most adroit. He constantly out-manoeuvred the Tories and often made Heath seem humourless and even foolish. One supreme example of Wilson's skill lay in finding a new Speaker when the existing one, Sir Harry Hylton-Foster, died. The new Speaker would now be his former deputy Horace King, a Labour member. Somehow Wilson had to avoid Labour's majority disappearing entirely. With exemplary skill he alighted on a quiet Welsh Liberal, E. Roderic Bowen, who became Deputy Speaker and thus left Labour's two-seat majority unimpaired. Bowen received modest rewards on public bodies in his later career. It was clear that Wilson was master of his party, and that Labour was able to weather its internal storms. The question remained whether Wilson could ever be master of the nation, and whether Labour could move out from its own bunker to take control of domestic and international events. The evidence of its first year-and-a-quarter in office was unconvincing on this level. Labour, and Wilson in particular, had prophesied boldly that a new community spirit would sweep the land when Labour was in power. In particular, its abiding links with the unions would create a harmonious, integrating national atmosphere as it had done under Bevin and Cripps in the past. Labour's early period of office, however, showed to the full the problems of corporatism, so far as it had had any reality since 1961. The period down to the end of 1965 did not witness any major strikes. But neither did it encourage any belief in the view that the unions would forgo their privileges or wage advances, or that the employers would collaborate if they did. The Wilson period saw the proliferation of a mass of quangos and public bodies designed to pronounce or reflect upon labour relations. But none had coercive power. The shambling structure of British industrial relations remained immune to reform of any kind.

Wilson's approach to the unions at first was tolerant and permissive. He declared that any kind of incomes policy would be voluntary in its conception, and that the pattern of incomes policy would be in no ways disturbed fundamentally. The government was quick to respond to TUC concern over the case of *Rookes* v. *Barnard*.[21] Here, a draughtsman for British Overseas Airways had sued two fellow-workers and an official in his union for conspiracy after resigning from it despite a closed-shop agreement. He had then had his case upheld in the Lords, despite the apparent protection afforded the union by the 1906 Trades Disputes Act. It was decreed that a threat to strike could constitute civil intimidation in certain circumstances. The Wilson government's Trades Disputes Act of 1965 was thus designed to close the loophole the unions had found opened by the Rookes case.

[21] *Rookes* v. *Barnard (1964) AC 1129*: see Donovan Report (Cmnd. 3623), 1968, para. 488.

In wage bargaining, Wilson struck a posture of moderation and smoke-filled-room diplomacy. In the talk of the time, strikes were settled over 'beer and sandwiches at Number Ten'. It was a reversion to the methods of Lloyd George's policy of settling strikes in 1919–21, when perhaps cold Welsh lamb and sugary tea provided the refreshment instead. There were always electoral considerations to remember, too. Thus his settlement of a wage claim by the National Union of Railwaymen in February 1966, in effect conceding their claim but covering up the cost through creative accounting, was typical of this expensive period of labour relations.[22] The TUC had reluctantly agreed to the setting up of a Royal Commission on the Trade Unions under Donovan in 1965, of which the TUC General Secretary, George Woodcock, was a member. But this was strictly on the basis that the voluntary system of wage bargaining would not be curtailed, and that the law would not intrude into labour matters. The Labour Party continued to operate a 'hands-off' posture towards the unions, and indeed towards the CBI as well, as the history of George Brown's abortive National Plan confirmed. European observers drew pained and pointed contrast between the adversarial character of British labour relations and the situation in Germany, the Netherlands, or Sweden, where unions were few (though levels of unionization were high), and the emphasis heavily on modernization, mobility, and the acquiring of new skills through industrial retraining. The British system continued with the mould unbroken.

The truth was that major structural changes within the British unions and procedures of industrial relations were occurring, as in due course the Donovan Report was to underline. Wage negotiations and bargaining on conditions of work were now largely localized and informal, the result of private, sectional agreements between shop stewards and individual managers. The image of private conclave at Number 10 between mass national unions

[22] *The Economist*, 19 Feb. 1966.

and nationwide employers, with the state holding the ring, obscured the sectional reality. In addition, the unions were increasingly propelled by white-collar clerical, administrative, and public service workers, with a different ethos from the old mass-based, manual-worker unions of the past. White-collar unions increased their membership from 1,964,000 in 1948 to 2,623,000 in 1964, a growth of 33.6 per cent.[23] Beyond this, the gulf between the state, as embodied in the somewhat quiescent figure of the Minister of Labour, Ray Gunter (known to the TUC as 'the ticket collector'), and the institutions that embodied the points of contact between unions and employers remained. The TUC had always adopted the spirit of voluntarism, the one unplanned area within their concept of a planned socialist economy being the one that they themselves inhabited. Voluntarism in the past, however, had been restricted within a framework of reciprocal relationships with the state; at least, it had been from the time of Bevin during the Second World War. Since the early 1960s, that was so no longer. George Woodcock presided placidly over a strike-ridden world in which shop stewards, plant spokesmen, and purely local representatives operated in a parochial context, one which made a mockery of the rhetoric of national unity and consensus.

These problems, however, were safely set aside when Harold Wilson called an election for 31 March 1966. The threat to sterling now seemed to have receded. Labour was advancing in the polls. The new Conservative leader, Edward Heath, aroused little enthusiasm. In these circumstances, the dramatic Labour by-election in Hull North in February 1966, when a marginal seat was converted into a safe Labour one, persuaded Wilson to call an election. The election this time concentrated on themes on which Labour felt relatively comfortable—the progress of the economy, the defence of the welfare state, the

---

[23] G.S. Bain, The *Growth of White Collar Unionism* (Oxford, 1970), 24ff.

relations with the unions.[24] The election itself was drab and
anodyne, though Wilson himself put up a strong, fighting performance. The most interesting feature of the campaign was the
conflict, not between Labour and the Conservatives, but between
Harold Wilson and the BBC, culminating in Wilson refusing to
give the BBC an interview in the aftermath of victory (not even to
W. John Morgan of 'Panorama' and the *New Statesman*). The
outcome was predictable. With 364 seats, Labour won a majority of 98 over the Conservatives and Liberals combined, with
striking gains in many areas. Oxford and Cambridge, Lancaster
and York, one of the Brighton seats (the first-ever Labour gain
in Sussex), distant rural seats like Cardiganshire or Caithness
and Sutherland, all went Labour's way. The party polled over
13 million votes, doing better amongst middle-class and women
voters.[25] It genuinely looked as if the party had captured its
second wind, with widespread gains in surban and commuter
constituencies. Wilson spoke of Labour becoming the 'natural
party of government'. It would fulfil the dreams of Keir Hardie
and the pioneers.

The euphoria of electoral success, however, did not last long.
Callaghan followed up with a budget in May in which, to much
surprise, he introduced a Select Employment Tax, designed to
encourage labour to move to manufacturing industry and away
from service employment. It proved to be a blunt instrument
indeed, hastily drafted by Callaghan's Hungarian advisers, Kaldor and Balogh. It could have potentially dire effects on banking,
insurance, shops, hotels, and the catering industry, all in their
different ways vital for the invisible earnings of the country. To
offer all workers in manufacturing industry indiscriminate support in this way was, some argued, an impressionistic policy. To
Samuel Brittan, the entire episode showed up Labour's lack of

---

[24] See David Butler and Anthony King. *The General Election of 1966*
(London, 1967).
[25] Report by Len Williams (Labour's General Secretary) on the 1966 General
Election. April 1966 (Labour Party archives, NEC Minutes).

feel for demand management.[26] It generated a nervous reaction in the markets.

It was followed by a damaging episode which showed that the disorder in labour relations was rampant, despite the euphoric rhetoric of the election campaign. On 16 May the National Union of Seamen began an indefinite strike. Over the next six-and-a-half weeks immense damage was done to Britain's export trade, and heavy pressure on sterling resulted. The traditional recourse to a tribunal of inquiry did not produce the kind of result that such a measure had done in the fifties, since the award of the Pearson Tribunal (which split the difference between the employers and the seamen's demands) was rejected by the NUS. With a drop of £38 m. in the reserves in May, Wilson had to abandon an air of detachment and to act. He did not do so very effectively. On 20 June he startled the Commons by a fierce polemical attack on the NUS executive, when he attributed the seamen's strike to sabotage perpetrated by 'a tightly knit group of politically motivated' extremists. This, together with his decision to name eight Communists on the NUS executive, only served to harden the seamen's resistance. It led to a clash on the Labour National Executive between Wilson and the Transport Workers' leader, Jack Jones.[27] After immense pressure on the reserves and on sterling, a settlement was patched up after six damaging weeks. But the aftermath was even worse. The government decided to deal with union indiscipline by introducing a Prices and Incomes Bill. No longer could credence be placed in the voluntary vetting operated by the TUC General Council. All wage, price, or dividend increases would have to be submitted to the statutory Prices and Incomes Board, with a four-month delay on any pay settlement. Penal sanctions were not yet included, however. But the same day that the text of the Prices and Incomes Bill was published, Frank Cousins, Minister of

[26] Sam Brittan, *Steering the Economy: The Role of the Treasury* (London, 1969), 210.
[27] Labour Party, National Executive Minutes, 25 May 1966.

Technology, resigned from the government.[28] Cousins had not been an effective minister and his performances in the House were often incoherent and unconvincing. Professor Patrick Blackett had been a disillusioned observer of a ministry he had helped bring into the world, and he concentrated increasingly on his work as President of the Royal Society instead. Cousins's resignation, nevertheless, marked a widening gulf in the historic alliance between the Labour Party and the unions. It was a declaration by the most powerful union boss of the day, to the applause of the left, that the state and the law should play no part in the regulation of labour relations. Inflation, the balance of payments, difficulties for sterling were all admitted as problems. But the voluntary tradition of labour relations, dating from Disraeli's time, based on the 'free-for-all' principle so derided under the Tories, was sacrosanct. Cousins's resignation was soon swallowed up by wider economic crises. But in its way, it marked an historic divide in British social history. It underlined the unwillingness of key union leaders to play the kind of bridging role that men like Bevin, Citrine, or Deakin had played (often brutally enough) in the past. Britain's public culture and declining economy were founded on the quicksands of sectionalism. So had they been even in the wartime triumphalism of 1939–45.

The more colourful and cheerful aspects of the otherwise somewhat drab record of this period came elsewhere. During the early Wilson years, the idea of 'the permissive society', focusing especially on images of 'swinging London', became common currency. Tourists came to London to gaze at an affluent society throwing off the Victorian shackles and the legacy of post-war austerity and puritanism, and expressing itself in a startling and revolutionary way. Here was a new El Dorado, perhaps a new Sodom and Gomorrah. It was hailed by *Time* magazine,[29] condemned by Mrs Whitehouse, but it made Britain international news in a dramatically new way.

---

[28] *The Times*, 4 July 1966.
[29] *Time*, 15 Apr. 1966, featured London as 'The Swinging City'.

The notion of 'permissiveness' was in itself ambiguous and many-sided. Indirectly, it reflected developments in the visual and plastic arts, with the current vogue for so-called Pop Art, associated with the free-flowing work of painters like David Hockney. It had echoes also in the architecture of the time, with the towering, post-Bauhaus office-blocks of the early sixties as a soaring gesture of revolt. Richard Seifert's Centre Point office-block skyscraper at the junction of New Oxford Street and Tottenham Court Road, commissioned by the property speculator Harry Hyams, became a controversial (and untenanted) symbol of this kind of work. But, beyond changes in artistic expression and design, 'permissiveness' in popular terms simply reflected the fact of full employment and a booming property and consumer market, with the new leisure and spending opportunities it brought for the working class, especially its young people. A more universal, apparently classless culture meant transformed consumer opportunities, notably with the growth of boutique-type fashion shops and cosmetic stores, for men as well as women. Mary Quant's fashion shops in the later fifties (starting with the King's Road, Chelsea, a Mecca for the apostles of the new age) were powerful market and style pioneers, as was the rise of Carnaby Street in North Soho, with its 'Mod' menswear appeal. The insistence and dominance of the new consumer culture aroused much head-shaking concern amongst public moralists. But it clearly also implied a gentler, less aggressive style of design and self-expression. In place of the staid 'teenagers' of the forties, or the 'macho' toughness of the fifties 'Teddy Boys', it was the more feminine and tolerant image of the Mods, with their bisexual fashion, that now predominated. It was they who proved, at least for the moment, the true heirs of the rock-and-roll revolution of the fifties.

The forms that the new consumer culture adopted were remarkable enough. Clothing, especially for girls, became *outré* and provocative, with the miniskirt as its omnipresent symbol, and King's Road, Chelsea as its forum. Journalists and photographers found new contemporary symbols of idealized beauty, varying from the model, Jean Shrimpton, to the pop singer, Marianne Faithfull. In pop music, the advance of updated rock and roll was irresistible. In place of the somewhat staid 'palais de danse' of the early fifties, exemplified by the ballroom style of the Lyceum, Hammersmith, there arose a flood of informal, hectic, and garish 'discos', in themselves a sign of changing generational conventions. The British pop-music industry developed at an extraordinary pace between 1964 and 1967. There was no more powerful symbol of it than the Beatles, those four Liverpudlians who became international leaders of a new folk culture. When they toured the United States, the world-wide ascendancy of Britain in this area of mass culture was confirmed by spontaneous hysterical receptions from American teenage girls. Their film, *A Hard Day's Night* (1965), with many surrealist techniques borrowed from Pop Art and ballet, was an astonishing success at the box office. Their records continued to sell by the million culminating in the album, *Sergeant Pepper's Lonely Hearts Club Band*, with its overtones of psychedelic experience and the drugs scene, in 1967.[30] The Beatles acquired for a time a unique national status; hence Harold Wilson's decision in 1965 that they should be collectively awarded the MBE (Wilson himself represented Huyton, a Liverpool constituency). The Beatles had stormed the citadel of the Establishment. At the same time, they were uninhibitedly working-class in accent, style, and folk-memory.

A closely associated area of mass public participation was popular sport. This was given an unexpected boost in 1966 when England won the World Cup in football, a competition in which the host country admittedly played at Wembley Stadium in London throughout. Much satisfaction was given by the fact that it was the West Germans whom England beat in the final by 4 goals to 2. Thus football became the basis for a new mass cult

---

[30] The sleeve of this album, a collage designed by Peter Blake, projected the satin-uniformed Beatles against a background of varied nineteenth- and twentieth-century personalities, ranging from Laurel and Hardy to Karl Marx.

linking the old and the new, the Victorian past and the youth culture of the 1960s, as a particularly English (rather than British) mode of self-expression. Harold Wilson tried hard to exploit it by being seen on the balcony of a West End hotel with Bobby Moore and the other victorious English footballers, to divert attention from the political and economic crises of July 1966. The results, however, were less pleasing. Football now became less of a traditional family pastime, and more an arena for young working-class 'fans', often of violent disposition. No area of public life more graphically showed the breakdown of the collective disciplines and sanctions of post-1945 than the violence that accompanied British football teams, at home and abroad, thereafter. The heroes of the football-field also suggested a new ambiguity. Old celebrities like Stanley Matthews and Tommy Lawton, model professionals with their short hair, lengthy shorts, and pathetically small maximum wage rates, were replaced by temperamental highly remunerated stars, frequently with their own agents or business managers. Archaic restrictions on footballers' pay had been removed after strike action. The Northern Irish and Manchester United footballer, George Best, with his long hair and highly publicized sex life (and eventual lapse into alcoholism) suggested very different values from the unpermissive sportsmen of the past.[31]

The common themes of 'permissiveness' in the mid-1960s seemed to be materialism, hedonism, and limitless freedom of self-expression. There was a particular emphasis on the cohesive pop culture of 'youth', considered as a collectivity now. It was, indeed, the generation of the 'baby boom' of the later 1940s, now growing into young manhood and womanhood, which was client and patron of the new culture. Sam Beer, a perceptive American observer of British society, has even seen in the rock culture of the 1960s, and the era of 'permissiveness' generally, harbingers of the end of an old civic culture which once made Britain great.

[31] See Michael Parkinson, *Best, an Intimate Biography* (London, 1973).

The Beatles, he wrote in Shelley-like terms, were 'the unacknow-ledged legislators of populist revolt'.[32] The aspects of revolt were were certainly omnipresent. Young people seemed less observant of traditional disciplines or the age-old sanctions conveyed by parents, policemen, church leaders, schoolteachers, employers, football referees, or other symbols of traditional authority.

Drug-taking, frequently of American inspiration, became far more prevalent too. Cannabis, 'by far the most important drug of the new youth culture',[33] originally of American or West Indian origin, became far more accessible, and 'pot parties' became a frequent form of teenage sociability. The hallucinogenic drug LSD (lysergic acid diethylamide) became more widespread from about 1965. The writings of the San Francisco LSD guru Tim-othy Leary, especially his book *The Politics of Ecstasy*, acquired a great vogue. Indeed, the cult of San Francisco, along with the 'flower-power' drugs cult, became widely fashionable amongst young Britons. The Beatles themselves became less purveyors of folk ballads and tradition, and more evangelists for the use of at least 'soft' drugs, frequently mixed up with Oriental religious mysticism. John Lennon and George Harrison were especially associated with this. The Beatles' tune, 'Lucy in the Sky with Diamonds' on the *Sergeant Pepper* album in 1967, was a parable of (or acronym for) the LSD drug experience. Harder drugs such as heroin also circulated far more widely. In 1968 it was recorded that there were 2,782 heroin addicts in Britain. Cannabis at least became so prevalent that in 1968 a committee headed by Bar-bara Wootton recommended that it be legalized: it estimated that there might be anything up to a million users of cannabis in Britain at the time.[34] Young people became experimental in other ways, too, notably in their sex life. The sanctions of

[32] Sam Beer, *Britain against Itself: The Political Contradictions of Collectivism* (London, 1982), 139.

[33] Kenneth Leech, *Youthquake*, 38.

[34] See the Commons debate on the Wootton Committee report 27 January 1969 (*Parl. Deb.*, 5th ser., vol. 776, 947ff).

marriage or inhibitions about premarital sex vanished in a tidal wave of permissive indulgence, homosexual as well as hetero-sexual. One-parent families, a huge boom in contraceptives, a crusade for sexual indulgence in whatever form, became accepted. The concept of marriage or life partnerships was replaced by the free-wheeling, ephemeral notion of the 'relation-ship', a 'quick fix' in a transient, uncaring world. 'Living together' became an accepted notion. The young, so older people felt, were more undisciplined, more addictive and self-regarding, potentially more disturbed and violent. It made a curious back-drop to Harold Wilson's replay of Victorian values and his attempt to revive an older patriotism in defence of the pound and an iron Britannia.

Britain certainly changed in spectacular fashion, visually and morally, during the mid-sixties. The transformations in relation to sex, clothes, relations between the generations, and the atti-tude to authority were dramatic. How far they implied a more fundamental revolution in society may, however, be doubted. It is true that the sixties did see public liberation in terms of the censorship of the arts, and in legislation on sexual issues. The authority of the Lord Chamberlain and others had already been undermined at the end of the fifties by such episodes as the Lady Chatterley case. The Lord Chamberlain was still busy as late as 1967 with the censoring of Edward Bond's *Early Morning* (not least because it depicted a lesbian Queen Victoria). But the tide was running against him, and in 1968 the role of the Lord Chamberlain was phased out altogether, by act of parliament. The censorship of the cinema also largely disappeared, though the British film industry, faced with the endless domestic chal-lenge of television, continued to decline. Changes in legislation on sexual matters arose from other factors, including the highly tolerant, enlightened, and influential approach of Roy Jenkins in his time as Home Secretary between December 1965 and November 1967. Penal reform was much accelerated, with cap-ital punishment finally being voted out by parliament in 1965, as has been noted. Henceforth criminal offences, it was hoped, would be examined not through the dogmatism of the moralist but through the hard-headed professionalism of the criminologist. Changes in the divorce laws eventually came in 1969, following much pressure from middle-class professional women for changes ever since the fifties.

The reform of the laws on homosexuality was pioneered by a Welsh backbench MP, Leo Abse, in 1967.[35] This followed much debate after the findings of the Wolfenden Committee. In the event, private homosexual acts between consenting adults, male and female, would be legalized, while soliciting on the streets or in public places was still prohibited. This chimed in with a wider publicizing of the viewpoint of homosexuals, notably through *Gay News* which began in 1962 and achieved a large circulation within a year. At this time, the American term 'gay' began to replace the old public-school term 'queer'. Here was a permissiveness which drew less on the new youth culture, and more on older ideas of a liberal society developed by John Stuart Mill in the 1850s, with his distinction between public and private life. The campaign to have abortion legalized made similar progress, and David Steel passed a bill to this effect in 1967, despite pressure from Roman Catholic and other religious lobbies. Henceforth, the terrors of back-street abortions and other nonprofessional ways of terminating pregnancies could be avoided.

In all these areas, the youth culture which attracted so much journalistic attention was only indirectly or marginally a factor for change. Genuinely radical public agitations like CND featured an older style of protester—Michael Foot, Sir Richard Acland, J. B. Priestley, the nonagenarian Bertrand Russell. It was noticeable, too, that young people managed to combine personal libertarianism with a staid, almost bourgeois attitude towards employment, the cash nexus, and professional advancement. After all, another key factor of the 1960s was the considerable expansion of education, especially technical and other

[35] See Jeffrey Weeks, *Sex, Politics and Society* (London, 1981), 263–8.

education in the wake of the Robbins Report. The growth of part-time education, too, the growing emphasis on technical and other qualifications in searching for a job in open competition, suggested a practicality and earthiness amidst the exciting drama of the romantic rebellion that the permissive pop culture seemed to be. A few of the leaders of the new art were people of some intellectual and cultural weight. Thus Mick Jagger, lead singer of the Rolling Stones, whose international fame as a pop group rivalled that of the Beatles, was himself a graduate of the London School of Economics with a sober, businesslike private demeanour and a passion for cricket.

Above all, the permissive era had no political implications at all. If anything, the very capitalism of the pop ethic widened rather than narrowed the class divide in Britain. Marxist writers like Stuart Hall persuasively used it as a key argument in defining the late crises of the collapsing capitalist order.[36] The Beatles may have originated in the clubs of the Liverpool back streets, but their rise to mega-stardom took them far from Penny Lane into a huge, promotional, image-building industry and a different level of experience. It was, sadly, one with which the Beatles themselves proved unable to cope. By the mid-seventies, the group had broken up in much acrimony and with some litigation, and their manager had committed suicide. In some other countries the youth revolt took the form of a genuine and creative challenge to authority. In France and West Germany the socialist critique offered by Rudi Dutschke or Daniel Cohn-Bendit was sharp and penetrating; among other things, it helped bring about much-needed reforms in higher education and civil liberties. The flower-power rebels of San Francisco and the drug-taking Provos of Amsterdam took up cudgels against at least some aspects of their society, including the problems of the homeless, public transport in congested city centres, and the inequality of women. British youth (with some significant exceptions in

---

[36] Hewison, *Too Much*, 146ff.

Scotland and in the Welsh-language movement) remained apolitical and self-absorbed. It represented neither an alternative nor an
echo to the political culture of Harold Wilson's Britain. Rather it
bypassed it completely. Thus, the radical theatre of the time,
especially Joan Littlewood's creative plays at the Theatre Royal
such as *Oh, What a Lovely War*, a merciless musical satire on the
generals of the First World War, had only limited popular appeal.
However revolutionary or shocking its public aspects, the culture
represented by the Beatles or Carnaby Street posed no questions
and operated within familiar social and economic parameters. If
it tried to penetrate beyond them it ran into difficulties, as when
John Lennon's observations on drugs and Jesus Christ brought
the four into some discredit. By the end of 1966 a particular
phase of pop music appeared to be over. The *Sunday Times*,
whose music critic, Richard Buckle had written in 1963 (apparently in all seriousness) that Lennon and McCartney were 'the
greatest composers since Beethoven', pronounced solemnly (and
perhaps prematurely) in November 1966 that 'Beatlemania is
over'.[37] The *Times* music critic, William Mann, who had praised
the 'pandiatonic clusters' and 'submediant switches' of 'I Want
to Hold Your Hand', now held his peace.[38] Like the 'angry
young men' of the fifties, the permissive pop artists of the sixties
were in many cases self-indulgent nihilists with no message for
society in general. It could hardly be otherwise since all you
needed was love.

The permissive rebels, whatever their cause, may or may not
have provided subterranean elements of Britain's erosion as a
civil polity. At the centre of power, however, the Labour government's standing rapidly went into decline after the successful
outcome of the March 1966 general election. Two particular
episodes mark the boundaries of this descent into the grave. Its
start came in the third week of July 1966, when Harold Wilson's
ministry was cast into disarray by a huge assault on sterling and

[37] *Sunday Times*, 13 Nov. 1966.   [38] *The Times*, 27 Dec. 1963.

on the gold and dollar reserves. The nation, Wilson warned darkly, had been 'blown off course' by an unspecified nexus of conspirators. All manner of options, including the resignation of the government and a possible coalition under political or even military control were mooted in an atmosphere of frenzy.[39] The end of this period came in the third week of November 1967 when Wilson had to announce that the pound was indeed being devalued, despite all his resistance for the past three years. What lodged in the public consciousness was that these calamitous crises were both projected by Wilson as some kind of triumph. In the devaluation crisis of November 1967 he emphasized that the government had charted a sure course and that, in any case, 'the pound in your pocket was not being devalued'. The episodes left jointly a feeling of impotence in controlling the economy and of cynicism and indifference towards the claims offered by political leaders. The legacy remained rooted in the public consciousness for a decade to come.

The events of July 1966 resulted from an alarming and turbulent period for the increasingly unsteady Wilson government. The flight from sterling and the worsening of the balance of payments generated by the seamen's strike continued apace even after the fudged settlement of the strike at the end of June. As noted above, it was followed by the resignation of Frank Cousins on 4 July in protest at the government's decision to go ahead with a Prices and Incomes Bill—a measure strongly opposed by large sections of the Labour left and the trade-union movement. On 14 July Wilson announced a rise in the bank rate to seven per cent, together with announcements of unspecified deflationary cuts to come. Coincidentally, on this same day the government lost a by-election in South Wales. The Labour vote in Carmarthen slumped badly, and Gwynfor Evans, the President of Plaid Cymru, the Welsh Nationalist Party, was returned with 39 per cent of the vote. It is probable that this

[39] Ibid. 4–22 July 1966; *The Economist*, 16, 23, 30 July 1966; *Financial Times*, 6–21 July 1966.

first-ever victory for a Welsh nationalist resulted largely from local economic and cultural causes;[40] but it added materially to the feeling that the government was on the run.

It was well known that there was widespread dispute in the highest levels of the government. The Chancellor, Callaghan, wanted a sternly deflationary policy to protect the pound, in some contrast to his budget two months earlier, whereas Brown sought to retain the remaining impetus of what little was left of his National Plan and to aim for more expansion. At this critical time also, it was known that key economic advisers of the government were in deadlock on whether or not to recommend devaluation of the pound.[41] Worst of all, at this terrible moment for his government, Wilson had accepted an invitation to visit Prime Minister Kosygin in Moscow to try to produce some kind of peace formula for the war in Vietnam. It was widely believed that this was a political gesture designed to win over left-wing support on other measures. Indeed, left-wing MPs like Michael Foot and Jack Mendelson were then induced to vote for the government on the second reading of the Prices and Incomes Bill on this basis. But the general impression was of a government out of control, leaderless at a crucial moment, with politics and economics taking second place to cosmetics.

During the two days Wilson was in Moscow, the run on the pound, and attendant city and political speculation, mounted apace. Briefed on these matters by his faithful bloodhound, George Wigg, Wilson returned on 20 July to try to salvage the mess. He was badgered on all sides, with Brown and Callaghan at odds, and Brown threatening resignation from the government, not for the first or last time. Economic advisers were divided as to whether the pound should be devalued, with eminent figures like Douglas Jay and Alec Cairncross advising that devaluation was still unnecessary because of the likely impact on the balance of payments. There were rumours that Jenkins,

---

[40] See Morgan, *Rebirth of a Nation*, 386ff.
[41] Cairncross and Eichengreen, *Sterling in Decline*, 164ff.

Crosland, and Crossman were engaged in a conspiracy to persuade the Cabinet to rush into devaluation, and that pro-Europeans like Jenkins were especially zealous in this direction.[42] It was, in any case, difficult to decide how far the run on the pound was the product of the short-term factor of the seamen's strike rather than the result of more deeply rooted weaknesses. The government then held twenty-four hours of frenetic and incoherent meetings, with Brown sulking in his tent like Achilles.[43] It was to result not in objective or calm assessment of the current state of the economy but in a series of nearpanic measures, extreme in their long-term impact on manufacturing industry and the social services, overlaid throughout by threats of ministerial conspiracy and the need to preserve socialist 'planning' as opposed to Tory deflation.

Wilson announced a series of massive restrictions on 20 July.[44] There would be a cut of £500 m. in the annual level of demand by the end of 1967. *The Economist* thought this might be 'perhaps the biggest deflationary package that any advanced industrial nation has imposed on itself since Keynesian economics began',[45] the equivalent of forfeiting about 1112 per cent of the national income. It would be achieved through cuts of at least £100 m. in defence and other forms of government spending; restrictions on hire-purchase and an increase of 4*d.* a gallon in petrol duty; a 10 per cent surcharge on surtax; a restriction of the overseas travel allowance to a mere £50 for the next 12 months; and a standstill in wage and salary increases for the next six months, with the Prices and Incomes Bill to become law in the near future. It was more severe than Selwyn Lloyd's deeply unpopular package in 1961, and was almost certain to mean a decline in the gross domestic product in 1967 and a likely rise in

---

[42] Jay, *Change and Fortune*, 346ff.; Callaghan, *Time and Chance*, 201; *The Economist*, 23 July 1966.

[43] Crossman, *Diaries of a Cabinet Minister*, i, 577 (entry of 20 July 1966).

[44] *The Times*, 22 July 1966, commented in its leading article: 'A stiffish dose at last.'

[45] *The Economist*, 23 July 1966.

unemployment. Four days later, the government announced cuts of a further £95 m. in the nationalized industries, and a further £55 m. of cuts in central and local government expenditure.

Some of the response was predictable. There were left-wing calls for further cuts in defence expenditure east of Suez, and abstentions on the unloved Prices and Incomes Bill. This finally passed through the Commons on 10 August, with a reduced government majority of 58. The threat to sterling moderated, helped by much assistance from the Bank of England and the New York Federal Reserve Bank. Harold Wilson recovered his spirits and began to enjoy the aftermath of England's winning the World Cup. His personal popularity remained strong in the opinion polls. Nevertheless, the general impact of the government conduct of affairs was disastrous, not least for the air of panic and personal recrimination with which the crisis of sterling had been surrounded. The issue of the devaluation of the pound, which many economists believed would be the essential concomitant of deflationary cuts, and the wage and salary 'severe restraint' was never tackled in a detached or objective way. Wilson himself, even when confronted on 13 July with temporary unity between Callaghan and Brown on the need for devaluation, was adamant on political grounds that devaluation was unthinkable.[46] The issue was never considered on its own merits, but was coloured by misleading or ill-recalled memories of earlier devaluations of 1931 and 1949 and the way in which they were thought to have had political effects adverse to the Labour Party. Callaghan's relatively expansionist budget of May lay in tatters and was made to look irrelevant. There were many who proclaimed the superior economic skills of Roy Jenkins, the Home Secretary. George Brown had behaved in an irresponsible and almost uncontrollable way. No one seriously believed in his planned regulation of wages and prices any more. Astonishingly, his reward was to rise even higher in the government when on

[46] Cairncross and Eichengreen, *Sterling in Decline*, 181.

12 August it was announced that he would become Foreign Secretary. How his combustible temperament would cope with the demands of diplomatic finessing with foreign diplomats and journalists few chose to speculate. His replacement at what remained of the Department of Economic Affairs was the retiring, schoolmasterly figure of Michael Stewart. It was, though, Harold Wilson who was to be the supreme casualty of the crisis in the longer term. His public professions of Walter Mitty-like optimism, combined with a paranoid fear of hostile journalists and broadcasters and the 'sell Britain short brigade' in the currency markets, aroused much derision. He retreated further into his private circle of advisers and kitchen Cabinet, itself a somewhat motley and frenetic group. The public culture of Britain, as identified with its institutions of government, suffered accordingly.

The twelve months that followed the July 1966 crisis were in some ways more stable for the government. There were no further resignations. The Prices and Incomes Bill became law and was reinforced by a twelve-month freeze on wage and price increases. The balance of payments showed a steady recovery in the winter of 1966–7, while Douglas Jay, President of the Board of Trade, was able to announce a sizeable reflation in December, with investment grants to be boosted to 25 per cent and from 40 to 45 per cent in areas of traditonally heavy unemployment.[47] The deficit on both the current and the long-term capital account showed a welcome tendency to fall, down to the time of the April 1967 budget. Politically, the government remained surprisingly secure. The Gallup poll showed Labour in the lead by 11½ per cent as late as mid-February 1967.[48] One major factor here was Wilson's easy debating ascendancy over Edward Heath in the Commons where the leader of the opposition's dour and humourless performances left the voters dissatisfied. Wilson's

[47] *The Economist*, 3 Dec. 1966.   [48] Ibid, 25 Feb. 1967.

Houdini-style ability to escape from impending disaster seemed to be confirmed.

At the same time, the state of public morale and indiscipline suggested a rapid decline from the enthusiasm with which Labour's election victory in 1964 had been widely greeted. The trade unions, pending the report of the Donovan Commission, showed little disposition either to respect the voluntary provisions of the Prices and Incomes Bill or to curb unofficial or other strikes. Britain's record of industrial stoppages grew steadily worse. Away from the cosmetic protest of the 'permissive' youth of the land, large sections of society seemed alienated or ignored. Surveys by sociologists like Peter Townshend and Brian Abel-Smith showed how the social services were less and less able to cope with demographic change and rising demand.[49] Poverty, notably amongst old people and disadvantaged groups like one-parent families, widows, and the disabled had actually increased under Labour rule. Labour party policy documents expressed widespread dissatisfaction with welfare and economic policies.[50] The social services were static and 'instruments of the *status quo*'. Inland Revenue figures showed that there had been relatively little redistribution of wealth and income since 1945. Less than 10 per cent of the population still owned over 80 per cent of all personal wealth. Ten million people still had incomes of less than £500 a year. The pattern of tax incidence was to throw the heaviest burden on those with the lowest incomes, especially families with young children. In industry, very little advance had been made towards any form of industrial democracy, despite some pressure from the Institute of Workers' Control and union leaders like Jack Jones of the Transport Workers

[49] See e.g. Peter Townsend and Dorothy Wedderburn. *The Aged in the Welfare State* (London, 1965); Brian Abel-Smith and Peter Townsend, *The Poor and the Poorest* (London, 1965).

[50] See paper on 'The Social Services' January 1968 (Labour Party Home Policy Committee) and paper on 'The Distribution of Wealth and Income'. March 1967 (Labour Party Finance and Economic Affairs Advisory Committee). Labour Party archives.

and Hugh Scanlon of the Engineers.'[51] Black opinion meanwhile showed a growing disenchantment with the current social provisions and state of the law as regards housing and employment, for all the benevolent intentions of the Race Relations industry. The rise of the National Front showed a worrying racism amongst predominantly working-class white males. 'Paki-bashing' was a growing trend in places like Bradford, Leicester, or Luton. As a progress report, it was all supremely discouraging.

There were different, but equally worrying, portents in Wales and Scotland. Here, the attractions of participation in the age-old structure of the United Kingdom seemed less and less obvious, with rising unemployment and industrial decay. In Wales, Gwynfor Evans's electoral victory in Carmarthen was far from an isolated phenomenon. It chimed in with growing working-class disaffection in the mining valleys with pit closures, with farmers' discontent at falling price levels, and with the activist dissent of the student members of the Welsh Language Society at governmental resistance to promoting equality for the Welsh language. The replacement of the veteran Jim Griffiths by the younger Welsh-speaker Cledwyn Hughes at the Welsh Office did lead to sympathetic developments such as the 1967 Welsh Language Act.[52] But the general feeling that the Welsh Office had aroused unfulfilled expectations, especially on the economic front, remained widespread. Plaid Cymru now began to make gains in the industrial valleys as well. In Scotland, too, the old Labour ascendancy seemed ageing and unpopular, with William Ross, a stern anti-Nationalist, a Stalinist figure almost, at the Scottish Office. Here the tide of nationalism was more powerful even than in Wales. The Scottish Nationalist candidate, Mrs Ewing, overturned a 16,000 Labour majority in a by-election in Hamilton in November 1967, and the SNP gained sweeping victories in local-government elections. Interestingly, unlike Wales where the

---

[51] See Jack Jones, *Union Man* (London, 1986). 211ff.
[52] Morgan, *Rebirth of a Nation*, 389ff. See *The Legal Status of the Welsh Language* (Cmnd. 2785), P.P., 1964–5, xxiii, 877ff.

strength of Plaid Cymru was most obviously rooted in the Welsh-speaking rural communities of the north and west, Scottish Nationalism was powerful almost everywhere, even in the cities of Glasgow, Dundee, and Edinburgh, and in the new towns of Cumbernauld and East Kilbride where SNP captured control of the local authorities. The disunion of the United Kingdom seemed in prospect, an eternal Celtic revolt against the central-ization and conformity of Labour rule.

In the course of 1967, Labour's fall from grace became even more acute. It was much hastened by failure in overseas policy, which added to the sense of national decline. Wilson, in fact, sought in 1964–7 to maintain the vestiges of Britain's position as a world power, both in strategic and financial terms. Thus it was agreed, almost without debate, that Britain would retain its Polaris missiles and indeed embark upon an even more expensive system, what became known in the 1970s as the Chevaline warheads, from 1967 onwards. Again, the decision not to devalue the pound was intimately linked with the wish to pre-serve Britain's role as a world banker and to keep sterling as a major reserve currency. Harold Wilson made much of his close relationship with President Lyndon Johnson, who in return pub-licly compared him with Shakespeare, Milton, Churchill and other national heroes. Closer to the reality was the pithy obser-vation of Walt Rostow in February 1967, at the time of attempted British mediation over Vietnam: 'We don't give a goddam about Wilson.'[53]

The general perception was of Wilson unsuccessfully acting as peacemaker between the Americans and the Soviet Prime Minis-ter, Kosygin, while in practice going along with a highly unpopu-lar US policy of the mass bombing of North Vietnam, in return for US financial aid. It was a deeply unpleasant vision of a client relationship. In effect, though, it confirmed the subordinate sta-tus of Britain in the transatlantic alliance dating from the 1957

---

[53] See e.g. Wilson. *The Labour Government*, 242–6; Ponting, *Breach of Prom-ise*, 226.

Bermuda Conference. One key aspect of the relationship, of course, was US financial assistance to bail out the ailing British economy and prop up the pound. This was broadly confirmed in talks between President Johnson and Harold Wilson in Washington in June 1967. The other was the pressure imposed by the Americans on Britain to maintain its defence commitment east of Suez. As a result of this, despite the moves towards economy in the defence budget promoted by the Minister of Defence, Denis Healey, aiming at reducing the budget to below £2,000 m. after 1970, British world-wide troop withdrawals proceeded at a slow pace. The 1967 Defence White Paper confirmed that British forces would be withdrawn from Aden and that the United Kingdom would not conclude a defence agreement with South Arabia when it became independent in 1968. On the other hand, a withdrawal from bases in Malaysia and Singapore was scheduled for 'the mid-seventies'. No date was given for a retreat either from Hong Kong or from the Persian Gulf, while there was also talk of maintaining island bases such as Bahrein, Cocos, and Aldabra in the Indian Ocean.[54] In the same region, the fishermen and farmers of Diego Garcia were, in effect deported to Mauritius to allow the Americans to use their island home as a nuclear base, humani-tarianism set aside. Britain's dependent status in the Atlantic alliance meant a maintenance of expensive post-imperial military commitments against the better judgement of the British government itself.

Nor was there much success elsewhere in overseas policy, despite the rumbustious postures struck by George Brown in his period at the Foreign office after August 1966. In Europe, Britain was continuing to meet with difficulties from its EFTA partners, still somewhat disgruntled by the 1964 import

---

[54] White Paper on Defence, January 1967 (Cmnd. 3203). Crossman records that there was a Cabinet vote on whether to maintain the Aldabra base, 28 July 1967. 'This was the first occasion when I've heard the P.M. after collecting the voices and finding he'd lost simply say. "There's a majority on my side" and we were committed to Aldabra.' (Crossman, Diaries *of a Cabinet Minister*, ii, 448–9).

surcharge being imposed without warning. In Commonwealth and colonial affairs, Labour's attempt to liquidate Britain's imperial heritage in a progressive fashion also had mixed results. The withdrawal from Aden and South Yemen was generally considered a diplomatic and military success. 'We want to be out of the whole Middle East as far and as fast as we possibly can', observed George Brown.[55] Conversely, in Nigeria a difficult civil war broke out in May 1967 with the Ibo majority in Biafra breaking away and engaging in bloody warfare with the central Nigerian government. Britain's broad support for the Nigerian government of General Gowon was controversial. News of mass starvation and genocide in the eastern region of Nigeria kindled much criticism of the government from Christian groups and old leftwingers such as Fenner Brockway. A powerful lobby built up to urge, unavailingly, that Britain should recognize the Biafran regime of Colonel Ojukwu as a sovereign republic.

The worst dilemma of all, however, was elsewhere in Africa, the almost insoluble problem of Southern Rhodesia. From the outset, Harold Wilson had spoken confidently of his ability to disentangle the mess in southern Africa after the winding up of the Central African Federation by Butler in 1963. However, discussions between Wilson and the new Southern Rhodesian Prime Minister, Ian Smith, including talks at the time of Sir Winston Churchill's funeral in January 1965, got nowhere, while the unwise statement by Arthur Bottomley, the Commonwealth Secretary, that there was no immediate intention to use British troops in Rhodesia encouraged hopes of independence.[56] Negotiations between Wilson and a variety of Rhodesian leaders, black as well as white, in Rhodesia in October 1965 failed to unearth a generally acceptable solution, and the following month Ian Smith declared unilaterally that Rhodesia was now independent. The Rhodesian problem rumbled on for the next fourteen years, with successive British governments finding it peculiarly

[55] Crossman, op. cit.. 462 (entry for 5 Sept. 1967).
[56] Blake, *Rhodesia*, 374ff.

difficult to impose, or negotiate, a settlement in this remaining legacy of Empire in southern Africa. Harold Wilson announced a policy of imposing oil sanctions upon Rhodesia to bring its economy to its knees. He blithely announced that this would bring a solution 'in weeks rather than months'. In practice this was an empty boast. South Africa maintained normal trading relations with Rhodesia throughout, while there was much evasion of sanctions through Laurenço Marques in Mozambique, which bordered Rhodesia. In addition European powers such as West Germany, Switzerland, and Portugal continued to ignore the more rigorous application of sanctions, while even British firms, such as Shell, BP, and other oil companies, openly contravened the sanctions policy with little restriction from the British Labour government.[57] In December 1966, Wilson met Ian Smith in private talks on HMS *Tiger* off Gibraltar. His aim was to put pressure on the Rhodesians to concede six fundamental principles, notably unimpeded progress towards black African majority rule, though he weakened considerably during discussions on 'A-roll' voting rights. As soon as the Rhodesian government delegation returned to Salisbury, however, any agreement was disavowed, including the immediate return to legality. Throughout 1967 the Rhodesian impasse continued. The British government argued that sanctions were working, that the unilateral declaration of independence by the Rhodesians was illegal, and that the beleaguered governor, Sir Humphrey Gibbs, who was under house arrest, was technically the voice of legal British authority. Short of military intervention, however, there was little that Britain could do. Rhodesia, which Wilson had blithely described as 'my Cuba' (another hostage to fortune, in effect), was another initiative which had gone horribly wrong. Many feared that the white minority regime in Salisbury was on the route to installing another apartheid-type system on the South African model.

---

[57] 'Analysis of Economic Sanctions against Rhodesia', Nov. 1967 (Overseas Department paper, Labour Party archives).

The worst of all the overseas disappointments came over the European Common Market. Labour's policy down to the summer of 1966 was to maintain the present policy of strengthening trading links with EFTA and the Commonwealth. However, the traumatic experiences of July 1966 had a powerful effect on civil servants and ministers in Whitehall. Key Cabinet members like George Brown and Roy Jenkins, joined by Richard Crossman, felt that joining the Common Market was the only practicable answer to the endless problems of the British economy, perhaps linking it with devaluation of the pound. Cecil King of the *Daily Mirror*, a newspaper proprietor close to Wilson at this time, was suggesting in his diary as early as February 1966 that the Prime Minister intended to get Britain into the Common Market.[58] Hugh Cudlipp, another prominent pro-Labour journalist, observed in November 1966 that this would deflect attention from troubles with Rhodesia and the economy: it was 'a gigantic red herring' in Cudlipp's view.[59] After lengthy discussion in Cabinet on the likely effect that joining the EEC would have on the balance of payments in April 1967, Douglas Jay wrote that the Cabinet had only the narrowest of majorities in favour of applying to join the Community, of 11 to 10, the majority including such very uncertain figures as Wilson and Callaghan. However, Tony Benn, a 'pro-Marketeer' who sought 'to cut the umbilical cord of Queen Victoria', listed a 18 to 8 pro-Market majority.[60] On 9 May it was announced that Britain was making a formal application to join the Common Market, the first since Macmillan's rebuff in early 1961. Yet President de Gaulle in

[58] Cecil King, *The Cecil King Diary*, 1965–1970 (London, 1972), 57 (entry for 11 Feb. 1966).

[59] Jay, *Change and Fortune*, 368. Cudlipp was chairman of Daily Mirror Newspapers at this time.

[60] Jay, op. cit., 387–9; Benn, *Out of the Wilderness*, 496. Also cf. Crossman, *Diaries of a Cabinet Minister*, ii, 336 (entry of 1 May 1967). which gives as his version ten unqualified supporters of entry, seven unqualified opponents and six 'in the middle' (Callaghan, Crossman, Gordon Walker, Greenwood, Silkin, Hughes) who might veer Wilson's way.

France was still a massive obstacle, while the overall British decline in its balance of payments and trading position made its bargaining position distinctly weaker than six years before. There were major figures in the Cabinet who strongly opposed the EEC still. They numbered most left-wingers, including Barbara Castle, and, most vehemently, the centre-right President of the Board of Trade, Douglas Jay. He voiced a range of objections, economic, political, legal, and historical, to the notion of joining the capitalist, cartel-dominated EEC. This led to his removal from the Wilson government in July 1967. There was much Commonwealth apprehension expressed on the effects on food and other imports presently given preferential treatment in British markets, while major groups at home pointed to the serious effect of the Common Agricultural Policy of variable levies on the British balance of payments.

In fact, here was yet another initiative that crumbled humiliatingly. On 16 May, seven days later, President de Gaulle firmly announced a second veto on British membership. His so-called 'velvet veto' took the form of a seris of *ex cathedra* statements about the role of sterling as a reserve currency and the British tradition of buying cheap food imports, which made British membership of the EEC impossible in his view.[61] He also observed that bringing EFTA into association with the Community would so radically change its character as to lead to paralysis. Britain's application to join had been vetoed in advance of its being formally put. Nevertheless, membership remained Cabinet policy, with Brown and especially Jenkins vehement exponents of the European idea. There was a background of pressure in the newspapers and in the City and much of industry from the so-called 'European movement'. But Britain was battering against a closed door, while de Gaulle's abrupt dismissal met with little protest from Germany and other EEC members. The whole episode left a continuing impression of Britain still searching

[61] *The Times*, 17 May 1967; *The Economist*, 13 May 1967.

for a role in international affairs. One role was dissolving in the heat and dust of central Africa; a successor had not yet arisen. Britain's prestige was further dented in consequence.

What led to the culmination of these varied pressures and disappointments for the government was a further lurch of the economy into disarray. Callaghan in his April 1967 budget had struck a mildly expansionary note, while leaving unemployment at the present level. He recalled the nautical words of command from his wartime naval service—'Steady as she goes'. *The Times* noted how he broke with 'the full employment standard'; it marked 'the end of the Keynesian era'.[62] Quite without warning, the outlook suddenly became most unsteady. The outbreak of the Six-Day War between Israel and Egypt in June 1967 led to the closure of the Suez Canal, a crisis for British exports, and sudden immense pressure against sterling yet again. Plans for British naval action to keep open the Straits of Tiran came to nothing. There was, in any case, a flight of gold and foreign exchange following a recession in the German economy, together with a downturn in US economic growth. Both of these hit British exports. The government was once again on the familiar rack of economic crisis, with unemployment rising to 2.4 per cent of the working population. The political response was muffled. Cuts in social-security benefits led to the resignation of the popular Scottish Minister of Social Security, 'Peggy' Herbison. The former chief whip, Herbert Bowden, also resigned, while, as noted, the anti-European Douglas Jay had been dismissed. Among key figures, Callaghan's prestige continued under challenge, while Brown commanded little confidence at the Foreign Office. Stewart lingered on at the remnants of the DEA as 'First Secretary', while Wilson claimed to be in overall charge of all departments. Quite remarkably, both Wilson and Callaghan achieved personal successes at the Labour Party Conference at the start of October. Callaghan, in particular, achieved a

[62] *The Times*, 12 Apr. 1967.

spectacular personal triumph in a speech which, among other things, appeared in retrospect to herald the monetarist philosophy dominant in the 1980s. Crossman noted how he seemed 'totally *en rapport* with the rank and file'.[63] Deflation and import controls were rejected. Yet otherwise the news was depressing. There were huge Labour losses in by-elections, including the old working-class strongholds of West Walthamstow in north-east London lost to the Conservatives on an 18.4 per cent swing. South-west Leicester followed on a 16.6 per cent swing, while, as noted, old Labour citadels in Scotland and Wales seemed likely to be stormed by the nationalists. Yet again the Wilson government was on the run.

The final nails in the coffin came in the familiar form of labour troubles, with the outbreak of serious strikes on the docks. In all, 7,000 dockers in the Port of London and many more on Merseyside went on indefinite strike for higher pay. October 1967 saw the worst-ever monthly trade deficit in British history, £107 m. higher than the previous record recorded in January 1964 under the Tories. Pressure on the pound now became relentless, and the challenge of devaluation could no longer be evaded. A heavy run on sterling led to a huge offer of support from the West German *Bundesbank*, while bank rate was raised to 16 per cent. Finally, persuaded by the massive flow of funds out of London and the conversion of a key Treasury adviser like Sir Alec Cairncross, the British Cabinet decided on 16 November that sterling should indeed be devalued. It was announced on Saturday, 18 November, that the pound would be devalued by 14.3 per cent to $2.40. Import controls had been rejected, while recourse to a huge IMF loan was turned down because it would reduce any remaining freedom of manoeuvre for the British government.[64]

Callaghan himself had always set his face against devaluation, with the exception of a brief interlude in July 1966. He told

[63] Crossman, *Diaries of a Cabinet Minister*, ii, 503 (entry of 3 Oct. 1967).

[64] *The Times*, 20 Nov. 1967; *The Economist*, 25 Nov. 1967; *Financial Times*, 20 Nov. 1967; Kenneth O. Morgan, *Callaghan: A Life* (Oxford, 1997). 268–80.

Crossman in April 1967 that the Tories would reap the benefit three years on.[65] Now he appeared humiliated, with British debts amounting to a record of $1,876 million. Devaluation would be accompanied by $3,000 m. of stand-by credits, much of it from the IMF. But the affair appeared unplanned and conducted without the rapture of optimism, despite Wilson's extraordinary chutzpah in his post-devaluation television broadcast. Callaghan took refuge in attacks on 'potentially sinister' right-wing business interests headed by Sir Paul Chambers, but there was an elegiac tone to his remarks.[66] The announcement by President de Gaulle, with exquisite timing, on 27 November, that France finally rejected the British application to join the EEC added to the sense of doom. On 29 November it was announced that Roy Jenkins, a staunch devaluer since 1964, would become Chancellor of the Exchequer, and that Callaghan would move to the Home Office instead, in place of Jenkins. The retiring Chancellor's genuine achievements—his considerable reform of the taxation system; his negotiation of drawing rights with the IMF; his more flexible view on the role of sterling as a reserve currency; important papers on public expenditure and the nationalized industries; even the introduction of decimal coinage on a sterling basis—were in danger of being forgotten. The government seemed at a low ebb. The publication on 30 November of Callaghan's letter of intent to the IMF caused further dismay for the pledges it contained. Much depended now on whether the genial Jenkins could kindle the same kind of stern recovery as the austere Cripps had done in the wake of Dalton's misadventures in 1947.

The devaluation affair set the seal on a depressing series of events. To some extent, the government suffered sheer bad luck. Britain was the victim of the economic uncertainty following the Six-Day War between Israel and Egypt, and of de Gaulle's narrow and self-centred stance on the Common Market. Rhodesia

[65] Crossman, op. cit., 335 (entry of 30 Apr. 1967).
[66] *The Times*, 23 Nov. 1967.

and Nigeria were areas where a feasible solution was hard to
detect. Incidental problems such as Scottish and Welsh nationalism, or the rash of unofficial strikes amongst the dockers were
marginal to the main problem. The fact remained that the way in
which devaluation had been agreed, amidst a paroxysm of press
speculation and a City atmosphere of near frenzy suggested deep
weaknesses in the conduct of economic management. For at least
three years, perhaps for six, Britain had been in almost constant
retreat, with repeated economic difficulties and no compensation
in its foreign policy or defence postures. Labour had come to
office with the credence attached to Wilson's pre-election cries
for scientific progress, planned investment, and expansive
growth. These pledges were in ruins. The reality to date had
been falling comparative growth despite rising domestic production *per capita*, repeated payments difficulties, and the
entrenched power of the Treasury in curtailing growth. Brown's
Department of Economic Affairs was but a memory. Even after
devaluation major answers were still required, for instance as to
what the correct rate for sterling should be, what kind of deflation or disinflation at home was necessary, and how an incomes
policy could be sold to a disgruntled and divided people. Wilson
took office against a background of pessimism that British institutions and social stability were in long-term decay, for all the
frivolous escapism of 'permissiveness'. After three disastrous
years, the nation was left with that black mood of foreboding
only reinforced.

8. Years of Hard Slog
1968–1970

IN the aftermath of the devaluation of the pound, the Labour government of Harold Wilson entered upon a grim period of deflation and austerity. In some ways it resembled the phase of retrenchment that followed the departure of Hugh Dalton in November 1947, when Sir Stafford Cripps imposed a stern and spartan regime of rationing and controls. The economic leader this time was a very different personality, Roy Jenkins, the son of a South Wales miners' agent who had progressed through Balliol and being Attlee's private secretary to create a public image of confidence, competence, and sociability. Jenkins, indeed, in many ways, seemed an unlikely spokesman for what he promised as 'two years of hard slog'. In time, his image of fastidious superiority and alleged taste for fine claret became the butt of journalists and clubland wits. He ended up as Chancellor of Oxford University. But Jenkins was also a tough operator, who had been a striking success at that traditional graveyard of reputations, the Home Office, where his liberal policies and attack on censorship and repression chimed in with the prevailing tolerant mood. He had also deepened his knowledge of political affairs through writing some notable works on political history, including studies of Sir Charles Dilke, Asquith, and the crisis between the Liberal government and the House of Lords in 1909–11. Indeed, the temperamental affinity between the ex-Gaitskellite Labour right and the Asquithian Liberals of a former era was often noted. Above all, Jenkins was a gifted and skilful economist, even though, surprisingly, he had not served on the Cabinet Economic

Committee prior to becoming Chancellor in late November 1967. As the custodian of the Treasury over the next few years, admittedly through a tough and perhaps needlessly severe regime of retrenchment, Jenkins boosted his reputation as a major public figure in a way highly unusual in the chequered history of British economic policy since the war.

His dominance at the Treasury coincided with a major remodelling of the administration. This came at a time when Wilson's own reputation was taking a battering in the media, especially the press. The catalyst was the final acceptance of George Brown's resignation, so often offered and so frequently rejected, in March 1968. The *casus belli* was the decision by Wilson, Jenkins, and Peter Shore to close the London Stock Market without consulting Brown.[1] This relieved Wilson of an impulsive and difficult, if in some ways inspirational, minister. His successor at the Foreign Office was Michael Stewart, who had been there before. Meanwhile James Callaghan, at the Home Office, began to repair a reputation somewhat dented by his difficult three years as Chancellor. But much of the energy of the government clearly lay elsewhere. Anthony Crosland, another ex-Gaitskellite on the right of the party, became Secretary of State in charge of Trade and Industry, and was in clear command of economic matters in partnership with Roy Jenkins. It marked, among other things, the final triumph of the Treasury over the concept of any kind of Department of Economic Affairs. To balance these right-wing advances, in typically careful Wilsonian manner, two old Bevanites also progressed in notable fashion. Richard Crossman became Secretary of State in charge of Social Services, while Mrs Barbara Castle, the only woman Cabinet minister, made a spectacular rise as Secretary for Employment and Productivity, in charge of key sensitive negotiations with the TUC on incomes policy. In other changes, Edward Short went to Education and George Thomas to the Welsh Office; Cledwyn

---

[1] Crossman, *Diaries of a Cabinet Minister*, ii, 713–14 (entry of 17 Mar. 1968). Brown in fact stayed on as deputy leader of the party.

Hughes went to Agriculture, and Patrick Gordon Walker left the government altogether. Significantly, Denis Healey, the Minister of Defence and one of the clear ministerial successes since 1964, was not promoted, but he had publicly disagreed with the Prime Minister both over cuts in defence expenditure and over arms sales to South Africa, which Healey at that time supported. He had also been at odds with his scientific adviser, Solly Zuckerman. In internal party terms, with men like Peter Shore moving up in the administration, the government shifted marginally to the left with these changes, so far as these factors had any meaning in the period of incessant financial crisis in which the government operated. But the dominant feature of all was probably the continuing pressure on Wilson's personal standing, with failure on the economy, Europe and Rhodesia, sagging support in the polls and a mood of almost psychotic apprehension throughout the party and the administration.

In this new ascendant position, Jenkins began to impose restrictions of a kind not experienced since the grim days of the Korean War. Following a rise in bank rate to 8 per cent at the end of 1967, Jenkins's budget of March 1968 rained blows on the consumer and industry alike. In all, £923 m. would be taken out of the economy in a full financial year, including £163 m. from purchase tax, £152 m. from Select Employment Tax, and higher duties on motor licences, petrol, cigarettes, betting, and drink. There would be also an exceptional 'one-year' levy on unearned incomes. Total priority was to be given to the balance of payments, Jenkins stating it as his objective that a balance of £500 m. would be achieved as soon as possible, to take advantage of the recent devaluation of the pound. There were commentators who praised the Draconian methods he was proposing in order to achieve this objective. Peter Jay in *The Times* declared, with perhaps misplaced euphoria, that the Chancellor had 'risen fully and magnificently to the occasion'.[2] Others soberly noted

[2] *The Times*, 20 Mar. 1968.

that the cost of living would probably rise by 1s. in the pound, and that the depressing effect on domestic demand would mean an end to promises that Labour could in any way expand the nation's economic growth. It was the most severe deflationary package of any post-war budget. Instead of stop–go, it would be stop-stop, at least for some time. It took a while for the medicine to show any positive effects. It was reported in June that Britain had its worst-ever balance-of-payments performance in the first four months of 1968, with the annual rate running at £1,352 m. in the six months to March, compared with the £776 m. left by the Tories in the mood of near-hysteria in 1964.[3] In addition to the usual increase in imports which accompanied attempts to expand the British economy, there was an alarming outflow of £183 m. in long-term private capital investment. The investors were voting with their feet.

Jenkins's stern regimen thus continued. Indirect taxes were raised by 10 per cent through the regulator, and hire-purchase controls were tightened still further. Currency restrictions largely abolished foreign holidays for sections of the population. At the end of the year, the benefits alleged to accrue from devaluation still had not materialized. Indeed, there was renewed talk that autumn of a further balance-of-payments crisis. A government committee, MISC 205 (Wilson, Jenkins, Crosland, Shore, Castle) prepared 'Plan Brutus', a contingency scheme for yet another devaluation, accompanied by import and exchange controls and massive further deflation.[4] There was still no real sign of a restructuring of the economy, and the diversion of resources from private consumption to exports and industrial investment was still not apparent. The capital account showed signs of improvement but, with a continued rise in the import bill, the visible trade balance continued to deteriorate. Economists confidently forecast another year of total economic stagnation in 1969.[5]

---

[3] *The Economist*, 22 June 1968.

[4] *The Economist*, 16 Nov. 1968; Ponting, *Breach of Promise*, 373–4.

[5] *The Economist*, 28 Dec. 1968.

The government's record in by-elections continued to be alarmingly bad in 1968, with a loss to the Conservatives in Sheffield, Brightside, and a near-defeat by Plaid Cymru in Caerphilly, both of them rock-solid industrial Labour strongholds over the past half-century. The Conservative lead in opinion polls soared to over 20 per cent. In a curious episode, the Minister of Power, Ray Gunter, resigned his post in July 1968, apparently because of the influence of unnamed middle-class intellectuals in the highest circles of government.[6] Gunter had not been an important or successful minister, but his departure had significance in that it marked the virtual elimination of the old style of trade-union leader in Cabinet office. Another resignation had come over the cuts in social services in January when Lord Longford resigned over the decision to defer the raising of the school-leaving age to 15. Jenkins's policy continued unabated in the first few months of 1969, and his budget of April showed little relaxation from the extreme severity of 1968. A further £340 m. would be taken out of the economy in tax increases in a full year, with £120 m. coming from increases in corporation tax and £130 m. in a 28 per cent rise in Select Employment Tax. There would also be large increases in employers' contributions to national insurance.[7]

Throughout the summer of 1969—a period marked, as will be seen, by deadlock with the Trades Union Congress over a proposed Prices and Incomes Policy—the economy continued to languish, and pressure resumed on the pound. The Treasury presented MISC 205 with 'Plan Hecuba', with the floating of the pound and huge attendant deflation. Yet a further plunge into indebtedness came in June when Jenkins negotiated a loan of up to $1,000 m. from Schweitzer of the International Monetary Fund. The Chancellor's letter of intent put economic growth only in third place of priority. It observed that, should the

---

[6] Crossman *Diaries of a Cabinet Minister*, iii, 112–13 (entry of 30 July 1968).
[7] *Financial Times*, 16 Apr. 1969.

balance of payments fall below target, it would be necessary either to intensify the squeeze on the British economy, or else float the exchange rate. This would mean further, and this time open-ended, devaluation of the pound.[8] At last, by the autumn of 1969, aided by a recovery in world trade and in North American markets, the balance of payments began to show clear signs of recovery, and a balance of payments surplus was recorded, for the first time for two years, from April to September 1969. The constraint of a prolonged payments crisis began to disappear at last. Jenkins's 'hard slog' showed signs of bearing fruit in time for the next general election. But the general mood of the time, while prepared to accept the intellectual rigour and consistency with which the Chancellor had pursued his balance-of-payments objectives, was nevertheless to see this as a period of decline and retreat.

This impression was strengthened by the major change in Britain's overseas defence posture that accompanied Jenkins's restriction of the economy at home. The government's position, and that of Wilson, on defence matters had remained uncertain. Cuts in expenditure under Healey had been accompanied by Britain's maintaining an east-of-Suez strategy from 1964 onwards. The only major shift had been the end of confrontation between Indonesia and Malaysia which would mean the removal of 60,000 British troops from Borneo and elsewhere in the Far East in the near future. After the vigorous debate in the Cabinet, Wilson was forced to announce in January 1968 that Britain's east-of-Suez imperial legacy would be rapidly wound up, with British troops removed from the Middle and Far East.[9] Forces would be withdrawn from Malaysia and Singapore by the end of 1971, and also from the Persian Gulf. Protests from Lee Kuan Yew, the Prime Minister of Singapore, were overridden, even though Malaysia and Singapore were major foreign holders of sterling, significant markets for British exports, and centres of

[8] *Guardian*, 24 June 1969; *The Times*, 30 June 1969.
[9] *The Times*, 17 Jan. 1968.

over £7,000 m. of British investment in rubber, tin, oil refineries, shipping, and insurance. The only real concession that Lee and the Malays could obtain was a delay in the British withdrawal to December 1971. Heath and the Conservatives criticized Britain's premature withdrawal from the Persian Gulf, with much turmoil surrounding the key states in that difficult region and the sensitivity of countries such as Kuwait and the United Arab Emirates for the British oil supplies.[10] So did the American administration. Even so, with the decision already announced for a retirement of the British military presence in Aden, this, too, had been foreshadowed. A key Cabinet problem, which caused angry and intense debate, was whether to proceed with the F111 aircraft which Healey himself strongly supported, as had Wilson also at one time. In the event, Jenkins vigorously outargued Healey on the cost aspect. By a majority vote, Healey, Brown, and Stewart apparently dissenting, the F111 disappeared, leading to the cancellation of an order worth £400 m.[11]

The outcome was not wholly clear-cut. British forces stayed on in the Middle East and the Persian Gulf until the end of the decade, and indeed were involved in hard military action in Aden and South Yemen. The exploits here of Colonel Colin Mitchell of the Argyll and Sutherland Highlanders, 'Mad Mitch', won some notoriety or celebrity which helped turn him into a Tory MP in 1970. When Edward Heath became Prime Minister in 1970 he tried to argue the case for a continuation of the British presence in the Persian Gulf. Healey himself remained attracted to the case for staying on in some form in Singapore and South-East Asia generally, quite apart from the special case of Hong Kong, a view strongly backed by the US administration which felt that Britain should not summarily evacuate and

---

[10] Douglas Hurd, *An End to Promises* (London, 1979), 40 ff.
[11] Crossman, *Diaries of a Cabinet Minister*, ii, 634–5 (entry of 4 Jan. 1968); Tony Benn, *Office Without Power: Diaries, 1968–72* (London, 1988), 1–5 (entries of 3, 4 Jan 1968). Benn records that Healey was very angry, 'and his language was full of f— this and f— that'.

liquidate its commitments in this sensitive area, still torn by American military and mass air attacks on the Vietnamese guerrillas. Military experts (along with scientists like Zuckerman) were heard to criticize Healey's 'Indo-Pacific assumptions'. In Europe, the offset of costs of the British Army on the Rhine was a continuing difficulty, fanned by the anti-Europeanism and anti-Germanism of some on the Labour left. British military expenditure remained at a high level, including as it did the so-called independent nuclear deterrent which Labour had promised in its 1964 manifesto to abolish. Meanwhile American submarines with their Polaris nuclear warheads remained in operational use at Holy Loch in Scotland, despite attacks from CND, the Scottish Nationalists, and the left generally.

Nevertheless, the general thrust of Labour's defence policy was clearly to wind up a decades-old policy of entrenched military involvement with the bastions in the Middle East, the Indian Ocean, the Pacific, and along the South-East Asian littoral, a policy dating from the imperial strategy of the Committee of Imperial Defence formed during the Balfour government back in 1904. It was clear that no significant military bases would remain in the 1970s outside Europe and the Mediterranean, with Cyprus as the most easterly base for deployment. Britain, flagellating itself at home in the aftermath of devaluation, extricating itself from the coils of sterling as a world reserve currency, was also at last adapting its defence and foreign policy commitments to the realities of economic constraint, local nationalist pressure, and strategic vulnerability. It was making a public statement that the last pretence of being a world power was being stripped away. But it was doing so, not in a controlled or considered fashion, but in a rush to disengage and economize, unheeded in Europe, a token head of the Commonwealth, a largely powerless client of the Americans, unable to retain what had for so long been its own.

These premonitions of external weakness were accompanied by, though not necessarily connected directly with, wider forces of turbulence and dissolution which made the later sixties a time of unusual racial, regional, and social tension. The optimism of the period of Wilson's election victory in 1964 totally dissolved. Some of the features of the time—the ethnic violence, the class conflict, the youth revolution—were very far from being peculiar to Britain. To some degree, they were imported from outside through the impact of the media in illustrating race riots, youth disturbances, and other manifestations overseas. These episodes marked the unhappy history of western Europe and the United States as well, where 'permissiveness' showed its hard, perhaps brutal, side. Social forces which brought down such mighty potentates as President Lyndon Johnson in the United States, or President Charles de Gaulle in France, which ended the domination of the Christian Democrats in Western Germany, and even threatened the fabric of a dictatorship like Franco's Spain, clearly went far wider than the specific endemic problems of Britain. Here, however, they were projected against a background of years of perceived decline and fall from eminence. Coming at this time, their impact on Britain was therefore peculiarly unhappy, though in some ways liberating and invigorating as well.

Britain, for instance, experienced the shock realization that the violent confrontations of black communities in New York, Detroit, or Los Angeles, were now becoming a feature of British society also, and producing a similar kind of so-called 'white backlash' in consequence. Commonwealth immigrants, mainly from India, Pakistan, and Bangla Desh in Asia, from Western and East Africa, and especially and in mounting numbers from the West Indies, had settled into ghetto areas of inner cities in an unplanned, uncontrolled way for nearly twenty years. The consequences now came savagely home to roost.

A variety of nativist organizations was formed at this period, in response to the alleged consequences of Commonwealth immigration, with the recent influx of Kenyan Asians a particular source of concern. The fact that the bulk of immigrants were, in fact, white-skinned—particularly Irish and Australian and other Dominions migrants—was seldom stressed. Such bodies as the Southall Residents' Association (close to Heathrow airport) ventilated white hostility to the presence of large concentrations of black and brown immigrants in older residential communities. A disturbing phenomenon in 1967 was the formation of the National Front, an amalgam of a variety of neo-fascist and racist groups, particularly fringe movements led by John Tyndall and Martin Webster which peddled a crude populist antagonism towards immigrants and Jews alike.[12] Although the numbers of National Front members were never great (their putative leader, Mosley, stayed in France in exile), they attracted much attention for their fanning of the flames of racial hatred especially amongst tough young 'skinheads' and other whites, and football supporters such as those associated with West Ham and other older working-class districts. There were alarming reports of racial violence in many urban areas, including outbreaks of 'Paki-bashing', physical assaults on young Pakistanis and their families in Bradford, Leeds, Leicester, Luton, and other centres of Asian migration. Less documented but certainly present were countless cases of racial discrimination in housing, employment, and social opportunity in pubs, clubs, and social organizations, widespread throughout the land despite the endeavours of the Race Relations Board.

A particularly potent stimulus to racial antagonism came in 1968 with a series of inflammatory speeches by Enoch Powell. He was a maverick former Conservative Minister of Health, now turned right-wing nationalist, who had quarrelled violently with the new Tory Leader, Edward Heath. From his constituency in Wolverhampton in the West Midlands, Powell now began to fan flames of racial and nationalist feeling associated in the area with Joseph Chamberlain in a previous era—even though Powell differed from the Chamberlain tradition in many key aspects of his political philosophy, including a strong opposition to imperial expansion or an independent nuclear deterrent. Powell's message

[12] See Richard Thurlow, *Fascism in Britain: A History, 1918–1985* (London, 1987), 275 ff.

was first heard in a pungent attack on Kenyan Asian immigrants at Walsall on 9 February 1968. More notorious was a pronouncement at Birmingham on 20 April when Powell openly raised the spectre of racial conflict and called for the repatriation of black and other Commonwealth immigrants. In language of classical obscurity, but with a clear underlying tone of violence, Powell recalled an ancient Roman who saw the prospect of the River Tiber 'foaming with much blood'.[13] Powell's approach appeared to be cerebral and intellectual in tone. Yet it contained openly inciting and emotional material about old ladies who suffered excreta being pushed through their letter-boxes, and vague allegations about the racial dangers resulting from 'wide-eyed grinning piccaninnies'. Powell's campaign undoubtedly raised the temperature of the discussion of racial questions substantially. He was vehemently attacked on the Liberal and Labour left, and disowned by Heath and the Conservative leadership too. But he clearly touched a chord in the increasingly demoralized British people, especially in working-class inner cities. The Monday Club and other far-right fringe elements in the Tory Party lent Powell support. In the East End of London, processions of dockers (joined by Heathrow immigration officers) marched on behalf of Powell's racial and cultural stereotypes as they had once done on behalf of the upper-class Oswald Mosley. At the Commons they clashed with the Jewish Labour MP, Ian Mikardo.[14]

The government attempted to respond with ameliorative and liberal policies, especially in the period when Roy Jenkins was at the Home Office in 1965–7. The 1968 Race Relations Act was a notable move in the attempt to institutionalize racial harmony. But the general anxiety about the extent of coloured immigration had its impact at all levels, especially in encouraging an official view that the entry of Commonwealth immigrants ought to be drastically curbed. James Callaghan—Jenkins's successor at the

---

[13] *The Times*, 21 Apr. 1968.   [14] *Daily Telegraph*, 27 Apr. 1968.

Home Office, proved to be less liberal than his predecessor in these matters.[15] The effect was that the Labour government tightened up the previous Conservative administration's 1962 Commonwealth Immigration Act. The Act of 1968 limited immigration to those who had 'patrial' ties with existing British residents. The definition of this idea led to a more and more restrictive approach being taken, and families from Africa and Asia were painfully split up as a result. Callaghan caused a particular furore by stopping the passport privileges of Kenyan Asians, in defiance of previous promises; a strict and discriminatory quota system would prevail. In due course, this told severely on Ugandan Asians also, seeking refuge in Britain from the atrocities committed against them by President Idi Amin in Uganda. Many Labour, as well as Conservative, politicians were heard to comment on the dangers accruing to Labour in its working-class strongholds through resentment amongst working-class people at the black intruder. A good deal of political bargaining resulted between the major parties as to who could be the more effective in pandering to white prejudice. The mood was enshrined in a popular television series 'Till Death Us Do Part'. This featured 'Alf Garnett', a traditional working-class Tory from London's East End who emphasized love of monarchy and fear of the blacks in equal measure. The popularity of this humorous production was a commentary on the ethos of the time. In general, British cities managed to avoid a racial explosion on anything like the American pattern. Areas like Brixton in south London remained tense, and the general mood in areas of mixed race was anxious with an underlying current of conflict. Black community leaders were vocal in protesting against harassment from the police in black areas, and the prejudice allegedly displayed by magistrates in their sentencing policy towards Afro-Caribbean offenders, but little public action was taken. As the economy showed signs of deterioration in the late

[15] See Callaghan, *Time and Chance,* 263 ff.

sixties, with rising unemployment and worsening social conditions afflicting black immigrants in unequal measure, the prospect for race relations in Britain was a disturbing one.

Elsewhere in the land, there was also rising conflict for other
reasons. In Scotland and Wales, the mounting tide of nationalist
resentment against an unsympathetic or remote Whitehall and
Westminster showed no sign of abating. In Scotland the Scottish
National Party (which had gained 5.0 per cent of the Scots vote
in 1966) reached unparalleled levels of influence in 1967–8.[16]
For a time it had the largest party membership in Scotland, and
showed immense gains in local-government elections. It spanned
a wide range of opinion, working men, small businessmen, and
housewives all being prominent in its ranks, and drew on Conservative but more particularly on working-class Labour support. Much glamour attached to the party after Mrs Winifred
Ewing's by-election victory at Hamilton in November 1967. The
vitality and youth of the SNP challenge contrasted with the drab
machine politics which was all that Labour Scotland could offer.
The Scottish protest mounted steadily with its effective cry, 'Put
Scotland first'. The other parties inevitably responded. Labour
produced a strong devolutionist fringe. One Scottish Labour MP,
Jim Sillars, eventually formed a one-man Scottish Labour Party
which sought to harmonize left socialism and Scottish nationalism as Jimmy Maxton and the Clydesiders had done in the inter-
war years. The Conservatives also responded, with Sir Alec
Douglas-Home chairing a party inquiry into Scottish constitutional devolution and Heath himself making remarkably sympathetic noises towards Scottish sentiment.[17] By 1969 the SNP tide
seemed to have passed its peak, partly because of the relative
ineptitude of Scottish Nationalist councillors in the business of

---

[16] See Ian Mclean, 'The Rise and Fall of the Scottish National Party', *Political
Studies*, 18, no. 3 (Sept. 1970).

[17] See *Scotland's Government: The report of the Scottish Constitutional Committee* (Edinburgh, 1970).

local government, but Scottish separatism remained a potent threat.

In Wales, some of the consequences were even more alarming. Plaid Cymru continued to grow.[18] Gwynfor Evans proved a dignified leader in Parliament. An astonishing near-victory over Labour in Rhondda West in 1967 was followed by another equally dramatic near-triumph in Caerphilly, another mining stronghold for Labour over forty years, in July 1968. All over Wales, not only in Welshspeaking mountainous areas but even in the valleys, those cradles of British socialism, Welsh nationalism had a new credibility. More disturbing, in time, was the activity of the Welsh Language Society, *Cymdeithas yr Iaith Gymraeg*, which favoured direct action against symbols of English rule. Thus attacks were launched on governmental offices such as Post Offices and the Inland Revenue. Television masts were damaged in protest against the failure to have more Welsh-language broadcasting. To the fury of road travellers in Wales, road signs were regularly defaced in protest at English place names such as Newtown or Cardigan being displayed. More sinister still were the paramilitary activities of a small guerrilla group, the Free Wales Army, which was believed to be associated with various bomb attacks on government buildings and also—a new phenomenon—on 'second homes' owned in Wales by English occupiers.

The government resorted to every kind of remedy, with some success. The royal family was given the maximum exposure, culminating in Prince Charles being invested as Prince of Wales at Caernarfon Castle in July 1969, in emulation of Edward VIII back in 1911. This was clearly a publicity measure directed against Plaid Cymru, as was a term's study spent at the University College of Wales, Aberystwyth, by the prince in the summer of 1969. There was much satirical response, including a pop song, 'Carlo', which poured scorn on the prince, and some uproar

[18]   Morgan, *Rebirth of a Nation*, 387 ff.

when he spoke in his recently learnt Welsh at the 1969 *Urdd* (League of Youth) eisteddfod. The prince himself responded with much dignity. On balance, the government achieved some success. As in Scotland, there were signs in 1969 that Plaid Cymru was passing its peak, and that the Welsh Language Society was annoying more people than it was converting by its strident and aggressive campaign. On the other hand, it was hard to dispute that the pressure of direct action, as with the suffragettes in the past, was achieving results where peaceful protest had failed. The advance of Welsh in official governmental business, the greater resources devoted to Welsh-language television, and particularly the popularity of the growth of many excellent all-Welsh primary and a few secondary schools indicated a potential fund of goodwill towards an ancient, persecuted language. The touchy regime of George Thomas, an amiable non-Welsh-speaking Secretary of State for Wales, who proved curiously impervious to Welsh-language claims, seemed out of touch with the new spirit of conciliation. What was beyond doubt was that the government had to respond in political terms. A variety of nominated and co-opted bodies in Wales, culminating in the Council for Wales wound up in 1966, had clearly fired no one's imagination.

In the aftermath of the Caerphilly by-election there were alarmist reports reaching Transport House from the Scottish and Welsh regional offices of the Labour Party.[19] The Wilson government then set up a broadly based commission on the constitution under Lord Crowther.[20] Its mandate was unclear, and the government clearly hoped that devolutionism or separatism in Scotland and Wales would simply peter out. But by 1970 it was still obvious that Scottish and Welsh nationalism remained vigorously alive. Celtic patriots were anxious that Crowther (later named Kilbrandon when its original chairman died and was replaced by Lord Kilbrandon) should not join previous inquiries on the scrap-heap of history.

[19] Crossman, *Diaries*, iii, 145 (entry of 18 July 1968).
[20] An excellent guide is Vernon Bogdanor, *Devolution* (Oxford, 1979).

Scotland and Wales, however, were mild enough distractions contrasted with the events in 'the other island', or more particularly Northern Ireland.[21] For over forty years, since the effective partition back in 1920, Ulster had been run in entrenched fashion by an inbred Protestant ascendancy, based broadly on backwoods landowners and the Protestant working class of the factories and shipyards of Belfast. Even Ulster, however, could not remain hermetically sealed from wider forces of change for ever. The first premonitions of trouble came in 1966–7 with some dissension within the Unionist majority over the relatively more liberal rule of Captain O'Neill. Extremist Protestant bodies emerged to protect the entrenched religious supremacy in jobs, housing, and education; one popular demagogue who achieved massive political influence was the Reverend Ian Paisley, who was briefly imprisoned for his inflammatory attacks on Roman Catholics. Conversely, alarming signs emerged of the prospect of renewed IRA attacks on persons and property in Northern Ireland, and perhaps on the mainland as well.

The main source of change, however, came with the growth of new forces of protest within the Roman Catholic minority and their creation of a civil rights movement in 1967. In October 1968 there came violent disturbances in Londonderry over housing and other Catholic grievances, and a series of civil rights marches, in which indeed some liberal Ulster Protestants also joined. A variety of Catholic organizations were formed. The most notable was the Social Democratic and Labour Party, led by Catholic politicians such as Gerry Fitt and John Hume; others were more socialist such as that led by the young Bernadette Devlin. After many acts of violence in civil rights demonstrations in Derry, Newry, and elsewhere, and much protest at the violence used by the Ulster constabulary, there was a change of premier in

---

[21] On these matters, see F. S. L. Lyons, *Ireland since the Famine* (London, 1973 edn.), 760 ff.; Paul Arthur and Keith Jeffery, *Northern Ireland since 1968* (Oxford, 1988); Padraig O'Malley, *The Uncivil Wars: Ireland Today* (Belfast, 1983).

Ulster, O'Neill being replaced by an Old Etonian landowner, James Chichester-Clark. The most powerful man in Ulster polit-ics, however, was the tough, business-like figure of Brian Faul-kner, Minister of Commerce and also an active Orangeman. Much violence and loss of life occurred in July and August 1969, especially in the Bogside region of Londonderry. Here the prominence of the Orange Order and the activity of the Protest-ant Apprentice Boys, echoing the suppression of the Catholics during the reign of William III in the 1690s, led to much Catholic counter-violence.

These alarming events, redolent of the tragic history of Ireland in earlier periods, led to vigorous and effective action by James Callaghan, the Home Secretary, in the most successful sphere of his departmental operations.[22] The 'Downing Street Declaration' of August 1969 committed the Northern Ireland government to speed up the process of civil rights and to extend housing and employment opportunities more fairly to the Catholic minority in the north. As a major palliative to Catholic sentiment, follow-ing the report of a commission chaired by Sir John Hunt, the Royal Ulster Constabulary was reorganized and disarmed. Its policing methods were severely condemned. More, the hated paramilitary B Specials (the part-time Ulster Special Constabu-lary) were abolished forthwith. By 1970, the processes of change in Northern Ireland were remarkable, and the entire scene trans-formed from the frozen ascendancy of the midsixties. Authentic Catholic political figures such as the ex-merchant seaman, Gerry Fitt, had arisen to challenge the stridency of men like Ian Paisley and the spokesmen of the Orange Order. Fitt founded the Social Democratic Labour Party as a vehicle for constitutionally minded Ulster Catholics. Even so, the outlook was a sombre one. The heartening evidence of reform had awakened, or rekin-dled, age-old sectarian and communal hatred. There seemed little moderate ground in Northern Irish politics, with such

---

[22] See his book, *A House Divided: The Dilemma of Northern Ireland* (Lon-don, 1973).

intermediate bodies as the Northern Irish Labour Party falling by the wayside. The constitutional progress of the SDLP and the Catholic minority went side by side with the growth of the Provisional IRA and its intensified campaign of assassination and incendiarism. On the Protestant side there were similarly violent extremist bodies such as the Ulster Volunteer Force. The Westminster government was forced to concede that local forces of law and order were breaking down.

From August 1969 the British Army was sent in some numbers to Londonderry, later extending its operations widely throughout the province. In the spring of 1970, the prospects of peace in Northern Ireland appeared bleak indeed, with Protestants and Catholics at each other's throats, the Provisional IRA fully active, the British Army under attack in Londonderry and in Belfast's Catholic strongholds such as the Falls Road, and replying with CS gas. The British troops, initially welcomed in many Ulster Catholic circles as liberators, soon aroused the traditional hatred when they were accompanied by a policy of internment and the stern measures of suppression of their commander, General Freeland. To many of the Catholic minority, the British were now invaders, an army of occupation designed to prevent for ever the desired goal of a united Ireland. The temper of Anglo-Irish relations deteriorated with the Dublin government of Jack Lynch's Fianna Fail party (the traditional ally of republicanism from the days of de Valera) apparently unable or unwilling to stem the flow of arms from IRA centres in the Republic (and often from the United States originally) to their brethren north of the border. Northern Ireland seemed aflame with carnage and sectarian hatred in 1970. The violence was being transferred to England as well, with bomb attacks on army property, and soon on shops and other English civilian targets, and with bitter anti-English resentment in the Irish population of such areas as Merseyside or the Kilburn area of north London.

Foreign relations were also inevitably affected, with the American government, now under President Nixon, voicing disapproval of British methods of suppression in Ulster, and apparently unable to prevent 'Noraid' and other bodies in the United States sending money to purchase arms and ammunition for the Provisionals in Northern Ireland. After being dormant for over forty years, Ireland returned to centre stage of British public life.

These varied elements of social and ethnic turbulence had at least one common factor. One element united the protest against racism and the bomb, the activities of the Welsh Language Society, and the campaigns of the Irish nationalists like Bernadette Devlin. This was the cult of youth, Indeed, the 'youth revolt' was much discussed in this period. It became associated with a particular style of adolescent protest hitherto unknown as a serious phenomenon in British society. As we have seen, the early sixties had seen much discussion of youth and its culture during the 'permissiveness' of pop culture, miniskirts, drugs, and generational rebelliousness. On the other hand, as we have also seen, this protest was largely personal, perhaps anarchic, certainly apolitical. In particular, the impact of consumer pressure, the Beatles, and new styles in dress and recreation had little or no impact in kindling wider social or political ideas among working-class young people.

In 1968 a new factor began to shake the public consciousness—the rebelliousness of the middle-class young, relatively well educated, highly articulate, and highly motivated, a generation of student rebels hitherto known only in countries on the continent or in Asia or Latin America which had a large shiftless student population with no common educational curriculum or immediate professional focus. The universities and even the sixth forms of British schools became, quite unexpectedly, cradles of something approaching revolution. In part, the causes were derivative. American universities had been aflame for some years, with a climax reached in the violent upheavals and disruption at the Berkeley campus, close to the centre of drug permissiveness in San Francisco.[23] In France, political conflict against

---

[23] Seymour Martin Lipset and Sheldon S. Wolin, *The Berkeley Student Revolt* (New York, 1965).

the Gaullist regime led to the violence of the student rebellion at the Sorbonne and Nanterre which threatened another French Revolution. Elsewhere in Europe, in Western Germany, the Netherlands, and other countries, student leaders of the type of Daniel Cohn- Bendit, Alan Geismar, and Rudi Dutschke, usually of the far Marxist left, became cult celebrities. Britain offered the exotic maverick figure of the Pakistani ex-President of the Oxford Union. Tariq Ali. It would have been surprising, no doubt, if these highly publicized and spectacular eruptions which saw university campuses aflame and engulfed in conflict with police and the military from the Latin Quarter to Lima had had no impact in Britain.

But there were also indigenous factors in Britain, especially within the universities where the student revolt most characteristically expressed itself. There was a growing tide of political resentment at the inadequacy of Wilson's Labour regime to provide inspiration or even competent leadership. This took the particular form of the traditional outlet of anti-Americanism, with massive disapproval of Lyndon Johnson's policy in Vietnam and the saturation bombing of the hapless Vietnamese peasants in the cause of American Cold War objectives. A group of Trotskyists and Maoists, with Tariq Ali prominent, formed a protest group called the Vietnam Solidarity Committee. Some of its members launched an 'underground' left- wing journal, *Black Dwarf*, so named after an early working-class publication suppressed in the 1820s, to suggest an appeal to native libertarian traditions. In the eyes of Marxist commentators like the historian E. P. Thompson, the national radical heritage was at least as important as international workers' and students' solidarity; however, the mysterious death of the legendary Marxist guerrilla leader, Che Guevara, in Bolivia in 1967 gave the student left renewed international inspiration. The Vietnam Solidarity Committee, with students heavily represented, as well as what was abusively termed a left-wing 'rent-a-crowd' (or -mob), organized a mass march on the American embassy in Grosvenor Square in October 1968. In preparation, *Black Dwarf* arranged a print run of 50,000 for a special pop song (banned by the BBC), 'Street-fighting Man'.[24] The Grosvenor Square demonstration led to a huge and violent confrontation with massed police, though with no fatalities. However, Callaghan, the Home Secretary, handled the Vietnam march and demonstration with much aplomb as an issue of civil liberties as well as of public order. The restraint and good humour of the police were widely commended in the press, though there were other interpretations of these events by the liberal left.

It appears that the tide of left-wing protest began to subside from this time on. But it did bring a kind of passionate political violence to the London streets unknown since the anti-fascist battle of Cable Street in 1936. There were factors that went beyond the efforts of agitators like Tariq Ali or left-wing inter-national gurus like the veteran American-based German philoso-pher, Herbert Marcuse, a cult figure comparable to Bertrand Russell. Indeed, left-wing politics were not the root cause of the disturbance of the time. The student protest was an upsurge of revolt by the heirs of the post-war welfare democracy, a rela-tively wealthy, secure, libertarian generation confronted with systems dating from an earlier era of conformity and revealed authority. This especially applied in universities where the pater-nalism and hierarchy of an older order still prevailed. It was not surprising that it was the newer universities, especially Warwick, East Anglia, and Essex, along with the old radical citadel of Houghton Street, the London School of Economics, where par-ticular disorder occurred, on issues great and small. There were student invasions of university offices, sometimes in vain pursuit of alleged political files or indexes of identification and censor-ship. Links with car-makers and other local capitalists were much denounced by E. P. Thompson in a fierce polemic.[25] The so-called

---

[24] Tariq Ali, *Streetfighting Years* (London, 1987), 222. Jagger, the author, was a rarity amongst pop musicians in his radical political commitment.

[25] E. P. Thompson, *Warwick University Limited: Industry. Management and the Universities* (Harmondsworth, 1971).

'repressive tolerance' of the university was viewed as a placid front for conformity and cultural hegemony, with the effective marginalization of dissent. The London School of Economics was closed after a student assault on the main building; a porter at the School died of a heart attack in these troubles. Even in the ancient cloistered world of Oxford there were sit-ins at the Clarendon Building and demonstrations on university and college property that sunny summer. There were protests against archaic university rules and procedures (for instance involving women guests staying overnight in colleges), and against old anomalies such as All Souls College, hugely wealthy, condemned by the 1964 Franks Report for 'infirmity of purpose',[26] and with no undergraduate or graduate students of any kind within its walls since its foundation to pray for the souls of victims of the Hundred Years War. The Robbins Report, it seemed, had reaped the whirlwind. Instead of a new generation of civic-minded scientists and professionals, it had spawned instead a strange breed of alienated, rootless, intellectual revolutionaries. It was a new demonstration of the uses of literacy. Oxford, like Yale in the United States, found that an intimate collegiate structure was not necessarily a guarantee that it would escape the deluge, though its deans and tutors might mitigate its effects.

By 1970, though, the so-called 'campus war' had begun to subside.[27] It had led to few enough casualties. Compared with the deaths in the Sorbonne, the beatings on the Berkeley campus, the use of the National Guard in Kent State, Ohio, or the class warfare in West Berlin, events on British campuses seemed relatively tame. The only known loss of life was the LSE porter mentioned above. Many of the students' 'revolts' were imitative and derivative, often straining hard, in relatively comfortable surroundings, to find a target for assault. Tariq Ali records in his memoirs that the original plan to storm and occupy the US

---

[26] *Report of Commission of Inquiry into Oxford University*, i (Oxford, 1966), para. 344 (147).
[27] John Searle, *The Campus War* (Harmondsworth, 1969).

embassy in Grosvenor Square in October 1968 was rejected for prudential reasons. He found himself outflanked and denounced by the even more extreme Socialist Labour League for 'revisionist' tendencies.[28] The student rebellion did not kindle a form of enduring left-wing critique comparable with those of the thirties. Indeed, more doctrinaire left-wingers such as those Marxists who published *New Left Review* viewed these often spontaneous movements of students somewhat as detached outsiders, as did the French Communist Party when it refused to make common cause with bourgeois students in the Sorbonne and Nanterre in trying to bring down Gaullism in 1968. For all the stridency of the new generation of student leaders and their vigorously expressed demands at the National Union of Students, and in a huge variety of protest movements dealing with the Greek colonels, South Africa, the regime in Chile, and other hated targets, it seemed that the majority of young voters in 1970, especially amongst middle-class students, either voted Tory or else took no interest in electoral proceedings at all. The Conservatives staged a considerable come-back in the National Union of Students. By the end of the 1970s, the spectacle of old student revolutionaries like Alain Geismar and Jerry Rubin turning to the successful exploitation of the world of capitalist self-advancement, with Tariq Ali surviving as a kind of exotic, itinerant talisman of self-indulgent protest, caused much satirical or ironic comment.[29]

Nevertheless, the deeper public significance of the student movements in the later sixties should not be underestimated. Politically, they played their important part in the mood of disillusion which did such damage to the standing of Harold Wilson and to the agencies of government in general, and which helped the disintegration of large sections of the Labour Party in the constituencies. Labour Party individual membership, as officially recorded (or invented) fell from 830,000 in 1963 to 680,000 in 1970. In the special case of Wales, the notable success

[28] Tariq Ali, *Streetfighting Years*, 228–9.   [29] <$$$>

of the Welsh Language movement owed much to the militant tactics pursued by students and other advocates of 'direct action'. Culturally and socially, the student revolts helped on a process of deracination and disenchantment which made schools and universities, like the police, the civil service, parliament, and much else, often-questioned embodiments of the abiding values of British life. In the public's estimation, they led to the vogue for higher education embodied on the Robbins Report rapidly losing its sheen. Especially with working-class people, long-haired, unemployed, student protesters were not popular. Car-workers in Cowley objected when Oxford students acted as pickets during a strike. The new universities, instead of being esteemed for their intellectual vigour and scientific research, became suspect for their inconsequence and self-indulgence. Protests by revolting students became regarded, however unfairly, as a kind of extension of 'rag week'. In the 1980s, with the many conflicts between the higher educational system and the Thatcher government, university spokesmen looked back to the student disturbances of the late sixties as the start of widening belief in government circles that universities were ineffective in the arts of management of men and resources. In generational terms, the sixties revolt is most notable for its articulate nature. It involved, clearly, a large proportion of students who were academically serious, idealistic, highly motivated. They were searching for the kind of 'great cause' for which the 'angry young men' had searched in vain a decade earlier, but with a range of learning, intellectual sophistication, and self-confidence denied their predecessors. They had some positive achievements, ranging from the overhaul of university disciplinary procedures to the lowering of the age for voting and of legal consent from 21 to 18.

But it was perhaps in their destructive endeavours, in the derision and discredit that was heaped upon the slow-moving institutions that selected them that the student rebels succeeded only too well. Beyond the world of campus politics, with its hothouse obsessions with such issues as student representation, personal files, and disciplinary tribunals, the student revolt was testimony to a wider dissolution. The civic culture of Britain had rested, even in the economic troubles of post-1945, on the strength of certain bases, the nuclear family, the cohesive neighbourhood, the benevolent virtues of professional advancement, respect for the rule of law. The existence of so strident a rejection amongst significant elements in teenage groups or young people in their twenties weakened all of these, without necessarily providing any obvious alternative view of society. Many of the main inspirational philosophies for the student movement came from remote areas of little direct relevance to the British scene. There was no native equivalent of the venerable Herbert Marcuse, so charismatic on Californian campuses six thousand miles away. E. P. Thompson's doctrinaire Marxism addressed only a small minority of the concerns of British students; in due course, he resigned his post at Warwick University to continue as a respected ideological guru in the elegant Regency ambience of Leamington Spa. The student revolt became a paradigm for the cult of the new, the rejection of moral conventions and social norms almost without thought, and for its own sake. In particular, the cohesion of the family, however defined, was rejected with contempt as part of a time-worn, middle- class strait-jacket. The advance in the acceptability of premarital sex, of relations (sometimes homosexual) unrelated to anything as formal as contractual processes of marriage, was much speeded up. Twenty years on, the image of the sixties seemed less liberating and more self-destructive, but by then the damage had been done. In the Commons debate on the proposed legalization of 'soft drugs' like cannabis by the Wootton Committee in January 1969, James Callaghan, the Home Secretary, proclaimed, to much Conservative applause, his wish 'to call a halt to the rising tide of permissiveness'. The latter was, he added, 'one of the most unlikeable [*sic*] words that has been invented in recent years'. The reaction of the 'silent majority' was already well under way.

The protests of middle-class students might generate newspaper headlines and endless sociological and philosophical diagnoses of the concept of 'academic freedom'. But they were peripheral to the more basic malaise of Harold Wilson's Britain. Basic problems of comparatively low increases in productivity, compounded by enduring social, regional, and class division, dogged any real attempt at national recovery. Nowhere was this more visible than in the vital field of labour relations. Indeed, this was the Wilson government's particular claim to understanding and authority, and ultimately by far its most disastrous failure.

The voluntary monitoring of wage claims and the regulation of trade-union behaviour under the 1966 Prices and Incomes Act had not brought much improvement. The government contemplated with gloom in 1967 and 1968 a continuing rash of unofficial and other strikes. The Ministry of Labour found its interventions to be ineffective, as the record of Ray Gunter, 'the ticket collector', showed. One basic strategy to curb the unions would have been a change in monetary and fiscal policy to undermine full employment, which formed the basis of the unions' and shop stewards' power in the market, but this was rejected. Alternatives, though, proved to be hard to devise. The Donovan Royal Commission on the trade unions reported in 1968.[30] But its thrust, influenced in great measure by two distinguished authorities on industrial relations, Hugh Clegg and Allan Flanders, of Warwick and Oxford Universities respectively, was to emphasize the voluntary reform of labour relations on the shop floor and the bargaining role of shop stewards. The majority on the Commission strongly rejected any form of legal or penal sanctions to enforce industrial discipline. While in many ways appropriate as a recognition of the localized, decentralized nature of wage-bargaining, the Donovan Commission offered no kind of programme for action. Nor did it in any way satisfy mounting popular concern with a pattern of industrial indiscipline amounting to chaos. The TUC, under its ageing General Secretary, George Woodcock, showed little capacity for exerting

---

[30] Commission report, July 1968 (Cmnd. 3263).

central direction or control over its affiliated unions. The transition from Woodcock to the much younger and more vigorous figure of Vic Feather in 1968 meant that this stance would only be reinforced, and the structure of British labour relations as it had existed since 1906 would be perpetuated indefinitely.[31]

Meanwhile, Wilson and his colleagues saw public concern about the role of the unions voiced in the opinion polls, and much unease expressed by investors and speculators against sterling. The Conservatives attracted much attention by their own policy document, *Fair Deal at Work* (April 1968), which proposed a sixty-day cooling- off period for certain strikes, the registration of unions, and the more precise definition of 'trades disputes' under the terms of the 1906 Act. The government well recalled the damage done to the economy and their own standing by the events of the seamen's strike in May- June 1966 which led to the sterling crisis, and the dock disputes which were the prelude to devaluation of the pound in the autumn of 1967. A particularly alarming episode which seemed to show how the power of the unions could be used gratuitously to feed widespread fears about British stability came on 'Mad Friday', 6 December 1968. There was a colossal run on the pound (a loss of $100 m. on that one day) and a mass of wild rumours were in circulation, including the resignation of Wilson and Jenkins, a further devaluation of the pound, and even that the Queen had abdicated in view of the calamitous state of the country.[32] Clearly, the government believed, something had to be done. More important, the IMF and Britain's many creditors held this view with even greater fervour.

A new watershed in these events came with the advent of Mrs Barbara Castle to the Department of Employment and Productivity, a much-expanded version of the old Ministry of Labour, in April 1968.[33] At a time when women's rights were entering the

[31] See Eric Silver, *Vic Feather, T.U.C.* (London, 1973).

[32] *The Times*, 7 Dec. 1968.

[33] See Barbara Castle, *The Castle Diaries, 1964–70* (London, 1984).

public agenda, she became the most prominent woman yet in the history of British party politics. Mrs Castle was an old Bevanite; like Bevan before her, she believed in order in labour relations. As a socialist she did not see why planning and regulation should be extended to every other aspect of social and economic affairs, but that labour relations should be left to the vagaries of the free market. Advised by the Oxford industrial-relations expert, William McCarthy, she interposed a new energy in discussions with the TUC. She was caustically critical of the negativity of the Donovan Commission, as she saw it, and at her first proper meeting with the TUC General Council she shook them by calling for an ordered system with possible legal penalties to enforce its provision.

With the encouragement of Wilson and Jenkins, Mrs Castle brought out a sensational White Paper in January 1969, *In Place of Strife*.[34] It was largely to dictate the course of events in the later period of the Wilson government. Some of its provisions, for instance over registration, notably strengthened the role of the unions. But what captured attention were three other proposals—that there should be a twenty-eight-day 'conciliation pause', that the minister could if necessary impose a settlement in inter-union disputes, and that there should be power to order a strike ballot if circumstances dictated. All these would be backed by 'discretionary reserve powers', with the threat of penal powers lying behind them. Individual strikers could thus be prosecuted before a new Industrial Relations Court. A Labour government was engaged in bringing the law into the world of industrial relations for the first time since the aftermath of the 1926 General Strike. A left-wing socialist, Barbara Castle, was boldly stepping in where a sequence of Tory Ministers of Labour between 1951 and 1964 had deliberately kept aloof. The events of early 1969 gave grist to her mill, being marked by more union troubles of the kind now dismally familiar. The Pearson Inquiry into a dispute in the steel industry was followed by the failure of

---

[34] *The Castle Diaries*, 560–2, for a good discussion.

injunctions by Ford Motors against two unions, the Engineers and the Transport Workers. Justice Lane concluded that the agreements between Fords and the unions had no legal force, while, of course, there was no statute in being to prevent the company being undermined by labour troubles. This increased the determination of Mrs Castle to legislate.

The government's proposals were widely popular, according to the opinion polls which saw a rise in Labour's standing for the first time in many months. But within the labour world, industrial and political, there was turmoil. The TUC under Vic Feather was strongly resistant to anything resembling penal sanctions, which carried 'the taint of criminality'. This especially applied to its two rising stars, Jack Jones of the Transport Workers and Hugh Scanlon of the Engineers, both on the left, and the main union spokesmen in fighting off the government's plans.[35] Within the Labour Party there was uproar, with an immense range of critics, from the usual dissidents on the left to wide sections of trade unionists normally on the party right. The chairman of the parliamentary party, Douglas Houghton, a usually cautious representative of a white-collar union, emerged as a particularly effective critic.[36] Within the government, opponents of Mrs Castle ranged from Mrs Judith Hart on the left to trade-unionist ministers like Richard Marsh and Roy Mason. Most unexpectedly of all, James Callaghan, now recouping much of his reputation at the Home Office and the senior minister most closely in touch with TUC opinion, made it clear that he was strongly opposed to the main drift of the bill proposed by the government of which he was a senior member. On 6 January 1969 the Home Policy Subcommittee, after meeting Mrs Castle, unanimously declared that it 'would regret any fresh statutory control with penal clauses on wages after the expiry of the present legislation': Callaghan was one of those present. On 26 March, in a keen

---

[35] See Jack Jones, *Union Man*, and Peter Jenkins, *The Bottle of Downing Street* (London, 1970), an excellent narrative and analysis.
[36] *Guardian*, 8 May 1969.

debate on the party's national executive, a motion by Joe Gormley of the Mineworkers, supported by Callaghan, was carried by 16 to 5 which rejected the main recommendations of Mrs Castle's proposed legislation. Jennie Lee and Tom Bradley were two other ministers who voted against the government's intended measure.[37] Labour now faced a growing crisis comparable to that of 1931, a precedent vivid in many minds.

The next few weeks were increasingly frenetic. Jenkins's budget in April announced that there would be implementation of some of the clauses of *In Place of Strife*, including penal sanctions and a compulsory twenty-eight-day conciliation pause. An inner Cabinet, including Jenkins, Castle, Crossman, Stewart, Healey, and Peart, was formed to try to reassert the government's authority.[38] But this was increasingly hard to achieve with a key minister like Callaghan in open revolt yet too important to sack, with frequent revolts against their own government by Labour back-benchers, and a general feeling in the country that the government was in a state of perhaps terminal crisis, with talk of threats to depose Wilson and perhaps create some form of Coalition government. Fifty Labour MPs announced that they would vote against Mrs Castle's bill and many more were likely to abstain. May Day 1969, that festival of labour hailed by Keir Hardie and others in the past as a day of liberation and fraternity, was marked by unofficial strikes by thousands of workers against the proposed Industrial Relations Bill of their 'own' Labour government. Meetings of Wilson with trade-union leaders at Downing Street led only to angry clashes, with Jones and Scanlon in particular. On 1 June 1969 the Prime Minister, increasingly a beleaguered figure, compared himself to the recently deposed Czech Prime Minister, Alexander Dubcek, and urged Scanlon and his trade-union troops to 'get his tanks off my lawn'.[39]

---

[37] Labour Party, National Executive Committee minutes, 26 March 1969 and Home Policy sub-committee, 6 January 1969 (Labour Party archives).

[38] *The Times*, 14 May 1969.

[39] Jenkins, *Battle of Downing Street*, 140.

A TUC unofficial congress at Croydon on 5 June saw a predictably huge majority against the government's bill by the massive margin of 7,908,000 to only 846,000. Vic Feather repeated the unions' total opposition to any kind of penal sanctions against strikes. The only prominent union leader to back the government was Les Cannon, a converted ex-Communist who led the Electricians and was now recognized as being on the far right of the movement.[40] A subsequent meeting of Wilson and Mrs Castle with TUC leaders was predictably fruitless. Jack Jones recorded that Wilson and Castle were 'basically academics', unable to see things from 'a shop-floor angle'.[41] Ironically, this was described by the press as an attempt by the government to get the union leaders 'off the hook'. In fact, it was clearly the elected government of the day that was desperate for a way out. The situation had arisen which Lloyd George had presented to Bob Smillie and the miners' leaders in 1919, namely an overt challenge to the government of the day by the unions who in themselves possessed the economic power to cause the country to come to a standstill. On that occasion, the miners' leaders felt that the Prime Minister's rhetorical demand had left the unions beaten and unable to challenge. This time, the TUC was far stronger and armed with powerful allies in parliament and Cabinet. This time, the unions would not be so timid.

To resist the Stalinists of the TUC, there were few divisions that the Pope of Downing Street could now call out. Labour's National Executive, with Callaghan a dominant figure, was in open revolt. The threat of revolts of a fatal kind from parliamentary back-benchers was ever more imminent. The replacement of the emollient John Silkin by the tough London docker Bob Mellish as Labour Chief Whip did not make the process of parliamentary discipline any easier for the government. On 17 June, Mellish bluntly told Wilson that not only had the bill no

---

[40] *The Economist*, 7 June 1969.   [41] Jack Jones, *Union Man*, 204.

prospect of passing the House of Commons but that he himself, as a loyal trades unionist, opposed penal sanctions anyway.[42] In theory, Wilson could still hope for the support of the Tory Opposition, but clearly Heath and his colleagues were aware that they had the government on the run and were unprepared to throw Harold Wilson, who had humiliated them for so long, any lifelines. In the Cabinet itself, apart from known opponents like Callaghan, Wilson found himself deserted by one ally after another. In the end, even the Chancellor himself, Roy Jenkins, left Mrs Castle high and dry, sensing that all hope of a political accommodation had gone. The best that could be hoped for was that the TUC would provide the government with a way of saving its face. At a lengthy meeting at Downing Street on 18 June, that is precisely what occurred. Following further deadlock over any kind of penal sanctions, and with Wilson deprived of a Prime Minister's main weapons of dissolving parliament or calling a successful general election, an obscure member of the General Council, Sir Fred Hayday, came up with the magic formula of a 'solemn and binding agreement' by which the TUC itself would monitor strikes and labour disputes and offer 'considered opinion and advice'. Mrs Castle and the Attorney General, Elwyn Jones, at once drafted a formula, and the 'solemn and binding undertaking' was revealed to the world the following morning.[43] The crisis, politically, was off.

The settlement was greeted with general derision—'Solomon Binding' became a popular figure for caricature. It clearly meant a colossal defeat for the Labour government and for Harold Wilson personally. All the key proposals of *In Place of Strife*, the 'conciliation pause', the penal sanctions, and the implementation of some kind of labour law in the chaos of industrial relations, were lost for ever. Instead there was an agreement that the TUC should be notified about strikes in breach of

[42] Crossman, *Diaries of a Cabinet Minister*, iii, 527–8 (entry of 18 June 1969); Jenkins, *Battle of Downing Street*, 151.
[43] *The Times*, 19 June 1969.

procedure and should use its moral persuasion to secure a settlement. Such moral suasion had never worked in the past and it defied credibility that it should do so now. The TUC had no realistic sanctions it could ever offer. The general interpretation was a total surrender by Wilson to the overweening power of the TUC. *The Economist* termed the episode, not unreasonably, 'In Place of Government'.[44] The disorder of labour relations for the twelve months after June 1970 if anything got even worse. Although 180 disputes were referred to Congress House in that period, little authority was exerted. A month after the so-called Downing Street Declaration, the TUC failed to get 1,300 blast furnacemen in the Port Talbot steelworks to return to work. An attempt at intervention with 11,000 workers on unofficial strike in Pilkington's glass factories in St Helens was an equal failure. The number of days lost in January-July 1970 was, at 6,054,000, almost double those lost for the same period in 1969.[45] The unions' power had never, it seemed, been more unrestrained. Vic Feather, the negotiator who brought about the 'solemn and binding' compromise, got his reward by being elected a member of Grillon's exclusive dining club in London.[46]

Politically, the Wilson government seemed to recover from the blow. Wilson presented the Downing Street Declaration as some kind of triumph and used the subsequent parliamentary debate for successful debating tactics directed at the Tories' 'thirteen wasted years' in the remoter past. The Cabinet recaptured something of its *élan*, for all the evident disappointment felt by Mrs Castle herself. James Callaghan, the villain of the piece to many during the debate over *In Place of Strife*, rose in stature, partly through his confident handling of Northern Irish matters, partly through his deft delay of the issue of the redrawing of parliamentary boundaries which would surely be to Labour's disadvantage at the next election. By the general election in 1970, relations between him and Wilson had been patched up and the Prime

---

[44] *The Economist*, 21 June 1969. [45] Eric Silver, *Vic Feather*, 163–4.
[46] Ibid. 169.

Minister could even ponder the prospect of his most disloyal lieutenant succeeding him in 10 Downing Street in due course. Generally, Labour supporters took some comfort from the thought that the crisis of 1931, with a huge and unbridgeable divide opening up between the TUC and the parliamentary leadership, had this time been averted, and the Labour alliance sustained. But only on the most narrow of political calculations could this interpretation be accepted. The entire episode suggested that, in key respects, Britain's social cohesion and very governability were now seriously in question. The epidemic of unofficial strikes would continue to rage. Key decisions could be taken elsewhere: withdrawal from east-of-Suez military commitments, devaluation of the pound, heavy retrenchment in public expenditure, a massive squeeze on credit. Yet internal labour relations, the key to improved productivity, a stronger trade balance, and a check to domestic inflation, remained impervious to change. The message, both amongst home electors and foreign creditors, was received and all too clearly understood.

The failure to reform industrial relations was only one, though much the most spectacular, of a series of episodes which seemed to suggest the inability of the nation to reform or update itself and its internal procedures. There seemed to be a current vogue for modernization and restructuring. But in reality there was only a series of disappointments. Relations with Wales and Scotland were left to the long-term rumination of the Crowther Commission, not due to report until the early seventies, with predictable division of viewpoints certain to follow. Another attempt at political reform came with the House of Lords which Wilson tried to restructure fundamentally in 1968. The one major reform of its composition hitherto had came with Macmillan's creation of life peerages in 1958. Hereditary peerages would now be replaced by a two-tier system of appointments, while all peers entitled to vote would be appointed by the Prime Minister. This aroused fears, not only on the Tory side but also on the Labour benches, of the unprecedented powers of patronage vested in a Prime Minister. Twenty-seven Labour MPs actually voted against the second reading on 3 February, and a powerful attack or perhaps filibuster was mounted by the unlikely partnership of the rightwinger Enoch Powell and the 'old left' spokesman, Michael Foot. There was much dislike of the measure in the Cabinet anyhow, compounded by distrust of Wilson and his immediate entourage. In due course the Chief Whip, John Silkin, had to admit to the Prime Minister that he could not guarantee a majority in the House, and on 2 April 1969 the Parliament Bill was formally withdrawn.[47] Whatever the merits of removing the ancient anachronism of the hereditary element in the Lords, it was yet another example of the government's inability to govern.

Another sphere that resisted institutional reform, at least for the moment, was local government, into which so many abortive inquiries or half-inquiries had been launched since the current framework was created in 1888. The Redcliffe-Maud report of 1969 proposed that the land be divided into eight provinces, with three 'metropolitan authorities' in Merseyside, the Birmingham area, and around Manchester and North Cheshire. This met with much resistance and in early 1970 the government announced the abandonment of the eight provinces proposed, but with the addition of two more metropolitan areas. The discussions in Cabinet, even though chaired by Anthony Crosland, were confused and ill-focused. In the event, local government remained strictly unreformed by the time Harold Wilson fell from power.[48]

Especially high hopes were entertained of the Fulton Commission on the civil service. A modernization of the administrative structure had been a major theme of the 'What's Wrong with Britain' critique of the early sixties, and one to which Wilson himself as a former Whitehall technocrat readily responded. The Fulton Committee report in 1968[49] appeared to depict much of

---

[47] Crossman, *Diaries of a Cabinet Minister*, iii, 441 (entry of 16 Apr. 1969).
[48] Ibid. 734–4 (entry of 17 Nov. 1969).
[49] *The Civil Service: Vol. 1 Report* (Cmnd. 3638) Parl. Papers, 1967–8, XVIII; see also the excellent discussion in Peter Kellner and Lord Crowther-Hunt, *The Civil Service: An Inquirp into Britain's Ruling Class* (London, 1980).

the civil service as élitist and dilettante, unduly dominated by Oxford and Cambridge graduates and attitudes, and dominated by the 'cult of the generalist'. It chimed in with demands for greater efficiency and an end to outdated class stereotypes being entrenched in the corridors of power. Fulton called for more professionalism, more scientific concern, more involvement with techniques of effective management; to this end, a Civil Service College was proposed. Fulton aroused some hopes, but in fact, the outcome was disappointing. Some of the more radical proposals, for a unified structure of classes within the service and a new Civil Service Department, were defeated by key civil servants such as Sir William Armstrong; the Chancellor, Roy Jenkins, anxious to sustain the strength of the Treasury as of yore, was concerned about other proposals. While there was reorganization and while the number of Civil Service entrants from 'provincial' universities, Wales, and Scotland did marginally increase, the main thrust was lost. The Civil Service Department lingered on through the seventies until it was finally abolished by Mrs Thatcher in 1981.

The civil service, therefore, remained largely unreformed. More fundamentally, perhaps, its sense of direction was being slowly modified, as a new uncertainty emerged. The frame of reference for the Fulton inquiries was that the processes of centralization in government should continue inexorably as they had done since 1945. In some ways, indeed, Fulton's arguments seem almost a recapitulation of the planning ethos of 1943–5 and the mood of reconstruction thereafter. A world in which the agencies of the state were losing their legitimacy, in which convention and authority were being increasingly questioned, and in which broad principles of policy, including the economics of Keynesianism and the politics of a kind of post-Fabianism, were being seen to be outdated, led to much uncertainty. Harold Wilson himself loomed perhaps unduly large as the main casualty of the time. Less conspicuously perhaps, the mandarin class, its patrician certainties slowly dissolving in the postwar world, was also to be the reluctant victim of change and national decline.

It was operating in the context of a period in which the nation, internally and externally, seemed to have lost its way. At home, the main fabric of the welfare state, with full employment, was being sustained, but at increasingly grave cost and as has been seen, the main lines of industrial and financial policy seemed hard to determine. Externally, Harold Wilson's conduct of affairs seemed to have lost its main signposts since the rejection of Britain's application to join the European Common Market at the end of 1967. Formally, Britain's application remained in being, and the pressure for membership in large areas of industry mounted, while the Conservative leader Edward Heath was an emphatic European in a way that such predecessors as Eden and Home had never been. But no progress was being made in these areas. The North Atlantic alliance, meanwhile, was being poisoned by continuing difficulty over the Americans' involvement in the war in Vietnam. The election of Nixon in place of Lyndon Johnson in the US presidential election in 1968 did not add to the closeness of the Anglo-American relationship on which Wilson had prided himself in his earlier years. Indeed, it was not until August 1969 that Nixon had a meeting with Wilson at all, and then it was a somewhat rushed affair, not in an official building in the centre of London but in the *ad hoc* surroundings of the US airforce base at Mildenhall in Suffolk.[50] Clearly no longer could Britain, declining and confused, consider itself 'first in the queue' in the NATO world as Sir Oliver Franks had confidently proclaimed at the time of the Korean War in 1950. The Foreign Secretary, Michael Stewart, was a quiet, withdrawn figure.

The most damaging aspects of the indirection of Britain's overseas role came with a series of bewildering problems concerning the old Empire. Commonwealth Prime Ministers' conferences became increasingly tense and marked by conflict. The

[50] Harold Wilson, *The Labour Government*, 866–9.

British withdrawal from east of Suez caused some tension with Singapore and Malaysia and clearly marked a public statement that the mother country could no longer sustain a military or strategic role of the first rank.[51] The naval base at Gibraltar caused long-running difficulties with Spain. Commonwealth immigration was another sore issue, especially with the limitation of black immigration under the Act of 1968 and Callaghan's decision to restrict the passport rights of Asians from Kenya and Uganda. The question of arms-sales to South Africa and trading with the Nationalist government there was another running sore. Only a major Cabinet row stopped the sale of Buccaneer aircraft there in December 1968 (which Brown, Callaghan, and other ministers favoured). In October 1969 Wilson managed to overrule Healey, his Defence Minister, over the sale of Wasp helicopters there.[52] The civil war in Nigeria between the Ibos in the eastern region of Biafra and the central government of General Gowon was an especial source of embarrassment, as full reports of the atrocities committed there, along with starvation and disease, came in. Roman Catholic elements were especially active in circulating such accounts. There was little that Britain could do directly, but its sympathy for the central Nigerian government did not add to its wider popularity on the left. The war in Nigeria dragged on until January 1970. The British government's view throughout was that it was in the interests of Africa as well as of Nigeria that the Federal Government should win against tribalism.[53] Colonel Ojukwu, the Biafran leader, fled to the Ivory Coast. In due course General Gowon was to read for a degree in politics at the no-longer rebellious Warwick University.

[51] *The Times*, 17 Jan. 1968.
[52] Crossman, *Diaries of a Cabinet Minister*, iii, 670 (entry of 9 Oct. 1969).
[53] Ibid. 779. This was also Tony Bonn's view, *Office Without Power*, 215 (entry of 27 Nov. 1969).

The worst problem of all was that of the remnants of the old Central African Federation, namely the illegal and effective declaration of independence by the Ian Smith regime in Southern Rhodesia. Economic sanctions having failed to bring the government down, and military intervention being ruled out, Wilson was forced to turn to the distasteful alternative of further negotiations with Smith. The two leaders, who had previously met on HMS *Tiger*, met on another royal-naval vessel, the *Fearless*, in August 1968. There were thirty hours of talks which, Wilson later recorded, were at least more agreeable in tone than those of the *Tiger* three years earlier.[54] Again the Prime Minister tried to insist on the 'six points' which would tend towards black African majority rule. Smith agreed to extend the B-roll franchise to a million Africans, but evasiveness over the registration provisions clearly made it a paper concession only. Talks with Smith in the autumn, held in Rhodesia by George Thomson, a British Cabinet minister, confirmed Smith's rejection of the six points, his refusal to accept external constraints on his sovereignty from Whitehall or Privy Council, and his inability to make any effective progress either in extending the African franchise on the A or the B roll, or in adding to the number of elected Africans in the legislature of Southern Rhodesia. The effect was that the problem of Rhodesia remained in limbo, with Britain under fire for imposing neither effective diplomatic or economic pressure. Like the TUC, Ian Smith, with his tiny population of resident whites, had been able to evade with impunity any pressure from the elected government of Great Britain. Wilson found himself assailed by those who complained of the failure of his diplomatic efforts and by those who said that they should never have attempted in the first place with an illegal and racist regime. British prestige duly went into further decline.

[54] Wilson, *The Labour Government*, 718.

Britain clearly no longer administered this recalcitrant portion of its old Empire. Nor, with the scrapping of the aircraft carriers and much else, did Britannia rule the waves. At home, there was a pattern of increasingly tense relapse into chaos and conflict. At the centre, the beleaguered figure of Harold Wilson symbolized the frustration and disillusion with a long-discredited system. Allies had disappeared. George Brown had resigned. Callaghan remained in a distant role after the fierce disputes over trade-union reform. Mrs Castle was glowering after defeat by the TUC. Roy Jenkins, an ardent European and on the right of the party, operated somewhere in a sphere of his own, along with other former Gaitskellites. There remained the frenetic, manic-depressive atmosphere in which Harold Wilson, his minders, and advisers operated, a world of constant plots and intrigues, with the press, the BBC, and sundry speculators as purported *dramatis personae*. In place of the measured, respected authority of Attlee, ministers and advisers found themselves engulfed in a private, masochistic world in which figures like Marcia Williams, an all-purpose secretarial aide of wide and perhaps sinister influence, and Joe Haynes, the press-relations officer, played distinct and apparently separate roles. Gerald Kaufman was accused of building up Wilson's megalomania.[55] Meanwhile, advisers who did have a genuine role and acknowledged expertise, like Solly Zuckerman, chief scientific adviser to the government, spoke openly of their frustration at the way in which decisions were taken or evaded, and the internal balance of power close to the court constantly shifted.[56]

In May 1968 there was talk of a '*putsch*' against Wilson to set up some kind of coalition government, in which Cecil King, head of the Mirror publishing group, and Lord Mountbatten, chief of the Defence Staff, were allegedly involved. In December 1968, as

[55] Benn, *Office Without Power*, 188 (entry of 23 June 1969).
[56] Zuckerman, *Men, Monkeys and Missiles*, 376 ff.

has been seen, there was talk of a further coup, with even the abdication of the Queen said to be imminent. Throughout there were rumours of coups, Northcliffe-Iike, by press lords, of possible military interventions in politics, of subversion and plotting against the government by right-wing elements in MI5 or MI6. Compared with this atmosphere of intrigue and decay, the later phase of Lloyd George's government in 1920–2, which after all really was a coalition, seemed relatively settled and successful. The British Broadcasting Corporation, now chaired by Lord Hill, a Tory peer whom Wilson himself had selected, was a particularly favoured target for fears of paranoia and conspiracy, with Wilson producing a long series of well-remembered complaints ranging from the refusal to show Mrs Wilson on television (the Tory leader, Heath, was a bachelor) to allowing personal criticisms on supposedly impartial news programmes. In December 1969, Wilson told Hill, 'The more he thought about it, the more he felt that the BBC was prejudiced against him and was failing to perform its duty as a public service.'[57] Underlying Wilson's grievances was a belief that the press was hopelessly prejudiced against him and that television, on which he had shown undoubted skill as a performer in interviews, offered him an unlimited opportunity of redressing the balance. Independent television, he felt, was more just in allowing this. As for the BBC, there was only a long catalogue of monitored and scrupulously recorded complaints.

Yet the government was showing some real signs of recovery in popular esteem in the early months of 1970. Some of the worst strains of *In Place of Strife* days had worn off. There were some apparent successes to record, notably the modernizing activities of Tony Benn, Frank Cousins's successor at the Ministry of Technology. His youthful enthusiasm for re-equipment and

---

[57] Lord Hill, *Behind the Scenes*, 146. Also see Michael Cockerell, *Live from Number Ten: Prime Ministers and Television* (London, 1988), 151–2.

adaptation to the world of the computer and the new electronics, gave a much-needed boost to a troubled government. New projects included the glamorous Anglo-French airliner 'Concorde', the high-speed train, and the planning of the Humber bridge. In Wales and Scotland, the more serious challenges posed by the nationalists seemed to be petering out. Labour's working-class strongholds no longer seemed at risk. The government had not lost its social *élan*, it seemed, either, with Richard Crossman now a vigorous Minister of Social Security intent on reforming pensions and superannuation arrangements which were little changed from where Beveridge had left them in 1942. The giant Department of Health and Social Security (1968) suggested a new organizational direction for the welfare state, with a revival of the wartime ethic of comprehensiveness, planning, and big government. There had also been extensive changes in the state educational system. Following Anthony Crosland's circular 10/65 of July 1965, local authorities in England and Wales had made rapid progress towards the creation of multilateral or 'comprehensive' secondary schools, and abolishing the hated 11-plus examination. The educationalist Robin Pedley's *The Comprehensive School* (1963) sold very widely.[58] Ironically, this was at a time when both major party leaders, Wilson and Heath, were products of the disappearing grammar schools. The private 'public' schools system from Eton and Harrow downwards only seemed to thrive as a result. These activities somewhat mitigated some other failures in government social policy such as that of the housing programme. This had led to the departure of Anthony Greenwood from the government, after defeat in July 1968 when he honourably attempted to win election to the secretaryship of the Labour Party. Wilson had pressed Greenwood to come forward,

---

[58] See Pedley's obituary in *The Independent*, 24 November 1988, written by Brian Simon.

but Brown, Callaghan, and others narrowly achieved the election of a senior TGWU official, Harry Nicholas.[59]

Above all, Roy Jenkins's policy at the Treasury was showing some real success with the balance of payments. Despite the growing failure of policies of wage restraint, by the end of 1969 Britain's balance of payments was again in the black, to the tune of £286 m., with surpluses in the trade balance for several months running.[60] The rate of economic growth continued to be slow, but at least the main public indicators, including the standing of sterling, were relatively stable in early 1970, with a general election generally felt to be close. In January, the strength of the reserves enabled Britain to pay off debts to the IMF and Bank of International Settlements ahead of schedule. Jenkins's April 1970 budget was a neutral one, designed to avoid charges of pre-election bribery, but the public seemed to approve, and the local-government elections of May 1970 showed a swing back to Labour. With Labour now ahead in the opinion polls (Callaghan having successfully delayed a reform of the boundaries until after the election) and the unions more or less tranquil, *The Economist* observed, following Labour leads in the Harris and Marplan polls, that the Conservatives now faced 'the apparent certainty of humiliating defeat' at the next election.[61] It now seemed that Wilson, bruised, humiliated, and long regarded almost with contempt, might rule for 'ever and ever'.

Thus, after carefully consulting all his colleagues and associating them firmly with the decision, Wilson called a general election for June 1970. The weather was exceptionally hot and sunny and the omens for Labour seemed set fair. Wilson was far ahead in the polls, the balance-of-payments surplus seemed likely

---

[59] National Executive Committee minutes, 24 July 1968 (Labour Party archives); private material from Lady Greenwood.
[60] *The Economist*, 13 Dec. 1969.   [61] Ibid. 16 May 1970.

to extend to £500 m., and there was much derision at the plodding efforts of Heath and the Conservative leadership. Indeed, the latter seemed to have saddled themselves with a deeply unpopular programme after the Selsdon Park Conference in January which promised, or threatened, lower personal taxation, a new law of contract for the unions, and some privatization of nationalized industry. Wilson quoted Cromwell at the battle of Dunbar: 'I thank God that this day the Lord has delivered the enemy into my hands.'[62] Yet observers noted that the campaign lacked the snap and punch of 1964 or even 1966. The *New Statesman* called it 'a safety-first election'. Ian Mikardo was a somewhat angular chairman of the party, while the NEC criticized the dull quality of the party manifesto.[63] Wilson himself seemed tired, his speeches repetitive. No longer was he the darling of the halls. There were many grumblings throughout the campaign. Pressure groups like Child Poverty Action pointed out the continuance of major pockets of poverty even after years of Labour government. There were critical comments by the CBI and the Bank of England, and an unexpected balance-of-payments deficit for May announced on 16 June, two days before polling. Heath's plodding campaign, which observers said had 'an air of incipient doom',[64] went on purposively, concentrating on rising prices and an appeal to women voters that the bachelor Conservative leader was surprisingly effective at making. On the eve of the poll, one opinion sampling showed a small swing to the Tories. In the event, there was a nation-wide swing of about 5 per cent, and opinion polls which had forecast a Labour victory of anything up to 80 found a Conservative majority instead, with 330 Conservatives, 288 Labour, 6 Liberals, and just 1 Scottish

---

[62] *The Times*, 18 June 1970.

[63] *New Statesman*, 29 May 1970; National Executive Committee minutes, 22 July 1970 (Labour Party archives).

[64] *The Times*, 18 June 1970.

Nationalist. Wilson's low-key, almost issue-less campaign had truly backfired. Most significantly, perhaps, the turn-out of voters was only just over 72 per cent, compared with 75.8 per cent in 1966 and 77.1 per cent in 1964. Labour voters in particular had voted with their feet, with Labour's vote falling by 930,000 since 1966. Indeed, the apathy and lack of enthusiasm from Labour partisans was the abiding impression of the campaign. Heath, a moderate figure who had already expelled the maverick Enoch Powell, aroused no strong feeling of alarm. In so far as he was proposing to curb the over-mighty unions, with whom Labour had dealt so ineffectively in 1969, he probably had widespread popular support. Labour went into Opposition, major figures like Richard Crossman leaving politics in the process, divided over incomes policy, Europe, devolution, and much else, brooding on the legacy of six wasted years.

In later years, the 'swinging sixties' evoked a *frisson* of levity and gaiety. Christopher Booker wrote of the 'collective fantasy' of the 'neophiliacs'.[65] In popular taste, this may have been justified. Young people became freer; taste in dress, food, and entertainment was more cosmopolitan and varied. The land shed many drab remnants of Victorianism. The BBC lost the Reith image, with programmes like 'That Was The Week That Was'. The theatre, music, film, architecture, and design were all exciting and innovative. Standards of living continued to rise.[66] Yet in most ways this was a grim period of dissolution and indiscipline. The promise of 1964 that science and reform would be brought to bear to produce a kind of planned new world, comparable

[65] Christopher Booker, *The Neophiliacs* (London, 1969), 57 ff. Booker had made his own contribution to the mood of the sixties when he was first editor of *Private Eye*. The book was dedicated to Timothy Birdsall, the *Eye*'s cartoonist, who had died young.

[66] See the excellent treatment in Trevor Noble, *Structure and Change in Modern Britain* (London, 1981), chap. 7.

perhaps to the United States of the New Deal or social-democratic Scandinavia, quite dissolved. The economy, far from being made more productive, had been largely out of control. Even the balance-of-payments success of 1969–70 was accompanied by a wage explosion that heralded further cost inflation, and an over-all decline in the growth of GNP to average barely 2 per cent a year in 1964–70. The National Plan and DEA of George Brown's dreams were on the scrap-heap of history, as were the proposed reform of land values, superannuation, and much else. Brown himself, indeed, was a casualty of the election since he lost his marginal seat at Belper. In the end, cosmetics had dominated politics in domestic and overseas affairs. Britain had curbed its overseas extravagances without any compensating growth at home. Worst of all was a loss of energy. The left had produced no analysis comparable to Crosland's *Future of Socialism*. Indeed, Crosland himself later confessed that his earlier work had been too complacent in trying to reconcile sustainable growth with the real demands of housing, health, education, and much else. He did, however, underline that public expenditure rose from 41 to 48 per cent as a percentage of the gross national product.[67]

The old intellectual ascendancy of the democratic centre-left was somewhat dented. But it was not destroyed. No other guidelines had clearly emerged. The right was still relatively muted in policy and philosophical terms, still reluctant to break with one-nation traditions. The most celebrated current exponent of 'philosophic conservatism', Michael Oakeshott, who had some-what remarkably taken over Harold Laski's old chair at the London School of Economics, specifically denied that philosophy could or should be used to promote social or political goals. The ageing Hayek remained a suspect outsider, though winning

---

[67] Anthony Crosland, *Socialism Now* (London, 1974), 17 ff.

support from financial journalists like Peter Jay. The history of the Namier school, with emphasis on structure and distrust of ideology, led to somewhat similar conclusions. The most famous historian alive, Namier's old Manchester colleague, A. J. P. Taylor, disavowed it.[68] It was 'taking the mind out of history', in the view of some critics. Meanwhile the centrist analysis of Jo Grimond and others, lively and analytical, with apostles like George Watson and the 'Unservile State' group did not command wide attention because of their political powerlessness. As has been noted, the student rebellion and other vanguards of 'permissiveness' were relatively uncreative in terms of ideas, as opposed to experiences.

Signs of progress in the sixties would, perhaps, be measured in other terms. Paul Johnson, bidding farewell as editor of the *New Statesman* in 1970, wrote perhaps elegiacally, since his journal was on the point of losing its old charisma under Crossman's editorship, while he himself was on the point of moving rapidly to the free- enterprise right. He took reassurance from the fact that Britain, though no longer a great power or an imperial presence, had become more civilized in its internal arrangements. 'We no longer terrorise homosexuals. We do not force mothers to bring unwanted children into the world. We have made it easier to end wrecked marriages. We have begun the true liberation of women. Children by and large get a better deal.... We do not murder by the rope.'[69] Most of these achievements, however, were achieved by a minority of middle-class reformers in defiance of the mass of public opinion. They were also somewhat negative, dissolving old Victorian standards of puritanical rectitude, without necessarily replacing them with anything equally durable. All these achievements, in any case, depended on Britain

---

[68] On this, see A. J. P. Taylor, *A Personal History* (London, 1983), especially 111–14.
[69] *New Statesman*, 26 June 1970.

continuing to remain economically viable and socially at peace with itself. After six years of the Wilson government, and a full decade of public criticism, disillusion, and cynicism, these desirable objectives seemed to have receded that much further from view.

9. *The Heath Experiment*
1970–1974

———

LATER commentators have not been kind to the government of Edward Heath between June 1970 and March 1974. Its very emergence was something of a surprise, with the polls confidently predicting a comfortable Labour victory for Harold Wilson until the very eve of the election. The government's course was marked by an increasingly intractable series of deadlock and disputes, over industrial relations, Northern Ireland, and finally the handling of the economy. The end of the administration was traumatic. The price explosion following the Arab–Israeli war of October 1973 and the oil blockade, led to the head-on confrontation with the National Union of Mineworkers and a lengthy national coal strike in February 1974 that was still unresolved when the government fell from office. Lastly, the fall of the Heath administration was confused, even undignified, with a desperate attempt at negotiation with the Liberals and their leader Jeremy Thorpe to keep a minority government in being since Labour, though the largest party, had failed to win an absolute majority. Heath seemed to be engaged in a sulky attempt to frustrate the verdict of the voters with covert diplomacy of the 'smoke-filled room' type. There was one major achievement of this government, claimed to be of supreme benefit and certainly of historic import, namely the taking of Britain into the European Economic Community on 1 January 1973. But even this excited little approval at the time. The distant bureaucracy of Brussels and the alien traditions of continental governments made the mood towards entry into 'Europe', as it was commonly termed, one coloured by fateful resignation rather than passionate enthusiasm.

After its downfall, the Heath government found few defenders. Naturally, the Labour Party spent much effort in pouring derision on a government which had presided over a record series of strikes, which had called more states of emergency than any other government in British history, and which had engaged in the first nationwide confrontation with the miners since 1926. But discontented Conservatives were even more venomous, especially after the success of Mrs Thatcher's 'coup' in defeating Heath as Conservative leader in 1975. She found herself obliged in the first instance to take a wide array of former Heath ministers into her administration, men like Lord Carrington, James Prior, William Whitelaw, Francis Pym, and Peter Walker who were of a very different stripe from herself. But her commitment to monetarism, privatization, rolling back the frontiers of the state, and undoing the collectivist work of the years since 1945 made her deeply hostile to the Heath government. After all, between 1970 and 1974, public spending reached new heights; even on areas like the NHS and education (ironically enough, Mrs Thatcher's domain), the Heath administration proved to be bigger spenders than the Labour government of the six preceding years. Control of the money supply was virtually ignored as M3 (a broad concept including bank notes, coins, and deposits) increased by 20 per cent in 1971–2, and inflation soared during the Barber boom. Rising personal incomes led to higher spending on cars and other foreign imports. Further, the Heath government, supposedly elected to undo the socialist works of the discredited Wilson administration, took collectivism much further, including more nationalization and extending the comprehensive schools. Its abolition of the old county councils under Peter Walker's aegis, and the creation of larger councils along with metropolitan and other super units infuriated a wide array of local Tory opinion, from opponents of the big socialism of large urban authorities to patriotic defenders of the historic autonomy of the Isle of Wight, Rutland, and the Soke of

Peterborough. With Heath himself a consistent and embittered critic of virtually every line of Thatcher policy after 1979, the Tory leadership in the 1980s used the Heath administration of the previous decade, even more than the Wilson governments of that period, as the yardstick of everything to avoid, as a period of mindless corporatism which had merely gone with the tide of statism and bureaucracy as understood after the Second World War.

In part, this later unpopularity must be related to the personality and style of Edward Heath himself.[1] He was an immensely hardworking man, a fierce critic of inefficient practices in government. Such initiatives as the overhaul of government agencies and the institution of a Programme Analysis and Review bore his technocratic stamp. He started the so-called 'Think Tank', the Central Policy Review Staff, under Lord Rothschild, in 1971. The frequently abused term 'managerial style' seems highly appropriate in this case. On a wide range of issues he proved to be a liberal, humane man; indeed, after 1979 he seemed much closer in ethos to the Alliance or even the Labour opposition. On race relations, corporal and capital punishment, policies towards South Africa, he fought courageously against the right wing of his own party. He had been firm in expelling Enoch Powell from the Shadow Cabinet after the 'rivers of blood' speech in 1968. He may reasonably be included within the old 'one-nation' tradition of Eden, Macmillan, and Butler of a somewhat earlier generation. He was also a highly cultured man artistically, with a deep love for, and genuine knowledge of, music. He delighted in conducting carol services and other choral events. On business matters, perhaps his most memorable *aperçu* was when he denounced the operations of 'Tiny' Rowland and the Lonrho group as the 'unacceptable face of capitalism'. For all that, and despite the genuine loyalty he inspired from Douglas Hurd and

---

[1] John Campbell's biography, *Edward Heath* (London, 1993). is the major source. There is valuable material in Douglas Hurd. *An End to Promises*, and, with reservations, in Andrew Roth, *Heath and the Heathmen* (London, 1972).

others who worked with him in 1970–4,[2] Heath, a bachelor, proved to be a lonely and isolated figure. Although he had been a highly successful Chief Whip, including during the Suez crisis, he proved to be a maladroit parliamentary leader, distant from the parliamentary party and presuming on his hold over the grass-roots—vainly so, as the Thatcher *putsch* of 1975 was to show. Heath's was an executive style that lacked personal warmth. His background—his time in the army, his experience of civil-service life, his years of being closeted away in the Whips' Office—had removed him from many of the natural channels of political communication. He was not a tea-room man, let alone a patron of 'Annie's Bar'. At the Ministry of Labour and the Board of Trade in 1960–4, his experience both of industrial and regional policy had entrenched him in a view sympathetic to corporate negotiations with business and union leaders rather than working through the grass-roots. Many MPs found him cold and unclubbable.

On some key issues he could be alarmingly distant from major elements in the party. Thus, in the abolition of resale price maintenance in 1964 he appeared to ride roughshod over traditional Tory sympathy for the 'little man', especially the grocer or family butcher in that revered image of village or folk life, transmitted in a thousand radio and television serials, 'the corner shop'. On Europe, while many Tories came to agree with his highly rational diagnosis of the case for membership, Heath's lack of concern for Commonwealth sentiment—a product of his distinctive background and involvement with European affairs since an Oxford undergraduate at the time of Munich—proved to be a handicap in promoting the cause. As Prime Minister he had few intimates. At first this seemed a positive advantage, since Heath, like Bonar Law in 1922 after the downfall of Lloyd George amidst the furore over the 'honours scandal', came in with clean hands. There was no paranoia over the press and no

[2] See Hurd, op. cit.

sinister kitchen Cabinet of aides and henchmen which had marked the later period of Harold Wilson's regime. But in time Heath's very isolation made for incommunicability and remoteness. Even his favourite outdoor hobby, ocean-going sailing, emphasized his wish to 'get away'. It lacked the folksy familiarity, say, of Lord Home's love of cricket or Harold Wilson's devotion to football analogies and the glorious history of Huddersfield Town. When the fall of Heath came in 1974, the supposed loyalty of the 'Heathmen' melted away. The fallen premier was to become a political Ishmael, treated with the same brutality as Balfour or Neville Chamberlain, other rejected party leaders in the past.

Heath's administration looked a somewhat frail one from the outset. It lacked the grandees of the past, men like Macmillan or Eden. It manifestly represented a new generation of Tories, men who had emerged in Macmillan's last, difficult period of 1961–3. A crushing blow came within a month when Iain Macleod, a formidable figure from the 1950s, Chancellor of the Exchequer and manifestly a 'man of government' as few of the leading ministers were, suddenly died, leaving a huge gap in the Cabinet. He was followed at the Treasury by Anthony Barber, who struggled for long to make an impression. Heath's main innovation was the appointment of John Davies, head of the Confederation of British Industries, as Minister of Technology. He proved to be a maladroit performer in the Commons, not least with tactless remarks about the need not to subsidize 'lame ducks' in industry. Davies was no more effective a politician than Labour's Minister of Technology, Frank Cousins of the Transport Workers, had been in the previous decade; in the end, his career perished sadly in ill health and he died young. The other major minister, Reginald Maudling, now Home Secretary, soon found himself fatally deflected into the labyrinthine affairs of Northern Ireland, and clouded by financial scandal. In the face of a highly formidable and articulate Labour front bench including Wilson, Jenkins, Crosland, Foot, Healey, Callaghan, Mrs Castle, and other major political operators, the government for long stretches seemed to lack conviction and not to be wholly in charge of events. Heath himself worked frenetically to plug the gaps in all directions, and indeed ministers like Prior and Walker emerged as effective departmental heads. But by the end of 1970 there was already talk that the Tories' traditional reputation for ministerial competence seemed to be sadly eroding.

The government's policies also showed an alarming shift of emphasis. Heath had been elected to promote a strictly anti-collectivist, 'hands-off' policy. Labour's Industrial Reorganiza-tion Corporation was abolished, and a policy begun of phasing down the subsidies of, and intervention in, failing or bankrupt industries. Regional policy also seemed distinctly less interven-tionist. Indeed, Heath had come to power with a prospectus of free enterprise of almost a doctrinaire character, with a pro-gramme that contained a degree of precision unusual for any opposition and almost unique for a Conservative opposition. The manifesto on which Heath had won the election had been specific and extremely lengthy.[3] Although not in any way a monetarist policy as that was understood in the 1980s, the Heath approach seemed to be strictly non-interventionist, and geared to the spirit of competition. When a dock strike broke out shortly after the government took office, the Minister of Labour, Robert Carr, caused something of a sensation by refusing to intervene with the Ministry's usual conciliation role. He stood back to allow the dockers and dock employers to fight it out amongst themselves. The logic was, of course, that repeated interventions by the Ministry, both in the Tory years of 1951–64 and the Labour period of 1964–70 had invariably resulted in surrender to trade-union muscle and acceptance of an excessively inflationary award.

Barber, Macleod's successor at the Treasury, seemed for long a model of free-enterprise innovation. He abolished such collectiv-ist structures as the Prices and Incomes Board and the

---

[3] David Butler and Michael Pinto-Duschinsky, *The British General Election of 1970* (London, 1971), 148–51, for its reception.

Land Commission, and instituted cuts in public expenditure to the tune of £330 m. in 1971–2. His first budget in April 1971 contained large cuts in taxation, including a reduction in the standard rate of income tax by 6d. in the pound.[4] Other Barber measures included cuts in the subsidies to council-house rents and in expenditure on school milk. Much of the odium here fell on the woman Minister of Education, Margaret Thatcher, who dealt robustly with the Labour-led uproar that followed. To Labour and other opponents, the Heath government was bent on a doctrinaire course that would undermine the welfare state, the mixed economy, full employment, and all the hallowed social achievements since 1945. The roots of this transformation were located in the Selsdon Park Conference back in January 1970 which committed the Conservatives to a vigorously anti-collect-ivist, right-wing programme. Selsdon Man, declared Harold Wilson, was ruling the roost and dividing the nation.

In fact, by mid-1971, Selsdon Man had been decently interred and the government's policy went into rapid reverse. This was largely because it was being accompanied by, or perhaps was causing, some alarming portents. Inflation and unemployment rose sharply at one and the same time. A new concept, 'stagfla-tion', was born. By the end of 1970, wage inflation stood at 14 per cent higher than a year previously while industrial produc-tion had hardly risen at all.[5] Consumer prices were rising fast and a hands-off approach in wages and prices policy seemed to be quite inadequate. By the time of Barber's budget in April 1971, it was hard to detect the anti-inflation side of the government's policy at all, with an annual rate of inflation in manual workers' wages of nearly 15 per cent, and a series of alarming surrenders to trade-union power in the docks and the motor industry. The more powerful unions seemed able to dictate the pattern of wage increases through industrial action; by contrast, a less powerful industrial group such as the postmen had to return to work after

---

[4] *The Economist*, 3 Apr. 1971.   [5] Ibid. 28 November 1970.

a lengthy strike in March 1971 almost empty-handed. But the general pressure on wage increases and price levels, fuelled by Barber's tax cuts and encouragement of a spending spree, meant that the government's policy of disengagement in wage policy was no longer sustainable.

Nor was the policy of non-intervention in industry. Indeed, the Heath government, committed as it was to rolling back state control, actually found itself forced to extend that control in the face of rapidly rising unemployment. Prognostications of steady growth in the economy were simply not being fulfilled. As a result, in a startling reversal, the government found itself forced to nationalize Rolls-Royce in 1971. So prestigious a firm, renowned throughout the world and a significant manufacturer of aero-engines, simply could not be allowed to go under for doctrinaire reasons. Its contract to build the Lockheed Tri-star RB 211 engine which brought in a major transatlantic connection was another important factor. John Davies, therefore, found himself miserably nourishing the very lame ducks he had witheringly scorned. When another major firm, Upper Clyde Shipbuilders, also threatened to go under, with the loss of 4,000 jobs, there was another crisis. A 'work-in' by the labour force began, led by two charismatic Communist shop-stewards, Jimmy Reid and Jimmy Airlie. The Chief Constable of Glasgow warned against possible violence if the yards were closed. In the event a large subsidy of £35 m. was granted to the yard, and to the glee of its Scottish and other critics, the government had engaged in another humiliating surrender.[6]

Indeed, the government now went from the extreme of non-intervention to new heights of corporatism. Perhaps this was a strategy more in tune with Heath's personal outlook and style. With the economy in deep recession, unemployment rising fast, and much disarray and discontent in Tory Party ranks, a new

---

[6] A helpful work on this theme is Gerald A. Dorfman, *Government versus Trade Unionism in British Politics since 1968* (London, 1979). For the Upper Clyde Shipyards, see Trade Union Congress Annual Report, 1971, 500–6.

kind of approach was proposed. This took the form of corporate management of demand and consumption, with new structures created in conjunction with the TUC and CBI, and the Treasury apparently losing its historic role as guardian of the public purse. The financial policy of the government now changed tack radically to allow much more relaxation in credit and monetary policy, and much larger increases in public expenditure. The government was also prepared to sacrifice the exchange rate, with fixed parities being abandoned in June 1972 and the pound being allowed to float. However, since this was not accompanied by attempts to monitor public expenditure or give any particular stimulus to exports to take advantage of the pound's reduced value, the effect was only to stoke up cost-push factors at first and to add to the inflationary pressures. As a result, the government took its Keynesian, almost neo-socialist policy of intervention to new heights. little was discernible of the ashes of Selsdon Man.

The area in which the reverse of strategy was most visible, and which impinged most directly and frequently on the general public, was industrial-relations policy. As has been seen, the initial assumption was for a policy of relative withdrawal and a less interventionist approach by the Ministry of Labour and the government in general. This, however, proved impossible to sustain as the soaring wage inflation approached 20 per cent by the end of 1971. Robert Carr got through an Industrial Relations Bill in 1971, designed to curb unofficial strikes. It followed the logic of Barbara Castle's *In Place of Strife* by setting up both an Industrial Relations Commission and a National Industrial Relations Court which would have penal sanctions to order a pre-strike ballot and also enforce a cooling-off period of up to sixty days in industries where there would be critical damage to the economy or the community.[7] This was intended as a major answer to the problem of moderating wage demands. But it

---

[7] *The Economist*, 5, 12 Dec. 1970. For a helpful summary, see E. H. Phelps Brown, *The Origins of Trade Union Power*, 179–81.

proved to be almost wholly ineffective, not least because of the difficulty of getting trade unions to register under the Act. The TUC threatened the expulsion of any union that complied with the Act's registration procedures; major problems of law enforcement now arose. Faced with the prospect of enforcing its edicts by sending shop stewards or ordinary union members to prison, the government proved hesitant, the more so as Lord Denning in the High Court proceeded to reverse two major decisions by the Industrial Relations Court. The Industrial Relations Act was invoked during a strike by the National Union of Railwaymen in May 1972, but was then frustrated since the union membership voted, by a 6 to 1 majority, to authorize the union to continue the dispute.[8] In the case of an unofficial dispute in the docks, some union members, the so-called 'Pentonville Five', were briefly imprisoned after the Chobham Farm Terminal affair. They had to be released in the face of continuing industrial action by militants in London, Liverpool, and Hull. A hitherto obscure public servant, the Official Solicitor, intervened to save the government's face. He applied successfully to the Industrial Court for the 'Five' to be released since it was against their union that action should be taken, and not five individuals. One notable feature of these events was that the employers in the CBI were almost as emphatic in condemning the government's approach to industrial relations, especially the threat of legal sanctions, as was the TUC. Indeed, the two sides of industry were probably closer to each other than either was to the government of the day. The decline in the authority and legitimacy of the central organs of government, so visible in the Wilson years, was being re-enacted now. In effect, the government decided to suspend further operation of its Industrial Relations Act and to cut its losses.

The most severe defeat that the government experienced came in a different industry, however, one with the greatest historic and emotional impact on the public consciousness. There had not

[8] *The Economist*, 3, 10, 24 June 1972.

been a nation-wide miners' strike since 1926 at the time of the
General Strike against the Baldwin government. Now, however, a
combination of the government's attempts at wage curbs in the
autumn of 1971, the emergence of new left-wing personalities on
the NUM executive such as the Vice-President Mick McGahey, a
Communist, and the secretary, Lawrence Daly, and a genuine
feeling on the part of the miners that their wages had lagged
disastrously behind other industrial workers in recent years, led
to a dramatic new departure.[9] Another factor, perhaps, was the
presence of a relatively new Coal Board chairman, Derek Ezra,
who lacked the authority and political experience of his predecessor, the former Labour minister, Lord Robens. There was also
an untried conciliation team at the Ministry of Labour, in place of
Conrad Heron and Andrew Kerr who had now moved to the
Commission on Industrial Relations and to Scotland respectively. An NCB offer of an 8 per cent increase was rejected by
the NUM executive. Joe Gormley, the miners' right-wing President, believed that the gap between the two sides was so narrow
that a strike was unnecessary, but that constant pressure by
Heath and Robert Carr upon the National Coal Board and
Ezra personally made a negotiated agreement impossible.[10] On
9 January 1972 a national coal strike began. Consequent severe
winter weather meant that it very rapidly had an impact. Homes
were plunged into darkness, and the government had to introduce a three-day week.

One factor that was very evident—and much in the Thatcher
government's mind in the later miners' strike of 1984–5—was
that the miners, remarkably, proved to be better organized and
more mobile and adaptable than either the police or the government. With every area of the nation's coal-fields solid in support
of what was felt to be a just wage claim, mass picketing was
easily arranged. The death of a miner, knocked down and killed

[9] See Tony Hall, *King Coal* (Harmondsworth, 1981), 166–96 and Andrew Taylor, *The Politics of the Yorkshire Miners* (London, 1984).
[10] Joe Gormley, *Battered Cherub* (London, 1982), 85 ff.

by a lorry driven by a nonunionist while picketing at Keadby power station near Scunthorpe, inflamed the strike further. A notable—many felt an alarming—novelty was the development of 'flying pickets' used with much success by the youthful Yorkshire Miners' official, Arthur Scargill, in denying the access of coal supplies from the Saltley coke depots in the Midlands. Here up to 15,000 massed pickets formed an impassable human barrier. The movement of coal across the country was effectively stopped. This was vital to the miners' calculations since there were 19 m. tons held by private and public consumers and a further 9 m. tons by the National Coal Board. The denial of coal supplies to power stations was a particularly important part of what came to be an increasingly ugly confrontation between a still-important industrial union and the elected government of the day and their appointed custodians of order, a conflict in which the latter lost most of the battles. Public relations were also handled with much skill by the NUM, and the calm and measured tones of Gormley and (especially) Lawrence Daly made a notable impression. In any case, the British public could be persuaded to feel guilty about the human cost of coal, whereas engineers and electricians had no such emotional appeal.

After three weeks, it was clear that the government desperately needed to take a new initiative. By now there was a three-day week in force, with huge cuts in coal available for domestic use, as well as a state of emergency with the possible use of troops. Fourteen power stations had closed down, with another seventeen having only a few days' supplies of coal. The initiative had passed to the miners long since. On 11 February, therefore, after the strike had been in progress for a month, the government decided to appoint a Committee of Inquiry under the chairmanship of a high court judge, Lord Wilberforce. He was already known for having awarded a 20 per cent increase to power workers a year before. In the two days that it conducted its rushed meetings, the miners' argument that they were 'a special case' who had fallen behind their traditional high place in the 'wages queue' made a considerable impact. It was assisted by the expertise of Professor Hugh Clegg of Warwick University, called in by the executive to present the miners' case.[11] As a result of this (and no doubt under moral and political pressure to settle a damaging strike very soon) the Wilberforce inquiry recommended, a few days later, a large pay increase of £5 a week for surface workers and £6 for underground workers. Wilberforce justified these on the basis of a singularly nebulous 'adjustment factor'.[12] The miners, however, were now in bullish mood, even a moderate like Joe Gormley being incensed by what he felt were extraneous pressures brought to bear on his talks with the NCB and also aware that the striking miners had not received any strike pay during the past five weeks. The NUM executive thus threw out even these highly favourable terms by 23 votes to 2.

With the Coal Board, and indeed the government, now desperate for a settlement, Gormley and his fellow negotiators applied tough tactics to win a series of other major concessions, notably increases in holidays and getting the unpopular Saturday 'bonus' shift incorporated, for pay purposes, into normal shift rates. Even then, some left-wing NUM executive members wanted more, but Gormley was able to win an 18 to 7 majority in favour of accepting terms which, by any definition, represented an extraordinary victory for the mineworkers. Black Friday and the General Strike had finally been avenged. In all, £116–117 m. had been added to the bill for coal—£85 m. for the basic Wilberforce award, plus a further £13.3 m. on overtime concessions, plus £6m. for holidays, £5–6 m. for further incidental rises, £4.5 m. in improved pensions arrangements, and £3 m. in improvements for wages for teenagers. The average miner's earnings, it has been calculated, would rise by 17 to 24 per cent, and the miners would rise dramatically to a high place in the table of wages for industrial workers.[13] On 21 February the

[11] Ibid. 109.   [12] *The Economist*, 19 Feb. 1972.
[13] *The Economist*, 26 Feb. 1972; *Financial Times*, 19–22 Feb. 1972; *The Times*, 19–22 Feb. 1972.

strike was called off, after six weeks. *The Economist* had blithely
commented earlier that 'the miners cannot stop the country in its
tracks as they once could have done'.[14] To most of the general
public this insouciant judgement flew in the face of the industrial
crisis of those winter months.

The miners' strike made a considerable impact upon the public
culture. It gravely weakened what was left of the post-war social
consensus. It made the Heath government seem weak and ineffective at a crucial time in its fortunes. It cast the gravest doubt
on the efficacy of the government's anti-strike procedures, especially in the case of a group of workers like the miners whose
work obviously could not be performed by troops or any other
auxiliary agency of strike-breakers. The police sensed their impotence in the face of military-style mass picketing, especially the
new phenomenon of organized 'flying pickets'. They began to
contemplate new strategies of countering picketing on so massive
a scale, activity which still remained nominally within the law
even if potentially alarming, since no adequate definition of the
nature or scale of picketing had been devised from 1906
onwards.[15] Conversely, for the trade-union movement, and especially for the miners, the strike of 1972 was a powerful impetus
towards militant direct action. It encouraged those within the
Labour Party, such as the newly radicalized Tony Benn, to lend
support to potentially violent measures of extra-parliamentary
action, even if Trotskyists and groups of outsiders, students, and
others were brought into a dispute that did not concern them at all.
In the NUM, it gave the left, and especially the forceful Yorkshire
Marxist Arthur Scargill, a new charisma. In particular, the 'battle
at Saltley Gates', the picketing which had prevented coke supplies
leaving the coke depot, came to acquire an almost legendary significance in the mythology of the coalfields, comparable with

---

[14] *The Economist*, 8 Jan. 1972.

[15] On this, see Jane Morgan, *Conflict and Order: The Police and Labour
Disputes in England and Wales, 1900–1939* (Oxford. 1987), chap. 6; Roger
Geary, *Policing Industrial Disputes, 1893 to 1985* (Cambridge, 1985), 73–7.

Tonypandy or Black Friday in the remoter past. For Arthur Scargill himself the Saltley episode became 'a magic moment' to treasure and emulate in strikes and disputes to come. He suddenly became, in his mid-thirties, a national figure. 'Saltley was the making of Arthur', recalled another Yorkshireman, George Wilkinson. 'I told him "You've got to be at the forefront, lad" and he went in where angels fear to tread.'[16] With his new celebrity, Scargill was easily elected President of the Yorkshire miners in succession to Sam Bullough in 1973. He thus led the largest group of working miners in Britain. The NUM executive as a whole swung markedly to the left.

With the miners changing their stance in this fashion, pressures built up in the TUC as a whole for similar militancy, with the engine-drivers' union, ASLEF, under a left-wing secretary Ray Buckton, likely to be the next to try its strength. In the nation as a whole, the sympathy that the miners received was a notable feature. The impact of the miners' case for a higher basic wage and an improved status in society generally was remarkably powerful. On television, in particular, the NUM's case shone in comparison with the relatively weak presentation by the Coal Board, while for the government neither Heath nor Carr was impressive as a communicator. It all added up to an episode which went far beyond public relations, and which questioned the very validity of the structure of central government. At a time when university students seemed again to be settling down to their studies after the aberrant 'revolts' of the sixties, and left-wing political protests were subsiding in the aftermath of President Nixon's decision to terminate US involvement in the war in Vietnam, this new impulse of direct industrial action within the trade-union world was a much more alarming phenomenon.

The Heath government, its credentials severely battered by the miners' strike and the manifest unworkability of its Industrial Relations Act, now turned, as in its industrial policy, to greater

[16] Michael Crick. *Scargill and the Miners* (Harmondsworth, 1985). 62.

interventionism. This meant another reversal of its approach, and a direct approach to the TUC and the CBI to try to work out a collective corporate strategy. Lengthy discussions were held with the TUC at the National Economic Development Council with the object of achieving some kind of voluntary policy of restraint on pay, with inflation in prices also central to the discussion. The government proposed a general flat-rate £2 a week pay increase for everyone; the unions presented alternative proposals. There was never much prospect of such talks reaching agreement, or indeed of Vic Feather and the TUC General Council having it accepted by individual unions if it were. The Heath government well recalled the ineffectiveness of the TUC's 'declaration of intent' during the early period of George Brown's National Plan in 1964, and the near-farce of the 'solemn and binding' commitment which had fudged the issue and prevented the Wilson government collapsing over the *In Place of Strife* proposals back in 1969. Heath wanted something much firmer; the unions, buoyed up by recent industrial successes, were in no mood to offer it. In early November 1972 it was announced, predictably, that the talks had broken down and that the government would now turn to a formal, statutory prices-and-incomes policy, much on the lines of that rejected under Barbara Castle's aegis in 1969.[17]

But the two most formidable of the union leaders, Jack Jones of the Transport Workers and Hugh Scanlon of the Engineers, both made it clear that they were unprepared to have formal wage controls, even though the rigid statutory control of retail prices was apparently acceptable to them. At the end of the year, the first stage of a three-tier Prices and Incomes Bill was passed, which meant a six-month standstill in wage increases. In the early months of 1973 phase II went through, which continued the wages freeze, and set up a new Pay Board. This was equally unpopular with the unions. It encouraged the Labour leader,

[17] *The Economist*, 4 Nov. 1972.

Harold Wilson, to sign a so-called 'social contract' with the TUC, which pledged that a future Labour government would never again introduce another statutory wages policy on the lines of that suggested in 1969.[18] Much trouble was forecast about the operation of phase II of the wages policy. In fact, the contrived 'Barber boom' introduced by the Chancellor, though highly inflationary, also meant substantial pay increases for the unions along with a fall in unemployment. The unions, therefore, found it hard to sustain the momentum to challenge a policy already so favourable to them.

Phase III of the prices-and-incomes policy emerged in the autumn of 1973. It meant a continuation of a pay standstill with an individual maximum increase in wages or salaries of £350 a year. Again it was loudly condemned by the unions. This time it seemed likely to produce much more difficulty. It was promptly challenged directly by the miners, who now called for large minimum wage increases of between £8 and £13 a week. Ironically, the government's phase III had been carefully devised to try to avoid the kind of damaging confrontation with the miners that had taken place in 1972. But, partly because of the big swing to the left on the miners' executive which saw men like McGahey and Scargill rising to prominence, partly because Heath placed excessive faith in the authority of the right-wing president Joe Gormley, the attempt to conciliate failed totally. At the end of 1973, another clash with the miners was looming. Gormley told Heath that things were going to be 'bloody difficult'. He added that 'the lads' chests were a mile wide and they thought they were the kings of the castle'.[19] In the light of this intelligence, Heath could only contemplate gloomily the imminent collapse of his approach to getting a statutory policy. But, as will be seen, by then a variety of other, appalling challenges were combining to erode the authority and will of his government anyway.

---

[18] Ibid. 3 Mar. 1973.   [19] Hall, *King Coal*, 201.

The Heath government devoted enormous time and much ingenuity to trying to find a way through the eternal thickets of industrial relations, conscious of rising inflation and flat records of production and productivity. Douglas Hurd later recalled that pay policy, and public sector wages in particular, occupied more time of the Cabinet than any other problem it faced.[20] Nevertheless, this vigorous (and in many ways innovative) policy proved to be a massive failure. In part this was because of growing pressures within an apparently irresistibly powerful trade-union movement for a more aggressive and militant approach. One group of major public unions after another, the power-workers, the electricians, the dockers, most crucially the miners, had taken on the government of the day and largely won the battle. Men like Jack Jones and Scanlon seemed to count for far more in terms of sheer power and muscle than the elected authorities. But, apart from this, the Heath government's policy simply lacked credibility. There were no effective instruments, administrative or even legal, to monitor thousands of wage negotiations and disputes, and none to give them effect. The one plausible alternative, a rigorous recourse to statute to regulate trade-union behaviour and try to impose some kind of order in wage negotiation was simply not tried. The Heath government was attempting to create a corporate industrial strategy in a situation in which there was no cohesion between the government, the CBI, and the TUC, the three elements of the putative strategy. Nor was there any authority by which the latter two could control or even persuade their members. However, neither was a policy of cash limits contemplated to try to curb pay settlements in the public sector; indeed, in the aftermath of the Plowden Committee's report on public expenditure the pressure was still towards expansion. The outcome was a series of postures, strong on rhetoric, weak on delivery, which weakened not only the industrial-relations policy but the authority of the government itself at the base.

[20] Hurd, *An End to Promises*, 95.

The government seemed in all these areas to be falling into disarray, even though there was as yet no compensating recovery from the Labour Party to replace it. The government's prestige was further depressed by a calamitous series of events in another, equally intractable, problem over the decades (and indeed the centuries) namely the problem of Northern Ireland.[21] A tense and difficult situation had been inherited, with growing sectarian clashes between Protestants and Catholics in Ulster, and an alarming tendency for bombing and other attacks to manifest themselves in the mainland as well. The Home Secretary, Reginald Maudling, a genial, easygoing man well-liked in the House and perhaps too casual in his contacts with the business world, tried to respond with a tough approach, designed to curb the excesses of the IRA. In August 1971, he introduced the policy of internment without trial, designed to separate 'the men of violence' from the peaceful majority of the Catholic population. In this, he repeated the errors of repeated British governments from that of Gladstone in 1880–5, since he alienated the Catholic population *en masse* without adding to the effectiveness of the security procedures. Such a policy ended any prospect of bipartisanship between the two communities in Northern Ireland and worsened relations between Westminster and the Dublin government of Jack Lynch, which was highly sympathetic to the Catholic cause in the north.[22] It also undermined agreement between the government and opposition front benches in the Commons since Labour declared itself strongly opposed to the internment policy. Even moderate men like Michael Stewart called for the British troops to be withdrawn from Ulster and a policy of a united Ireland to be openly aimed at. Despite the progress made in civil rights, indeed, the IRA was increasingly active in violent

[21] For events in Northern Ireland after 1970, helpful works include: Arthur and Jeffery, *Northern Ireland since 1968*; O'Malley, *The Uncivil Wars*: Kevin J. Kelley, *The Longest War: Northern Ireland and the IRA* (Westport, Conn., 1988 edn.). James Callaghan's *A House Divided* contains some critical comments on Maudling's policy; the latter's memoirs are not very informative.

[22] O'Malley, *The Uncivil Wars*, 208 n.

acts in the north, finding its parallel in the rise of a series of paramilitary organizations operating under the umbrella of the extremist Protestant Vanguard organization. In August 1971, following repeated clashes between the British troops and the Catholic population, Ulster yet again seemed to be ablaze.

The key episode which confirmed the disastrous course that Northern Ireland was now taking occurred on 'Bloody Sunday', 30 January 1972, in the Catholic Bogside area of Londonderry.[23] This was a largely Catholic city which had been under local Protestant rule, effectively, since the reign of William III in the 1690s, and where the 'Apprentice Boys' were a Protestant organization that had a violently inflammatory effect on Catholic opinion. A civil rights march in Londonderry, which had been officially prohibited, led to clashes with troops of the Parachute Regiment. As a result, thirteen Catholic civilians lay dead, and many others were wounded. A tribunal of inquiry under Lord Widgery gave a somewhat guarded exculpation of the troops but also contained some material sympathetic to Catholic ears. Relations between London and Dublin now deteriorated alarmingly, and tensions rapidly rose in the north as well. Ulster politics, always Byzantine, now became increasingly multi-faceted. In addition to splits in the Catholic ranks between the Provisional IRA and the constitutional followers of the Social Democratic Labour Party and its leaders Gerry Fitt and John Hume, there was now a pattern of disintegration amongst the Unionist majority. The Official Unionists who endorsed the cautious, reformist policy of the Northern Ireland premier, Brian Faulkner, faced a breakaway group of more zealous Protestants, the Democratic Unionists. Their loudest voice was the vehemently anti-Papist minister, the Revd Ian Paisley, a fundamentalist demagogue of much populist appeal in Belfast. In addition a small breakaway movement of moderate Unionists led to the formation of the non-sectarian Alliance Party, seeking for the middle ground of

[23] *The Times*, 31 Jan. 1972.

community co-operation—which proved, as in the past, to be a wholly mythical terrain. With Ulster seeming ungovernable, in March 1972 Heath took the brave step of suspending (in effect abolishing) the Northern Ireland government at Stormont altogether. He thus reversed the policy of Lloyd George in the 1920–2 period which had at least brought peace of a kind to Ireland from the 1920s to the late 1960s. In place of Stormont and its parochial politicians there was to be direct rule from Westminster, with William Whitelaw, a singularly emollient man, to serve as Secretary for Northern Ireland.

From that time on, the position in Northern Ireland became increasingly tense and polarized. The imposition of direct rule from Westminster, even under as genial a minister as Whitelaw, had the effect only of emphasizing the alien nature of the government of the north. The British troops or 'security forces', hated by most of the Catholics, came under verbal (and sometimes literal) fire from Protestant zealots as well for being too mild. The Provisional IRA continued to escalate its campaign of violence, with random attacks on civilians in Belfast and other towns and cities in Ulster reinforcing a sense of tension and ungovernability. New elections were held for the new Assembly in Northern Ireland in July 1973, but the outcome was only to confirm the broad division of Ulster as it had endured over the decades, with an entrenched Protestant majority, and the minority Catholic SDLP refusing to participate in the Assembly's affairs. In Dublin, the British embassy was burnt down. Finally, buoyed up by the good fortune of the election of a Fine Gael-Labour coalition government in Dublin, less hostile to Britain than the Fianna Fáil of Jack Lynch, Whitelaw negotiated the power-sharing agreement at Sunningdale in December 1973.[24] Under this, both Brian Faulkner of the Official Unionists and Gerry Fitt would take part in a joint power-sharing executive, representative of both communities, henceforth. For the first time

[24] *The Times*, 9 Dec. 1973.

since 1920 the Catholic minority would play some direct role in the government of the north. On the other hand, to placate Protestants, it was agreed that no change in their relationship with the United Kingdom would take place without the consent of the majority. A long-term project of some kind of Council of Ireland with the Dublin government was also specified, though it was not until the Anglo-Irish Agreement concluded, somewhat surprisingly, by Mrs Thatcher and the Fianna Fáil Premier of Ireland, Charles Haughey, in late 1985 that any further progress was made in this direction.

On paper, then, aided by the remarkable diplomatic skill of Whitelaw and much gut common sense from Heath himself, progress had been made in providing some kind of viable executive administration for the north, free from Westminster, and with some openings to the government of the Republic. Some attempt had been made to bridge the gap between the two communities, while the operations of the security forces had also been tightened. After a climax of horror in 1972, when 146 security-force members and 321 civilians died or were killed, and nearly 5,000 others were injured, the saga of atrocity and violence showed some mitigation, with 1973 a relatively more peaceful year, though still marked by horror enough.

For all that, the reality in Northern Ireland by the end of 1973, when the Sunningdale Agreement and much else was swallowed up by other, wider crises, was of the faltering control of the authorities over an increasingly violent pattern of events. The basic social and economic problems of the Catholic minority, in terms of employment, jobs, and education, had still not really been met; many still found their salvation in emigration to England. The Provisionals found ready support amongst a population which felt that constitutional, peaceful, pressure had led nowhere for half a century and more. The forces of 'law and order' were themselves compromised and suspect, since the end of the B specials had led instead to local policing being handled by the Royal Ulster Constabulary, an overwhelmingly Protestant force under hard-line chief constables. They were regarded by many Catholics as little more than the detested B specials under another name. British troops, welcomed by the Catholics as saviours from a Protestant holocaust in 1969, were now hated figures and targets for snipers in Catholic areas such as the Bogside of Londonderry or the Falls Road and the Cregan estate in Belfast, or much of Tyrone and Fermanagh with their majority Catholic population and border with the south. It was known that they were infiltrated by unpopular units such as the SAS for training in 'anti-terrorist' techniques.[25] Much resentment was caused by the implementation of the government's anti-terrorist policy, especially the operation of internment, the handling of political prisoners in prisons such as the Maze block, and the operation of the so-called 'Diplock courts', non-jury courts where suspects were tried in secret before a judge sitting alone in order to prevent violence or intimidation towards witnesses or members of a jury.

Political indirection was further reinforced by the failure of the constitutional SDLP to command the allegiance of Sinn Fein-inclined Catholics and by the myriad sectarian divisions within the Protestant ranks which branded Paisley as an extremist, ruled out a former militant like William Craig after he had held secret parleys with the SDLP, and left the Official Unionists under their leader Brian Faulkner remote and isolated. Meanwhile the Alliance perished for lack of real support from a genuine middle ground. There was a background, too, of the economic difficulties of the United Kingdom being felt with special force in Ulster, with the decline of textiles and other industry, and over-dependence on a few giants such as Harland and Wolff shipyards and Short Brothers aircraft. In all of these, of course, the key skilled jobs were inevitably captured and monopolized by Protestants. After the high hopes with which the progress of the civil rights movement in the North of Ireland had been greeted in the late 1960s, and the joy with which the abolition of the B specials had

---

[25] Kelley, *The Longest War*, 248 ff.

been received, the condition of Northern Ireland was grim indeed. It was an embittered, divided, economically declining province, regarded by most of the British population as an incomprehensible backwater only marginally a part of the United Kingdom at all. Its connections with the other problems of the time were tangential. But it markedly increased the sense of impotence, ungovernability, and endemic disintegration which was driving the Heath government, and perhaps even Britain itself, to its doom.

It was, perhaps, in foreign affairs that some hope of a new departure could be found. Like Macmillan and Wilson before him, Heath could reasonably hope to find comfort in overseas success, or at least prominence, to compensate for difficulties and failures at home. It took some time, however, for the hope to find its appropriate outlet. Heath at first was concerned that Britain should retain a more ambitious defence posture overseas than the outgoing Labour government had prescribed. The ending of the 'east-of-Suez' policy meant a rapid withdrawal of British troops from Asia. Heath tried to resist this policy, both with regard to the Persian Gulf and Singapore and Malaysia. He was especially concerned about the pledge to withdraw from the sensitive Persian Gulf with its major oil supplies, and Britain's pledges to such governments as that of Kuwait and the United Arab Emirates. The Foreign Office, however, was resistant, the Treasury and Ministry of Defence unenthusiastic, and the economy failing to move ahead. By mid-1971 Heath had accepted defeat and Britain's withdrawal east of Suez went ahead.[26] There were some Commonwealth protests at this, notably from Singapore, but Heath was not a natural Commonwealth man himself, as has been noted above. On the difficult issue of Rhodesia, he formally continued the oil and other sanctions policy, even though it was clear that many breaches were in fact occurring and no signs

[26] Hurd, *An End of Promise*, 40 ff. For the background to this, see the special 'Britain East of Suez' issue of *International Affairs*, 42, 2 (Apr. 1966), especially Hugh Hanning, 'Britain East of Suez—facts and figures', 253 ff.

emerging of Rhodesia's government being brought down by economic pressure in weeks, months, or even years. Unofficial exploratory talks with the Smith regime led to no new initiatives. Proposals offered by Douglas-Home, the British Foreign Secretary, were deemed by the Pearce Commission in May 1972 to be unacceptable to black African opinion, and the impasse continued.[27]

Towards South Africa, the Conservatives pursued a somewhat less hostile policy than Labour had done. Some arms sales to South Africa were resumed, while Douglas-Home announced that Britain would renew the agreement over the Simonstown naval base, which allowed for Anglo-South African naval co-operation. However, South Africa remained excluded from the Commonwealth, with its isolation reinforced by a growing sporting and cultural boycott. British cricket teams had refused to play tests against South Africa after the Nationalist government of the Republic refused admission to Basil d'Oliviera, a coloured South African by origin who had been chosen to play for England where he had settled with his family. Curbs on immigration from Commonwealth countries were stepped up by the 1971 Commonwealth Immigration Act and a new definition of 'patriation' extended to the family backgrounds of coloured immigrants from Commonwealth countries. Some modifications came, however, in 1972 when the grandparentage as well as the parentage and the place of birth was also taken into account, and Commonwealth citizens given priority over other immigrants, while Ugandan Asian immigrants, whose status had been in doubt, were now admitted in modest numbers.

The Commonwealth, however, did not thrive during the Heath years. Nor did the Anglo-American relationship which became more and more distant. President Nixon manifested no special warmth for Britain, regarding the West German government as of much more consequence, while developments in Ulster caused

[27] Robert Blake, *Rhodesia*, 402–5.

continuing difficulties with Washington. Even the relationship between Lyndon Johnson and Harold Wilson at the time of the latter's supposed attempts at exploratory mediation in Vietnam in 1966–7 now seemed very distant.

However, it was elsewhere that the Heath government was committed to change in Britain's overseas role. Edward Heath had always been a strong supporter of British entry into the Common Market; his maiden speech in 1950 had been made in support of the Schuman Plan for a European Iron and Steel community. His role as chief European negotiator under Macmillan in 1961, though frustrated by de Gaulle's veto, had done nothing to mitigate his zeal for membership. Such emotional issues as New Zealand butter or memories of Gallipoli meant relatively little to him. Negotiations got under way from the outset of his government focusing on such difficulties as Commonwealth food imports, and especially British contributions to the community budget to support the highly unpopular Common Agricultural Policy, which ran counter to a century of British experience in a policy of cheap food imports. This time, however, the progress of negotiation went far better than in the past. Apart from Heath's much more wholehearted commitment to Europe, and growing support from industrial and commercial circles in the light of Britain's seemingly endless economic difficulties, there was also the major factor that de Gaulle was no longer on the scene. Talks between Heath and the new French President, Pompidou, in May 1971 were notably cordial and removed many of the obstacles to British membership.

Heath now faced the problem of getting acceptance of membership of the Common Market through parliament. There were important dissenters in his own party, particularly those devoted to the relationship with the Commonwealth. The Labour Party was deeply divided, with passionate pro-marketeers like Roy Jenkins and David Owen balanced by hostile figures like Michael Foot and Tony Benn, with Harold Wilson and James Callaghan in the middle anxious at all costs to preserve party unity. Labour's NEC declared strongly against British participation in the Community on the traditional political, economic, and legal grounds, with figures like Douglas Jay on the right being as vehement as left-wingers like Foot and Mrs Castle. For all that, in the decisive vote on 28 October, acceptance of the entry into Europe was passed by a comfortable 112 votes, with sixty-seven Labour MPs defying their party's instructions and voting with the government. A further twenty abstained. These rebels included the party's Deputy Leader, Roy Jenkins.[28] During 1972 the European Community Bill made a difficult passage through the Commons. The second reading was passed by a majority of only eight votes. During the Committee stage, Labour turned to endorse a proposal, originally emanating from a Conservative member, Neil Marten, that there should be a consultative referendum before British membership of the EEC was endorsed. This led to the resignation of the party Deputy Leader, Roy Jenkins, and his replacement by Ted Short. The new prominence of the leading anti-Marketeer, Michael Foot, as Shadow Leader of the House, emphasized Labour's repugnance towards joining the alien institutions of Brussels and Strasbourg. Labour, however, seemed hopelessly divided on the issue, since the decision to accept a referendum on British membership of the EEC was accepted by the parliamentary party by the margin of only 129 to 96. Callaghan, who could appeal emotionally to conference delegates to defend 'the language of Chaucer and Shakespeare' from the threats of European foreigners, could also edge towards a compromise position on diplomatic grounds (he was now Shadow Foreign Secretary). Harold Wilson seemed ambiguous and evasive on the whole issue, and concerned mainly to preserve party unity at a time of growing internal bitterness between the left and right in Labour's warring ranks. After all, he had been the Prime Minister who endorsed a second British application to join Europe in 1967. The third reading of the European bill was passed through the House by 17 votes in

---

[28] *The Times*, 29 Oct. 1972.

July, and Britain became a member of the European Economic Community on 1 January 1973, Heath himself presiding over the formal celebration.

The sense of rejoicing at what was undoubtedly a historic shift in Britain's role in the world was, however, distinctly muted. Edward Heath had emerged with far more consistency than Wilson or other leading politicians; but no obvious political advantage had accrued. The mood with which Britain had entered into these final negotiations about the community had been reluctant, almost resigned. The main feeling that determined public attitudes was that Britain's economic weakness was so endemic and prolonged that exclusion from a growing European market would be dangerous, almost fatal. One major obstacle to membership of the Community had been removed in 1972 with the 'floating' of the pound, which ended the old post-war difficulty of sterling being a reserve currency. On the other hand, as *The Economist* observed, Britain was still 'Europe's economic invalid'.[29] Industrial investment was flat, unemployment at $3\frac{1}{4}$ per cent and rising, inflation rampant. The Barber boom in 1973 had led to a dramatic expansion of output but the balance of payments had not benefited since, unlike the 'hard slog' of the Jenkins period of 1968–70, resources were being frittered away in a consumption spree including an explosion of house prices, and not protected in long-term investment. The question, therefore, arose whether the bracing experience of competition with Europeans in their own market would not be more fatal than the original disease, with the prospect of a huge flood of foreign imports. The Common Agricultural Policy, since it challenged the concept of cheap food with which the Liberals had triumphed over the tariff reformers back in 1906, was remorselessly unpopular, as it deserved to be. A vision was created of inefficient and grasping French and German farmers sucking in endless subsidies from a Britain which for decades

[29] *The Economist*, 30 Dec. 1972; cf. F. T. Blackaby (ed.), *British Economic Policy, 1960–74* (Cambridge, 1978), 62 ff.

had benefited from its own efficient agricultural production, from 'deficiency payments' from the Treasury, and cheap imports from friendly Commonwealth countries. The Common Market's governmental and bureaucratic aspects also did not add to its popularity since the dictatorship and strength of the non-elected Commission, the relative feebleness of the European parliament, and the expensive juggernaut of bureaucracy at Brussels were quite at variance with British tradition and experience. In fact, for all the enthusiasm amongst most Conservatives, not all associated with the party right, opinion polls repeatedly showed a public indifferent or openly hostile to the idea of joining this alien and oppressive foreign organization.

There were practical reasons, political, legal, and above all fiscal why the British should be wary of joining the Common Market. But in emotional terms also there was little popular enthusiasm for 'Europe' as embodied in the sprawling structures of the EEC. The sympathy for Anglo-American mid-Atlanticism, fired briefly by the youthful enthusiasm of Kennedy's New Frontier in the early 1960s, had long since passed. The war in Vietnam, the presence of Nixon in the White House, and, most of all, the growing feebleness of Britain within any viable Anglo-American partnership had undermined what little credibility it ever received. Heath himself has been described by Andrew Gamble as 'the least Atlanticist British premier since the war'.[30] The Commonwealth was also an organization that inspired little genuine affiliation amongst the British; it existed, it seemed, mainly in terms of test matches against West Indians, Australians, Indians, and others. Nor did sporting contacts necessarily draw the bonds of Commonwealth much closer. The concept of the multi-racial Commonwealth of Nations increasingly formed the theme of the Queen's public pronouncements, including Christmas Day broadcasts on television, but beyond mere sentiment it was hard to see substance in the concept.

---

[30] Andrew Gamble, *The Free Economy and the Strong State: The Politics of Thatcherism* (London, 1988), 74.

But neither were the British in the full sense 'Europeans'. They travelled abroad in greater and greater numbers, mostly to continental Europe. Over seven million holidays were taken overseas by 1971; by the end of the decade it was close to ten million—though it should be said that the most popular destination of all, because of its cheapness, was Franco Spain, which was not an EEC member at all. Continental food and cuisine became increasingly popular at delicatessens, and supermarkets offered a far wider variety of fare than in the past. 'Pizza parlours' flourished, as did 'espresso bars'. British wine consumption, especially of hock and claret, rose dramatically, despite taxation by successive governments. 'Wine bars' began to mount a challenge to the old-fashioned pub. Intellectually and culturally, of course, there were notable links with continental Europe as there had been since the Norman conquest. Foreign orchestras performed in British concert halls to great acclaim. British playwrights such as Harold Pinter showed a more experimental approach to writing, often of continental inspiration. In academic life, the 'structuralism' associated with French intellectuals such as Althusser, Barthes, Saussure, and Lévi-Strauss had a considerable impact on British literary criticism, as later did the 'post-structuralism' of Derrida and Foucault.[31] Althusser provoked a memorable attack from E. P. Thompson in the *Poverty of Theory* (1978) for his negative effects on the would-be Marxist intelligentsia. Amongst the historians, the French *Annales* school, with its attempt to define the underlying psychology or *mentalité* of past societies, had its disciples, notably amongst the Welsh. British culture seemed generally more outward-looking now, from the cinema to the study of semantics, than in the days of the robust Englishness of the 'angry young men' of the fifties.

Yet in any serious respect, 'Europe' still seemed to the insular British a distant and relatively unattractive concept. On balance

---

[31] See Martin Dodsworth, 'Criticism Now; the Abandonment of Tradition?' in Boris Ford (ed.). *The New Pelican Guide to English Literature*, vol. 8, *The Present* (Harmondsworth, 1983), 82 ff.

the transatlantic influence was far greater, both on intellectuals and on popular mass culture. Bob Hope was far more familiar to film-goers than Jacques Tati or Fernandel. The gulfs of language, geography, history, legal and constitutional development between Britain and Europe were still formidably wide, far wider than the puny obstacle of the English Channel. Idealists might expound, in terms of a latter-day Charlemagne, the wide cultural advantages of the free movement of travellers, business-men, students, and workers without having the barriers of pass-ports and frontiers to contend with. Even on the left, there were those who urged, unavailingly, that the concept of the brother-hood of man had to start somewhere. Genuine collaboration with socialist comrades in France, Germany, the Netherlands, and Italy, most of whom passionately wanted Britain to join the Community, would be beneficial to the workers and the unions in an increasingly multinational world economy. But it made slight impact. The mood when Britain joined was one of wary acceptance, since no obvious alternative could be found. It even appeared a kind of surrender, a recognition that the loss of Empire and the breakdown of an equal partnership with the Americans had left Britain as an enfeebled and divided offshore island with nowhere else to turn. It was not an invigorating mood in which to celebrate the ending of what Hugh Gaitskell had once termed 'a thousand years of history'. Indeed, 1 January 1973 came and went with little sense of historical change at all.

In the latter part of 1973, the Heath government seemed increasingly under siege. It had never, at any time, looked par-ticularly in charge of events. Even the entry into Europe seemed more a triumph for bureaucratic allies of the Prime Minister and smoke-filled negotiations by Geoffrey Rippon than a genuine definition of the national purpose or reassertion of national will. The Heath government had started badly in June 1970. It never really recovered its morale or sense of self-esteem. In part this was due to bad luck. The death of Macleod at the outset was followed by further blows. Its next most senior figure, Reginald Maudling, had to resign from the Home Office in mid-1972 in the wake of accusations of his corrupt involvement with a gaoled architect, John Poulson (which also resulted in the imprisonment of Labour's boss in Newcastle, T. Dan Smith). Two minor members of the government, the Lords Jellicoe and Lambton, were compelled to resign in 1973 after being implicated in a sexual scandal with London prostitutes. The Cabinet had always to face the formidable sniper fire of Enoch Powell, expelled from the Shadow Cabinet by Heath in 1968 and now a constant critic of the government. In 1974 he was to become Ulster Unionist member for South Down. As has been seen, in industrial relations and Northern Ireland—admittedly two of the most intractable and longest-lasting dilemmas of British life—there was little but deadlock and heartache to record. There was, above all, repeated evidence that the economy was not properly under control; Barber at the Treasury seldom inspired confidence. After an early period of stagnation, he committed the country to a very rapid boom, running to 5 per cent annual growth. In 1973, prices and wages rose fast, and unemployment, which in 1971 had reached the one million mark for the first time since the war, fell by 20,000. The press poured scorn on 'an unloved government', nevertheless, since the effect was to promote rapidly rising inflation and the devotion of resources to a consumer spree rather than to building up the economic infrastructure.[32] Public expenditure continued to rise fast.

Naturally, this moderated the government's loss of esteem since it freed resources for desirable social and other objectives. In particular, it enabled a large increase in the educational budget. Mrs Thatcher, later the sternest incarnation of monetarist curbs on public spending while Prime Minister, was able to introduce such costly innovations as raising the school leaving age to 16, a long-term capital investment programme in school building, and considerable support for nursery school building as recommended by the Plowden Report. She also managed to

[32] *The Economist*, 19 May 1973.

1. VE Day celebrations: rolling out the barrel, Piccadilly Circus, 8 May 1945

2. Lord Mountbatten discussing Britain's plans for the transfer of power in India with Pandit Nehru, Lord Ismay, and Mohammed Ali Jinnah, 7 June 1947

3. The worst of austerity: housewives queuing for horse-meat, 1949

4. The Earls Court Motor Show, 21 October 1952: a Sunbeam Talbot 90 coupé admired by girls from the Windmill Theatre

The first CND Aldermaston March on its way through Maidenhead, 13 April 1958

5. Harold Macmillan and Nikita Khrushchev at Moscow airport, 21 February 1959

7. Symbols of the Permissive Society: the Beatles in concert, 1965

8. Bobby Moore, England's captain, holding aloft the World Cup, June 1966. Other
in the picture are Jack Charlton, Stiles, Banks, Ball, Peters, Hurst, Wilson, Cohen,
and Bobby Charlton

9. Kenyan Asian immigrants arriving at London airport, 26 February 1968

10. 'Bloody Sunday' in Londonderry, 30 January 1972: a demonstrator chased into custody by a soldier from the Parachute Regiment

11. The miners' strike, 1972: police clashing with flying pickets at Saltley coke depot, 9 February

12. Science in the Seventies: Texaco's Zephyr oil rig in the North Sea, 26 June 1973

13. The birth of the Social Democrats: Roy Jenkins, David Owen, William Rodgers, and Shirley Williams at a press conference in London, 26 March 1981

14. Tony Blair greeted by a flag-waving crowd of supporters as he enters Downing Street after Labour's election landslide, 2 May 1997

15. Mourners outside Kensington Palace in the lead-up to the funeral of Princess Diana, September 1997

16. Boris Johnson's controversial 'Vote Leave' Brexit bus in Exeter, May 2016

salvage the popular 'Open University', or 'university of the air', whose future had been in doubt. Sir Keith Joseph, Minister of Health, James Prior, Minister of Agriculture, and Peter Walker, Secretary for the Environment, also spent freely from the public purse, at a time when the Defence budget was being trimmed back. Yet these only added to the built-in inflationary pressures surging up in the economy long before the Arab–Israeli Yom Kippur War in October 1973.

The main element of hope for the government, as always, lay in the weakness of the opposition. The Crowther Commission (later the Kilbrandon Commission) on Wales and Scotland did not report until the end of 1973. This kept the nationalist threat relatively dormant, while in any case it was Labour that had far more to fear from this threat in its Celtic heartlands. The Liberals continued to form a buoyant third force. After defeating Labour at Rochdale through Cyril Smith, they added a notable by-election victory over the Conservatives in Sutton and Cheam in December 1972; others followed in the Isle of Ely, Ripon, and Berwick-on-Tweed during 1973. But the Liberals hardly seemed to represent quite the same kind of sustained, persistent threat that they had done at the time of the emergence of Orpington Man in 1962.

The main challenge to the Conservatives, of course, came from Labour. It was, therefore, a comfort to Heath and his Cabinet that the Labour Party was in extreme disarray on almost every issue between 1970 and 1974, with Harold Wilson a less and less commanding leader. On perennial problems such as the bomb and industrial relations, on Celtic devolution, on public ownership, and most of all on entry into Europe, Labour presented a pathetic spectacle of division and confusion, with able and eloquent figures like Jenkins and Crosland, Benn and Foot, unable to make an impression on the Conservative enemy because of their internal feuds. A particular feature of these years was the swing to the left in the party, focusing on the dynamic but disturbing personality of Anthony Wedgwood Benn, now recycled as plain Tony Benn, his *Who's Who* entry duly amended.

Like Stafford Cripps in the 1930s, here was an upper-class radical of rare charisma. Like many others in the Labour Party, Benn concluded that the Wilson governments in 1964–70, in which he had latterly been Minister of Technology, had proved the failure of opportunist, consensus politics. Unusually, however, this moved him from being a broadly centrist, Gaitskellite-type social-ist to becoming a zealot of the far left. He now called for extensive public ownership, unilateralism, 'an alternative economic strat-egy' embracing much state direction, and opposition to the Com-mon Market. This was mingled with a populist strain which led him to support the Upper Clyde 'work-in' and forms of workers' co-operative or decentralized models of industrial organization in general. As chairman of the party in 1971–2 he launched the exercise 'Participation '72', in which a variety of programmes ranging from the popular election of the party leader and Shadow Cabinet to democratic participation in industry, freedom of the press, accountability of the police and civil service, and other themes were proposed.[33] Precisely why Benn shifted his ground politically in this way is not clear; neither was it apparent how much coherence a *mélange* of Marx and Rousseau, state direction and industrial democracy, with the unreformed trade unions central to both operations, really could have. But there is no doubt that it led to a mighty left-wing upsurge amongst the ranks of the left and within the trade unions. Thereafter, Benn embraced a wide variety of other causes including attacks on the Official Secrets Act, feminism, abolition of the Lords, a neutralist foreign policy and leaving NATO, and support for Sinn Fein on Irish questions. The Labour Party was now engulfed by turmoil and inner tension even deeper than the fateful Bevanite movement of the early fifties. In particular, Benn pressed hard for a pro-gramme of widespread state control of the economy, including the nationalization of twenty-five major companies.

[33] See Tony Benn, *Office without Power, passim*, and especially 392 (entry of 31 Dec 1970).

These issues were superimposed on a party already looking jaded after the disappointing sixties, and with only the pragmatic leadership of Wilson and Callaghan to give them any sense of direction. The Common Market rent the party severely in 1971–4, with Roy Jenkins resigning his Shadow Cabinet position as has been seen, and Michael Foot (for the first time in his career a front-bench spokesman) emerging as a valuable parliamentary voice for the anti-European, CND left. More and more, Labour looked like an ageing party in this period. The import and extent of its socialism was unclear. It was internally divided as never before while the links with the unreformed, and almost unreformable, trade unions were more and more of a liability. Apart from a rare by-election gain at Bromsgrove in 1971, Labour slipped back in public support. One of its main ideologues, Tony Crosland, ironically enough in a book entitled *Socialism Now* (1974), vigorously attacked the failures of the 1960s governments in which he had served, especially for failing to regenerate the economy or promote economic growth.[34] Talented figures like Jenkins and Shirley Williams now seemed isolated over defence, Europe, and incomes policy. The left was torn between the 'old left' parliamentarists like Foot and the populist campaigns of Benn. Wilson himself, in the centre, now seemed an inert figure, mainly concerned to keep the ship afloat whatever the cargo forced upon it. He had the uncertain achievement of the so-called 'social contract' negotiated with Vic Feather of the TUC. More important, he pursued a skilful campaign designed to frustrate and neutralize the influence of Benn, notably when he declared that Benn's plan for nationalizing twenty-five major companies, accepted by a left-led NEC by a one-vote majority, would not form part of Labour's next manifesto. At the party conference in early October 1973, Labour looked more than ever a nostalgic party, promising a better yesterday rather than a more

---

[34] Crosland, *Socialism Now* (London, 1974), especially 23 ft.

fruitful tomorrow. Soon after, the Conservatives went ahead in the opinion polls for only the second time.[35]

But what really triggered off the social and political change was a series of external and internal events which brought the Heath government to its knees. In early October, the Yom Kippur War between Israel and Egypt led to a damaging oil embargo, and a colossal increase, four-fold in all, in the price of oil. Britain, like other industrial nations, was suddenly threatened with huge inflationary pressures and a massive cut in its energy supplies, some years before the projected North Sea oil reserves could come on stream. There was a 10 per cent cut in oil supplies and talk of rationing. Retail prices suddenly soared by 10 per cent.[36] At the same time, policies in Northern Ireland were reaching deadlock. Industrial relations remained as big a mess as ever, with the National Industrial Relations Court threatening to sequestrate the funds of the Engineers for disregarding its edicts, and a go-slow on the railways threatened by the Railwaymen's union just before Christmas.

Worst of all, relations between the government and the miners, simmering since the strike in early 1972, now suddenly deteriorated. The NUM executive, as has been seen, put forward a large wage demand in November 1973, and by a majority of 20 to 5 declined to put an offer by the NCB to a ballot of members. An overtime ban had already been called on 8 November.[37] Heath, mindful of his defeat in 1972, now promptly called a state of emergency on 13 November to keep essential industries going. On the 28th talks between him and the NUM executive broke down, with, as a background, the doubling of the price of oil and long queues of motorists developing at petrol pumps. On 13 December Heath told the nation that a three-day week was

---

[35] *The Times*, 2–4 October 1973. However, Tony Benn's proposal for nationalizing the twenty-five major companies in the land was defeated by 5,600,000 to 291,000.

[36] *The Economist*, 8 Dec. 1973.

[37] Gormley, *Battered Cherub*, 128 ff.; Hall, *King Coal*, 206 ff.

being declared. Apart from his extreme anxiety about the effect on the economy of this threat to a central component of the energy supplies, Heath was also convinced (erroneously) that Communists like Mick McGahey on the NUM executive were trying to overthrow the elected government of the day for purely political purposes.

The Prime Minister and close advisers like Sir William Armstrong, the head of the civil service, were now under extreme pressure, with rising inflation, a drying-up of oil from the Middle East, and a threatened national miners' strike occurring simultaneously. In the period just before Christmas, Heath, almost exhausted, had also to cope with the Sunningdale Agreement over Northern Ireland and the European summit meeting at Copenhagen. In February 1974, Sir William Armstrong suffered a nervous breakdown. Douglas Hurd rightly observes of this period that historians, calm, remote, and Olympian, neglect at their peril the 'pell-mell of politics'.[38] One possible, but highly unpredictable, way out was to call an immediate general election on the theme of 'Who governs Britain?' to cash in on trade-union unpopularity. This option remained in play that Christmas-time. In the mean time, the more secure strategy was pursued of trying to negotiate out of a crisis. While Peter Walker held amiable talks with Sheikh Yamani and friendly Arab oil suppliers in Switzerland, William Whitelaw was transferred from the Irish Office to become Secretary for Employment. There was here the vain hope that the man who had worked the miracle of getting Ulster Protestants and Catholics to co-operate over the power-sharing arrangement might also make an impact on moderates on the NUM executive such as Len Clarke, Sid Vincent, and President Joe Gormley himself.

It was not to be. In the weeks after Christmas, the pressures upon the Heath government and the Prime Minister and his personal entourage mounted remorselessly as in some Greek

---

[38] Hurd, *An End to Promise*, 113.

tragedy. Whitelaw's very amiability, a distinct asset when dealing with the prickly Ulstermen, now proved something of a snare when negotiating with the hard-headed miners, who found him 'too gabby'. A meeting between Whitelaw and Gormley at Brown's Hotel on 20 December (later transferred to an Italian restaurant after a bomb scare) appeared to produce a promise by Whitelaw of extra payments to miners to cover time spent washing up after work and also waiting around to go on shift. Gormley took this seriously, but the Pay Board largely undermined it after which Whitelaw himself turned against his own proposal.[39] The miners now felt they could turn for real support only to the TUC. Its new general secretary, Len Murray, was a quieter figure than his extrovert predecessor, Vic Feather, but a man of strong will. Heath, in particular, feared him as a more dedicated socialist than his amiable, pragmatic predecessor, 'a cynical person given to devious conspiracy'.[40] On 9 January a national strike became inevitable. Whitelaw's final proposals were abruptly rejected by the NUM executive, while Len Murray's counter-proposal that the TUC would use its authority to prevent any other union taking advantage of treating the NUM as a 'special case' was rejected out of hand by the Chancellor of the Exchequer, Barber. Heath agreed with this view, and both sides now dug in amidst a deepening atmosphere of crisis.

The resolve of both sides was not in doubt. Gormley told the government that a ballot had given him an 81 per cent vote in favour of a national stoppage. Even the traditionally moderate men of Nottinghamshire and Leicestershire supported one now. Heath and his advisers, by contrast, were adamant in defence of phase III of the Prices and Incomes Policy.[41] Robert Carr at the Home Office seemed better prepared to deal with the problem of mass picketing than in 1972, and had prepared mobile squads of police to protect such key areas as docks and power stations.

---

[39] Gormley, *Battered Cherub*, 132–8.
[40] Dorfman. *Government versus Trade Unionism*, 100.
[41] *The Economist*, 12 Jan. 1974; *Financial Times*, 22 Jan. 1974.

The Labour Party rested contentedly on the sidelines, seeing a possible political advantage, while being anxious to distance themselves from NUM Communist leaders like Mick McGahey who were said to speak of using the strike emergency to bring the government down. The background to these developments was a rapid deterioration in the nation's finances in the wake of the oil crisis plus a growing shortage of coal. It was announced in early February that in 1973 Britain had suffered a balance-of-payments deficit of £112 billion, the worst figures on record.[42] Yet the full impact of the oil-price increases had still to be felt.

The one major initiative that the government could take was political, namely to call an immediate general election on the 'Who Governs Britain?' theme and thereby to confirm and renew its mandate from the people. There were many divided voices in Cabinet circles. Ministers such as the Chancellor, Anthony Barber, were amongst those who wanted the earliest possible appeal to the country, perhaps as early as 7 February. Many subsequently argued that a quick election, timed just before the strike was due to begin on 9 February, would have given Heath a victory. Conservatives' private pollsters, however, indicated that the electoral prospects were uncertain and that, as in 1972, the public was by no means unsympathetic to the miners' case. After much dithering, Heath opted for an election to be held on 28 February. Many later argued that the three weeks' delay in effect ruined his premiership and his future career as party leader, but the argument is, of course, impossible to prove either way.[43]

What is clear is that the government gave an unimpressive showing during the election campaign, even though the opinion polls at first seemed to show the Conservatives well in the lead. The strike which began on 9 February lacked the drama and potential violence of the 1972 dispute. Gormley, the NUM

[42] The Trade deficit for January 1974 was a further £383 m. (*Financial Times*, 26 Feb. 1974).

[43] See Denis Kavanagh, 'The Heath Government', in Hennessy and Seldon (eds.), *Ruling Performance* (London, 1987), 231.

President, had failed to get the strike called off in the interests of Labour's campaign prospects; but at least he and his colleagues did ensure that the strike was a low-key affair, with no mass picketing, and careful collaboration with chief constables and other police chiefs to ensure that there would be no physical provocation or intimidation. The government's handling of the issue seemed wayward to the end. On the very day the election was called, Whitelaw referred the miners' case to the Pay Board, which he had previously refused to do. This proved to be a disastrous move, since the hearings of the Board, which continued to be held during the election period of 18–22 February, showed again much support for the miners' claim on the key relativities issue. Indeed, it appeared that the government's figures were in any case incorrect, and that the miners were entitled to a further 8 per cent on the Wilberforce award of 1972. Heath blundered badly by not regarding the pay relativities mechanisms as appropriate to industrial disputes such as this. The Conservatives' campaign was low-key, with Heath's own image to the electors, according to *The Times*, 'brusque and unsmiling'.[44] The Tories' prospects were not helped by disastrous trade-deficit figures of £383 m. in February, the worst in British history. Of course, this was mainly due to a 70 per cent increase in crude-oil prices, and a huge rise in the import bill accordingly, but the electors naturally thought the government was to blame.

The campaign also enabled Labour to cast aside its divisions and internecine quarrels, and gave Harold Wilson himself new impetus, especially in raising the issue of rising prices. A succession of events gave Labour's campaign some stimulus. Wilson managed to persuade Ray Buckton of ASLEF, the engine-drivers' union, to call off a threatened strike. The trade statistics, with their endemic gloom, buoyed Labour further. Fringe attacks on Heath by Enoch Powell, who actually advised the electors to vote Labour because of that party's opposition to entry into Europe,

[44] *The Times*, 23 Feb. 1974.

brought further succour, while an even more unlikely ally was Campbell Adamson, Director-General of the CBI, who appeared to call for the repeal of the government's 1971 Industrial Relations Act because of the trouble it had caused between unions and employers. 'It has soured the industrial climate', Adamson declared with a magnificent disregard of the political impact of his remarks, delivered just two days before polling day.[45]

Conservative leads in most opinion polls continued to the end, but the position was more and more insecure especially in a key area like the West Midlands. Heath looked less and less like a winner. In the end, the result was a small swing to Labour. Nor could this be attributed to voter apathy, since the turn out was 78.8 per cent in February 1974 compared with only 72.0 per cent in June 1970, the fact of a winter election notwithstanding. The election saw Labour returned as the largest party, with 301 seats to the Conservatives' 296, with 14 Liberals, and 23 other parties. One irony was that the Ulster Unionists, firm allies of the Conservatives since 1920, were now quite disaffected and in no mood to back their old allies after the abolition of Stormont and the experiment of power-sharing with the Ulster Catholics. A few days of political confusion resulted, with Heath making approaches to the Liberal leader, Jeremy Thorpe, for a possible coalition. Thorpe was tempted, but grass-roots opposition in his party ended these overtures. On 4 March, four days after the poll, Harold Wilson, to his apparent surprise, returned to Downing Street. His new Employment Secretary was the old Tribunite and Bevanite, Michael Foot, who made it clear that he would impose no veto or curb on the miners' negotiations, and that in any case the Tories' Prices and Incomes policy was to be set aside.[46] A settlement was promptly reached, at the cost of £103 m. to the NCB wages bill, and the nation's pits at once resumed work, with surface workers' pay rising to £32 a week,

[45] *The Times.* 27 Feb. 1974.
[46] Simon Hoggart and David Leigh, *Michael Foot: A Portrait* (London, 1981). 165 ff.

underground workers to £36, and men at the coal-face to £45.[47]
The miners yet again appeared triumphant, indeed in the
euphoric view of young left-wingers like Arthur Scargill virtually
invincible.

The miners' strike ended a somewhat sad three-and-a-half
years of Edward Heath. There was little enough success to report
on any front, other than the Common Market which had yet to
prove its popularity with the voters by February 1974. The
government fell at a time of a record trade deficit and inflation,
with near-chaos in Northern Ireland, and a country polarized
socially after years of industrial conflict. The Conservative Party
itself seemed almost demoralized, with a large and growing gulf
emerging between a distant and insensitive leadership which
lacked major personalities or forces of inspiration, and an anxious rank and file. The Tories' famous secret weapon—loyalty—
seemed to be missing now, and Heath's own position as leader
could not be taken for granted. It seemed in retrospect that
Heath had won by default in 1970 and that over the next four
years the mood of the country was not supportive.

More alarming than the political fortunes of one man and one
party, though, was mounting evidence that the cohesive civic
culture which had sustained Britain during the Second World
War and in meeting difficult internal and external readjustments
in the next two decades was beginning to disintegrate. From
striking trade unionists and mass pickets to nationalists in Ireland, Scotland, and Wales, there was a mounting pattern of
sectional disarray amounting to lawlessness. The general public,
who had benefited in cash terms during the Barber boom but at
the cost of constant disruption to public services and of soaring
prices, reacted with more cynicism. There seemed to be fewer
agreed norms and values to which the community would
respond. What had given the nation direction since 1945 was
centralized planning of a Keynesian/social democratic kind.

---

[47] *Financial Times*, 7 March 1974.

It reached in some ways its apotheosis under Heath. The Barber boom was a kind of Keynesian pump-priming gone mad. The budgets of 1972 and 1973 were perhaps the last to be based on the classic demand-management pattern. Heath's own methods of government involved a high degree of intermeshed corporate planning, with close links between the Cabinet Office and ministers and major civil servants like Sir William Armstrong, politicized as never before. It was to be noted that Sir Douglas Allen (Lord Croham), Armstrong's successor as head of the civil service after March 1974, had a less intimate contact with Downing Street. Behind the scenes was an apparatus like Lord Rothschild's Central Policy Review Staff which brought in vigorous young men like William Waldegrave, and several younger high-flying civil servants. Whitehall seemed to be energized and invigorated as never before since 1945, with old Keynesians like Douglas Wass, Ian Bancroft, and Frank Cooper giving fresh dynamism to the old orthodoxies, the British style of paternalist rule ought to have worked with greater efficacy, just as the Raj reached its peak of governmental effectiveness after the Montagu-Chelmsford reforms at the end of the First World War.

But it did not work that way, either in India or in Britain. The general public witnessed only uncontrollable public expenditure and devalued money, an overloaded governmental machine (now attached to an even more enormous one in Brussels), and a greater and greater detachment of the community from the processes of administration. Symbolically, the reforms in the machinery of government that Heath patiently, almost lovingly, put together, were all to be scrapped—along with the giant departments like Trade and Industry established by the Wilson government of 1974-6—as the Thatcher governments of the eighties stamped with glee on the ashes of the discredited Heath and the Heathmen. Indeed, Heath and his colleagues did not seem to have much faith in their own creations either—witness the desuetude into which the Industrial Relations Act fell after 1971, the low-key role of the Pay Board and the Industrial Relations Court, and the reluctance to call further states of emergency. Even the architect did not believe in his own grand design. Conservative supporters lamented the social cost. They complained that Barber's dividend limitation had penalized those dependent upon an income from savings, that price controls had undermined business profitability, while orchestrated inflation threatened everybody. The only enduring legacies were an over-hauled local-government system and, of course, entry into 'Europe'. Both were unpopular.

Many changes were taking place in these years, both in British public debate and in the tone of daily life. In each case, the notion of society as something that could be clinically defined and regulated suffered a setback. In each case, disorder and discomfort resulted. In the realm of ideas, there were a growing number of Tory critics sceptical of the whole intellectual basis of post-war social and economic policy, including politicians, such as Powell, John Biffen, and Jock Bruce-Gardyne. But the main dialectical challenge came from the centre or right-wing newspapers, a force for a change now, just as the left-wing journals had fuelled new ideas in the inter-war years. Now it was argued strongly by influential publicists that full employment and demand manage-ment, coupled with the growth of institutional power amongst the unions and other key pressure-groups, only led to a vicious spiral of inflation and inflationary expectations. Social disequilibrium resulted. These views were propounded by ex-Keynesian journal-ists such as Samuel Brittan (formerly of the *Observer*) in the *Financial Times* and Peter Jay (son of a former Labour Cabinet minister) in the columns of *The Times*. Brittan quoted with approval the belief of the American monetarist, Milton Friedman, that 'the authorities have no more than a temporary power to influence output and employment'. He urged the need for flexible exchange rates and a firm attitude towards what he called 'the unions' employment-reducing behaviour'. Earlier, in *Left or Right: the Bogus Dilemma* (1968), he had insisted that right-wing views on economic enterprise were wholly compatible with liberal views on such matters as sexual permissiveness. Sam Brittan was no Edmund Burke. His views were controversial, but have been not unreasonably described as 'setting the intellectual agenda for the next decade and more'.[48] Journalists like Jay and Brittan found support amongst leading Conservative ministers like Sir Keith Joseph and even a little, surprisingly, on the Labour side with the advent of Denis Healey as Shadow Chancellor (and actual Chancellor from March 1974).

The intellectual mood of post-war Britain, still relatively homogeneous down to 1970, was changing fast. In its wake was a growing disillusion with the Keynesian economists, the Fabian planners, the post-Beveridge social engineers, the consensual liberal positivists who had governed the realm like so many conquistadors for a quarter of a century. Economic and social science reached its zenith in public esteem and funding in the late sixties, with a surge of growth in the social science departments of universities, in journals such as *New Society*, and in the patronage lavished by the Social Science Research Council. Nuffield College, Oxford, presided over by an urbane Mancunian, Norman Chester, an expert on public administration who had begun his career working for the Beveridge Committee, enjoyed an exalted public status as the Mecca of post-war faith. But it was the kind of power and influence that trembled on the brink of eternity.

The temper of public and private life also seemed to be changing. Events like the miners' strikes of 1972 and 1974 suggested a growing mood of confrontation, with more than an undercurrent of violence. British society seemed to be losing that fabled tolerance and gentleness, of which Orwell had affectionately written in the thirties. The student revolts of the 1968 period had been transient affairs, with only a limited impact beyond the narrow, cloistered confines of the universities. The public mood of the young in general still conformed to the gentle nihilism of the 'permissive' age. The Vietnam War had ended. Now something

[48] David Kynaston, *The Financial Times: A Centenary History* (London, 1988), 368–9; William Keegan, *Mrs. Thatcher's Economic Experiment* (London, 1984), 41 ff.

more fundamental appeared to be happening. Living in Britain appeared to be becoming an altogether harsher experience. Home Office crime statistics reflected a pattern of greater violence, with the police recording year by year a growing tally of cases of personal assault, reaching a total of 89,599 in 1974. Of these, woundings and assaults totalled 62,000.[49] There was also a declining proportion of 'clear-up' cases by the police, especially in relation to sexual assaults. As a result, the dangers lurking for peaceable citizens in inner-city areas were widely discussed. In 1974, Sir Keith Joseph was to declare that British cities were becoming unsafe for the first time since Peel set up the Metropolitan Police. He drew a fanciful parallel with the fall of Rome— 'destroyed from the inside'.[50] One feature in this mounting wave of crime was a growing popular hostility towards the police, not only from the black community. The familiar stereotype of the friendly 'copper on the beat' was at odds with the reality. Previously peaceable leisure activities were being scarred by violent confrontation. Thus the national game of association football, a focus for patriotic mass participation as recently as England's World Cup victory in 1966, was being marred by marauding gangs of hooligan youths, less concerned with the game on the field than with settling scores with rival supporters inside or outside football grounds, and terrorizing local inhabitants in the process.

Not all the violence was public or contrived. Indeed, a notable feature of these statistics is the steady rise in domestic violence, including rape and wife-battering. A factor here (one which undoubtedly stimulated the rate of divorce or the break-up of marriages) was the new form taken by the feminist movement for women's rights. In place of traditional campaigns for such issues as equal pay, or the stereotype of sixties' permissiveness which again treated women as symbols of sexual admiration or

---

[49] Roy Walmsley, *Personal Violence*, Home Office Research Study, No. 89 (HMSO, 1986), 3 ff.

[50] *The Times*, 21 Oct. 1974; see Geoffrey Pearson, *Hooligan*, 4–6.

exploitation, the feminist movement from 1970 adopted a much more aggressive approach. Taking its cue from the United States, it crusaded not only against old forms of gender discrimination in job opportunities or legal status, but against marriage, motherhood, and other totems of a heterosexual, male-dominated world. Thus it was in 1970 that a major impact was created by Germaine Greer's *The Female Eunuch*, a bible for the new feminists. It was followed by the underground publication *Spare Rib*, the women's publishing house Virago, and a rich variety of social and cultural pressure-groups.[51] The newly active women's movement had a very rapid impact on public opinion, male as well as female. It had many beneficial consequences, both in public perceptions and in legislation to remedy aspects of sexual discrimination following on from similar measures dealing with race relations. Yet one wider effect was to generate social and personal tension. The price individuals paid often included domestic unhappiness and perhaps violence, as men and women tried to come to terms with a new range of relationships within a world turned upside down. All too often, it was defenceless young children who bore the brunt of adult failure.

In many ways, therefore, the years of the government of Edward Heath formed an important transitional period. They showed that the external world was changing with the huge inflationary wave and the industrial slow-down of 1973, leading in turn to a questioning of post-war social policy. They indicated that the sense of community was changing too, with not much left of the solidarity of the forties and fifties, let alone the 'Dunkirk spirit'. The Heath government found itself unable either to persuade employers to invest or trade unionists to abate their wage demands, or even to obey the law.[52] Values that, in their different ways, Attlee, Churchill, and Macmillan had taken for

[51] For these matters, see David Boucher, *The Feminist Challenge: The Movement for Women's Liberation in Britain and the USA* (London, 1983).

[52] See Graham Wootton, 'The Impact of Organized Interests', in William B. Gwyn and Richard Rose, *Britain: Progress and Decline* (London, 1980), 105 ff.

granted, and to which they had readily appealed at times of crisis, were now in doubt or the subject of derision or satire. In private life, the stability of neighbourhood, the family, and parenthood was visibly less assured. Significantly, one of the rare branches of sociology that was to expand in the intellectual crisis facing the social sciences in the seventies was that of criminology, both in terms of the theoretical analysis of the sociology of crime and of the empirical investigation of deviant behaviour. Instead of being the pioneer work of a handful of European émigrés such as Max Grünhut at Oxford or Leon Radzinowicz at Cambridge, the subject mushroomed in university graduate schools and institutional centres of research. The 1970s have been given the dubious accolade of being 'the Golden Age' of British criminology.[53] There were wider issues at stake here.

The turbulent events of the winter of 1973–4, then, saw much more than the decline and fall of Edward Heath as premier, more even than the demise of 'one-nation Toryism'. They witnessed also the erosion of an ethical system. Conceived in an age of intellectual confidence, institutional strength, and instinctive patriotism, it was now withering away in confusion and doubt.

[53] Paul Rock (ed.), *A History of British Criminology* (Oxford, 1988), especially 61–2.

10. *Challenge to Consensus*
1974–1976

═══

'BLEAK HOUSE rather than Great Expectations' was how a budget earlier in the century had been greeted. The mood was not dissimilar when Harold Wilson returned to 10 Downing Street at the head of a minority Labour administration on 4 March 1974. The new Cabinet contained a rich array of very talented people, but its main characteristic was the need for internal checks and balances, to prevent either left or right, pro- or anti-Europeans (not at all identical categories) gaining the upper hand. Thus Denis Healey at the Treasury and Roy Jenkins at the Home Office were countered by the central role of Michael Foot as Secretary for Employment and by other figures on the left such as Barbara Castle and Peter Shore. Tony Benn had to be given a major portfolio at Trade and Industry, but a watchful Prime Minister hedged him around with political and civil-service restraints to keep his socialist zeal well in check. A key figure in the administration was James Callaghan, now firmly restored to favour and placed in the Foreign Office. But he was a senior figure not obviously related with policy innovation, whose zeal for high politics had been shown to be qualified when he came close to being appointed managing director of the International Monetary Fund in May 1973. The main symbol of caution, even inertia, was Harold Wilson himself, a jaded, dispirited figure for much of the 1970–4 period, now quite unexpectedly propelled into office a third time in the wake of the miners' dispute. Wilson had learnt some sad lessons from his excessive prominence as political chief in the years after 1964.

This time he was a more measured figure, his political advisers such as Marcia Williams less in evidence, his own flanks less exposed. In place of his Paymaster-General George Wigg, to feed fears of conspiracy, he now sought guidance from an urbane and wealthy socialist, Harold Lever, and found companionship from businessmen prominent in the Jewish community. A former academic historian, Bernard Donoughue, was called in to head the Downing Street Policy Unit. Using a favourite football metaphor, Wilson told his parliamentary followers that he intended not to play as centre forward but rather as 'deep-lying centre-half' on the model of Herbie Roberts in the successful Arsenal football team of the thirties.[1] It suggested a less frenetic, less paranoid style of government than in the sixties. But it also implied a general absence of initiative. On all the troubled areas of policy—industrial relations, Welsh and Scottish devolution, defence, above all Europe, the need was to avoid rocking the boat and to ensure that the government remained in office. It was an unheroic recipe for epic times, but at least Wilson's particular skills were well attuned to such an emergency.

The government, of course, began as a minority administration. It was even possible that it would be thrown out of office immediately. However, the Conservatives, with commendable constitutional caution, decided not to force an amendment to the Queen's Speech on prices and incomes policy. It was not clear what the outcome would have been since the Conservatives might have captured the votes of the 14 Liberals, making a potential total of 310, whereas the 7 Welsh and Scottish Nationalists and 1 SDLP would have voted with Labour, a tally of 309, leaving everything dependent on the uncertain whims of the 11 Ulster Unionists whose concerns were wholly parochial. The government, buoyed up by a sparkling debut ministerial speech by Michael Foot, survived.[2] But it was clear that everything

---

[1] Harold Wilson, *Final Term: The Labour Government, 1974–1976* (London, 1979), 17.

[2] *The Times*, 19 Mar. 1974.

would be dictated by the need to prepare the ground for another early election and a prospective overall majority for Labour. Issue after issue was delayed or defused. Most centrally, Michael Foot made it transparently clear that the government would provoke no crisis with the unions, on whose support it depended, that the Industrial Relations Act would be set aside, and the Pay Board abolished. Over Europe, devolution, and Northern Ireland, as will be seen, major decisions were deferred. On the social side, Anthony Crosland, Secretary of the Environment, similarly postponed a major recasting of housing policy, an area widely acknowledged, including by Crosland himself, to have been a relative failure in the 1964–70 government. He decided to freeze private and council rents, while £55 m. was made available to the building societies from the Treasury to enable them to keep interest rates stable for another year and thus hold back inflation.

The main need, though, was to try to stave off disaster on the economic front in the aftermath of the massive price explosion and inflation pressures after the oil crisis, still working themselves through the economic system. The main actor here was Denis Healey, the new Chancellor of the Exchequer. He was a relatively untried figure in the economic field, though with a reputation as a determined and systematic manager of the Ministry of Defence in the 1960s. His main advisers were a group of three Cambridge economists, Nicholas Kaldor, Sir Robert Neild, and Wynne Godley, with Maurice Peston from Queen Mary College, London. This suggested that a broadly interventionist approach would be resumed after the 'hands-off' policy of the former Chancellor, Anthony Barber (who had now left politics for the City). Healey's first budget was a relatively cautious affair in March 1974, designed to ward off excessive deflation and not to annoy the unions. There would be increases in taxation including a 3p rise in income tax, increases in VAT and petrol duty, a rise in Corporation Tax and an increase in the prices to be charged by nationalized industries. However, broad tax increases of £1,400 m. were countered by higher pensions, increased food subsidies to the tune of £500 m., and some redistribution in taxation, largely to keep the TUC content. The main emphasis in meeting the deficit would come from overseas borrowing, notably an increase in the 'swap' facilities from the New York Reserve Bank to $3,000 m., plus another large loan raised by the London clearing banks.[3] It was a carefully designed package, with much political content. Labour partisans could bemoan the absence of major defence cuts or any kind of wealth tax, but rejoice in the social and redistributive aspects of Healey's programme.

A further budget in July added £900 m. to consumers' purchasing power and added up to further pump-priming on broadly Keynesian lines.[4] That summer, Healey could therefore point to a reasonable stability in the balance of payments, and as yet no serious cuts in public services. Short-term oil money even meant a rise in Britain's reserves. All the main questions were begged; inflation remained very high and manufacturing production was stagnant, but no disasters had occurred. The Labour Party remained comparatively stable, with Benn's proposed socialist experiments such as planning agreements set on one side. Wilson's watchfulness ensured that the minority administration survived all tests with some ease. The continuing malaise in Tory ranks under Heath's leadership added to a reasonably tranquil atmosphere that summer.

A general election was inevitable, and the 'short parliament' came to an end with an election in early October. The campaign was a dull one, with little passion evoked on the mainstream issues. The polls were most encouraging for Labour with leads of over 11 per cent shown, and a prospect of gains in the Midlands and the South. Heath's campaign, in which he mysteriously urged the merits of a putative 'government of national unity', fell largely flat. On balance, he still seemed to be associated in the voters' minds with the three-day week and deadlock with the

---

[3] *Financial Times*, 27 Mar. 1974; *The Economist*, 30 Mar. 1974.
[4] *Financial Times*, 23 July 1974; *The Economist*, 27 July 1974.

miners. Labour, however, failed to arouse much enthusiasm either. There was a reduced turn-out compared with February, from 78 per cent to 72 per cent. More damaging for Labour, the Liberal vote fell by almost a million and there were reduced inroads into the Tory vote in Southern England as a result. The outcome was the narrowest of overall Labour majorities on a swing of 2 per cent, with Labour winning 319 seats, the Conservatives 277, the Liberals 13, the Welsh and Scottish Nationalists 13 between them, and 12 others, mainly Ulstermen. The main uproar after the election came from within Conservative ranks, calling for the deposition of Heath as party leader since he had actually lost three elections out of the four he had contested. But it was not an election that, either in prospect or in retrospect, aroused much passion. To the large bulk of the population it seemed almost marginal in the face of the massively increasing economic problems confronting the nation, notably inflation rising to over 20 per cent. The most that could be said was that the election was at least over and a more stable period of administration might now emerge to confront the social and economic challenges of the time.

The main strategy of the Wilson government, domestically, was clearly directed towards self-preservation rather than innovation. This was also apparent in overseas policy, although the emphasis showed a distinct change after the approach adopted by the Heath government. The frostiness of the Atlantic alliance evaporated. After all, the Vietnam War was now increasingly distant, while President Nixon resigned the US presidency following his involvement in the Watergate scandal. His successor, Gerald Ford, was a much more neutral figure.

Callaghan, the British Foreign Secretary, struck up a good working relationship with the US Secretary of State, Henry Kissinger, himself something of an Anglophile since he had in the past written an academic treatise on the diplomatic policy of Lord Castlereagh after 1815. He told Callaghan early on that the United States would view Britain's economic plight sympathetically, whatever the outcome of efforts to renegotiate

Britain's relationship with the European Economic Community.[5]
He and Callaghan were to work closely on a number of issues.
Notable among them was an attempt to handle the difficult
dispute which broke out in Cyprus in the summer of 1974 with
the threat of war between Greece and Turkey in a region where
tension had continued long after the independence settlement
worked out for Cyprus in 1960. In a plot instigated by the neo-
fascist Greek government in Athens, the long-serving president of
Cyprus, Archbishop Makarios, was overthrown; at first it was
thought he had been murdered. In his place was installed Nicos
Sampson, a former leader of the EOK A terrorists. Turkish
troops then invaded the island and Anglo-American attempts at
mediation were frustrated thereafter. Turkish troops remained
on the island for years afterwards and hopes of a federal solution
were dashed repeatedly. Nevertheless, Callaghan was felt to have
conducted himself ably in this crisis, not least by minimizing the
degree of British military involvement. As against those who felt
he ought to have invoked the Treaty of Guarantee and acted
against the usurper President Sampson in Cyprus, others felt
relieved that Callaghan had avoided another Suez, with the
highly armed Turks, a NATO ally, as the adversary this time.
Callaghan's stature at the Foreign Office by the end of 1974
seemed somewhat greater than that of Herbert Morrison in
1951, with whom he was freely compared—and, indeed, than
his own standing at the Treasury in the dark days of 1964–6.
Other crises such as difficulties with South Africa and a 'cod war'
caused by a fishing dispute with Iceland were also handled in
measured fashion. Among other things, Callaghan's credentials
as a possible future Prime Minister were much enhanced, though
the agreement to go ahead with the Chevaline nuclear weapons
system in 1974–6 (as discussed in the next chapter) left an
ominous legacy.

[5] Callaghan, *Time and Chance*, 319–20.

The main issue in foreign policy, clearly, lay in dealing with the European Economic Community. It was in this field that Wilson's and Callaghan's instincts for survival were stretched to the limit. Labour's policy, at least on paper, was to negotiate anew the terms of entry, especially on such contentious issues as agricultural policy, the community budget, and Commonwealth food imports, and then to put the renegotiated terms—if any, indeed, emerged—to a referendum of the people. But, underlying these formal provisions was the well-known public dilemma that the Cabinet was hopelessly divided on the issue, with passionate pro-marketeers such as Shirley Williams and Roy Jenkins being opposed by fervent anti-marketeers like Benn, Foot, and Shore, and a centre group including Wilson, Callaghan, Crosland, and Healey moving warily towards acceptance of the *status quo*. The issue of Europe was thus less of a debate about Britain's international role or economic and political needs than an exercise in political equilibrium which would neither destroy a fragile government nor provoke extremes of dissent in a troubled people. What was lacking throughout, as in Britain's approach towards the concept of European unity since the days of the Schuman Plan in 1950, was a head-on engagement with the issues of principle involved in attaching Britain to a wider entity and breaking down centuries of insularity. The one major novelty was the intensified feeling of national weakness, even impotence, prevalent throughout the nation in the wake of the oil crisis and the inflationary explosion as never before.

In theory, the Labour government was engaged from March 1974 onwards in renegotiating the terms of entry into the Common Market. Labour had voted against the EEC in 1972 as has been seen, and TUC opinion was overwhelmingly hostile. On the other hand, opinion in Britain had moved steadily towards a reluctant acceptance of membership of the Community, fear of foreign encroachments on British sovereignty being nullified by the alarm kindled by British economic weakness. Even in Wales and Scotland, where most opinion had seemed to be hostile, partly through fear of the Community nullifying an effective regional policy and its threat to such groups as hill farmers, sentiment was becoming more sympathetic to remaining in the Community. The Community and its negotiators were thus pushing at something of an open door. James Callaghan, the main British negotiator as Foreign Secretary, had himself moved towards wary aceptance of 'Europe' since 1972. The very notion of 'renegotiation', therefore, was something of a misnomer since, as Chancellor Helmut Schmidt observed to Wilson in December 1974, the discussions never implied revision of the Treaty of Rome. The outcome was, therefore, not in doubt. What was, however, uncertain was the capacity of a precarious and somewhat despairing Labour administration to stand the strain.

Callaghan found the climate amongst the members of the community sympathetic, especially Helmut Schmidt, the recently elected German Chancellor and head of a mainly Social Democratic government. The French President, Giscard d'Estaing (who spoke English well), was also far more amiable than de Gaulle ever was. Callaghan was careful to balance Peter Shore, an anti-European adviser, in his delegation to Brussels, with Roy Hattersley, an equally enthusiastic supporter of Market membership. The British negotiators were much assisted by the distinctly limited view of the Community that existing members such as the French already took. Visions of political union were set aside. Most of the discussion concentrated on more mundane aspects of international housekeeping such as budgetary contributions and the financing of subsidies to continental farmers. There was some modification of the budgetary provisions where contributions would be somewhat phased down to allow for countries such as Britain with balance-of-payments difficulties. It was recognized that, in the eighties, with British oil from the North Sea due to come on stream in great quantities, these problems might well diminish if not disappear. There was also set up a regional fund to assist relatively underdeveloped areas like Brittany, southern Italy, and parts of Callaghan's own Wales. But no significant modification of Britain's relationship with the community had really been achieved by the end of 1974. It was simply that the mood in Britain itself, and in the Labour Party, had changed. On that flimsy basis, Harold Wilson told his Cabinet in December that they were moving towards acceptance, and that, as promised in the election manifesto, a referendum ought to be held. A final settlement, of a kind, was achieved in a summit at Dublin in March 1975. At this, after much bargaining, a formula was proclaimed by which Britain's budgetary contribution would be reduced, and a verbal construct invented to try to placate New Zealand and other Commonwealth food producers. Harold Wilson then announced the end of the negotiations and the government's intention of offering the nation a chance to give its opinion in a referendum. The Prime Minister very fairly observed to the House: 'the Government cannot claim to have achieved in full all the objectives that were set out in the manifesto on which Labour fought. It is thus for the judgement now of the Government, shortly of Parliament and in due course of the British people.'[6]

The subsequent referendum campaign was a unique episode in British history.[7] The government provided £125,000 from public funds to finance both the pro- and anti-market campaigns. The Cabinet itself operated on the basis of a free vote for each minister, the collective responsibility principle being set aside. The analogy usually quoted was the unhappy one of the Imports Duties Bill in 1932, but that had been introduced by a Coalition government consisting of Conservative, Liberal, and National Labour. The main role in the campaign, in fact, was not taken by either of the party leaders. Wilson and Callaghan remained largely aloof, while the newly-elected Conservative leader, Mrs Thatcher, was far from being what contemporaries termed a 'Euro-fanatic'. Her philosophy seemed, if anything, a British version of Gaullism. On the Labour side, the main role was

---

[6] *Parl. Deb.*, 5th Ser., vol. 889, 821–38 (7 Apr. 1975). After a four-day debate, the government's motion was carried 396 to 170 on a free vote.

[7] See David Butler and Uwe Kitzinger. *The 1975 Referendum* (London, 1976) and Philip Goodhart, *Full-hearted Consent* (London, 1976).

taken by passionate pro-Europeans such as Roy Jenkins, Mrs Williams, and George Thomson in the 'Yes campaign', with the Conservative Edward Heath equally vehement on their behalf, along with virtually all the Liberals. The Labour 'noes' were headed by Michael Foot, Tony Benn, Peter Shore, and Mrs Barbara Castle, with many trade-union leaders also prominent. The main Conservative dissentients were mainly back-bench figures such as Neil Marten and Teddy Taylor, along with the Scottish Nationalists and the maverick figure of Enoch Powell. The Welsh Nationalists were divided in sympathy, but moving towards acceptance.

What did not take place was a proper debate. The result was a foregone conclusion, with the vast bulk of the press pro-market and powerful 'Britain in Europe' campaigns mounted by finance and industry. On the other hand, the anti-marketeers did manage to get equal time on radio and television which somewhat redressed the balance. In addition to the £125,000 from the government, the pro-marketeers, well funded from the Stock Exchange, spent a further £1.5 m. which dwarfed the 'Keep Britain Out' campaign. At a televised debate at the Oxford Union, Edward Heath was able to make a powerful personal impression, while Mrs Castle was in difficulties having to explain whether or not she would stay in the Cabinet if the vote in the referendum went against her. Kitchener-like, she proclaimed: 'My country needs me.'[8] The general impression was left, perhaps unfairly, that the anti-marketeers were either left-wing 'little Englanders' or old-fashioned Tory imperialists, xenophobic and insular, living in the past. To be pro-'Europe', however, appeared to imply modernity, enterprise, expansion, internationalism, and the road to the future. The 'Yes' campaign thus easily won the public-relations battle. The Labour Party itself had voted 3,724,000 to 1,986,000 in favour of a 'Yes' vote, with many large unions having changed their minds. The stamp of failure

[8] *The Castle Diaries, 1974–76* (London, 1980), 404–6 (entry of 1–5 June 1975).

was thus evident in the 'No' campaign from the start. The result of the referendum was a massive 2 to 1 majority for remaining in the Common Market. The poll on 5 June showed a vote of something over 17 million in favour of remaining a member of the Community, and just over 8 million against. It was, exulted Peter Jenkins in the *Guardian*, a 'Euroslide victory'.[9] The vote in favour was equally emphatic in all parts of Britain, with Wales voting in favour by 2 to 1 and even Scotland also showing a 'Yes' vote. It was an intriguing constitutional exercise, one which kindled more interest in the referendum in academic and other circles as a form of testing popular opinion.[10] Some commentators were sufficiently impressed by the spectacle of the Labour man, Roy Jenkins, the Conservative Heath, and the Liberal leader Thorpe participating in the same campaign on the same platform to urge the need for more coalition-minded or bipartisan politics in place of sterile conflict between time-worn and somewhat discredited parties. Coalition-mindedness was widespread at this time, with perhaps Callaghan as a possible unifying figure. But this talk got nowhere while Callaghan himself, with party memories of Ramsay MacDonald well in mind, was in no mood to commit political suicide.

The Common Market referendum appeared finally to settle a major dispute about Britain's present and future. In practice, it certainly did so, and British representatives merged into the structure of the Community over the coming years. Shortly, Roy Jenkins, in disillusion with the anti-Europeanism of many of his Cabinet colleagues, was to become President of the European Commission in 1977 and (although technically a native of South Wales) was to strike a very English, Oxonian posture there. But the commitment to 'Europe' by the public and by the Labour government remained indirect and half-hearted for years to come. The intermeshing of Britain with the processes of the

---

[9] *Guardian*, 7 June 1975.
[10] See e.g. David Butler and Austin Ranney (eds.). *Referendums: A Comparative Study of Practices and Theory* (Washington, 1978).

EEC seemed only to mean endless disputes over agriculture support and community budget contributions, with little of the idealism and internationalism that the referendum campaign had foretold. The Labour government had negotiated with some success, but the Labour Party remained formally hostile, including at the elections of 1979, 1983, and even 1987. Leading figures in the party like Benn, Foot, and Shore were implacably opposed to the Market in all its forms, while the choice in 1976 of John Silkin, a notable 'Tribunite' and anti-marketeer, as Minister of Agriculture, to confront his European ministerial colleagues in abrasive exchanges, ensured that the presentation of British membership would be jarring and disagreeable. Such wider developments as British entry into a European Parliament (with Euro-elections scheduled for 1979) were not greeted with enthusiasm, while the Labour Party and the TUC urged a boycott. Further developments still, such as a single, united European market (finally to be achieved in 1992) or such a development as Britain's entry into a European monetary system, were strongly resisted by Labour and Conservative governments alike in the 1970s and 1980s. The most that could be said was that the issue was apparently settled, and a long-running conflict put to one side. More important for Wilson and his colleagues, it had been settled without bringing down the Labour government and by the adoption of a skilful mechanism which enabled the Labour Cabinet to continue in being despite the widest possible gulf between its members on such a key issue. Britain and the Wilson government had survived. The wider implications of Britain's relations with any kind of Europe, or the public's perception of them, were swept briskly to one side.

The same tendency to provide a short-term pragmatic solution and to sweep wider questions to one side also governed policy towards the Celtic nations, the now burning issue of devolution in Scotland and Wales, and the alarming situation in Northern Ireland. The Kilbrandon Commission on the constitution had reported in October 1973. At the time, it was overshadowed by the impending oil embargo and the Yom Kippur War, followed by the miners' strike and the general election. But it was clear that a Royal Commission originally set up in 1968 to avert damaging defeats for Labour in Scottish and Welsh by-elections might eventually lead to crisis. At the very least, the presence after the October 1974 election of three Plaid Cymru MPs and no fewer than eleven Scottish Nationalists in the House, at a time when the government had an overall majority of only six, would concentrate the minds of the administration. The Kilbrandon Commission had reported in confusing terms, with no fewer than four models of Scottish and Welsh devolution proposed. But most notable was the proposal, supported by eleven out of thirteen members of the Commission, that there ought to be an elected Scottish parliament and also an elected Welsh assembly, with more limited powers but also some executive jurisdiction. A major constitutional dilemma was thus in the making.

British public opinion, not least in Scotland and Wales, was deeply uncertain about the Kilbrandon proposals and what to do about Celtic devolution.[11] The prevailing unionism that had governed the structure of the United Kingdom since the merger of England and Wales with Scotland in 1707 was now in question. Of course, there had been devolution in Northern Ireland between 1920 and 1973, but no one thought that was a safe model to follow. The entire issue of devolution, indeed, was a curious and unexpected one to become a major political priority. In England, the dominant partner, no serious discussion about the formal structure of the United Kingdom had taken place since the end of the First World War. There had been a gradual accretion of power for the Scottish Office and notable local developments such as the Highlands and Islands Development Corporation after 1945; in Wales, the modest creation of the Ministry of Welsh Affairs by the Conservatives in 1951 had been capped by Labour, somewhat unexpectedly, with the emergence of a Secretary of State for Wales in 1964. But most English

[11] See Bogdanor, *Devolution*.

people took no interest at all in such matters, while academic proposals for some form of regional devolution in the different areas of England aroused little enthusiasm or debate.

Even in Wales, the passion for governmental devolution was somewhat limited. Plaid Cymru won three seats in October 1974, as has been seen, but all were in mainly rural, Welsh-speaking areas, Caernarfon, Merioneth, and Carmarthen. The advance of Welsh nationalism in the mining valleys of the south, so marked in the later 1960s, seemed to have been checked. The main thrust of nationalist passion in Wales focused on the Welsh language, but even that had been somewhat defused since the sixties with the growth of Welsh schools and other concessions to linguistic nationalists. The Welsh Labour Party had moved towards a more devolutionary position since the 1960s, and the new Secretary of State, John Morris, was a staunch devolutionist. Rut, even so, the bulk of the party in the industrial and urban strongholds of south and south-east Wales was manifestly resistant to what most Welsh socialists saw as a pandering to nationalism and inward-looking parochialism.

Only in Scotland did devolution have a real head of steam. In Scotland, not only were eleven SNP MPs returned in 1974, but four seats were gained from the Tories apart from the gains already made from Labour. The Scottish Nationalists claimed 30 per cent of the Scottish vote, only 6.4 per cent behind Labour and far ahead of the Scottish Conservatives' 24.9 per cent. Although Labour's Secretary of State, William Ross, was sternly resistant to any concessions to nationalism, there were prominent figures such as Jim Sillars and Alex Eadie in Labour's ranks who also favoured a strong impulse towards a self-governing, socialist Scotland. The rising unemployment and economic decay of the infrastructure north of the border gave nationalist demands a wide currency in all parts of the country from the Western Isles to new towns such as Cumbernauld and East Kilbride.

The government thus found itself compelled to formulate an approach if only to prevent massive defections from the Labour

Party in its Scottish heartland. A White Paper, *Our Changing Democracy: Devolution in Scotland and Wales*, published in November 1975, outlined major changes in the constitutional structure of the United Kingdom.[12] There would indeed be a Scottish elected assembly with widespread legislative powers. However, to the fury of nationalists, it would have no powers of revenue-raising or over major economic aspects of industrial or agricultural policy while the Secretary of State for Scotland would have significant powers to veto or override the assembly's measures. In Wales, the elected assembly would be much weaker. Its powers would be confined largely to the executive aspects of social policy, with a block grant of £850 million provided by the Treasury for expenditure on local administration. A bill designed to give broad effect to Scottish and Welsh devolution finally passed its second reading in December 1976 by 292 votes to 245, with much cross-voting by both Conservative and Labour MPs.

The debate over devolution, however, was largely unreal and provoked a good deal of cynicism. There was the utmost confusion over what the government really intended. Broad issues such as the number of Welsh and Scottish MPs to remain at Westminster (vital as they were to any possible Labour majority in the future), the role of the Secretaries of State for the two nations, the constitutional and legal relationships between the new proposed assemblies and Westminster were cloudy in the extreme. There was much resentment amongst English MPs at the favoured treatment given Scotland and Wales. Hence the government issued a White Paper, *The English Dimension*, intended, unsuccessfully, to reassure English doubters.[13] It became increasingly uncertain whether there was a genuine majority in the House for devolution. Pro-devolution Conservatives like Edward Heath were matched by a wide range of Labour MPs, on the left and right of the party, who rejected devolution as a barrier to

[12] *Our Changing Democracy: Devolution in Scotland and Wales* (Cmnd. 6348), Parl. Papers, 1975–6, XIV.
[13] *Devolution: the English Dimension* (HMSO, London, 1976).

cohesive nation-wide socialist planning. There were many important dissenters in Welsh Labour ranks, sometimes making use of (or trying to create) tension between Welsh-speaking and non-Welsh-speaking communities and forecasting a putative Welsh Ulster emerging. One highly effective critic of devolution was a youthful Gwent MP, Neil Kinnock. The Scots Labour MPs were more enthusiastic, but there were critics here too, including Tam Dalyell and a London-based Scotsman, George Cunningham, who was shortly to scupper the government's entire plans by ensuring that devolution would take effect only with a 40 per cent majority of the voters after separate referendums were held in Scotland and in Wales. The debate in Scotland and Wales, according to some idealists or wishful thinkers, involved a profound reassessment of the nature and balance of power within the United Kingdom, a satisfying of the centuries-old cry for national equality from the 'internally colonized' subject Celtic nations of the periphery. It is clear that nothing so fundamental occurred, and that the proposals for devolution were marked by political manœuvring, procedural muddle, and a good deal of cynicism. The main objective was to fudge a solution which would ensure continuing Scottish and Welsh support for Labour in the House and in the country without producing a lasting separation. No long-term programme evolved. The devolution debate, profoundly uninteresting to a great mass of the population especially in England, was deeply anti-climactic and yet another facet of the Labour government's essay in survival. For all that, it carried enough momentum as a parliamentary issue in the later 1970s for an enormous amount of energy to be devoted to it, and for it to act as a further element of division and frustration within the United Kingdom.

Devolution in Wales and Scotland, however, was essentially a parliamentary dispute. Northern Ireland, as since 1968, had far more damaging implications. Here again was an unresolved dilemma which continued to undermine social and political stability. The Labour government confronted the problem with a series of contradictory attitudes. The party claimed to be more committed to creating a new relationship with the Republic to the south than the Tories could be; at the same time. Labour was anxious to stress that any change would both rest on a fundamental reappraisal of the Ulster situation and be no change at all, at one and the same time. Again, the Labour government constantly spoke of the need to reduce the British military presence, and the new Secretary for Ireland, Merlyn Rees, and his deputy, Stan Orme, both spoke in 1974 of the desirability or prospect of withdrawing British troops. On the other hand, Labour remained committed to preserving order and security, at least to prevent conflict between the communities and restrain the IRA, at worst to prevent a holocaust at the expense of the Catholic minorities of Ulster. The British security forces thus became guardians of the peace and an occupying neo-imperialist army at one and the same time. As usual, the Labour government, like all British governments since the time of Gladstone if not of Cromwell, saw the Irish dimension essentially in British terms, as a tiresome political bog to avoid rather an issue of mediation and reconciliation to be met by constructive statesmanship. In the background was the fact that Northern Ireland had suffered more than any other part of the realm from mounting unemployment and industrial recession since the mid-1960s. After March 1974 this did not change.

Nevertheless, the Labour government, with Merlyn Rees a dedicated and courageous executive at the Irish Office, did try to provide a new political initiative in this unpromising situation. One hopeful sign was that the Republic of Ireland now had a Fine Gael/Labour government under Liam Cosgrave which might be expected to prove far more conciliatory towards London than Fianna Fáil and the ex-Taoiseach (Prime Minister) Jack Lynch. There were, therefore signs of a new energy devoted to trying to resolve the Irish dilemma in a more basic way after the comparative success of the Whitelaw initiatives under the Conservatives.

The Labour government was anxious to emphasize the community rather than the security side of British policy in Ireland, and to replace direct rule with a more effective form of devolved government. One moderating move was the gradual abolition of the internment of members of the IRA and the ending of the jury-less so-called 'Diplock courts', the extra-judicial system set up following a report by the English judge, Lord Diplock. But the basic structure inherited from the Conservatives, the implementation of the Sunningdale Agreement and the power-sharing executive of Protestants and Catholics set up at the end of 1973, remained. Catholics were deeply suspicious of these developments; conversely, militant Protestants were openly hostile to a policy which they regarded as the first stage of imposing the yoke of Dublin and of Rome on the Protestant Unionist population. The birth of the Ulster Defence Association, a Protestant extremist body of similar temper to the Catholic 'Provos', marked a rise in tension and a sign that the Unionist leader of the power-sharing executive, the former right-winger Brian Faulkner, no longer spoke for Protestants as a whole. A huge strike was organized by the Protestant-run Ulster Workers' Council on 15 May 1974.[14] Within a few days, it was clear that the economy of Ulster was grinding to a halt, with power stations and other key installations closing down. An attempt by Len Murray to lead a demonstration of the British TUC to persuade Irish workers to give up their politically motivated strike resulted in his being abused and spat upon by Protestant women in Belfast's Shankill Road. The Labour government found itself powerless in the face of determined industrial action which, by persuasion or intimidation, made Ulster ungovernable. A total climb-down followed. On 28 May, amidst the lighting of bonfires by Protestants up and down the province, Brian Faulkner resigned as head of the power-sharing executive. That very short-lived body thus collapsed. The Sunningdale Agreement, six months after it was signed, was moribund. Yet another attempt to build bridges between the two Ulster communities and between London and Dublin had led nowhere, and total deadlock resulted in which the

[14] *The Times*, 16–23 May 1974. Also see Merlyn Rees, *Northern Ireland: A Personal View* (London, 1985), 65–90.

violent men of the IRA and the Protestant 'Defence' organizations had the field to themselves.

Despite some ministerial talk of 'pulling out' British troops, the Labour government attempted yet another political initiative in the endless cycle of abortive gestures. A White Paper on 4 July now called for a Constitutional Convention to be called, with no blueprint or agenda, in which the local politicians would meet and decide for themselves on the next step forward, untrammelled by Westminster or Whitehall. To ensure that such a move would be frustrated, the IRA now extended its operations openly to the British mainland. Savage bomb attacks followed in such places as a public house in Birmingham and two pubs in Guildford frequented by British soldiers. After a short-lived 'truce' called by the Provisional Sinn Fein forces in February 1975, a renewed pattern of murder and violence was resumed that summer with gun battles common in Catholic areas of West Belfast. More violent attacks took place in Britain also, notably in London. There were gruesome episodes such as the murder at his home in Middlesex of Ross McWhirter, a right-wing journalist prominent in the 'National Association For Freedom', who had campaigned publicly against IRA bombers. In this atmosphere, the Constitutional Convention inevitably proved to be yet another Irish initiative that led nowhere. Although a reasonable poll of 64 per cent was achieved in the Convention elections, with Unionists of various shades winning 47 seats out of 78, against 17 for the SDLP and 8 for the moderate Alliance Party, there was no meeting of minds between Protestant and Catholic politicians on any major issue. The Convention failed to produce an agreed solution of any kind. After a few months of ghostly existence it, too, disappeared from history in early 1976.

Throughout 1976 the pattern of violence seemed complete, with renewed determination by an apparently invincible Provisional IRA met by tougher measures by the British government, including applying a new criminal status to political Republican prisoners interned in the camp at Long Kesh. Some hope was kindled by a new 'Peace Movement' started by two Catholic

Belfast women in the summer of 1976 following the accidental death of three children in a violent incident in Belfast. This aroused optimism in Catholic ghetto areas and much international acclaim for the two women leaders involved, Betty Williams and Mairead Corrigan. In 1977 they were to receive the Nobel Peace prize. But in reality, for all the courage and idealism of this short-lived upsurge of 'peace' in the ghettos of West Belfast and the Bogside of Derry, the gulf between the two communities was wider than ever, with no political bridges in existence at the end of 1976. The security forces were using tougher and tougher measures of reprisal, while the tendency to rely increasingly on the Royal Ulster Constabulary, together with the part-time Ulster Defence Regiment, both overwhelmingly Protestant and seen as committed and sectarian by most Catholics, made the preservation of an agreed system of security harder and harder to achieve. Northern Ireland was frankly seen as a military rather than a political problem now, as the injuries and funerals multiplied. A sign of the times was the replacement of the moderate Merlyn Rees at the Irish Office by a former miner, Roy Mason, who took a tough view of security matters, and who began to end remission for good behaviour by Republican prisoners in the H block in the Maze.

How deeply Northern Ireland impinged on the British consciousness, is hard to say. In most respects it seemed to the English, Welsh, and Scots a world apart, which impinged on them only in incomprehensible and brutal bombings and assassinations in their cities, without warning and seemingly without purpose. The Ulster political culture and social mood were so utterly distinct from that in the rest of the United Kingdom that it hardly related to the governability or peaceableness of British life in general. A common reaction was boredom with the ritual killing of each other by Irishmen. A notable literary renaissance in Ulster was inevitably coloured by its political and sectarian context. Its leading poet, Seamus Heaney, resigned a lectureship at Queen's University, Belfast, and moved to Wicklow and then

Dublin in the Republic. In *North* (1975) Heaney wrote sadly (and perhaps with some guilt) of how:

> I am neither internee nor informer
> An inner emigré, grown long-haired
> And thoughtful; a wood-kerne
> Escaped from the massacre.

Elsewhere, he wrote:

> No treaty
> I foresee will salve completely your tracked
> And stretch-marked body, the big pain
> That leaves you raw, like opened ground again.[15]

But, however removed it may have seemed, these violent events added to the sense of unease and insecurity about British civic culture. They meant that the army was being built up and being used in frequent action as it had not been regularly since wars in Cyprus and Aden in the fifties and sixties. It also meant a steady drain on British resources, and much tension with the United States, with its large Irish immigrant population in major cities. There was also difficulty with the International Court of Human Rights where British policy such as internment without trial frequently met with condemnation. Dictating government responses, as elsewhere, were the political realities—efforts made by the Wilson government to conclude deals with the Unionists over their representation in Westminster, as a way of finding some reliable fragment of Unionist opinion on which a new settlement could be based. The endless cycle of violence and political impotence that Ulster generated added to the feeling of helplessness and failure that marked British life in the seventies.

More hope, perhaps, attached to a quite different area of society where the Labour government could reasonably claim to start on a more positive basis than the outgoing Conservatives,

---

[15] Seamus Heaney, 'Exposure', in *North* (London, 1975), 73, and 'Act of Union', ibid. 50.

that of industrial relations. As has been seen, the trade unions were growing rapidly at this period, notably in such areas as public-service employment in local government and health, and in white-collar unions such as ASTMS. NUPE membership grew from 265,000 in 1968 to 712,000 in 1978, a product of burgeoning bureaucracy. Alan Fisher of NUPE, Ken Gill of TASS, Clive Jenkins of ASTMS were the rising stars of the trade-union world. Yet, at the same time, polls repeatedly showed that trade unions as institutions enjoyed diminishing respect and esteem. Public perceptions linked them directly to the low productivity and cost inflation that marked British economic performance. In 1976 it was reported that 66 per cent of trade unionists themselves felt that unions enjoyed excessive power.[16] The Conservatives had manifestly failed to deal with this problem through legislation or court action, and had crashed from power in the chaos of the miners' strike. Labour, with such dominant union figures as Jack Jones of the Transport Workers and Hugh Scanlon of the Engineers, both mighty figures in the party, and with the old Bevanite, Michael Foot, in charge of labour policy, could surely hope to do better.

Labour's claim to offer a new departure rested on the so-called 'social contract' concluded between Harold Wilson and Vic Feather in 1972 in which the unions agreed to voluntary restraint on wages in return for congenial social and industrial policies and an agreement by the Labour Party not to offer legislative or legal interference with collective bargaining when it returned to government. It was the product of the labyrinthine processes worked out by the party's Liaison Committee. From the outset, its implications—and even more its enforcement—were clouded by doubt and uncertainty. Wilson himself argued that the essence of the contract lay in productivity agreements.[17] As in 1969 there was little evidence to show that either the will or the machinery existed to restore order to the wage market, with local bargaining

---

[16] See Denis Kavanagh, *Thatcherism and British Politics* (Oxford, 1987), 292 ff.
[17] Jack Jones, *Union Man*, 286.

by shop floor representatives and the 'drift' effect on wage levels driving inflation upwards. By the end of 1974, with union after union, culminating in the moderate NUR led by Sid Weighell, achieving wage increases well into double figures, it was recorded that wage rates had risen by 26.4 per cent in the year. Other built-in pressures such as oil and petrol increases and rising food prices under the European Common Agricultural Policy led to an over-all inflation rate of over 28 per cent.[18] The miners, buoyed up excitedly by their two triumphs over the Heath government, were now proposing further demands that would boost the pay of surface workers by no less than 94 per cent. Even friends of the unions like Michael Foot were constrained to admit that this was no basis for a planned or orderly increase in wages.

Nevertheless, in 1975 the indiscipline in the wages market continued to frustrate the government; indeed, it was openly encouraged by at least one Cabinet minister, Tony Benn. In a notable coup, Harold Wilson managed to transfer him from the Trade and Industry Department to the Department of Energy in June 1975, just after the Common Market referendum. Benn was replaced at Trade by the mild and moderate figure of Eric Varley, and his wings in the administration continued to be clipped.[19] Nevertheless, in his new portfolio—where he had at least the prospect of announcing repeated good news about North Sea oil supplies coming on stream—he continued to encourage massive wage increases, backed up or extorted by industrial action.

Increasingly within the TUC itself alarm began to be felt as one 20 per cent wage increase followed another at the behest of a powerful union, threatening the economic life of the nation. There was at least a prospect of a change favourable to the unions under a Labour government, with Michael Foot carrying through a notable innovation such as the conciliation service, ACAS, and the proposal of an Employment Protection Bill. All this would be set aside in the event of uncontrollable inflation

---

[18] *The Economist*, 14 Dec. 1974.
[19] Wilson, *Final Term*, 144; Barbara Castle, *Castle Diaries, 1974–76*, 410.

and the widespread social disorder that was likely to result if it occurred. It is symptomatic of the mood of the time that a new initiative came neither from within a relatively paralysed government, nor from within the civil service, but from the most self-interested part of all, the TUC, and its famous left-wing champion, Jack Jones, the Secretary of the giant Transport Workers' union. Since the 'social contract' was clearly worthless, Jones proposed instead, at a union rally in Bournemouth in March, a policy of voluntary restraint based on a flat-rate rise of identical amount for everyone, of no more than £6 a week. The TUC General Council voted this in by 19 to 13 in June and on 3 September the TUC conference accepted the wage-restraint policy, carried by the remarkably large majority of 6.9 million to 3.4 million.[20] How effective in operation such a policy would be remained to be seen. But it was at least the clearest indication to date that the unions were aware that excessive wages led to rising inflation and diminishing employment, and that their monopolistic control over the job market was proving self-defeating, most of all for the ill-organized and low-paid.

This policy was accompanied by a series of ministerial pronouncements, starting with a notable speech by Denis Healey in his Leeds constituency in January 1975[21] to the effect that wage inflation was a prime cause of unemployment, and that cash limits needed to be imposed on public expenditure. The spectre of supply-side monetarism was abroad in the land. Attempts were made by minister after minister to curb public spending, fuelled as it was by unions' wage demands. Anthony Crosland, Secretary of the Environment, imposed vigorous controls on the spending by local authorities, most of them Labour-controlled. 'The party', Crosland declared ominously, 'is over.' Healey's latest budget in April 1975, the fourth in a rapid sequence,

---

[20]   *The Times*, 4 Sept. 1975.

[21]   *The Times*, 16 Jan. 1975, including Peter Jay's article 'Into Battle with Mr. Healey'—'the most controversial inversion of post-1944 conventional wisdom about the management of the economy'.

concentrated on taking money out of the economy, and imposed new taxes to the tune of £1¼ billion a year, with a big rise in VAT and in income tax, along with cuts of over a billion pounds in public spending.[22] With inflation continuing to rise throughout the winter, the centre-piece of Healey's next budget in April 1976 was the imposition of a 3 per cent maximum for wage increases, very much in line with the formula worked out by Jack Jones and Michael Foot. Indeed the unexpected axis between two very different personalities, Michael Foot and Denis Healey, now became fundamental to the government's strategy. Healey's aim was for inflation to be reduced from over 20 per cent to 5–7 per cent in 1977. Yet there remained doubt in government circles as to how effectively the TUC could be persuaded to accept this limit, tantamount to no more that £2 a week for everyone at a time of rising prices. Michael Foot, in somewhat traditional words, was quoted by Barbara Castle as observing that 'we have got to fight like hell for agreement with the trade unions and what they are prepared to recommend'.[23] In the interim, though, inflation fell steadily in 1975 and 1976, and so, incidentally, did the rate of strikes. Comparative industrial peace was certainly a feature of this period.

How successful the government's *démarche* in industrial relations policy really was remained doubtful. Within the labyrinths of government there remained intense doubt and suspicion of the unions. As has been noted, the presence of Communists and Marxists in the NUM such as McGahey and Scargill had hardened the attitude of the Heath government in the miners' disputes of the early seventies. Major union figures like Jack Jones and Hugh Scanlon (a Communist in his earlier years but now a fairly centrist Labour supporter) were under secret surveillance by MI5. Secret reports were sent by security agencies to the Prime Minister Harold Wilson (ironically enough, himself a supposed subject of security scrutiny at this period) and the Home

---

[22] *The Economist*, 19 Apr. 1975.
[23] Castle, *Castle Diaries, 1974–76*, 717.

Secretary, Roy Jenkins, but not to either of the left-wing ministers, Michael Foot at Employment and Benn at Trade. When
Jack Jones was proposed as chairman of the National Enterprise
Board in late 1974, and again when Scanlon was offered a
directorship of the British Gas Corporation, in each case MI5
sent in a negative report. Sir Arthur Hetherington, Chairman of
British Gas, observed: 'As far as Scanlon is concerned, I want to
be sure the man we have is loyal to the country.'[24] For years
ahead, these two major union leaders continued to be viewed as
potential or actual security risks.

But the real doubts about the new industrial relations
approach of the government concerned not the patriotism of
union leaders but their operative effectiveness. Whatever the
virtues of the new flat-rate limit devised by Jack Jones, such a
policy of restraint and self-abnegation had come too late. Nor
was there any guarantee of its duration. It had emerged in very
rushed circumstances, with a variety of figures bandied about. It
was the product, not of objective calculation by government or
public servants of the appropriate kind of industrial policy for a
time of external difficulties but of political, pragmatic calculation
by unions and ministers of the minimum agreement that would
be credible in the light of the traditional relations governing the
unions and the Labour Party. Since Michael Foot was hardly
another Cripps to evangelize for the cause of austerity and a
wage-freeze, the policy rested squarely on the personal prestige
of Jack Jones himself, something of a poacher turned gamekeeper
after his central role in defeating Mrs Castle's proposals back in
1969. His personal stature was considerable, though it was
dented by growing criticisms on the left, notably by Ian Mikardo
at an angry *Tribune* meeting in September 1975.[25] But it all
meant a comparatively frail basis for long-term industrial planning with all the main questions bearing upon the relationship of

[24] Mark Hollingsworth and Richard Norton-Taylor, *Blacklist: The Inside
Story of Political Vetting* (London, 1988), 124.
[25] Castle, op. cit., 512 (entry of 1 Oct. 1975); see *Guardian*, 2 Oct. 1975.

the unions with the government and the community still to be answered.

The wider policy of industrial reconstruction associated with this agreement on collective bargaining was also uncertain. As over Northern Ireland, the government had come to office with conflicting postures. On the one hand, they were committed to a wider involvement with the direction of the economy and investment in industry. On the other hand Wilson, Callaghan, and others were anxious to evade the excesses of intervention associated with Tony Benn. His original scheme for planning agreements, the compulsory acquisition of shares by a National Enterprise Board, and a growing policy of nationalization was watered down or simply evaded. Apart from political considerations, Benn's advocacy of 'an alternative economic strategy' was much discredited by his association with endorsing a series of workers' co-operatives which concerned plants threatened with closures. The *Scottish Daily News*, the Scottish *Daily Express*, Norton Villiers Triumph motorbikes at Meriden, Kirby Engineering in Liverpool (which, extraordinarily enough, produced orange juice along with car parts), became derided in Cabinet as 'Benn's follies', commercial fiascos one and all.[26] The attempt to inject £3.9 m. into Kirby Engineering led to an embarrassing public row between Benn and his high-profile civil-servant adviser, Sir Anthony Part. Further efforts to inject public funds into failing concerns such as Bear Brand stockings and Triang children's toys also failed to get much support. Benn's advocacy of a vigorous policy by the National Enterprise Board was neutered by Wilson, and its chairman, Donald Ryder, ensured that it played a relatively modest role. Later came the resignation of Eric Heffer from the government, though Benn himself fatalistically stayed on.

Denis Healey argued consistently against excessive state intervention and for a more collaborative approach to private

[26] See Joel Barnett, *Inside the Treasury* (London, 1982), 35 ff.

enterprise. The main government strategy was to curb public intervention, cut back public spending, and introduce cash limits. On the other hand, the National Enterprise Board had been created with powers that could theoretically be extended. Its very presence encouraged the growth of monetarist thinking amongst the government's free-market opponents at the time, while the evidence of growing Labour sympathy with nationalization, after three decades of tranquillity and preservation of the existing mix of the economy, alarmed defenders of free enterprise. So did the nationalization of aircraft and shipbuilding in due course. The decision to rescue British Leyland, which was on the brink of bankruptcy, meant a virtual take-over by the state in return for the massive injection of public funds. The government seemed to be adopting postures simultaneously of both increasing and relaxing state involvement in industry, of both curtailing and extending public investment at one and the same time. Meanwhile unemployment and inflation both rose to record post-war levels and the government seemed to travel in the wake of events.

At this critical and pivotal time, there was quite unexpectedly a change of premier. Harold Wilson, whose energy had seemed somewhat diminished in his last term in office, announced on 16 March his departure from office. The reasons led to feverish speculation, although it would appear that ill-health probably played its part. As noted, his final term in office had been less frenetic and more placid than the 1964–70 period, though the condition of the nation had not improved. His reputation, however, was further sullied by a final honours list which, in Lloyd George style, honoured old cronies such as Lord Kagan, Sigmund Sternberg, James Goldsmith, Sir Eric Miller, and Lord Weidenfeld. More than one met an untimely end: Lord Kagan of 'Gannex' fame was shortly to be imprisoned for fraud, while others committed suicide. Perhaps unfairly many of the old doubts about Wilson's style of government and range of associates were rekindled, while his links with Jewish financial circles kindled a covert anti-Semitism.

His successor was not in doubt. James Callaghan had emerged as a central cohesive force in the party since 1970 and had played a major consolidating role over Europe, industrial policy, the unions, devolution, and much else since 1974. In a generally courteous leadership contest, he defeated Michael Foot, the main left-wing candidate, with some ease (176 to 133 on the second ballot), leaving Jenkins, Healey, Benn, and Crosland trailing. Callaghan ensured that a thoroughly professional style of politics would now prevail. He carefully remodelled his government, leaving Benn isolated as virtually the only real voice of the left. Callaghan lost Roy Jenkins as a pillar of the right. On the other hand, he also removed Barbara Castle of the old left, a vehement anti-European. Callaghan's own stature now rose considerably. There was renewed press talk of his emerging as some kind of leader of a coalition. On a wide range of matters, from incomes policy to education, he spoke with new authority. He also won the respect of Tessa Blackstone and others in the 'Think Tank', more so than either Heath or Wilson, since he showed more capacity to listen and discuss matters openly. Talk of *putsches* and conspiracies vanished. Callaghan, according to William Rodgers, saw himself (reminiscent of his naval service during the war) as 'the able seaman, the man who understands the common man'.[27] Conversely, Callaghan was associated at best with a policy of quiescence, and with all the main range of policies over the past twelve years. His ideas had been formed during the Attlee years after 1945. He was not in general a voice for innovation or reform. His presence was a guarantee that much the same, familiar methods would be adopted to face an emerging crisis.

As noted above, Callaghan was confronted with almost intractable problems on devolution and Ireland which taxed all his ingenuity. But his resources were stretched to the very limit by a new and alarming crisis in the economy which threatened to bring his administration crumbling down after only a few months in Number 10. *The Economist*, ironically enough, had prophesied in January that 'whatever happens, 1976 will be a

[27] Phillip Whitehead, *The Writing on the Wall: Britain in the Seventies* (London, 1985), 256.

better year for Britain than 1975', with North Sea oil to boost the balance of payments and a revival of world trade as the economies of the leading industrial nations pulled out of recession.[28] In fact, circumstances continued to deteriorate. Healey was compelled to bring in yet another mini-budget in July in which he declared his wish to keep the growth in the money supply to 12 per cent for the rest of the year. Callaghan himself took a boldly monetarist line at party conference two months later—'You cannot now, if you ever could, spend your way out of a recession'[29]—words popularly attributed to his son-in-law, Peter Jay, a leading financial journalist (shortly to go to the embassy in Washington). But there were endless problems. There was strong left-wing pressure on the NEC to reject the government's cuts in public expenditure. Labour's fortunes in the polls and in by-elections were disastrous, culminating in a by-election at Walsall which saw a record 27.3 per cent swing against the government. The government indeed only remained in office through the courtesy of the 3 Plaid Cymru members, 2 representatives of the 'Scottish Labour Party' and 2 Irish Roman Catholics, including Frank Maguire, a publican from Fermanagh whose attendances at Westminster votes were erratic in the extreme and who favoured 'abstaining in person'. The National Union of Seamen called an all-out strike, and the pound sank to a low point of near $1.70. Bank rate climbed to 15 per cent in October and there was again pressure on the reserves. In a humiliating episode, Denis Healey was called back at Heathrow from a flying visit to the IMF Conference at Manila.[30]

The government thus faced a crisis of extreme severity, far worse than any experienced since the oil crisis in 1973, and there appeared to be no alternative other than recourse to the International Monetary Fund. How to do so, however, and on

---

[28] *The Economist*, 10 Jan. 1976.   [29] *The Times*, 29 Sept. 1976.
[30] Ibid., 27 Sept. 1976. As a result, Healey appeared at party conference where he made a pugnacious, much-heckled speech in the five minutes allowed him.

precisely what terms, raised highly contentious political and economic issues. Callaghan decided, in contrast to Wilson's established practice, to conduct the debate on the basis of old-fashioned collective Cabinet government. No fewer than twenty-six Cabinet meetings were held in October–December 1976 to consider the precise terms of an IMF loan.[31] Clearly massive public expenditure cuts would be involved. Indeed, the IMF called for no less £2–3 billion. Healey was predictably attacked by Benn and Shore on the left. But unexpectedly he faced vigorous assault from more right-wing colleagues as well, notably Crosland, Shirley Williams, and Harold Lever, at the cuts in public spending and the social injustices that would result. Healey found himself at times with very little Cabinet support at all, with only a few ministers like Edmund Dell and the maverick figure of Reg Prentice backing him. There was also tension on occasion between the Prime Minister and his Chancellor, although in general Callaghan threw his backing behind his colleague in a way he felt that Wilson had not done behind him in the somewhat similar crises of 1966–7. The very severity of the crisis, however, forced a solution through, however unpalatable. The left-wing 'alternative strategy' propounded by Benn failed to carry much support, with figures like Foot, Shore, and Silkin moving to back up the Chancellor. A crucial element was Callaghan's ability to sway the Foreign Secretary, Anthony Crosland, the main intellectual voice of the Keynesian dissenters, along with Harold Lever, an influential figure since he understood market finance in much detail.[32] In the end, Callaghan threw his own support behind a package of £2 billions of cuts, distinctly less than some of the figures bandied about, and agreement was reached. Healey announced that a huge loan of $3.0 billion from the IMF would be made available in three instalments,

---

[31] See Whitehead, *Writing on the Wall*, 193–201; Callaghan, *Time and Chance*, 434–46; Bernard Donoughue, *Prime Minister: The Conduct of Policy under Harold Wilson and James Callaghan* (London, 1987), 96 ff.

[32] Callaghan, op. cit., 434 ff; cf. Susan Crosland, *Tony Crosland* (London, 1982) for Crosland's opposition to the cuts.

the first tranche of £1.5 billion to come in early 1977. In return, Healey announced a cut of £1 billion in public spending estimates in 1977–8 and a further £112 billion in 1978–9. In addition, a further £ 500 m. would be raised by the sale of most British Petroleum shares. Healey thus became incidentally the first privatizer.

The pound thereafter was stable, and the markets were calm. Amongst Labour supporters, who had feared another 1931-style holocaust, there was even relief. Some of the more extreme forms of public expenditure measures such as reduced social-security benefits or cuts in housing benefits had not materialized. There was no government resignation, not even that of Tony Benn, who contacted his Bristol supporters just to make sure. Callaghan's skilful and protracted handling of the Cabinet discussions was beyond reproach and greatly enhanced his reputation for statesmanship. His adviser, Bernard Donoughue, later praised his 'remarkable' achievement. 'He had delivered a much smaller IMF cuts package than expected to his Cabinet, and he had delivered his Cabinet's approval to the IMF.'[33] It would be hard to argue that an international capitalist cartel like the IMF had cut the ground away from under a Labour government and its trade-union supporters. There was general hope that the balance of payments would now improve substantially, with the impact of North Sea oil becoming more evident and more buoyancy in international trade. The election of the Anglophile Jimmy Carter as US President was a cheerful portent. Britain would indeed be about 60 per cent self-sufficient in oil by the end of 1978. Falling unemployment, reduced inflation, and resumed growth were foreshadowed in the years to come, prophecies which were generally borne out in the later seventies.

Nevertheless, the IMF crisis was a traumatic and damaging episode. It shook the cohesiveness of the government to its foundation. Jack Jones, who played a generally loyalist role, also spoke of his shock at hearing Denis Healey 'speak with the

[33] Donoughue, *Prime Minister*, 99.

voice of the IMF'. Britain's debtor status was humiliatingly exposed to a sceptical and critical world. Fellow-members of the EEC were heard to wonder aloud precisely what kind of lame duck they had admitted to membership. Worst of all, the IMF crisis, conducted in the full glare of world publicity, and with much incidental sniping from the US Treasury and its minister, William Simon, severely undermined the intellectual self-confidence of the Keynesian establishment who had dominated economic and social policy-making for so long. Critics like the Oxford economists, Roger Bacon and Walter Eltis, now attacked the damage done to the economy by Keynesian government-led booms over the past twenty years, and also basic errors in Keynes's ideas including a relative ignoring of international trade and thus of the balance of payments.[34] Outsiders like the monetarist critics acquired much credibility as old orthodoxies crumbled, and apostles of the traditional view like Crosland and Shirley Williams seemed to lose their way. There were now signs of monetarism making inroads at the highest levels of the Labour Party through Healey's cash-limits policy. There was also the influence of Harold Lever, whose 'seminar' of top civil servants in 1977–9 was one consequence of the monetarists' alternative to the Keynesian treasury. Callaghan himself presided over a major push from public resources to private during the IMF crisis. Bernard Donoughue later wrote of how the doctrines later known as 'Thatcherism' were first launched in late 1976 'in primitive form' by Callaghan, the Treasury, the Bank, and above all the IMF and sections of the US Treasury.[35]

Everything that was vulnerable about the British position was epitomized by the IMF negotiations—an overvalued pound still bedevilled by prospects that sterling could play a world role;

---

[34] Roger Bacon and Walter Eltis, *Britain's Economic Problem: Too Few Producers* (London, 1976). They focus especially on the growth in public-sector employment in the 1961–76 period. Also see Walter Eltis, 'The Failure of the Conventional Keynesian Wisdom', *Lloyd's Bank Review*, 122 (October 1976).

[35] Donoughue, *Prime Minister*, 94.

excessive wage costs driven up by the unions, alongside ineffective, timid management; public spending beyond Britain's means
to sustain it with any confidence: all were thrown into stark
relief. Britain appeared on centre stage as an incompetent beggar,
with few friends in the Commonwealth, though much residual
goodwill—on approved terms—from the EEC, through individual figures like Helmut Schmidt. There seemed to be an indirection with few parallels in other major countries. Reflecting on
previous industrial disputes and Britain's high rate of inflation,
American politicians observed, with absurd exaggeration, that
the old country had become 'as ungovernable as Chile'. Previous
crises—the withdrawal from Palestine in 1948, Suez in 1956, the
withdrawal from 'east of Suez' in 1968, repeated rebuffs in the
attempt to join Europe prior to 1973, had shown up the contours
of external weakness. The IMF crisis, skilfully handled by Callaghan though it was, and although greeted by a stunned British
public with an almost neurotic sense of relief, showed a much
more damaging erosion from within by a nation that had (some
commentators argued) ceased to believe in its destiny or in itself.

After the IMF crisis, there was much talk of internal dissolution, of the centre failing to hold, where (to quote W. B. Yeats
in his poem 'The Second Coming') 'the best lack all conviction'
while 'the worst are full of passionate intensity'. A famous Dimbleby Lecture on television by Roy Jenkins in November 1979
became a point of reference for this kind of diagnosis.[36] The old
leadership élite, weaned on Beveridge, Keynes, and imperatives
of planning was losing the intellectual initiative. The weakness of
the Labour right wing—many of whom later re-emerged in the
Social Democratic Party when it was created in 1981—was a
sharp reminder of the decline of consensus. In its place came new
surging extremes of left and right, with the land seeming to be
increasingly polarized.

---

[36] Roy Jenkins's Dimbleby Lecture was printed in *The Times*, 23 Nov. 1979.

The new movement to the far left had been foreshadowed since 1970, after the humiliating circumstances in which the Wilson government had fallen from power, and the general feeling on the left that it had failed through opportunism and lack of policy or programmatic guidelines. The new left that emerged was very different from the Bevanite old left of the fifties. *Tribune* was now supportive of the party, if not always of the Labour leadership, under the longterm editorship (1961–82) of Dick Clements. This was not surprising since many of its main platforms, including nuclear disarmament and opposition to membership of the Common Market, had become official party policy. CND was nothing like the mass movement it had been in the early sixties, and the ritual of the annual Easter march to Aldermaston attracted diminishing attention. The classic voice of the Bevanite left, Michael Foot, was a crucial member of the Cabinet whose support for Healey and Callaghan had been a major factor in preserving cohesion during the IMF crisis. His alliance with Jack Jones had kept the government's industrial relations policy afloat. Other traditional Bevanite figures such as Jennie Lee and Barbara Castle were also generally within the party mainstream. In their place came a variety of new forces, not so much the product of Marxism as of pressures for workers' democracy and industrial and political populism. The Communist Party was largely a small, detached observer. A dissatisfaction with the kind of Morrisonian corporatism which Callaghan embodied was central to the new socialist upsurge. In part, it found its expression in the unions, as shown in the many industrial disputes of the early 1970s. The older unions, indeed, spawned the growth of a variety of local movements under shop stewards or other plant spokesmen, notably the Transport and General Workers in a series of successful strikes in the car industry, in British Leyland and elsewhere. Jack Jones, the TGWU General Secretary, a champion of industrial democracy, had openly encouraged movements of this kind, though the emergence of such openly Trotskyist shop stewards as 'the Mole' (Alan Thornett) in the Cowley Works in Oxford and 'Red Robbo' (Derek

Robinson) in Longbridge alarmed him. In the Miners, there was a steady drift to the left, away from the old-style 'Labour alliance' approach of Joe Gormley. Arthur Scargill, the militant Marxist who led the Yorkshire miners, was the natural voice of this kind of movement.

But there were wider movements of militancy, too, especially among the public-service unions such as NUPE, NALGO, COHSE, and ASTMS which grew so rapidly in the late sixties and early seventies, with angry demands for industrial action amongst groups like nurses, hospital workers, and school-teachers not previously thought of as symbols of militancy. Women also figured far more prominently and aggressively in union affairs, and women union leaders emerged such as Brenda Dean in SOGAT, the printers' craft union. No 'angels of mercy' here. In strikes or other disputes, there was increased aggression on the picket lines and a lessened disposition to accept the edicts of a Labour government or the TUC General Council in observing wage limits or pay norms. Even an honoured leftist like Jack Jones, a hero of the International Brigade, was dismissed as 'fascist' by one angry worker in Barbara Castle's constituency.[37] Conversely, the Labour government gave renewed life to the Civil Contingencies Unit, the strike-breaking apparatus devised by Heath in 1972. Its secretary, Brigadier 'Dick' Bishop, remained in office throughout the period of Labour government, indeed down to 1981.[38] His Unit kept in close liaison with the Home Office and Ministry of Defence to prepare plans to defeat industrial action by key men such as power engineers or water workers. It was to see early action in the use of 'green goddesses' by the army in combating a strike by firemen in 1977.

Within the Labour Party, constituency parties, which had lost membership alarmingly in the seventies (an official total of barely 600,000 individual members was recorded at the end of the decade), found themselves taken over by younger elements.

---

[37] Barbara Castle, *Castle Diaries, 1974–76*, 687 (entry of 12 Mar. 1976).
[38] Peter Hennessy and Keith Jeffrey, *States of Emergency*, 237–8.

Often they were single-issue groups such as Irish republicans, black activists, or advocates of 'gay lib'. The feminist movement, increasingly influential in the seventies, developed an important Marxist wing which also moved into local Labour parties, especially in London boroughs such as Lambeth, Brent, or Tower Hamlets. Many of their leaders were young products of the abortive student movements of the 1960s. An important body that acted as a focus for them all was the Campaign for Labour Party Democracy, founded in 1973, much influenced by an émigré Czech, Vladimir Derer, and a young unemployed ex-Cambridge graduate, Jon Lansman.[39] Corrupt and decaying Labour parties in the inner cities were, indeed, uninspiring and all too ripe for take-over. They were notorious citadels of unthinking male 'chauvinism'. A report by Reg Underhill on 'entryism' in local parties mentioned ominous signs of far-left activity by Militant Tendency and other neo-revolutionary groups. But the NEC suppressed it and no action was taken in the Wilson–Callaghan period, until it was too late.

There was consequently a curious phenomenon which showed up the divided consciousness and inner weakness of the Labour movement. As the party in Cabinet moved away from socialism, neutralizing the doctrinaire demands of Benn, and towards monetarism, cash limits, and a total accommodation with capitalism, the Labour Party as entrenched in local government, as in the new metropolitan council and in Greater London, became associated with far-left postures, open resistance to demands for expenditure cuts, and association with Marxist and other groups not at all attracted to the pragmatic Labour tradition of Attlee, Gaitskell, and Wilson. As black flags of solidarity with South American Marxist guerrillas flew from Labour-run town halls (Oxford was 'twinned' with a town in Nicaragua) and declarations of support were made on behalf of Sinn Fein, CND, or lesbian activists, ratepayers and indeed traditional Labour

---

[39] See David Kogan and Maurice Kogan, *The Battle for the Labour Party* (London, 1982), chap. 3, for the CPLD.

supporters began to wonder how their old party had become a Trojan horse for a miscellaneous coalition of the discontented. In the national party, these movements now dominated the constituency parties, as well as a growing number of unions. Party conferences now became far more tense affairs than in the days of Attlee, with delegates enthusiastically passing motions in support of mass nationalization, total nuclear disarmament, the withdrawal of British troops from Ulster, and removing Britain from the Common Market. When leaders like Wilson and Callaghan tried to negate or circumvent these demands, they provoked cries for more 'inner party democracy' from the CLPD, including the election of party leaders and members of the Shadow Cabinet, the popular drawing up of the manifesto, and reselection (or de-selection) of members of parliament to ensure that they kept firm to the edicts of the party and its local management committees. They found an excellent target in Reg Prentice, a far-right-wing Labour minister under fire from his constituency in Newham. Prentice was indeed to be disowned by his local party; he was later to oblige them by turning Conservative and serving in Mrs Thatcher's government.[40]

Labour at the grass-roots, then, seemed to be moving to the fundamentalist left. The demands at bottom were political, a cry for a fundamental shift of economic power to the working class and to their chosen political voices in the constituencies, in the face of a changing economy in which multinational companies and hydra-headed capitalist organizations of all kinds undermined the power and wealth of the worker at the point of production. These demands gained the more credibility because of the appalling series of blows that the economy received from the sterling crisis in July 1966 to the IMF affair a decade later. But it had also a charismatic voice in the remarkable personality of Tony Benn, who combined technocratic enthusiasm with Congregationalist zeal reminiscent of a latter-day Savonarola. In his

[40] *The Times*, 13 Sept. 1975.

new guise as socialist fundamentalist after 1970, he became the voice of populist, extra-parliamentary protest in a way remarkable for a member of the Cabinet, far more intensely so than the Bevanite spokesmen of the fifties. Much ingenuity had been spent by Wilson in 1974–5 in ensuring that Benn's pressure for an 'alternative socialist economic strategy' was nullified, including appointing an economist, Richard Graham, as a 'Benn-watcher' within the central administration.[41] Callaghan successfully faced out Benn's challenge in December 1976 by suggesting that he resign, and thereby calling his bluff. But Benn's prestige as a voice of socialist purity was nevertheless much enhanced by the IMF affair. In the later seventies, there was much talk of the transformation of 'the Labour Party I joined' by senior activists, of how this new 'bed-sit brigade' of youthful, far-left, middle-class zealots, often women, or Irish or black activists, seemed radically different in character, outlook, and allegiance from the mass working-class movement of the old days. A fundamental prop of social order and political continuity seemed to be transforming itself, with possibly revolutionary implications. A young militant like Ken Livingstone found it all too easy to move through the largely Irish echelons of the Brent constituency.[42] With vocal support for violence on the picket lines, covert support for the murderous campaign of Provisional Sinn Feiners, endorsement of black power or the alternative sexual scenarios of lesbians and homosexuals, the Labour Party in the localities seemed to be turning into an alienated and irreconcilable cabal of full-time revolutionaries.

Less visible, but perhaps of even more fundamental importance, were signs of seismic movement in Conservative ranks also. In this case, as in Labour's, they arose from deep discontent with the policies of continuity and consensus, and the weakness of the party leadership over a long period. The Heath government had

---

[41] Whitehead, op. cit., p.129, citing an interview with Graham himself.
[42] See Ken Livingstone, *If voting changed anything, they'd abolish it* (London, 1987).

left a sour legacy of failure and incompetence. Heath himself, the architect of three electoral defeats in four attempts, was never a lovable figure. The monetarist approach to economic policy, calling on Tories to renounce inflationary public spending and increased state encroachment, had made some progress in the 1970–4 period. One important vehicle for it, founded in June 1974, was the privately funded Centre for Policy Studies, led by a maverick ex-Communist, Sir Alfred Sherman. The most powerful voice of dissent proved to be Sir Keith Joseph, previously a typical 'one-nation' Tory Cabinet minister in the early 1960s and early 1970s. It was Joseph, along with Margaret Thatcher, who had founded the CPS as an instrument of anti-Heathite Toryism. In a series of controversial speeches in 1974 he appeared to challenge the very basis of Conservative economic and social philosophy. On economic policy, in a speech at Preston, he attacked the very premises of Keynesianism, pump-priming, deficit finance, and the rest, and came near to advocating a rise in unemployment as a cure for inflation. Inflation, he declared, was 'a self-inflicted wound'.[43] Certainly, he was close to what later came to be the established monetarist position. He was on popular ground, since the inflationary pressures of the 'Barber boom' of 1972–3, along with the rising wage inflation resulting from trade-union power and 'threshold agreements' to allow wages to rise in the period of Heath government, had provoked much Tory discontent. In another controversial speech, at Edgbaston, Joseph appeared to advocate not only immigration restriction but even a form of restraint on the breeding capacities of the poorest social classes, 4 and 5, along with possible sterilization, and some kind of public experiment in eugenics to prevent miscegenation and undermining of the race.[44] Heath himself kept his distance from these calls also, but they clearly struck a powerful chord in right-wing nationalist or racist ranks.

[43] *The Times*, 5 Sept. 1974.
[44] Ibid., 21 Oct. 1974. Also see his collected speeches, *Reversing the Trend* (London, 1975).

The decisive event, as time was to show, was the overthrow of Heath as party leader in February 1975. He was defeated, not by Joseph, who withdrew from the contest for somewhat private reasons, but by the little-known Margaret Thatcher. She had been the Minister for Education in the previous Heath government but was not considered one of the giants of the party. With the discrediting of Heath, the withdrawal of Maudling, and the diffidence of Joseph, Mrs Thatcher naturally became the symbol of right-wing protest against the Heath regime and style.[45] Later she was hailed as leading a 'peasants' revolt' against the party grandees and the mandarin establishment, and there was always a populist aspect to her programme and appeal. Her campaign was adroitly managed by Airey Neave, a successful intelligence figure and escapee of the Second World War, and she polled 130 votes against 119 for Heath in the first ballot. Heath promptly resigned as leader. In the final ballot, Mrs Thatcher easily defeated William Whitelaw, the representative of the Toryism of the sixties and the values of the shires, by 146 to 79. The implications of this major change were not immediately clear. Mrs Thatcher, once the excitement of having a woman as party leader was absorbed, proved to be less adroit than either Wilson or Callaghan in the House. She owed her election, clearly, to a grass-roots upsurge by the party's centre and right-wing against a patrician approach that had, in fact, lost the Tories four out of the last five general elections. On the other hand, her Shadow Cabinet was still dominated by Heathite moderates, figures like Carrington, Whitelaw, Pym, Prior, Gilmour, and Howell. In her first year as party leader, she revealed herself, in the view of *The Economist*, to be 'a strikingly cautious politician', keeping her

[45] For good books on the emergence of Mrs Thatcher, see Denis Kavanagh, *Thatcherism and British Politics*, (Oxford, 1987); Andrew Gamble, *The Free Economy and the Strong State*; and Robert Skidelsky (ed.), *Thatcherism* (London. 1988).

distance from ideologues such as Sir Keith Joseph, keeping her options open on such matters as prices-and-incomes policy.[46]

Nevertheless, the movement towards a much more radical version of Toryism, cutting adrift from the 'mixed economy' statism of the era since 1951, was certainly apparent. Younger Conservatives, anxious to espouse the cause of monetarism, denationalization, tax cuts, and the control of the money supply through the establishment of fixed target, found a more and more ready response from the party leadership. The doctrines of Professor Milton Friedman, the archangel of monetarism from Chicago, were espoused by economists of the London Business School and the Institute of Economic affairs. The famous anti-statist tracts of the venerable Professor Friedrich von Hayek, with his dirge against collectivism, became increasingly popular. One leading Conservative after another declared his rejection of old doctrines, notably Sir Geoffrey Howe, who had been much alienated by the corporatism and incomes-policy failures of the Heath government in which he had served. He now became a leading economics spokesman. With such allies as Nigel Lawson, Sir Keith Joseph, John Nott, and David Howell, he began to draft a Conservative alternative to the current discontents, far more rigorously anti-statist than even the Selsdon Park document of early 1970. Lawson later identified the IMF crisis as marking the Tory break with existing consensus.[47] The senior personality of Lord Thorneycroft, something of an early martyr for monetarism when he resigned from the Macmillan Cabinet as Chancellor back in January 1958, now became Party Chairman, another pointer to the new direction of party policy. As Labour moved rapidly to the fundamentalist left, so the Tories seemed to be marching back to the neo-Liberal private enterprise of the mid-nineteenth century, an equally stark alternative. It was Marx versus Adam Smith, a hundred-and-twenty years on. In each case, it was perhaps the weakness of the existing ideology that

---

[46] *The Economist*, 19 Jan. 1976.
[47] Whitehead, *Writing on the Wall*, 333.

fuelled revolt. The very inability of key figures in Heath's regime of 1970–4 to defend the corporatist intervention of that era with any conviction, plus a general perception that the unions were too powerful and directly linked with the encroaching menace of inflation, made the critics all the more effective.

With an increasingly left-wing Labour and a strongly right-wing Conservativism thus pulling the nation apart, the credibility and the confidence of the defenders of the middle ground, as has been seen, rapidly waned. Keynesianism, welfare, and the mixed economy could, it could reasonably be claimed, be associated with at least twenty years of growing affluence after 1945. But after the traumas of the late sixties and early seventies, its glowing record seemed dimmed. Apostles of the centrist or consensus position, from the discouraged Labour right (soon, sadly, to lose its main intellectual force with the premature death of Anthony Crosland, after a brief spell as Foreign Secretary, in January 1977) through the miscellaneous ranks of the small Liberal party, on to the Heath faction in the Tory Party, were losing ground. In the press and in the media also, amidst a growing mood of national discouragement, the centrists were in Steady retreat.

The irony was that, for all the industrial and monetary troubles of 1974–6, most of the population still seemed to be thriving. The general level of personal incomes had risen substantially, even ahead of soaring inflation, since 1970. Home-ownership had risen steadily, despite the high mortgage-interest rates of the early 1970s. Town and cities continued to expand, especially Greater London, though at the expense of inner cities where housing in particular fell into decay.[48] In Wales and Scotland, enough survived of the old regional policies (as, for instance, in the Welsh Development Agency) to ward off mass unemployment on the old pattern. Agriculture in particular thrived in the 1970s. Britain's entry into the Common Market

[48] *The Economist*, 1 Jan. 1977.

seemed to portend a further advance, especially for wheat farmers, perhaps less for dairy farmers and hill farmers in the north
and west. There was a growing tendency for farming to be taken
over by inorganic, mass-production techniques, often with the
pulling down of hedgerows and the obliteration of traditional
rights of way and bridle paths, along with the introduction of
harmful chemical methods of fertilization and soil nourishment.
The massive growth of conservationist and environmental movements, seen in the growth of the Council for the Preservation of
Rural England (and Wales), and the rapid development of the
National Trust, to protect historic buildings and landscapes, was
in part a voluntary protest at the very prosperity and advance of
agricultural Britain. East Anglia, in particular, was being transformed, and proved to be a magnet for a rapid growth in population. Cities and towns like Norwich, Cambridge, Ipswich, and
Chelmsford grew spectacularly, while new ports emerged in
Harwich, Felixstowe, and Lowestoft, free from the labour
demarcation problems of old ports like Liverpool and Hull.
The growth of protest movements concerned with ecological
matters was in part a regional challenge to developments that
threatened to merge town and country into one tarmac unity. It
was a feeling caught in Philip Larkin's nostalgic poem 'Going,
Going', published in 1974: 'all that remains/For us will be concrete and tyres'. But they also indicated another phenomenon of
the age—the growing articulateness of the affluent middle class,
fostered by the educational boom of the 1963–76 period, by
growing home-ownership, and the rise of new professional and
occupational opportunities.

While press and media were full of lamentations of woe, the
quality of life of large sections of the population seemed to
advance steadily even in an age of 'stagflation', especially in
southern and eastern England. Here, too, the arts continued to
thrive, with a flood of festivals, and music and opera prospering
mightily. The National Theatre finally opened on London's South
Bank in March 1976. Even the long-depressed British film industry showed marked signs of recovery as popular cinema-going

became fashionable for the first time since the mid-fifties. In part this was due to such novelties as the multi-screen presentation of several films within the same cinema building. On the other hand, in several respects the arts suffered from the economic constraints of the decade like everything else. Many of the theatres constructed in the heady expansion of the sixties were in financial trouble a decade later; one additional handicap was the imposition of value added tax on theatre takings by Anthony Barber when Chancellor in 1972. The Royal Court in Sloane Square, the epicentre of the socially realistic theatre of the fifties, by 1975 faced a financial crisis, with the Arts Council subsidy falling at least £100,000 short of its needs. Indeed, the Council's funding of the arts in general showed a decline in real terms after the heights reached under the chairmanship of Lord Goodman in the late sixties. The introduction of museum charges by Margaret Thatcher while Minister of Education, although rescinded by Labour in 1974, had been a sign of the times.

On balance, popular discontent was not obviously apparent either in external decay or social or cultural collapse. There were no riots on the streets other than occasionally in Ulster. A succession of deals and settlements of strikes and monetary crises probably left most of the nation temporarily satisfied. But much of this prosperity and progress had rested on broad, unchallenged assumptions about sustained public spending and the public discipline that underpinned the civic culture. By the end of 1976, after the IMF crises and endemic decay, these could no longer be taken as assumed. If the social and cultural objectives remained much the same, the instruments of order commanded less credibility. In particular, quite apart from the particular problems of communities such as the Northern Irish or the black community, the answer to social progress and cohesion no longer seemed to lie in the hands of the state. There were only a handful of enthusiasts who felt that the bracing shock of membership of the European Community would provide the stimulus for reform. In a disillusioned society, the solution could only come from within. In the final analysis, what the crises of 1974–6 generated was a rejection of a style of leadership, not the aristocratic leadership of the Victorian age, nor again the business corporatists of the First World War, but the planning technocracy of post-1945. The main movements of protest in the mid-seventies took the form of populism, a revolt against post-war 'national efficiency'. The Bennites on the left urged the causes of workers' and citizens' participation on behalf of a socialist economy. The monetarists associated with Mrs Thatcher marked the rise of equally new and challenging forces, part intellectual, part sociological (as in the dominance of the grammar-school educated, Methodist grocer's daughter who now led the Tories and the prominence of *arriviste* entrepreneurs and journalists, including Jews such as Joseph, Brittan, Lawson, and Alfred Sherman). On each extreme, 'conviction politics' predominated. One-nation Labourism and one-nation Conservatism, the centrism of the Fabian planner and the Tory grandee, were equally under fire. The 'Establishment', that ill-defined bundle of sensations that formed the target of the playwrights and the leftish journalists of the fifties, was now under closer scrutiny and more sustained and effective attack. The British still respected old norms and cherished institutions. They could still be enthralled by the magical concept of a national 'heritage'. But they also wanted a prospect of dynamism and hope of escape from a self-destructive cycle of decay.

11. *The Years of Discontent*
1977–1979

BRITAIN after the IMF crisis had an air of being a nation after the deluge. The cuts had been agreed without the collapse of the government or immediate catastrophe in the economy. The unions were acquiescent; other than in Northern Ireland, there was no overt social conflict. The Labour government, it is true, did suffer an immense personal blow soon after the IMF negotiations were completed, with the sudden death of Anthony Crosland, recently appointed Foreign Secretary. Apart from disturbing the balance in the Cabinet, this removed the only major socialist theoretician of the day. His *Future of Socialism* in 1956 had provided a point of reference for the party, and progressives throughout the nation, over the past twenty years with its emphasis on social equality rather on public ownership as the instrument of change. He was replaced, not by the senior figure of Denis Healey, who was chained to his oar at the Treasury in the aftermath of the IMF cuts, but by the youthful and little-known figure of David Owen, Crosland's junior minister at the Foreign Office. The Cabinet, however, even though shorn of Crosland, and also of Roy Jenkins on the right and Barbara Castle on the left for different reasons, still remained credible as an agent of authority, and in the early months of 1977 Britain slowly emerged towards a plateau of greater tranquillity and modest economic recovery. The revival was in many ways only a relative one. Unemployment continued to rise to reach over one-and-a-half million by mid-1977. The people's standard of living was further depressed as both the longer-term effects of the oil-price increase of 1973 and the post-IMF cuts of the immediate past began to sink in. Nevertheless, by the time of the Queen's jubilee that summer there was some sense that a good deal of the worst might be over.

The custodian of this mood of growing calm was the new Prime Minister, James Callaghan, who imposed himself on the public consciousness as a new Baldwin, the apostle of peace in our time. His press soubriquet 'Sunny Jim' was rather misplaced since it concealed a somewhat touchy disposition, just as Henderson's unwontedly benign term of endearment, 'Uncle Arthur', had been in the past. But he commanded general respect as an authoritative voice, in tune with the need for social order, sensitive to the needs of the unions and his own party, but also with a genuine cross-party appeal. 'You can trust Jim', was Labour's appeal, reminiscent of a friendly village bobby or a family doctor of the old school. He proved to be the most effective Prime Minister since Macmillan's first phase. In the Cabinet, Callaghan's open methods and refusal to countenance conspiracies made for a more harmonious atmosphere than ever prevailed under Harold Wilson (now Lord Wilson of Rievaulx). Even the left-wing Tony Benn was relatively quiescent, not least perhaps because he was now the bringer of good news at the Department of Energy, as North Sea oil began to flow in large quantities. No doubt, Callaghan had his limitations. Although an advocate of open Cabinet discussions, he also firmly believed in the principle of confidentiality or plain secrecy in key areas. Thus, defence policy was kept in the hands of a small group of ministers (Callaghan, Healey, Owen, and Fred Mulley). A major consequence was that the development of the extremely expensive 'Chevaline' warheads went ahead despite all the economic difficulties of the period, with no Cabinet discussion at the time. Even David Owen was later to admit that they should have been scrapped during his time at the Foreign Office in 1977–9. Chevaline in all had risen in cost from £350 m. in 1974 to over £1 billion by 1982, on top of the Polaris missile programme—even though by this time US-Soviet arms limitation agreements had made Chevaline redundant.[1] It was the price of maintaining Britain's posture as a supposedly independent nuclear power, under Labour as under the Tories. Equally, exchange rates and aspects of market economics were kept for close-quarter deliberation, notably within Harold Lever's so-called 'economic seminar'.

Along with this, Callaghan was not by instinct an institutional radical. He had been a trade-union official, in a white-collar civil-service union, in his young days, and he regarded as sacrosanct maintaining the liaison between unions and party at all costs. Thus, in 1969 he had been the main Cabinet instrument of dissent in rejecting Wilson and Mrs Castle's proposed statutory incomes policy. Many, therefore, blamed Callaghan for the explosion in union wage claims that followed in the early seventies. In the Home Office, he had demonstrated broadly conservative views on crime, drugs, and racial issues, not surprisingly so perhaps for one who served as parliamentary spokesman for the Police Federation. Over such key issues as the European Common Market he had followed a prudent, unadventurous course, only moving to endorse membership at the last moment when political circumstances seemed so to dictate. In his years in Number 10, he showed limited interest in social or institutional reform. The changes wrought by the Heath government were allowed to survive, to be left for Mrs Thatcher gleefully to dismantle in the eighties.

But this cautious, adroit, enigmatic leader seemed for long to be very much what the nation and the times required. The country seemed to be on a knife-edge, with a minority government, the economy poised on the edge of collapse, and potential disorder in industrial relations, racial matters, and the affairs of the Celtic fringe. Callaghan proved to be an imperturbable and shrewd pilot for these storms. Further, he was not unwilling to show enterprise. The move towards cash limits, cuts in current

[1] Zuckerman, *Men, Monkeys and Missiles*, 386 ff.; Whitehead, *Writing on the Wall*, 270–1, quoting Owen.

expenditure, and a generally monetarist policy were heralded by a speech to the TUC in September 1976, which (as noted) reflected the influence of his son-in-law, Peter Jay. Again, on education, Callaghan attempted to promote new standards of literacy and numeracy, based on an agreed core curriculum in schools. In foreign policy, while seldom innovative, he did try to carve out new relationships with Britain's new European partners, especially through his close personal association with Helmut Schmidt, the West German chancellor and a fellow social democrat, as well as maintaining his contacts with the new US Democratic administration of Jimmy Carter. In 1977 and 1978, indeed, Callaghan showed the ability to do more than survive, and emerged with a stature which perhaps surprised his many jaundiced critics in the party and press. He became the personal embodiment of a new solidarity, a new *ralliement*, nudging his fellow-countrymen towards a new accommodation to changing circumstances at home and overseas. The new Conservative leader Mrs Thatcher, was finding it hard to assert herself, especially with a Shadow Cabinet consisting largely of followers of the defeated Edward Heath. In Sir Ian Gilmour's *Inside Right*, a defence of the post-1945 political consensus, it was clear that the Tory centrists could fight back, and the monetarist radicals had, therefore, to be wary.[2] With little pressure from that quarter for an early general election, Callaghan almost imperceptibly emerged with growing command. Until a sudden decline from September 1978, he seemed almost unchallengeable.

He was fundamentally assisted by political accommodation, and by evidence of growing economic recovery. The first was his own work, the latter the somewhat ambiguous achievement of Denis Healey, with incidental assistance from the IMF, the central banks, and Jack Jones of the Transport Workers. The

---

[2] Ian Gilmour, *Inside Right: A Study in Conservatism* (London, 1977). The same approach appears in his *Britain Can Work* (London, 1983). See also his *The Body Politic* (London, 1969) and Lord Blake and John Patten (eds.). *The Conservative Opportunity* (London, 1976).

political accommodation stemmed from the 'pact' concluded between the Labour government and the tiny Liberal Party. The latter had a mere twelve members but nevertheless carried weight in a situation where the Callaghan government was in a technical minority in the House and in danger of imminent defeat. In March–April 1977, however, the so-called 'Lib–Lab pact' was concluded between Callaghan and the new Liberal leader, David Steel.[3] The leader of the parliamentary Labour Party, Cledwyn Hughes, himself a 'Lib–Lab' figure of noted moderation and an admirer of Lloyd George, was an important go-between. The upshot was that the Liberals promised to support the Labour government in the House by their votes. The conditions included a joint consultative committee being set up to consider future legislation, chaired by Michael Foot, the leader of the House, and regular meetings between Cabinet ministers and Liberal spokesmen to consider government measures. The government agreed to press on with devolution, and also to advance direct elections to the European Parliament, to which Labour had been hostile, while the Local Authority Works Bill, perhaps Labour's last instalment of socialism, was watered down. On balance, it was a package strongly in favour of the government. No major concessions were made; in particular, no ground was given to the Liberal demand for proportional representation to give minor parties a more enhanced position in the country. The government, in effect, was guaranteed perhaps an extra two years in power. For the Liberals, they gained an indirect foothold in government for the first time since 1931 in peacetime circumstances, and it flattered their self-esteem as a small third force to become part of the governing process. David Steel, the Liberal leader, was anxious to enhance his, and his party's, authority following the damaging departure of the former leader, Jeremy Thorpe, in a series of scandals involving accusations of homosexuality, fraud, and even attempted murder. Steel himself was a

[3] See Alastair Michie and Simon Hoggart, *The Pact* (London, 1978).

noted tactician, more concerned with manœuvre than with pol-
icymaking, a style appropriate for the parliamentary situation.
The government thus gained a new foothold on power relatively
painlessly, apart perhaps from the consultations between Denis
Healey and the Liberals' economic spokesman, John Pardoe, two
combustible personalities whose stormy meetings (or shouting
matches) provided amusement and entertainment throughout
Whitehall.

With its political basis ensured, the government could now
settle down to consolidate and enjoy the fruits of recovery.
There was much to enjoy in 1977. The benefits of North Sea
oil were now coming through strongly. The first oilfield to come
on stream had been the small Argyll field in mid-1975, followed
by pipeline deliveries from the Norwegian 'Ekofisk' field and the
massive British Forties field later that year. Five more oilfields
were producing oil from the North Sea continental shelf in 1976,
including the massive Brent and Alpha fields. By the end of 1978
nine were in production and several more on course for development. It was evident that by the end of the seventies Britain
would be self-sufficient in oil and was likely to remain so,
depending on depletion policy, until at least the end of the
century. By 1980, Britain would be producing 100 million tonnes
a year, with 500,000 barrels a day from the Forties field and
370,000 from the Brent field, putting the United Kingdom on a
par with Kuwait, Nigeria, or Iraq as a major oil producer.[4] With
a growing number of nuclear power stations (the old Magnox
reactors such as Calder Hall in Cumbria or Wylfa and Trawsfynydd in North Wales being supplemented by stations such as
Sellafield, despite the opposition of environmentalists and the
anti-nuclear lobbies); with hydroelectric power in the Scottish
Highlands and North Wales; and a still important, if aged, coal
industry, together with another huge energy bonus in the shape
of North Sea gas, Britain's energy position seemed remarkably

[4] See Colin Robinson and Jon Morgan, *North Sea Oil in the Future: Economic
Analysis and Government Policy* (London, 1978).

secure. Many of the problems faced by other industrial nations thus disappeared. Among other things, the successful strikes of North Sea oil proved a notable bonus for British technology, reinforced in the seventies by other achievements such as the Anglo-French Concorde transatlantic airliner, and the emergence of the 'high-speed train' capable of speeds of up to 130 miles per hour. Clearly the native resources of scientific talent and ingenuity had not run dry, for all the disappointment caused by the failures of the 'science and government' campaigns of the early 1960s.

External improvement in the balance of payments was accompanied by a steady fall in the rate of inflation from a peak of 25 per cent at the end of 1975 to around 7 per cent by mid-1978. The precise cause was open to debate. Labour partisans hailed the effectiveness of the Jack Jones 'flat-rate' formula which had introduced a virtual wage freeze until mid-1977, and which the government then continued with a year-long pay-restraint policy. Critics claimed that a more likely cause of the fall in the rate of inflation was the stagnation of the British and international economy, with the loss of manufacturing output and rising unemployment. This took pressure out of the economy by reducing demand. For all that, the decline in inflation was undeniable.

By August, after Healey's latest mini-budget had been passed through the Commons with surprising ease, there was a glow of good news, with bank rate falling to 7 per cent, the stock market rising strongly, the pound being sustained, and the balance of payments showing impressive recovery. The month of August 1977 showed a balance-of-payment surplus of £316 m., the largest ever recorded in numerical terms for one month. Share prices soared, although some of this was due to falling interest rates that followed the unhooking of the pound from the dollar, stimulating gilt-edged, rather than a major increase in manufacturing output or exports.[5] Healey was able to pay back the first

---

[5] *The Economist*, 13 Aug. 1977.

instalment of £2 billion to the IMF with some ease, and indeed the full IMF loan proved to be unnecessary, while income-tax allowances were raised and a bonus for Christmas could be afforded for old-age pensions. A balance-of-payments surplus of £206 m. in October meant a surplus of £758 m. for the past three months, much helped by North Sea oil cutting the fuel deficit, and a strong pound.[6] Exports showed some improvement, although the rise in the import of finished manufactures such as motor cars and other vehicles was continuously alarming. At the end of the year, Britain seemed much revived from the black days of the IMF crisis twelve months earlier. The market soared, especially in government gilt-edged stock, and the pound emerged ever stronger. Denis Healey himself, a long-established whipping boy, now became almost popular, with his chairmanship of the International Monetary Fund inner steering committee making him a figure of greater eminence. Alongside his Chancellor, Callaghan emerged with more credibility in the international arena, especially through his pact with the West German Chancellor, Helmut Schmidt, and the partial decline in the reputation of the French President, Giscard d'Estaing. Britain seemed in almost bullish mood as 1977 went out. It seemed well on the way to revival, with the balance-of-payments surplus rising to £1,000 m. in 1978 and the pound, now a petro-currency, rising to not far short of $2 on the foreign exchange. Douglas Jay observed that the later 1970s were a time of genuine recovery—'one of the few examples of any Western governments in the seventies reducing both inflationary pressures and unemployment' at one and the same time.[7]

The revival continued for much of 1978. Indeed, by the middle of that year critics were saying that the cuts imposed at the time of the IMF crisis may have been too harsh, and that fixed investment in manufacturing capacity needed to be stepped up, even though it actually rose by 8 per cent in 1978. Sir Brian Hopkin

[6] Ibid. 29 Oct. 1977.
[7] Douglas Jay, *Sterling* (London, 1985), 162–3.

was later to describe the relaxation of monetary targets at this time as 'the last dying kick of Keynesian demand management',[8] but clearly there was life left in the old orthodoxy yet. Denis Healey, nevertheless, had to contend with a wide range of critics, from socialists such as Benn who claimed that his successes resulted from such right-wing nostrums as a wage freeze and cutting public spending, to the monetarists of the Policy Studies Committee who attacked him for being far too *dirigiste*. In the spring of 1978 there were signs of the happier times coming to an end, with the pound under pressure and Healey himself attacked for anticipating tax cuts that summer in the budget he introduced in April. Under some pressure from the Liberals, he agreed to accept amendments to reduce the standard rate of income tax in his Finance Bill, but his alternative scheme of including a 2 per cent surcharge on employers' National Insurance contributions was much attacked in the City.[9] There were, indeed, tremors both in the markets and in the strength of sterling that summer. But, on balance, the government seemed able to claim that it had turned the tide, albeit with the aid of £2 billions from North Sea oil to swing the balance into surplus. After a steady series of by-election blows throughout the seventies (including a calamitous defeat at Ashfield in April 1977), Labour was cheered by a decisive defeat of the Scottish Nationalists in the Hamilton seat (May 1978), one of the markers in the SNP advance in the 1960s. After lagging as much as 15 per cent behind the Tories in the opinion polls in 1977, Labour was actually level with them in July 1978 and threatening to pull ahead. Whether by luck or careful management, Callaghan's administration looked much more credible now, and many expected him to call an autumn election in 1978 to cash in on favourable economic and political trends and, against all the odds, snatch another term of power.

---

[8] Brian Hopkin, 'The Development of Demand Management', in Frances Cairncross (ed.). *Changing Perceptions of Economic Policy* (London, 1981), 47.
[9] *The Economist*, 8, 15 Apr. 1978.

The significance of the economic recovery, such as it was, in 1977–8 caused much debate and some perplexity. Some genial foreign observers claimed that it illustrated that gloomy predictions about Britain's demise, like that of Mark Twain, were much exaggerated. Keynesian apologists partially recovered their confidence. The North American economist, John Kenneth Galbraith, took a distinctly positive view, claiming that the crisis had shown both the revival of industrial technology and the reimposition of civic discipline as demonstrated by the pay pause, in the face of difficulties which might have led feebler nations to buckle under, or even lapse into military or other dictatorships. The American journalist, Bernard Nossiter, even saw Britain's decline of manufacturing output as a sign of advance and of maturity, since the British, civilized and civic-minded as they were, were proclaiming the need for more leisure and less regimented ways of living.[10]

Without lapsing into the complacency, or even euphoria, of some of these judgements, there was certainly evidence of a nation enjoying the fruits of prosperity, however deceptive. Public spending had risen from 40 per cent to 45.5 per cent of gross domestic product in 1974–6, partly through heavy industrial subsidies and the cost of maintaining the 'social wage' through the social security system. Despite the severe cuts imposed in late 1976, public spending continued to rise in absolute terms. There was, in particular, a renewed surge of spending on state schools, part of it to finance the rapid completion of the comprehensive secondary education system now being finished under the aegis of Shirley Williams, a right-wing member of the government but also a critic of private schooling. Expensive new capital projects were under consideration including a vast new British Library to replace the Georgian splendour of the British Museum. One spectacular monument of much value to historians opened in 1977 was the glossy, computerized Public Record Office at

[10] Bernard Nossiter, *Britain: A Future that Works* (London, 1978).

Kew, to supplement the venerable Victorian legacy in Chancery Lane. Elsewhere, in Scotland and Wales, regional policies continued to thrive, as if the economic hammer blows of the 1970s had never been. The Welsh Office and the Welsh Development Agency were active in extending financial aid for a variety of local causes from advanced factories in decaying mining villages to Welsh-language schools and the Welsh National Opera. Throughout Britain there was an extensive road-building programme, including a rapid growth of the motorway system and such impressive developments as the new bridges across the Humber and the Severn.[11] The arts generally continued to thrive through public subsidy, to orchestral music above all, and new forms of partnership were being developed between the Arts Council and local authorities and industry and finance. Much of this artistic creativity was more innovative than before. In the world of youth or pop culture, Britain, without reaching the frenetic heights of the years of the Beatles and the Rolling Stones in the sixties, remained a market leader, with rock festivals taking place in such unlikely locations as Windsor Great Park and Stonehenge.

Even so, there was broad agreement that this evidence of innovation and vibrancy was being achieved at the cost of institutional inertia, a reluctance to champion enterprise, and an avoidance of any deep-seated restoration of the national economy. The linchpins, after all, were such traditionally unsocialist (or even anti-socialist) policies as a very severe incomes policy, a move from direct to indirect taxation, and swingeing cuts in public expenditure in both 1976–7 and 1977–8. Under the shield of North Sea oil and gas, the endemic problems of the economy in the sixties—low productivity, backward manufacturing capacity, immobile and inadequately retrained labour, and excessively cautious unions and management—remained untouched.

---

[11] The Ministry of Transport's *Highway Statistics* show that private motor cars and light goods vehicles increased in number from 11,643,000 in 1968 to 15,166,000 in 1978.

On balance, the general reaction to the greater social tranquillity was one of relief rather than euphoria. Britain was proving itself to be better than the ungovernable 'banana republic' of hostile critics in 1975–6, but still an ailing ex-imperial giant lacking focus and perhaps even faith. There was much national rejoicing at the jubilee to celebrate Queen Elizabeth II's reign since 1952. But it was countered by the somewhat cooler attitude towards the royal family that had emerged in recent years, some of it captured in an 'anti-jubilee' number of the *New Statesman* edited by Anthony Howard. The jubilee, like, indeed, the royal wedding of the then Princess Elizabeth and the Duke of Edinburgh back in 1947, was less than unbridled in its lavishness. The Department of the Environment confined itself to spending £175,000 on banners and other adornments along the Mall and in Trafalgar Square. For all the obvious potential of the pageantry in attracting tourist income from America and the Commonwealth, official expenditure on flags and bunting in the City of London came to just £150, while, to save money, the cleaning of the floor of St Paul's Cathedral before and after the jubilee service was done by an army of volunteers.[12] Like George VI and the then Queen Elizabeth eating spam from a gold plate during the Second World War, this was pageantry on the cheap rather than an unrestrained recapitulation of the glories of the first Elizabethan Age.

Many of the major issues confronting government and nation remained unsolved, or at best marginally confronted in the 1977–8 period. In the Commonwealth, Callaghan (previously a supporter of arms sales) took a firm line in promoting a ban on sporting and other contacts with South Africa, and enforced the so-called Gleneagles Agreement with other Commonwealth countries, amongst whom the Conservative Prime Minister of Australia, Malcolm Fraser, proved an unexpectedly vigorous opponent of apartheid. But the abiding issue of Rhodesia, still in the unilateral and technically illegal control of the minority

[12] *The Economist*, 11 June 1977.

white government of Ian Smith, despite strong black guerrilla opposition from supporters of the rival Nkomo and Mugabe factions, remained undisturbed. The main new initiative attempted by Callaghan was the dispatch of the much-respected former Cabinet minister, Cledwyn Hughes, to southern Africa in 1978, partly to facilitate a continuing rapport with the Carter administration in Washington on relations with the illegal Smith regime. Hughes's talks with black African leaders such as Robert Mugabe and Joshua Nkomo, and the heads of the so-called 'front-line' African states, Zambia, Malawi, and Mozambique, suggested, however, that there was no common ground or any possible basis of negotiation with the Smith government. Remarkably, however, the seeds of change emerged in Rhodesia itself. Under pressure from the South African government, and in the face of growing guerrilla warfare, Ian Smith unexpectedly announced on 24 September 1976 that there would be majority rule in the country within two years. In May 1978 he reached agreement with the more moderate African leaders, Bishop Muzorewa and Ndabaningi Sithole. In April 1979, on the eve of a British general election as it happened, Bishop Muzorewa's United African Council received more than 60 per cent of the votes in a general election, and the Methodist Bishop became Prime Minister of 'Zimbabwe-Rhodesia', although in the face of the opposition of the Nkomo/Mugabe forces. It was an astonishing climax to the long-running Rhodesian crisis. But it owed everything to political manœuvres and economic pressures in southern Africa, and nothing to British influence.

Elsewhere, the legacy of Empire was allowed to decay. Gibraltar, whose importance as a naval base was now much diminished, caused continuing diplomatic embarrassment with Spain, although the local population made clear their wish to remain British. In the Far East, the future of Hong Kong, an immensely important financial and manufacturing centre, where the British lease was due to run out in 1997 was left in abeyance by both the British and the Chinese governments, in the post-Mao era. Only in one remote, unnoticed, and unreported area did imperial authority ring out with any confidence. This was the Falkland Islands in the distant southern Atlantic, where Callaghan managed to deter, or dissuade, the Argentine military junta from taking naval action in the vicinity of the Falklands or occupying South Georgia. The British vessel, *Endurance*, an ice-patrol ship reinforced with helicopters and missiles, was kept in Falklands waters despite pressure from the Ministry of Defence. Callaghan not unreasonably claimed in his memoirs that the Tories won the Falklands War but that Labour had kept the peace. On the other hand here was again a problem where a settlement was postponed rather than achieved. Meanwhile, the dispatch of a Foreign Office minister, Ted Rowlands, to Port Stanley to try to persuade the Falk-landers of the merits of starting up diplomatic negotiations with the Argentine government, which claimed the islands as their sovereign 'Malvinas', had an ominous ring to it.[13]

Nearer home, Northern Ireland only produced renewed deadlock. There was, in truth, little initiative that any British government could offer in the unpromising circumstances of 1977–8. The return of a Fianna Fáil government under Jack Lynch meant something of a decline in Anglo-Irish cordiality or willingness to collaborate in security matters, while the end of the constitutional assembly in early 1977 had removed any prospect of finding any viable Ulster administration to modify the picture of direct rule from Westminster. Under Roy Mason, the tough ex-miner who had succeeded Merlyn Rees as Home Secretary, a strong policy was adopted against the violence of Sinn Fein. This was foreshadowed by the appointment of Major-General Timothy 'Bull' Creasey as General Officer Commanding in Northern Ireland in late 1977, along with the increasing use of SAS forces and a freer hand given to the RUC police. The government's policy was formally one of 'Ulsterization', namely allowing a wide range of local programmes and policies to be

[13] Callaghan, *Time and Chance*, 370–8; Lawrence Freedman, *Britain and the Falklands War* (Oxford, 1988), 22–8; Eric Grove, *Vanguard to Trident: British Naval Policy since World War Two* (Annapolis, 1987).

taken over by local leaders. But the realities were spelt out mainly in military terms. Indeed, in 1978 there was some evidence that the British security forces, coupled with divisions amongst the Provisionals, were swinging the balance away from the IRA. The year 1978 saw only 81 deaths, the lowest annual total since 1970.[14] The 'men of violence', it was claimed, were truly against the ropes. But these successes were achieved by military and legal means which did Britain's international reputation much harm, including the use of the 'Diplock courts', stern methods of interrogation and arbitrary imprisonment, and severe conditions of detention or confinement amongst political prisoners in the H block and elsewhere. A new wave of IRA attacks then broke out early in 1979, including several on the British mainland. The most spectacular of them (April 1979) was the assassination through a car-bomb attack of the right-wing Tory MP, Airey Neave, a close friend and confidant of the Conservative leader, Margaret Thatcher. This was claimed to be the work not of the IRA proper, but of the Irish National Liberation Army, an offshoot of it. Clearly as a military phenomenon alone Ulster would continue to trouble the conscience of the British in the 1980s.

In political terms, there was no sign of breakthrough. Indeed, 1977–9 with Roy Mason at the Northern Irish ministry, was the most unproductive period that Ireland had known, in political or constitutional terms, since the troubles began in the late 1960s. The tenth anniversary of the civil rights movement was celebrated on 1 January 1979 amidst a growing alienation of the minority Catholic population, a rising toll not only of violence but also of poverty and unemployment in the six counties, and an increasingly unbridgeable gulf within the majority Protestant ranks, with the Official Unionists and the so-called Democratic Unionists under the Revd Ian Paisley vying with one another in intransigence and extremism. Relations on security matters between the Westminster government and the Dublin Fianna

---

[14] Kelley, *The Longest War*, 272 ff.

Fáil government of Jack Lynch were never close or cordial. In short, Ulster remained more of a violent backwater, removed from the mainstream of British social development, at the end of the 1970s than it had been at the start of that troubled decade. The irony was that, for all their political ineffectiveness, the Ulster Unionists exercised a matchless political influence for quite fortuitous political reasons. Their existence, like that of other nationalist splinter groups, was vital to the continuance of a Labour government, and private negotiations with them (amongst whom was now numbered Enoch Powell) ensured that their numbers in the new House of Commons would be raised from 12 to 17. But this was the only positive outcome of an otherwise peculiarly negative and dismal phase, even by the standards of Northern Irish history.

The issue of governmental devolution for the other Celtic nations of Scotland and Wales made more headway. The Scottish and Welsh Devolution Bills made steady progress through the Commons, until both became law in 1978. But there was much evidence of divided counsels on both the Labour and Conservative sides, as has been noted above. Indeed, the government had to make major concessions during the committee stage, especially to Labour critics. The amendment by an expatriate Scot, George Cunningham (Labour, Islington), by ensuring that a 40 per cent vote of the electorate (not simply of those voting) would have to be achieved for a devolution bill to go through and for a repeal order not to be tabled, made devolution, at least for Wales, virtually an impossibility. Even when the Scottish and Welsh Bills became law in July 1978 it was clear that the issue was very far from settled and that the referendums, finally announced for 1 March 1979, would be the decisive factor.[15]

The 'great debate' over the structure of the United Kingdom and the relations of the Celtic nations to the predominant English partner, was likely to be diverted from the outset. It was achieved

[15] For the referendums, and the events leading up to them, see Bogdanor, *Devolution*.

in a mood of almost stunned boredom amongst English opinion, confident that the dismantling of the United Kingdom as it had endured since 1707 or 1536 would not in fact take place. There was much criticism of the time taken up in the Commons by these devolution measures, and also of the careless drafting of two bills which were likely to produce a legal and constitutional nightmare if they ever took effect. The devolution campaigns began in the winter of 1978–9 when, as will be seen, the public was far more concerned with the 'winter of discontent' with the trade unions and the likely approach of a general election. In Wales there was not much doubt that the result would be negative. The dominant Labour Party included large sections of industrial South Wales which was openly hostile, fearing that devolution would separate Wales from the economic and social structure of England and perhaps become a paradise for linguistic nationalists. Plaid Cymru itself was distinctly half-hearted on the issue. There was never any prospect of a 'Yes' vote being recorded, and the treasured plans for a Welsh assembly to occupy a derelict coal exchange in Cardiff docks were put on ice. In the event, on 1 March 1979 there was a 4 to 1 majority in Wales against devolution, 243,048 votes in favour and 936,330 against. In Glamorgan and Gwent the votes were overwhelming, but even in Welsh-speaking Gwynedd, with its two Plaid Cymru MPs, there was a 2 to 1 majority against devolution. Self-government disappeared from Welsh history amid universal derision, and attention now concentrated on further building up the Welsh Office instead.[16]

Even in Scotland, the huge majorities in favour of devolution once recorded steadily diminished in the opinion polls in 1978 as the Scottish economy appeared to recover and Labour regained much of the ground lost to the Nationalists. Two of the main Labour devolutionists had been lost, Professor John Mackintosh, an eloquent and gifted academic advocate of devolution, by death, James Sillars through defection to a minority splinter-

[16] See Morgan, *Rebirth of a Nation.* 403–7; D. Foulkes, J. B. Jones, and R. A. Wilford (eds.) *The Welsh Veto* (Cardiff, 1982).

group, the Scottish Labour Party. (Sillars later married the Scottish Nationalist ex-MP Margo MacDonald and became SNP member for Govan in November 1988.) Labour's devolution campaign in Scotland lacked force and credibility and Scottish enthusiasm waned steadily. On 1 March 1979, devolution did, indeed, gain a majority amongst the Scottish voters, by 1,240,937 to 1,153,502, 51.6 per cent to 48.4 per cent, but over 36 per cent of electors did not vote at all. Even Scotland was far removed from the necessary 40 per cent margin. The decade ended with Scottish Nationalism as a political force decidedly on the wane, and devolution discredited. The issue was clearly much more buoyant than in Wales, and Scottish Labour circles continued to be sympathetic. But in general, here, too, was a major issue in which the 1970s had been wholly unproductive, in which Celtic nationalism had been enflamed but left impotent and dissatisfied, and real questions about accountability and democratic participation left unanswered.

Devolution, even in Ulster, was a relative sideshow. The main issue, undoubtedly, lay in the sphere of industrial relations. This would decide whether the hard-won economic recovery of the post-IMF phase would be destroyed by rampaging wage demands and raging inflation. Between the Labour government and the unions there was an uneasy *détente* at the start of 1977. An interlude of social peace had been forged of which Jack Jones of the Transport Workers' Union was the architect.[17] Jones was now in the twilight of a complex and often controversial career. In 1977 the campaign was already afoot to choose the successor to him as General Secretary, with Moss Evans as the favourite. Certainly, such peace as prevailed owed an immense amount to Jones's personal stature in the movement, as one of the old-style union leaders who had, nevertheless, taken an outward-looking and creative role in trying to relate union demands to a wider pattern of economic stability and also, incidentally, the wellbeing

[17] Jack Jones, *Union Man*, 303 ff.

·of a Labour government. Jack Jones was an interesting, transitional figure. He was an old leftist who had fought in Spain in the International Brigade. He had grown up in a quasi-syndicalist tradition in the Liverpool docks, and his influence in the sixties had been thrown behind the growth of the shop-stewards movement and local plant bargaining on a devolved basis very much on the lines of the 1968 Donovan Report. He was far removed from the centralism embodied by his predecessors Ernest Bevin and Arthur Deakin. On the other hand, he had played a nationally constructive role also, especially since he and Hugh Scanlon helped the TUC defeat Barbara Castle's incomes policy in 1969. Jones had then worked closely with the docks employer, Lord Aldington, in getting a new wages agreement for the docks including a settlement for the problem of casual labour which drew on him the fire of many militant shop stewards amongst the stevedores. He was also the leader of a pressure-group to improve the lot of old-age pensioners. Jones emerged in 1975 and 1976 as the unique champion of a policy for wages which reconciled voluntary bargaining with a national perspective.

Until the autumn of 1976, the £6 flat-rate increase for wages and salaries below £8,500, agreed by the TUC General Council by a narrow margin in July 1975, held firm and clearly played a major part in the sharp reduction of inflation that year. As a testimony to one trade-unionist's authority and stature, carried through in the face of some hostility within the administration and somewhat glacial relations with Denis Healey at the Treasury, it was a remarkable accomplishment. But the achievement was always precarious and was maintained only with some difficulty. With the mounting balance-of-payments crisis, the TUC was reluctantly persuaded in the summer of 1976 to renew a virtual wage-freeze policy with a limit of 5 per cent increases for the next twelve months. The financial atmosphere was dire at this period. Even so, the new relationship between government and the unions was unlikely to last, at least on the present basis. Jack Jones told Healey that summer: 'We will have to get back to normal collective bargaining. The most you can expect from us is an attempt to organize an orderly return with emphasis on some priorities.'[18] Clearly, the optimism in some quarters that the unions were moving towards any long-term incomes or anti-inflation policy was quite unfounded. Jack Jones himself remained poised, perhaps torn, between his traditional stance as a union negotiator committed to autonomy and his wider view of the need to recast an adversarial industrial-relations system. Somewhat remarkably, he gave strong support to the proposals emanating from a committee under Lord Bullock for co-determination or industrial partnership as a basis for management.[19] But the horizons of most trade-unionist leaders were much more limited.

In 1977 the skein of any agreement on wages policy began to come apart. Trade-union leaders, hailed in the press as industrial statesmen during the period of the flat-rate wage policy, were now denounced as over-mighty tyrants. Jack Jones found himself assailed by Paul Johnson, the ex-editor of the *New Statesman* who had moved to the far right, as 'The Emperor Jones', almost a fourth estate of the realm in himself and the symbol of overweening trade-union power. Despite the warnings of Callaghan and Healey, the TUC at its conference in September 1977 voted for a return to 'unfettered collective bargaining', with Jones and Scanlon taking the adverse view. Although the TUC also, and somewhat contradictorily, endorsed a twelve-month gap in pay settlement, the banks of wage agreements were being burst again. The pressure for an increase in wage levels, at least as agreed at the local branch or shop-floor, steadily mounted, and in the 1977–8 pay round settlements averaged over 15 per cent.[20] TUC support for a national limitation steadily eroded, not least because a so-called 'Top People' pay-review inquiry under Sir Edward Boyle recommended large rises for already well-paid

---

[18] Ibid. 308.   [19] Ibid. 314–16.

[20] As early as 16 July 1977. *The Economist* pronounced that 'Wage restraint is dead—again!'

professions such as High Court judges and top civil servants, while the police, the armed services, the dentists, and doctors also benefited from substantial salary rises. This was not helpful to TUC advocates of wage restraint. Len Murray, the General Secretary, worked solidly on behalf of the government's 5 per cent policy but, unlike his predecessor Vic Feather, had no illusion of his power or ability to dictate to autonomous and all-powerful national unions.

Anxiety about trade-union power was rife at this period, as the personal attacks on Jack Jones indicated. National unions like the Miners seemed able to advance almost any inflationary proposition with some real hope of success. In the NUM a left-wing spokesman like Arthur Scargill advocated a broad pay increase of up to 80 per cent, and denounced local incentive schemes accepted in most coalfields as a means of increasing productivity. Although nationwide strikes diminished in 1976–7, such disputes as did occur caused the maximum of attention, most of it highly unfavourable in tone. When the firemen went on strike in 1977, a state of emergency was called by the Callaghan government and the army was employed in a strike-breaking capacity with the use of 'green goddess' fire-fighting vehicles. A similar occurrence came when NHS ambulance drivers also stopped work.

An episode which attracted particular concern was a strike that occurred at an obscure photo-processing plant in North London, the Grunwick works. This saw mass picketing by the unions after the employer, George Ward, a member of the 'National Association for Freedom', sacked some Asian workers following his dismissal of employees who were members of unions. After almost a year of dispute, mass picketing began in June 1977. The union involved was APEX, a notoriously moderate union with a right-wing General Secretary, Roy Grantham. In addition, the mass picketing outside Grunwick's works was intended to publicize the dispute rather than cause violent obstruction, as with Arthur Scargill's massed legions at the Saltley coke depot in 1972. Nevertheless, violence outside the

Grunwick works rapidly escalated, culminating in a so-called 'day of action' (11 July 1977) when about 18,000 people turned up to picket and there was much fighting with the police, resulting in seventy arrests and several injuries. Daily scenes of confrontations outside the Grunwick works between the pickets and their supporters (sometimes not members of unions at all) and police cordons dominated television news coverage. Right-wing members of the Labour government like Roy Hattersley and Shirley Williams felt it their duty to show solidarity with the pickets. In the end, picketing was much reduced from the summer of 1977. But the entire episode promoted anti-union sentiment, not only amongst Conservatives, and led to many cries for legislation on picketing to clip the power of the overmighty trade unions once and for all. The TUC had now the dilemma of wondering how far to authorize secondary action, for instance by calling out water workers or electricity power-station personnel. In the event, the General Council drew back from this extreme policy and the outcome was that, after months of violence and intense bitterness, George Ward won his point and unions were excluded from the Grunwick plant. The workers on strike found jobs elsewhere. But, even in defeat, the unions had succeeded in imprinting the notion of workers' power on the minds of the public. They had reinforced international criticism, not always well founded, of the 'British disease' of chaotic and adversarial industrial relations and endless strikes.[21]

The industrial scene thus looked much more alarming in the early months of 1978. The government's hard-won economic plateau seemed unlikely to last. Len Murray of the TUC worked hard but was unable to exert power that he did not possess. A major factor was that the two famous left-wing union leaders, both to some degree poachers turned gamekeepers, Hugh Scanlon and Jack Jones, were now removed from the scene through retirement. Scanlon's successor as President of the Engineers'

---

[21] For Grunwick, see Joe Rogaly, *Grunwick* (London, 1978).

Union, Terry Duffy, was, in fact, a strongly right-wing figure anxious to reach an accommodation with the government, but naturally it would take him time to build up his authority. Jack Jones's successor was Moss Evans, a Welshman who had worked in the car industry as TGWU National Organizer. He was a man with a limited grasp of wider economic or political implications who had set his face against wage restrictions, or even any notion of a social contract. Indeed, it was largely because of this stance of old-fashioned industrial unionism that he had been elected in the first place.

The government's reaction pivoted on the response of the Prime Minister, James Callaghan. As noted, his prestige had steadily risen since his accession to office. In particular, as an old union man he was thought to have a particularly sensitive, almost intuitive, understanding of the unions and how best to sell a policy of wage restraint to them. In the crisis, quite unexpectedly, Callaghan seemed to lose some of his touch, with fatal results. In July 1978, he announced bluntly that the government would commit the unions to a pay-increase norm of just 5 per cent for the next twelve months. This proposal, unexpectedly small and unexpectedly rigid, took the unions aback. It was by no means clear how the figure arose in the first place. Callaghan later stated that it 'popped out' at the end of 1977 and then became firmer following a television broadcast.[22] It was argued that 5 per cent on paper would mean nearer 8 or 9 per cent in reality through wage-drift effects. Even so, to proclaim so dogmatically a single-figure norm (instead of something attainable such as 10 per cent) was widely perceived to be a mistake. The previous year, a more credible figure had been achieved without the need of a formal agreement at all. Defending the increasingly indefensible policy of a 5 per cent pay norm led the government into growing difficulties.

---

[22] Callaghan, *Time and Chance*, 519–20.

Closely related to this was the prospect of a general election. Labour had actually moved ahead of the Tories in some polls at the start of August 1978. Many in the Cabinet felt that Callaghan would be in a uniquely favourable position, both politically and in terms of the balance of payments, to call an election in October. Nicholas Kaldor urged him: 'It is a peak. Maybe a submerged peak, but a peak nevertheless.' The Prime Minister wavered throughout the summer with the contradictory signals coming from his colleagues and closest advisors. Some trade unionists later felt that they had been misled by private assurances from the Prime Minister that there would be an early election. In the end, Callaghan backed down because his private information suggested that Labour prospects were too precarious.[23] The Tories had again moved ahead in the polls at the start of September. In part, perhaps, this was because of an effective advertising campaign on their behalf by Saatchi and Saatchi who published posters of the alleged army of unemployed people (recruited, in fact, from the affluent ranks of the Young Conservatives) which claimed that 'Labour isn't working'. Private polls in the constituencies conducted by Robert Worcester also suggested that in seventy marginal seats in England Labour would do badly, partly because a decline in the Liberal vote there was likely to assist the Conservatives. Callaghan, therefore, decided against an early election. But he did so in the most unfortunate manner. At the TUC conference, which was intended by its chairman, David Basnett, to be a pre-election rally, the premier displayed some unwonted frivolity, singing an old music-hall song about 'There she was, waiting at the church'. On 7 September he delivered a television broadcast in which he claimed that, for the sake of the economy and the national wellbeing, the election would be postponed to some time in 1979. It was altogether a mysterious episode. The Liberals had decided to

---

[23] Ibid. 516–17; Whitehead, *Writing on the Wall*, 276–9; David Butler and Denis Kavanagh, *The British General Election of 1979* (London, 1980), 43–4. Whitehead, loc. cit., attributes the 'peak' remark to Thomas Balogh.

end their pact and so the government had no firm majority in the House on which to rely. Their policies on devolution seemed to be going awry. There was every indication that the economic prospects would be much less favourable in 1979, with industrial trouble of a major kind looming up. A mood of excitement had been allowed to build, followed by a feeling of let-down. It made Callaghan seem untypically fragile and lacking in confidence.

There followed an alarming period in which the carefully contrived economic recovery and social peace created under the Callaghan government disintegrated. This became enshrined in popular memory as the 'winter of discontent' in which all the components of the British malaise emerged in heightened colours.[24] The manœuvring ability left to the Callaghan government was now slight, following the decision not to call an early election. In the Labour party, as in the TUC, the policy to impose a 5 per cent norm had provoked much fury, and the party conference in October heavily rejected the policy, even though Callaghan and Healey made it clear that they would ignore the views of the delegates. The party continued to swing to the left, with the prestige of Tony Benn, albeit still a Cabinet member, rising ever higher, and new left-wing figures like Neil Kinnock and Dennis Skinner elected to the constituency section of the NEC. At the same time the party continued to contract and disintegrate, even in its old mining and inner-city strongholds. The official figures showed the party membership to be around 650,000; the real figures were well known to be far below that number, possibly below 300,000, with an undue proportion being middle-class activists who had taken over old and decaying working-class parties or management committees. Transport House was, in terms of its organizing capacity, under-financed and distinctly run down. On the Conservative side, the decision of Callaghan

[24] There is much helpful material on the winter of discontent in the symposium in *Contemporary Record*, 1, no. 3 (autumn, 1987), 34–43. Also see Donoughue, *Prime Minister*, 167 ff, and William Rodgers, 'Government under stress; Britain's Winter of Discontent', *Political Quarterly*, 55, no. 2 (1984).

not to hold an election came as a shot in the arm. Mounting industrial unrest gave the party new heart after internal disputes over incomes policy, immigration, Rhodesia, and much else. Mrs Thatcher found it more possible to assert her own right-wing views as against those of moderates like Prior or Walker, with a strong thrust towards monetarism emerging in the party's *The Right Approach to the Economy*.[25] She now called, with increasing confidence and with the backing of a sophisticated advertising campaign, for 'a change of direction' and an attack on the monopolistic powers of the state and the crushing incubus of the trade unions. The suburban middle class were fighting back, in the wake of the economic setbacks and union advances of the 1970s. A new mood of aggressive support for 'privatization' and economic liberalism resulted.

The union troubles mounted apace that autumn, partly as a sign of growing strength. Union membership continued to rise steadily, especially in service employment, to reach a peak of over 13 million in 1979. The flash-point came, as so often in the past, in the car industry, with Ford workers, members of the TGWU, deciding to smash the 5 per cent guideline with calls for a minimum pay rise of £20 a week and associated fringe benefits. By the end of September, all twenty-three plants were lying idle, the management's offer of talks on productivity deals being abruptly rejected. Moss Evans, the new Transport Workers' Union leader, made no effort to rein in his members' demands, while the Ford company itself, worried by loss of profits, was in no mood for a prolonged fight. A Tory vote in the Commons on the Ford dispute in November helped defeat any form of incomes policy. After two months, a settlement of 17 per cent was agreed, but the green light had been given for others to follow on. There followed a

---

[25] William Keegan, *Mrs. Thatcher's Economic Experiment* (London, 1984), 99 ff. The authors of *The Right Approach* were Geoffrey Howe, Keith Joseph, and David Howell, with some assistance from James Prior. There was, interestingly, nothing on legislation to deal with the unions.

22 per cent pay rise for the firemen, a 14 per cent deal for the bakers, and no less than 30 per cent, in two stages admittedly, for heating and ventilation engineers.[26] It was in the Transport Workers, above all, that the main battle was taking place, with the Ford dispute leading to another threatened strike by British Oxygen workers, and finally a conclusive dispute amongst the drivers of long-distance lorries and oil tankers. A nation-wide strike by lorry drivers was declared for early January, starting in Scotland, with also an overtime ban, and another threatened strike by oil-tanker drivers early in the new year. Britain faced the prospect of a winter without food and without energy, at the mercy of powerful unions and ineffective employers.

The Cabinet did what it could both to promote talks and also to set up emergency procedures under the Civil Contingency Unit chaired by Merlyn Rees, the beleaguered Home Secretary. But the sheer impossibility of providing a national network of food and oil delivery made these efforts relatively ineffective, especially in the absence of legal or financial sanctions against the unions. The situation was worsened by the ineptitude and intransigence of the oil companies. No doubt the threat of national paralysis seemed much worse than it was: after all it would take many weeks for the full effects of a national strike to have an impact. But the prospect was alarming enough and it was a gloomy festival at Christmas 1978.

Early in the new year there was a meeting of the leaders of the main industrial nations, Carter, Schmidt, Giscard, and Callaghan, on the attractive island of Guadeloupe in the French West Indies to discuss both economic and defence matters. From this, Callaghan, sun-tanned and confident, returned to cold, strike-torn Britain. At the airport, he replied to interviewers with words that were memorably misreported as being: 'Crisis—what crisis?'[27] Certainly, he

---

[26] *The Economist*, 30 Sept. 1978 and subsequent issues.

[27] *The Times* and *The Guardian*, 11 Jan. 1979. Callaghan's actual words were: 'I don't think that other people in the world would share the view that there is mounting chaos.'

failed to respond immediately to the gravity of the situation, and his authority slumped accordingly.

On 19 January the lorry drivers' strike ended with an almost total victory for the unions. A rise of between 17 and 20 per cent was agreed, amounting to £64 a week, a dramatic demonstration of workers' power. But the malaise of discontent was now spreading fast. Public-service workers in such unions as NUPE and NALGO objected to the effects of the 5 per cent pay norm on low-paid workers, and on 22 January a national strike of 24 hours was declared by public-service workers. It was followed by a rash of local selective strikes by health-service workers, dustmen, even the grave-diggers of Liverpool. Rotting rubbish piled up in the streets. Schools were kept closed because their caretakers stayed away, as did cleaners, cooks, and deliverers of fuel. In the end an agreement on St Valentine's Day 1979 was cobbled together of 9 per cent plus an extra £1 a week, but the stakes were going up all the time. Some COHSE hospital workers told Bernard Donoughue, the Prime Minister's personal adviser: 'We'll tell you straight. Our purpose is to get more than you offer and whatever you offer it won't be enough.'[28] Formally, the main crisis was now over, even though strikes by civil servants and many local groups continued in February and March. The government and the TUC were now committed to a concordat to bring inflation down to 5 per cent over three years, while new TUC guidelines were issued over picketing and the operation of the closed shop. But this hardly carried credibility in view of the collapse of three attempted wage-restraint initiatives by the Labour government since 1974, and the failure of the 1969 'solemn and binding' covenant, the 1974 social contract, and a myriad other scraps of paper in the past.

Correctly or not, the public interpretation was of an industrial system out of control and a government in a state of near-paralysis. Literally this was not so, since the emergency procedures

---

[28] *Contemporary Record*, loc. cit., 43.

of the Civil Contingency Unit were kept in being and it felt able to cope with almost every dispute other than that of council grave-diggers. But it was obviously impossible to deal with a nation-wide emergency such as lorry-drivers' strikes, and equally impossible to respond properly to a rash of major disputes all at the same time. The evidence also suggests that, in the two weeks between the Prime Minister's return from Guadeloupe and the subsequent attempts to settle the public-service strikes, there was a remarkable absence of initiative in the Cabinet and Whitehall and an unusual mood of despondency in Number 10 Downing Street. Callaghan told Joel Barnett that he had never felt so depressed, and the news spread.[29]

The Callaghan government never recovered from the sense of ungovernability and social chaos heralded by the winter of dis-content. In a vote of confidence on 28 March about the govern-ment's handling of the industrial crisis, the Liberals, the Scottish Nationalists, and most of the Ulster MPs voted with the Conser-vatives, while the government enlisted the support only of the 3 Welsh Nationalists, 2 Scottish Labour, and 2 Ulstermen. One Labour MP, Sir Alfred Broughton, was away sick and that proved decisive. The government lost by one vote, 311 to 310, and for the first time since October 1924 an administration had been voted out of office through a Commons vote. The general election followed, in which Labour fought a vigorous but undeniably defensive campaign. Callaghan himself followed a staid and dignified, but uncharismatic, course. The main excite-ment, apart from the concerns of Ulster, came with disputes between Tony Benn and his NEC colleagues over the future direction to be pursued by a socialist government. In the end, Callaghan managed to remove such policies as unilateralism, abolition of the House of Lords, and nationalizing the 'big four' banks from Labour's manifesto. The polls showed a drift back towards Labour during the campaign and an NOP poll,

---

[29] Joel Barnett, *Inside the Treasury*, 170 ff.

extraordinarily, even showed a Labour lead of 0.7 per cent at the end of April, though this was not confirmed elsewhere. Peter Jenkins in *The Guardian* opined that 'it would no longer be amazing to see Mr Callaghan win by a whisker'.[30]

In general, though, it was notable that Labour, as in 1951, fought a negative and backward-looking contest, offering no new initiatives, and reiterating its well-known support for the National Health Service, public education, and fuller employment. What Labour could hardly claim was that it had a magic formula for preserving peace with the unions, although the St Valentine's Day 'concordat' with the unions was milked for what it was worth. The radicalism of the campaign came wholly from the Conservatives, redolent of the shift in the political and intellectual climate of the period generally since 1974. The overall expectation was that the Conservatives would win and in the event they did so with rather more comfort than the polls had tended to suggest. There was an overall majority for them of 44, which guaranteed a full term in office, with 339 Conservatives. 268 Labour, and only 11 for the Liberals who had clearly not benefited from their quasi-governmental experiences of the Lib-Lab Pact. Even though its vote was slightly up on that of October 1974, Labour's share of the poll had fallen to 36.9 per cent, the worst since 1931, while the Tories had risen to 43.9 per cent. With the Liberals in decline and nationalism in retreat (only 2 SNP and 2 Plaid Cymru members were returned), the discontent with Labour had flowed strongly towards the Conservatives. Under the leadership of a woman Prime Minister for the first time in western European history, the forces of the right, of private business, and the beleaguered middle class regrouped to redesign their nation before it was too late.

The 'winter of discontent' and the subsequent return of the Conservatives for what proved to be a very lengthy period of rule seemed to most observers to mark a profound watershed. It

[30] *The Guardian*, 2 May 1979.

seemed to provide an *envoi* to the policies and economics of consensus, which had coincided with decades of calamitous financial and international decline. Few doubted that Britain's position had eroded substantially.

This was powerfully expressed in a valedictory message from the retiring ambassador to Paris, Sir Nicholas Henderson, who was about to succeed Peter Jay at the British embassy in Washington.[31] The gloomy terms of his report to the then Labour Foreign Secretary, David Owen, were widely leaked. Henderson drew a sharp contrast with the years after 1945 when Britain was still a major and respected force in world affairs, the dominant power in the Middle East down to the time of Suez, the second most important power in the Far East at least down to the 1954 Geneva Conference. More controversially, Henderson linked subsequent failure with the inability of Britain to involve itself in 'Europe', either in the Schuman Plan or in the Messina Conference. This meant, he argued, that in the 1960s the members of the EEC were able to develop a large and sophisticated market with much technical innovation as a result, while Britain continued to trade in its traditional markets, still partly obsessed with its Commonwealth relationships. In the 1970s, Henderson argued, Britain was clearly not in the front rank, even as a European power, with its declining economy and lack of investment in managerial and engineering resources. This diagnosis, that linked national decline so closely with non-membership of the European Common Market, was open to much debate. But the broad facts of internationally diminishing status, linked with economic weakness and social division at home, was generally accepted. They were underlined by Labour's Defence Review of 1974–5 which committed Britain's ground forces solely to the defending of continental Europe, and stripped away the last fragments of the country's global pretensions.

[31] *The Economist*, 2 June 1979.

There was, indeed, a broad sense that the gloomy seventies had brought about a transformation not only in Britain's external status but also in the main instrument and agents of planning and social policy, after the oil-price explosion, the IMF crisis, and the winter of discontent. The mandarins were losing their charisma. Sir Alec Cairncross, himself a distinguished practitioner of the Keynesian policies of the 1950s and 1960s, ruefully recalled in 1981 that the standing of economists, which was at its peak just after the war, was now back 'at its pre-war low'. He added: 'We live in a society in which all forms of management and leadership, however advised, are under constant challenge. . . . Consensus and cohesion in the execution of policy are increasingly hard to achieve.'[32] The sense of common purpose and common direction that governed the war years had been lost, perhaps for ever. In place of the Fabian imperatives of post-war planning and the corporate outlook of the 1944 White Paper, there had come sectional interest and a declining confidence in the public sector. A nation unsure of its standing in the world was also unclear in its internal lines of direction and command structure.

No doubt, in many ways this gloom about the condition of Britain in the seventies was exaggerated. The partial recovery of the economy after 1983 was to show that some of it was misplaced, and that fears about national ungovernability and inability to adapt were ill-founded. The seventies came to an end with somewhat contradictory signposts of national advance or regression. The arts continued to flourish, amidst growing argument over the role of the Arts Council, the right balance to be struck between the metropolitan and the regional, and between private and public funding. British higher education remained another source of national pride and complacency, with the high international standing of British universities and polytechnics generally assumed, even though the differential fees imposed on

[32] Alec Cairncross, 'Academics and Policy-Makers', in F. Cairncross (ed.). *Changing Perceptions of Economic Policy*, 20.

overseas students in Britain, first by the Callaghan government, and later by the Conservatives after 1979, somewhat eroded this appeal.

Above all, there was a general belief that, after three decades of social welfare and redistributive taxation, the spirit of Beveridge and 'fair shares' was not dead, and that Britain was a far more equitable society than before the war, with more genuine opportunity for different classes and races. Thus, the marked advance of women in education and in the professions in the seventies was a notable, if belated testament to social advance, even if some of this progress owed much to the belligerent assertiveness of the feminist movement as well. The Royal Commission on the Distribution of Income and Wealth, chaired by Lord Diamond and originally set up by the Wilson government in 1974 to appease the unions over a wealth tax, made a series of oracular judgements which confirmed the progress which was generally assumed.[33] Reporting between 1976 and 1979 it showed how the share of the before-tax distribution of wealth of the top ten per cent had fallen from nearly 30 per cent in 1959 to 26.6 per cent in 1974–5. The effect of taxes and social benefits had achieved 'a substantial redistribution towards equality'.[34] Even at the poorer end of the scale, the effect of the distribution of benefits in cash and in kind had been substantially to equalize the wealth of older and poorer people. The 20 per cent of the poorest households, who had claimed only 0.9 per cent of the 'original income', rose through welfare benefits and other supplementary assistance to a 'final income' share of 9.0 per cent. A social wage had been provided for those unable for whatever reason to earn,

[33] *Royal Commission on the Distribution of Income and Wealth in Britain*, Reports 3 and 4 (Cmnd. 6838 and Cmnd. 6626), 1975–6, Reports 5 and 6 (Cmnd. 6999 and Cmnd. 7175), 1977–8. The last includes a valuable background paper on 'The Causes of Poverty' by Richard Layard and others. Excellent use is made of the material drawn from the Royal Commission by one of its members. Sir Henry Phelps Brown, in *Egalitarianism and the Generation of Inequality* (Oxford, 1988), 305 ff.

[34] Report, No. 5, 204.

or those whose earning capacity had been interrupted by illness, injury, and unemployment. Beyond aspects of redistribution, almost all classes of the community showed a picture of greater affluence and comfort over the past thirty years. Aided by substantial tax relief on house mortgages, the proportion of owner-occupiers had risen from 29.5 per cent of dwellings in 1951 to 52.8 per cent at the end of 1975. Conversely, privately rented dwellings had fallen in proportion from 44.6 per cent at the former date to 16 per cent in 1975. Clearly, a large and growing majority of occupiers owned their own home. Their assets had improved in other ways also. For instance, building-society deposits, bank cash accounts, and National Savings holdings all rose sharply throughout the period, especially with high interest rates prevailing for parts of the 1970s. It was a good decade for the *rentier* and (to a lesser extent) the small investor.

In many ways, then, it seemed that the pressure of welfare policy and social planning had indeed led both to greater equality and to more diffused prosperity as pioneers like Beveridge and theorists like Titmus had long forecast. In one important respect, the Beveridge legacy had been notably extended in the seventies. Barbara Castle pushed through a far-reaching reform of the state pension system which took effect in April 1978. This provided an earnings-related pension for some twelve million people not covered by good occupational schemes. For the low-paid, the new pension would represent at least half pay on retirement; further, it was protected against inflation. This measure, which Crossman had tried unsuccessfully to put into law in 1969–70, recognized that the original Beveridge scheme of flat-rate pensions in return for flat-rate contributions was out-of-date, not least because of the burden placed by the contributions on the low paid. Labour and Conservative governments had promoted social provision, income maintenance, and (down to 1973) full employment, in contrast to the social misery after 1919. Yet there was cause for anxiety even here. This affluence was disproportionately concentrated in south-east England. Even in the seventies there was awareness of a 'north–south' divide. In 1978,

42 per cent of all personal income went to 33 per cent of households concentrated in south east England, especially Greater London. The new patterns of the economy, the steady decline of manufacturing industry (in which 6.5 m. of the population were directly employed at the end of the seventies) as against the rise of the service and transport sector (which employed 7.25 m. at the start of 1980) also told in favour of the redistribution of resources in favour of particular regions and occupational groups. Managers, technicians, and other 'lower professionals' expanded in number with especial rapidity.[35] Again, the welfare state had in many respects advanced equality of opportunity, but not equality of outcome. It was above all the white middle class who benefited from a free health service, earnings-related pensions, and the growth of larger secondary schools. The new comprehensive schools, educationalists complained, seemed to have less social mixing than the old grammar schools had done. Less than ten per cent of the university or other higher-education student population came from working-class households.

The welfare state, then, had not closed the gap between classes, despite the growth of supplementary and other benefits under the 1974–9 Labour governments. There had been some redistribution of income. But in terms, say, of residual wealth and capital, educational mobility, or occupational status, even in everyday terms such as dress, hobbies, or accent, British social divisions remained unusually pronounced by European or transatlantic standards. Some of the social and economic assumptions on which Beveridge and other pioneers had based their welfare schemes had been proved to be over-optimistic. There had been steady, if slow,

[35] Comparing the censuses of population of 1971 and 1981, it emerges that the 1970s saw the greatest drop in the proportion of manual workers in the century. In 1971 the proportions were: non-manual workers 44.3 per cent: manual workers 55.7 per cent. In 1981 the proportions were: non-manual workers 52.3 per cent: manual workers 47.7 per cent. The category of non-manual workers designated as 'managers' rose from 9.8 per cent to 13.7 per cent in 1971–81, while 'lower professionals and technicians' rose from 7.7 per cent to 10.6 per cent in that period, as a percentage of the total occupied population.

economic growth down to the 1970s. The national income had doubled since 1948; in the period 1951–73, the average annual rate of growth was 2.3 per cent. But, apart from being a relatively poor performance by international standards, national resources had not grown sufficiently to take account of total need. There had been weakened competitiveness, endemic balance-of-payments problems, cyclical stop-go movements in the economy, and a falling off of the rate of capital accumulation. This weakness had become far more pronounced since the oil crisis of 1973 with a severe cut-back in output and demand, and the annual percentage rate of growth in 1973–9 a mere 0.7 per cent.[36]

The welfare state was a particular casualty. Pensions and benefits had not risen to keep pace with the rate of inflation, especially in the 1970s. Hopes that private and voluntary agencies, along with the nuclear family, could supplement the welfare state did not apply with equal validity to a society with more dislocation, more one-parent families, a growing divorce rate, and less active involvement by religious and other charitable bodies. The army of social workers had indeed risen sharply. At the start of the 1970s, at least 135,000 people were employed in local authority social service departments.[37] But the task was increasingly beyond them, as social surveys showed the inability of the welfare services to cope with the specific needs of the aged, the disabled, and one-parent families. Divorces rose steadily, though the real acceleration in the divorce rate was to come after the Matrimonial and Family Proceedings Act of 1984 which allowed petitioning for divorce after only one year of marriage. Especially disadvantaged were children, whose needs were dramatically highlighted by the Child Poverty Action Group and similar organizations. The ending of the former

[36] An admirable guide here is R. C. O. Matthews, C. Feinstein, and R.C. Odling-Smee, *British Economic Growth, 1856–1973* (Oxford, 1982). Also see Angus Maddison. *Phases of Capitalist Development* (Oxford, 1982).

[37] Eric Butterworth and Robert Holman (eds.), *Social Welfare in Modern Britain* (London, 1975), 119 ff.

child allowances and their replacement with tax-free child benefits in 1975 meant an increase in the problem of dependency,
with only about half the 750,000 one-parent families in 1976,
for instance, able to rely on their income as means of support. An
unduly high proportion of such families were black.

The rising toll of unemployment was another alarming problem,
involving as it naturally did the families and children of the
unemployed man or woman as well. Over a million people found
themselves dependent on supplementary benefit to eke out an inadequate existence as regards food and drink, with inflation taking its
toll of what was provided. Relative poverty, more markedly than
absolute poverty, clearly rose rapidly throughout the 1970s.

On balance, social scientists glumly concluded, the welfare
state, in spreading its net so wide, was often avoiding the needs
of specifically targeted groups and individuals who needed help.
The social provision that had been Britain's thank-offering to an
expectant postwar world after 1945 had left the problem of
poverty, in some respects, remarkably and alarmingly
unaffected. It had also generated complacency and an insuffi-
ciently productive, administratively-oriented work-force. In most
respects, Britain spent a smaller proportion of the annual budget
on welfare than did continental European countries with a system financed from contributory sources or with a greater mix of
public and private provision. Nor could it be said that the British
welfare system identified, or even defined, let alone assisted, the
genuinely needy groups as effectively as did some systems prevailing elsewhere. In short, quite apart from economic or foreign
policy considerations, the social momentum which had sustained
the British throughout their difficult experiences since 1945 was
not being maintained.

Underlying these themes was the belief that the problems of the
British system were being thrown into stark relief by the endless
economic difficulties of the 1970s. The Oxford economists,
Bacon and Eltis, found a receptive audience across the political
spectrum for their diagnosis that Britain was generating far too

few producers of wealth.[38] In their stead came a new intermediate breed of service operatives working in administration, in finance, or in the professions. University graduates became accountants, solicitors, or stock-brokers instead of entering industry. One consequence in industrial terms was the greater bargaining power of professional and white-collar groups, especially focusing on their trade unions as during the 'winter of discontent', able to use their bargaining muscle to claim a growing share of the national income for themselves without much compensation in manufacturing or investment. Eltis linked this with the basic errors he detected in Keynesian ideas, as propounded by such recent disciples as Harrod or Kaldor, who gave full employment and job creation the priority over price stability.[39] Demand management had been given priority in preference to profitable or productive work. Rather than being the workshop of the world, Britain was becoming one of the world's secretarial colleges, with priority given to non-manual clerical and service occupation. While the drift out of industrial employment was common to all developed countries after 1945. in Britain in 1975 the ratio of non-industrial to industrial employment was 41 per cent, compared with 32.8 per cent in Germany, 27.9 per cent in the USA, 22.5 per cent in France, and just 4.5 per cent in Japan.[40] One pointer was the way that a growing percentage of the workforce was employed in the various activities of tourism, much of it of necessity on a shortterm or seasonal basis.

This disparity loomed ever larger in the rescue of the balance of payments. It affected not only rural or seaside communities (some of which were now facing a crisis with the growing attractiveness of continental holidays and the inroads made by car and caravan into the traditional domain of the seaside

[38] Bacon and Eltis, *Britain's Economic Problem: Too Few Producers* (London, 1976).

[39] Walter Eltis, 'The Failure of the Keynesian Conventional Wisdom', *Lloyd's Bank Review*, 122 (Oct. 1976), 1–18. There is a rebuttal by G. D. N. Worswick, 'The End of Demand Management?', *Lloyd's Hank Review*, 123 (Jan. 1977).

[40] Bacon and Eltis, op. cit., 11 ff.

landlady), but even industrial areas, where such attractions as Big Pit at Blaenavon in South Wales paid testimony to the passing of the age of coal. The so-called 'heritage' industry brought large numbers of foreign and other tourists to old centres of attraction like country houses (now increasingly taken over by the National Trust), towns like Stratford, York, or Bath, and also to monuments of industrial or other archaeology. But the entire heritage concept was an ambiguous one, culturally and financially. It had an educative purpose, and it brought in some cash to hard-pressed regions. But it also increased the focus on unproductive, marginal, service employment, and perhaps encouraged a pervasive, discontented nostalgia, in which the inheritance of the glorious past was either unrelated to, or else unhistorically contrasted with, the bleak, discontented present.

Survey after survey in the 1970s pointed both to growing public expenditure (much of it on defence) and yet also to a run-down public sector. Trains and telephones broke down, cities and highways were grubby and unhygienic. There was a failure to invest, an inability to sustain science which led to renewed talk of a 'brain drain' of British scientists to American and other campuses, an inherent suspicion and division which prevented effective collaboration in industry. Britain's social engineers had prided themselves on the ability to plan as they had done during the war. But compared with the Monnet ideal in France, or the corporate strategy of Japan, Britain had scarcely planned in any meaningful sense at all. Harold Wilson's 'white heat' talk of 1963 seemed in 1979 extraordinarily dated. Michael Shanks, author of the powerful *Stagnant Society* of 1961, bitterly criticized fifteen years later the sterile failure of the planning imperative.[41] In 1976, at the time of the Bullock Committee on remoulding industrial relations, Chancellor Helmut Schmidt of West Germany had been brought in to instruct the Prime Minister, Callaghan, and Britain's industrial leaders and trade unionists on the

[41] Michael Shanks, *Planning and Politics: the British Experience, 1960–76* (London, 1977).

need to frame a new industrial climate as a basis for productive growth and a revived influence in the world. Callaghan and some of the CBI, at least, were duly impressed. But the consequences were abuse from the unions, hostility from the CBI, caution in Whitehall and Westminster, and no real change at all. Bullock's call for worker-directors was generally derided as utopian.[42] The very lack of dynamism, or pro-active vision in British industry, government, and scientific development, while widely perceived and understood, resisted efforts at reform.

The 'winter of discontent' thus encouraged a wider sense of national enfeeblement and decline. There was a tidal wave of pessimistic literature on this theme—*The Future that Doesn't Work: Social Democracy's Failures in Britain* (1977); *The Politics of Economic Decline* (1979); *Britain: Progress and Decline* (1980); and, most evocatively of all, *Is Britain Dying?* (1979).[43] History text-books invariably included in their titles such keywords as 'Decline', 'Downfall', and 'Eclipse'. Turmoil in industrial relations, ethnic disturbances, the growth of violent crime, even the dismal competitive record of British footballers, cricketers, and tennis players, were all grist to the commentators' mill. The roots of all this, it was agreed, lay deep in British history— perhaps in the moral nihilism of the 1960s, perhaps in the collectivism of the 1940s, perhaps in the decline of the entrepreneurial spirit in the late Victorian period, perhaps even in the many centuries of geographical isolation and freedom from foreign occupation behind the barrier of sea power. The point of reference for the origins of Britain's eclipse could be placed almost anywhere from 1968 back to 1066. But, however sketchy

---

[42] Private information. Both the CBI and the TUC objected to proposals that shop stewards should sit on boards of directors.

[43] R. Emmett Tyrell, Jr., *The Future that Doesn't Work: Social Democracy's Failures in Britain* (New York, 1977); James E. Alt, *The Politics of Economic Decline* (Cambridge,1979): William B. Gwyn and Richard Rose, *Britain: Progress and Decline* (London, 1980): Isaac Kramnick, *Is Britain Dying? Perspectives on the Current Crises* (London, 1979). Americans were especially prominent in this kind of diagnosis or pathology.

or plain foolish the history and social anthropology might be, the existence of long-term degeneration, in some key respects at least, commanded widespread assent.

One demographic factor, much noted, was that the British, an old nation, were an increasingly elderly people. The proportion of the population over 60 rose to nearly 29 per cent by 1980, most of them women. At the other end of the age-scale, renewal was less in evidence. In the seventies, after a rise in the birth-rate from the mid-fifties to the mid-sixties, creating a 'bulge' in the school and student population in the 1970s, there was a gradual decline in the birthrate in the seventies. The Registrar-General's statistics showed a low point of 11.8 per cent of live births per 1,000 of the population in 1977, with a slight rise thereafter.[44] In part, this was because of rising affluence, and a sense of financial and other independence among women. Working women were delaying or curtailing their capacity to bear children, marrying later or perhaps being reluctant to have children at all. The rise of a new stratum of child-minders and crèche facilities, public or private, was testimony to the wish of women to lead more relaxed, interesting, child-free lives, accentuated by the fact of more women being middle class in status or perhaps aspiration. The classic working-class 'mum', living at home to look after her numerous children with the man as the bread-winner, while a folk myth sustained by the Inland Revenue and the population census amongst others in the 1970s, conformed less and less to the reality. These factors might well be seen as socially beneficial. But many commentators saw only a decline in the desire to rear or look after children, a weakening of the cohesive effects of the family, and an associated diminution of the buoyancy of the stock in terms familiar at least since the Boer War. The partial compensation found in the fertility of the black and brown

---

[44] See D. A. Coleman, 'Population', in A. H. Halsey (ed.), *British Social Trends*, 36–50. The birth-rate in England and Wales was 11.6 per cent in 1976, 12.1 per cent in 1977, and 12.9 per cent in 1978. The figures were somewhat higher for Scotland and Northern Ireland.

immigrants of the Commonwealth countries who had sent over 3 million people into Britain since 1962 did not meet with universal enthusiasm, as the evidence from the Race Relations Board frequently suggested. Afro-Caribbeans huddled in ghetto areas like Brixton or Southall. Non-white Britons were having a growing impact, notably in mass sport and entertainment; commercial advertisements to an increasing degree focused on a poly-ethnic consumer market. But only an enlightened few saw this as a symbol of national renewal.

In the face of this varied sense of internal malaise, the return of the Thatcher government, with its young-Turk generation of monetarists and entrepreneurs, marked at least a change of gear, even if the privatization of publicly-owned enterprises was a very minor feature of the Conservative manifesto in 1979. An updated welfare state was linked with 'strengthening family life'. As yet there was no great sense that the policies of welfare and social egalitarianism since 1945 needed to be reversed. The recasting of economic policy in a supply-side direction still remained the faith of a minority. But that there was need for a substantial change in British society was a widespread conclusion. The British in 1979 were poised between a reverence for old historic symbols which had provided order and cohesion over the centuries, and an uneasy awareness that such reverence had become a recipe for immobilism and devotion to the outdated totems of the past. Polls in the state of public opinion and attitudes offered contrary findings. They suggested that, despite everything, most British people remained calm. They continued to prefer (and, indeed, to expect) a quiet life. A poll commissioned by the EEC in 1977 showed that 82 per cent of the population declared themselves to be broadly satisfied with living in Britain, compared with 68 per cent in France and 59 per cent in Italy.[45] Compared with

---

[45] William B. Gwyn, 'Jeremiahs and Pragmatists: Perceptions of British Decline', in Gwyn and Rose, *Britain: Progress and Decline*, 25, basing this on *World Opinion Update* (January 1978). Also see Rolf Dahrendorf, *On Britain* (London, 1980), 29–30, and Alt, *Politics of Economic Decline*, 48 ff.

most continentals and, indeed, Americans, the British by this crude test were a relatively happy people. Their democracy had remained secure. Suggestions in 1975 of a military coup by Colonel Stirling's 'non-party, non-class organization of apprehensive patriots' or General Walker's 'non-class Militia' met with almost universal derision. So, too, did the alarmist outpourings of the National Association for Freedom, a far-right pressure-group directed by a clutch of ex-army officers and Norris McWhirter, better known as the author of the *Guinness Book of Records* and apologist for South Africa.

At the same time, the British were in distinctly worried mood. Since 1961 (to be precise, since Selwyn Lloyd's 'pay pause' that summer) British people had given sustaining the economy the priority over foreign affairs among their concerns. They had become increasingly introspective. In the sixties, polls showed that, even if they believed that they themselves were doing rather well, most British people felt that their country was doing rather badly, and falling further behind foreign competitors. By the late 1970s, both private and public expectations were in parallel decline. Britain in mid-1979 was unlikely to lurch into any drastic transformation, let alone a dictatorship. Record inflation would not reproduce the panic of the Weimar Republic in the twenties, nor the 'winter of discontent' the pre-Vichy, neo-fascist despair of the French Third Republic in the later thirties. The British had no wish to move elsewhere. Emigration to Australia or New Zealand, let alone the United States, which had its own extreme problems of crime and racial violence, was little more than a trickle. Like the immortal 'Old Bill' in Bruce Bairnsfather's First World War cartoon of the trenches, the patient British urged their neighbours that if they knew of 'a better 'ole' they should go to it. For all that, it was a dismal phase in the chequered history of postwar Britain. The urge for a redirection of effort to repair national self-esteem was predominant as the unpermissive, unproductive seventies came to their close.

III

Thatcherism and its Aftermath

1979–2001

12. *The Foundations of Thatcherism*

1979–1983

MORE than any change of government since 1945, Margaret Thatcher's election victory was taken as marking a decisive shift in the national mood, politically, intellectually, and culturally. The fall of James Callaghan in the summer of 1979 meant, according to most commentators across the political spectrum, the end of an *ancien régime*, a system of corporatism, Keynesian spending programmes, subsidized welfare, and trade-union power.[1] To enthusiasts, it meant the passing of 'the dependency culture' in favour of a new wave of enterprise and individualism. After forming the core of a post-war consensus for over three decades since the Attlee period, the bitter legacy of the old order was now seen in the uncollected refuse bins and undug graves which popular credence (somewhat exaggeratedly) identified with 'the winter of discontent'. On all sides, both in the government service directly and in its associated echelons of closed institutions, corporations, committees, and 'quangos', there had been evidence of a loss of national confidence. The conventional wisdom of the pre-1970 period had perished in the 'stagflation' and social strife of the recent past. In place of the chastened, latter-day apostles of Keynes and Beveridge, a new generation of

---

[1] See, for instance, Geoffrey Goodman, 'Goodbye to 1945 and all that', *Guardian*, 27 Mar. 1989.

hard-headed spokesmen of free enterprise emerged, taking their cue from the dogmas of the new Prime Minister herself. Certainly there was abundant evidence as to how the centre-left had lost its entrenched intellectual and ideological ascendancy. As the Thatcher government gradually recovered from a shaky and difficult start to retain power by a hugely increased majority in 1983, followed by another overwhelming electoral triumph (in seats if not in votes) in 1987 and as the spectacle was observed in 1989 of a Prime Minister remaining in unchallenged power for over a decade, comparable to Lord Liverpool if not yet Robert Walpole in the past, the belief took hold that the values and style of modern Britain had been transformed. More than any Prime Minister since Lloyd George, Mrs Thatcher appeared justified in proclaiming after some years in office, 'I have changed everything'.[2] To adopt her favourite adverbs, everything had been 'totally and utterly' transformed, or so it seemed.

By the mid-1980s, this became increasingly the accepted view of what the Thatcher years had meant for Britain as a society and a polity. On the political right, this implied the triumph of the market philosophy, the private ethic, and the imperatives of early-nineteenth-century liberalism in place of the dead hand of state-directed corporatism which Attlee, Macmillan, Wilson, and Heath had variously created. Mrs Thatcher appeared to see herself as the embodiment of revenge upon a whole generation of social engineers. She committed herself to the view that 'there was no such thing as society', only individuals and families.[3] an extraordinary reaction against the outlook of the past forty years. On the political left, a popular approach was to adopt the terminology of the long-dead Italian Marxist, Antonio Gramsci, to argue that Thatcherism was more than a governmental system, more even than an ideological banner. It was truly a hegemony that

---

[2] See *The Times*, 19 Jan. 1985, in which she stated that she wished her government to be remembered as one that broke with a 'debilitating consensus'.

[3] A. H. Halsey, 'The Paradoxes of Thatcherism', in Robert Skidelsky (ed.), *Thatcherism*, 173 ff.

extended the market ethic beneath the shelter of an increasingly powerful state apparatus, at the cost of both social cohesion and personal liberty.[4] It penetrated the very substructure of national culture, with the message of traditional capitalism proclaimed in an unusually explicit and aggressive form.

Between the ideologues and monetarists of the New Right, and the revisionist Marxists of the New Left, defenders of what they took to be the post-1945 social order floundered unhappily. One after another, down to the end of 1988 at least, attempts to reform or redefine the old consensus on 'one-nation' lines proved ineffective. Hopes attached to the new Social Democratic Party of right-wing Labour Party defectors in 1981 collapsed after the internal divisions that followed electoral disaster in June 1987. By mid-1989 the centre in British politics, split between the renamed 'Democrats', the remaining Social Democrats, and 'green' environmentalists, seemed weaker than at any time since the leadership of the old Liberals by Jo Grimond at the time of 'Orpington man' in the early 1960s. The Labour Party, riven by schism and self-doubt, seemed in long-term, inexorable decline, for sociological as well as ideological reasons. The long march to 1945 and beyond had truly been halted. Large sections of the community, especially the blacks in the urban ghettos, young unemployed in urban areas of the north, and a considerable swathe of the people of Scotland, seemed almost to contract *out* from traditional forms of participation and civic involvement.

The cultural activity of the land remained vigorous, with a notable revival, for instance, in British sculpture. But the new generation of novelists and playwrights in the 1980s were somewhat more inward-looking in finding their cultural stimulation than, say, their predecessors in the fifties and sixties. They were increasingly prone to introspective analysis without a social cutting edge. Successful, Booker Prize-winning women novelists such as Anita Brookner or Penelope Lively, for example, did

---

[4] For an interesting treatment of this point, see Andrew Gamble, *The Free Economy and the Strong State*, chap. 1.

not reflect the feminist awareness of the time to any marked extent. Aspects of class, race, or nationalism passed them by, though this was less true of another distinguished author, Margaret Drabble. John Osborne's *Look Back in Anger* was presented in a new production in 1989 as a study of a failed marriage rather than of the playwright's early ideological concerns. Truly, there were now 'no great causes left'. Meanwhile, significant groups of intellectuals and artists, often in a somewhat modish, self-conscious way which attracted derision in the press, seemed to move away from identification with their society, so alien to their instincts did what they saw as the unacceptable, philistine face of Thatcherism appear to be.

In the face of the self-confident panache of the new monetarists, the Policy Studies group, and the apostles of the marketplace, significant numbers of British intellectuals seemed to lose heart. There was open, if despairing, resistance in the plays of David Hare, Howard Brenton, or David Edgar, or in a realist film like *My Beautiful Laundrette*. Critics tried to rescue older notions of 'community' or 'citizenship' to set against the competitive values of the Thatcher government—only to discover that the latter was highly adept in taking over these themes itself in such areas as housing, education, and 'neighbourhood watch' crime-prevention schemes, partly as a weapon against left-wing local authorities. In the summer of 1988, a group of writers and other intellectuals, ranging from Alliance supporters to Euro-Communists, formed a new journal, *Samizdat*.[5] It openly evoked the example of the Soviet dissidents, and voiced the despair of liberals of varying shades at what had happened to the fabric of British society since 1979. Not until the spring and summer of 1989 when, for the first time, the Thatcher government showed clear signs of frailty, with electoral defeats, economic difficulties, and internal acrimony which recalled the later years of Macmillan's government in the early 1960s, did the critics begin to regain their confidence. For the first time in a

---

[5] Its editor was Professor Ben Pimlott, author of a distinguished biography of Hugh Dalton.

decade the Thatcherite crusade seemed to be faltering, though how permanently it was too early to judge.

The new regime took its cue, to a truly extraordinary extent, from the personality and outlook of the new Prime Minister. Margaret Thatcher was remarkable, of course, for being the first woman Prime Minister, and she could use this factor to persuade or beguile male colleagues on occasion. But it was very seldom her femininity, but rather her image of toughness, determination, and ruthless single-mindedness that dominated public perceptions. She took office in May 1979, proclaiming on the steps of Number 10 Downing Street the healing words of St Francis of Assisi—'where there is discord, may we bring harmony.' Yet it was not the message of saintly benevolence but the jarring note of conflict, belligerence, and confrontation which marked her style from the outset. Moderates or doubters were dismissed as 'wets' or sometimes 'wimps'. From the outset, Mrs Thatcher had the sense of being a political outsider. It went far beyond her role as a woman in public life. She was the self-conscious product of a grocer's shop and a frugal Methodist background in Grantham in rural Lincolnshire. Her exemplar was her father, a local patriarch and evidently an apostle of Samuel Smiles-type individualism: she omitted reference to her mother in *Who's Who*. A minister in the Heath government, she had rebelled totally against its corporate style, and joined with Sir Keith Joseph in forming the Centre for Policy Studies in 1974 as a forum for proclaiming the cause of market individualism and monetary discipline. She was elected as Tory leader in 1975 as the voice of *petit bourgeois* protest in the constituencies, as against grandees like Whitelaw, Carrington, or Pym. It has been perceptively written that her victory was the product of a kind of 'peasants' revolt' within the Tory Party.[6] She rejected the complacent, paternalist inactivity of the 'common ground'. Her ability, like that of Lloyd George (a previous premier for whom she

---

[6] The author of this description is Julian Critchley, MP.

had no affection) to project herself as an outsider, detached from her party leadership, her civil service, even the Cabinet which she led, was a vital key to her effectiveness and impact. When she was attacked by her venerable predecessor Harold Macmillan (now elevated to the Lords as the Earl of Stockton) for 'selling off the family silver', it added to her proud sense of detachment.

Mrs Thatcher was usually termed 'a conviction politician', most at home with others of that stern, unbending creed. Moderates, liberals, 'wet' Tories of the old school, were witheringly dismissed as 'not one of us'. She was not an intellectual; her philosophical baggage was comparatively light. The abiding influence, it appeared, was that of the venerable Austrian anti-statist, Friedrich von Hayek, a critic of encroaching government since before the 1945 election. Mrs Thatcher claimed to have read Hayek's *Road to Serfdom* while she was still a student at Somerville College, Oxford, just after the war; but it was not until the 1970s, while in opposition, that she seems to have read Hayek's writings more generally.[7] In any case, her main ideological inspiration, like that of Lloyd George, came from people rather than from books. One ideological guru was Sir Alfred Sherman, founder with her of the Centre for Policy Studies in 1974. Even more did she rely on the guidance of Sir Keith Joseph, another rebel against the Heath interlude, whose speeches in 1974 first traced the clear lines of monetarism and market strategy which by 1979 had become the orthodoxy in many Conservative circles. The main thrust of Thatcherite social and economic philosophy was far from clear when she took office in May 1979, so entrenched were key figures of the Heathite past in the party; but the general thrust would clearly lie in pursuing the monetarist approach of the Chicago economist, Milton Friedman, in which control of the money supply through M3 indicators, and identifying inflation rather than unemployment as the central enemy, were the fundamental themes. The central issue was seen to be the relationship between the

[7] Hugo Young, *One of Us* (London, 1989), 407.

growth or contraction of the money supply and the pattern of national income and expenditure.

In general, though, Mrs Thatcher's approach was not really philosophical at all. Indeed, instinct rather than inductive reasoning marked her approach to life. In the Burkeian sense, she followed prejudice and (sometimes) prescription. Time and again, she would turn to simple, homely precepts drawn from the grocer's shop in Grantham, embellished with strongly held views about human nature. On one famous occasion, these were defined as 'Victorian values'. This implied a distinctly selective view of the nineteenth century which omitted Dickens, Disraeli, Arnold, and Ruskin among others. More than any Prime Minister, perhaps, since Douglas-Home, she had little interest in the development or clash of ideas. It followed that her associates and most admired colleagues were invariably businessmen or entrepreneurs rather than intellectuals, writers, or artists, doers rather than talkers or thinkers. She formed a distinctly close relationship with some business figures prominent in the Jewish community, though this did not unduly colour her view of the state of Israel. She symbolized her down-to-earth philosophy in her own busy persona, ceaselessly active, endlessly combative at home and abroad, hardly ever taking a holiday, never relaxing with music, books, or in the world of the arts. She apparently read every civil-service memorandum, personally confronted or abused officials, and intervened in departmental affairs as few premiers had done since Sir Robert Peel. In time she also found allies in a handful of civil servants like Charles Powell and Sir Percy Cradock and an occasional diplomat like Sir Anthony Duff and Sir Crispin Tickell. On all issues, she appeared formidably well-informed. A politician of intuition not of intellect, she served as the perfect antidote to the cerebral doctrines of the Keynesian planners of the 1945–79 period, against whose dominion she had so memorably rebelled. It was not endearing, comfortable, or perhaps attractive. But for many years after 1979 this approach seemed to embody many of the qualities which a depressed, declining nation yearned for and acclaimed.

The real essence of 'Thatcherism', indeed, lay not so much in its ideas, which proved to be increasingly malleable as the years went by, and especially when Nigel Lawson took over the Treasury in 1983. It lay rather in the company it kept, the classes with which it was associated. As noted, Mrs Thatcher came from a relatively humble, unprivileged background, though a degree at Oxford and later marriage to a millionaire businessman gave her a distinctly *haut bourgeois* status in time. But her outlook was subtly different, say from that of Edward Heath, whose father was a carpenter in a small town in Kent and who, like Mrs Thatcher, went to a local grammar school rather than the private boarding schools favoured by most Tory leaders. The Heath background was one of constructive, but deferential, working-class Toryism. The Thatcher background was one of entrepreneurial, upwardly-mobile, self-sufficient, middle-class neo-liberalism. It followed that her main associates and the figures to whom she was most naturally attracted, and who in turn revered her ascendancy, were self-made businessmen and smaller entrepreneurs, usually from the fields of finance, speculation, and investment. The roots of Thatcherism lay in acquisition rather than in production. It sought to create a business, perhaps a *rentier*, culture. Its spokeswoman imposed on the Conservative Party values very different from those of industrialists like Peel, Bonar Law, or Baldwin in the past. She was liable to propel into the governmental system men associated with business success, of whom Lord Young became the prototype from 1984 onwards. She was truly a distinctive phenomenon, linked neither with the patrician values of the grandees in the shires, nor with the manufacturing Tories of northern England cherished by Disraelian Tory Democracy in the last century, nor again with the suburban Toryism dominant in the party in the interwar years and after 1951. Mrs Thatcher gloried, among other things, in being a provincial, whose Lincolnshire origins would sometimes come out unexpectedly in her rhetoric. Such time-honoured Conservative themes as reverence for the Church and the gentry, for 'one-nation' cohesion in the romantic style of the Primrose

League, made little impact on this perpetually embattled leader. Her relationship with Queen Elizabeth II was believed to be frosty and her regard for the Commonwealth, now dominated by black-and brown-skinned leaders from Africa and Asia, slight. She made precious few concessions to the old orthodoxies. Her detachment from her own party as well as her nation added to her strength and sense of invincibility.

The nation expected a radical new impetus from Mrs Thatcher in May 1979, but it was curiously long in coming. For, alongside the conviction politics, and the violent rhetoric, was in practice an ingrained pragmatism. After all, Mrs Thatcher was also a supreme politician, not just an evangelist. She could eat her words, while denying with the maximum of emphasis that she was ever 'for turning'. In fact, her first administration down to June 1983 showed the impact of Thatcherite policies to be somewhat muted, with even so single-minded a Prime Minister apparently lacking in direction. There are many reasons for this. No doubt it was hard to dismantle, or even dent, the consensus policies of thirty-five years at a stroke. There were also inherited pledges which no new Prime Minister could disavow. Thus, the Conservative attack on inflation and public-sector wage explosions was in part nullified by the Clegg awards on pay comparability. This meant a huge rise of £114 billion in public-sector wage settlements in 1979–80 and drove inflation up far higher than the Callaghan government had ever done previously.

The decisive factor, though, was that Mrs Thatcher, for all her election triumph, was far from being mistress in her own house yet. With far more reason than Harold Wilson in 1964, she could claim to be running (*mutatis mutandis*) a Bolshevik revolution with a Tsarist Cabinet.[8] The domination of the old Heath Conservatives in her first Cabinet was overwhelming. Lord Carrington, a consensual aristocrat of the old school whose experience of government went back to 1951, had to be

[8] See above, p. 231.

Foreign Secretary. The Home Secretary was Willie Whitelaw, another traditional practitioner of one-nation ideas, and a major influence on party and government. James Prior went to the Department of Employment; in the words of one critic, Jock Bruce-Gardyne, he was to make this key department a citadel of 'unrepentant corporatism'.[9] Francis Pym went to Defence; Peter Walker to Agriculture; Sir Ian Gilmour also to the Foreign Office; Norman St John-Stevas became Leader of the House. Against these powerful Heathite figures, there were indeed very few colleagues whom the Prime Minister could safely regard as 'one of us'. The minority included Sir Keith Joseph, who took his bleak monetarist outlook to the Department of Trade and Industry, and John Biffen, an early apostle of Enoch Powell's financial credo, who became a Treasury Minister (and who also shared the Prime Minister's lack of enthusiasm for 'Europe'). Lower down in the government were such potential agents of 'Thatcherism' as David Howell and (more doubtfully) Nigel Lawson. The rogue figure of Angus Maude became Paymaster-General, another symbol of revolt against Macmillan-style politics and an opponent of the consensus approach. But, in general, fully three-quarters of her first Cabinet were identified with the mainstream Toryism of post-1945. They were welfare democrats and public spenders, not at all in tune with Mrs Thatcher's awkward imperatives. This was the supreme limiting restraint upon her ascendancy. Not until the end of 1981 did she begin to fight free of their domination.

The real test of Thatcherite radicalism would surely lie with its economic and financial policies. Here, the appropriate leader of change had been in some doubt. Some Conservatives, astonishingly enough, had even visualized the return to the Treasury of Roy Jenkins, a Labour minister until 1976 and now President of the European Commission in Brussels.[10] In fact, though, the new Chancellor turned out to be the emollient figure of Sir Geoffrey

[9] Jock Bruce-Gardyne, *Mrs. Thatcher's First Administration* (London, 1484), 18–19.
[10] Young, *One of Us*, 141.

Howe, once a vaguely progressive Heathite minister too, but a notable convert to monetarism in the later 1970s. His yielding to the edicts of Number 10 on financial policy eventually enabled the main thrust of Thatcherite innovation to show itself here, even though it was often the moderation as much as the radicalism which was to impress observers. Certainly, the Treasury was to be a major battle ground between contending philosophies. Its respective champions were personified by the Permanent Secretary, Sir Douglas Wass, an entrenched mandarin prone to statements like 'We're all Keynesians here', and Mrs Thatcher's new army of private advisers, monetarist apostles like Terry Burns and, from 1981, Alan Walters. Not until two years had passed was the outcome of these disputes at all clear.

Geoffrey Howe's first budget on 14 June 1979, only three weeks after the government had been in office, marked out the early objectives of the monetarist advance.[11] It included a sharp attack on public spending, with cash limits on the public sector, the raising of minimum lending rate to 14 per cent, some sale of public assets to help finance the public-sector borrowing requirement, and a major switch from direct taxation to taxes on spending. The standard rate of income tax was lowered to 30 per cent, whereas the raising of Value Added Tax and other indirect taxes switched tax policy to focus on expenditure. The supply side was elevated in contrast to Keynesian demand management. Exchange controls were also notably relaxed; in the autumn they were to be abolished altogether. This strikingly different budget was clearly intended to spearhead a monetarist assault on cost inflation. Yet, in fact, inflation continued to rise sharply, partly through the effect of the Clegg awards. Howe's budget deflated the economy and seriously added to unemployment. Yet it managed to raise prices and to add to inflation at one and the same time. For the next year and a half, the attainment of the monetarist objectives proved exceptionally difficult. For the

[11] *The Economist*, 16 June 1979.

nation as a whole, the visible effect was a huge rise in unemployment and a vast drop in the gross domestic product, with factories, mills, and pits closing down all over the country. In 1979–81, while other nations saw their GDP rise by 5.3 per cent, Britain's fell by 2.5 per cent. Unemployment rose to 13.3 per cent, the highest in Western Europe.[12] Britain's productive capacity was falling more rapidly than at any time since the dawn of the industrial age. Howe's second budget of March 1980 assumed a drop of 2 per cent in the real national income, and continuing and rising unemployment.[13] After a year in office, the Thatcher government found itself presiding over mass de-industrialization, inflation of more than 20 per cent, a rise in public spending, and the prospects of a slump. Only the blessings of a continuing income from North Sea oil kept the balance of payments in reasonable condition, but even here the emergence of the pound as a 'petro-currency'(along with high interest rates) led to its appreciation in value to the cost of British exports. A government elected to cut public spending and reduce inflation as the basis for economic recovery had achieved, it seemed, exactly the reverse.

The arguments within the Thatcher administration went on apace over whether to swing the axe fiercely into public spending in the winter of 1980–1, with ministers like Prior, Pym, Walker, and Carrington arguing the case for maintaining public expenditure and investment, monetarists outside the government like Alan Budd urging far more stringent monetary restraint, and Sir Geoffrey Howe at the Treasury buffeted about in between. The bleakness of the government's economic approach was never more apparent. The Heathite ministers effectively won the Cabinet debates over the public-spending round in the autumn of 1980, but their victory was short-lived. The Howe budget of March 1981 marked a clear triumph for the monetarists and a

[12] William Keegan, *Mrs. Thatcher's Economic Experiment* (London, 1984), 203.
[13] *The Economist*, 29 Mar. 1980, which described it as a 'dog days budget'.

new level of austerity.[14] In the face of the open dissent of Prior, Pym, Walker, and Gilmour, and even some resistance from the Chancellor of the Exchequer himself, the Prime Minister, urged on by her newest economic adviser, Professor Alan Walters, forced through the most resolutely anti-Keynesian budget of modern times. It imposed Britain's biggest-ever tax increases, including a rise of 20p in petrol tax, and heavy taxation on smokers and drinkers. A total of £3,500 million was taken out of the public-sector borrowing requirement. Never before had there been so savage a fiscal squeeze; not since the thirties had there been a comparable increase in unemployment, now approaching 3 million. There were widespread murmurs in Tory ranks, and the government's standing fell to only 27 per cent in the polls of March 1981. A total of 364 economists, almost one for each day of the year, dispatched a formal letter to *The Times* denouncing the government's economic approach as ruinous—though they were soon matched by a similarly large number of economists who were prepared to endorse it. Both the city and the CBI were strongly critical of the budget: Sir Terence Beckett of the CBI spoke of the need to have a 'bare-knuckle fight' with the government, though this aggressive posture later disappeared. The government seemed to be presiding over massive industrial contraction; Mrs Thatcher at this time was the most unpopular Prime Minister since Neville Chamberlain in 1939. At the 1980 Tory Party Conference she pronounced stubbornly that 'the lady's not for turning'. There would be no 'U-turns' in financial policy. But the cost of such rigour, both in economic and political terms, seemed almost unacceptable.

In fact, the government's policy from 1982 onwards became somewhat less rigid. This was in part because it was simply not working. The effect of high interest rates and a 'petro-pound' was to strengthen sterling; the consequences were for exports to sag and for inflationary pressure to increase rather than diminish.

[14] Ibid. 14 Mar. 1981; *The Times*, 11–12 Mar. 1981.

Government ministers tried to stem the tide of mounting public expenditure: John Nott's replacing Francis Pym at the Ministry of Defence in January 1981 was thought to be a pointer in this direction. Public spending continued to rise nevertheless, not least because of the colossal bill of social-security payments to relieve the rising number of unemployed. But after this period economic policy showed some moderation. Attempts to claim that M3 was a precise yardstick of the money supply were abandoned; after all, it had actually expanded by 20 per cent with high inflation. The much more limited test of MI, 'narrow money', including non-interest-bearing deposits, was favoured instead. New curbs on wage settlements reminiscent of Selwyn Lloyd's 'guiding light' of the early 1960s replaced the doctrinaire 'hands-off policy of 1979–81. As production began to recover somewhat during 1982, and inflation to fall (partly because of an improvement in the US economy), a less rigorous approach was adopted towards the money supply in the 1982 budget, while £1.3 billion in taxes were prudently 'given away'.[15] By the end of the first Thatcher administration, even Geoffrey Howe was scarcely to be identified as a strict monetarist, and the 'medium-term financial strategy', was in retreat. Mrs Thatcher, ironically, now found herself criticized by the Chicago sage, Milton Friedman, for failing to apply the monetarist remedy with sufficient consistency or determination. The major achievement that could be claimed by March 1983—a notable one indeed—was that inflation had fallen from a peak of 22 per cent in early 1980 to a mere 5 per cent. On the other hand, this was partly the result of huge unemployment depressing demand and consumer pressure, while the sharp fall of sterling against both the dollar and the deutschmark was also not what was intended. It also reflected the passing of the second OPEC price shock of 1979–80. At the time of the June 1983 general election, with Geoffrey Howe widely believed to be destined for transfer

[15] *The Times*, 13 Mar. 1982.

to the Foreign Office, the financial strategy unveiled in his first budget of June 1979 was being quietly buried. Its major advocate, Professor Alan Walters, was back in the United States teaching economics. While far from being a 'wet' herself, Mrs Thatcher was presiding over a distinctly watered-down form of Tory economic policy by the summer of 1983.

The relative caution of her first administration was equally confirmed in industrial and social policy. For all the anti-statist rhetoric of the 1979 campaign, privatization, or the dismantling of public enterprise, was not seriously on the agenda down to 1983. The sale of part of the assets of BP oil owned by the government in Howe's first budget did little more than continue the policy of Denis Healey's Labour budget of 1976. There was little or no attempt to denationalize the giant state monopolies thereafter. Privatizing Cable and Wireless, Amersham International, even Britoil, excited only limited controversy. There were, indeed, large subsidies still being paid to state-owned industries such as British Leyland, Rolls Royce, and the coal and steel industries, even by that apparently doctrinaire minister of Trade and Industry, Sir Keith Joseph. The discipline of cash limits was repeatedly disregarded, with political factors often intervening to soften the government's monetarist convictions. Thus the political decision was taken to keep all five major steel plants in operation, including the distinctly vulnerable plant in Ravenscraig in Scotland. Celtic nationalist passion certainly was a factor here.

On the trade unions too, the Thatcher government again proved to be more cautious than its language might imply. Under the aegis of James Prior, the Department of Employment was unlikely to go in for strongly anti-union policies. Prior's Trade Union Act of 1980 was a moderate measure intended to forestall further attacks on union power. There would be public money to provide union ballots on strikes and leadership changes. Closed-shop arrangements would be made more difficult and secondary picketing outlawed, to avoid the kind of violence that had disfigured the Grunwick dispute. On balance, the least inflammatory of the available options were selected. More rigorous was the measure introduced by Prior's right-wing successor at Employment, Norman Tebbit, in 1982. This went further by challenging the immunity that the unions had enjoyed from any financial damages incurred during strikes, a privilege dating from the Liberal government's Trade Disputes Act of 1906.[16] Henceforth unions could be fined very heavily for conducting what were deemed to be unlawful strikes: several of them were to suffer accordingly, starting with the National Graphical Association. Tebbit's bill also applied firmer penalties to secondary picketing, and gave compensation for those dismissed as a result of closed-shop agreements.

Even so, the unions' power to strike and picket remained substantial; Tebbit found himself unable to outlaw the closed shop entirely. Despite the Act of 1982, Mrs Thatcher was obliged to give some ground to the unions on a number of occasions. Thus, in February 1981, in the face of a series of lightning strikes in parts of the coal industry, notably in the Welsh mining valleys, the government had to retreat and extend a subsidy for this struggling industry in a way totally at variance with its basic philosophy. A similarly timid attitude had to be taken with regard to strikes by ASLEF, the train-drivers' union, and the bailing out of British Rail. Certainly, the government's rhetoric towards the union was much harsher, with the replacement of Prior by Tebbit at Employment a symbol of it. Len Murray and the TUC General Council found themselves frozen out from communication with government to an extent unknown since before 1939. But what was really neutralizing the power of the unions was the growing economic crisis and resultant unemployment. The number of strikes fell dramatically; in 1981 only

[16] For a right-wing view of these trade-union reforms, see Martin Holmes. *The First Thatcher Government, 1979–1983: Contemporary Conservatism and Economic Chanye* (Brighton, 1985), 132–53; for a left-wing view, see Tony Lane, 'The Tories and the Trade Unions', in Stuart Hall and Martin Jacques (eds.), *The Politics of Thatcherism* (London, 1983), 169 ff.

4.2 million days were lost in industrial disputes compared with an average 13 million per year throughout the seventies.[17] Union membership had fallen from over 13 million in 1980 to below 10 million three years later. The TUC itself, and especially Len Murray, repeatedly threw its influence, such as it was, against militancy and against challenging the government through industrial action. In industries like British Leyland, workers were disavowing their own shop stewards; the star of such local firebrands as 'Red Robbo' and Alan 'The Mole' Thornett seemed to have set. It was really wider economic and sociological factors which were expunging memories of the 'winter of discontent' and uncontrolled union power, rather than the policies of the Thatcher government, which in this early period were broadly non-confrontational.

Social policy showed the same relatively moderate trend. In one important area, indeed, the Thatcher government did launch a bold change of course, and one that had widespread popular backing among working people. This was the conscious policy of furthering the sale of council houses, promoted by Michael Heseltine's Housing Act of 1980. This was attacked by Labour as dismantling the housing welfare programme as it had existed since 1945, or perhaps since the Addison Act of 1919. But amongst many working-class Labour voters, the prospect of emulating their middle-class neighbours and owning their own homes on tax-subsidized mortgages proved irresistible. This break with post-war social assumptions proved relatively easy to initiate: by the end of 1984, 800,000 council tenants were buying their own homes. Elsewhere, the government proved to be surprisingly cautious. The National Health Service, though evidently under-funded, was to survive as the basis of the

---

[17] *The Economist*, 6 Feb. 1982. A critical view of the government's failure to stick to its monetary objectives appears in Patrick Minford and David Peel, 'Is the Government's Economic Strategy on Course?', *Lloyd's Bank Review*, 40 (Apr. 1981), 1–19. Also cf. Sir James Ball, 'Demand Management and Economic Recovery: the United Kingdom Case', *National Westminster Bank Quarterly Review* (Aug. 1985), 2–17.

healthcare system of the nation. Radical plans to remodel the education system, especially anything which resembled the undermining of the comprehensive secondary schools against which Tories had long since railed, were scrapped. So, too, were proposals to end the state-funding of higher education and charge full-cost fees, or alternatively abolish the system of grants for university students (a particularly unpopular idea amongst middle-class Tory voters). On the other hand, Britain's universities were afflicted from 1981 with very severe cuts in their funding, amounting to a 2 per cent drop in income for most universities. The era of the 1963 Robbins Report had truly come to an end. With memories of the student 'unrest' of the late sixties still part of the living past, Sir Keith Joseph was able to impose a stern monetary discipline upon British higher education with the prospect, many feared, that some universities and polytechnics might disappear entirely. Nevertheless, the conclusion must be that, down to 1982, Mrs Thatcher was anxious not to give many hostages to fortune by breaking too openly with the one-nation traditions of Butler and Macleod. She bowed to Scots nationalists over Ravens-craig steelworks and to Welsh nationalists over the Welsh television channel, 'Sianel Pedwar' or S4C. Bizarrely, even Mrs Thatcher became a kind of Bevanite now. 'The National Health Service', she had to proclaim in 1982, 'is safe with us'.[18]

This same pragmatism showed itself also in many aspects of Commonwealth and foreign policy. Here again, the apparently abrasive style of Thatcherite 'conviction politics' proved less robust in reality, at least on one occasion. Her government began with a huge surrender, the quite unexpected settlement in which she acquiesced which ended the long-running saga of British relations with the former Southern Rhodesia, now renamed Zimbabwe. When Mrs Thatcher took office in May 1979 it was assumed that southern Africa would cause a massive

---

[18] Dennis Kavanagh, *Thatcherism and British Politics* (Oxford, 1987), 98.

rift between her and the black African states of the Common-wealth. It was expected that she would show sympathy with the white settler minority associated with Ian Smith's Rhodesia Front and propose a deal between him and the near-puppet govern-ment of Bishop Abel Muzorewa. In the event, under heavy Foreign Office pressure which she secretly resented, Mrs Thatcher gave way completely. A conference at Lancaster House in August 1979 saw the British government make conces-sion after concession to the Black nationalists. Both Muzorewa and the white minority had to undergo severe pressure. It was agreed that elections would be held in Zimbabwe, despite the activities of various black guerrilla forces led by Joshua Nkomo and Robert Mugabe, and a constitutional convention was to be held in London. At this conference in November, an agreement was laboriously worked out to the effect that Zimbabwe would shortly gain its legal independence.[19] Sanctions would cease to be applied from 15 November, while the senior patrician figure of Christopher Soames (Winston Churchill's son-in-law, no less) was sent to Zimbabwe to act as temporary governor to supervise new elections and restore the country's trade. Much to the British government's surprise, the elections in early 1980 resulted in a massive victory for the Marxist Robert Mugabe, whose party gained 57 seats, as against 29 for Joshua Nkomo and only 3 for Bishop Muzorewa. A legally elected Zimbabwean state now came into being.

In fact, Britain's relations with black African states and the Commonwealth generally greatly improved, not least because the long-turbulent figure of Ian Smith was finally forced off centre-stage. Mrs Thatcher's own demeanour at the Common-wealth Conference at Lusaka that August had certainly helped, as in the good relationship she struck up with President Kenneth Kaunda of Zambia. On the other hand, the main credit for resolving the dilemma of Rhodesia / Zimbabwe really belonged

---

[19] *The Economist*, 17 Nov., 15 Dec. 1979. More generally, see Anthony Verrier, *The Road to Zimbabwe* (London, 1986).

to Commonwealth leaders such as Julius Nyerere of Tanzania and Malcolm Fraser of Australia, and especially to Lord Carrington and the mandarins of the Foreign Office. Indeed, the very success of the Zimbabwean settlement, in line with repeated British withdrawals from colonial territories since the late 1950s, encouraged a growing impatience on Mrs Thatcher's part with the consensus men of the Foreign Office and with Lord Carrington, its grandee incumbent. The *bien-pensant*, anti-colonialist, 'Euro-speak' Foreign Office, in Mrs Thatcher's view, was distinctly not 'one of us'.

Otherwise, the Commonwealth relationship remained more tranquil under Mrs Thatcher than might have been expected. Her differences with other Commonwealth states over economic sanctions in South Africa did not prevent collaboration with them on other issues, notably in maintaining a boycott of cultural and sporting links with South Africa under the Gleneagles agreement, which the British government faithfully observed. Perhaps the truth was that for Mrs Thatcher, the Commonwealth, like 'Europe' was relatively low in her priorities. She was no more a disciple of Churchill than she was of Heath. Meanwhile the media kept the imperial mystique well to the fore, especially India. Such notable films as *Gandhi* (a severe treatment of the Raj), A *Passage to India*, and *Heat and Dust*, even the James Bond spectacular *Octopussy*, kept the Indian subcontinent securely in the public's imagination. One of the most triumphant television productions of the decade was ITV's dramatization of Paul Scott's 'Raj Quartet' under the title, 'The jewel in the Crown', a testament to the uneasy, Forster-like, imperial conscience of a pre-Thatcherite age.

In foreign affairs, Mrs Thatcher's experience was slight, and her responses at first simple and superficial. She had built up a reputation as 'the Iron Lady' with some stern condemnations of Soviet Communism and its imperialist designs, before she became Prime Minister. Her prevailing stance in foreign affairs was one of cold-war hostility towards Eastern Europe, and an aggressive self-sufficient nationalism, almost Gaullism. She adopted an abrasive stance towards the European Common Market, for which she had never been a strong enthusiast. Her clashes with other European heads of state over Britain's budgetary contribution to the Community aroused all her basic emotions: here, indeed, she had strong support in Britain itself where sympathy for the bureaucrats of Brussels, with their butter mountains and wine lakes, was distinctly muted. At the Dublin summit of the EEC countries in December 1979 she took a highly belligerent, insular line.[20] She claimed that the British contribution to the budget was 'our money' which foreigners were taking away. She came close to threatening the Community with a repetition of de Gaulle's policy of 'the empty chair' in the sixties. Her relations with Helmut Schmidt, the German Chancellor, and Giscard d'Estaing, the French President, were glacial. Yet here too the practice of Thatcherism proved less abrasive as time went on. By mid-1982, an acceptable compromise had been reached over European affairs, including the budget and agricultural policy. Mrs Thatcher was at least in a functional sense, beginning to show greater capacity for involvement in the life of the community, if without the passion of Edward Heath in the past. On Europe, she was an agnostic rather than an unbeliever.

Indeed, surprisingly enough, Mrs Thatcher's reputation, in the doldrums at home at least to the end of 1981, began to grow in foreign affairs as she became more self-assured. Ultimately, though, her success lay neither in Commonwealth nor in Common Market affairs, but in the North Atlantic alliance. She struck up an effective rapport with the new Republican President of the United States, Ronald Reagan. At last the 'special relationship' seemed to have some meaning, perhaps for the first time since the days of Macmillan. There was accord over trade policy and over regional policy in such areas as Latin America. Most important of all, on defence issues, the needs of Britain and the United States came closer together. A deal was struck under

[20] *The Times*, 1 Dec. 1979.

which Britain would allow US Cruise missiles to be sited on British soil. In return, Trident would be offered as a replacement for the ageing Polaris submarine-based missiles as the basis of the so-called 'British independent deterrent'.[21]

This provoked furious controversy. Trident was hugely expensive—£10 billion at the first assessment alone. The Campaign for Nuclear Disarmament found in Cruise and Trident a stimulus it had not had since the early 1960s. The campaign against the Cruise missile bases, in particular, led to passionate demonstrations. One of the most notable protest movements of the early Thatcher years was the series of demonstrations by feminist and other women supporters of unilateral nuclear disarmament at Greenham Common in Berkshire, where the Cruise missiles were to be based (along with Molesworth in Cambridgeshire). Clashes between the Greenham Common women and the police were prolonged and often violent. On the other hand, the general theme was one in which Mrs Thatcher was able to tap reserves of nationalist sentiment, as could her flamboyant, flak-jacketed Defence Secretary, Michael Heseltine. On balance, the Cruise missile demonstrations embarrassed the left, and turned much to Mrs Thatcher's advantage. The Prime Minister could strengthen her growing reputation as a tough, determined champion of British national interests, one whose role in the transatlantic alliance was testimony to the growing influence of her nation after decades of consistent decline. Her firm stance enabled her to speak to the Russian government with greater authority also. As Helmut Schmidt was defeated in the German elections in 1982, following Giscard d'Estaing's failure in the French presidential elections in 1981. Mrs Thatcher, to general surprise, emerged as a strong and respected world leader. Yet she was one whose reputation was in reality based on dialogue rather than on sabre-rattling.

---

[21] 'Defence Policy', in Peter Byrd (ed.), *British Foreign Policy under Thatcher* (Deddington, 1985), 159 ff.

The same tendency to compromise showed itself in a facet of internal policy much closer to home, one whose violent impact threatened life and property on the British mainland herself. Mrs Thatcher's sentiments were staunchly Unionist. A close political ally was Airey Neave, a former intelligence officer who was to be murdered by the IRA in the precincts of Westminster. Relations between Mrs Thatcher and the new Irish Fianna Fáil premier, Charles Haughey, were at first tense. Horrific events continued to scar Anglo-Irish relations, as terrorist attacks, mainly by Provisional Sinn Fein, continued. In the summer of 1980, an indefinite hunger-strike by Republican prisoners in the Maze prison in Belfast was followed in May 1981 by the death, after a lengthy hunger-strike, of the recently-elected Sinn Fein MP and convicted terrorist, Bobby Sands. Violent events both in Ulster and in Britain itself continued to escalate, with the murder of Lord Mountbatten on his yacht at the hands of the IRA. Attempts by the Northern Ireland secretary, Humphrey Atkins, to promote a representative assembly, proved a complete failure. Nevertheless, the prospect of a dialogue between London and Dublin remained, and the prospect strengthened when Fine Gael returned to power. The result was a summit meeting between its leader, Dr Garret FitzGerald, and Mrs Thatcher in November 1981, with the objective of exploring the idea of a kind of inter-governmental council. This would clearly imply some involvement by the Dublin government in the internal affairs of Northern Ireland for the very first time. The dispatch of James Prior to the Northern Irish office, in place of Atkins, in the government reshuffle of September 1981, also presaged an attempt at further negotiation. Prior came forward with the idea of a form of 'rolling devolution', with an elected assembly of seventy-eight members and a thirteen-man executive.[22] This was inevitably rejected by the Catholic SDLP as perpetuating Protestant rule in Ulster, while the Paisleyite Unionists condemned any form of

[22] See Prior's government statement, 'Northern Ireland—a Framework for Devolution' (1982).

power-sharing with the 'Papists'. Yet, while the background of terrorist violence remained, and the gulf between the two communities in the North hardly seemed to narrow at all over the years, the stance of the Thatcher government was clearly one based on diplomacy and compromise. It would inevitably lead to a closer relationship between the government of the Republic and the people of Ulster. Here again, the practice of the Thatcher government by 1983 was less strident and aggressive than its rhetoric suggested.

In many areas, then, the Thatcher government in the period 1979–83 was not far removed in many respects from the post-war outlook of the kind familiar to British experience since 1945. And yet, to many British people and social groups, the Prime Minister and her colleagues appeared to be not moderates but extremists. Their legacy was seen in rising unemployment, a growing gulf between a prospering, high-tech south-east and the squalid and declining towns and cities of the north, Scotland, Wales, and Ulster. The 'north-south divide' became a familiar part of popular folklore as in the days of Mrs Gaskell. Thus, in its first two years, the government's reputation slumped sharply; Mrs Thatcher's ability to impose her personality upon it suffered accordingly. By the end of 1981, she seemed almost a Prime Minister at bay. Throughout 1980 she had battled against a largely hostile public opinion and formidable critics in her own Cabinet such as Ian Gilmour, Peter Walker, and James Prior. She won one victory in January 1981 when a palpable 'wet', Norman St John-Stevas, was removed as Leader of the House (where he had been a conspicuous success), while younger men like Leon Brittan and Kenneth Baker were promoted, the latter having been one of Heath's campaign managers in 1975. But there still remained immensely powerful ministers who led the fight for increased public investment and spending measures to cut unemployment. Men like Prior, Gilmour, Pym, Walker, and perhaps Heseltine seemed to be challenging the very premisses of monetarism.

In the summer of 1981, Mrs Thatcher was at her lowest ebb, very far from the invincible leader she was later to appear. There was open talk of revolt in sections of her party. The economy continued to lapse into decline, with manufacturing output having fallen by no less than 10 per cent in the past twelve months. At this time, too, there came violent racial disturbances in black ghetto areas like Brixton in London, Toxteth in Liverpool, and Moss Side in Manchester. The subsequent Scarman Report on the Brixton riots spoke eloquently of the despair of unemployed young blacks, and their sense of alienation from the community and especially from the police, whose intolerance and insensitivity were deplored. Britain, it appeared, was threatened with a racial explosion on American lines. Although the Commonwealth immigration acts since 1962 had slowed the inward flow from Commonwealth countries to a trickle, the problems of assimilating the black population now resident were as acute as ever, especially during the period of rapidly rising unemployment.

From all these matters the embattled Prime Minister seemed strangely detached. It was noted that she kept herself almost isolated from her own colleagues. She had no senior heavyweight figure like Cherwell or Swinton to advise her, and indeed no close colleague at all.[23] Even Peter Thorneycroft, the veteran proto-monetarist of 1958 whom she had made Party Chairman, proved to be a 'one-nation' man at heart, and she was eventually to sack him in favour of a little-tried new favourite, Cecil Parkinson, the Paymaster-General.

Almost in desperation, Mrs Thatcher seized the initiative with a political purge. It evoked comparisons with Macmillan's bloody 'night of the long knives' in July 1962. On 14 September 1981, she removed three major Heathite ministers, Christopher Soames (the patrician Churchillian with whom she had clashed over civil-service pay), Mark Carlisle (Education), and Ian Gilmour (Lord Privy Seal). The last-named issued a furious resignation statement in which he accused the Prime Minister of steering the ship of state 'straight on to the rocks'. More traumatic still,

[23] *The Economist*, 10 Oct. 1981.

James Prior, with the greatest reluctance, was forced to move from Employment to the exile of Northern Ireland, even though Mrs Thatcher had to keep him on the Cabinet's main economic forum, the E Committee.[24] In their place, new, rightish figures emerged—Nigel Lawson at the Department of Energy; Norman Tebbit in place of Prior at Employment; Nicholas Ridley, the driest of dry monetarists, as Financial Secretary to the Treasury. For the first time, it appeared, Mrs Thatcher had some measure of command over her own Cabinet. Its centre of gravity had shifted markedly to the right. But Carrington, Pym, Walker, and, of course, Prior were there still, as was the equivocal figure of Whitelaw. Throughout the autumn, even with the economy beginning to show signs of bottoming out and inflation falling fast, Mrs Thatcher was still under siege.

The turning-point—and in many ways the great divide of British politics since 1979—came totally unexpectedly in March 1982. It arose from a crisis in a disregarded part of the world, of no consequence to the British since the days of Captain Cook, namely the South Atlantic. On Good Friday, 1982, it was announced that the government of Argentina had invaded and occupied the British colony, the Falkland Islands, long coveted by Argentinians as 'I as Malvinas'. This episode followed a period in which the Thatcher government had shown reluctance to maintain such meagre defences as the Falkland islanders possessed. It had recently withdrawn the ice-breaker *Endurance*, generally taken as a clear sign of retreat. This *demarche* by the Argentine government of General Galtieri, however, provoked a furious political reaction. The House of Commons met on a Saturday for the first time since the war. There were violent condemnations of the British government for its weakness, including from the leader of the Labour Party, the veteran near-pacifist, Michael Foot. Three Foreign Office ministers, headed by Lord Carrington, had to resign from the government, though Carrington was

---

[24] *The Times*, 15 Sept. 1981.

replaced by the hardly more resolute figure of Pym. The Defence Secretary, John Nott, narrowly retained his office. The Prime Minister, however, responded with the instinctive nationalist belligerence that came most naturally to her. On 10 April it was announced that a 'task force' of 10,000 men would be assembled under the command of Rear-Admiral 'Sandy' Woodward, to sail into the South Atlantic, whatever the hazards, and recapture the Falklands for the British Commonwealth.

It was a dramatic approach, but one which was recorded as having the support of 83 per cent of the British people. Conservatives disliked the Argentine government for being aggressive foreigners; Labour men attacked it as 'a tin-pot fascist junta'. A mood of bellicose jingoism, unknown since the days of Suez in November 1956, swept the land, directed against 'the Argies'. But it was a most risky strategy. The task force was only made possible by cobbling together the remnants of the battle fleet, including the two last aircraft-carriers, *Invincible* and *Hermes*. The latter had been intended for the scrap-yard a short while earlier. There would also be amphibious assault ships, notably the *Fearless*, while troops would be carried in tourist passenger vessels headed by the *QE II*. The logistic capacity of the Royal Navy would be stretched to the very limit, as would that of the RAF to provide air cover and defence against missile attack. The diplomatic context was also highly uncertain, with much opposition in the United Nations to the British action, not only from Latin Americans. It so happened that the UN Secretary-General, Perez de Cuellar, was himself a Peruvian. Most vital, and also most uncertain, was the support of the US government, whose radar detector services would be crucial to any British victory. There were abortive attempts at a settlement by the American Secretary of State, General Alexander Haig, and discussions over a Peruvian peace plan which would bypass the British contention that it possessed sole sovereignty over the Falklands. In the end Mrs Thatcher had to gamble that her friend, President Reagan, would, despite anti-British feeling from Irish-Americans, Hispanics, and others, throw his weight behind his old ally in the alleged 'special relationship'. In the event, through the use of a US air-base on Ascension Island, the gift of anti-radar weapons and Sidewinder missiles, and much intelligence information, the Americans materially helped the British to win the war.[25]

Mrs Thatcher's gamble, which might have caused a huge crisis and the fall of the government, came off triumphantly. A War Cabinet, consisting of Mrs Thatcher, Whitelaw, Pym, Nott, and Cecil Parkinson, assisted by civil servants such as Sir Robert Armstrong, Sir Anthony Acland, and Sir Frank Cooper, along with Admiral Sir Terence Lewin of the Chiefs of Staff, directed operations, At this kind of uncomplicated executive command, the Prime Minister excelled: her instinct for isolated decision-making was now a strength, not a weakness. Information to the public was carefully processed and censored by the Ministry of Defence. As the task force made its slow way towards the Falk-lands exclusion zone, hostilities began in earnest on 2 May when a torpedo from a British nuclear-powered submarine sank the Argentine cruiser, *General Belgrano*, with the loss of 360 lives; it was a highly suspicious episode, since the *Belgrano* appeared to be leaving the exclusion zone and heading back to Argentina at the time. Mrs Thatcher's later versions of the affair showed much uncertainty over the facts. Two days later, in reply, an Argentine Exocet missile sank the British vessel, HMS *Sheffield*, with the loss of twenty sailors. Then, on 26 May, British troops landed near San Carlos Bay in East Falkland. The early experiences were disastrous since there was only limited defence against persistent Argentine air attacks. The *Coventry, Ardent*, and *Antelope* were all sunk; many Welsh Guardsmen, waiting to land, were killed or maimed in an air assault on the *Sir Galahad* at Bluff Cove. But in the end the British troops managed to land successfully and soon proved their technical superiority over the poorly trained and equipped Argentine conscript army. A British parachute batal-lion won a notable engagement at Goose Green, despite losing

[25] Lawrence Freedman, *Britain and the Falklands War* (Oxford, 1988), 71–2.

their commander, Colonel H. Jones (who gained a posthumous V.C.), with the capture of 1,200 Argentine troops. There was a final assault by 7,000 British forces, including Nepalese Gurkhas, on Port Stanley, and on 14 June the Falkland capital was easily recaptured. A tally of 14,000 bedraggled, disillusioned Argentine prisoners of war were taken. It was a triumph beyond all expectations. In three weeks, the British had re-evoked past imperial triumphs over inadequate opposition. Omdurman and Mafeking had come again. Mrs Thatcher urged the nation to 'Rejoice! Rejoice!' The British tabloid press, notably Rupert Murdoch's somewhat pornographic *Sun*, reached extraordinary levels of distasteful jingoism. The Governor returned to Port Stanley from which he had been expelled, and huge defence installations were then erected to prevent any further Argentine attacks, including a massive new airport at Port Stanley. As a military exercise, however, many gaps in British naval and air provision had been shown up; but it was a spectacular triumph, the first that Britain had known since the 1950s.[26]

The Falklands War totally changed the public and political climate. Its mood of self-confident chauvinism galvanized the nation, however little the British knew of the culture, economy, history, or even postage stamps of the distant Falklands and its population of just 1,200 sheep-farmers and their dependants. Mrs Thatcher turned from being the least popular Prime Minister of modern times to becoming an Iron Britannia, a new Boadicea, the very embodiment of toughness, triumph, and grim resolve. For the first time in her premiership she had won a knock-out victory. The opinion polls, which had shown a small move towards the Tories in the early months of 1982, now showed a large and growing Conservative majority. From the time of the Falklands War, it was certain that the Tories would win the next general election, and that Mrs Thatcher would gain new stature as Prime Minister.

---

[26] 'The Falkland Review: Report of a Committee of Privy Counsellors' (HMSO, 1983), chaired by Lord Franks, virtually exonerated the government from blame for the initial Argentine attack through unpreparedness.

Within six months, the war had receded from most people's minds. A service of thanksgiving in St Paul's Cathedral was marked (to Mrs Thatcher's displeasure) by a distinctly muted and moderate sermon from the Archbishop of Canterbury, Dr Runcie, himself certainly no jingo. It now seemed extraordinary that so remote and irrelevant a place should ever loom so large in national and international affairs. And yet, after the war in the Falklands, the triumph of 'Thatcherism', however that ambiguous concept be defined, was assured.

The political and social landscape was now transformed. From this time onwards, commentators who had speculated on the Prime Minister's early removal from office, now assumed confidently that Thatcherism was here to stay. One major factor, of course, was that the possible alternatives seemed enfeebled and lacking in conviction. The Labour party showed little sign of recovering from its election defeat in 1979. Indeed, it became increasingly torn apart by sectarian and ideological division. The tension between the traditional, consensual centre-right and the doctrinaire, neo-Marxist left in the constituencies and many unions, who saw Tony Benn as their charismatic champion, became more acute. The resignation of James Callaghan as party leader in November 1980 added to the party's disarray. Indeed, by a somewhat surprising decision, the parliamentary party elected not Denis Healey, the last of the centre-right heavyweights, but the deputy leader Michael Foot, ex-Bevanite and present unilateralist, the authentic voice of the old left. He was unlikely to suppress the Bennites however little he sympathized with their methods. In a disastrous party conference at Wembley in January 1981, new constitutional procedures were adopted to form a hybrid 'electoral college' to elect the party's leader and deputy leader. This followed proposals from a left-dominated 'committee of inquiry' at Bishop Stortford in 1980.[27] In addition,

---

[27] Helpful works on these matters include David Kogan and Maurice Kogan, *The Battle for the Labour Party*, and Paul Whiteley, *The Labour Party in Crisis* (London, 1983).

the compulsory re-selection of all parliamentary candidates, including sitting MPs, had already been agreed, to give spokesmen of the far left in constituency management committees the power to remove right-wing or moderate figures. Only the drafting of the manifesto still remained precariously in the hands of the leader and the NEC. In disgust, Shirley Williams, David Owen, and William Rodgers of the Labour right left to form a new Social Democratic Party. Twenty-nine Labour MPs were eventually to join it.

With Michael Foot installed as party leader, his position was temporarily secure. But Labour was shaken to the core by a passionate battle for the deputy leadership (a post originally created to placate Herbert Morrison after 1951) between Denis Healey and Tony Benn. It was a battle of social leadership as much as of ideas. Healey was the spokesman of the centre-right, the older unions, and the more traditional 'broad church' sections of the party. Benn was the voice of the far-left, middle-class zealots in the constituencies, unilateralists and radicals of all persuasions, extra-parliamentary as well as parliamentary, college lecturers, and the newer public-sector unions. The very identity of the party and the movement was at stake. In the September 1981 party conference it was revealed that Healey had indeed won, by the narrowest of margins, with 50.3 per cent of the popular vote; the star of Tony Benn began to dim somewhat thereafter, not least because Michael Foot was able subtly to mount a movement of the old (or 'soft') constitutionally-minded left against the 'hard left' of the neo-Marxist, unilateralist fringe. But the entire episode left the party looking damaged and fragile. Its support began to crumble alarmingly even in its own working-class strongholds. Far from being a challenger for power, it could not even hold on to its old citadels. In a disastrous by-election in February 1982 in Bermondsey, a docks constituency in east London, Labour since 1918, Labour's youthful, far-left candidate, a Marxist homosexual from Australia, was crushingly defeated by the Liberals. Labour's support in the polls, partly it is true as a result of the Falklands War, steadily languished.

Beyond electoral matters, there was growing belief that, for long-term sociological and historical reasons, Labour was in terminal decline. The Marxist historian Eric Hobsbawm, in an important lecture entitled 'The Forward March of Labour Halted?' (the question-mark was often mischievously omitted), argued that the old, historic, back-to-back working class based on mass labour-intensive industries and the distinct proletarian culture associated with the older industrial and urban areas, was rapidly eroding.[28] A much more flexible and pro-active strategy was needed, unless Labour was to pass into total oblivion. Professor Hobsbawm's remedies included electoral reform and alliance with environmentalists, the peace movement, Scots and Welsh nationalists, and other dissenters. The belief that Labour was a relic of an older past, of the first industrial revolution rather than its successor, took hold. It seemed to be in permanent decline, possibly for some of the same reasons as the Liberals after 1918. The idea of socialism, so passionately affirmed by the Bennite multitudes, attracted less and less support amongst the population at large. The links with the unions, increasingly unpopular, dispirited, and losing membership, were no longer a source of strength. The nostrums of statism, centralization, and planning had lost much of their thrust with the stagflation and popular disaffection of the 1970s. No new Crosland seemed likely to emerge to give them a fresh charisma. Neither sociologically nor ideologically did Labour have much to offer. Instead, under an amiable leader, Michael Foot, who was savagely pilloried by a largely right-wing press, it was compelled by constituency pressures to have a far-left programme hostile to NATO, to membership of the Common Market, and to a system of national nuclear defence; it would also be committed to mass nationalization, reinforcing further the power of the unions, and a variety of other proposals unlikely to have much popular appeal. The manifesto Labour finally adopted in the 1983

---

[28] This theme is taken further in his *Politics for a Rational Left* (London, 1989); also see Peter Jenkins, *Mrs. Thatcher's Revolution* (London, 1987), 103 ff.

election paid deference to the wishes of 'greens', unilateralists, Irish republicans, homosexuals of both sexes, and feminists. It included demands for ending the House of Lords and abolishing fox-hunting. It was a very lengthy document, wryly termed, with some reason, 'the longest suicide note in history'.[29]

If Labour suddenly seemed old and unelectable, a real youthful challenge to the Thatcher regime seemed to come from the new Social Democratic Party. It was formed after the 'Limehouse Declaration', issued from David Owen's home in February 1981. This seemed a refreshing attempt to 'break the mould' of British politics.[30] It could appeal to old Gaitskellites like the 'gang of four', Owen, Williams, and Rodgers, joined by Roy Jenkins whose Dimbleby Lecture in 1979 had first outlined the prospect of a new centrist movement. It could also draw in apolitical idealists alienated by both the extremism of the far left and the abrasiveness of the Thatcherites. For much of 1981 and early 1982 the Social Democrats seemed to carry all before them. An exciting new prospect of political transformation was opened up. The SDP won an extraordinary by-election success at Crosby in Liverpool in November 1981, when Shirley Williams turned a Tory majority of 19,000 into an SDP majority of 5,000. There was another gain from the Tories in Croydon in the south London suburbs. Roy Jenkins, who had fought a striking campaign at Warrington that summer, won Glasgow Hillhead in March 1982, just before the Falklands War. For a time, the Social Democrats seemed able to appeal to disaffected middle-class Tories and to moderate opinion of all shades. Twenty-nine Labour MPs joined the new party, along with a reformist Conservative MP from East Anglia, Christopher Brocklebank-

---

[29] The author of this phrase is said to be Gerald Kaufman, MP.

[30] For the birth of the SDP. see Ian Bradley. *Breaking the Mould? The Birth and Prospects of the Social Democratic Party* (Oxford, 1981) and Ivor Crewe and Anthony King, *SDP: The Birth, Life and Death of the Social Democrats* (Oxford. 1995).

Fowler. The mould was being broken and the two-party system left in fragments, so the SDP exultantly claimed.

But the momentum did not last long. The Falklands factor was an element in pushing Mrs Williams and Jenkins from the forefront of the stage. The SDP did not and could not have a good war. The new party was also demonstrably vague in its ideological position—whether it was a reborn version of Attlee / Gaitskell-type social democracy, a humane version of Butler-style Toryism, or a completely new variant of political programme which transcended all known political categories. It was in many ways a mood rather than a movement, a transient phenomenon with shallow roots in the constituencies, and particularly weak in local government. Working-class voters were suspicious of its patrician, incurably middle-class image. The main problem bedevilling the SDP, though, was its relationship with the old Liberal Party led by David Steel. This problem was to plague the new party until its virtual disappearance from the scene after the 1987 general election. The SDP claimed to have its own tradition and style, and to be more governmentally orientated than the decentralized, almost anarchistic, community-based Liberals. It also had a tougher, pro-Trident stance on defence. On the other hand, the Liberals were undeniably out there in the country, and it would be electorally suicidal to have two smaller centrist parties fighting for leadership of the middle ground. The Liberals had powerful grass-roots strength and an historic identity in much of the Scottish Highlands, rural Wales, and especially Devon and Cornwall. In early 1983, therefore, a somewhat difficult pact was concluded, the so-called 'Alliance', between the Liberals and the SDP, in which they would agree to choose one Alliance candidate in the different constituencies, and fight a joint election campaign with Roy Jenkins as leader and putative Prime Minister. But the tense negotiations over the formation of the Alliance, debate over what precisely it meant in terms of policy and tactics (did it support a coalition, for instance, and if so, with whom?), left the SDP hamstrung from the start. In the winter of 1981–2, at the time of the Crosby by-election, the Conservatives had been terrified by SDP threats to their support in south and east England and suburbia generally. Roy Jenkins and Mrs Williams gave the impression of governmental timbre, with the Napoleonic figure of David Owen, an ex-Foreign Secretary after all, as the likely heir-apparent. In the spring of 1983, with the public mood changed by the Falklands War and the fragmented nature of the Alliance already evident, the threat from the new party was manifestly beginning to wane. Its novelty was wearing off.

The general election of June 1983 reflected all these factors.[31] With the consequence of the Falklands still exerting its potency, the economy showing distinct signs of recuperation, and inflation falling fast, Mrs Thatcher had been able to call an early election. The outcome was never in doubt. Labour was still in deep disarray, its campaign badly led and generally disorganized. The Alliance failed to make a distinct impression. For the Tories, the issue was simply Mrs Thatcher's leadership, and she banged the election drum with fierce attacks on 'pacifist' unilateralists like Michael Foot, and 'the dark, divisive clouds of Marxist socialism'. The campaign showed few issues and, with the Conservatives overwhelmingly backed up in the popular press, was wholly one-sided. Labour ended up with only 209 seats and 27.6 per cent of the popular vote, its lowest since 1918. It finished only just ahead of the Alliance poll of 26 per cent (which produced for them only seventeen Liberal and six SDP seats). Less than 40 per cent of trade unionists had voted Labour; even less than half of the unemployed. They too had imbibed the market culture, it seemed. The Conservatives, with 397 seats, had a huge majority of 142; the legacy of 1945 had indeed been reversed.

The victory for the Thatcherite ethic seemed overwhelming. The evidence is less convincing on closer examination. The Conservative Party won only 42.9 per cent of the popular vote, less than they had achieved in any election between 1945 and 1979,

[31] See David Butler and Dennis Kavanagh, *The British General Election of 1983*, (London, 1984).

and did badly in Scotland and much of northern England. It won because of its residual strength in southern and eastern England, and also greater London, where most of the constituencies were located. As has been seen, the progress of Thatcherism had been erratic, even hesitant, since 1979, though the Falklands victory had given the record of the past four years a spurious consistency. In large areas of Britain the results of the Thatcher government had been mass unemployment, collapsing public services, and urban decay. In Merseyside or Tyneside there had been almost a general deindustrialization. Britain's economic fortunes generally had fallen sharply compared with other western European countries since 1979.[32] In Brixton or Toxteth, the black ghettoes of the inner cities, alienation from the police, the government, and the social structure generally left a potentially combustible debris of explosive material. Northern Ireland had deteriorated in its social and economic fabric too since 1979. For most British people, certainly, living standards showed some absolute overall improvement since 1979; but there was also a popular sense that the quality of life had degenerated, and that in particular violent crime had risen sharply.

Thatcherism, however, triumphed because of its political and social roots.[33] It had coincided with rising prosperity in the expanding towns of southern England and East Anglia. High-tech industries, based on computer software and the like, had meant near-boom conditions for such places as Cambridge, Basingstoke, Winchester, and especially Swindon, the outstanding growth town of the decade. Along the so-called M4 corridor, as far west as Newport in Gwent, new, technically sophisticated smaller industries were mushrooming. The legacy of four years of Thatcherism, therefore, was an intensification of social division

[32] OECD figures showed the average growth of the British GDP after 1979 to be substantially below those of the USA, Japan, Germany, France, and Italy, while Britain's inflation was notably higher until late 1982 and after 1986.

[33] An interesting discussion is by Simon Jenkins in *The Economist*, 21 May 1983, 29 ff.

and varied economic expectations in different parts of Britain. It went further than the much-discussed 'north–south divide'. Prosperity, too, had been the product of small enterprises and a lengthy consumer boom financed by credit. The decline in Britain's manufacturing base was indisputable, though the causes were open to scholarly debate. But for the clients of the Thatcher order in the south and east of the nation, it was more than enough. The dispiriting memories of the seventies were fading. Mass unemployment had lost its old political potency. For the next four years, it was the suburban conquerors of southern Britain, not the decaying and dispirited north and west, who would pay the piper and call the tune.

13. High Noon For the New Right—Resurgence or Retreat?
1983–1990

GOVERNMENTS often lose momentum in their second term. Many Conservatives still recalled the disarray into which the Macmillan administration had plunged after its striking election victory in 1959. Mrs Thatcher was determined that this would not happen to her. On the contrary, from the Queen's Speech of November 1983 onwards, she turned her second term into a crusade of increasing radicalism, the doubts and hesitancies of the first administration mostly shed. It was in these years that the main contours of 'Thatcherism' as a phenomenon were firmly established. It is on these years that the government's historical reputation will surely be based. Faint hearts were summarily dispatched. Francis Pym, who had given a somewhat hesitant performance at the Foreign Office in the Prime Minister's view, was removed from his post immediately after the election. He was replaced by the safe, if decidedly dull, figure of Sir Geoffrey Howe, a diplomat not a policy-maker. In his place at the Treasury came the younger, almost reckless, figure of Nigel Lawson, an able former financial journalist and apparently still a nominal enthusiast for monetarism. To an increasing degree, the government and its outlying establishments bore the Prime Minister's stamp; her press secretary, Bernard Ingham, seemed more powerful than most Cabinet ministers, somewhat on the pattern of Lloyd George's use of 'Bronco Bill' Sutherland in 1918–22. There were personal setbacks, as when her close political confidant, Cecil Parkinson, had to resign from the government in October 1983 after a sex scandal involving his former secretary. But this caused little permanent difficulty for the government. Parkinson's successor at Trade and Employment, Norman Tebbit, a working-class Tory and former trade-union official, emerged as a key performer in this high noon of renascent Conservatism.[1] He urged the unemployed of the north to 'get on your bike' and look for work, as his window-cleaner father had done in the thirties. No social compassion here. The Thatcherite band-wagon rolled on relentlessly, though with crises, errors, and 'banana skins' aplenty littering the route.

In many key directions the new radicalism now showed itself in full. Much the most notable of these novelties was the policy of the privatization of industries and utilities.[2] After 1983, the 'frontiers of the state' were, in this respect at least, rolled back as they had not been since 1945. There had been only piecemeal policies of denationalization in 1979–83, and indeed the Conservatives had been reluctant to replace state monopolies with privately-owned ones. The turning-point came with the triumphantly successful privatization of British Telecom in 1984 for almost £4 billion. This was not argued particularly in terms of service to the consumer, indeed, the efficiency of a denationalized, deregulated British Telecom somewhat declined thereafter, and led to complaints about poor service and rising telephone bills. It was rather a huge success in sociopolitical terms, in vastly expanding the range of the shareholding classes. It made privatization part of a wider cultural shift among the British people, including wide swathes of the working class. Many hundreds of thousands of trade unionists were among those who became

---

[1] See his autobiography, *Upwardly Mobile* (London, 1988).
[2] See particularly, the *Observer* supplement, 'Privatisation Survey', 25 Oct. 1987.

shareholders for the first time. Even more important, the sale of public assets made possible large cuts in taxation in the 1985 and 1986 budgets. There followed the privatization of British Aerospace and Britoil, and finally the huge sale of British Gas for £5,434 million in December 1986. This was another enormously successful sale. The government's cartoon publicity telling the British public to ask 'Sid' made its point. Rolls-Royce and British Airports followed, and there was talk of electricity and even coal being privatized in due course. The legacy of the Second World War and the Attlee government, the very notion of the mixed economy as familiarized by 'Butskellism', was being dismantled. On the other hand, the thrust for privatization somewhat lost its appeal as the public came to realize that share values could fall as well as rise. The aftermath of the stock market crash of October 1987 was to make the sale of British Petroleum shares (over £7 billion in all) much less successful. Many of the share purchasers now were large institutional buyers rather than the small saver or investor, the 'little man' or aged widow beloved of government propaganda.

Even so, the advance of privatization was a notable shift in public debate, a great reversal of the growth of corporatism as it had rolled on, government after government, since the centralization of the First World War. It chimed in with a mood of *antiétatisme* in many countries, notably in France where the Chirac government used the Thatcher policy as a model in its privatization of state banks and other enterprises in 1984–6.[3] It is notable, too, how few tears were shed for nationalization and state control. Trade unionists seemed reluctant to defend the 'bureaucratic monoliths' that Herbert Morrison had created after 1945.[4] The Labour Party, under a youthful new leader, Neil Kinnock, elected in October 1983, was significantly hesitant in proclaiming its zeal

[3] See supplement on 'Privatisation', *Financial Times*, 16 Sept. 1987, 6, for a discussion of French privatization.

[4] John Carvel, 'Labour turns away from Nationalisation', *Guardian*, 7 July 1986.

to renationalize, even in cases such as British Gas where state-run industries had been clearly successful. Down to the 1987 general election and beyond, nationalization on the old pattern played an increasingly smaller role in Labour's priorities. Even the Euro-Communists of *Marxism Today* welcomed the end of the old order. There were few to oppose the pattern of denationalization and deregulation on strict efficiency grounds. Here the Thatcher revolution was considerable, almost complete.

Financial policy, which deviated increasingly from monetarist orthodoxy, also pursued a more distinct course with Nigel-Lawson as Chancellor. Finally abandoning M3, the medium-term financial strategy, and other totems, he strongly urged major cuts in public expenditure and extensive cuts in personal taxation to offer incentives for the rich or the would-be rich. Under his aegis, the gulf in personal resources between rich and poor became very much wider than it had been in the period 1945–79. By 1985 it was recorded that the top 6 per cent of the population in income terms now received 25 per cent of national income, while for the poorest 20 per cent their share had actually fallen from even the 5.9 per cent they enjoyed in 1979.[5] As it happened, largely because of a world-wide expansion in trade, the British economy advanced considerably down to 1987. There was an annual growth rate of some 4 per cent, while inflation continued to fall. The balance of payments, much helped by oil of course, was comfortably in surplus down to 1986. It could be claimed that Lawson was the custodian of success, however risky his strategy appeared to be. Unemployment remained high by historic standards (a peak of 3.2 million being reached in April 1985); but somehow it appeared to have been defused as a major political issue during the eighties, partly through redundancy payments. Despite much popular resentment at the effects of cash restraints on public services, the government's continuing popularity largely rested on its claim to have been the architect of

---

[5] See European Commission on *Trends and Distribution of Incomes: An Overview* (1988).

new prosperity, based on finance, credit, and consumer pump-priming rather than on mass manufacturing industry as in the past. How long it would last, however, when precisely inflationary pressures would build up, and how much the entire façade rested on Britain's possession of North Sea oil and associated export revenues, were unanswered questions.

Lawson remained confident and buoyant in his commitment to tax cuts. His budget of March 1987 took the standard rate of income tax down to 27p, and in all a huge budget surplus of over £16 billion was recorded.[6] Less noted was the fact that taxes other than income tax were, in fact, rising steadily under the Conservatives. The main reason for buoyant government revenues lay in the increasing returns from VAT and other taxes on the consumer, and on increasing Corporation Tax returns from business profits. Lawson ran a high-risk strategy at the Treasury. It rested, in part, on an ability to neutralize international pressures. At various times, notably from midsummer 1985, these threatened the value of sterling and seemed likely to cause an old-fashioned 'run on the pound'. By 1987 there were clearly long-term problems emerging for the balance of payments. But, in his distinctly supply-side programme of aiding the wealthy and 'achievers' in general with tax cuts, his relative disregard for social inequality and the mounting costs for the unemployed and other socially disadvantaged groups, and his hedonistic endorsement of private gain, Lawson's financial methods became the pivot of government policy. Social commentators noted, in a transatlantic usage, the rise of the 'yuppy' (young upwardly-mobile professional) whose girl-friends and families took over older working-class areas such as Limehouse, Islington, or Hackney. Lawson himself, while neither tactful nor popular, was astonishingly successful for a long period. He came to be regarded as the major reason for the government's post-

---

[6] *The Economist*, 21 Mar. 1987.

Falklands electoral strength, its reputation for competence, enterprise, and success.

The government's new abrasiveness showed itself especially in industrial policy as it related to the trade unions. After 1983, Norman Tebbit's Act of 1982 on strikes and other industrial practices came to be much used. Strikes rapidly disappeared as union after union either found their members unwilling in union ballots to risk strike action which might mean unemployment, or else felt wary of running up huge costs through fines in the courts. The TUC itself contributed to a mood of defensiveness. Thus, in December 1983 it was made very clear that other unions would not encourage the small National Graphical Association when it defied the law over Eddie Shah's nonunion printing operations in Warrington and insisted on conducting a strike deemed by the high court to be illegal. The outcome was huge financial damages for the NGA and a sharp defeat for the restrictive practices by which traditional craft-workers such as the printers had hamstrung British newspaper and book publishing. The stranglehold of 'the closed shop', the 'British disease' of strikes, official or unofficial, prolonged or 'wild-cat', seemed under Mrs Thatcher to have been finally loosened.

There was one supreme test of the government's resolve in 'standing up to the unions', as the phrase went. This was the miners, whom Harold Macmillan had once bracketed with the Catholic Church and the Brigade of Guards as institutions with which no Conservative government ought ever to tangle. In April 1984 the National Union of Mineworkers called a national strike against pit closures, including that of the lately closed pit at Cortonwood in south Yorkshire, and in favour of a vastly increased basic wage.[7] Whether this momentous event, the first

---

[7] Good accounts of this strike include Martin Adeney and John Lloyd, *The Miners' Strike* (London, 1985); Huw Beynon (ed.), *Digging Deeper: Issues in the Miners' Strike* (London, 1985); Raphael Samuel, Barbara Bloomfield, and Guy Boanas (eds.). *The Enemy within: Pit Villages and the Miners' Strike of 1984–85* (London, 1986); and David Howell, *The Politics of the NUM: a Lancashire view* (Manchester, 1989).

national coal strike since 1926 was the result of accidental circumstances or a long-term conspiracy between the National Coal Board and the Department of Energy was subsequently fiercely debated. Much attention focused on the aggressive personality of the vehement Marxist, Arthur Scargill, a Yorkshireman who had succeeded the moderate, Joe Gormley, as president of the NUM in 1982.[8] There was also much emphasis on the personality clash between the youthful Scargill and the new chairman of the NCB, Ian MacGregor, an elderly Scots-American of Thatcherite persuasion. But the miners' sense of anger at the prolonged destruction of their industry is also worthy of note. Support for the strike was virtually solid not only in old militant areas such as South Wales, Scotland, Yorkshire, and Kent, but also (at first) in traditionally moderate Lancashire, Durham, and Northumberland. The deep disillusion of the mining community (including miners' wives who played an unprecedently prominent role in the strike) at the erosion of their pits, their villages, and their way of life since the 1950s was spontaneous and genuine.

The strike lasted for virtually a year, ending in April 1985. It was a battle that Mrs Thatcher, recalling Heath's humiliating climb-down in 1972 (and her own in 1981), was determined not to lose. The government, indeed, had made careful preparations, both in conserving fuel stocks and protecting the power network with the aid of other European nations, and also in building up the co-ordinating powers of the police nationally to deal with mass picketing. In 1972, at the time of the Saltley flying pickets mobilized by the young Scargill, the miners had held the upper hand; not so this time around. There were violent clashes between police and pickets, notably at the Orgreave coking depot in Rotherham in the summer of 1984. Britain seemed at times to be close to open class war; Mrs Thatcher denounced 'the enemy within'. There were several times in 1984 when the government seemed fairly near to defeat, notably in November 1984

---

[8] See Michael Crick, *Scargill and the Miners* (Harmondsworth, 1985), *passim*.

when the pit deputies' union, NACODS, seemed likely to strike also. This would mean that safety procedures would not be carried out and all the nation's pits might have to be scrapped in a mass act of collective suicide. There was much public sympathy for the miners in general, however rebarbative the personality and creed of Arthur Scargill himself. In October 1984, *The Economist*, remarkably enough, committed itself to the view that 'Mrs Thatcher is not now going to win the miners' strike outright.'[9] It based this false judgement on the need for conciliation and for restoring the fabric of industrial relations.

But there could be only one winner, in 1985 as in 1919. The miners themselves were deeply divided, not least because Arthur Scargill had refused to carry out a ballot prior to calling a strike. In Nottinghamshire and adjacent Warwickshire and Leicestershire, pits continued to operate, despite physical intimidation by mass pickets. The eventual result was the breakaway from the NUM of a new union, the Union of Democratic Mineworkers, with a membership of close to 30,000. After the turn of the year, with victory nowhere in sight, more and more miners returned to work in Lancashire and Scotland. In early January, 71,000 out of 187,000 miners were back at work.[10] The personality of Arthur Scargill, with his apparent willingness to receive money from the terrorist regime of Colonel Qadaffi's Libya and his condoning of violence, alienated many, including the leader of the Labour Party, Neil Kinnock. Himself the son of a South Wales miner, Kinnock compared Scargill with a world war general who wanted 'another Gallipoli'.[11] The police were far better organized than ever before, with the National Reporting Centre to co-ordinate police movements and intelligence and a high degree of latitude given to police in the handling of pickets, however violent the methods used. The government, in the confident person of Peter Walker, the Energy Secretary, had a carefully worked-out policy of safeguarding power supplied through the national grid. He forbade the Electricity

---

[9] *The Economist*, 6 Oct. 1984.   [10] Ibid. 12 Jan. 1985.
[11] Robert Harris, *The Making of Neil Kinnock* (London, 1984). 164.

Board to order voltage reductions, since this would give comfort to the NUM leadership.[12]

A major turning-point came at the start of 1985 when Peter Walker announced that there would be no power cuts at all in the coming year, however long the strike lasted. It was a kind of public dethroning of King Coal. The winter was mild, which also told against the miners' cause. The trade-union movement was reluctant to help, and there was relatively little sympathetic action from the railwaymen, dockers, or others. Imported coal continued to be unloaded, some of it from Communist countries. A general strike was never remotely on the agenda, especially after the harsh treatment received by Norman Willis, the new TUC General secretary, from miners' meetings in militant areas. Coal no longer dominated the national economic scene. The industry employed barely 150,000 men. It supplied only a fifth of the nation's energy supplies, far behind oil, and was now challenged by nuclear power. No longer had the miners, the shock troops of the British working class, the power to dictate to a British government or to hold the community to ransom by sheer industrial muscle. Nor, in truth, had they done so often in the past. The era of class confrontation in Britain's coalfields had been confined mainly to the short period 1910–26.[13] In early April, in fine spring weather, the miners went back to work, 'their heads held high', with brass bands blaring and ancient banners on display. There was proud talk of Tolpuddle, Tonypandy, and Jarrow. But they knew that it was a humiliating defeat. Mrs Thatcher, who had routed President Galtieri of Argentina, had achieved a similar defeat of another president nearer home, Arthur Scargill of the miners. Further contraction, pit closures, and industrial erosion would certainly follow. The membership of the NUM, already attenuated by the defection of the UDM, fell drastically to total a mere 60,000 by the end of 1989, and

---

[12] Adeney and Lloyd, *The Miners' Strike*, 154.

[13] See Kenneth O. Morgan, 'Joe Gormley, Arthur Scargill, and the Miners', in *Labour People*, 289 ff.

they even lost their automatic right to a seat on Labour's national executive. There was talk of the NUM being absorbed by the Transport and General Workers. By late 1989 the labour force in the Welsh pits, once a quarter of a million men in those proud valleys, had fallen to less than 5,000. In both Scotland and Lancashire it was barely 3,000, while the militant Kent coalfield had been totally wiped out with the successive closures of Snowdon, Tilmanston and Betteshanger pits. As in 1926, so in 1985 the old legend of the impact of workers' solidarity and union power had been exploded. It was the climax of a long, and indeed largely popular, campaign by the Thatcher government to undercut union monopoly in the labour market, and to exorcize memories of the 'winter of discontent'.

Along with privatization, supply-side finance, and 'union-bashing', the government expressed its radicalism with a series of assaults on major segments and institutions within British society. In effect, the security and strength of major professions were undermined for ever.

This meant in particular a direct attack on public-sector institutions and their custodians. The enclosed world of the 'quango', the public board, and the corporation came under fire in various guises. Thus, in the Bank of England a series of clashes between the premier and the governor, Gordon Richardson, resulted in his replacement in 1983 by Robin Leigh-Pemberton, a banker of enterprise outlook and, politically, a known Conservative. The stock market was fundamentally reformed by the 'big bang' (27 October 1986) which ended old restrictive practices.[14] Henceforth the old spectacle of brokers milling around on the Stock Exchange floor was replaced by silent, almost invisible, computerized networks for dealers, reflecting the new internationalism of the stock market. In the Treasury, Keynesian critics such as Sir Douglas Wass were winkled out of their positions of influence, and new monetarist advisers such as John Hoskyns, Alan Walters, and Brian

---

[14] *The Times*, 28 Oct. 1986; Nicholas Terry, 'The "Big Bang" at the Stock Exchange', *Lloyds Bank Review*, 156 (Apr. 1985), 16–30.

Griffiths emerged elsewhere, with the Policy Unit under first Ferdinand Mount and then, in 1985, John Redwood, assuming greater prominence. The civil service found itself penetrated and politicized in the mid-1980s in a manner unknown since the days of Lloyd George. The Civil Service Department, invented by Lord Crowther-Hunt in the Wilson years, was merged into the Treasury scheme of things in 1981. A popular television series, 'Yes, Minister' (later 'Yes, Prime Minister') only parodied the consensual, complacent ways of the permanent secretaries and under-secretaries. It was said to be Mrs Thatcher's favourite television programme—indeed, she actually took part in a rehearsal.

A particularly important sacred cow to slaughter was local government, to which the Thatcher government devoted much attention. Since 1945 there had been repeated inquiries into the structure and finance of British local government, but until the 1970s no reform at all. In the Wilson-Heath period of corporatism, local government had swollen in power and importance, especially after the massive six metropolitan authorities set up by the Heath-Walker reforms in 1973. Local authorities like the Greater London Council were spenders on a massive scale. They were employers of a huge new group of middle-class employees, lecturers, social workers, local-government personnel of all kinds; local-government unions such as NALGO had expanded massively since 1970. More, the major local authorities were usually in Labour hands, frequently those of the far left. Thus, men like Derek Hatton, the leader of Merseyside, and Ken Livingstone, who led the Greater London Council (after a brutal coup which removed the previous Labour leader, Andrew McIntosh) became symbols of ideological extremism and financial extravagance at one and the same time. Of all the local authorities, however, it was, above all, Liverpool which marked out the challenge.[15] Once the happy city of the Beatles and 'pop' permissiveness, home of the most consistently successful football

---

[15] See Michael H. Parkinson, *Liverpool on the Brink: One City's Struggle against Government Cuts* (London, 1985).

team in the land, Liverpool was now a visibly decaying city. Its massive cathedrals towered over a community whose port and commercial infrastructure had collapsed as investment declined and union power encroached. Some of the least attractive features of Liverpool society emerged in May 1985, when a riot of Liverpool football supporters at the Heysel football stadium in Brussels led to the death of many Italian football fans at the European Cup Final between Liverpool and Juventus of Turin. It was Liverpool's housing and employment problems which had sparked the Toxteth race riots, and which led Michael Heseltine to launch a much-publicized new initiative at inner-city regeneration through more inward private investment. The far left totally controlled Liverpool's city council, with Militant Tendency figures like Derek Hatton and Tony Mulhearn in command. (Militant was a group of far-left activists working with constituency parties since the late 1970s.) Liverpool inevitably became the centre for disputes about rate-capping for excessive expenditure, and then for surcharging when it tried to defy the government over expenditure cuts.

In the end, the government's 1986 Local Government Act ended the problem by, in effect, abolishing the metropolitan authorities, and indeed greatly curbing the power of local councils in general. Despite popular laments for the great days of Herbert Morrison and 'municipal socialism' on the LCC, such Tory bugbears as the Merseyside authority and the Greater London Council disappeared from the scene. A story of local democracy and participatory initiative dating from the reforms of the later 1880s came to its sad close. It was a victory for Mrs Thatcher—though a debatable one since it largely snuffed out the power of British local government at a time when many other European countries were trying to decentralize and devolve. It was also a problem which enabled Labour's new young leader, Neil Kinnock, to make his mark, perhaps for the first time since his election in October 1983. His passionate onslaught at the 1985 party conference against the Militants of Merseyside (whom he accused of hiring taxis to hand out redundancy notices to their workers) appealed to the unions and gave him new public stature. But the longer-term victory was one for central government and its determined custodians.

Other public institutions were put to the sword elsewhere. The Arts Council found its ability to provide patronage made more selective—perhaps rightly so, though the effects proved a serious blow to many theatres and galleries. Its new chairman, Lord Rees-Mogg, showed an enthusiasm for applying the market approach to museums, art centres, and the like. The American model of private funding of the arts was much cited. In effect, this meant a steady decline in public funding, problems in finding support for artistic experimentation, and financial crises for such famous museums as the Tate Gallery in London and the Ashmolean in Oxford. Some theatres had to close, though the opening of the Barbican Centre in the city of London provided yet another boost to musical and dance performances in the metropolis—which hardly needed it. The BBC found itself embroiled in a long series of disputes with the government, partly over its financing, partly over alleged anti-government reporting of such episodes as the Libyan bombing raids in 1986 (covered by an able woman reporter, Kate Adie). There were frequent clashes over the reporting of Northern Ireland, ending with a ban on interviews with members of Sinn Fein. The BBC found itself increasingly demoralized, the proud corporate ethic of the days of Lord Reith under constant challenge. Once again, a chairman sympathetic to the Thatcher regime was chosen, in this case 'Duke' Hussey, while a policy of supplying franchises to a variety of new commercial television and radio companies, exploiting the potential of satellite transmission, again threatened the BBC's position. Many observers were disturbed by the way in which the high standards of service and integrity associated with the BBC as a public corporation were being compromised. The commercial ethic meant some deterioration in standards, while the cutbacks in the Overseas News department, one of the glories of Bush House, caused much dismay in the public communications world.

The press was another estate of the realm cut down to size. This was partly by governmental pressure and the constraints placed on it by Bernard Ingham of the Prime Minister's press office. More, it was the result of the involvement of large multi-national concerns like the newspaper empire of the American-based Australian, Rupert Murdoch, which took over not only the downmarket *Sun* but also *The Times*. The partisanship of both organs was not in doubt. Whether press standards declined after this was a matter for debate. What was clearer was that the range of opinion in the press tended increasingly to favour the government. In both the 1983 and 1987 general elections the government had strong press support, with only the erratic Maxwell-owned tabloid, the *Daily Mirror*, to support Labour, along with the Alliance-inclined *Guardian* and the *Observer* on Sundays. An impressive newcomer was the *Independent*, a centrist newspaper which emphasized finance, higher education, and other middle-class concerns. The prospects of significant dissent from Fleet Street no longer existed. Indeed, 'Fleet Street' itself was a misnomer from 1985 onwards, as modern technology and high unit costs led major newspapers to move out of central London to the eastern inner suburbs, to avoid the unions' stranglehold. The long, sometimes violent, dispute with the print unions over the relocation of *The Times* plant at Wapping marked a notable step both in the new financial and technological independence of the press and its ideological separateness from the union-corporate approach of the past.

The Church of England was also, to some degree, a victim of the Thatcherite attempt at hegemony. The Church had continued to lose members in the 1970s and 1980s, yet it remained a powerful source of social criticism. Its 1985 report on the inner cities, *Faith in the City*, was attacked by government ministers for its allegedly 'Marxist' inspiration. The implied condemnation by Archbishop Runcie of the jingo spirit of the Falklands War, and the open, if confused, critique of the government's handling of the miners' strike by the Bishop of Durham, David Jenkins, caused a widening breach between government and the established Church. The latter, it was claimed, was now in effect 'the SDP at prayer'. Mrs Thatcher herself made appearances at Church and Methodist assemblies to rebuke bishops and non-conformist leaders for their hostile approach towards material gain, their over-involvement with issues such as poverty and urban decay, and their over-zealous support for black African nationalists in South Africa. She rapped their collective knuckles (along with those of the Church of Scotland, which showed nationalist tendencies as well) for their inability to see wealth creation as an essentially Christian act. The good Samaritan with his non-mercenary values, it seemed, was not 'one of us' either. In return, the Church cut a somewhat uncertain figure. It was hesitant about its role, and indeed divided within itself over doctrinal issues like the significance of the Resurrection, and over such indicators of change as the ordination of women. Wags commented on a search for 'closet Christians' among the bishops. But here again was a major institution in the land in clear conflict with the determined woman who bestrode government—and actually appointed bishops and archbishops as well (though they often disappointed her). The doctors, the architects, and, after 1987, the legal profession were all to face the same mood of antagonism.

No group in society, however, symbolized the alienation of key institutions from the government more clearly than did the university teachers. The wheel had come full circle since the heady days of expansion after the Robbins Report in 1963. In the sixties, the universities acquired a public esteem unique in British history. Now, in the bitter 1980s they found themselves facing the impact of annual cuts in real funding, and pressures to apply new codes of managerial techniques and short-term profit-making out of tune with the traditional practices of British universities.[16] They also

[16] The cuts in the U.G.C. grant to universities ranged from 5.7 per cent to St David's University College, Lampeter, to 46.3 per cent at the University of Salford between 1980/1 and 1986/7; the average cut was 12.5 per cent (*Public Money*, Dec. 1986, 53–7).

faced a loss of morale, with the drain of talented staff to the United States and Canada. No group in Britain better illustrated the gulf between the old professional order and the new Thatcherite ethos. To Mrs Thatcher, the universities were an enclosed, complacent guild, managerially incompetent, with little interest in wealth creation and lacking in accountability to government. The University Grants Committee had acted as a buffer against change. She herself, though a product of Oxford University, identified with wealth-producers and businessmen rather than with academics and intellectuals. They in turn responded with incomprehension and then with anger. In a famous episode in February 1985, Oxford University congregation voted by a 3 to 1 majority to deny the Prime Minister an honorary degree, a rebuff previously extended only to the late President Bhutto of Pakistan. The cause, it was stated, was the 'systematic damage' she had wrought on higher education—and indeed education in general. It was a vigorous gesture, but also a risky one, since it emphasized the yawning gulf between the traditional pattern of autonomous free institutions within a plural culture and the new centralizing regime. Universities continued to languish through the eighties. Research programmes, especially in medical and other science, continued to be under-funded. A revamped University Funding Council, directed by a former Cambridge don, Sir Peter Swinnerton-Dyer, threatened to impose much more severe financial disciplines on universities that were already struggling; on the other hand, the 1985 Jarratt Report resulted in complex new structures of planning, resource management, and managerial accountability.[17] Partly by way of compensation, the government lent its favour increasingly to the allegedly more cost-effective polytechnics (now made independent of local authorities), and to more practically or vocationally orientated institutions such as business schools. They were more in tune with the thinking of a managerial

---

[17] See *Times Higher Educational Supplement*, 5 Apr. 1985 for the Jarratt Report.

government than were the traditional scholarly citadels of unproductive, useless learning.

In all these areas—the unions, the local authorities, the Church, the media, the universities and schools—the paradox was that a government notionally dedicated to extending individualism and the private ethic became a champion of greater centralization and state control. Indeed, the central state built up its authority, directly and indirectly, in the Thatcher years more decisively than in, say, the Attlee period, which was by comparison a model of high pluralism, evidence by the retreat from 'planning' in 1947–50. This new centralism was in part because the Thatcher government perceived these institutions as potentially so damaging that they needed the maximum of intervention to suppress them. It was also the case that the conversion of the population to the market philosophy needed direction on a massive scale. Thatcherism was philosophy teaching by encroachment rather than by example. It was thus the very strength of the state, the power of major government departments such as the Environment or Education and Science over the somewhat ragged army of local-government officials, dons, bishops, editors, and men and women of letters that contemporaries noted. In the universities, where in the sixties rioting students and the educated tele-celebrities of the 'chattering classes' had commanded public attention, there were now dormant, apolitical students anxious only for their future employment, and embittered lecturers suffering a crisis of morale and lamenting the bureaucratic invasion of time traditionally left for teaching and research. The freedom and autonomy guaranteed for universities by the old University Grants Committee were no more.

It was a centralization that was not only institutional in its forms. It was also highly personal in its focus. The Thatcher Cabinet after 1983 radiated from the woman at the centre. It was personalized and identifiable in a way unknown since Lloyd George's heyday. The Thatcher Cabinet had become crystallized as a system of conviction politics all on its own. The Prime Minister relied in part on close advisers like Charles Powell,

Robin Butler, and her press secretary, Bernard Ingham, a 'garden suburb' no less than in 1918.[18] Indeed, she had a talent for implying that somehow she did not belong to her own Cabinet. She communicated instead with a small group of trusties like Lord Young, and advisers within her policy unit. Her relations with both her Foreign Secretary and Chancellor of the Exchequer became somewhat cool, not least because she attempted to run both foreign and financial policy herself. The dangers to the Thatcher regime, it appeared, came not from revolts or putsches on the back benches. Dissidents like Francis Pym came and went: his banner of revolt, *The Politics of Consent* (1984), a cool, rational argument in favour of 'consensus',[19] failed to spark a Heathite revival. Still less did the danger lie in overthrow by Labour or by assorted dissidents or intellectuals. It lay rather in its rigidity, in the way that centralization was hardening, some felt, into something approaching personal dictatorship. Like Louis XIV before her, Mrs Thatcher might provoke an eventual revolution.

It was this growing tendency after 1983 which almost brought the government to its knees. The crisis arose from an extraordinarily parochial subject, namely whether the Westland group of helicopter manufacturers, situated in Yeovil in the West Country, should be purchased by a European consortium or by the US-dominated Sikorsky–Fiat group.[20] There were thus foreign-policy implications as well as business issues at stake. There was a furious row over the negotiations in Cabinet between Michael Heseltine, Minister of Defence, and Leon Brittan, Secretary for Trade and Industry, which soon became embarrassingly public.

[18] See Richard Norton-Taylor, 'The face of foreign influence'. *Guardian*, 30 June 1989. Butler, a career civil servant, was her private secretary.

[19] Pym helped set up a new moderate pressure group within the Conservative Party, 'Centre Forward', in 1985, but it soon disintegrated. His book, however, was a bestseller. A notable feature (pp. 196–201) was a lengthy, historical, coded attack on Joseph Chamberlain who demonstrated, in Pym's view, the danger of 'ideological obsession'.

[20] See Magnus Linklater and David Leigh, *Not with Honour* (London, 1986).

By November 1985 it became apparent that the real antagonists were neither the Westland company nor British Aerospace, but Michael Heseltine, as a vigorous champion of the European link, and Mrs Thatcher. On 9 January 1986 Heseltine dramatically walked out of a full Cabinet and resigned in the full glare of televisual attention. He accompanied his resignation with biting public criticisms of the dictatorial style of the Prime Minister.[21] Nor did the matter end there. In increasingly bizarre circumstances the Attorney-General, Sir Patrick Mayhew, discovered that a letter of his, partially rebuking Heseltine, had been selectively leaked to the press without his permission or knowledge by a young female official in the Department of Trade, one Colette Bowe. After denying knowledge of the leak to the House, apparently to protect the Prime Minister, Leon Brittan, the Secretary for Trade, also resigned on 24 January.[22] Whether Mrs Thatcher herself was implicated in the leak is not known, but it was widely believed that Brittan resigned to save her skin. It was also known that Mrs Thatcher's closest advisers, Charles Powell and Bernard Ingham, were implicated in the leak, and it seemed improbable that the Prime Minister should have been totally ignorant. There was a real threat that she might have to resign.[23] In the event, she just survived, partly because Neil Kinnock made an inadequate speech in the Commons debate, but perhaps really because helicopters were really too parochial an issue to involve the fall of governments.

But the Westland affair lingered on for some time to come. It showed up the Achilles heel of the government—its excessively dictatorial tendencies. Collective responsibility seemed to be disappearing. At this time Mrs Thatcher looked somewhat less in command, with coded criticism of her style coming from such ministers as Douglas Hurd and, more surprisingly, John Biffen, a previous admirer of hers. Younger men like Kenneth Clarke, Kenneth Baker, and John MacGregor were less identified with

---

[21] *The Times*, 10 Jan. 1986.   [22] Ibid. 25 Jan. 1986.
[23] *Guardian*, 28 Jan. 1986.

the Prime Minister personally. In the summer of 1986, the legacy of Westland and local-government losses led to a relatively low point for the government. A defeat by an Alliance candidate in the Ryedale by-election confirmed this. As in the autumn of 1981, it seemed to be losing its way, with doubts over government support for British Leyland, ministers attacked over repeated strikes by secondary school teachers, and criticisms also over Britain's support for President Reagan at the time of bombing raids on Libya. The government had to retreat over a plan to sell British Leyland trucks to America's General Motors—partly because of a rooted popular affection for Britain's 'Land Rovers', partly because it had the air of a Westland mark II. The very parliamentary strength of the government and its consequent lack of accountability, were proving its weakness.

For most people, unaware of the implications of an obscure West Country helicopter firm, it was in other ways that the government's problems showed themselves. One of the notable features of the mid-Thatcher period was a revival of the civil liberties movement, as governmental pressures against individual right of expression impressed themselves on the public consciousness. There was some pressure for a Bill of Rights, notably from the 'Charter 88' group. The use of the Official Secrets Act against government employees and others became more widespread. One civil servant, at least, managed to escape the net when Clive Ponting, a Ministry of Defence official who had leaked documents about apparent ministerial lies on the sinking of the *Belgrano* during the Falklands War, was acquitted by a jury when the case came to court. Another official, Sarah Tisdall, was not so fortunate. Otherwise, the pressure exerted by the security services, aided by the police, caused much concern. The free-ranging behaviour of the police during the miner's strike, for instance, provoked some alarm, since it appeared to negate the traditional approach to freedom of movement around the country. That the police should stop law-abiding Kent miners at the Dartford tunnel on the grounds that they were thought to be destined for the Yorkshire coalfield two hundred miles away was remarkable indeed. More concern was caused by the abolition of free trade unionism in the GCHQ security establishment at Cheltenham; this appeared to equate trade unionism with disloyalty, even treason. There was also a strange security operation against a journalist following disclosures about espionage devices ('Zircon') in the *New Statesman*. In addition, there was the matter of John Stalker, the Deputy Chief Constable of Manchester, who was flagrantly obstructed within the police service when he attempted to inquire into abuses by the Royal Ulster Constabulary. In disgust, Stalker left the police force altogether. Aspects of the Westland case also showed the dangers of a government monopoly over the dissemination of information and its resultant debate.

One, more entertaining, episode was the lengthy attempt to suppress the publication of the book *Spycatcher*, the memoirs of an elderly ex-member of MI5, Peter Wright, an emigrant to Tasmania. Among other things, he alleged that MI5 had tried to destabilize the Wilson governments. The Secretary of the Cabinet, Sir Robert Armstrong, who had stonewalled successfully on Mrs Thatcher's behalf during the Westland inquiries, was sent to Australia in a vain attempt to stop the book being published there. Armstrong's patrician Oxbridge performance was not very successful in the brash atmosphere of the Australian courts—significantly less so than his performances before House of Commons committees. In a near-fatal *aperçu*, Armstrong's comment on the civil servant's need to be 'economical with the truth' seemed to set the seal on a growing process of encroachment on individual freedoms by a strong-minded, centralist government. Meanwhile, travellers abroad found no difficulty in buying *Spycatcher* in airport bookstalls.

Whether civil liberties or freedom of expression really languished in this period is open to debate. The Thatcher government's strong stance on many issues won much popular support amongst a people weary of attempts to defy the law by left-wing local authorities, strike pickets, or disaffected journalists. The emotion roused by the murder of a policeman in late 1985 during

racial disturbances at Broadwater Farm, a dismal sixties high-rise
housing estate in Tottenham, north London, confirmed much
public endorsement of the role of the police in a public-order
capacity. It also showed up the disasters of previous patterns of
so-called neighbourhood planning. The Labour Party seemed to
sense that it had gone too far in criticism of the police, perhaps in
response to the far-left, middle-class activists of sociological
inclination, and had been too tender towards violent criminals
and other deviants. It turned its attention to 'victim support', of
children especially.[24] From 1985 onwards, 'law and order'
became a watchword for the British left, too. Artists of various
kinds complained of the restrictions under which they laboured.
Yet, compared with the literary censorship of the sixties, these
were in most areas minuscule. The long moralistic campaigns of
Mrs Mary Whitehouse directed at BBC television had not made
much headway. It was lack of funding rather than lack of freedom that was the main burden for British writers and artists in
this period. For all that, the Thatcher high noon seemed to show
the balance between state power and individual self-expression,
in some key episodes, tilting against the individual or the dissenting minority. The police and the security services grew stronger;
the press and media generally were more subject to control. It
made dissent, social criticism, and alternative scenarios more
difficult to articulate.

The image of the government was one of strength in domestic
affairs. So, too, was it overseas, though in a less belligerent mode
as time went on. Mrs Thatcher herself emerged with greater
international stature now, in large measure because of her relationship with President Ronald Reagan. This went through some
crises, as when the Americans dispatched marines to put down a
left-wing government in the British island of Grenada in 1984,
without communicating their intentions to the British government. But on the main episodes, Anglo-American collaboration

[24] See Neil Kinnock's statement, 'Volunteers in a Caring Community', in
Victim Support, no. 32 (Dec. 1988).

stood firm. During the Falklands War, as has been seen, American support, including missiles, materially assisted towards a British victory. In the bombing of sites in Libya in April 1986, in the face of much criticism at home, Mrs Thatcher strongly defended the right of the Americans to use British bases such as Upper Heyford for long-range attacks. The bombing was, she argued, intended to dislodge the Qaddafi regime in Libya—even though it was civilian property as much as air-bases that were bombed, with much loss of life amongst children and others. One major result was the confirmation of a long-term American commitment to maintain the British nuclear deterrent, including the use of Trident missiles. Mrs Thatcher had emerged with much more confidence on the world stage by 1987. On the one hand, she was able to temper President Reagan's willingness to engage in longterm negotiations over intermediate-range and other missiles based in western Europe. She remained dedicated to the American nuclear umbrella over the west. At the same time, through a somewhat unlikely relationship with the emergent Soviet leader Mikhail Gorbachev, she was able to present herself as no longer an 'iron lady' but an instrument of greater international co-operation. She 'could do business with Mr Gorbachev', she told the world.

She also appeared more convincing in a European role. The old abrasiveness over the community budget had for the moment disappeared. The British Prime Minister emerged as a much more accommodating personality; at the Fontainebleau summit in June 1984 she was deemed to be now 'a good European'. But on longer-term issues such as membership of the European Monetary System she remained hostile. The British attitude to Europe remained as functional and piecemeal as it had been in the time of Ernest Bevin after 1945. One symbolic breach with age-old insularity came with the decision, confirmed in a ceremony in Canterbury Cathedral in February 1986, for Britain and France to build a channel tunnel to provide a rail link between the two countries. The ceremony in this Anglo-Norman setting was replete with references to Charlemagne, Napoleon, and

Churchill.[25] But in fact it rested on more pragmatic considerations of Anglo-French trade common to both Mrs Thatcher and
President Mitterrand, along with the need to boost employment
in south-east England and along the Pas de Calais. Despite this,
Mrs Thatcher's European sympathies remained distinctly moderate. In time, both Howe and Lawson were to prove more
sympathetic to the notion of monetary and economic union
with the Community. But at least since 1984 the major flash-
points of conflict between Britain and her European partners had
disappeared, while Mrs Thatcher found, with the departure of
Schmidt and Giscard d'Estaing, a greater eminence as both a
European and a world statesman.

This image of statesmanship also held true nearer home. In
Ireland the tide of murder and violence continued, though the
IRA felt increasingly desperate in the stranglehold maintained by
the security forces. In one terrifying episode, Mrs Thatcher and
her ministers came close to being collectively murdered in the
bombing of the Grand Hotel, Brighton, in October 1984. Many
felt that a grand gesture of statesmanship was required in relation to Northern Ireland. It was Mrs Thatcher who appeared to
supply it. The situation in Ulster in 1985 was as bleak as ever. In
addition to the background of violence and sectarian division
which had ruined Prior's plan for 'rolling devolution', there was
growing economic decay. Northern Ireland's was heavily a public-sector economy; its rate of unemployment, at 21 per cent, was
the highest in Britain. In Catholic working-class areas like
Newry, Londonderry's Bogside, and parts of West Belfast, it
rose to even 30 or 40 per cent. Major giants in the Ulster
economy like Shorts Aircraft were in difficulties, while the Harland and Woolf shipyards were making heavy losses. Without a
political initiative, however, it was hard to see how economic
progress could be made. Much was owed here to the new Northern Irish Secretary, Douglas Hurd, and to Robert Armstrong on

[25] *The Times*, 13 Feb. 1986.

the British side, and to the genial presence of the Fine Gael premier, Garret FitzGerald, in Dublin. But Mrs Thatcher, too, lent her moral support to what resulted.

The outcome was the Hillsborough agreement of 15 November 1985.[26] Under this Mrs Thatcher and Dr FitzGerald agreed that Northern Ireland would remain a part of the United Kingdom according to the wishes of its majority, but that ministers from Britain and the Republic would meet regularly to review political and security aspects. In effect, for the first time since 1922, the direct interest of the Dublin government in the internal affairs of Northern Ireland was explicitly set out. It caused uproar in Ulster Unionist ranks where all fifteen Unionist MPs, other than Enoch Powell (South Down), decided to resign their seats in a mass protest. The Prime Minister's Housing Minister and former personal secretary, Ian Gow, also resigned. The agreement, however, passed the House of Commons by 473 votes to 47 and received a similar endorsement in the Irish Dáil. As a symbolic act it was of much importance since it offered the prospect of a framework for a wider Anglo-Irish settlement and provided a hope of genuine political involvement for the Catholic minority in Northern Ireland, not in a failed local assembly but through their co-religionists in the south. But the question remained whether it could really mean much in practice. The Protestant majority in Ulster totally refused to acknowledge, let alone operate, the Hillsborough Agreement. The truth, indeed, was that the agreement was conceived essentially in a British context.[27] It marked a fresh stage in the process of the isolation of the Ulster Unionists from the British political scene—and indeed from the Conservative Party itself which had once proudly named itself 'Unionist' in the days of Balfour and Bonar Law. The security problem remained acute, not least because the Royal Ulster Constabulary, which had suffered grievously in

---

[26] *The Times*, 16 Nov. 1985.
[27] See George Boyce, *The Irish Question and British Politics, 1868–1986* (London, 1988), 122–5.

various shootings and bombings, was clearly seen as a Protestant ascendancy force. Only 3 per cent of its members were Catholic. But the Hillsborough Agreement made Mrs Thatcher look credible and constructive over Northern Ireland in the eyes of world opinion, and especially in the United States. In this, at least, it succeeded, however limited its success as a settlement for the endemic, historic problems of Ireland.

In this period there was much journalistic talk of Britain's world reputation having recovered after decades of decline. Mrs Thatcher herself claimed to have 'renewed the spirit and solidarity of the nation'. There was, indeed, some truth to this. Her varied responses in the North Atlantic alliance, in the European community, in Irish affairs, and in attempting to mediate in the Middle East as broker between the Arabs and Israel added to this impression. At the same time, this belief in British national strength owed much to short-term factors. Military victory in the Falklands gave Britain a new stature for a time, but by 1987 the impact of this had disappeared. The strength of the British economy in the mid-1980s, the signs of growth and rising prosperity, helped dispel the old image of 'the sick man of Europe'. As long as the balance of payments remained boosted by North Sea oil and the pattern of growth continued, so Britain's international credibility would continue to grow. Above all, there was Mrs Thatcher's uniquely close link with President Reagan—but this, too, could only be a temporary phenomenon. Even in this area, notably over the Americans' 'Star Wars' defence system, there had been rifts as well as accord in the transatlantic relationship. The Reykjavik summit, when President Reagan met Mr Gorbachev for the second time, led to a notable strain between Washington and London. The world reputation of the Prime Minister provided grist for the mill of the Conservative Party managers by 1987, but it was invariably presented in terms of the traditional imagery that Thatcherism meant strength, secure defence, and freedom from the defeatism of socialism and the unilateralists. Mrs Thatcher's approach to world affairs remained in key respects significantly insular, her approach to full European collaboration notably hesitant. To the extent that her position was based on a reputation as a creative world leader or participant in great events, it was a partial deception.

In the spring of 1987, with the economic omens still cheerful, Mrs Thatcher decided to call another general election.[28] The campaign was not without its strains, not least because of tactical disagreements between Lord Young and the Party Chairman, Norman Tebbit. The latter also diverged from the Prime Minister, with whom he had latterly differed over Westland, Libya, and other issues. For all that, the result as in 1983 was not in doubt. Neil Kinnock fought, personally, a highly effective and energetic campaign. He succeeded amply in Labour's main objective of defeating the Alliance as the main alternative to the Conservatives. Yet Labour still operated against a background of long-term decline. It was based essentially on the old industrial areas of Scotland, Wales, and the North, on the public-sector unions, and on client electors on council housing estates and in the local-government services. It had less and less to say to a home-owning, share-owning, bourgeoisified population, at least so it seemed. Labour seemed happiest when proclaiming its undying support for the National Health Service and the state education system of the post-Beveridge era. It continued to celebrate the glories of the Attlee years. On the issues of the future, especially on wealth creation and technological change, Labour had little to say. It was muffled on trade-union reform and taxation policy. It was confused on Europe, and on defence still caught in the grip of an unpopular unilateralism. The spectre of Bennery haunted it still. In much of southern England, Labour hardly existed. Outside parts of inner London, it held only two seats now in the south and east, below a line drawn from Bristol to the Wash. In the metropolis, its seats were largely dilapidated older boroughs; it held none of the thriving suburban seats or commuter constituencies. The movement begun in 1945 had indeed come full circle.

---

[28] See David Butler and Dennis Kavanagh, *The British General Election of 1987* (London, 1988), and Rodney Tyler, *Campaign* (London, 1987).

If Labour offered only a feeble challenge, the Alliance was scarcely more than a rabble. The Alliance campaign, with the differing emphasis posed by Liberals' David Steel, who was of the centre-left, and the Social Democrat, David Owen, who contemplated a possible coalition with the Tories, was a disaster. At no stage did the Alliance make any serious impact or strike any distinctive note. In the end, the Tory majority remained virtually intact. The Conservatives, with 42.3 per cent of the vote, won 376 seats; Labour, with 30.8 per cent, won 229, only a small improvement on the débâcle of 1983; and the Alliance won a mere 22 seats, with 22.6 per cent of the vote. Election experts could legitimately point to the fact that a system of proportional voting could have given a very different result. Once again Mrs Thatcher won a huge majority with the support of well under half of the British people. But this was, in every sense, academic. After another successful campaign, apart from some setbacks in Wales and near-disaster in Scotland, the Thatcher regime seemed as impregnable as before. The new mood established in 1979 seemed amply confirmed.

The 1987 election marked the high noon of the government of Margaret Thatcher. All its major innovations—the sale of council houses, the reform of the unions, privatization of industry, tax reform—had met with popular acclaim and substantially added to the Conservatives' constituency. There was a genuine public image of national strength and rising prosperity, though the latter was distinctly variable in its regional impact. Even though opinion polls might show that 'Butskellite' or 'Labourish' attitudes prevailed among the people on such issues as health, housing, education, and pensions,[29] the main thrust of the election was clearly to give backing to the anti-socialist, anti-planning revolt which had gathered momentum since 1979. For several years, a sustained attempt had been made to inject the institutional and

[29] Ivor Crewe, 'Has the Electorate become Thatcherite?', in Skidelsky (ed.), *Thatcherism*, 35–49, and John Rentoul, *Me and Mine: The Triumph of the New Individualism?* (London, 1989).

cultural life of the nation with market philosophies and business values, to galvanize national complacency with the short, sharp shock of enterprise. One after the other the main adversaries, local authorities, the miners, the universities, the bishops, dissidents of various shades, had retreated in disarray. As Mrs Thatcher reflected on her sweeping victory in the aftermath of the polls, urging her weary troops to yet more frenetic endeavours in the future, with the inner cities (and their Labour-led councils) as the next target, she could contemplate a major sea-change in the national consciousness. No less plausibly than Attlee and his colleagues in 1945, Mrs Thatcher was entitled to declare: 'We are the masters now.'

After the 1987 election, the battle went on with new intensity. Radical measures heralded by the Queen's Speech proliferated as the momentum of change was kept up. No one by 1989 could doubt the Prime Minister's stamina as, politically, a long-distance runner. The question now was whether she was going too far, straining the responses of an ancient nation beyond what was acceptable or practicable. Indeed, in the very aftermath of the elections, a series of government initiatives all ran into some difficulty. They suggested perhaps that more remained of the pre-1979 order than Thatcherite zealots had imagined. There were limits to the extent to which the post-1945 consensus could be overturned. Thus, in local government, attempts to curb the spending and pretensions of local authorities from Liverpool to Lambeth, especially when they could be designated 'loony left', were widely acceptable. Much less so were efforts to remodel the existing rating system by a new local tax, imposed without regard to the ability to pay. The proposal for a community charge—or 'poll tax'—put forward by Nicholas Ridley in 1988 ran into furious local opposition, not least among the Scots who were to be the first to pay this new imposition, After all, freeborn Englishmen, led by Wat Tyler, had revolted against a poll tax as long ago as 1381, and its bluntness and social inequity helped fuel a considerable popular protest, including in the Conservative shires. The advent of the poll tax in Scotland in 1989 and in England and Wales in 1990, with its heavy burden on working-class families in urban areas, enormously added to the government's unpopularity. When the poll-tax came into force in April 1990, there were immense protests all over England and Wales; some of them led to violence between protesters and the police. Edward Heath and many other leading Conservatives voiced their opposition; Tory local councillors in areas such as Witney in West Oxfordshire resigned from the party; the poll-tax was primarily responsible for a huge swing against the government which saw Labour win the Mid-Staffordshire by-election. It was noticeable that November that Michael Heseltine's remarkably effective campaign against Mrs Thatcher for the party leadership laid heavy stress on the need for a 'fundamental reform' of the poll-tax, perhaps the government's most signal claim to national unpopularity.

Again, the relatively popular policy of the privatization of industry fell on stony ground when it was proposed for extension to the electricity supply industry and to water services. The case for efficiency in each case was not made out, and there was a clear prospect, at a time of rising inflation, of large increases in charges for both, especially for water supply, with privately metered arrangements likely to increase the cost to the domestic consumer. The environmental advantages of privately-run water supply services were also far from clear, with European reports drawing attention to the pollution of Britain's rivers and beaches. There were early signs that the proposed £7 billion flotation of water shares was going slowly.[30] Some felt Mrs Thatcher was now denationalizing out of dogma, without making out a case on managerial or cost grounds. Labour recovered its confidence here and firmly promised that a future Labour government would return both electricity and water to public ownership and control. Privatization was losing its magnetism with the public, as

---

[30] *Observer*, 2 July 1989. The eventual sale was a success.

the government's decision to delay the electricity measure until late in 1990 seemed to confirm.

Aspects of the government's attempts to infuse the welfare state with the spirit of competition and the market-place also ran into difficulties in both education and health. Kenneth Baker, the Secretary of State for Education, met with opposition to his proposals to alter the structure of state education, notably by allowing comprehensive schools to opt out of the secondary system, and by giving more powers to parents in running schools, a latent veto for the middle-class. The 1988 Education Act was much criticized. So, too, were its features relating to universities and higher education generally. The government found itself having to make concessions to normally docile bodies like the House of Lords and the Committee of Vice-Chancellors and Principals, over such matters as security of tenure for academics and the universities' powers to raise their own finance.[31] Government ministers now boasted of having increased spending on higher education and struck an expansionist note in calling for doubling student numbers over the next twenty-five years. It was increasingly difficult for the government to rely on popular hostility towards the teachers' unions in getting through what many saw as a direct attack on quality in the schools. The attempt to achieve a national core curriculum, while widely supported as a way of improving literacy and numeracy amongst schoolchildren, was also feared as yet another turn in the ratchet of state control over local experimentation. It was also a comment on years of under-funding, by international standards, in the nation's schools.

Amongst the most strongly opposed of all the government's innovations was its challenge to the National Health Service in February 1989. The NHS had long become a totem of bipartisan welfare provision, Bevan's conflict with the BMA long forgotten. Mrs Thatcher had been constrained to observe in 1982 that the

---

[31]   *Guardian*, 30 June 1988, and personal knowledge.

NHS was 'safe' with her. Labour's attack on the under-funding of hospitals and long waiting lists for patients awaiting operations had been effective in its otherwise ineffectual 1987 election campaign. Kenneth Clarke, the Minister of Health, now proposed to introduce the market mechanism, to give doctors more control over their own budgets and, perhaps more alarmingly to many, to create a purchaser/provider split between hospitals and health authorities. This seemed to many privatization run mad. A notable feature of the resultant controversy was that the British Medical Association, the vehement opponent of Aneurin Bevan in 1946, was now most forceful in defending the health service, in denouncing the government for threatening its existence and failing to fund it as was properly required. Clarke engaged in a vigorous debate with the doctors but found public sympathy running against him. Despite years of Thatcherism, both deep-rooted sympathy for the NHS as a bulwark of the welfare state, and the professional strength and influence of the doctors as a pressure-group were still remarkably strong. It was widely believed that the Conservatives' heavy defeat in the Vale of Glamorgan by-election in May 1989 was partly due to the campaign of local general practitioners against the government's health plans. Labour had now the most natural of themes, invoking the almost sacred name of Nye Bevan. Conservative attempts to find new radical impetus seemed to have backfired. Other unpopular new measures were the deregulation of private rented housing and the 'targeting' of social security benefits, with disadvantage to many.

There seemed grounds for believing that the Thatcher government was, at least for a time, losing direction. The loss of William Whitelaw, who suffered a stroke and had to leave the government, was a blow to the Prime Minister.[32] He had chaired major Cabinet committees, including that for home affairs and the 'star chamber' on public expenditure cuts. More, he was almost the

---

[32] See *The Whitelaw Memoirs* (London, 1989). There is a perceptive review of it by Robert Skidelsky in the *Sunday Times*, 7 May 1989.

last representative of Tory paternalism of the old one-nation type, an important source of consolidation within the Cabinet. Mrs Thatcher had no one else like him. All the old Heathites, save for Peter Walker (a highly individualist and quite effective Secretary of State for Wales) were on the back-benches. Norman Tebbit had also fallen out with Mrs Thatcher and left the government, while Leon Brittan, recently knighted, found a new niche at Brussels. A symptomatic problem came with a ministerial wrangle over salmonella in egg production which cost the government the presence of Mrs Edwina Currie. By early 1989 the Prime Minister was at odds with several colleagues, not only Nigel Lawson with whom she quarrelled incessantly, but also with Sir Geoffrey Howe whose sympathy for European monetary union and generally benign approach to foreign affairs came increasingly to jar with her. She had no Cabinet intimate and seemed increasingly isolated on her lofty eminence. Another former confidant, John Biffen, in effect removed himself from the government after coded criticism of the Prime Minister's strident, dogmatic style. The administration became more and more centralized and the civil service enmeshed with it, notably after Robin Butler became Secretary to the Cabinet in 1988. Something more fundamental than the 'banana skin' of Westland seemed to be happening. The government was plunging on into uncharted waters without a pilot or perhaps a map.

But the main reason why the tide of Thatcherism seemed to ebb after the 1987 election was that its main claim to popular support, the apparent revival of the economy and the stimulus to productive growth, was beginning to lose credibility. There was a huge stock-market crash in October 1987 which wiped 24 per cent off stock prices.[33] Yet Nigel Lawson continued with a vigorous supply-side policy of tax cutting. This reached a climax in the budget of March 1988 which reduced the rate of income

---

[33] *Bank of England Quarterly Bulletin*, Nov. 1987, 485. In the United States, the Dow Jones index recorded a loss of 15 per cent, and the Nikkei index one of only 13 per cent in Japan.

tax to two bands only, 40 per cent for the rich and 25 per cent for all other income-tax payers.[34] This was hard to justify on either monetarist or public equity grounds. Left-wing critics furiously attacked the Chancellor's cynicism and blatant inegalitarianism. More orthodox critics feared that he was only stoking up a consumer boom which would reap the whirlwind in a vast price inflation. Mrs Thatcher tried to respond to social critics by emphasizing the government's caring image in help for the elderly and programmes for schools. But the latter charge concerning domestic inflation appeared to be correct. By the summer of 1989 the old evils of 'stagflation' seemed to have returned to haunt the government. Non-oil imports had been rising steadily throughout 1987 and 1988. The current-account deficit in the year following the March 1988 budget was to reach nearly £20 billion, easily the largest figure on record.[35] The pound came under pressure and fell steadily against the dollar and the deutschmark in the spring of 1989; in the autumn, the slump in its value became far more alarming. Worst of all, the conquest of inflation, the government's main boast, seemed undone as inflation rose to reach 8.3 per cent by June 1989. Nigel Lawson, it seemed, was neither holding the pound steady abroad nor keeping down prices at home. This time it was a consumer-credit and spending boom, not government borrowing, that was causing the problem. Critics dated this from the controversial tax-cutting budget of 1988. Lawson's chosen weapon was the most politically damaging that he could have selected—successive increases in interest rates, to reach a minimum lending rate of 15 per cent by October 1989, on the eve of the Tory party conference. With Britain a nation of mortgage-holders who operated in an economy based in large measure on the credit system, this brought home the immediacy of the government's difficulties with the economy to almost every householder in the land. Indeed, as the indices stubbornly refused to improve, there seemed little

[34] *The Economist*, 19 Mar. 1988.   [35] *The Economist*, 4 Mar. 1989.

prospect that interest rates would not remain at this historically high level for a long period to come. Hope of a 'soft landing' for the economy were at least deferred, and the stock-market plunged downwards that troubled autumn. The crisis deepened when Nigel Lawson resigned as Chancellor in October after a disagreement with Professor Alan Walters. John Major replaced him.

The main Conservative claim to national support, therefore, namely that they had worked an economic miracle, seemed increasingly shallow. Monetarism had run into the sands long before Lawson himself effectively buried it, along with the medium-term strategy, in 1985. But his alternative, more flexible approach had proved fallible also. Evidently he had rejected the Keynesianism of the past, though the course of economic debate now suggested that apostles of the old orthodoxy were beginning to recover their confidence. It would be hard, though, to call Lawson a strict monetarist either. Control of interest rates loomed far larger than control of money supply. On balance, it was his wish to defend sterling by interventionist methods, to check activity at home and keep down the sterling price of imports, rather than curb the flow of money, that dictated much of his policy. But what kind of post-monetarism he was espousing was uncertain, too. This uncertainty was reflected in unprecedented levels of argument within the government, conducted in the full glare of public attention. The Prime Minister came close to accusing the Chancellor of starting the inflationary spiral by an attempt to link the rate for sterling with the value of the German deutschmark. Nigel Lawson rebutted this with some vigour. It seemed that the Prime Minister was unable to dismiss her Chancellor, but was unable to invest him with full confidence either. On the approach to the European monetary system, Prime Minister and Chancellor were more at odds. Mrs Thatcher, in effect, did not anticipate being linked to the monetary system of an increasingly interventionist Europe in her political lifetime. Nigel Lawson, by contrast, saw the EMS as a potential brake against violent fluctuations in the rate of exchange. The debate between them oscillated, sometimes violently. Britain was indeed committed to entering a free and open European market in 1992, but it could well do so with the highest inflation rate in western Europe, the worst balance of payments, and the sharpest contraction in the manufacturing base. Whether or not Britain joined the EMS in due course, it would be operating against a background of some endemic weakness. Without exactly being in the 'stop-go' cycle of Selwyn Lloyd or the 'hard slog' of Roy Jenkins in years gone by, Britain's posture in the later Thatcher period still seemed to reflect the historic structural weakness of former years. The Prime Minister, after all, had been unable to change everything 'totally and utterly'.[36]

Arguments over the EMS confirmed that in overseas affairs the country had not really recovered the proud international stature that had been proclaimed. The nation's foreign policy remained highly personal, with Downing Street bypassing the Foreign Office time and again. Mrs Thatcher was still highly visible at international summits, but often now as an obstructive, quarrelsome figure. Her main claim to influence had been her close association with President Reagan. His retirement in January 1989 left, inevitably, a much more indirect relationship between London and the new incumbent, President George Bush. The special relationship looked more formal and detached, with Mrs Thatcher in danger of being sidelined, with her suspicion of long-range missile agreements that might mean the end of Trident and a potential British nuclear presence. Instead of her more bellicose approach, the somewhat more neutralist stance of the West Germans loomed larger in NATO, and indeed it was Bonn rather than London that seemed to have the closer relationship with Washington in 1989. Mrs Thatcher's international stature also rested on the curious chemistry of her relationship with President Gorbachev of the Soviet Union, but the rigour of the Prime Minister consorted somewhat uneasily with the fluid

[36] See the leader, 'Summer of Discomfort', *Sunday Times*, 28 May 1989.

world of *perestroika*, democratization throughout eastern Europe, German reunification, and moves towards international disarmament. It seemed, in the wake of rival expulsions of alleged spies from London and Moscow, that Anglo-Russian relations were not as buoyant or as important as the British Prime Minister had claimed.

Meanwhile in the European Community, even with old arguments over the budget and farm policy removed, the British government looked like a somewhat negative force. The Prime Minister argued strongly against any form of federalism that would undermine the sovereignty of the nation-state. Her Bruges speech in the autumn of 1988, drafted by Charles Powell, which attacked the notion of 'a United States of Europe', aroused much controversy, though the 'Bruges group' of right-wing historians and others declared their support for Mrs Thatcher's stand. The irony was that it was the British Labour Party which now responded more sympathetically towards Europe, since the social charter of the Community, drafted by its French socialist president, Jacques Delors, was in most respects highly congenial to the British left. On the other hand, Mrs Thatcher was wont to see in the Delors Charter the kind of creeping state socialism and patronage of the trade unions which she hoped to have dispelled in Britain itself. Within the Common Market, Britain in 1989 seemed as much the odd nation out as it had been in 1979 at the time of the rancorous Dublin summit, unable to prevent major changes within the Community by responding in a negative, bad-tempered way. Britain as a committed member of the European world was not a wholly credible concept at the time of the Madrid summit in June 1989, or in the Strasbourg conference that November.

Ten years of vigorous overseas promotion, therefore, left Britain somewhat isolated in Europe and outweighted in NATO. Within the Commonwealth, Mrs Thatcher's hostility towards trade sanctions on South Africa had long weakened ties with the African and Asian states so fruitfully built up at the time of the settlement in Zimbabwe in 1979. As Dean Acheson had commented back in 1962, Britain had indeed lost an empire yet failed to find a post-imperial role. The years of decline had not really been reversed. In 1989 the agreement concluded some years earlier with the Chinese government for the peaceful winding-up of the 150-year lease on Hong Kong suddenly seemed hard to defend. It was clear that the free-enterprise (indeed, Thatcherite) peoples of Hong Kong were likely to be swallowed up in a huge Marxist empire of uncertain direction. But there was nothing Britain could do. It could expect to defeat a lesser power like Argentina, but taking on Communist China was unthinkable. With the British government unable to contemplate much immigration of Hong Kong holders of British passports to these shores either, the posture struck was a weak one. Abroad, therefore, as at home, the future of 'Thatcherism' looked in some doubt, and the vision of 'the strong state', based on free enterprise and nuclear defence, that much feebler. The replacement of Geoffrey Howe by the little-known John Major at the Foreign Office in July 1989 added to the uncertainty, as did Major's replacement by Douglas Hurd three months later.

Much of the electoral strength of the Thatcher government was based on the claim that 'there was no alternative'. In the summer and autumn of 1989 it seemed possible that this might no longer be true. The threat from the Alliance had evaporated since the division of the Social Democrats in 1987. Two of its five MPs (the Scots, Kennedy and Maclennan) joined the Liberals in the newly named Social and Liberal Democrats, while the other three, headed by Dr David Owen, remained independent. By the time of local elections, it was apparent the the SDP of 'claret and chips' mould-breaking fame at the time of the Limehouse Declaration in 1981 was disintegrating.[37] It still had some major figures but no broad base. Three of the 'Gang of Four' (Jenkins, Rodgers, and Mrs Williams) had left front-line politics. The Democrats had yet to attain anything like the rooted strength

---

[37] After the local elections, Dr Owen announced that the SDP would no longer take part in contests on a nation-wide basis. In 1991 he retired from politics.

of the old Liberal Party. In the Euro-elections of June 1989 they polled disastrously, and actually did much worse than the new and untried Green Party concerned with environmental issues. The Democrats now seemed in much disarray, and presented a dismal prospect for their new leader, Paddy Ashdown, who had succeeded David Steel. The centre ground of British politics remained the same uncertain terrain it had been ever since 1918. One major Democrat theorist, David Marquand, a former Labour MP, wrote an important book, *The Unprincipled Society* in 1988. In this he argued powerfully for a revival of social citizenship and the 'developmental state'. With the Tories moving on to more radical positions, and the Labour Party now much more centrist, logic seemed to dictate that this kind of Alliance supporter should move back to a Social Democratic outlook identical with that of old Gaitskellites.[38] Much of the intellectual *élan* of the Alliance moved with him. One sign of the times was that Lord Young of Dartington, a founder member of the SDP in 1981, moved back to rejoin the Labour Party. He had been the head of Labour's Research Department at the time of the 1945 election. His odyssey thus brought the history of an important part of the British intellectual left full circle.

The mould thus stubbornly remained unbroken. The real and only alternative to Thatcherism, at least for the foreseeable future, was a return of the old two-party system, with Labour moving back towards credibility. Neil Kinnock had by now established his leadership strongly in the party. He dominated the National Executive with his 'soft left' allies. In 1988 he crushed a vain attempt to challenge his leadership by the veteran Tony Benn, with an 8 to 1 majority, while Roy Hattersley comfortably held on to the deputy leadership. In the 1989 party conference, Ken Livingstone was thrown off the NEC. There were many signs of the so-called 'new realism' now. Labour's

[38] The author quoted approvingly the examples of Sweden and West Germany, whose proportion of public expenditure to GDP was much higher than that of Britain (loc. cit., 97 ff.).

economic programme accepted the thrust of the market in allo-
cating social goods and advocated an obviously mixed approach
towards economic planning in place of the stereotyped nationalization of 1983. On Europe, as has been seen, Labour was by
1989 much more committed to developments within the Community. Jacques Delors actually was warmly received at the
Trades Union Congress as 'frère Jacques'. Labour also moved
towards more concern for the consumer, towards an acceptance
of the need for legal curbs on the power of the unions, and the
party's need to confirm itself as the defender of the law and order
sought by working-class citizens. After all, it was they who tended
to be the main victims of burglary, assault, and other forms of
violent crime. Roy Hattersley's testament, *Choose Freedom*
(1987), emphasized Labour's commitment to equality as the
guarantee of pluralism, tolerance, and personal freedom.[39]
Above all, over a unilateral nuclear policy, a stance previously
adopted with fervour by Kinnock and Michael Foot before him, it
was now accepted that this was a programme unpopular with the
mass of the British people, and actually rejected by the *glasnost* of
President Gorbachev as well. Labour's foreign-affairs spokesman,
Gerald Kaufman, was anything but a unilateralist. In 1989,
therefore, Neil Kinnock made it explicit that he was rejecting
the unilateralist approach of his youth. Labour, in effect, was
reverting to Gaitskell's (and Bevan's) stance of 1959 and going
multilateralist once again. On this basis Polaris, and even Trident,
could be retained as at least a bargaining counter. Unilateralism
was formally renounced at the party conference in October 1989.
There were real signs that Labour's new strength, confirmed
by a growing lead in the polls, was more solidly based now.
The unions, so dormant in the 1980s, were now more positive
in their approach, through leaders such as Gavin Laird (Engineers), Tom Sawyer (NUPE), and John Edmonds (Municipal
Workers), representatives of the older craft industries and

---

[39] Roy Hattersley, *Choose Freedom* (London, 1987), especially chap. 7,
'Choose Equality', 129–47.

some of the newer high-tech, white-collar workers, too. There were signs that the onward march on which Labour prided itself would be replaced by something differently constituted but no less rooted in British society.

In the autumn of 1989, therefore, the evidence for a permanent revolution in British public and private attitudes as a result of ten years of Mrs Thatcher's rule was far from conclusive. The comparatively muted way in which the Thatcher decade was celebrated in May 1989 suggested some hesitancy amongst the Conservatives themselves. Over ten years the market philosophy had undoubtedly penetrated the social services, education, the professions, and a whole range of public institutions. Changes such as extensions of working-class home- and share-ownership had been accepted as part of the norms of British life. Much of Britain in the Midlands and the south relished the new prosperity the Thatcher years had brought. The glossy shops and building societies of towns like Swindon and Basingstoke, the proliferation of 'leisure centres' and recreational amenities in much of the south, appeared to be firm signs of the enjoyment of the good life. The reaction against 'society' voiced by the Prime Minister herself was also in evidence, from the disappearance of a once influential weekly like *New Society* to the criticism of social workers resulting from the 1987 Cleveland cases of alleged child sexual abuse.

On the other hand, the despair and decay of much of the northeast or Merseyside had left their mark, too. In Scotland, especially, the rejection of the Conservative Party and the Thatcherite ethic was almost total. In the Euro-elections of June 1989 the Tories were wiped out north of the border. The revival of the campaign for Scottish devolution—indeed, for Scottish nationalism, as shown in Jim Sillars' by-election victory in Govan—was a notable feature of the later phase of Mrs Thatcher's regime. Here and elsewhere, the government strove to identify itself with new themes. In particular, the 'green' argument advanced by environmentalists, fanned by the importance of themes such as land conservation, acid rain, and the protection of the ozone layer and 'the greenhouse effect' in the 1989 Euro-elections, suggested that the message of Thatcherite consumption and wealth creation failed to mesh with wider concerns for the quality of life. The rise of 'green' issues, indeed, was more naturally appealing to Labour or Alliance politicians, and a powerful reminder of the rich variety of resistance to Thatcherism that British society could release. It led to Nicholas Ridley's removal from the Environment department in July 1989, in favour of the notoriously 'wet' Chris Patten. The government was not omnipotent after all. A surrender to the farmers over the egg controversy, hesitancy in confronting the brewers, and some retreat in the face of the judges' opposition to legal reform indicated that there were lobbies and vested interests which even the all-conquering Prime Minister could not challenge with impunity.

In the summer and autumn of 1989, Labour led strongly in the opinion polls again. By-election victories for them in the Vale of Glamorgan, Glasgow Central, and Vauxhall confirmed the trend, with black pressure from an ethnic candidate in the last-named constituency failing totally. The European elections saw Labour capture forty-five seats to the Conservatives' thirty-two, the first major defeat for Mrs Thatcher in ten years of premiership. The Democrats, significantly, finished well behind even the Greens and won no seats at all. There appeared to be some similarity with the decline of Macmillan's regime in the early sixties—Cabinet reshuffles; acute balance of payments' difficulties, a shaky pound, and high interest rates; a renewal of strikes on the railways, the docks, and in local government services;[40] a somewhat disaffected public apprehensive at Britain's declining power in the world. The truth or otherwise of this diagnosis would be revealed in the future. The electoral and sociological

---

[40] The docks strike concerned the government's decision to abolish the National Dock Labour Board scheme, a legacy of the Wilson years. Only a minority of dockers were in the scheme, in fact, and the strike collapsed that August.

omens favoured the Conservatives still, with their entrenched position in the prosperous and populous southern half of Britain. It seemed unlikely, however, that a more abrasive or divisive programme would be the way for them to recover their position. The enduring strength of post-war social and economic policy, for all its frequent and perceived failures, still commanded enough allegiance for the Conservatives to fight it with only danger to themselves. A series of appalling disasters in the public services, notably the Kings Cross underground fire and the rail crashes at Clapham and elsewhere underlined the damage that could result from the public sector being run down. As the Conservatives themselves hesitantly took up the theme of citizenship in response to opposition challenge, it was argued that only a more flexible, compassionate style of Toryism could be their route to safety.[41] Mrs Thatcher herself remained an imperious figure, respected, perhaps feared, but rarely viewed with affection. In December 1989 a backbencher, Sir Anthony Meyer, actually challenged her as party leader, gaining 33 votes. For all her professed populism, she was seen as remote from ordinary people, hardly ever catching a train, watching a film, or relaxing in a British holiday resort, turning instinctively to privileged private treatment in educating her children or adopting health-care systems for herself. She was unduly prone to use of the royal 'we'. As a phenomenon, the most triumphant premier since Lord Liverpool in 1812–27, she was unique. But the essence of the nation, its temper, its geology flowed on beneath her.

Throughout 1990 the pressures on the Thatcher government mounted remorselessly. Although John Major's first budget as Chancellor was reasonably well received, rapidly increasing inflation and the rise of interest rates to a peak of 15 per cent made the government deeply unpopular with mortgage-holders and others. Attempts to squeeze inflation out of the system led

---

[41] See in particular, John Biffen, 'Now it's time for a change', *Guardian*, 30 Apr. 1989, which calls, *inter alia*, for Conservatives to be 'explicit about the virtues of a publicly financed social policy'.

inevitably to a slow-down in industrial production and a rise in unemployment. By the autumn it was pronounced by the CBI that Britain was clearly in a recession with no obvious relief likely in early 1991. These economic discontents spilled over into foreign policy with the continuing arguments over whether or not Britain should enter the European Exchange Mechanism. Nicholas Ridley, Secretary for Trade and Industry, declared his strong opposition in an interview for *The Spectator* in July, lacing his remarks with sharp anti-German prejudice. Reluctantly, Mrs Thatcher had to dismiss him as a result. Thus Europe cost the Cabinet yet another prominent member, as it had cost it Heseltine, Brittan, and Lawson in the past. Nor could it be assumed that the government's disarray in Europe would end there. The Thatcher government appeared to regain its credibility somewhat in the conduct of foreign policy that summer when it strongly backed up President Bush's decision to send American troops to the Persian Gulf in response to the occupation of Kuwait by President Saddam Hussein of Iraq. Britain also sent some battalions of troops, Centurion tanks, Tornado bombers and other weaponry to the Gulf, and struck a more resolute posture than Germany, Italy, or other continental powers. The Tory press wondered whether another 'Falklands factor' was in the making, to rescue Mrs Thatcher from her domestic troubles. But, in the face of rising interest rates and unemployment, the poll-tax and public alarm over declining standards in education and the Health Service, a forceful stance in foreign policy seemed unlikely to bring the government any significant reprieve.

In the autumn of 1990, Mrs Thatcher appeared increasingly beleaguered, however vigorous her defiance. At home, her electoral fortunes seemed at their lowest ebb. Labour enjoyed a massive lead in the opinion polls, of up to 20 per cent. Scotland seemed almost lost to Toryism, the Conservative Party there racked by internecine dispute. The IRA continued to be hard to suppress, making their presence felt with the assassination of Ian Gow, a close political confidant of the prime minister. In February 1991 they were even to launch a mortar attack on Downing

Street. In the resultant by-election at Eastbourne after Gow's murder, the Conservative campaign collapsed, and a huge majority melted away, leaving the revived Liberal Democrats victorious. A comfortable Labour majority in Bradford North followed. As before, it was Europe that proved the most embarrassing cause of weakness, with the Cabinet in continued disarray. Perhaps against her will, Mrs Thatcher was persuaded to agree to British entry into the Exchange Rate Mechanism during the Conservative Party conference, but the wider issue of entry into the European Monetary Union, vigorously championed by Jacques Delors for the Community, remained a festering sore.

In November, these pressures finally proved overwhelming, even for a leader as resolute as Mrs Thatcher. Her antagonistic approach towards EMU and any suggestion of European federalism led to the dramatic resignation of Sir Geoffrey Howe as leader of the House. He followed it up with a fierce assault on the prime minister's diplomatic style in his resignation statement to the House, perhaps the most forceful personal onslaught since Leo Amery's on Neville Chamberlain in May 1940. The nation sensed that now, as then, the future of a once all-powerful Tory prime minister was at stake. Michael Heseltine, in the wings since his resignation over Westland in 1986, now announced his intention of challenging Mrs Thatcher for the party leadership—and thus the premiership. In a fiercely contested campaign, in which he emphasized the need to reform the poll tax as well as pressing home European themes, Heseltine gained 152 votes to Mrs Thatcher's 204 in the first ballot, on 20 November. Although Mrs Thatcher had come close to winning the necessary votes under the rules (208), it was clear that a tide of opinion was running hard against her within her own party. After words of defiance in Paris on how she would 'fight on', sombre advice from virtually all her Cabinet colleagues led, early on 22 November, to her dramatic announcement of her intention to resign as soon as the second ballot was concluded. The so-called Iron Lady, the very paradigm of toughness and determination in eleven years of astonishing personal ascendancy, was driven to

Buckingham Palace to announce her intentions to the Queen; journalists noted that there were tears in her eyes and that she suddenly looked much older. Not through parliamentary or electoral defeat, but through a grass-roots movement within the Conservative Party finally reflected in the Cabinet itself, the Thatcher years had, with breathtaking speed, suddenly come to an end.

The second ballot, without Mrs Thatcher, was a far more tranquil contest, between Michael Heseltine again, and two new candidates, Douglas Hurd, the Foreign Secretary and a centrist force, and John Major, the Chancellor, a relatively young man of 47, representing Thatcherite economic views but with a social conscience and a tone of reason and moderation. It was a sign of the social and ideological changes of the Thatcher years that Major's 'classlessness'—the humble boyhood home in Brixton in south London, a limited educational background, and graduation not from Oxbridge but in 'the university of life'—was held to give him a distinct edge. By contrast, Douglas Hurd, a product of Eton and Oxford, almost had to apologize for his comfortable, patrician origins. Commentators sensed that, with Mrs Thatcher removed, Michael Heseltine's support might not hold up, and so it proved. On 27 November it was revealed that Major had received 185 votes, Heseltine 131, and Hurd 56. The party organizers then declared that a further ballot was unnecessary. John Major became Prime Minister after barely twelve months' experience of high office. The Tories at once improved their standing in the opinion polls. Labour complained, like old Tories, that 'they've shot our fox'. Commentators spoke of a new sense of centrist moderation after years of abrasive confrontation at home and overseas. There seemed little doubt that in 1990, as with the downfall of Lloyd George in 1922 and the resignation of Neville Chamberlain in 1940, the Conservative rank and file had appropriately reflected a wider national mood. The logic of Mrs Thatcher's programme since 1979 had been to reverse the main lines of her country's history as it had evolved since the Second World War—the conventional wisdom, the corporatism, the 'debilitating consensus'. Through ceaseless activity and a triumph of will-power, she had by 1987 come as near to success as was possible for one self-sufficient human being. The nation had formally rejected neither her nor her policies by the end of 1990. But, below the surface, it had defeated her, just the same.

14. *Fin de Siècle:* New Labour in Power

1990–2001

THE fall of Mrs Thatcher was generally felt to be a defining moment in modern British history. People would ask each other where they were when they heard the news on the morning of 22 November 1990, much as an earlier generation had responded to the news of the assassination of President Kennedy in 1963, also on 22 November, as it happened. After years of storm and stress, from the war in the Falklands to the battles over the poll tax, the advent of John Major appeared to usher in an era of greater tranquillity. When he spoke of creating a 'nation at ease with itself', this familiar promise by an incoming prime minister perhaps had more substance than usual. His new Cabinet seemed to confirm a new mood of moderation. While Norman Lamont succeeded Major himself as Chancellor, the most striking new appointment was the return of Michael Heseltine to the Cabinet as Secretary of State for the Environment. His main role would be to find a substitute for the hated poll tax. John Major's early experiences were alarming. On 7 February 1991 the entire Cabinet came close to being murdered when the IRA launched a mortar attack on 10 Downing Street. But the Prime Minister gave an impression of calm imperturbability. His popularity was enhanced by an immediate crisis in the Middle East which he inherited from his predecessor. Following the invason of Kuwait by the Iraqi president, Saddam Hussein, Britain gave strong support to the UN response led by the American government. After the UN deadline to Iraq expired on 15 January 1991, the RAF was heavily involved alongside American warplanes, with Tornado and Jaguar bombers launching air strikes on Baghdad. In the brief land war of 24–8 February which rapidly liberated Kuwait from Iraqi occupation, the British First Armoured Division under General Peter de la Billière was prominent in the rout of Saddam Hussein's forces. The professional efficiency of British arms, despite repeated defence cuts, was amply confirmed. The only British losses were at the hands of the Americans. For a fleeting moment, the prospect was held out of the Conservatives benefiting from another 'Falklands factor' as in 1982–3, and perhaps calling an early election in consequence.

But the advent of a new, likeable prime minister did not cure the unpopularity from which the Conservatives had been suffering since the later Thatcher period. The deep-rooted problems of the previous decade would not disappear. In particular, the economy continued to go badly after the slump of the later Lawson years, with falling output and unemployment rising to well over 2 million during 1991. Britain was in recession, and this time it was the Conservative heartland which was suffering most acutely. The middle class of southern England found itself confronted with insecure employment, high interest rates, and a collapsing housing market. Many who had purchased their homes in the high noon of Thatcherite prosperity were now faced with negative equity and unsustainable mortgages. In the City, so recently the safe haven of the 'yuppy', merchant bankers, investment brokers, accountants, and law firms had now to lay off staff. The electoral impact on Conservative fortunes remained as severe as in Mrs Thatcher's twilight period with the Liberal Democrats conspicuous beneficiaries. In a by-election in March 1991 they captured Ribble Valley in Lancashire on a 25 per cent swing: this apparently deterred Major from calling a snap general election. The first budget of Norman Lamont was also inauspicious for his party. While it was made clear that the poll tax would disappear in 1993 in favour of a council tax, a modified version of the old domestic rates, in other respects it was attacked for sharply increasing taxes: in particular, VAT would rise from 15 to 17.5 per cent. Lamont himself did not prove a popular advocate of his policies with the general public. He was attacked for saying that unemployment was 'a price well worth paying' and later derided for claiming to detect the 'green shoots' of economic recovery at a time of prolonged recession. The voters responded with a Labour by-election gain in Monmouth on a 13 per cent swing and a loss of 900 seats for the Conservatives in local elections in May. It was widely expected that Labour under Neil Kinnock might well return to power in the near future.

In fact, for all these problems, Britain still appeared to be an essentially Conservative country as for most of the period since the First World War. The Prime Minister was an enigmatic figure, hard to classify; attempts to define 'Majorism' as an ideological creed distinct from 'Thatcherism' led nowhere.[1] On the other hand, his calm and measured style, and some success in presenting himself as a relatively classless figure, did seem to make some impact. Throughout the summer and autumn of 1991 if there were no great novelties of policy, there were no disasters either. The main economic indices showed some sign of improvement: interest rates fell to single figures and inflation to 4 per cent. The opinion polls indicated that the Conservatives were gaining ground and actually showed them in the lead in the autumn. There was still public doubt about Labour on grounds of economic competence, and also about the capacity of its leader, Neil Kinnock, widely suspected in middle England for being Welsh, wordy, and working-class.

Above all, John Major appeared to have won a kind of truce in the long-running debate about membership of the European Community. This had dogged the Tories relentlessly since the

---

[1] For Major, see Anthony Seldon, *Major: A Political Life* (London, 1997) and Sarah Hogg and Tim Hill, *Too Close to Call: Power and Politics—John Major in Number 10* (London, 1995).

mid-1980s and by provoking the successive resignations of Heseltine, Lawson, and Howe, had led to the ultimate downfall of Mrs Thatcher herself. Europe, indeed, was what British post-imperial foreign policy was largely about. The European heads of government conference at Maastricht in Holland in December 1991 was a key moment for British policies towards Europe. It marked an 'irreversible' path towards political and economic coherence in the EU, with the prospect of a single unified currency by 1 January 1999, an independent European Central Bank, and general moves towards greater integration, if not federalism. All this was anathema to many Conservatives and the bulk of British opinion. They noted with dismay the words in the first clause of the Maastricht Treaty that it intended 'to create an ever-closer union among the peoples of Europe'. In the event, it was widely felt, therefore, that John Major had come reasonably well out of the Maastricht conference. He managed to sustain his view, proclaimed in a speech at Bonn, that Britain now lay 'at the heart of Europe'. But he did so in a way that gave only limited ground to the federalists. Britain stood aside from the goals, timetables, and mechanisms of Maastricht. It gained what was called an 'opt-out' over future monetary union, and also over signing the so-called Social Chapter of workers' rights plus a minimum wage which Labour warmly supported. The powers of the European Commission over British social legislation were also curtailed. John Major had preserved party unity for the moment. Some even proclaimed Maastricht as a great diplomatic triumph, 'game, set and match to Britain'.[2] In practice, of course, it only meant that all the key answers to Britain's policies towards Europe would be deferred until an uncertain future. The country's attitude towards its role in Europe remained profoundly ambiguous. But at least Britain had some kind of policy, however tentative. Most key members of the government, such as Michael Heseltine and the Foreign

[2] *The Times*, 11 Dec. 1991.

Secretary, Douglas Hurd, were regarded as pro-European. For the moment, with Mrs Thatcher and the Euro-sceptics holding their fire, the government could put up a façade of fragile unity.

The general election in April 1992 was a curious affair. The public mood was not heroic. Neither the Conservatives nor Labour seemed especially confident and the public displayed some apathy towards both. Intellectual and cultural opinion appeared strongly in favour of a change after 13 years of Tory rule; the silent majority were less committed. The Conservatives' decision to delay an election until almost the latest possible date did not suggest hopeful prospects. On the other hand, much of Labour's support in the polls seemed to be 'soft'; to achieve victory, a gain of ninety-seven seats and an 8 per cent swing were required, higher than any party had achieved since the war. When the campaigning began, it was Labour which seemed to hold the initiative. The polls almost universally showed a strong and rising lead. The party combined attacks on the social consequences of Thatcherism with an emphasis on its own moderation. It was no longer a party committed to high taxation, massive public spending, more public ownership, or the defence of the unions. The party presented itself as a modern social democratic party; its communications officer, Peter Mandelson, ensured that the red flag image would disappear, with the party's new symbol being the gentle emblem of the red rose. The class war was over, if indeed it had ever begun. Neil Kinnock himself threw himself into the fray with gusto, projecting himself as the leader of a team, a latter-day Attlee, and Labour's television broadcasts were much the more effective. By contrast, the Conservatives' campaign appeared indecisive and confused. A political change seemed increasingly inevitable; in Scotland, where devolutionist sentiment remained powerful, the pro-Union Conservatives appeared especially beleaguered. John Major seemed destined for the fate of Douglas-Home in 1964, a short-term leader rejected by the voters at the first attempt.

In fact, the outcome was a surprise, one that provided a remarkable commentary on British social attitudes in the post-Thatcher period. The polls were simply wrong. Much was later made of John Major's own personal style of street-corner campaigning, using a loudspeaker on a soap box in a way that evoked his Brixton boyhood. But the real feature of the campaign was not so much public confidence in the Conservatives but distrust of Old Labour. The campaign itself, and Labour mistakes during it, confirmed long-held doubts. Labour's shadow chancellor, John Smith, somewhat rashly produced his own shadow budget. What caught public attention was the admission that, to increase state benefits, there would be markedly higher taxation. While Labour claimed that only 'the rich' would pay higher taxes, it was noted that they would apparently include all those earning the relatively modest income of £21,000 a year.[3] The precise definition of those considered to be 'rich' was singularly unclear. Fear of Labour as a 'tax and spend' party was therefore revived. In any event, the party put itself needlessly on the defensive. There were echoes, too, of a less savoury political style. If the union leaders were kept in the wings and less appetizing figures such as Gerald Kaufman concealed from public gaze, a rally at Sheffield on 1 April attracted much criticism by its shallow and triumphalist tone, reminiscent some felt of events at Nuremberg. At the same time, Labour allowed itself to be placed repeatedly on the defensive by Tory tabloid newspapers, of which the Murdoch-owned *Sun* was the most strident. Its personal attacks on Neil Kinnock undermined his and his party's morale. Although the polls continued to the end to suggest a Labour victory—a view even confirmed in exit polls on election night itself—Labour headquarters sensed some days before polling day on 9 April that its momentum was dribbling away.

From the start, the results confirmed the continuing Conservative ascendancy. Labour never looked like achieving the 8 per cent swing required for victory. An early Conservative victory in Basildon, a new town stronghold of the 'Essex man' type of voter

[3] David Butler and Dennis Kavanagh, *The British General Election of 1992* (London, 1992), 103–5.

allegedly appealed to by the Tory *Sun*, told its own story. The Conservative vote held up more strongly than commentators had forecast; indeed in Scotland the Conservative vote actually went up by 1.7 per cent compared with 1987. Although Labour still made gains in its old heartlands of the north of England, Scotland, and Wales, its total of seats advanced only to 271, well below the Conservatives' 336. The Liberal Democrats, who had been expected to undermine the Conservative vote in many parts of England, had a disappointing election, with only twenty seats from 17 per cent of the vote. Labour's defeat, indeed, was worse than it appeared. Its share of the poll, at 34.16 per cent was almost 8 points below the Conservatives' 41.85 per cent. Less than half the working class had voted Labour. The Tory vote had risen to over 14,000,000, the highest poll any party had obtained since 1945 and their own highest ever. Had it not been for the quirks of the way that the vote was distributed, Labour's performance would have looked much worse. Despite everything, it seemed the voters still saw the Conservatives as the party of greater prosperity and national unity, Labour that of higher taxation and divided counsels. Neither it nor its leader inspired ultimate confidence. The party of change and of a better future, it seemed, was identified rather with a stagnant past, certainly not with the opportunity state. Labour had argued that it was time for a change. But the voters felt that this had occurred eighteen months earlier, with a change of prime minister. The 1992 election, therefore, proved to be a turning-point at which British politics obstinately refused to turn. Neil Kinnock promptly resigned as Labour leader. His torment in defeat was somewhat cruelly captured afterwards in *The Absence of War*, a play by the leftish playwright David Hare, with hints of ideological betrayal. Kinnock was succeeded by the shadow chancellor, John Smith. A sharp Edinburgh lawyer, he gave a greater sense of intellectual self-confidence than Kinnock had been able to convey. But, in his way, Smith was also a conservative, cautious politician who still reflected the rejected values of Old Labour.

The general election of 1992, therefore, apparently confirmed the continuing dominance of British Conservatism. Major perhaps might prove to be another Baldwin, offering one-nation, post-Thatcherite peace in our time. Yet in fact his victory was to herald a long and almost unrelenting phase of crisis and decay. The election results had masked far more powerful forces of change, and the seeds of one of the great upheavals in British political history. The campaign had taken place in a mood of public doubt, against a background of uncertainty about both the economy and policy towards Europe. For a long period thereafter these raced together towards a point of crisis. They raised fundamental issues about post-Thatcher Conservatives and whether her party still retained the will or the capacity to govern.

The origin of these crises can be pinpointed with remarkable precision. They exploded on 'Black Wednesday', 16 September 1992. The Conservatives' reputation for economic competence and John Major's reputation as a political leader were never to recover. As Norman Lamont was to put it in a bitter speech when dismissed as Chancellor in May 1993, the Conservatives gave 'the impression of being in office and not in power'. *Fin de siècle* Tory Britain showed a government and an ethic barely surviving, and no more. It provided a context for public disillusion and cynicism about the institutions and policies which had galvanized British history since the Second World War. It was known in the summer of 1992 that the economy was in recession and that the pound was weak. The British government hung on indecisively, refusing to take such tough decisions as raising interest rates or devaluing the pound. It chose to denounce its European partners for failing to act; the Germans, whose Bundesbank was unwilling to reduce interest rates at a time when the reunification with the former East Germany was imposing heavy financial strains, were a convenient target. In the first days of September pressure against the pound became overwhelming. The Italian lira was devalued on 12 September. The British government, which regarded sterling as a national totem, a badge of pride, refused to respond, and a mood of frozen impotence resulted. On

Wednesday, 16 September, the pressures on the pound became a torrent. Panicstricken, the government raised interest rates to 12 per cent and then to 15 per cent but the pound continued to fall in value. In twenty-four hours, the Bank of England sold over £30 billion from its reserves: in effect the British currency reserves 'went negative'. In a mood of desperation, Major and Lamont decided that Britain would have to leave the European Exchange Rate Mechanism (ERM). The pound in effect was devalued. For the rest of the year, it bumped along far below its previous floor. Since everything else about the British economy appeared to be weak—output, investment, training—sterling could not take the strain. As in 1949 and 1967, devaluation was seen as a massive national defeat.[4]

The trauma of Black Wednesday 1992 had enduring effects. It not only tore the government's economic and financial policies into tatters; it massively dented its overall reputation for competent management, an area in which Conservative governments had always been thought superior to Labour. The opinion polls showed Labour's lead soaring to over 15 per cent. It remained at a continuously high level, sometimes touching 30 per cent for the next four and a half years. John Major himself naturally bore most of the blame. He had personally been identified with the ERM as Chancellor and had claimed it was no soft option that would lead to devaluation. Although he withdrew an apparent decision to resign immediately after Black Wednesday, he now became the most derided and despised prime minister since Neville Chamberlain, a byword for a failed leadership. The previously supportive Tory press savaged him for being grey and indecisive, and lacking the attributes of leadership. His Cabinet appeared hopelessly split between pro-European centrists like Hurd, Clarke, and Heseltine, and disciples of free-market Thatcherism like Portillo, Lilley, and Redwood. The Chancellor, Norman Lamont, who apparently had responded

[4] Philip Stephen, *Politics and the Pound: The Conservatives' Struggle with Sterling* (London, 1996), 240 ff.

to Britain's leaving the ERM with relief by cheerfully singing in his bath, became a derided figure, accident-prone in both his political and his private life. In retrospect, it seems surprising that he was not immediately moved elsewhere, perhaps to the Home Office. Previous Chancellors who had been forced to devalue, Cripps in 1949 and Callaghan in 1967, had retained residual political strength to bounce back from defeat; Callaghan indeed was nine years later to become Prime Minister. Lamont, by contrast, stayed on for eight more months, the hapless emblem of humiliation and defeat. His next budget in March 1993 only caused his government's and his own reputation to slump still further. Inevitably, it involved major new taxation to the tune of £10.3 billion to try to meet a public sector borrowing requirement rising to £50 billion in 1993–4.[5] The battered middle-class mortgage-holders of middle England suffered further blows. Most unpopular of all, Lamont proposed to raise VAT duty on fuel to 17.5 per cent, a measure vehemently attacked by the elderly. The government appeared incompetent and heartless at the same time. The pound sank a few more points.

Britain and its system of government now entered a strange twilight period, a kind of malaise. John Major's government plunged into apparently endless unpopularity on grounds of its competence. On many fronts its capacity for legislative initiative petered out. Even more damagingly its reputation for integrity also appeared to dissolve. On the policy front, crisis followed crisis. Michael Heseltine appeared seriously to misjudge an announcement to close over thirty collieries involving the dismissal of over 20,000 miners at a time of rising unemployment. Commons pressure, along with popular sympathy for the miners and even for their Marxist leader Arthur Scargill, forced him to retreat. In foreign affairs, the ambiguous policy of Douglas Hurd towards the civil war in the former Yugoslavia, with its refusal to send arms to beleaguered Bosnia, aroused much criticism. One

---

[5] *The Economist*, 20 Mar. 1993.

aspect was the danger thus posed to British troops serving under the UN in the former Yugoslavia. More serious, the very standards of government now seemed tacky and corrupt: the antique word 'sleaze' (originally applied to textiles) gained a new currency. There were echoes of the Profumo period thirty years earlier. A long series of sexual and/or financial scandals involving Conservative MPs began in September 1992 when David Mellor, a confidant of John Major, had to resign from the government after an affair with an obscure Spanish actress, best known for a pornographic video. Soon after, a long-running scandal about the alleged illegal export of arms to Iraq in the late 1980s led to the appointment of the Scott Inquiry which threatened to expose several Conservative ministers as having ignored the guidelines and deceived parliament. There was an unsavoury suggestion that they had known of breaches in the arms policy but had been happy to let the directors of a private firm, Matrix-Churchill, go to prison to cover up their own misdeeds. Commentators observed that a lengthy period of one-party rule, allied to the opportunities afforded by privatization and deregulation, and liaisons with private lobbyists, were introducing an endemic corruption into British government. Public cynicism towards the government and indeed all politicians gathered pace.

If there was one issue, however, above all others that characterized this period of impotence and indecision, it was undoubtedly Britain's relationship with Europe. It soon emerged that the Maastricht Treaty, far from being a diplomatic achievement which had given Britain breathing-space, was a long-running disaster for the Conservative Party. A hard core of right-wing so-called Euro-sceptics, hostile to Maastricht and perhaps to membership of the EU altogether, emerged to harry the government at every turn and even to threaten its very existence. The vote to confirm the treaty on 4 November 1992 was a desperate affair, the government clinging on by just three votes, with twenty-six Conservatives voting against their own government and others abstaining. Only the support of the Liberal Democrats averted defeat. The long process of fighting the treaty, clause by clause, meant a war of attrition in the Commons with Tory pitted against Tory. The Opposition parties watched with incredulous glee as the Conservatives' alleged 'secret weapon', party loyalty, disintegrated amidst intense personal bitterness.[6]

Involvement in 'Europe', however defined, had seldom been a popular cause in recent British history. Even after the referendum of 1975 had confirmed British membership of the old EEC the British had been apathetic, suspicious of the Brussels bureaucracy and of the power of a now reunified Germany in particular. This was not hankering for the glories of a defunct empire, but an innate insularity, fanned by memories of the 1939 war and of an indomitable island race 'fighting alone'. On the other hand, in the 1980s there did appear to be a kind of accommodation towards the European Union, especially when Mrs Thatcher was able to remove the long-running grievance over British budgetary contributions. British institutions gradually became enmeshed in the European scene. British businesses found their major markets for manufactures on the continent; the City was able to reassert its dominance in European money markets; British universities became increasingly drawn towards European partnership in student exchange and research projects. An old debate, founded on an innate historic sense of British insular exceptionalism, seemed to be drawing to a close.

Of the two major parties, the Conservatives had always been the more obviously pro-European. Macmillan had launched the initial overtures back in the early 1960s; Heath had negotiated British entry into Europe a decade later. Even Mrs Thatcher, for all her ingrained suspicion of foreign entanglements and her personal ties with President Reagan, had approved the economic philosophy behind European moves towards a Single Market. She had even reluctantly been persuaded to join the ERM. By contrast, Labour had long been suspicious of a capitalist cartel which seemed to constrain socialist planning at home. Despite

[6] *The Times*, 28 Sept. 1992.

the successful referendum put through by Wilson and Callaghan in 1975, Labour remained sceptical; as it moved to the left, Bennite anti-Europeanism took charge. As late as 1983, in the famous 'longest suicide note in history', Labour was committed to withdrawal from Europe. Now in the early 1990s there was a massive change. Under Neil Kinnock, the party moved to embrace European membership as a platform for economic advance; the social integration, 'Social Chapter' and all, advocated by Jacques Delors and other European socialists, was popular with Labour and TUC alike. After the 1992 election, John Smith was an enthusiast for Europe, as were most of his leading lieutenants like Gordon Brown and Tony Blair; the one leading dissident, the anti-European Bryan Gould, left the front bench in disgust in the autumn of 1992 and departed to his native New Zealand.

By contrast, the growing Conservative fear of Europe, manifested in Mrs Thatcher's Bruges speech in 1988 and voiced repeatedly by her after she left Downing Street, became increasingly strident. Europe as an open competitive free market for British exports was an acceptable concept. Europe as an integrating, federalizing superstate, bringing in Delors-style socialism by the back door even as Thatcherite Britain rejected it at home, was anathema. In the post-Maastricht world, as the EU assumed an increasingly close-knit form after the ending of the Cold War, Europe became an endless torment for the British Conservative Party. It became for many on the party right an object of near-hatred. To them it threatened the basis of British sovereignty; it flouted what Gaitskell in 1962 had called 'a thousand years of history', Empire and all. A European common currency, the anticipated 'euro', would banish the pound, and threaten long- or short-term instability. European law would undermine the role of Parliament and the prerogative of the Crown. Suggestions by commentators such as David Marquand,[7] along with the Scottish Nationalists, that British institutions would have to be

---

[7] David Marquand, 'Reinventing Federalism', in *The New Reckoning* (London, 1997), 125 ff.

remodelled in a European direction, with greater devolution and decentralization, electoral reform and coalition governments, led to fears of a break-up of the United Kingdom at home alongside its emasculation by a European superstate overseas. A remorseless civil war thus developed, a relatively small band of right-wing Eurosceptics finding voices in the Cabinet like Michael Portillo and John Redwood, with the pro-Europeans in the Cabinet such as Kenneth Clarke and Michael Heseltine fighting vigorously back. John Major wavered almost helplessly in between, occasionally venting his anger to journalists against those he called the Euro-sceptic 'bastards'. Not since the debates over tariffs and imperial preference early in the century had the Tories been so divided. John Major's position seemed an uncanny echo of Arthur Balfour's wobbling equilibrism then—and Balfour's unhappy premiership had led in 1906 to a record Conservative electoral defeat.

Throughout 1993 the Tory torment on Europe continued unabated. There were endless crises in the Commons as the Maastricht Treaty wound its tortuous way through Commons committee. Major and the government found themselves forced increasingly to give ground to Euro-rebels of various shades and to offer a referendum on British adherence to a single currency, EMU, should it come about. On 22 July 1993, twenty-three Conservative MPs voted against their party and the government squeaked home on the final Maastricht vote by 324 to 316. Even more alarming was the collapse of Conservative support in the country. The local election results of May 1993 were calamitous. All the flagship bastions of the Thatcherite heyday, Kent, Surrey, even Essex, home of the legendary *Sun*-reading, lager-drinking C1 skilled worker, 'Basildon Man', fell as Labour or the Liberal Democrats captured their county councils. The Tories suffered 452 net losses; only Buckinghamshire of English county councils remained in Conservative hands; in Scotland and Wales the party seemed close to extinction. In by-elections, the Liberal Democrats were still the main challengers—scoring a remarkable victory in Newbury, where a local proposed bypass through open country had led to much environmental protest.

The inevitable scapegoat had to be Norman Lamont. He could claim to have cut back inflation and raised the economy from the darkest depths of recession. But an accident-prone Chancellor who proclaimed, Edith Piaf-style, during the Newbury by-election that he regretted nothing, was manifestly a political liability. Tory spirits were lifted by the succession to the Treasury of Kenneth Clarke, a combative pro-European with far superior presentational skills and self-confidence.[8] But the bitter circumstances of Lamont's departure and his condemnation of John Major's lack of leadership confirmed the Tories' trauma. Those with a longer memory compared his sacking with the panic induced by Macmillan's 'night of the long knives' in July 1962, and the malaise that accompanied an earlier period of extended Conservative rule.

There were hopes that, with the advent of Kenneth Clarke and growing signs of economic recovery, the government and the country would recover their standing and their confidence. In fact, there followed a prolonged, depressing period of discontent. It was frequently claimed that the government's fortunes had 'bottomed out' with Major regaining credibility. Then a further decline would occur with a renewed plunge in the opinion polls. It heralded a long phase of public cynicism, a culture of despair. National institutions became the butt of public ridicule. The conduct of government became a cause for contempt as one misfortune after another, personal or political, struck Major and his Cabinet. A climax of a sort was reached in early January 1994. In the period up to that month a government which had proclaimed its attachment to 'family values' saw a junior minister, Tim Yeo, resign after fathering an illegitimate child; another government aide resign after a shady property deal; a Tory member being shown to have slept with another man on a holiday in France; Lady Caithness, the wife of another government minister, shoot herself after her husband's sexual infidelity; and

---

[8] *The Times*, 28 May 1993.

Westminster Conservatives, headed by Lady Porter, shown to have pursued improper housing policies for the sake of electoral gerry-mandering. Yet more personal scandals followed in succeeding months and years. Two PPSs, Riddick and Tredinnick, resigned after receiving 'cash for questions', while the *Guardian* reported cases of ministers enjoying free hospitality at the Paris Ritz from the Egyptian owner of Harrods. With all these bizarre events, satirists on television or in *Private Eye* had a field day unknown since the stirring time of the Profumo affair. *The Economist*, usually a moderate enough organ, declared that the government had 'convinced much of Britain that the nation is governed by clowns and hypocrites'.[9] Labour's lead in the polls soared to 25 per cent and there was worse to come.

Every yardstick of opinion underlined the government's deep unpopularity. The local elections in May 1994 were another disaster. The European elections in June resulted in Labour winning 64 seats to the Conservatives' 18 and the Liberal Democrats' 2. The local government elections in May 1995 and May 1996 were merely to confirm the collapse of the long dominant Conservative Party in the localities. In 1995 no fewer than 1,800 seats were lost, many of them in traditionally Tory areas of middle-class southern England; in much of the north, the party seemed virtually to have disappeared. The home-owning C1 skilled and semi-skilled workers won over in the 1980s were deserting in droves. After the 1996 elections, there were only 4,700 Conservative councillors throughout the land, as against 5,100 Liberal Democrats and 10,800 Labour.[10] All this meant that British Conservatism was withering at the grass roots. Bye-lections told the same story. As a series of Conservative MPs died or resigned for a variety of often bizarre reasons, the party proved incapable of holding any seat anywhere, however large its previous majority. The Liberal Democrats as usual were

---

[9] *The Economist*, 15 Jan. 1994.
[10] David Butler and Dennis Kavanagh, *The British General Election of 1997* (London, 1997), 13.

powerful challengers (a record 35 per cent swing to them in Christchurch in Hampshire in July 1993 being particularly remarkable); but there were increasing signs of disillusioned Tories moving straight over to Labour now. In Dudley West in the West Midlands in December 1994 Labour captured the seat easily on a 29 per cent swing, another record. Clearly a seismic shift in opinion was under way. It continued unabated until by the start of 1997 the Conservatives had lost their overall Commons majority and had to rely on a few Ulster Unionists. In Wirral South, a highly prosperous commuter constituency that was home to some of the wealthier Merseyside and Mancunian bour-geoisie, in March 1997 within a few weeks of a general election Labour swept home to victory yet again. One variation came in Scotland, where Tory fortunes had slumped to new levels, with a victory for the SNP in Perth and Kinross in May 1995. In no part of the United Kingdom could the Tories find safe haven. Not since 1989 had they been victorious in a by-election anywhere. Another sign of the times was that three Tory MPs actually left their party during the session. Emma Nicholson and Peter Thurnham joined the Liberal Democrats, while Alan Howarth became the first sitting Conservative MP in history to cross the floor and join Labour.

It was always Europe that was the supreme source of torment, with Chancellor Helmut Kohl of Germany a popular target. Issue after issue seemed to emerge to inflame Europhobes on the Tory backbenches and the tabloid press. Opinion polls showed a hardening of British attitudes towards the EU in general and the single currency in particular. Even when it became clear that a single currency, pushed on by the German and French governments, would come into effect by the end of the decade, Conservative ministers, headed by John Major, continued to claim that its prospects were in doubt, and that in any event Britain, which had refused to commit itself about joining in any foreseeable future, held a unique diplomatic advantage. The fear of a threat to British sovereignty was treated in a simplistic way; the implications of being in the single market or being bound to

European social and labour legislation had simply not been understood. Euro-scepticism received an endorsement in 1995 in a book by Bernard Connolly, a British official who had worked in the monetary division of the European Commission. He described EMU as 'a dangerous confidence trick'.[11] On one front after another, European policies came under fire. British lamb and veal were variously under threat when they entered French ports. European fisheries policy was passionately attacked by British fishermen for threatening their livelihood by the reduction of quotas and allowing Spanish and French fishermen into traditional British waters. It reached a crescendo in 1996 over another food product, British beef. As a result of deregulation of animal feeds in the Thatcher era, it was discovered that British beef was contaminated with BSE, or 'mad cow disease'; as a result, some consumers had died from the related CJD disease. The European Union, with the Germans in the lead, promptly banned British beef imports until diseased herds had been slaughtered and scientific tests showed that all trace of disease had been eradicated. The Agriculture Minister, Douglas Hogg, did not inspire confidence in his handling of the issue, while the crisis inflamed the beef producers and Europhobe sentiment in general. A vote of censure on Hogg in the Commons was defeated only with the reluctant votes of Ulster Unionists (who had their own grievances over BSE). In the summer of 1996 John Major briefly toyed with a policy of blocking EU business at Brussels, his Foreign Secretary Malcolm Rifkind was denounced by all the other fourteen foreign ministers for 'blackmail', and cartoonists evoked the First World War with British farmers 'going over the top' in defence of British interests.[12] It seemed impossible for John Major to pacify his warring factions. Eight Tory rebels had the party whip removed in December 1994 for voting against an increase in British contributions to the EU. Norman Lamont actually suggested leaving the EU altogether,

---

[11] Bernard Connolly, *The Rotten Heart of Europe* (1995).
[12] *Independent*, 23 May 1996.

while a group of far-right Tory backbenchers flirted with the Referendum Party financed by Sir James Goldsmith as a vehicle for anti-European sentiment at the next election.

But the torment of Europe did not stand alone. In one area of policy after another, the Conservatives seemed to plunge into disarray. The economy, under the handling of Kenneth Clarke, was in fact showing distinct signs of recovery in 1994–6 with output going up 4 per cent in 1994 and disposable personal incomes rising steadily. But to the consumer this was translated into higher taxes and a stagnant housing market with negative equity on properties house-owners had been encouraged to buy on easy terms in the 1980s. What was called by journalists 'the feel-good factor' obstinately refused to emerge. After all this, recovery was based in part on cuts in public spending which showed up in long waiting lists in the National Health Service, excessive class sizes in schools, and inefficiencies on the railways and other forms of transport. In part, too, it rested on taxation levels which continued to rise under the Conservatives: one of the most unpopular of the new taxes proposed was added VAT on fuel, rising from 8 to 17.5 per cent, a hard blow for the elderly. In a backbench revolt in December 1994, the government was defeated, leaving a hole of £1 billion in the national finances. Much hope was invested in a consumer spending boom, but lack of confidence amongst taxpayers meant reluctance to spend or to invest.

Nor did other aspects of the government's policies fare well. Privatization of the railways did go through, but public criticisms of the delays and poor services of the rail system continued as before. The railway service disintegrated into a myriad individual companies, with a separate body, Railtrack, in control of the lines on which trains ran. Serious accidents, including one at Southall, appeared to imply a threat to passenger safety as a result. Indeed, privatization seemed less obviously a panacea. To the general public it was symbolized by the cuts in supplies from Yorkshire Water during dry summers, and enormous pay rises for executives in privatized utilities, such as Cedric Brown of British Gas awarding himself a 75 per cent pay rise when consumers' bills were going up. When Michael Heseltine proposed selling off the local post offices, a popular outcry, notably in rural areas, forced him hurriedly to withdraw. Three other areas, it was felt, might restore the government's fortunes—deregulation of business, education, and law and order—but in the event none did so. Deregulation had led directly to the deaths caused by mad cow disease. Gillian Shephard's tenure of the Education portfolio was marked by complaints by teachers at growing bureaucratic burdens and excessive class sizes, although the new national curriculum was carried through successfully. As for law and order, Michael Howard, the Home Secretary, found his policies rejected almost with contumely by the criminal justice system, the police, and the legal authorities. Champions of civil liberties were up in arms when he was defeated in case after case in the high court, especially in instances involving those seeking political asylum, and appalled by a bill that threatened new sanctions against rebels such as New Age travellers or hunt saboteurs. His Police Bill in 1994 was attacked for proposing to transfer control of the police from elected councillors to more of those nominated 'quangos' (quasi non-governmental organizations) that flourished in the Conservative years. The Lords rebuked Howard over proposals to change compensation schemes for crime victims without consulting parliament, and to alter criminal sentences without reference to the courts. The prisons inspector, Judge Stephen Tumim, ferociously condemned his penal policy. A clash with the director of prisons, Derek Lewis, who was sacked in October 1995 after problems in Strangeways gaol, led to accusations that Howard was trying to evade his own responsibility for a struggling penal system. Proposals to extend police powers of surveillance, bugging, or intruding into people's homes were attacked not only by former home secretaries like Jenkins and Callaghan, but even by the police themselves.[13] Here again was a minister under siege and a government at bay.

[13] *Guardian*, 13 Jan. 1997.

It was the tone even more than the policies of government that now aroused public concern. An endless series of cases involving impropriety of one kind and another by legislators and ministers suggested a moral decay at the heart of British governance. An unwise claim in 1993 that the government were going 'back to basics' as new moralists was followed by a stream of Conservative MPs caught up in sexual misdemeanours of one kind and another—Mellor, Yeo, Hughes, Ashby, Milligan, Rod Richards. Others were caught up in embarrassing financial liaisons—Michael Mates, Tim Smith, Neil Hamilton. The last two illustrated the new role of lobbyists who could influence Tory back-benchers or even ministers prepared to ask questions in parliament for cash, without publicly declaring an interest.[14] More legitimately, disgraced or deposed Tory ministers slipped effortlessly into business appointments to enrich themselves. David Mellor after resignation promptly landed twelve consultancies, four with defence manufacturers, apart from lucrative commitments on radio as a commentator on football. Norman Lamont followed his departure from the Treasury with a directorship at Rothschilds. Douglas Hurd, without apparent embarrassment, was to work for a bank that had profitable dealings with Serbia during the Bosnian crisis while he was Foreign Secretary. These intimate liaisons of government and business aroused much cynicism. The Nolan Committee on standards in public life which reported in early 1995 called sternly for closer monitoring of interests and for cleaner government all round. A new Commissioner, Sir Gordon Downey, was appointed to oversee MPs' behaviour. He soon found himself busy, first in censuring yet another minister, David Willetts, for trying to influence the Commons privileges committee. There followed Neil Hamilton, another ministerial casualty after he had received favours from an omnipresent Arab businessman, the owner of Harrods, Mohammed el-Fayed (who threatened briefly to become the

---

[14] See David Leigh and Ed Vulliamy, *Sleaze: The Corruption of Parliament* (1997) for an account of the Hamilton affair by two *Guardian* journalists.

father-in-law of Princess Diana). Political standards were tarnished in perhaps even more profound ways. Government ministers such as William Waldegrave and Sir Nicholas Lyell were severely criticized by the Scott report for their behaviour in the Arms for Iraq affair, for secretly changing the guidelines on arms sales and misleading parliament. The Whitehall culture of secrecy was damagingly uncovered here. Soon after, Jonathan Aitken, who had been surprisingly appointed Minister for Defence Procurement by John Major, was exposed in the press in connection with his activities in arms-trafficking in the Middle East. Despite claiming to be armed with 'the sword of truth',[15] he was to lose a libel action against the *Guardian*, and stood publicly condemned as a liar. In 1998 he was prosecuted for perjury. Over all these misdemeanours John Major presided in insouciant fashion, almost suggesting that either he did not know or did not care about the standards of public life under his command.

In all this period, only one aspect of policy looked like a success for the government. This came in the unpromising area of Northern Ireland. John Major had had little connection with the province previously—indeed he had not actually been to Ireland before 1990. In this area, his particular skills of quiet diplomacy appeared to bear fruit. With the Irish prime minister, Albert Reynolds, a kindred soul of pragmatic outlook, he produced the Downing Street Declaration of 15 December 1993.[16] This went a considerable distance in meeting the constitutional grievances of the Nationalists in the North, and placed the entire issue in an Anglo-Irish context. The British government, remarkably, declared that it had 'no selfish or strategic interest in Northern Ireland'. For his part, Albert Reynolds acknowledged that any change in the status of Northern Ireland must require the full consent of the majority there. After covert negotiations with Sinn Fein representatives, the IRA declared a cease-fire at the end of

---

[15] *The Economist*, 15 Apr. 1994.
[16] Tim Pat Coogan, *The Troubles: Ireland's Ordeal 1966–96 and the Search for Peace* (London, 1995), 354.

August 1994. For nearly two years the province knew a rare interlude of tranquillity. A visit by President Clinton to Belfast was claimed as a triumph. But attempts to take the issue further towards a political solution made little headway: the British government imposed conditions about a 'decommissioning' of IRA and other weapons which Sinn Fein could not be expected to accept. Orange and other loyalist marches continued to inflame local opinion. In any case a government which by the start of 1997 was dependent on Ulster Unionist MPs for any kind of Commons majority was not seen as even-handed in its treatment of the two communities. Early in 1996 a huge bomb blast in Canary Wharf in east London followed by another in a shopping centre in the middle of Manchester indicated that the IRA cease-fire was indeed at an end. With a general election pending and the government majority now resting on the support of a few Ulster Unionists, no further progress in Northern Ireland could be expected. John Major in this sphere had shown a remarkable degree of ingenuity and political courage. But the inevitable out-come was that Ireland frustrated his hopes of political recovery, as for so many before him.

In the summer of 1995, harassed beyond reason by Europhobe and other critics in his party, John Major took the remarkable step of resigning as party leader and challenging his critics to oppose him. Unexpectedly, one Cabinet colleague, John Redwood, the Secretary for Wales and a far-right Thatcherite Euro-sceptic, did so. After a short, intense campaign, John Major predictably triumphed. But his victory over Redwood by 218 votes to 89 with another 20 abstaining showed an alarming degree of Tory coolness towards their prime minister. It did not still party discontent; indeed the fact that Major had felt it necessary to challenge his critics at all merely underlined his weakness.

These years, then, were ones of cynicism and indirection as the long period of Tory rule seemed to be entering upon its death agony. Many critics pondered the roots of this national malaise, what the state of the government revealed about the state of the nation. Indeed the mid-1990s rivalled the early 1960s with its flood of literature on the lines of 'what's wrong with Britain?' Two of these critiques bear particular scrutiny. Will Hutton's *The State we're in* (1995) was a fightback by a distinguished Keynesian economic journalist, which caught the mood of the times. He urged an attack on widening social inequality with a revival of communitarianism and a new sense of citizenship and republican solidarity. A complex work of applied economics, Hutton's book headed the best-seller lists for about six months. It sold, remarkably, over 40,000 copies in hardback and almost 150,000 in paperback. Equally striking was *Accountable to None*, written by a Conservative former editor of *The Times*, Simon Jenkins. He launched a fierce attack on the Thatcherite 'nationalization' of Britain, the way in which local government had been emasculated, and privatization and government regulation had led to a massive leviathan of central control by appointed 'quangos' in housing, health, education, the police, and many other areas.[17] Hutton and Jenkins in their different ways reflected the disillusion of middle opinion at the effects of prolonged Conservative rule. Hutton showed how a government committed to reducing expenditure and a more enterprising society had in fact massively raised taxes and undermined much of manufacturing industry. A married man with two children had lost 32.2 per cent of his income to tax and insurance contributions in the last year of Labour government, 1978–9; but in 1995–6 the loss was 35.9 per cent.[18] Government spending as a proportion of GDP had gone up sharply under Mrs Thatcher, rising to 44 per cent in 1994–5, as a result of higher unemployment and resultant social security payments. Simon Jenkins meanwhile argued that a regime dedicated to rolling back the frontiers of the state had introduced centralized control unknown in British history, and in

---

[17] Simon Jenkins, *Accountable to None: The Tory Nationalization of Britain* (London, 1995). Thatcher's approach is called 'democratic centralist', p. 21.

[18] *The Economist*, 29 Jan. 1994; Will Hutton, *The State we're in* (London, 1995), 172 ff. I am grateful to the author for information on his sales.

a grossly undemocratic fashion. For both, the decline of Britain as a community and a polity of free institutions was a result. Their works testified both to the disillusion with Tory rule and the abiding uses of literacy.

Much of the public debate of these years focused on politics; a great deal of it was of a singularly sterile kind. Political theory appeared defunct as an intellectual exercise. The left had produced no major work since Crosland's *Future of Socialism* in 1956, the right none since Michael Oakeshott in 1962. The paradox was that in many ways this was a nation coming fruitfully back to life. Without doubt, Britain remained a profoundly unequal country; all the indices from OECD and others showed how the gulf between classes, income groups, and regions had widened since 1979. Britain in the 1990s showed a great gap between those in work and the 3 million unemployed, between those flourishing on higher incomes and those (often women) stuck on low pay in low-status jobs, between those able to accumulate capital and those who could not. The gap between the highest and lowest wage levels was the greatest since records began. Will Hutton wrote of a 30 : 30 : 40 society with the first two categories forming a disadvantaged or marginalized near-underclass. The position had become markedly worse since 1979, partly through the effect of tax changes with the switch to indirect taxes on consumption and lower taxes on capital, partly through the cut-backs in the equalizing social wage deriving from the welfare state. In 1993, 10 per cent of the population owned no less than 48 per cent of the nation's wealth.

The disparities were there for all to see. In the nation's capital, the traditional roles of the East End and the West End were reversed. Spectacular property development around Wapping in east London by the Docklands Development Corporation, with its monumental tower at Canary Wharf, ecological park, and marina, was juxtaposed against a ragged army of mainly young homeless people, sleeping in doorways in the Strand, Kingsway, or Lincoln's Inn Fields, a phenomenon unknown in the capital since 1945. The government had begun a Rough Sleepers

Initiative, costing £96 million, to move the homeless into hostels or more permanent accommodation, but it had to be extended to meet an enduring need.[19] Tawney's 'Religion of Inequality' had been revived with the policies of the Thatcher era, with serious implications for lifestyle and opportunity. The relative fall in incomes of the poorest individuals and families meant vast discrepancies in health and welfare. For the affluent majority, private medicine flourished, as did the public schools and personal pensions schemes (subject to a *frisson* after the scandals associated with the funds run by the media tycoon Robert Maxwell). For the poor, by contrast, there was a pattern of deteriorating health provision amidst signs of a demoralized NHS. Hospital wards were being closed, and even an entire famous hospital like St Bartholomews in London was scheduled for closure. Diseases like tuberculosis, long thought to have been conquered by modern medicine, returned as a scourge of the vulnerable minority.

Regional and social differentials in lifestyle were very marked: the prevalence of liver disease and heart trouble in a city like Glasgow was evidence of wider cultural contrasts. So, too, was the prevalence of smoking amongst the working-class young, especially girls, despite all the evidence of its damaging effects. Other features of the time added to a sense of social instability. More and more young people were the product of broken homes. In 1993 the divorce rate was seven times what it had been in 1961, and Britain comfortably headed the divorce rate in all the countries of the European Union. 'Partners' became more fashionable than spouses. Middle-class divorce or marriage breakdown became more widespread, partly through the greater professional opportunities open to women, partly through the impact of long working hours on marital relations. The Child Support Agency tried to force absentee fathers to support their children but this led to a huge outcry when others faced impoverishment; many people blamed an uncaring government.

---

[19] *The Economist*, 6 Feb. 1993.

More than a quarter of British households consisted of one person living alone (which meant, among other things, a revival in popularity for the radio to ease the lonely silence). A variety of factors took their toll on stable family life. The impact of hard drugs amongst young people in inner cities was vividly recaptured by the Scottish novelist Irvine Welsh in a disturbing trilogy—*Trainspotting* (1993), written in a strange Edinburgh patois, *The Acid House* (1995), and particularly *Ecstasy* (1996). There was also the growth of long-term youth unemployment in areas such as the Welsh valleys or Merseyside, the rising number of single mothers living off state benefit on bleak housing estates, the abiding difficulties of black (more particularly Afro-Caribbean) people in semi-ghetto areas such as Brixton or Manchester's Moss Side, which all took their toll. At the other end of the demographic scale an ageing population (the number of people over 80 more than doubled between 1961 and 1994 to reach 2.3 million) added to strained public services and diminishing resources. It was an ugly picture of a divided society.

For all that, John Major's Britain had many positive features. Overall, the wealth of most families had steadily risen. Average incomes rose through the 1980s; one factor that enhanced family incomes was the greater range of employment for women, which increased their financial independence, even if much of it was part-time. One curious outcome was that domestic service, long thought of as a relic of Victorian times, showed an increase, with the growing demand for nannies and child-minders to act as substitute mothers in double-income households, along with cleaners and gardeners. Small savers had windfall gains from free shares or bonuses as building societies floated as limited companies; tax-free nest-eggs were easily accumulated in saving schemes like PEPs or TESSAs; supermarkets offered financial services like cheap loans or instant credit. Earlier retirement commonly meant more leisure and comfort for the elderly. For them and others, foreign holidays became the norm, with America as common a destination as the Costa Brava had been thirty years earlier. Travel to the continent was commonplace, especially with the opening of the Channel Tunnel in May 1994 and Eurostar rail services to Paris and Brussels. Almost every family had a car, frequently two or more, with hazardous consequences for a polluted environment. In England in 1993 there were 369 cars per 1,000 people. The average home invariably featured leisure facilities like a video (77 per cent), kitchen conveniences like a microwave (67 per cent), comforts like central heating, and increasingly such working aids as a home computer.[20] In 1997 there were 8 million mobile phones. Surveys of regional trends showed that these were distributed comparatively equally throughout the different parts of the country.

Britain had its ageing urban areas and troubled housing estates: these were unflatteringly depicted in the television series 'EastEnders' and 'Brookside', set in London and Merseyside, which became popular as the warmer neighbourhood values of Salford's 'Coronation Street' looked more dated. The long-running radio series 'The Archers', an 'everyday story of country folk' when first broadcast in 1950, now featured crime, rape, and racialism. But Britain also had areas of spectacular growth, including many previously run-down inner London suburbs. The Docklands development around Canary Wharf did feature distinguished postmodernist buildings designed by architects like Norman Foster and Richard Rogers. At the other end of England, Newcastle upon Tyne became a new metropolis of the north-east. Leeds and Manchester thrived as business and commercial centres; Harvey Nichols struck roots in the former, Selfridges in the latter. Old Yorkshire mill or mining towns like Huddersfield and Barnsley became models of civic contentment. In East Anglia, Norwich was a boom town. There was spectacular development in Cardiff, for which the National Lottery provided a rugby stadium though not an opera house. After the dereliction and racial troubles of the 1980s, cities were manifestly back in favour. Their pubs, now usually freed from brewery

---

[20] *Social Trends*, 1996, 119; *Regional Trends*, 1997, 113.

control, enjoyed a renaissance; their eating-places were more cheerful and cosmopolitan, and sometimes architecturally innovative, as with the 'minimalist' Conran restaurants. Much more provision was offered to the disabled. The growth of out-of-town shopping centres and leisure centres made inroads into rural areas but also added to consumer comfort and convenience. The newer microchip industries meant a rapid growth for areas such as Cambridgeshire and parts of the Thames Valley: smaller railways like the Cotswold Line, once condemned to near oblivion under the Beeching Axe, attracted new demand. One part of Britain showing particular vitality was Scotland. Cultural vigour in the resurgent city of Glasgow (designated European city of culture in 1990) went alongside the devolutionist enthusiasm of the multi-party Constitutional Convention for governmental reform, chaired by Canon Kenyon Wright, as part of a putative Europe of Nations.[21] Elsewhere a university for the Highlands and Islands was projected, while the inspirational fiction of the film *Braveheart* offered Scots everywhere a patriotic kick. The vitality of Scottish life contrasted with the more subdued mood in Wales and some of northern England at this time.

Many aspects of mid-1990s Britain therefore testified to a more cheerful and affluent lifestyle. There was more money, more choice, more fun. One of the government's truly popular initiatives proved to be the National Lottery, where the excitement of possible riches went alongside resources raised for charitable causes, and for a variety of cultural, educational, and social objectives. Money was also set aside for projects to celebrate the millennium in the year 2000. Mass sport remained intensely popular, for observers rather than for performers perhaps, and a legacy to the Thatcherite ethic of enterprise. Football benefited from massive finance from Sky television, with large all-seater stadiums built in previously struggling towns like Derby, Middlesbrough, and Sunderland; immense funds became

---

[21] Chris Harvie, *Scotland and Nationalism* (1994 edn.), 206.

available to buy star foreign players from Europe, Africa or South America. There was success on the field of play, England performing strongly to reach the semifinal of the European Cup at Wembley in 1996 (defeat in a penalty shoot-out by Germany unfortunately coinciding with the xenophobic passions released over mad cow disease). The Premier League, launched in 1993, illustrated the huge gulf between affluent and successful clubs like Manchester United and Arsenal, many of them floated on the stock exchange, and the journeymen teams of lower divisions, often in old industrial towns. The people's game impacted on culture through Nick Hornby's *Fever Pitch* which laid bare the adolescent agony of an Arsenal fan. One positive effect of modern football was its effect on race relations. Outstanding black footballers playing for major clubs provided new role models for the young and for commercial advertisers. Rugby football was also transformed in 1995 with the advent of the professional era, and new money invested by wealthy individuals. The character of the game changed, with English teams like Saracens, Richmond, or Newcastle able to pay for outstanding players, but such bastions of the game as the Welsh teams in old mining communities or Scottish former pupils' clubs unable to compete. Professionalism meant that sport in Britain had resources previously undreamt-of, but also that it was less obviously a popular mass-participatory exercise. Tickets at major events went increasingly to business guests enjoying sponsored corporate hospitality rather than to genuine sports fans. Cricket suffered from being still run by the antiquated, all-male Marylebone Cricket Club. In tennis, Wimbledon ran perhaps the biggest tournament in the world, but only limited funds were released to encourage young people to take the game up. One more heart-warming event was the London Marathon, where tens of thousands of amateur athletes (including the disabled) took part each Easter in a mass public festival to raise immense sums for charitable causes. Here was a rare British sporting event where class was irrelevant.

In the arts and design, Britain remained innovative and distinctive, even if the Heritage department proved a somewhat muted source of support. Architects like Richard Rogers became international celebrities. British novelists remained distinctive, sometimes alarming as with Irvine Welsh, revolutionary as in Martin Amis's *Time's Arrow*, which experimented with narrative in reverse. The most discussed novelist of the day, however, may have been Jane Austen, whose works were much filmed and televised. The controversy that surrounded the work of artists like Damien Hirst (which featured a cow and a sheep pickled in formaldehyde) at least testified to their originality. Several new art galleries opened up, including in seaside towns such as St Ives and Llandudno. Some artistic centres suffered long-term funding troubles: more than one London orchestra and the Royal Opera House in Covent Garden went from one financial crisis to another. Several provincial theatres had to close, although experimental productions flourished, as in the Almeida, tucked away in an Islington side-street. One particularly thriving art form in the 1990s was the British film, whose producers and actors were patronized by international companies or the media. Some of the successful British films of the day followed popular class or imperial stereotypes as the Ealing Studio comedies had done in the late 1940s. *Four Weddings and a Funeral*, made by Channel Four television, replayed old idioms of upper-class whimsy which went down very well in America; *The Madness of King George* was a classic historical drama; *The English Patient* chronicled the tragic love-affair of a wealthy woman on a British archaeological survey in the desert before and during the war; Kenneth Branagh's *Hamlet* renewed the ageless appeal of Shakespeare. But other films were startling in their originality. *Trainspotting* was a powerful and disturbing analysis of youthful drug culture in the slums of Edinburgh, *Secrets and Lies* offered a subtle study of lower middle-class suburban anomie, while *The Full Monty* (1997) was the bracing odyssey of six unemployed steelworkers in Sheffield who turned their talents to striptease. A Welsh-language film, *Hedd Wyn*, a study of a Welsh bard killed during the First World War, was nominated for the Cannes film festival awards. It was another sign of Celtic renewal, along with the successful Gaelic television channel in Scotland and S4C in Wales.

With rising youth affluence, pop culture remained vigorous and thriving as in no other country. Its icons varied from Oasis, a gruff working-class Mancunian replay of the Liverpudlian Beatles, to the five (later four) multi-ethnic Spice Girls, who made much of 'girl power' and of Union flag-waving patriotism. A feature of the pop scene was its roots in the Celtic nations, such as the Irish band Boyzone, or the Welsh-speaking Catatonia. More generally, the emergence of a rekindled British nationalism in popular art, music, and design, paralleled in some ways the English nationalism of the Euro-sceptics and defenders of the Union. In music, clothing, and design, London appeared to hark back to the cultural heyday of the 'swinging sixties'. There was journalistic talk (at first encouraged by the government) of 'cool Britannia', of British style conquering western Europe markets even in France, and a mood of national self-confidence fostering a distinctively British brand of 'chic' and 'retrochic'. Despite the exchange problems of a stronger pound, foreign tourists flooded in.

It should have been a happy country, perhaps, freed from past traumas of war or mass unemployment. But in fact the prevailing mood at this period was one of discontent. Opinion polls showed an abiding pessimism even if other nations seemed no more attractive and emigration rates were low. City dwellers were fearful of increasing burglaries or muggings. Country folk complained of the varied threats to their way of life from French farmers, speculative builders, or hunt saboteurs (most people now wanted fox-hunting abolished). A more prosperous nation mostly in full employment positively refused to 'feel good' simply because the government told it to. The current budget deficit was caused in some measure by the fall of tax receipts as wary consumers, lacking in confidence, refused to spend or consume. In part, this disgruntlement was a reflection of the dissatisfaction generated by John Major's government and the crumbling ethic of the Tory Party. But there was a wider sense of decay within long-established institutions. Well-publicized sleaze cases undermined faith in the governmental processes. The Maxwell pensions scandal and problems in Lloyd's insurance shook confidence in the City, for all its success as a world financial centre. There was evidence of the police engaging in corruption or falsifying evidence, as in the case of the wrongly convicted Birmingham Six. Universities lost their élitist reputation after former polytechnics were accorded university status, but also some of their claim to excellence as government insisted that their major role was 'wealth creation'. The abiding feature of the growth of participation in higher education was expansion on the cheap, with growing student indebtedness and inadequate maintenance of fabric.

The Church of England was an institution under particular pressure, trying desperately to modernize its appeal, but still failing to establish a clearly defined role in society. Under Archbishop George Carey, it offered courageous critiques of government policy on such issues as poverty or race, but it remained marginalized. Bruising internal battles over women clergy or the admission of homosexual priests did not add to its sense of dignity or self-confidence. Appealing mainly to the elderly, it was in no realistic sense a national church. A few called for its disestablishment along the lines of the Welsh back in 1920. Even the Roman Catholic Church, with its strongly Irish clientele, found the going difficult, with its dated views on issues such as divorce, contraception, or abortion. The Nonconformist conscience was a thing of the past. In Yorkshire and Wales, historic chapels rotted away, their denominations too impoverished to find the resources to knock them down. Christianity as a body of doctrine seemed to be eroding and lacking in self-confidence.

Above all else, the monarchy, for long veiled from public controversy, became a weathervane for popular discontent with tradition and institutional orthodoxies. In part, this was because of the aberrant behaviour of its members. The long-running difficulties of three of the Queen's four children, all of whom became divorced, undermined confidence in the institution as a focus of family values. The bitter public separation and later divorce of Charles, Prince of Wales, and Diana, his glamorous but distinctly wayward wife, with rival authorized biographies launched, further diminished public esteem, even if Diana, part-victim, part-client of the paparazzi, launched a thousand tabloids like a latter-day Helen of Troy. Only the aged Queen Mother, now in her nineties, remained unquestionably popular with the general public. But there were wider doubts about the point of a monarchy and its ability to relate to a mass democracy. The Queen seemed unable to adapt her style, and the public relations of the royal family were lamentable. The Christmas broadcasts were widely derided although a proposal that they be scrapped met with implacable opposition; the turn to public funds when part of Windsor Castle was burnt down in 1992 was badly received, and Buckingham Palace had to be opened to tourists to raise money.[22] The Queen spoke of an *annus horribilis* in 1992, but truly it was only one of many such. Diana's mainten-ance of a kind of alternative, media-centred, populist court of her own after her divorce added to the sense of strain. Her public embrace (often literally so) of minority groups such as Aids sufferers, the Muslim community, and the homeless in Centre-point made her seem more responsive to contemporary needs than the cocooned House of Windsor. Her nervy, brittle persona as a beautiful but unhappy single mother, breaking up marriages and suffering from eating disorders, seemed to enhance her appeal amongst the young, women, and ethnic minorities. Public debate about the point of the monarchy acquired a force unknown since the 1870s, with the BBC now far removed from the old Reithian air of awed deference. However, open advocacy of a republic (as in Australia) did not make headway if only for lack of any clear view of an alternative system or the choice of president. Desperate attempts were made to modernize. The Queen began to pay income tax; some details of her vast wealth

[22] Ben Pimlott, *The Queen* (London, 1996), 558–62.

were made known; royal visits were made marginally less stilted; more sensitive press advisers were used. But the debate on the monarchy dragged on right up to the 1997 general election. There were doubts expressed as to whether Prince Charles, already middle-aged as his mother lived on into her seventies, would ever succeed at all. This testified to a wider sense of malaise with public institutions—but also a fierce public determination to challenge and to question. There was talk of an aggressive English nationalism emerging in the wake of debate over Europe and over devolution at home, to fight for Queen, country, and the pound sterling. But the new questions asked of the monarchy suggested a more iconoclastic kind of patriotism, an anxiety to preserve historic badges of identity, but to ensure also that they were relevant and alive.

With all these discontents, 1990s Britain looked for new inspiration. This could only come from within the traditional public culture. In practice this meant a reformed and modernized Labour Party. Despite the disappointments of the 1992 general election, much progress had been made in the nine years of Neil Kinnock's leadership to make the party credible and electable once more. Labour had spanned the whole odyssey of post-1945 Britain. It had launched its own social democratic utopia in the Attlee years; it had sought to promote modernization and personal liberation in the 1960s; it had lapsed into atavistic class-consciousness and traditional leftism in the turbulent 1970s. It had moved from hegemony to internecine decay. The advent of the SDP in the 1980s had almost extinguished it entirely. But if new leadership and values were to be found for a troubled society, there was no viable source for it other than an updated Labour Party.

Under the leadership of John Smith from 1992, progress was made in modernizing and redefining the party, building on the achievement of Neil Kinnock in moving his party to the centre ground and expelling the extremists of Militant Tendency. The party was in good heart, with the growing disarray of the Tories and a sense that, with the problems of the British economy, 1992 might not have been a bad election to lose. Smith was a more cautious, less confrontational leader than Kinnock, but he too was a modernizer, anxious to change his party's image. The transformation of Labour policies went on apace in 1993–4. The shadow chancellor, Gordon Brown, emphasized that Labour no longer aimed at higher public expenditure, taxing the better-off or the broad principle of state planning. Much effort was devoted to improving Labour's relations with the CBI; several influential figures in the business world announced their Labour sympathies. The shadow home secretary, Tony Blair, strove to change an impression of Labour being anti-police or soft on law and order issues. Labour, he declared, in a pregnant if obscure phrase, would be 'tough on crime, tough on the causes of crime'. Another Labour figure, Jack Straw, openly campaigned for the abolition of Clause Four. Few believed that nationalization played much part in Labour's thinking any longer.

John Smith himself concentrated on internal democracy, and in particular removing the hold of the unions over party decision-making. No longer would a 'social contract' dictate Labour's approach to power. He came into conflict with the TUC leaders in the summer of 1993 in his efforts to promote 'One Man, One Vote', which meant creating individual trade unionists as party members and ending the trade union block vote at the party conference.[23] He managed to get his way at the TUC and then, very narrowly, at the party conference in October. His margin of victory was only 0.2 per cent but it was enough. No longer could it be claimed that Labour was the sectional creature of the unions rather than an unfettered party representative of the nation as a whole. Beyond that, Smith seemed unwilling to go. He seemed happy to present himself as a consensual figure, well able to work harmoniously with former leftists such as Margaret Beckett, John Prescott, and Michael Meacher. With Labour over 20 points ahead in the opinion polls in the spring of 1994, a return to

---

[23] Andy McSmith, *John Smith* (London, 1994), 294 ff.

power seemed well within its grasp. Then John Smith suddenly died of a heart attack on 12 May, leaving his party's fortunes again in the melting-pot.

In fact, his death led to a far more dramatic period of change. Its catalyst was the new Labour leader, the 42-year-old Tony Blair.[24] He managed to leapfrog over his senior rival, Gordon Brown, in running for the leadership, showing a good deal of ruthlessness thereby. He also weaned away from Brown that subtle party strategist, Peter Mandelson, in effect his campaign manager and image-maker. Blair more than any other Labour leader came without obvious roots in the party; not for him Arthur Henderson's sentimental attachment to 'this great movement of ours'. Indeed his ideological inspiration, if any, came not from Britain at all but from the reformist politics of Australia conjoined with a spiritual attachment to Christian meta-physics. He came from neither the philanthropic social background of Attlee or Gaitskell, the wartime technocracy of Wilson, the union background of Callaghan, the radical journalism of Foot, the leftist student politics of Kinnock, nor the Scottish socialism of Smith. On the contrary, he emerged via an affluent home in which his father was a card-carrying Tory, Fettes public school, and St John's College, Oxford, and a career at the bar. As a student his interests veered towards rock music rather than political commitment. But his very freshness and air of youthful vitality, in a campaign in which all candidates showed a mood of reason and comradeship, were in themselves massive virtues. It soon became clear that in all wings of the movement he had immense support. In the electoral college on 21 July (the last such election to be fought via that cumbersome mechanism), Blair won an easy victory with 57 per cent of the vote to John Prescott's 24 per cent and Margaret Beckett's 18.9 per cent. Blair was victorious everywhere, with 60 per cent of the MPs' vote, 58 per cent of the party membership, and 52.3 per cent of the

[24] See John Rentoul, *Tony Blair* (London, 1995) and Jon Sopel, *Tony Blair, the Modernizer* (London, 1995).

union vote. It was in every sense a dramatic transformation for so new a party. Blair went on to speak not of Labour but of 'New Labour', leading a 'New Britain' with patriotism and compassion. Confronted with a crumbling Tory government constantly on the point of disintegration, Labour responded by ditching Keir Hardie's cloth cap and discreetly burying socialism in our time.

Over the next few years, the ascendancy of Tony Blair was the key to British politics. Long before the general election of 1 May 1997, he was regarded by the media, the Civil Service, and the general public at home and abroad as a leader in waiting. He built up a moral ascendancy as Opposition leader without parallel in British history. He imposed himself in a spectacular first speech as leader at the Brighton party conference in October 1994, preaching the gospel of ecumenism, moderation, and patriotism. Britain, he declared, was not only a great historic nation, but also a young country. It was Labour's mission to recapture that youth. The language was evangelistic and imprecise (the word 'new' appeared thirty-seven times), but it registered powerfully with the electorate, especially those voters in southern or 'middle' England with no previous attachment to the Labour Party. Over half the electors were middle-class in 'democracy's second age'. In the House and in the country, it seemed hard for Blair's opponents to damage him. He made no mistakes, his personal rectitude was beyond question, and his generalized appeal to 'values' rather than precise policies made it difficult to pin him down. The mood of politics and of the nation was suddenly transformed. After years of disgruntlement, from 1995 onwards a new mood of self-confidence was abroad in the land.

In three main respects, Tony Blair imposed himself on Labour in quite new ways. First, there was a dramatic emphasis on his personal leadership, this in a party which had been apprehensive of overmighty leaders since the days of the alleged 'treachery' of Ramsay MacDonald back in 1931. He built up a total ascendancy over the hybrid ranks of the Labour movement, notably by appealing directly to a growing party membership over the heads of party activists. He did this most dramatically in calling for the scrapping of Clause Four; this old totem, which had defeated Gaitskell before him back in 1959, was overwhelmingly rejected in a national party ballot in the spring of 1995 as an irrelevant survival from Old Labour days. He cut himself free from any sense of dependence on the trade unions, who became increasingly marginalized. Through his personal machine, headed by Peter Mandelson as strategist and Alastair Campbell as a combative press officer, the image of the leader swamped possible rivals in the shadow Cabinet. Any dissent therein, for instance when Clare Short appeared to make sympathetic noises about legalizing cannabis, was ruthlessly slapped down. No dissident would be allowed to stray 'off message'. Over time, Blair's power as leader extended itself to dominance over the National Executive and the annual party conference. No longer could they threaten the leader, as they had once harassed Gaitskell, Wilson, or Callaghan. Their powers were strictly circumscribed by a leader who seemed more presidential than a product of the more collegial British political style. Blair himself made a virtue of his commanding role. He scored heavily in the Commons when he told John Major, labouring under internal disputes over Europe and other issues, 'You follow your party, I lead mine.'

Secondly, Blair and his entourage of advisers revolutionized the techniques of politics. Their methods reflected a global political context, and the new force of information technology. A party which had once favoured the lumbering amateurism of Transport House, called by Harold Wilson 'a penny-farthing in the jet age', now emerged as ultra-modern. It used the full range of sophisticated high technology from its control centre in Millbank. The primeval Labour carthorse now surfed the Internet. It followed shifts in voter opinion through the sophisticated use of focus groups rather than the traditional processes of constituency-based party democracy. It conveyed its edicts through a layer of message-makers and spin doctors who controlled the media and in effect themselves made the news. The political scientist David Butler felt it to be the greatest change in British politics since the advent of television during the 1959 election.[25] The modernizing impact then had been nation-wide: now it was global. And a Labour Party, desperate for power, dazzled by the charisma of its young leader, accepted it all without demur. The occasional grumble from a union leader seemed irrelevant, an echo of a dying era.

Finally, the Blair era saw Labour's policy transformed in every detail.[26] All the traditional policies—public ownership, state planning, higher public spending, redistributive direct taxation, universalized welfare benefits, full employment, active regional policies, egalitarian policies in education, sociological approaches to law and order—were all ruthlessly jettisoned. Instead there emerged a party which proclaimed its closeness to business and the CBI, which said that it had no intention of exceeding Tory spending programmes or raising higher taxes in the lifetime of the next parliament, which spoke of toughness on crime, and kept its distance from the trade unions to the point of invisibility. The unions played virtually no part in Labour's pre-election campaigns, which served to confirm their weakness since the suicidal frenzy of the 'winter of discontent' in 1979. From a peak of nearly 13 million members, they now claimed only 6.75 million, and those were mostly unmilitant. Renewed dock troubles in Liverpool remained strictly local. Labour's priorities were few and undoctrinaire; no far-left 'suicide note' this time, not even the damaging shadow budget put forward by John Smith in 1992. Its most powerful notes were promises to rebuild the National Health Service and to promote 'Education, education, education.'

The models for Labour revisionism in the 1950s had been the Bad Godesberg programme of the German Social Democrats, or perhaps the amalgam of socialism and Keynesianism practised by

[25] David Butler, R. B. McCallum memorial lecture, delivered at Oxford, Nov. 1997.
[26] See Brian Brivati and Tim Bale, *New Labour in Power* (London, 1997).

the Swedish government. Yet Gaitskell and Crosland still considered themselves socialists and felt close to the historic roots of
the party; Gaitskell himself cherished his early experiences with
the Workers' Educational Association amongst the Nottinghamshire miners, while Crosland deferred to the fishermen of
Grimsby. With Tony Blair it was goodbye to all that. He spoke
not of the left, but of the centre-left, or (more puzzling) of 'the
radical centre'. He was happy to put out feelers to the Liberals
and to welcome collaboration with Roy Jenkins and others who
had once defected to the Social Democratic Party. He employed
in his Policy Unit young men like David Miliband who had close
connections with inter-party bodies such as Charter 88 or the
Demos group. In his speeches, including one notionally to celebrate the fiftieth anniverary of the 1945 Attlee government, Blair
seemed consciously to keep his distance from the state intervention and egalitarianism of the past: the National Health Service
seemed almost his only point of contact with the pioneers of
1945. In that respect only, Nye Bevan appeared a more sympathetic figure than Herbert Morrison, Labour's old orchestrator
and also the grandfather of Peter Mandelson.

Blair's rhetoric made a point of being inclusive. Where earlier
Labour leaders had paid their meed of praise to the founding
fathers, from the Tolpuddle Martyrs to Keir Hardie, Blair
declared that Lloyd George, Keynes, and Beveridge were
amongst his heroes, too. He looked back not to an exclusive
socialist pantheon but to a kind of rainbow coalition on the lines
of the Progressive Alliance of Liberal and Labour under Asquith
in 1908–14. Even Conservatives were not ruled out by Blair's
inclusive style. He showed no embarrassment in establishing
relations with the media tycoon Rupert Murdoch, whose *Sun*
had wrecked Labour hopes in 1987 and 1992. Addressing Murdoch's empire in Australia in early 1995 he declared that Labour
in the previous period had simply been unelectable. More startling still, he frequently spoke with respect of the commitment and
patriotism of Mrs Thatcher. Indeed his own view of the promotion of enterprise and curbing back the restrictive powers of

central government seemed little different from hers. It was no surprise that, soon after he became Prime Minister in May 1997, he welcomed Mrs Thatcher to Downing Street, whereas he made little effort to approach his predecessor, Lord Callaghan, the epitome of the union alliance and the corporatism of Old Labour. A striking volume, part-authored by Peter Mandelson, *The Blair Revolution* (1996) made a point of discrediting the records of the Labour governments of 1964–70 and especially of 1974–9.[27] They allegedly belonged to the failed past. Wherever New Labour began, it would never start from there.

The model for the Blairite project was hard to define. When expressed in a particular formulation such as the 'stakeholder society', or the 'Third Way' it seemed lacking in much precision. If anything, Blair's New Labour was an amalgam of Thatcherite economics with Lib-Lab social compassion. It was allied to admiration for Australian 'market socialism' or even the ambivalent conservative/liberalism of President Clinton, which carried him to victory in the American election of 1992. It was noticeable that whereas Major and Clinton had had a distant relationship (partly because the Conservatives gave some assistance to the Bush campaign in 1992), Blair appeared wholly at ease in a transatlantic setting. In a world of elderly men in grey suits, he strolled around in blue jeans and used Americanized vocabulary. On the other hand, he was also broadly pro-European and was the first party leader to speak passable French. Like other Labour leaders, he holidayed in the Dordogne and Tuscany; Mrs Thatcher had never seemed to take holidays anywhere. On all fronts, therefore, Blair dominated public debate. He galvanized an old country with the cult of the new.

In March 1997, a weary, battered John Major called a general election for 1 May. He had delayed the election until the last possible moment, so desperate had his position been in the opinion polls. He had also given himself the dubious benefit of

[27] Peter Mandelson and Roger Liddle, *The Blair Revolution* (London, 1996).

an unusually long election campaign, presumably in the hope
that Blair would somehow make a mistake. In fact, the campaign
and the outcome were wholly predictable. The tidal wave of anti-
Conservative emotion, suppressed in the 1992 general election,
but released in full flood after Black Wednesday on 16 September
1992, swept all before it. The election campaign was dull, the
Conservative machine inept and party workers in the constituency depressed if they were not actually voting with their feet.
But even had the Conservatives had the most streamlined and
sophisticated of campaigns and a party chairman more charismatic than the dour Ulsterman Brian Mawhinney, nothing could
have saved them from a débâcle. One traditional source of help
was denied them this time. For once, the newspaper press overwhelmingly favoured Labour. Even Rupert Murdoch's *Sun*
declared in Blair's favour. Labour forgot its attacks on monopoly
control of the media by press empires. Evidently Blair's peace
mission to the Antipodes had not been without effect.

But, however predictable from the evidence of the polls, the
results of the general election were astonishing. The Conservatives suffered the worst defeat in their history, worse than 1945
or 1906, indeed the worst since the Duke of Wellington had led
his party to a political Waterloo after the 1832 Reform Act. Like
the Duke, they might indeed complain, 'Damn democracy'.
There was a 10.9 per cent swing to Labour. It ended up with
419 seats as against the Conservatives' 165, while the Liberals
with 46 seats scored their best performance since the days of
Lloyd George, the Scots and Welsh Nationalists netting 10
between them. Five Cabinet ministers were defeated, among
them the Foreign Secretary, Malcolm Rifkind, and the Defence
Secretary, Michael Portillo. The Conservatives did worst in
southern England, which had swung to them most heavily
in the Thatcher years. There were swings of up to 20 per cent
in some London suburbs, including Finchley, the former seat of
Mrs Thatcher won by a Dutch university lecturer, and Enfield
West, the seat of the right-wing Euro-sceptic Michael Portillo,
defeated by a young acknowledged homosexual, which caused a

particular sensation. The Tories were virtually driven out of the cities. They lost over 60 seats in London, and ended up with none in Birmingham, Liverpool, Manchester, Leeds, or Sheffield. All the new towns from Milton Keynes to Crawley went strongly Labour. In the Celtic fringe the Tories' performance was calamitous; they could not win a single seat in either Scotland or Wales. For the moment, the Conservatives, the party of the nation and the Union, were forced back into a few redoubts in the English countryside and wealthier suburbs. The results did not show enormous passion for Labour, whose poll of 44.4 per cent was lower than in 1945–66; the turn-out of 71.4 per cent was the lowest since the war. The 1997 election, said the Nuffield survey, 'attracted less interest than any other in living memory'.[28] Instead, there was a massive determination to drive out the Tories. There was much evidence of tactical voting, with the Liberals benefiting in seats such as Harrogate, Winchester, or Oxford West from anti-Tory Labour votes. Euro-scepticism was not helpful to the Conservative cause; xenophobic attempts during the campaign to depict Tony Blair as a puppet of Helmut Kohl were quite unsuccessful, while all the 547 candidates of the far-right Referendum Party under Sir James Goldsmith were heavily defeated. One factor that perhaps did the Conservatives particular harm was the issue of 'sleaze': cases of financial malpractice dogged them during much of the campaign. In a symbolic contest in Tatton in affluent Cheshire, Neil Hamilton, whose 'cash for questions' and stays at the Paris Ritz had dragged him and his party into disrepute, was heavily defeated, by an independent candidate, Martin Bell. He was a television news reporter who ran on an anti-corruption ticket with Labour and Liberal support and sported a white suit as a symbol of purity.

The seismic nature of the shift in the electoral landscape astonished observers. A political scientist on television shouted excitedly that it was not so much a landslide as an asteroid hitting

[28] David Butler and Dennis Kavanagh, *The British General Election of 1997*, 299.

the planet. It was a victory for a distinctly bourgeoisified Labour Party, with far fewer working-class or union members than before. But there was innovation of another kind, almost equally startling. Of the 419 Labour members, 101 were women, all middle-class, many remarkably young. A total of 120 women MPs in all, almost three times the previous tally, testified to a gender revolution that had already permeated many professions but had yet to manifest itself in the mother of parliaments. The tabloid press contented itself with celebrating the advent of 'Blair's Babes'. Feminist writers, who had lost some *élan* since the heady liberationist days of the 1970s were modestly triumphant.

The new Labour hegemony, initially more overwhelming than either the Labour landslide of 1945 or Mrs Thatcher's ascendancy after 1979, would clearly provide the parameters for British society at the dawn of a new millennium. What the early phase of that government brought was a transition that, compared with all previous Labour administrations, was trouble-free. Blair started with a bustling 'hundred days' reminiscent of Franklin D. Roosevelt in 1933, but at a pace that remained disciplined. Through good fortune and the economic legacy of Kenneth Clarke, here was the first ever Labour government in history to enter office with no economic crisis in sight, a happy outcome denied its precedessors in 1929, 1945, 1964, or 1974. Average earnings were growing at 4.75 per cent annually, yet there was a steady, non-inflationary growth, which Gordon Brown clearly intended to sustain with prudent fiscal management. Stock market prices rose sharply; after Brown's budget in March 1998 the FTSE index (standing at 4300 in May 1997) climbed to over 6100 points. Nor had Labour lumbered itself with a Department of Economic Affairs to rival the Treasury as it had in 1964. One shrewd initial move was for the Bank of England to be given independence in the determining of interest rates. On the other hand, the financial regulation of banks was taken away from the Bank and placed with the Securities and Investment Board. In effect, the Bank's role was confined to managing monetary policy and ensuring financial stability. The Chancellor's first budget in July 1997 was far removed from old 'tax and spend' policies of former Labour governments, although a £5.2 billion windfall tax on privatized utilities to assist in retraining and combating youth unemployment was a novelty.[29]

The economy continued to perform with remarkable strength throughout the remaining period of the Blair government down to 2001. Gordon Brown presided over a prolonged period of economic stability, making him perhaps the most successful Chancellor of the Exchequer since the war. He retained strict controls over expenditure and kept to his pre-election promise not to increase personal taxation. Employment rose steadily while inflation remained comfortably below the government's own public target of 2.5 per cent. The public debt was rapidly eroded. On the other hand, increasing budgetary surpluses, allied to his own commitment to 'entrepreneurial welfarism', enabled Brown in his budgets in 2000 and 2001 to increase investment substantially in state education and the National Health Service, and address family and child poverty. He was, however, criticized for tardiness in raising pensions for Britain's increasingly large elderly population. The major concern with Labour's economic policy, though, lay in the continuing high value of the pound which shackled exports to Europe particularly. It was this uncompetitive value of sterling that was said to be a fundamental cause of lay-offs in the car industry, notably at Vauxhalls in Luton, and a serious loss of jobs in the steel industry by the Corus company in south-east and north-east Wales and in the north-east of England announced in February 2001. These would test Tony Blair's declared intent to 'restore the capacity of the state'.

In foreign policy Britain was able to take more of a lead, with Robin Cook as Foreign Secretary showing more enthusiasm for involvement in Europe than the Conservatives had done in

[29] *Guardian*, 3 July 1997.

eighteen years. On the other hand, the government's European stance was fundamentally a cautious one, to the disappointment of some observers. Britain confirmed that it would not seek to join the European single currency in January 1999, even though it met nearly all the convergence criteria. Britain's six-month presidency of the EU in January was accompanied by rhetoric about a 'people's Europe', but since the main objective of the EU was to prepare for the single currency from which Britain had excluded itself, the country still appeared isolated from its Continental partners. The British presidency turned out to be unremarkable. The most natural thrust of Labour foreign policy was still largely transatlantic as it had been since the days of Ernest Bevin. When President Clinton threatened bombing raids on Iraq in February 1998 in reprisal for Saddam Hussein's refusal to allow UN inspectors to examine biological and other weapons sites in his country, Britain was the one country to show enthusiastic support. British warplanes were dispatched to the Persian Gulf as under the Conservatives in 1991, but this time they were not used. Tony Blair himself sought to play an active role in Europe. He worked closely with the new German Social Democratic Chancellor, Gerhard Schröder, in pressing the model of a free-market system, and in trying to dispel the legacy of Delors-style *dirigisme*. The remarkable zeal of Britain's Labour government for deregulated free-market capitalism was, however, resisted by other European leaders, especially the French socialist prime minister, Lionel Jospin. A more fruitful area for British involvement turned out to be pressure for a collective European defence force where British and French views were closer. Britain also pushed hard for the enlargement of the European Union and claimed to be well satisfied with the outcome of the heads of government conference at Nice in December 2000. While William Hague and the Conservatives moved consistently towards a negative, even hostile, approach to the entire European project, so that pro-European figures like Clarke and Heseltine became completely marginalized, Britain's Labour government appeared to be the most sympathetic towards Europe since that of Edward Heath thirty years before.

On the other hand, the government's approach towards joining the 'Euro', the new European currency created in 1999 which Britain refused to adopt in the first instance, was hesitant. It still revealed much of the old ambivalence and caution towards the European relationship typical of so much of British history since 1945. Blair announced that Britain would eventually hold a referendum on whether to join the EMU, within two years after the next general election. British public opinion appeared to be consistently hostile to the whole idea of the Euro and saw it as a precursor of a European 'superstate', though this was perhaps not surprising since Blair, Brown and other ministers declined to argue the case for it. Instead they declared that adopting the Euro should be determined by 'five tests' for the British economy. Four of them seemed largely subjective; only the need for sustained convergence of the British and European economies was critical. Up to the 2001 general election, Eurosceptics made much of the running in debate while Blair reserved his most important statements on European policy for continental locations such as Aachen, Ghent or Warsaw. Not until the issue of Britain's membership of the European monetary system was resolved would overseas policy shed the indirection so frequently shown in the years since 1945.

In most respects, New Labour appeared moderate if not positively conservative, anxious not to offend business interests or middle-class home-owners and savers in southern England. While £3 billion was taken from the contingency reserves to assist health and education (Barts Hospital was to be saved), overall public spending was strictly controlled. The welfare budget was to be pruned: the new message was 'welfare to work', supply-side training in place of managed demand. When this resulted in reduced benefits for such social victims as single mothers and perhaps the disabled, there was the first sign of rebellion from Labour idealists in the constituencies. 'Welfare to work' had a stern transatlantic ring to it, as had 'zero tolerance' as a guide to Labour's attitude to street beggars and other social victims. Truly this was the 'hard edge' of New Labour's view of community. Again, the pattern of financial caution in education led to university students being charged for tuition fees for the first time in British history and maintenance grants being abolished. Labour was stealing the Conservatives' clothes, just as had happened in reverse in the Butskellite phase in the 1950s.

However, while cautious over public spending and over committing itself to significant policies of redistribution of the kind embraced by Labour in the past, the Blair government did show signs of traditional social concern.[30] In particular, it dealt with key aspects of poverty, brought now on to centre-stage of public debate, albeit under the somewhat ambiguous heading of 'social exclusion'. The problem of low pay was addressed in the government's embracing the European Social Chapter, including a range of rights for individual workers and the important commitment to a national minimum wage. This last, however, was received by the unions with muted gratitude since the initial wage level was only £3.60 an hour, with a level of £3.00 for young people aged between 18–21, in each case well below the rates sought by the TUC. Still, the minimum wage, said by the Conservatives and the CBI before the election to be unaffordable and inflationary, was generally welcomed. The hourly rate was raised to £4.10 in March 2001. The Working Families Tax Credit, was another important contribution to relieving poverty by guaranteeing any family with a full-time worker payment of £214 per week. A New Deal programme for training in skills made some progress in addressing another basic cause of deprivation, namely long-term unemployment amongst young people, while child poverty was significantly reduced, notably through the Children's Tax Credit. The Child Poverty Action Group's 'audit

---

[30] See *Political Quarterly*, 72, No. 1 (2001), special issue, 'Auditing New Labour'.

of deprivation' in February 2001 reported that the number of children in poverty had fallen by 1.2m. since May 1997.

Even so, the government's own inquiries showed how deep-rooted social and economic inequality remained in Britain. Indeed, in some key respects, the disparities between classes and regions (including perhaps a much-debated 'north–south divide') remained intractable in the four years that followed the 1997 general election. Amongst young women, for instance, while an ever growing proportion went on to some form of higher education or professional training, the daughters of unskilled parents were nine times more likely to end up as teenage mothers with no pay and no job. The government's approach placed a reliance on work and individual effort in reducing poverty, but the evidence suggested that much more effort was still required, including a greater commitment to the role of the state for egalitarian and social purposes.

In Northern Ireland, the removal of the Unionists as a prop to an ailing government necessarily meant some progress. A revived 'peace process' instituted by the first woman Irish Secretary, Dr Mo Mowlam, saw Sinn Fein, Loyalist, and government representatives (from Dublin as well as London) sitting around the same table in Belfast for the first time since 1921. Repeated violent acts in the province, bombings and murders, by both Loyalist and IRA extremists meant that progress towards any kind of political agreement was erratic. However on Good Friday, April 1998, the various parties did, remarkably, achieve agreement on a document drawn up by the former US senator George Mitchell. This included a 108-member elected assembly for Ulster on the model of that proposed for Scotland; a North–South ministerial council dealing with cross-border security and other issues; and a British–Irish Council of the Isles to regulate relations between the Republic and the various nations of Great Britain. The Republic undertook to remove any territorial claim to the North from its constitution. It was the closest that Northern Ireland had been to any kind of consensus since the Sunning-dale agreement negotiated by the Heath government in 1973, indeed the closest since the partition in 1922. Among other things, it represented a considerable diplomatic achievement for Tony Blair who took charge of negotiations at a critical stage. Selling it to the hard men, Loyalist and Nationalist, on the streets of Belfast and Derry remained a massive challenge to statesmanship in the years ahead. However, the endorsement of the settlement by a 71.12 per cent majority in a referendum in Northern Ireland in May was a hopeful portent.

But the sectarian and tribal divisions of Ulster remained as deep-rooted as ever. Large caches of weapons remained in the hands of the IRA and of various loyalist groups, and there were many violent incidents. The progress of the new Northern Ireland Assembly was, therefore, distinctly chequered. The elections for the new assembly in June 1998 saw strong votes (18% first preference votes) cast for the more extreme parties, Sinn Fein and the Democratic Unionists, as against the more centrist official Unionists and the SDLP. Although a new administration for the devolved province began to take shape in July 1998 with the Unionist leader David Trimble elected as first minister, the omens remained unpromising. The following month there was a huge bomb explosion at Omagh that killed 29 people and injured scores of others, planted by a splinter group, the so-called 'Real IRA' who rejected any settlement. The unwillingness of the IRA to hand in or 'decommission' any of its arms, as called for under the Belfast Agreement, led to a total impasse and after a few weeks the new Northern Irish Assembly was suspended.

After tense negotiations, with the further involvement of Senator George Mitchell, the assembly began its life again in November 1999 under a strange, scarcely credible, executive including three official Unionists, two Democratic Unionists, three SDLP and even two Sinn Fein, one of them being the former terrorist, Martin McGuinness. But the issue of arms decommissioning remained in deadlock and in February 2000 the new Irish Secretary, Peter Mandelson, had to suspend the assembly a second time. Whereas his predecessor, Mo Mowlam, had been thought too favourable to the Nationalists, Mandelson was attacked for supposedly leaning towards the Unionists. In May 2000, powers were restored to the Assembly and it resumed operations a second time. However, the credibility of the devolved administration in Belfast remained doubtful. David Trimble found his authority as Unionist leader endlessly challenged. The overhaul of the security forces led to immense argument. The abolition of the old Royal Ulster Constabulary, as proposed by the Patten report, infuriated almost all Unionist Protestants. On the other hand, Sinn Fein and other Nationalists attacked the British government for preventing a more fundamental reform. In the spring of 2001, the claim that something called 'a peace process' was still in being and that the devolved executive of the new Assembly actually functioned as a credible government was in doubt. The Blair government, like all its predecessors over the decades, had yet to make a breakthrough here. The resignation on personal grounds of Peter Mandelson as Irish secretary in January 2001 added uncertainty, as did official Unionist losses in the general election five months later.

However, in mainland Britain, New Labour, cautious in so many respects, proved to be remarkably adventurous in one key area, which indeed chimed in with devolution in Northern Ireland. This concerned constitutional reform, which had provoked much debate from Charter 88 and other bodies since the later 1980s. Some of Labour's reforms took time to finalize. A distinctly cautious Freedom of Information Act did not pass through parliament until the end of 2000. Reform of the House of Lords proved to be a massive quagmire. A curiously British compromise was reached in late 1999 under which all save 92 of the 650-plus hereditary peers (elected from amongst their own number) were removed from the upper house for ever. However, the ultimate form of a reformed House of Lords, whether it would indeed contain an elective element as cautiously proposed by the Wakeham committee, was left in limbo until after the next general election. Other areas, however, were more positively addressed. Thus the incorporation of the European corpus of human rights into British law was a potentially massive

transformation which would reshape the operations of government. The resultant Human Rights Act handed over to the judges
massive powers in relating British legislation to the European
Convention. A. V. Dicey's theories in the late Victorian era of an
inviolable parliamentary sovereignty had been overturned for ever.

More public attention, however, focussed upon devolution in
Scotland and Wales, which had attracted passionate support in
the former nation at least. Here, unlike its predecessor in the late
1970s, the Labour government went ahead promptly and referendums were held in September 1997, only four months since
Labour had taken office. In Scotland, where a 129-member
parliament would have powers of primary legislation and raising
or lowering taxes, there was a roughly two-thirds vote on 11
September both for a parliament and for powers to raise revenue.
The possibility, indeed, was that a parliament at Edinburgh
might demand further powers, especially since Scottish opinion
tended to favour more radical economic and social policies than
in England. However, the presence of Donald Dewar, an experienced and widely respected Labour figure, as First Leader was
thought to be reassuring. In Wales, which had voted resound-
ingly against devolution in 1979, the referendum of 18 September 1997 saw a sufficient swing in the old mining valleys for a
very narrow majority of 50.3 per cent to be registered for devolution on a low poll. On the other hand, enthusiasm for anything
resembling separatism was historically tepid in Wales, while the
60-member Welsh elected assembly would only be an executive
body and perhaps not a very strong one since it had no financial
powers. Not until six months after the election was its waterfront
location in Cardiff Bay confirmed, while the Welsh Secretary,
Ron Davies, resigned in scandalous circumstances. His successor,
Alun Michael, was criticised in some Welsh Labour circles as a
less committed devolutionist and a creature of Millbank.

Nevertheless, devolution, especially the more daring Scottish
version, would surely affect the future course of the United
Kingdom, its multiple identities and the whole ambiguous notion
of 'Britishness'. With a stronger Nationalist presence in both the

Scottish and Welsh assemblies, there could be a prospect of endless constitutional deadlock and a legislative nightmare from which neither Labour nor the country might benefit. Finance could lead to conflict, with disputes over the 'Barnett formula' under which Scotland and Wales received extra funding from the Exchequer. The United Kingdom, critics feared, could become more disunited, turn into a kind of federation or even conceivably break up entirely. On the other hand, devolution could be looked at more positively, as a way of preserving the union while recognising the pluralism of British culture. It could reverse centuries of centralization and modify the kind of unaccountable 'quango' regime which had added to Conservative unpopularity in the Major years. It could even encourage regional government in England, perhaps in the north-east, Merseyside or the north west, and mesh with the reform of London government and the election of a Lord Mayor there, to produce a more centralized, vibrant and locally sensitive system of administration. It could revive the civic ideal of Victorian times. Within a Europe of Nations and a globalized economy which challenged traditional ideas of the nation-state, Britain might be stumbling towards a revamped partnership of the national and local, more appropriate for the modern age.

Uncertainty over the long-term implications of devolution was demonstrated by the Blair government at an early stage, its tendencies towards *dirigisme* at odds with its support for devolution. Thus, in Wales, the Labour machine worked hard to ensure that Alun Michael, Tony Blair's candidate, succeeded Ron Davies as head of the party in the principality, in preference to the clear choice of the party's grass-roots, Rhodri Morgan, who was thought by Millbank to be erratic and/or unduly nationalist. Michael's narrow election, via the aid of the discredited electoral college and much trade-union manoeuvring of the traditional kind, alienated many of the Welsh rank-and-file. In somewhat similar fashion in London, Millbank devoted much effort to campaigning against the maverick left-winger, Ken Livingstone, when he sought the Labour nomination for

the mayoralty contest, and used highly dubious (and spectacularly unsuccessful) tactics to promote the cause of the official
candidate, Frank Dobson.

The elections to the Welsh and Scottish devolved bodies in
May 1999 illustrated all these expectations or forebodings to the
full.

In Wales, the Labour Party polled unexpectedly badly, its
members perhaps angered by the methods used to keep out
Rhodri Morgan. Under the PR system adopted, Labour failed
to win a majority in the Welsh Assembly, losing seats in such old
industrial strongholds as Llanelli, the Rhondda and Islwyn to
Plaid Cymru, and ending up with only 28 seats out of 60. Plaid
Cymru polled far more strongly than before and, with 17 seats,
was clearly the challenger to Labour. Alun Michael soldiered on
with a minority government but, after some delay in obtaining
European 'Objective One' funding for deprived areas in south
Wales, he had to resign. The advent of Rhodri Morgan as the
new First Secretary brought new momentum to the Assembly as
did the decision in October 2000 to form a coalition with the
Welsh Liberal Democrats, and a period of greater stability
ensued. One result was a Children's Commissioner for Wales
which was the first item of primary legislation to go from the
Assembly to Westminster. Even so, there was discontent with the
relatively weak powers of the Welsh assembly, a body operating
on a corporate basis with no powers over finance or of primary
legislation, compared with Scotland. When nearly 3,000 steel
workers lost their jobs in Shotton in north Wales, and Llanwern
and Ebbw Vale in the south-east, the Welsh national assembly
was merely a by-stander.

Scotland made a stronger start, even though Labour failed to
dominate the 129-strong Parliament in Edinburgh, winning just
56 seats, with 35 for the Scottish Nationalists, 18 for the Conservatives and 17 for the Liberal Democrats. Donald Dewar was
elected First Minister and his decision to form a coalition with
the Liberal Democrats from the outset gave the new legislature a
much-needed stability. A blow was suffered when Dewar died in

the autumn of 2000, to be succeeded by Henry MacLeish. Never-theless at the start of 2001 the potential of a devolved Scottish parliament was increasingly evident, as policy decisions taken north of the border began to diverge significantly from those pursued by the government of Westminster. A series of specific Scottish policies—the abolition of tuition fees for students from Scotland in Scottish universities, a staged pay rise of no less than 20 per cent for local schoolteachers, and a remarkable decision to provide free nursing and personal care for old people living at home or in residential homes, as suggested in the Sutherland report—all suggested a distinctive and socially radical agenda north of the border.

On the other hand, the confusions introduced by devolution, with different policies prevailing in different parts of the United Kingdom, and varied outcomes for, say, university students or elderly people, depending on the accident of their birth or domi-cile, led to anxiety. A vague and diffuse debate on 'Britishness', its possible meanings and its very existence, arose. It chimed in with a report from the Runnymede Trust in 2000, written from the standpoint of ethnic minorities, to the effect that the conno-tation of Britishness was imperialist and racist, and that the concept might well be abandoned. Historians such as Linda Colley or Norman Davies deconstructed old Whiggish notions of 'British' history to give new emphasis to multiple identities and plural cultures. English nationalism as such remained relatively dormant, other than in football or rugby matches, with the vast majority of English people oblivious to the problems posed by the 'West Lothian question'. (Perhaps they were following the Lord Chancellor's advice not to ask the question at all). In any case they saw themselves as 'British' rather than 'English'. But people in parts of England began to voice worries at being left behind by developments in Scotland. There were signs that in areas such as Tyneside or Merseyside the local regional bodies, the RDAs, set up to co-ordinate local industrial and social devel-opment, might in due time foster a move towards a more fully-fledged regional government, even on an elected basis. The

Labour Party, John Prescott in particular, showed more interest in an idea which evoked memories of the Heptarchy of Anglo-Saxon times. It was another move away from old Labour's centralist view that the 'the gentleman from Whitehall knew best'.

Easily the most striking feature of the new Blair government was the effortless ascendancy of Tony Blair himself. His power was unlike that of any of his predecessors, even of Lloyd George or Churchill in wartime. In the words of Peter Hennessy, his presidential style made him almost 'an elective monarch'.[31] If there were problems, over cigarette sponsorship or arms to Sierra Leone, he appeared on television to reassure the viewers that he remained the 'pretty straight kind of guy' they had come to know and love. He dominated his Cabinet, which was less a deliberative or policy-making forum than a body initially bypassed by a big four of Blair, Brown, Cook, and Prescott. In addition, a nexus of committees orchestrated by the Lord Chancellor, Lord Irvine (who rashly compared himself to Cardinal Wolsey), a range of policy reviews dominated by the Downing Street Policy Unit, and a powerful communications agency to provide instant rebuttal and the spinning of news, all boosted 'the man in the saddle', as Lloyd George had once been called. They left Cabinet, parliamentarians, and party trailing in their wake. It seemed unlikely that Blair would, for some considerable time, face the kind of challenge that Mrs Thatcher faced from Heseltine, Lawson, or Howe and which in the end brought her down. Indeed after his role in the signing of the agreement for a settlement in Northern Ireland on Good Friday 1998 his dominance seemed even more emphatic.

So, too, was his new authority in foreign policy when he appeared to take personal charge of events when the British airforce led the NATO bombing raids on Serbia during the Kossovo crisis. It was noted that parliament, so prominent as a forum as recently as the Falklands war in 1982 or the bombing

---

[31] Peter Hennessy, 'The Blair Style of Government', *Government and Opposition*, 33: 1 (Winter 1998), 19, and his *The Prime Minister* (2000).

of Libya in 1986, was by-passed entirely. Of course, like all prime ministers, not even Tony Blair was totally omnipotent. He had to be cautious on some key areas of policy—the approach to Britain's adopting the 'Euro' in foreign policy, relations with the Liberal Democrats and suggestions that there might be a referendum to consider proportional representation or other forms of electoral reform. Within his Cabinet, Gordon Brown was a formidable presence, and it was believed that his influence grew after the resignation of Peter Mandelson early in 2001. Nevertheless, the quality of Blair's leadership was of a different nature from that of any other postwar prime minister. It was indeed remarkable for the Labour Party which had distrusted overmighty leaders since the alleged 'betrayal' of the party by Ramsay MacDonald back in 1931, and whose history from Keir Hardie to Tony Benn had often been one of internal division of the most unfraternal kind.

Tony Blair's authority seemed less constitutional than moral, almost metaphysical. The Prime Minister's dominance was projected in a highly personal way. He headed an irresistible juggernaut of power. Aware of the power of distance and spatial control, he was less head of government than symbol and megaphone of the people's aspirations. With focus groups and the media at the ready, he was the ultimate populist, as powerful as an American president, but instrumentally far more effective, with the Commons and the civil service totally at his command. One remarkable aspect of this came in the most dramatic event of New Labour's early months, the death in a car crash in Paris in August 1997 of Princess Diana, the divorced wife of the future monarch. This led to an extraordinary outpouring of grief, amongst a people for whom Diana was both a glamorous show-business icon and also a kind of establishment outsider who challenged the conventions of monarchy and showed empathy with excluded groups in society. It was also fanned by the tabloid press, which Diana had herself manipulated with great tactical skill. Diana's funeral had powerful emotional impact throughout the nation and indeed the world; the family home in Althorp became a kind of ersatz shrine. It was claimed by journalists that all this suggested Britain becoming a more compassionate, caring society after the money-making ethos of the Thatcher years and the brief era of the yuppy. This seemed impossible to prove, and was perhaps unlikely. It was also unclear that the monarchy would benefit from the new mood. While Diana's death meant a truce in the warfare between the royal family and the popular press, it was not clear that her particular qualities could easily be transferred to the more reclusive, introspective figure of Charles, the heir to the throne. He had his own personal problems through admitting to long-term adultery with Mrs Camilla Parker-Bowles. This led to some *sub rosa* clerical criticism as once with Edward VIII in 1936. The general public, however, saturated in 'permissiveness' and no longer cleaving to the marital vows, seemed rather more relaxed.

What was self-evident, however, was how the emotional populism of Diana's funeral naturally transferred itself to Tony Blair. He, too, was youthful and glamorous, without any of Diana's personal complications; he coined for her the masterful description, 'the people's princess', but it seemed also that he was anointing himself as 'people's prime minister', a beacon of authority rather than a candle in the wind. When the fiftieth wedding anniversary of the Queen and the Duke of Edinburgh took place in November 1997, it was noted how the Prime Minister enjoyed an almost patronizing intimacy with his monarch, as though he was extending his own popularity and mastery of public relations to protect her. Even towards the monarchy, perhaps, Tony Blair was a constitutional revolutionary. Still, he seemed to offer a wary nation the kind of reassuring leadership that it required.

As the century came to its close, there were signs that the ascendancy of New Labour was becoming less secure. Results in 1999 in the Scottish and Welsh elections, in the European elections and in local government, showed a marked slippage. In the first London mayoralty election in May 2000, the left-winger, Ken Livingstone, running as an independent candidate, humiliatingly defeated Labour's Frank Dobson. The main challenge did not come now from the established parties. The Liberal Democrats, cowed by the huge Labour majority, could not make their former impact as a force of protest, while the resignation of Paddy Ashdown as leader in late 2000 and his replacement by the youthful Charles Kennedy did not improve their fortunes. The Conservatives still remained unpopular and trailed far behind in the polls. Their attempt to pursue populist policies—anti-European, critical of government policies on crime or the admission of asylum-seekers from Kossovo, Kurdistan and elsewhere—had limited impact. Their new leader, William Hague, a Yorkshireman elected after the 1997 election at the age of only 36, an able debater who perhaps lacked charisma, found it hard to impose himself on a party still somewhat demoralized in its post-Thatcher phase. Hague did manage to reform its method of electing a leader, but for the moment he made only a limited impact. Disraeli's Taper had once spoken of 'Tory men, Whig measures'. In the late 1990s, with a pattern of 'Labour men, Tory measures', in such areas as business, welfare, and law and order, a similar era appeared to dawn. One portent of change in early 2001, following the second resignation of Peter Mandelson, was that the government made rather less use of the term 'New Labour', along with its supposed ideological underpinnings such as 'the Third Way' or 'the Stakeholder Society'. It now spoke more clearly of the traditional values of the Labour Party, emphasising community, social justice and the public service.

The difficulties now encountered by the government were both internal and external. Its air of pristine cleanliness, in contrast to Tory 'sleaze' was harmed by its involvement with rich men, often of doubtful financial credentials. A Treasury minister, the millionaire, Geoffrey Robinson, had to resign, while the influential figure of Peter Mandelson, had to resign on two occasions, for alleged half-truths first over a housing loan, secondly in January 2001 for appearing to involve himself in passport applications by rich Indian businessmen. But more damaging were complaints that the government was too slow in meeting its pledges to modernize the country and its public services. Complaints continued to surround the National Health Service, despite the government's attempts to cut waiting times and improve working conditions for hospital staff. Even more criticism attended the privatized railways with responsibility variously scattered between Railtrack and the private railway companies. Complaints of poor service turned into anger when a horrific train accident at Hatfield (October 2000) revealed a record of poor maintenance of a track where long-established cracks in the line had led to several deaths. The chairman of Railtrack later resigned and there was a saga of delays, lengthy railway repairs and passenger frustration right through the winter. Somehow the railways had seemed to function more effectively in the years after 1945, even with more passengers and far more tracks in those pre-Beeching days. To the dismay of environmentalists, the roads became ever more crowded and the air of cities ever more polluted. High fuel taxes had scant effect.

If these assaults could be deflected by the government on to the privatization policy put through by the preceding Tory administration, others were targeted directly on Labour and the prime minister. One interest group, long dormant, that surfaced in the later nineties, was that of country people, feeling neglected and marginalized in a largely urbanized nation. Their pressure group, the Countryside Alliance, allied farmers, aggrieved at falling prices, rising fuel taxes and the effects of BSE (and later foot and mouth disease), with the particular viewpoint of the fox-hunting community, angered that this traditional, if controversial, rural pursuit was likely to be banned after a large Commons vote to that end. Only the Lords, with their many landowners, provided a bulwark against abolition here. Since Labour had won a remarkably large number of rural constituencies in 1997, it had to pay heed. It was rural groups who largely endorsed an unexpected series of fuel blockades by road hauliers in September 2000, angered by the high fuel tax imposed by the Treasury which made British petrol the dearest in Europe. For a time, Tony Blair personally came under fire. Foreign commentators fancifully compared the fuel tax campaign with that against the poll tax which had so weakened Mrs. Thatcher in 1990. However, the government was able to make some concessions to defuse further protest. The road hauliers made a psychological error in launching their demonstration in Jarrow, which offended people who cherished the role of the Jarrow hunger marchers of 1936 in their folk memory. The crisis for the government passed by.

The advent of the Millennium in 2000 might have seemed an opportunity to raise Labour's profile in leading nationwide rejoicing on the lines of the Great Exhibition in 1851. The Millennium Dome, a spectacular construction designed by Richard Rogers, was built at Greenwich, close to architectural masterpieces by Inigo Jones and Christopher Wren. It was intended to provide a focus for national celebration as had been done with the highly successful Festival of Britain in 1951. The original concept lay with the Conservatives, and Michael Heseltine in particular. However, its immediate planner was Peter Mandelson, whose grandfather, Herbert Morrison, had planned the Festival fifty years earlier. But whereas the Festival then had provided a sense of excitement, innovation and national pride in marking the 'national autobiography' which Gerald Barry planned in 1951, the Dome was dismissed as little more than a politically correct, virtual-reality theme-park with none of its predecessor's sense of history. It met with fierce press and public criticism from its ill-starred opening on 1 January 2000; it failed to attract anywhere near the 12 million visitors anticipated (only just over 6 million came in the end); its financial management was poor with several additional injections required from public funds; the eventual sale of the Greenwich site was plagued with uncertainty after the Dome came to its unhappy end on 31 December. The Dome was a public relations disaster, despite the best efforts of the government minister, Lord Falconer, an intimate of Tony Blair, to present it as an exciting project to regenerate a rundown area of the Thames riverside. Indeed, for a time the very word 'Millennium' appeared to attract derision and disaster. A Millennium footbridge crossing the Thames close to St. Paul's had to be closed to the public after only one day when it swayed excessively as a few hundred people walked across. It stayed closed for the next 18 months. In addition, the Millennium Eye, a spectacular ferris-wheel on the south bank of the Thames almost opposite Parliament, while widely praised, also suffered frequent stoppages for safety reasons.

However, many other features of the Millennium celebrations, mostly financed from the National Lottery, did much better. The opening in May 2000 of the Tate Modern art gallery within the brilliantly re-designed Bankside power station on the south bank, was hugely successful, and attracted millions of visitors. Other projects in London were also remarkable triumphs for British architects, designers and engineers, inviting comparisons with showpiece public projects in Paris or New York. The refurbishment of Somerset House as a series of art galleries to open up William Chambers's original building of the 1770s to the general public, was matched by Norman Foster's redesigning of the newly glass-topped British Museum, whose Great Court evoked comparisons with the Louvre in Paris. Edinburgh could boast its new National Museum, Cardiff its futuristic Millennium Rugby stadium. In older industrial locations, the new art galleries at Salford (to house the collection of L. S. Lowry's paintings) and another in Walsall, along with landmarks such as the dramatic suspension bridge at Gateshead, close to a towering new sculpture named 'The Angel of the North' were all widely acclaimed.

Complaint about the public services, therefore, was poised against artistic innovation and much consumer comfort elsewhere. As Britain entered the new millennium, indeed, the public mood appeared relatively tranquil. Its economy was more robust, its role in Europe less contentious. An old society was in the process of relatively peaceful readjustment. Some of the more striking artistic work at the turn of the century reflected aspects of cultural change and rebirth as they affected particular groups. The film *Billy Elliot* described a working-class boy brought up in the industrial north east who overcame prejudice to become a ballet dancer. Two young women novelists wrote powerfully on the problems of identity and heritage as they affected ethnic minorities. Zadie Smith, a black writer, explored in *White Teeth* the experiences of Jamaican and Bengali immigrants to London, while Linda Grant's *When I lived in Modern Times* analysed the identity crisis of a postwar woman emigrant to Israel. Much the most popular children's books, the successors to Enid Blyton or Roald Dahl in the past, were the Harry Potter stories written by J.K. Rowling. They concerned even greater problems of identity, namely entering the world of wizardry and witchcraft, though they were criticised in some quarters for their social implications.

Deep inequalities remained within British society, without question. But some of the worst were being tackled. Outside the ageless quagmire of Northern Ireland, the land appeared stable, even secure, as surveys of popular opinion consistently showed. Even in Northern Ireland, indeed, there were signs of progress since a 'peace process' still existed in some form. Many of the discontents of former years—the union troubles of the later 1970s, the mass confrontations of the later 1980s—raised fewer problems now. Ethnic minorities were enjoying greater mobility; racial tension in the inner cities had receded; black sports men and women and pop stars became role models of the young. The multi-ethnic Notting Hill festival, first launched in 1970, had now become an acclaimed landmark in the national calendar. Zadie Smith's *White Teeth* commanded attention in part because of its optimistic view of race relations. One remaining problem area was the police whose failures in following up the Stephen Lawrence murder showed them, in the view of the MacPherson report, to be guilty of 'institutional racism'. Race riots in Oldham and Leeds during the 2001 election were followed by strong polls for the British National Party in a few northern towns. There were abundant press stories about illegal immigrants and asylum-seekers on the loose. But there was no great evidence of the anti-immigrant neo-fascism visible in France, Germany or Austria.

There was adjustment to change elsewhere. Gender inequality was publicly recognised and was narrowing in key respects, even as the older style of feminism lost its impact. Most women had far more fulfilling lives. In two-thirds of families in 2001, both parents were at work. Over half the university student population was now female. The Scots and the Welsh were expressing their national identities in laying the foundations for a successful local devolution, with little evidence of separatism. In most places, an increasingly affluent consumer society testified to popular contentment and the enjoyment of leisure. Some of the entertainment remained home-based, notably the popularity of computerized games (which aroused some concern for the physical well-being of the unathletic, obese young) and the enduring appeal of Americanized television. While long-established soap operas like *Coronation Street* and *Eastenders* retained their popularity, a new *genre* was voyeuristic programmes focussing on the individual tensions within small isolated groups. The characters of 'Big Brother' became briefly national celebrities.

But more and more the British pursued their pleasures outdoors. Increasingly, people went to the cinema, while mass sport, especially football, had never been more popular, affluent or cosmopolitan. The marriage of David and Victoria Beckham, a famous Manchester United footballer and a member of the celebrated 'Spice Girls', aroused media frenzy. The presence of continental footballers or managers, invariably well-spoken and more fluent in English than their working-class British colleagues, helped the populace adjust to Europeanism in their midst. Although, especially in football, the fortunes of national teams on the field of play were often a disappointment, in rugby and even in cricket English fortunes improved as the new century dawned. In the Sydney Olympics in September 2000, Britain won 11 gold medals, the oarsman Stephen Redgrave (subsequently knighted) actually winning his fifth in successive games. It was noted that many of these successful athletes (a number of whom were black) benefited from assistance from the National Lottery. This all helped to promote a mood of patriotic contentment. Meanwhile, many British successes in the Para-Olympics in

Australia focussed attention on the achievements of disabled people, whose needs and rights had risen rapidly up the social agenda.

After a delay caused by a serious outbreak of foot and mouth disease, the general election was called for 7 June 2001. The opinion polls consistently showed a huge Labour lead of up to 20 per cent or more. Perhaps for this reason, the campaign was widely seen to be uninspiring, with much talk of political apathy, especially among the young. Labour concentrated on its key themes of the public services, especially health, education and law and order, whereas the attempt by Hague and the Conservatives to emphasise joining the Euro or an influx of asylum-seekers seemed a mistaken strategy. In the event, there was a second Labour landslide, with results remarkably similar to those of four years earlier. Labour won 413 seats, a record for a second term, with an overall majority of 167, only 12 down on 1997. The Conservatives held just 166, doing badly in London and its suburbs (other than Essex), registering only one seat in Scotland and again none in Wales, while the Liberal Democrats, under their new leader, Charles Kennedy, went up to 52, their best performance since 1929. Celtic nationalism showed no advance, the SNP ending up with 6 seats and Plaid Cymru 4. Labour's share of the poll was 42%, two down from 1997, with the Conservatives on 32.7% and the Liberal Democrats 18.8%. Perhaps the most notable statistic was the steep fall in the number of those actually voting: the turn-out of only 59%, down 12 from 1997, was much the lowest since 1918, although whether this reflected complacency, contentment or sullen distrust of all politicians was much debated. The number of women MPs fell from 121 to 115, although the new 23-strong Blair cabinet included a record number of seven women. Still, for the first time in its history, Labour had won a full second term, with every possibility of a third, whereas the Conservatives were left marginalized, as they had been after 1846 and 1906. William Hague immediately resigned as party leader.

Millennial Britain seemed, for the moment, to have chosen a style and a leadership with which it felt comfortable, if not enthusiastic. It appeared finally to have moved on from the insularity and complacency generated by a victorious world war fifty years earlier. Only on rare public occasions, one being the ever-popular Queen Mother's one hundredth birthday in August 2000, were the old nostalgic notes struck. Outbursts of the former imperialism were confined to quaint survivals like the flag-waving choruses on the last night of the Promenade concerts in the Albert Hall. External crises such as that in Iraq or Serbia were far removed from the jingo mood of Suez or even the Falklands. Nobody expected Britain to be at war with anyone. Membership of Europe, if comparatively unloved, was taken for granted. The new millennium would undoubtedly produce new threats and tensions. The unpredictable impact of globalization would have its alarms for old industries and settled communities, as evidenced for example by some of the former mining areas. The slump in the major Asian economies in 1997–8 posed a threat to British trade and inward investment. Signs of an American recession in 2001 could be even more worrying and the stock market turned bearish. Despite a series of rhetorical conferences at Kyoto and elsewhere, unrestrained environmental forces could menace generations yet unborn as heavy flooding in the winter of 2000–1 suggested. But for once Britain appeared ready to face these challenges in good heart. The continuing popularity of history, British and other, in print and on the television screen suggested a robust cohesion and unity. William Shakespeare was declared to have been man of the millennium. The welfare state, and especially the National Health Service, with all its problems, provided a symbol of social solidarity. Episodes like the advent of Tony Blair, the death of Princess Diana, charitable campaigns on the model of 'Band-Aid' or Save the Children, Olympic success, patriotic reflections on the meaning of 'heritage', could at times bring the nation more closely together. A people's peace, tentatively launched in 1945, so fragile for so long, might finally have taken root.

IV

The New Millennium

2001–2020

15. *Millennial Perspectives*
2001–2008

THE British entered the new millennium in sober and unheroic mood. There was none of the imperial bombast that greeted the dawning twentieth century at the height of the South African War, nor the social patriotism when the country emerged from world war in 1945. And yet Britain under Blair's New Labour appeared stable, tranquil, even content. This mood was founded on steady economic growth and popular consumerism reflecting a rise in affluence amongst the mass of the population. Blair was indeed the first ever Labour Prime Minister not to be challenged by overwhelming economic difficulties. Attlee's government in 1949 and Wilson's in 1967 had been shaken by devaluation of the pound. Now the pound sterling was strong, perhaps too strong for comfort. Blair's powerful Chancellor, Gordon Brown, presided over a steady annual growth of more than 2 per cent. Unemployment, so central a theme in Britain's recent past, was the lowest for twenty-five years, with inflation falling to 1.8 per cent, the lowest in Western Europe, and interest rates in November 2001 standing at a forty-year low of 4 per cent. Well might the Labour Party, founded a century earlier to defend the working class and underprivileged, claim that it was 'the party of business', from which the capitalist classes had nothing to fear.

Britain's was now overwhelmingly an economy based on finance and credit. In the one-time workshop of the world, manufacturing output had fallen to well under 20 per cent of the total, whereas services contributed up to 75 per cent, with business services, banking and other finance, and computer

technology predominant. London remained a massive international magnet in the world financial system, as it had been
since the 'Big Bang' of 1986. A globalized capital market, so
much feared, was much to its advantage. Other European countries, notably Germany and France, with their economies now
falling into difficulties, looked on ruefully at the rapid progress
made across the Channel by the one-time sick man of Europe. In
some ways Britain's economic stability was superficial. It rested
heavily on high levels of consumer spending at home, especially a
buoyant housing market which allowed heavy personal borrowing, perhaps used for a second or third car or a holiday home in
Spain. Spending through credit cards soared into the billions. A
notable feature was the boldness with which citizens plunged
heavily into debt, especially to finance housing mortgages, or
perhaps school or university fees for their children. Old Victorian
precepts about spending beyond your means were discarded. In
2007 it was calculated that the average adult owed around
£33,000. Much therefore depended on stability in interest rates.
A slump in house prices or a downturn on the stock market
could plunge huge numbers into negative equity and financial
distress. But at the start of the millennium these perils seemed far
off. One ironical feature of New Labour policies was that they
largely followed the market-led policies of deregulation, privatization, free capital movements, and low direct taxation inherited
from the Conservatives. Under Tony Blair's Labour administration, it almost seemed that, economically though not socially, we
were all Thatcherites now. It was noticeable that Labour politicians always referred to 'the market', never to 'capitalism'.

It followed that, in such an economic climate, much that
embodied Old Labour—public ownership, controls on industry,
redistributive taxation, comprehensive welfare, or support for
the trade unions—withered on the vine. New Labour's 'Third
Way' implied structures of managerialism as a substitute for
ideology. Analysts described an expanding 'demi-monde' of
quangos, 'czars', task forces, private finance initiatives, and the
like, with a concomitant emphasis on unelected management

consultants, special advisers, and spin doctors at the expense of Whitehall and Westminster. David Marquand's *Decline of the Public* (2004) argued that, since 1979, free-market Thatcherites followed by Blairite managerialists, often adopting an anti-intellectual populist style, had undermined Victorian ideals of the public realm and disinterested public service. In this unfamiliar political climate, Blair's was the first Labour government to face no challenge from the left, Marxist or otherwise. Socialism as a coherent idea lacked conviction—as, indeed, did any ideology of Conservatism after Mrs Thatcher. No worthwhile book on socialist theory had appeared since Anthony Crosland's *Future of Socialism* (1956) which now looked very dated. Meanwhile, the trade unions, whose membership was little more than half their peak membership of 13 million in 1979, seemed marginalized or ignored, and many amalgamations resulted. Unions of identifiable people like miners or transport workers had been replaced by bodies with cryptic titles such as Unison and Amicus (later absorbed into Unite). The old intimacy of their partnership with the Labour Party had gone, though it still mattered in the party's finances. The government seemed centrist and consensual, in no sense philosophically driven. The ideological gulf between Labour and the Conservatives was trivial compared with 1945, or indeed 1983, but no one much seemed to care.

Politics was dominated by the personal charisma of Tony Blair. He had made a virtue of transcending the old left–right divisions of the past, and showed an effortless mastery of the media. Assisted by a cadre of personal advisers far larger than for any previous prime minister, truly he was the master now. Thus in the general election of June 2001 (delayed for a month because of an outbreak of foot and mouth disease) Labour scored another landslide victory with an overall majority of 167, scarcely diminished from that of 1997. The Conservatives still seemed demoralized in their post-Thatcher trauma. Their tally of 166 seats showed an advance of just one, while they lost some seats in southern England to the third-party Liberal Democrats. The most striking feature of an extraordinarily dull election, however, was the meagreness of the poll, just 59 per cent, the lowest level of voting since 1918. Britain, which prided itself on its commitment to participatory democracy and to its parliamentary constitution, where 'Big Ben had rung out for freedom' in 1940, as Mrs Thatcher once put it, seemed to be abdicating its historic role. Crusades for the vote and secret ballot by Chartists and Suffragettes, apparently, need never have been.

The public, however, still required its heroes. It found them in Britain's past not its present. In particular, Britain, far more than any other major nation, still looked back to heroic legends of the Second World War. The year 1940 in particular, when Britain purportedly 'fought alone' during its 'finest hour', a hinge of history symbolized by Dunkirk, the blitz, and the Battle of Britain, was endlessly rehearsed on cinema and television screen. They would feature on Christmas Day just after the Queen's broadcast, with traditional anti-Germanism well to the fore. In particular, the cult of Churchill rose to new heights, as biography followed biography. It achieved a global scope with even President Bush in the White House, no historian, keeping a bust of 'Winston' in his private office. Churchill's values, his passion for empire and attachment to a lost social hierarchy, might be remote from Britain in 2001, but he embodied strength and international greatness in a way none of his successors appeared to do. He enjoyed a far broader appeal than Lloyd George, leader of the nation during the First World War. If crises of terrorism or environmental disaster occurred, people naturally referred to the Dunkirk spirit, never to Gallipoli or the Somme.

Churchill, 'man of the millennium', remained an iconic rallying point. In this he superseded the royal family whose prestige had been dented in their domestic upheavals of the 1990s. Public perceptions suggested a basic confusion between the royal family as individuals, the monarchy as a constitutional concept, and the Crown as a legal one. Arguments over royal finance and taxation reflected this confusion. Whose, for example, were the royal pictures? Yet the Queen managed to sustain her position, perhaps more as a survival than a revered icon. The fiftieth jubilee of her reign was celebrated in style in June 2002. The flower beds of Buckingham Palace resounded to the Beatles' hit song of the sixties, 'All you Need is Love'. A little earlier, the funeral of the centenarian Queen Mother, revered as a kind of heroine of the blitz, saw an outpouring of mass emotion. Prince Charles, heir to the throne, married Camilla Parker-Bowles, his also divorced long-term mistress previously referred to in The Times as his 'companion', with relatively little controversy in 2004, a sign among other things of a more relaxed, tolerant mood on moral issues. Unlike Australia, republicanism in Britain was a distant threat. A revival of old loyalties came with the film, *The Queen* (2005) which depicted in sympathetic, though not fawning, terms the dilemmas posed for the Queen by Princess Diana's death in 1997. The actress who played Queen Elizabeth, Helen Mirren, already a Dame, duly won an Oscar. Where peoples such as the Americans and the French took pride in seeing themselves as citizens, the British (more particularly the English) were reluctant to challenge their lesser status as subjects of the Queen.

This was broadly a time of social peace, with few parallels since the high Victorian era. There was none of the tensions of the recent past—no major strikes, no poll tax protests, no race riots. The police, accused by its own senior officers of 'institutional racism', had adopted more conciliatory strategies towards ethnic communities in the inner cities, and this yielded results. While concern was expressed at campaigns by the neo-fascist British National Party and its ability to appeal to white working-class males, initially in northern cities, Britain showed nothing resembling the potent racism associated with Le Pen in France or Haider in Austria, even though memories of black slavery, the basis of the wealth of revered eminences like Gladstone tended to be erased from popular memory. Even in Northern Ireland, always deeply riven by sectarian division, there was far less tendency to recourse to violence. A peace process in some form continued to hold, even if disputes about weapons remaining in the hands of the IRA (and some extremist Protestant groups as well) prevented the devolved Northern Ireland assembly from actually sitting. But even Ulster appeared to be approaching a normality not experienced since the partition of Ireland back in 1922, as well as benefiting from the prosperity of its republican neighbour to the south.

The only social protest of any significance at the start of the millennium came, rather improbably, from the rural community. The Countryside Alliance flourished, with marches and large demonstrations in Parliament Square. Its grievances were a compound of genuine protests from country people at declining local amenities such as post offices and bus services, farmers' complaints at the mishandling of foot and mouth disease, and the more specific protests of fox-hunters at proposals in Parliament to end hunting with dogs. But in an overwhelmingly urban or suburban society, the protests of rural people were unlikely to be decisive, any more than they had been over the Corn Laws in 1846. Even fox-hunting was finally defeated, when the ending of hunting with dogs was carried through a recalcitrant House of Lords, improbably through the use of the 1911 Parliament Act. However, in typically British fashion, after all the passion expended by both sides, the bill proved hard to enforce. The practice of country hunters maiming and killing foxes, hares, stags, and other wild creatures continued much as before.

Beyond fox-hunting, Britain in the millennium was fighting no class wars. On the other hand, class division was as pronounced as ever. Social stability in Britain resulted from a broad unwillingness to challenge a social structure that remained inegalitarian. The broad mass of the population in the middle tiers of society—often located in that mythical territory 'middle England'—moved towards a rough equality, more homogeneous in living standards and lifestyles. Yet a feature of the Blair years, as of the eighteen years of Conservative government before them, was that Britain became more and more unequal. The trend towards greater equality of wealth and income of the 1970s had been sharply reversed in the thirty years since then. Certainly Labour successfully targeted many of its social policies on the poor in the inner cities. It offered them redistributive tax credits for families and individuals, New Deal programmes to generate employment, campaigns designed to halve and then eliminate child poverty, and strong investment in primary education in deprived areas. It also endorsed the European Social Chapter and implemented the minimum wage that the Conservatives had previously opposed, even if the wage was initially at a modest level. These measures certainly had a positive impact, as did strong voluntary bodies such as Shelter, Save the Children, and Help the Aged.

And yet the reports from the Joseph Rowntree Foundation in 2007 showed that in fact the proportion of poor people had stubbornly remained the same, or perhaps had even grown. Households of what those reports called the 'breadline poor', where people lived below the poverty line, rose to 17 per cent. A total of 12.7 million people lived in what was defined as 'relative poverty' (incomes below 60 per cent of the median) in 2007. In cities in Scotland and northern England, or deprived communities like former mining areas in South Wales or the North-East of England, they might include almost half of the households. Inner cities still had their almost irredeemable 'underclass'. Conversely, the very rich grew disproportionately in biblical fashion. 'Asset wealthy' individuals benefited from huge rises in the value of housing, especially in southern England, and from a steady rise in the value of investments in stock markets. The share of national income enjoyed by the richest 1 per cent, which had stood at 5 per cent in 1979 had more than doubled after 2000. City bonuses soared, as did the rewards from private equity companies. In 2007 the average pay for chief executives had risen to £2.85 million, yet, through adroit management, many of them paid a lower rate of tax than did their office cleaners. The directors and owners of multinational concerns found London a congenial place in which to live, given its cultural vitality and benevolent tax regime. Rich and poor increasingly lived in different locations identifiable by postcodes, they sent their children to different schools, and scarcely knew each other within a land in which leftish intellectuals had once proclaimed that 'socialism was about equality'. A relaxed policy on inherited wealth and capital transfer meant that ingrained inequality divided individuals after death as it had segregated the living. With life chances so dominated by family background and education, social mobility in millennial Britain was limited. Meanwhile a leading minister, Peter Mandelson, declared that his party were not bothered about the filthy rich. New Labour rivalled Disraeli in putting 'two nations' on display. Only in October 2008 could OECD conclude that Britain's social inequality was now diminishing a verdict strongly contested.

But, for all this class divide, no revolution followed. This was because the great majority contentedly accepted their lot, and believed that for their children things would probably be better. Three-quarters of the population owned their own homes, ran one or more cars, enjoyed often more than one overseas holiday through cheap holiday flights, made use of technical advances such as mobile phones, video-recorders, or personal computers, enjoyed foreign cuisine, and relaxed by watching on television (though less commonly actually playing) sport and games. If Concorde airliners, now technically obsolescent after thirty years, stopped flying the Atlantic in 2003, British-built Airbuses took wing in 2007. More adventurous souls could buy a ticket for future space travel on the website of Virgin Galactic. Education was a powerful social solvent, with higher education expanding rapidly to embrace almost half the post-school age group. It no longer ended at 21 in a society which supported 'lifelong learning'. Women in particular benefited from this, and indeed over half the university population was now female. As a result, women achieved steady progress in gaining professional advancement (though not equality in pay). Even the head of MI5 was a woman. Both marriage and childbearing were deferred as educated young women gave priority to their careers, with a consequent negative impact on the birth rate. The average age for having a first child rose to 30. Contraceptives like the morning-after pill were readily available over the counter at chemists. In addition, abortion had for decades been legal, despite Roman

Catholic 'right to life' opposition, and offered free choices in the life patterns of women. The feminist movement of the 1970s might have lost its edge, but here it had left a powerful and permanent legacy.

All this meant that public debate no longer focused so much on the welfare and egalitarian themes that had preoccupied social thinkers since the New Liberalism of Lloyd George's day. Debate now turned far more on quality of life issues, a healthy environment and sustainable development, personal well-being and individual freedom. There was much concern with obesity amongst overfed inactive adults and, even more, children. Smoking was subjected to ever greater pressure on health grounds, and by 2007 was forbidden in workplaces, restaurants and pubs, places of entertainment, and public transport. There was also anguished debate about the effects of alcoholism, internet and other gambling, and the traffic in drugs. At the same time, government policies in allowing all-night drinking in city centres, promoting casinos in inner cities (a super-casino was defeated in the Lords), and uncertainty in distinguishing between soft and hard drugs (cannabis was first downgraded then upgraded as a danger), tended to have the opposite effect. When a fashion model, Kate Moss, was found to have been taking cocaine, her career temporarily suffered, but as a role model her public standing, if anything, improved.

One part of the population that manifestly benefited from the new social agenda was the 'gay' community, as homosexuals and lesbians were now generally known. Public attitudes had become increasingly tolerant and less censorious since the decriminalizing of homosexual activity between consenting adults in the sixties. Only some of the religious communities waged ineffective campaigns against it. A notable landmark in 2004 was legislation sanctioning civil partnerships—in effect, gay marriages—while gay people also claimed new legal rights in adopting children. Public figures confidently declared their sexual preferences. The old puritan persecution which had claimed so many victims from Oscar Wilde onwards, was being exorcized, but now without drama. Heterosexual relations, too, were never more open and diverse, with 'partnerships' increasingly replacing formal marriages, and half of the latter ending in divorce.

Among other things, all this indicated the declining influence of the churches who had resisted sexual equality for gays and easier divorce. The Church of England, itself tormented by the issues of gay clergy and women priests, seemed to be losing authority, with well under 10 per cent of its purported communicants attending church on any given Sunday. The Catholics and Muslims far outstripped them in zeal. Popular Protestantism, a central thread of Britishness for 400 years, was waning fast. Over 70 per cent of the people may have declared their belief in God, 'faith schools' (several Muslim) might be pressed forward, and hard secular atheism was the creed of only a small minority. But, for most practical purposes, Britain was ceasing to be a religious country. Puritanism and chastity were in full retreat. When Alastair Campbell, Tony Blair's press secretary, was asked to expand on the premier's strong religious views, the crisp reply came—'We don't do God'. Perhaps in contradiction, Blair was to convert to Roman Catholicism at the end of 2007, after leaving office.

By far the most visible of the social changes, one which provoked anxious debate, was that Britain's 60 million population was being transformed by heavy immigration. The United Kingdom was, of course, a polycultural union state of different native peoples, English, Welsh, Scottish, and Irish. After the earliest Saxon incursions, there had been invasions by Danes and Normans. In later centuries, Flemish weavers under the Tudors, French Protestant Huguenots under the later Stuarts, Jews from Eastern European 'pogroms' and then immigration from the black Commonwealth from 1950 onwards had introduced new ethnic minority cultures. By the year 2000, large populations from the Indian subcontinent, Africa, and the Caribbean were well established, largely in major cities. They were increasingly joined by refugees or other immigrants, legal or illegal, from the Middle and Far East and the Balkans. There was anguished debate, which some politicians sought to exploit, at the 'flood' of immigrants seeping into Britain. Attention focused both on their treatment in detention centres like Campsfield in Oxford-shire, and their right to be here at all. The plight of many asylum-seekers was particularly harrowing, if they faced perils at home after deportation.

A report on multiculturalism chaired by the British-Indian political scientist, Lord Parekh, in 2000 argued powerfully that Britain should acknowledge, and celebrate, the fact of its being a multicultural, multi-faith society quite openly and positively. This applied not only to employment, welfare, and housing policies, but in its education and even its view of British history, which should be reinterpreted in a far broader multicultural context. While this received wide support, the Commission for Racial Equality preferred laying the emphasis on integration rather than multiculturalism. Even if some of the old racial tension withered away, there were complaints about how an enforced politically correct polyculturalism was threatening old cultural landmarks such as children's toys, nursery rhymes and children's stories, hot cross buns at Easter, and the sending of Christmas cards ('Winterval' was one suggested alternative name). Jack Straw, a leading government minister and member for Blackburn, caused controversy by suggesting that Muslim women should not wear the veil. Sikh demonstrations caused the closure of Kaur Bhattis's controversial play, *Behzti*, in Bir-mingham Rep.

But the Asian immigration was now an immense entrenched social and cultural force. A Cabinet minister, Robin Cook, sug-gested that chicken tikka masala had become as much a British culinary speciality as Yorkshire pudding. In 2007, with almost a tenth of the population foreign born, Indians were the largest cohort with 570,000, followed by the Irish (417,000) and the Pakistanis (274,000). When England played cricket against India or the West Indies in home Test matches, the sympathies of the crowd would be equally divided: Conservative politicians had called for a 'cricket test' to be imposed as a criterion of citizen-ship. Nevertheless, popular culture was manifestly less obviously white and Anglo-Saxon. English and Scottish football teams featured an array of talented black players, alongside Europeans and South Americans, also often black. Major teams like Arsenal and Chelsea might contain hardly one home-born player. Yet tribal loyalty towards the 'local' team remained as passionate as it had ever been. Club, not country, really mattered.

The problems of racial and cultural integration became more complicated after 2004. The European community was already changing British society through its movement of peoples. There was significant out-migration, notably to France and Spain. Conversely, Britain, with its welfare state and vibrant economy and culture, was a magnet for many. London, with over 300,000 French inhabitants, was now, in effect, the fourth largest French city after Paris, Marseilles, and Lyons: French presidential candidates canvassed votes there in 2007. Things took a new turn with the accession of ten mainly Eastern European countries to the European Union in 2004. Bulgaria and Romania followed on 1 January 2007, making a total of twenty-seven countries. Poles, in particular, often equipped with technical skills, flocked over in large numbers. In the three years 2004–7, an estimated 630,000 Poles came to London, with Slovaks, Hungarians, and Lithuanians not far behind. The cultural complexities of several London suburbs were extreme. However, Poles and others usually found jobs, often in vital domestic trades such as plumbers and electricians, paid their taxes, kept out of trouble, and made major contributions to the economy. It helped them that they were also white as were 92 per cent of the population. One intriguing change came in Northern Ireland where the Polish immigrant influx tilted the balance of population in favour of the Roman Catholic minority, while the hiring of Poles in the Northern Ireland police service further modified the composition of that traditionally Protestant force. In all, there were estimated to be a million and half immigrants that had come to Britain since 1997 (the real number was almost certainly greater). The implications for Britain's social structure, religious composition, popular culture, and indeed sense of history had still to be fully explored.

Overseas immigration was one of two highly visible changes in millennial Britain. The other was the restructuring of the constitution. There had been a dramatic programme of constitutional reform in the early period of the Blair government in 1997–9, under the leadership of a forceful Lord Chancellor, Lord Irvine. The House of Lords had lost all but ninety-two of its hereditary peers. The Human Rights Act had provided for powers of judicial review in monitoring legislation and public policy. And in 1999 a new Scottish Parliament and elected Welsh Assembly had come into being in Edinburgh and Cardiff respectively. The process of reform continued, though in a more piecemeal way after the millennium. Thus after 2004, the Law Lords were destined to move from their location within the palace of Westminster and would now form a separate American-style supreme court, under the jurisdiction of the Lord Chief Justice. Also the historic, if anomalous, Lord Chancellor would no longer preside on the woolsack in the Lords as a member of the government and the legislature and yet also head of the judicial system, despite the separation implied in the 1701 Act of Settlement. His role was, in effect, transferred to the Commons and in 2007 exercised by Jack Straw as head of a new Department of Justice. Thus it was that the historic unwritten British constitution, governed by custom and convention rather than written edict, increasingly resembled the American, with statutory human rights, a supreme court to monitor the government, and the separation of powers between legislature and judiciary. There was also an American-style Freedom of Information Act and a culture of greater disclosure within government circles, from which historians amongst others were greatly to benefit.

Most important of all, the devolution settlement took firm root as Scotland and, to a lesser extent Wales, proceeded on a different path from England. The Labour-dominated Scottish government followed distinct policies on such matters as free tuition for university students and medical care for the elderly. Although it was claimed that nationalism in Scotland had been assuaged thereby, in fact, the Scottish National Party continued to progress, raising the prospect of governments of different party stripe cohabiting in Westminster and Edinburgh. Wales, where the Assembly had no powers of primary legislation and none of the financial powers of the parliament in Scotland, remained in a somewhat indeterminate state, and many called for the Welsh Assembly to acquire the powers of the Scottish body. In the end, the Government of Wales Act in 2006 largely conceded the point by giving the Welsh Assembly far greater power of legislation albeit through the cumbersome device of an Order in Council. By 2009 it was manifestly clear that British domestic policy was diversifying through devolution, and the United Kingdom seemed less united in form year by year. There were, for instance, four quite different health systems operating in the British Isles. After centuries of enforced Unionism with the tone set by Westminster and Whitehall, a huge shift was under way. The gentleman from Whitehall no longer obviously knew best. The cultural distinctiveness of both Scotland and Wales became more pronounced. In Scotland, in effect the domestic political discourse was entirely determined by the Edinburgh Parliament (a striking, if expensive, modern building at Holyrood by a Catalan architect). The Union flag was largely jettisoned in favour of the Scottish Saltire, while 'God save the Queen' was seldom sung north of the border, despite the Queen's residence in Balmoral in Deeside and her kilt-wearing son. In Wales, devolution brought new policies on education and children, and a new boost for the native language, which the 2001 census showed had gained ground for the first time since 1911. Welsh culture, long chapel bound, now embraced the world of pop. In the 1960s, Welsh folk singers had sung mournfully 'Dy ni yma o hyd' (We're still here), the language of stubborn survival. In 2000 the sexy blonde soubrette of the band Catatonia told the world that 'Every morning I wake up and thank the Lord I'm Welsh'.

In England, by contrast, nothing much happened, and plans for regional English assemblies collapsed. Constitutional experts called England 'the black hole' of constitutional reform. There were, indeed, worrying signs of English resentment towards

Scotland in particular. No one had answered the 'West Lothian' question by Tam Dalyell about why Scottish MPs could vote on English affairs, whereas the reverse was forbidden. The Barnett formula, a temporary provision of 1978 which provided greater per capita funding for the population of Wales and Scotland (and even more for Northern Ireland), was criticized for unduly favouring them at the expense of England. Also prominent Scottish MPs like Gordon Brown and Robin Cook dominated Westminster, whereas, to the English, Scotland was an excluded territory. Some Conservatives called for an English Parliament. There were visible signs of a long-dormant English nationalism, shown by the greater use of St George's flag. Englishness appeared to gain a temporary boost from the unexpected success of the English rugby union team in winning the world cup in Australia in 2003. However, with the consistent failure of England's footballers, no enduring popular enthusiasm for it would take root.

The purpose of all this constitutional change was to diffuse a sense of transparency and accountability. Ultimately, Gordon Brown declared, the objective was greater liberty, much as John Stuart Mill had expounded in the mid-Victorian era. But, despite the popularity of devolution in Scotland and Wales there was a widespread feeling that Britain still remained in essentials a polity marked by secrecy and control. The closet method in which key decisions were taken in government, especially during the lead-up to the Iraq war in 2003, led to widespread criticism; inquiries such as the Hutton report were condemned as establishment cover-ups. Britain was still failing to provide a sense of open, transparent government as, to a degree, prevailed across the Atlantic. Its citizens could not claim ownership of their constitutional arrangements, as Americans had done in 1787. There was particular controversy over human rights legislation, with the judges criticizing government policy over control orders, anti-social behaviour orders, threats to a jury system which had endured since before Magna Carta, and the treatment of immigrants and asylum seekers. Judges and government seemed to be often in conflict about the very meaning of the Human Rights Act, and public confusion resulted. Constitutional change had brought many benefits, but the consequences had been piecemeal and incoherent. The introduction of devolution in Scotland, Wales, and Northern Ireland had been made deliberately asymmetrical. It had been introduced in self-contained fashion to deal with the particular problems of each country, without proper mechanisms for intergovernmental co-ordination. Bodies like the Joint Ministerial Council and the Council of the Isles, intended to pull the United Kingdom together, seldom ever met. The reform of the British governmental system, therefore, had created as many problems as it tried to solve. It remained unfinished business.

In major respects, Britain was buoyant and a beacon for the world. Much of its primary science was pioneering, notably in genetics: thus in 2000 British scientists mapped a strand of human DNA for the first time in history. Britain's cultural life also flourished in most of its modes, spectacularly in London which perhaps outstripped Paris and even New York. Musical life was active, with four symphony orchestras resident in London. A popular move in 2007 was the refurbishment of the Royal Festival Hall, nostalgically using the same pastel shaded decor of the Festival of Britain in 1951. A host of local festivals testified to the importance of music for the British. Edinburgh, Glasgow, and Cardiff opened major new concert halls, while Liverpool was the 2008 European capital of culture. London was also a hub of the art world, not least through the innovative Tate Modern on London's South Bank and the annual Turner Prize.

The theatre was buoyant with new resources released after the Boyden report in 2000. The West End enjoyed a protracted boom, while there were also exciting developments in Birmingham and Sheffield's three theatres. Two small local theatres in London, the Almeida in Islington and the Donmar Warehouse in Covent Garden, were thriving, often featuring Hollywood celebrities in lead roles. One sign of the times was a surge of 'factual theatre' from 1999, the theatre perhaps serving as a substitute forum for political debate, beginning with 'Colour of Justice', based on the Macpherson inquiry into the police handling of the murder of a black boy, Stephen Lawrence. Others plays covered variously the Potters' Bar rail crash, the Hutton report on the death of the scientist, Dr David Kelly ('Justifying War'), 'Bloody Sunday' in Belfast, and the treatment of terrorist suspects in Guantanamo Bay. In a category of its own was David Hare's 'Stuff Happens' on the Iraq war, which mixed drama with verbatim dialogue from figures such as George Bush and Donald Rumsfeld. It was a tribute to freedom of expression that the subsidized National Theatre should be used to criticize the government on so fundamental an issue. A highly successful play of the period was Alan Bennett's 'History Boys' (2004), dealing with a homosexual history teacher's relations with his pupils, but above all raising basic issues about the value of education for its own sake as opposed to crude materialist standards. Even Bennett was transcended by the most popular and successful playwright of the time—William Shakespeare. Tragedies like Macbeth, Othello, and King Lear, comedies like Much Ado About Nothing, drew vast audiences, frequently to the renovated Globe Theatre, and attracted leading actors like Ian McKellen and Judy Dench. The Bard retained his timeless authority in the second Elizabethan age as he had done in the first.

The literary scene was also very lively, notably for children's books, where J. K. Rowling's much-filmed Harry Potter stories, sagas of school and sorcery, sold by the million. While printed books were challenged by electronic media, publishing houses benefited from online marketing and produced constant new titles, with history well to the fore, sometimes boosted by television series as with books by David Starkey and Simon Schama. History also featured in major novels, with Pat Barker, Sebastian Faulks, and Giles Foden, amongst others, pursuing aspects of the First World War. Ian McEwan's intricate novel *Atonement*, by contrast, was partly set in the Second World War, and featured the retreat from Dunkirk. One indicator of a multicultural society was the prominence of writers from the ethnic minorities, heralded already in Zadie Smith's *White Teeth* (2000). Monica Ali's *Brick Lane* (2002), an account of a young Bangladeshi woman forced into an arranged marriage with a much older man and resident in London's East End, won praise, as much for its treatment of gender issues as of race. The ethnic communities themselves were not so enamoured at what they saw as negative portrayal. When *Brick Lane* was made into a film in 2006 it had to be filmed somewhere else in the face of local opposition. An appealing 'ethnic' film was 'Bend it like Beckham' (2002), dealing with two girl footballers, a Sikh rebelling against Punjabi parents, and an English girl challenging her mother's notion of feminity. The combination of race, sex, and football was irresistible.

Architecture of all the art forms was the most visible and triumphant, with striking new buildings such as Norman Foster's revolutionary 'gherkin' (Swiss Re tower) soaring up amidst other modern landmarks in the City of London. The Welsh Millennium Centre on Cardiff's waterfront, was a multi-purpose structure featuring local slate. Great publicity was attracted in late 2007 by the rebuilt St Pancras station, linking London via Eurostar to Paris and Brussels. Its design by Nick Derbyshire harmonized remarkably sensitively with the engineering and architectural wonders of George Gilbert Scott's mid-Victorian hotel and W. H. Barlow's railway shed, which had for decades stood almost derelict. Modern innovative British design thus gave due reverence to the Victorian heritage. Appropriately, St Pancras featured a seven-foot-high statue to the poet John Betjeman, an enthusiast for Victorian Gothic, who had long campaigned to preserve the station and its hotel as gems of vernacular patriotic Englishness.

Much British culture, as always, was the preserve of white middle-class enthusiasts and intellectuals. The price of opera and theatre tickets alone tended to keep the working class away. On the other hand, culture more broadly was democratizing. Indeed many critics complained of 'dumbing down' of the BBC, taking it far away from the style and tone of its creator, Lord Reith. 'Reality television' was one novelty, with ordinary citizens pitched into an artificial milieu, a closed house or a desert island, to provide voyeuristic entertainment for the masses. A cautionary note was struck when the TV show 'Big Brother' saw a young Indian woman racially abused by female inmates: she was invited to tea in 11 Downing Street in compensation, and in the end was the show's winner anyway. The digital revolution made radio, video, and television far more accessible and interactive, just as 'ipods' or laptop computers allowed music enthusiasts to download and enjoy music they liked, without needing to frequent record shops. Online networks such as 'facebooks' enabled invisible chains of friendships to be created through the internet. Communication took the most direct of forms. Thus journalism and writing of the traditional kind was being invaded by the 'blog' when ordinary individuals used electronic dialogue to create a kind of random, unstructured public forum for themselves and anyone else interested. Pedants complained that proper grammatical English was being corrupted by the demotics of the 'blogosphere', while the omnipresence of the internet, assisted by the spread of broadband, was undermining more considered forms of writing. Others protested that genuinely popular forms of cultural expression were being invaded, or still worse, bourgeoisified. Thus the Glastonbury pop festival, a long-established forum of liberation for the free-thinking, free-living young, was increasingly a middle-aged and middle-class *récherche du temps perdu*. Young radicals seeking more exciting forms of drug culture or sexual experiment had to look elsewhere, which was not difficult. However improbably, Glastonbury was following Benjamin Britten's Suffolk base in Aldeburgh and Edinburgh as a fixed festival landmark on the establishment's cultural calendar.

Most of British public debate for many decades had focused wholly on domestic affairs. British foreign policy had been increasingly cautious since the 1980s, a result of diminishing resources and indeed the more tranquil world heralded by the end of the Soviet Union and the Cold War. The Trident nuclear 'deterrent' floated unused in Scottish waters. Tony Blair, like Mrs

Thatcher earlier, handled much of foreign policy himself, and the Foreign Office was more marginalized. The main area of overseas preoccupation was the European Community. Blair seemed anxious to play a far more overtly European role, but he was constrained by the continuing suspicion and scepticism of the British people towards 'Brussels'. The Treasury led pressure within the government to keep Britain out of the euro, the single currency which began its life in 2001. There was concern at Britain's being deprived of its own financial powers, notably in the setting of interest rates. There was also much insularity; tabloid journalists deplored the possible removal of the Queen's head on banknotes. In the event Britain remained outside the euro without mishap. There was Eurosceptic alarm, too, at proposals for a new European constitution, with more clearly defined roles for a European foreign minister and intergovernmental agencies. Tony Blair had to promise a referendum on the point. In the event, defeats for the European constitution in France and the Netherlands in 2005 ensured that no British referendum would take place—much to the relief of the government since it would certainly have been lost. Britain signed a diluted version of the constitution at Lisbon in 2007, amidst some protests that a referendum should still be called.

But British foreign policy suddenly lurched into a far more interventionist and controversial phase with the catastrophe of '9/11', 11 September 2001, the attack by Al-Qaeda terrorists who flew into the US Trade Center building in New York and also the Pentagon in Washington, causing in all almost 3,000 deaths. Among those killed were sixty-seven British citizens: it was the largest overseas loss of life Britain had suffered in any such incident since the Second World War. Blair, who had already indicated his wish for close relations with the newly elected American President, George W. Bush, took a strongly emotional line in his address to the Labour Party conference at Brighton a few days after 9/11. He declared his passionate support for the Americans in their suffering, and also in their determination to root out terrorism. Britain would stand 'shoulder to shoulder' with them. His speech raised an evangelical prospect of liberal interventionism by the great powers to sort out the world's problems, whether it be terrorism, poverty, or environmental disaster. It was inspiring, in the way Gladstone's speeches had once been, but it also aroused global hopes that could hardly be fulfilled. At any rate, Britain was the only country to send significant detachments of troops to fight with the Americans in Afghanistan to throw out the Taliban regime, and, it was hoped, eliminate the Al-Qaeda bases in the mountains of that notoriously dangerous country. Some warned Blair and Bush of the immense difficulties invasions of Afghanistan had encountered in the past, notably in the British imperial Afghan wars of 1839 and 1878, and experienced by the Russians also very recently. But the Taliban regime was soon evicted, British troops were stationed in Helmand province and other difficult parts of the country, and Blair was acclaimed in the American Congress and by President Bush as a transatlantic hero. He was even awarded a Congressional Medal but postponed accepting it while prime minister. He was apparently inspired by his success in persuading President Clinton to take armed action against Serbia in Kosovo four years earlier. He saw Afghanistan as a morally valid form of liberal intervention, as well as of further cementing the 'special relationship' with the Americans.

Hitherto the British people, stunned by the horror of 9/11, had broadly applauded Blair's bold approach. But then matters took a very different turn. In a meeting with President Bush in Crawford, Texas (April 2002), Blair secretly agreed to back an invasion of Iraq, whose tyrannical leader, Saddam Hussein, was believed to be an instigator of terrorism and himself a threat to the world with long-range biological and chemical weapons and perhaps nuclear weaponry to follow. Thereafter, there were repeated statements by Blair about the threat that Iraq posed and the need to remove its weapons, preferably it was said via the United Nations, but, if not, then unilaterally. There was support that was tepid at best for the work of the UN weapons inspector in Iraq, Hans Blix. Two dossiers of September 2002 and February

2003 were produced to make the case that Saddam Hussein had within his country weapons of mass destruction: Blair repeatedly adopted the mantra that they could be deployed 'within forty-five minutes'. The slipshod analysis of the latter led to its being christened 'the dodgy dossier': part of it had been plagiarized from an obscure doctoral student. By February 2003 it was clear that Tony Blair, who had already sent British troops to Sierra Leone, the Balkans, Iraq, and Afghanistan in earlier wars, was planning to send British forces again to invade Iraq alongside his American allies, the only European leader to do so to any significant extent. There were 35,000 British troops heading for the Gulf. The tone from Downing Street was warlike on how Saddam Hussein was an international threat. Though the term 'regime change' was disavowed, it appeared that that was being planned. With no military background, Tony Blair, returned on a basically domestic agenda in 1997 and 2001, now resembled our most warlike prime minister since Palmerston.

The outcome was an explosion of popular anger such as had not been seen since Suez back in 1956. On 15 February 2003, over a million people took to the streets of London in the largest political demonstration in British history; there were similar marches in other cities. It was in the old 'trouble-making' tradition of dissent against British foreign policy going back to Charles James Fox during the French Revolution, and caused a massive impact at a time when British public opinion was supposed to be apathetic, feeling that there were no great causes left. The demonstrators were not at all Marxist or Muslim fanatics; they included many elderly people, middle-class churchgoers, and plenty of schoolchildren. The Attorney-General's avowed change of mind on the legality of invading a foreign country in this way without UN sanction caused much controversy. On the eve of war, in a forced parliamentary division, 139 Labour MPs voted against the government, despite much pressure from the whips. It was the largest ever backbench revolt. The ex-Foreign Secretary, Robin Cook, resigned office and delivered a powerful statement from the backbenches. Military men asked anxiously whether the government had provided for an effective restoration of order after hostilities had ended. They also pointed out the over-stretch for British troops, with 7,000 deployed operationally in Afghanistan along with others variously engaged in Bosnia, Kosovo, Northern Ireland, Gibraltar and the Falklands, and even briefly in manning 'green goddess' vehicles during a fireman's strike. Others with a longer historical perspective noted how difficult Britain had always found it to evacuate after invading overseas: thus Gladstone's invasion of Egypt in 1882, intended as temporary, started a British military commitment that lasted until 1954. Blair, however, was adamant and on 19 March American and British aircraft pounded Baghdad, Basra, and other cities. Without UN sanction, the war had begun.

The actual fighting was soon over. After five weeks, the outnumbered, outgunned Iraqi forces were rapidly defeated and Saddam Hussein overthrown. He was later discovered in hiding, and hanged. But Blair's problems had only just started. It seemed clear that there had been no serious planning about a post-war restoration of order. Local police and army units were dissolved, while the Americans pursued the control of Iraqi oil and other economic rewards. For the next four years a catalogue of violence continued in Iraq, with some British casualties, until by 2006 there appeared to be almost civil war as Iraq descended into near-chaos. For Tony Blair himself, Iraq was apocalyptic. He lost for ever his position of apparent invincibility, as the war became extremely unpopular. By September, 61 per cent of the voters were said to be dissatisfied with him as prime minister, and his press secretary, Alastair Campbell, resigned. A particularly damaging episode was when a government scientist, Dr David Kelly, saw a journalist privately to express doubts about the government's claims; soon afterwards, his dead body was found in an Oxfordshire wood. It was said to be suicide and Blair was widely condemned.

Thereafter the Prime Minister was haunted by Iraq. The economy continued strong, with Britain's inflation rate in 2003, at 1.6 per cent, the lowest in the European Union. Labour's huge parliamentary majority remained intact. But Iraq superseded them all. Two inquiries were held. The Hutton report on the death of Dr Kelly was derided as an official whitewash, though the documents it included made for startling reading including on the views of the Attorney-General. The Butler report on the intelligence background to the war was far more critical, albeit in a somewhat veiled fashion. It included astonishing material on the closeness of the intelligence agencies of MI6 to 10 Downing Street, including Alastair Campbell. It also commented sceptically on sofa-style managerial government, by which informal conclaves of advisers took decisions privately. The Cabinet as a formal body of elected ministers was too often ignored. Thus Tony Blair's very dominance had proved to be a major handicap as he bypassed Parliament, Cabinet, and the civil service in favour of personalized rule. He discovered, as Lloyd George and Mrs Thatcher had done before him, that the British public did not take kindly to the Napoleonic style. From the most popular prime minister since Churchill, he became the most unpopular. Some MPs even suggested that, for taking the country into an illegal war on a bogus prospectus, he should be impeached, a procedure unused since the case (unsuccessful) of Henry Dundas, Lord Melville, back in 1805.

Iraq, therefore, proved to be a turning point. It showed the land to be wary of overseas ventures, as well as fearing an over-involvement in the alliance with America. Britain's militarist ethic had long departed with the end of empire. The nationalism of Mafeking, Suez, or even the Falklands was no more. Just like Joseph Chamberlain in 1906 and Anthony Eden in 1956, Tony Blair was its tormented victim.

The general election of May 2005 mirrored this post-Iraq disillusion. There was not much public debate about issues. Few expected the Conservatives to make much more impact under Michael Howard than they had done under William Hague and Ian Duncan Smith in the past few years; nor did they. The Liberal Democrats took a stance strongly critical of the Iraq war, but they were clearly a minority party. The war overshadowed the campaign; Blair himself had the embarrassment of the father of a British serviceman killed in Iraq standing against him in his Durham constituency. The poll was just 60 per cent, little improvement on last time. The Conservatives' tally of seats rose to only 198, below even Labour's dismal total under Michael Foot in 1983. But Blair's majority fell by around 100, and a majority of just 66 suggested that the climate was turning autumnal. An unprecedented third Labour victory felt almost like a defeat.

Tony Blair could still demonstrate astonishing persuasive skills, as in April 2007 in finally brokering a peace settlement in Northern Ireland between Sinn Fein and the Democratic Unionists. With the aid of financial douceurs from the British government, an election in Northern Ireland was called after which, after years of suspension, devolved government could finally come into being. In May 2007 an extraordinary coalition government was set up in the province, with the hitherto irreconcilable veteran Unionist, the Revd Ian Paisley, as first minister and the Sinn Feiner, Martin McGuinness, as his deputy. Orderly local government began. For the first time, perhaps, since Cromwell, the entire island of Ireland seemed to be in for a lasting time of peace. Only Blair, perhaps, could have worked this particular miracle. His personal magnetism was crucial again when London's bid for the 2012 Olympic Games was successful in Singapore. But these individual coups could not neutralize a wider sense of disillusion and unease.

This unease was markedly heightened on 7 July 2005 when, the day after London's successful Olympic bid, there were huge terrorist explosions in different parts of the city, three in the London underground (Russell Square, Edgware Road, and Aldgate) and one on a bus in Tavistock Square. Three other attempted explosions in underground stations failed. A total of 52 people, most of them commuters, were killed in the blasts, and over 700 injured. Four Muslim bombers were also killed. The perpetrators were extremist Muslim zealots, devotees of Al-Qaeda, further inflamed by the invasion of Iraq. Two weeks later, a further bombing attempt on the London tube miraculously did not cause casualties. The British public remained typically stoical, and the medical and fire-fighting services coped astonishingly well. But the ongoing effect on public life was considerable. A range of protective barriers and electronic security devices was installed outside Parliament and other public landmarks. Passengers at airports and even train stations, along with spectators at sporting events and other mass gatherings, were subjected to searches of property and person. A new regime of surveillance prevailed. Liberty of movement, threatened by the Luftwaffe during the war and again by Sinn Fein terrorists in the eighties, was now permanently affected. After a deceptive lull, an abortive attempt by a few Muslims, working in hospitals in Scotland, to drive a car full of explosives into Glasgow airport in June 2007 brought new reminders of the sense of threat. British people would henceforth have to live within a culture of imminent personal danger. The question was how best to respond. One consequence was an ongoing passionate debate about the balance to be struck between guarding ordinary citizens against a terrorist threat and preserving traditional guarantees of personal freedom such as habeas corpus going back to before Magna Carta. The proposed reintroduction of Identity Cards for ordinary citizens, for the first time since the immediate post-war years, was highly controversial. Especially passionate argument was caused in the summer of 2008 by a proposal by the Brown government to extend police powers of detention without charge to forty-two days. This failed in the Lords. Between the authorities and champions of civil liberties there was little meeting of minds. Clashes of priorities and principle were set to continue.

Tony Blair's successor was his long-serving Chancellor of the Exchequer, Gordon Brown, with whom there had been long-term tensions ever since Blair became party leader in 1994. Brown had a difficult process of consolidation and reassurance ahead of him. At first the omens were favourable. He had to face a series of crises in his first few days. The attempted bombing of Glasgow airport, and a recurrence of foot and mouth disease in farming districts in Surrey were followed in late July 2007 by an immense downpour of rain which left the Severn and Thames valleys, and several ancient towns in central England inundated under massive floods. The consequences of climate change were thus terrifyingly displayed. But Brown and his new ministers coped with great competence. The Conservative leader, David Cameron, who had given a good impression of youth, charm, and moderation in his first year as Opposition leader, was somewhat caught at a loss when parts of his own Oxfordshire constituency disappeared under the floodwater. Brown also sought to give an impression of greater openness and collegiality in handling his colleagues and parliament. One proposal was that decisions to make treaties and go to war should be approved by parliament, another nail in the royal prerogative and a retrospective comment on the invasion of Iraq in 2003. By the time of the Labour Party conference, it was widely believed that Labour might call a snap election, but Brown, after damaging hesitation, decided not to take the risk. It could be argued that his reputation never recovered after this display of faintheartedness.

This was accompanied by a sudden slump in the prestige of parliament with the revelation of MP's exploiting the system of remuneration for working expenses, or perhaps simply cheating on matters like mortgages for second homes. The House of Commons slumped in public esteem, with several ministers and shadow ministers caught up in the scandal. There was an angry public response. The Speaker of the Commons, Michael Martin, who was felt to have exercised insufficient vigilance overall, was forced to resign, the first such event since Speaker Trevor back in 1694. A new system of external regulation of MPs' expenditure was set up, with an Independent Parliamentary Standards Authority to determine the payment of MPs, monitor their financial activities, and impose new rules about paid advocacy and outside interests. The reputation of parliament and government suffered. In 2010, three MPs and a peer were charged by the police.

The result was the ventilation of a wide range of constitutional reform issues, many of them not obviously connected with the issues of corruption. Advocates were vocal on many proposals, including a new voting system with proportional representation in place of the first past the post system, a partially or wholly elected House of Lords, reduced powers for the prime minister through an axing of the royal prerogative, stronger powers for the Commons and backbench MPs, the enhanced separation of powers, and perhaps even the long-term objective of a written, codified constitution. The Brown government came up with a revised Constitutional Reform Bill which would include the removal of the few remaining hereditary peers. The debate that followed was far from ordered or rational, but it implied that textbook accounts of the British constitution, little changed from pronouncements on parliamentary sovereignty dating from the Victorian jurist A.V. Dicey, were no longer meaningful. The long-venerated 'mother of parliaments' was in the melting-pot.

This atmosphere damaged the repudiation of the Labour government under Gordon Brown. In 2009, the local government election results brought heavy losses for Labour with the loss of its last four councils in England. It came third overall with only 23 per cent of the vote. The European elections were even worse: Labour ended up with a mere 15 per cent, behind the Conservatives and even the new anti-European party, UKIP. In Wales, the Tories headed the poll for the first time since the heyday of Gladstone in the election of 1868. Much alarm was caused by the success of the hitherto dormant British National Party in winning Yorkshire Humberside and the North-West, through exploiting fears about European immigration amongst white working-class males in northern cities.

But the period also had several more positive features. Overseas, British troops were withdrawn from Iraq. The Chilcot inquiry limited public inquiry into the origins, conduct, and aftermath of the war; it was later to report with devastating effect for Tony Blair's reputation. There continued to be mounting controversy over British losses in an apparently unwinnable

war against the Taliban in Afghanistan, where every invading
force, British or Russian, had failed since the disastrous retreat
from Kabul in 1842. At home, environmental issues were prominent in the public agenda as never before in history. The government embarked on an ambitious programme of policy to
combat global warming and other perceived aspects of climate
change. There were plans to generate far more energy from
sustainable, renewable sources in place of fossil fuels, and new
'carbon budgets' for greenhouse gas emission. It was proposed to
generate 15 per cent of Britain's energy needs from wind, wave,
sustainable biomass and solar power by 2020. Coal had more or
less disappeared from use in Britain; oil and petrol might eventually follow. Large noisy wind turbines decorated or desecrated
(according to choice) mountain areas of natural beauty in the
Lake District or Mid Wales, although the Scottish government
found itself frustrated in this respect by the inhabitants of some
of the western isles. To help curb carbon emissions, ministers put
forward a programme for a high-speed rail network to link up
major British cities. At the time, Britain had only 68 miles of such
lines (the line connecting London to the Channel tunnel); the
French nationalised TGV had 1,100. A new golden age for a
revamped Victorian railway system was trumpeted. Conversely,
a new threat came from 'swine flu', an alarming influenza epidemic originating in Mexico initially predicted to strike half the
population and perhaps lead to a possible 65.000 deaths in the
winter of 2009–10 (a forecast later much reduced to 19.000).
The latest in a series of historic pandemics from the Black Death
of 1348 to the Spanish influenza of 1918–19, it could have
seriously weakened Britain's society and the economy, although
the eventual impact was not severe,. By contrast, statistics
revealed that Britain's population, swollen by immigration from
eastern Europe, had soared during hard times to reach over 61.4
m. with a considerable baby boom since 2002.

But the central problem confronting the nation's leaders went
beyond these economic, social, political, and physical difficulties.
It was rather how to keep an ancient country, caught up in rapid

cultural and demographic change, in any sense coherent and united. Gordon Brown was an ambiguous figure, with his adaptation of 'supply-side socialism', neither obviously left nor right; a survivor of over ten years of New Labour government, yet seeking to embody something different and more democratic. An overriding anxiety was the elusive concept of 'Britishness'. Brown, a history Ph.D. from Edinburgh University, brought a trained historical mind to it. With quotations variously from Voltaire, Montesquieu and Adam Smith, he attempted to link 'Britishness', a benevolent creed, with 'British values', even with proclaimed pride in the heritage of Empire (in which his native Scotland had so effectively participated). But these values, including such admirable qualities as tolerance, civil liberty and equality before the law, were hard to differentiate from the values of decent people anywhere on earth. Brown also sought to use plans for constitutional renewal to promote national integration including symbolic gestures such as more flying of the Union flag on public buildings. Here a crucial issue was growing pressure for greater independence from his native Scotland. This increased with the advent of a minority Scottish National Party government, headed by Alec Salmond in May 2007, foreshadowing perhaps a fundamental breach in the country 300 years since the Act of Union in 2007. The kind of problems that could ensue were vividly depicted in August 2009 when the Scottish government decided to release on compassionate grounds a Libyan convicted of involvement in a terrorist bombing back in 1988. This had brought down an American airliner at Lockerbie, near Solway Firth, with the loss of all crew members and 243 passengers, most of them American. The tensions that emerged between a Scottish parliament which controlled its own judicial system, and a British government with overall authority over foreign policy, were thus laid bare. The Americans and the French looked to their constitutions as a focus for citizenship. In Britain, an unwritten, uncodified constitution, and the shibboleth of being subjects of the Queen, rather than citizens, made such an approach impossible. The British could never say of their constitution, as did the Americans at the start of their formal document in 1787 'We the People of the United States'. The British national anthem celebrated a family, whereas the *Marseillaise* (and, indeed, *Yr Hen Wlad fy Nhadau* in Wales) paid allegiance to a nation. Proposals for a written, democratically envisaged constitution, a bill of inalienable rights or Declarations of the Rights of Man, had hitherto appeared to be too mechanistic and formal, or simply 'unBritish'.

After two thousand years, how could national coherence be sustained in a venerable country variously challenged by Celtic separatism, mass immigration from Europe and Asia, and the forces of globalisation? What remained of the social citizenship and the public realm of post-1945 in a society fragmented by individualistic consumerism? How meaningful a term was Britishness anyway, so penetrated by other peoples from distant continents and a worldwide Commonwealth? Might not the future lie in a new structure in which the British union-state would transform itself into a federal system or even a ruptured series of fragments including the severance from the European Union which many increasingly advocated? So many of the fundamental historic components of the so-called 'island story'—a commitment to a patriotic Protestantism, the challenge from a continental 'other' (notably France), command of the open seas and free trade, the heritage of empire—had disappeared. Nationwide institutions such as the BBC and the Royal Mail were diminished; the Crown was but a symbol, though one of profound historical influence. Perhaps the post-war welfare state remained as an integrating idea, but its future shape, notably the role of the internal market, was in flux, especially after the devolution settlement in the Celtic nations of Scotland and Wales. The United Kingdom had been devised in 1603, the Union with Scotland in 1707, Great Britain and Northern Ireland as recently as 1922. They all looked fragile now, in varying degrees. Britishness had long been conflated with Englishness, reflecting the imperial dominance of much the largest country. But that was a term that defied definition. The notion of English nationalism that emerged during the devolution debate was a baffling one whose essence had still to be defined. The idea of an English parliament, which could theoretically challenge the supremacy of Westminster, seemed most unlikely. 'Constitutionally' the *Encyclopaedia Britannica* had declared, 'England does not exist'. England seemed almost a geographical expression, as Metternich had once described Italy. After two millennia of brilliant, tumultuous history, the British people had still to work out precisely who they were.

16. *From Crash to Brexit*

2008–2020

TOWARDS the end of the first decade of the twenty-first century, the course of British history alarmingly changed. Gordon Brown had become prime minister in 2007 in a mood of relative tranquillity. The government had a secure majority, while the angry passions kindled by the invasion of Iraq in 2003 were beginning to fade away. New Labour, combining most of the free-market economic policies of the Thatcher period with progressive ventures in social and constitutional reform, had governed in the main without challenge. Most citizens had appeared content with the mantras of 'the third way' even if the meaning of this opaque term was far from clear. In particular, it had been the first Labour government to rule without serious economic difficulties such as a balance of payments crisis or a run on the pound. MacDonald, Attlee, and Wilson had all suffered some loss of authority through a devaluation of sterling. Not so Tony Blair. The economy, during Gordon Brown's ten-year period at the Treasury, had proved to be sufficiently robust to allow for major increases in public spending, somewhat to the alarm of conservative economists. The National Health Service, in particular, received a major boost in spending. In the years 2001–6, businesses and workers enjoyed a growth rate of 4%. which helped the economy to thrive as in the housing market. Brown claimed, with some danger of hubris, to have ended the long saga of Britain's having a boom and bust economy.

Twelve months later, it was all over. Brown faced declining tax receipts and rising unemployment, with a growing prospect of a collapse of the British banking system. Along with other western nations, Britain faced a huge economic collapse, with a rapidity and force that recalled the great depression of the 1930s. It was to place its stamp on social and political developments for at least the next ten years. Economic forecasters were left stunned and uncomprehending. The Queen asked the fundamental question 'Why did nobody see it coming?' No-one could provide her with a sensible response. There had been premonitions of serious problems in the banking system for at least a year. There was huge volatility in the stock market in August 2007. The new chancellor, Alastair Darling, was told that the Northern Rock bank, which had pushed its reserves into dangerous investments in an imprudent and incompetent way, was on the point of collapse. Its debts by the start of 2008 ran to £24bn. and panicky savers were queuing up in their tens of thousands to withdraw their savings. After a hectic few weeks, in which the government backed a projected sale of government-guaranteed bonds to pay lenders' debts, in February 2008 legislation was passed for Northern Rock to be nationalized. To the ironic amusement of many on the left, the old 1918 socialist recipe of nationalizing the means of exchange, along with production and distribution, long denounced on the right as mere Marxism, was beginning to come about, and it was followed by other measures of public ownership. Northern Rock was the forerunner of other hapless financial institutions, deemed by the government as being 'too big to fail'. Public bewilderment was followed by anger, at the banks and their overpaid, self-remunerated chief executives, all of whom managed to evade retribution, let alone legal action. A particular target was Sir Frederick Goodwin, popularly known as 'Fred the Shred', chief executive of the calamitous Royal Bank of Scotland, for which the government had to pay out £45bn. to try to rescue it. The biggest bank in the world in 2007, a year later it threatened to go out of business in just one day unless it received an immediate hand-out of £12bn. Goodwin was stripped of his knighthood in 2012 for his incompetence in running Royal Bank of Scotland but kept his £700,000 annual pension together with huge bonuses from them. Andy Hornby, a key figure in another major bank, HBOS (Halifax Bank of Scotland), was condemned in 2013 for 'colossal failures of management' but remained immensely wealthy, including the lead directorship of a large bookmakers.

The most alarming period of financial collapse came after a massive crisis in the American sub-prime mortgage housing market. After months of eerie calm, one giant investment bank in New York after another announced that it was in grave trouble. The climax was reached on 18 September 2008 when Lehman Brothers, America's fourth biggest bank, which had run a colossal loan book in commercial property, announced that it was bankrupt. A day or two later, AIG, the world's biggest insurance company, saw its stock market value collapse, and other desperate news followed. The global capitalist system, unstable to the core, was on the point of disintegrating. Its major players like Ben Bernanke, head of the US Federal Reserve, seemed overrun by bewilderment and complacency, having declared for years that the world economy had created its own well-developed techniques and institutions to protect it against extreme shocks. There was no Keynes around to educate them this time. In Britain the repercussions were cataclysmic. HBOS, the Royal Bank of Scotland, Bradford and Bingley, Alliance and Leicester, and other major finance houses were on the brink of going the same way as Lehman Brothers. Britain was certain to suffer more than most countries from this collapse in the business world for several reasons. House-price inflation in the United Kingdom was even more rapid than in America, with household mortgage debt 125% of disposable income. The financial sector, and erratic phenomena such as hedge funds, were unusually central to the British economy. Terms of trade could decline exceptionally rapidly here. Household income would become weakened and government spending dry up. The deficit in 2009–10 could soar to 65% of GDP.

Most of 2009 was taken up by the British government and the Bank of England governor trying to clear up the mess, with limited help from the financial regulators which had totally failed to act in time. Brown's initiative and Darling's calm reactions did much to help. Broadly, money was poured into ailing banks and other financial bodies through the deceptively named 'quantitative easing' of large transfers of electronic money. Lloyds Bank stepped in to rescue the collapsed Royal Bank of Scotland, but then had itself to be rescued by effective public ownership, as with Northern Rock. The stock market somewhat stabilized over 2009 and Gordon Brown won acclaim from President Obama among others for his rapid action on the international front in protecting the global banking system. By the late spring of 2010 the British economy was again growing, albeit very modestly. This did not prevent Brown and the Labour government receiving immense flak for its policies in trying to ward off a global collapse not of its making. If Brown had received credit for the boom, he received blame for the bust. But while the financial crisis stabilized a little, its aftermath in terms of social division, political fragility and the rise of populist, nationalist protest movements like the anti-European UKIP in Britain left a legacy of instability and unrest that cast its shadow in a way unknown since the 1930s. Henceforth it would be an apprehensive bewildered, socially divided country, very different from the confident heyday of New Labour. When the ten-year anniversary of the Crash of 2008 was commemorated in 2018, many economic commentators gloomily speculated that the fundamental problems of the world economy had not been properly dealt with, that the banks were still in urgent need of proper regulation. Another, even more serious crash, was always on the table. Ironically, it was in 2018 that the Royal Bank of Scotland for the first time made a profit since its troubles had threatened to pull the entire British economy crumbling down.

This turmoil showed itself in the political field. Brown's government became an increasingly unhappy one, torn by personal recriminations and tensions over the aftermath of the 2008 credit crash. Brown himself lacked the emollient qualities of Blair (Iraq always excepted). New Labour had passed its peak.

The amorphous Middle Way of such centre-left writers as Anthony Giddens and Geoff Mulgan had lost its sheen and degenerated into a shallow managerialism. Socialists deplored the fact that the government at home largely adopted the neo-liberalism of the Thatcher era, with a benevolent tax regime for the rentier and privatisation continuing. The basic problems of social inequality seemed unchanged after thirteen years of reformist Labour government. The Iraq invasion had been a bitterly contested source of Labour division, one which had tarnished Blair's reputation for ever. Perhaps the one New Labour achievement which appeared to have the most enduring impact was the Good Friday agreement, which had launched the peace process in Northern Ireland, even if it was followed by great problems in trying to form a stable power-sharing government. On the personal side, Brown himself, a gruff reclusive figure, lost his early popularity while the credit crunch, even if of non-British origin, inevitably damaged the reputation of the government, which lagged badly in the opinion polls.

However, a general election was due and, with much foreboding, it was held on 6 May 2010. It was an uninspiring exercise. Labour's campaign was solemn, with Brown appearing tired and morose after thirteen years in government. One unfortunate event for him was a confrontation with a woman in Lancashire, a Labour voter, who berated the prime minister for the steep rise in European immigrants, an increasingly powerful complaint after the credit crash. Brown was heard complaining about 'that bigoted woman'. The Conservatives, under their new leader, David Cameron, were distinctly more cheerful, with Cameron giving an air of youthful liberalism on social and moral issues. By far the most effective party leader seemed to be Nick Clegg, recently elected Liberal Democrat leader. He did especially well in the televised debates, and young supporters thereafter wore sweaters bearing the slogan 'I agree with Nick', a phrase of which Brown had made liberal use in the debates. The party also benefited from the reputation of their economics spokesman, Vince Cable, who appeared to be the one politician who had correctly forecast and understood the credit crash. The polls forecast a Conservative victory, though not by a large majority.

In fact, the polls left Britain with a relatively new experience, the first general election since 1929 in which no party had an overall majority, and the first hung parliament since Callaghan in 1977. The Conservatives ended up with 306 seats, a rise of 96. Labour fell to 258 seats, a fall of 91. Only in Scotland where it polled 42% of the vote did it put up anything like a strong performance. More surprising, due to the vagaries of the first-past-the-post voting system, the Liberal Democrats' tally of seats actually fell from 62 seats to 57, despite Clegg's lively campaign, which saw the Liberal Democrats gain 23% of the vote (over 6.8m.). There was much debate by commentators over the causes of all this; Ed Balls shrewdly pointed to immigration as a factor that had led voters to distrust the Labour government. The only possible outcome was a two-party coalition, of which Britain had had no experience in peacetime since Lloyd George's in 1918. The week after polling day was spent in secret discussions between Brown, Cameron, and Clegg about forming a coalition. Clegg, the leader of much the smallest party, was the key element. His own preference, unlike that of previous party leaders like Charles Kennedy and Menzies Campbell, was for an alignment with the Conservatives. More crucial was the arithmetic—a Lab-Lib coalition would only have the barest of majorities, perhaps only one or two, whereas a Conservative-Liberal government would be secure with a majority of over 50. Cameron was able to placate the Liberal Democrats over their main concern, a vote on proportional representation which could greatly increase their Commons membership. The Labour negotiations with Brown seemed far less positive, even with a younger leader like Ed Miliband who favoured voting reform. So Cameron moved into No. 10 with no manifesto such as the Unionists and Liberals had offered to the people in 1918. Instead, he had a document called 'the coalition agreement', the best common denominator on hand, but a document which made collective bi-partisan responsibility in the Cabinet very speculative. After a cheerful press conference in the rose garden of No. 10 with Clegg at his side, Cameron declared that it was a new era for Britain with the old politics cast aside.

This was wishful thinking. In fact, the new Coalition government ran into party political problems at a very early stage. It received a major psychological boost from the 2012 Olympic Games in London, a great organizational success with many victories for British athletes, male and female, who won a plethora of medals. But the impact politically was short-lived. Some key Liberals, notably Paddy Ashdown and Menzies Campbell, had been unhappy about a coalition with the Tories from the outset. They were aware that, historically, coalitions with the Conservatives had been catastrophic for Liberals. Their party had been divided into two in 1918 and into three in 1931. William Hague privately predicted this new coalition could quite possibly destroy the Lib. Dems. for all time. Problems soon emerged. The Lib. Dems. had to project an almost untenable position of voting for Conservative policies while indicating that they did not actually favour them, as though being in government and opposition at one and the same time. Problems soon emerged on both social and constitutional policy. Many Lib. Dem. activists in the country had strongly opposed being in alliance with the old Tory enemy in the first place, and tensions soon emerged. The most serious disagreement came very early in the history of the Coalition, over higher education policy. Clegg had rashly declared before the polls that as a matter of honour his party would never vote for higher tuition fees for university students, and large numbers of students in constituencies around the land voted Lib. Dem. accordingly. There was mass dismay when the new Chancellor, George Osborne, insisted on dealing with the problems of university funding by almost tripling tuition fees, from £3,000 to £9,000. Of the 57 Lib. Dem. MPs, 21 voted against it in the Commons and a further eight abstained. Students, already hard-pressed by the cost of re-paying loans over a long period of decades to come, responded with much anger, shown in many demos in university towns and cities. Clegg himself was reviled as a hypocrite who had broken his clearly stated word, Lib. Dems. around the country denounced the Coalition, and the reputation of both them and their leader never recovered.

More difficulties came on constitutional issues. The Lib. Dems. had been dogmatically committed to a radical reform of the largely nominated House of Lords, supposedly fulfilling promises made in 1911 by a Liberal prime minister at the time of the Parliament Act. The government came up with a patchwork bill which would halve the number of peers to 450 and have 80% of members of the Lords elected by proportional representation, but then to continue in post unelected for fifteen years. This aroused much opposition. Labour were inclined to oppose an elected upper house which might challenge the legitimacy of the Commons, while many Conservatives thought it a time-wasting triviality which would nevertheless damage the constitution. In the end, the government withdrew the bill when the timing arrangements fell through after a rebellion of 91 Conservative MPs. But it left the Lib. Dems. bitter and humiliated, and unwilling to endorse constituency boundary changes by a government of which they were members. Soon afterwards, came another setback. To fulfil a pledge made to the Liberal Democrats when the Coalition was formed, Cameron offered a referendum on an alleged form of proportional representation, the alternative vote, with members of the government free to campaign on opposing sides as happened over import duties under the national Government in 1932. It was another disaster. There was little popular interest, the public seeing it as a scheme to have permanent coalition. Cameron and the Conservatives campaigned strongly against it. While the new Labour leader, Ed Miliband, favoured PR as a way of unifying the anti-Tory vote, most of his party were hostile. The vote was predictably one-sided, with a majority of almost 70% voting against PR, which meant that it would disappear from the political agenda. The stability of the Coalition thus suffered a further blow.

The worst problem for the government, however, was that the weaker partner, the Lib. Dems., were inescapably identified with harsh social policies to which most of them were opposed, and their reputation suffered grievously for it. By the start of 2011 their opinion poll rating had fallen ten points to 13%, and they were shedding local government seats across the country. Cameron and Osborne's reaction to the effect of the credit crash was to blame much of the sovereign debt crises in so many countries on public spending, when politicians were desperate at the time to call in the state and even to nationalize banks. This policy, in Britain as elsewhere, was officially termed austerity, a grim programme of cutting back the national debt. Osborne's first emergency budget, after only a month in office, swung a mighty axe to welfare benefits, notably housing, child, out of-work and disability benefits. VAT would rise sharply. At the same time, banks were said to 'breathe a sigh of relief' after the bank levy was raised by a small amount despite the banks' disreputable role in the Crash.

It was followed by a Welfare Reform Act which set a firm maximum of benefits that could be paid to each household. and seriously added to working-class inequality. The most evocative cut of all was a new tax on 'spare room subsidy' often used for elderly relatives or their carers; which imposed harsh limits on rooms deemed to be surplus to needs. This new measure, reminiscent of the hated means test provision in the 1930s, became derided as the 'bedroom tax' and was a prime target for critics of the government. Experts claimed it was based on incorrect statistics of those moving into rented accommodation, and of the savings that would accrue. It was accompanied by £26bn. cuts in National Health Service spending. Liberal Democrats were highly critical of this but nevertheless found themselves trooping through the lobby in docile support in both Commons and Lords. Labour, under their new leader, Ed Miliband, naturally benefited greatly as a result, although the most effective setback from the opposition came from the House of Lords, where delegated legislation signifying major cuts in tax credits which would have severely affected many of the poorest, was voted down by peers as seriously unjust, Osborne later giving way to this rebuff.

Overall, the effect was a marked rise in social inequality. The effects of the deindustrialization in the 1980s now came home to roost. Employment held up but it was noticeable that many of the poor deemed to be living on or below subsistence level were actually in work. Child poverty also rose, with such New Labour initiatives as Sure Start being cut back. It was partly to provide for around 400,000 children in need that one embarrassing symbol of the Cameron era arose—food banks. These schemes, organised by charitable bodies such as the Tressel Trust in conjunction with high street stores, became as much of a public landmark as the dole queues of the thirties or the people sleeping rough outdoors in shop doorways in the eighties (these last also becoming more prevalent now). The government's policies did make slow progress in reducing the public deficit but at a grave, publicly visible cost to social justice, which undermined the welfare state and struck at the sense of communal provision since the 1942 Beveridge Report. It was all highly damaging to any sense of unity or collective responsibility for the Coalition, and for the heirs of Lloyd George, Keynes and Beveridge to be identified with such a programme.

The disaffection that the years of austerity brought merged with another fundamental source of division, the movement for the independence of Scotland. Ever since the Scottish National Party (SNP) assumed government in the Scottish Parliament at Holyrood in 2007, separatist sentiment had been growing. In a gloomy, depressed phase of its history, the United Kingdom itself seemed in danger of disintegration, just as Catalonia's separatist movement threatened the integrity of Spain. Wales, where much of the nationalist impulse was cultural and linguistic, was gradually warming to the idea of devolution, especially when the Welsh assembly acquired reserve powers comparable to those of the Scottish parliament. Plaid Cymru, the nationalist party, found it hard to win support away from the thinly-populated Welsh-speaking areas in the far west and north. Scotland was very different. The seeds had appeared ever since the creation of the Scottish parliament in 1999. Although the voting system was supposed to guard against any party winning an overall majority, the Scottish National Party, led by Alex Salmond, achieved this in the 2011 Scottish elections by claiming 69 seats. Here indeed were winds of change. Thereafter the politics of Scotland were a continuing story of a long-dominant Labour Party, with much Irish immigrant involvement, lapsing into decline, seen as traditional, uninspiring and, to a degree, corrupt.

As a result of this, an historic landmark occurred north of the border. Cameron had to give way on a key issue of principle. For the first time since the Union of Scotland in 1707, the Scottish people would be asked if they wanted to continue in it. Alex Salmond achieved his wish with a referendum on independence in Scotland, to be held symbolically on 18 September 2014, near the anniversary of the rout of the English at Bannockburn back in 1314 (23-24 June). It was a fierce contest with threats of civil disorder in places. The polls suggested that it would be very close, perhaps just a handful of votes in it, and much alarm was expressed in the media. Cameron, the prime minister, campaigned hard, as he had done in the AV referendum, and with some effect. Labour dominated the cross-party group 'Better Together', headed by the former Chancellor, Alastair Darling, but Ed Miliband, Labour's leader and a Londoner, seemed to have limited impact, even though the secession of Scotland would make it almost impossible for Labour to win power again without one of its great strongholds. Gordon Brown who returned to front-line politics was far more effective with several powerful speeches. Many considered him the man who saved the union.

But in the later stages of the referendum campaign the nationalist momentum appeared less powerful. The SNP in the past had argued that an independent Scotland would be more prosperous than if it were chained to the union, with revenue from its great reserves of oil ('It's Scotland's Oil') and its strong financial sector. Now the price of oil had fallen substantially while Scottish banks such as the Bank of Scotland had fared disastrously in the credit crash. It looked as if an independent Scottish government would be in serious deficit for a long period with Scottish incomes £300 a head less p.a. than those in the rest of the UK, while public spending (boosted by the controversial 'Barnett Formula') was £1,500 a head higher. In 2013–14, Scotland was performing far less well economically than the rest of the UK: its public deficit as a percentage of its GDP was 8.1%, whereas the UK as a whole showed one of 5.6% An independent nation seemed a far less attractive prospect for Scottish taxpayers now. Alternatively, nationalists said that unionists were relying on 'project fear'. In the end, the movement for Scottish independence lost its sheen, and the 'No' to independence vote carried the day by 55.3% to 44.7%. a larger majority than many had forecast. No Bannockburn this time around. An independent Scotland was off the agenda for the immediate future. It was significant that while Glasgow voted for independence (53.45%), along with North Lanarkshire (51.07%) and West Dunbartonshire (53.9%), only four out of 30 voting districts voted 'Yes' Edinburgh opposed independence by a wide margin. It was a decisive if not overwhelming majority. But the Scottish argument would not go away. The issue re-emerged with equal force during the debates on the European Union that were about to explode. It seemed possible that one act of disunion could lead to another.

The following year, the May 2015 general election was emphatically to confirm the power of Scottish separatism. The SNP, now led by Nicola Sturgeon, achieved an extraordinary sweeping triumph, winning no less than 56 of the 59 Scottish seats, polling over 50% of the votes north of the border. Labour were shattered, losing 40 seats and ending up with one, Edinburgh South. The Liberal Democrats fared just as badly, losing ten of their eleven seats and retaining only Orkney and Shetlands, while the Conservatives, in a land where Unionists had won the majority of seats as recently as 1955, also clung on to just one, despite the emergence of an impressive young woman leader, Ruth Davidson. It was an extraordinary performance, marking, it seemed, the possible demise of the creed of unionism in the United Kingdom. One symbolic result was the heavy defeat in Paisley and Renfrewshire of Douglas Alexander, once considered as a future Labour leader, by a Sottish Nationalist woman aged only twenty.

All over Scotland, from the remotest western isles and the highlands, through industrial Clydeside and down to the border, separatist sentiment was overwhelming, with Scottish civil society in the professional classes converted to the cause. Working-class opinion, too, for so long solidly Labour (the party of Keir Hardie which had bred the Clydesiders and waged the class war with unrelenting passion), was also affected by the economic decline and social injustices of the era of austerity. But the crisis here took the form not of class protest but of political nationalism. Gordon Brown argued that there were fundamental economic causes of the sweeping nationalist tide, but there were broader ideological and historical reasons for this too. Disaffection with the political system, and with the casual rule of a distant metropolitan elite located mainly in faraway south-east England and currently headed by public-school products like Cameron, Osborne, and the maverick mayor of London, Boris Johnson, was sharpened. In Scotland this was expressed through the call of nationalism. Working-class discontent with the union was now shown by the great city of Glasgow becoming a powerful centre of nationalism, while Edinburgh remained more favourable to the union. With Scotland emphatically supportive of membership of the European Union, and Euroscepticism or Europhobia heavily concentrated in southern England, the gulf between the two nations grew ever wider.

The Battle for Brexit

For the rest of the decade and beyond, British politics was convulsed by intense and bitter argument on Europe and little else. Almost all other domestic issues were put on hold. British foreign policy was to consist of disputes on Europe and little else. Indeed, Britain had scarcely had much of a foreign policy since the invasion of Iraq. When in 2013 there was a question of Britain sending forces to Syria, torn by civil war and mass atrocities, parliament voted it down, to the humiliation of Cameron and his Foreign Secretary, William Hague, amid a popular mood of isolationism. But deep-seated passions had lain beneath the surface for forty years over the EU. The 1975 referendum had avoided key aspects of joining the EU, notably the political urge for an 'ever closer union'. It reached a bitter climax over Maastricht during John Major's troubled years in 1992–3, but was dormant in the New Labour era. Britain had remained a semi-detached member of the EU. It had kept out of the Eurozone to popular rejoicing, it had insisted on opt-outs on the Social Chapter and the Schengen agreement on movements across boundaries. Yet the tabloid press kept up a barrage of derision against Jacques Delors and other 'Eurocrats', 'Brussels' became a term of popular abuse, the symbol of tyrannical control over the country by faraway unelected bureaucrats who flooded struggling Britain with hordes of unwanted immigrants from central and eastern Europe. The European question now dominated public life and divided the country as no issue had done since 1945.

This was first foreshadowed in the general election of May 2015. Outside Scotland, it had produced a mostly dull campaign which led commentators to forecast a close result. Despite the unpopularity of austerity, the Conservatives had held their ground and reduced the public debt. Labour had moved a little to the left, with Ed Miliband making a stirring attack on 'predatory capitalism' at the 2014 party conference, but the post-Blairite party still appeared uninspiring and searching for a cause. Yet few predicted the decisive swing to the Conservatives that occurred. There were three notable features. One, as noted above, was the astonishing SNP sweep throughout Scotland. Second was the near wipe-out of the Liberal Democrats, whose tally of seats crashed from 57 to only eight, with a mere 7.9% of the vote. As many party strategists had prophesied, the junior partner in the late Coalition suffered horrendously for their association with Conservative austerity policies, which most of them opposed anyway. And thirdly, the Conservatives held their own indirect conflict with Labour throughout England, with the exception of parts of London. As usual, Labour did particularly badly amongst the over-65s, gaining only 23% of their vote. There was every prospect, the first time since 1987, of a secure Conservative government, with 331 seats as against Labour's 232, and perhaps a new hegemony as the aftermath of the 2008 Crash began to pass into history. Cameron could hope to establish an historical reputation as a Macmillan-style One-Nation Tory. It marked the zenith of a swift and successful career.

But events turned out very differently. The most important result of the election was that of a small party which won no seats at all. Its influence on British public life was to exceed that of almost all the other parties combined, even though Europe had been not been a central issue in the campaign. This was UKIP, the UK Independence Party, a strongly anti-European nationalist movement with the sole purpose of having a referendum on membership of the European Union and then securing Britain's withdrawal from it. Formed in 1993, UKIP had made progress mainly in European elections. It particularly flourished under the leadership of a right-wing propagandist, Nigel Farage, who was known to engage in rough verbal assaults on immigrants from Europe and elsewhere and Muslim and other ethnic minorities more generally. It was a British nationalist party with populist overtones and an extremist fringe. In the 2015 general election it won over 3.5 million votes (12.5 per cent of the total) and also gained seven seats in Assembly elections in traditionally Labour Wales. It won no parliamentary seats (Farage was defeated in Thanet in Kent where anti-immigrant animus was strong), but it came second in over 100 other seats, along with several successes in local government elections. It targeted white working-class voters in run-down industrial constituencies in old Labour strongholds like the Durham coalfield and the South Wales valleys, and Labour lost votes to them. But so, too, did Conservatives when UKIP proved sympathetic to older white voters with conservative social and moral opinions, even if they lived in areas with very few immigrants at all. After the polling in 2015, UKIP and its sympathizers became an increasingly dangerous threat to the Conservative government. The arguments mounted by Eurosceptics (or in the case of UKIP Europhobes) changed the course of British political life.

Cameron soon found himself on the defensive like Major in 1993.The Conservative manifesto, after all, had promised another referendum on British membership (to which Liberal Democrat ministers had meekly agreed), at a time when Cameron did not seem to be under much pressure on the issue: he himself was marginally Eurosceptic but with no powerful convictions. The months after the general election were fateful. There was a growing contact between Conservative and UKIP grass-roots members, along with a core of some dozens of well-established backbench MPs, UKIP personnel and the organiser of a new body, 'Vote Leave', Dominic Cummings, a former Conservative party aide. Pressure inside his party compelled Cameron to attempt to redefine Britain's relations with EU, including on such issues as Britain's rebate on contributions to the EU, the impact of EU regulations on British national sovereignty, and the rights of immigrants to claim welfare provisions such as child benefits, a sore point with many voters. The prime minister, on the defensive, sounded increasingly critical of the EU and its procedures. Before the election he had called in a speech before the Bloomberg company for fundamental reforms in the Union. He had openly voiced his dismay at the election as new president of the European Council of Ministers of Jean Claude Juncker, a controversial Luxemburger and an arch federalist in Europe. A key episode was a meeting of Cameron with EU leaders in February 2016 when the British premier attempted to persuade the Europeans to adopt a less centralist approach and pay more heed to objections in Britain to the way Europe was run. Despite his confidence beforehand, Cameron returned with nothing to show.

An even more serious phase now followed. Cameron, showing signs of losing control of his party, was now facing serious resistance even in his Cabinet.[1] In particular, two key members declared themselves to be Leavers, to general surprise. One was Michael Gove, until recently Education Secretary and respected as an intellectual force in the government. The other was a maverick figure, long believed to be a Remainer, Boris Johnson, former twice elected mayor of London and a colourful figure in the media. His position was indeed ambiguous as he had apparently written newspaper articles both for and against being in the EU. But his relations with Cameron were not good, and he came out forcefully as a Leaver, citing the threat he believed the EU posed to British sovereignty. When, after a Cabinet meeting in February 2016, Johnson colourfully announced his determination that Britain should leave the EU, it caused a sensation. Newspapers speculated that this might herald a challenge to the prime minister's leadership speculation which Johnson noisily did nothing to dampen. It was known that six other Cabinet ministers, including the former party leader Ian Duncan-Smith, Chris Grayling and Priti Patel were similarly committed leavers. These were far more significant adversaries than long-running backbench critics like Bill Cash and Bernard Jenkin. Cameron challenged them all and went ahead with a referendum on Europe fixed for 24 June. Close advisers had wanted him to delay, but the prime minister, fresh from triumphs in the AV referendum in 2011 and the Scottish referendum, was full of self-confidence. Hubris was soon to descend.

The personnel of the party leadership was now important. Cameron had become over his six years in office an acquiescent European like Wilson, Callaghan, and Major before him. Even the critical Mrs. Thatcher had worked hard to create the single market. Cameron was never a warm advocate of the European Union, but it became clear to him that British trade and

[1] Tim Shipman, *All out War* (London, 2016), p. 345 ff.

employment depended on the links with Europe. He encouraged George Osborne to spell out the economic dangers that leaving Europe would mean. At the start of the referendum campaign the polls showed Remain ahead, though not decisively so, and suggested the wisdom of this approach. But a complicating factor was the leadership of the Labour Party. The party vote for a successor to Ed Miliband (who resigned immediately after the general election) resulted, to great surprise, in a near landslide for an elderly left-winger, Jeremy Corbyn, who easily outstripped his three centre-right opponents with a 59% share of the vote. He benefited by an influx of new party voters, who joined Labour under Ed Miliband's new rule which allowed sympathisers to join if they paid a three-pound membership fee. These were mostly young people and they formed a new pressure-group in the party called Momentum who pressed for left-wing causes including more deselection of sitting (centrist) members. For the first time since the early 1980s, Marxism played a part in political debate. But, while the young were mostly pro-Europe, Corbyn himself was a long-term Eurosceptic who had consistently opposed EU membership since the 1970s. He was still unsympathetic and took little part in the Brexit campaign in May-June. He said nothing positive on Europe. The success of the Leave campaign vote in June owed much to Corbyn's calculated refusal to assist the Remainers. In the end, 70 per cent of Labour constituencies were to vote Leave, contrary to the views of a large majority of Labour MPs. UKIP's decision to focus its attention on disgruntled white working-class voters had drawn dividends.

The Brexit referendum campaign was not distinguished. Hardly anyone, Remainer or Leaver, reflected on what life would be like after Brexit, or what the pattern of global trade would be like. Cries of 'take back control' had an ironic tone when so much of the British economy, industrial and financial, was already under the direct ownership of overseas companies and corporations. Half the London stock market was foreign owned. In the debate, such as it was, the most striking feature was the lifeless quality of the Remain campaign. There was none of the cross-party collaboration that characterised the referendum in 1975 which saw Edward Heath and Roy Jenkins joining forces for Yes, and Michael Foot and Enoch Powell for No sharing the same platforms. Neither Corbyn nor, to a lesser degree Cameron wished to associate publicly with rival parties. The debate was strident and often dishonest. Remainers focussed complacently on the economic damage that Brexit would do— 'project fear', which had worked in the Scottish referendum. Cameron made a bad error in implying that a refusal to vote Remain might lead to World War Three. Leavers, notably Boris Johnson, claimed falsely that ending EU membership would release £350m. a week for the National Health Service, that there might be a massive invasion of Turkish migrants, and that an unfettered post-Brexit Britain could easily trade with the rest of the world, which it was presently unable to do. While the Remain campaign, 'Stronger In', focussed on economic arguments ('project fear' again), Brexit arguments focussed on EU controls on British sovereignty (hence 'No more control'), and had an emotional flavour increasingly made more bitter and racist by the theme of immigration. A Leave battle bus and posters featured a long stream of migrants at a border post (in fact between Croatia and Slovenia). Remain supporters became increasingly nervous as the polls showed rising support for Leave. Their strategic belief that threats to the economy would have far more impact as a campaign issue than immigration was being shown to be false: a pro-Brexit Conservative, Penny Mordant, offered electors alarmist talk of 88 million immigrants likely to enter Britain from the Balkans and Turkey. A frightening indicator of how much racial bitterness had been stirred came near the end of the campaign when a young pro-Europe Yorkshire MP, Jo Cox, was brutally murdered by a racist constituent, a supporter of a fringe fascist body called Britain First. Politicians called for a truce in campaigning but this predictably lasted about a day and the campaign went on apace.

On referendum day, Remainer fears were amply confirmed. Contrary to predictions at the start of the campaign, Leave totalled 51.9% of the vote, and Remain just 48.1% It was a close result but a definitive one. The poll of 72.2% was relatively high. While Scotland voted clearly for Remain (although on a lower poll than expected), as did Northern Ireland, where Catholic and Sinn Fein voters were heavily pro-European, Wales unexpectedly voted for Leave, a strong vote being recorded in the depressed post-industrial valleys of the South. In England there was clear evidence of that English nationalism, long detected by commentators. Leave voters predominated equally in old Labour industrial areas in the north east, heralded by a 61% vote in Sunderland for Leave, and among older middle-class voters in southern England. Most major cities, London especially, Manchester, Liverpool, Leeds and Newcastle, backed Remain with their large body of young, better educated, more ethnically mixed electorates. But it was not enough: even London had a relatively low poll. British people had voted in numbers to sever their ties with Europe. Satirical commentators compared Cameron's legacy in breaking with Europe with that of Lord North in losing the American colonies in 1783.

The Prime Minster was the greatest and most immediate of the casualties. He resigned immediately, apparently anxious to avoid an outbreak of civil war in his party, or at least be involved in it himself. There was a brief but bitter contest for the leadership. Boris Johnson's noisy efforts were promptly torpedoed by his campaign colleague Michael Gove who publicly cast doubt on his judgement and leadership credentials. There was a brief flurry by another right-winger, Angela Leadsom. In the end there was elected unopposed Theresa May, the former Home Secretary, who had voted Remain but played virtually no part in the campaign. Sceptical colleagues christened her 'the Submarine' for her invisibility. She was a cautious, uncharismatic figure, a vicar's daughter who would inevitably face severe challenges within in her party for her position on Brexit, especially from Brexiters in the grass-roots who argued that the referendum had given them the popular mandate for which they had contended. The Conservatives were now torn into three, ex-Remainers like the Chancellor Philip Hammond, 'hard Brexiters' who followed Johnson and the back-bencher Jacob Rees-Mogg, and, the largest group, milder Brexiters like the Prime Minister. With the country divided or simply muddled about its view, May had to stagger on from June 2016 until the resolution of the Brexit negotiations with the European Union, fixed for 29 March 2019. Undermined at home, frustrated by the Europeans, with bleak economic news and anger on the streets, where some immigrants were physically assaulted for doing nothing worse than speaking Polish in public, May faced the most severe tensions within the Conservative Party since Robert Peel had split them over the repeal of the Corn Laws in 1846. Beyond that, the country faced its most severe and divisive political conflict since the second world war. Neither Suez nor the poll-tax riots compared with this.

May's unhappy plight soon got a great deal worse. After a prolonged deadlock in her party, she quite unexpectedly called another general election, despite having a perfectly workable majority in the Commons. She hoped to appeal to the kind of nationalist instincts that had carried Brexit in the referendum and thereby win a strong base during the negotiations in Brussels. The outcome for her was catastrophic. The Conservatives lost their majority, ending up with 315 seats, a loss of 13, Labour won 262 seats, a gain of 30 (and a rise of 9.5% of the poll), while the Liberal Democrats stayed in the doldrums with just 12 seats. UKIP support fell dramatically and the party won no seats. A very revealing result was in Scotland where the SNP lost 21 seats in total, to Conservatives, Labour and Lib. Dems., to end up with 35. This suggested that, despite having a popular leader in Nicola Sturgeon, the tide for independence had receded. In England and Wales, far from achieving a solid hold on power after the Brexit victory, May lost much ground to Labour. Her majority disappeared in a hung parliament. The Conservatives had fought a listless campaign, focussing mainly on the unimaginable horrors that would result from a Labour government headed by the old-fashioned left-winger, Jeremy Corbyn. Theresa May herself did little to enthuse supporters and attracted derision for her mechanical repetition of the phrase 'strong and stable government'. The electors seemed to be more impressed by the spectacle of interminable Conservative divisions over Brexit, with Boris Johnson an unpredictable freebooter on the fringes. May's personal advisers, Nick Timothy and Fiona Hill, were attacked for aggressive high-handedness and later dismissed.

Labour performed far more strongly than the analysts had expected. The polls, having overstated the Labour vote in 2015, now had seriously underestimated it in 2017. It benefitted from the tens of thousands of mainly young people who had joined the party via Momentum since Corbyn's election as leader. With over half a million members, Labour was now the largest Social Democratic party in western Europe. The election results showed that Labour voters in areas such as Wales and the north-east had returned to the fold in the aftermath of austerity. At the same time, while Jeremy Corbyn had largely kept his peace over Brexit, Labour clearly benefited from the mass support of younger pro-Remain voters, notably university students who were strongly pro-European. This emerged in such constituencies as Sheffield Hallam, (where Nick Clegg lost his seat), Reading, and Cardiff. There were some remarkable results: Labour narrowly won wealthy Kensington and Chelsea, with a high quota of millionaires, many of them coming from abroad such as Russian oligarchs. They also improbably gained Canterbury, the first time the Conservatives had lost it since the election of 1832. Significantly, the constituency contained 20,000 university students, who voted in numbers. The outcome for Brexit now was unpredictable, even perilous. May faced the prospect of difficult negotiations with the EU representatives, with a disunited Cabinet (she placed the leading Brexiters David Davis, Liam Fox and Boris Johnson in the key posts of Trade, the European Exit department and, however improbably, Foreign Secretary, where Johnson was to prove a highly erratic minister) and no majority in the Commons. The last problem was resolved with a difficult pact with the ten-strong Democratic Unionist Party. This proved to be an expensive deal, with the Treasury having to hand over £1.1bn. in subsidies to the government in Stormont. The status of the Irish border now became a huge stumbling-block in the Brexit negotiations with the EU. May faced an almost impossible position, and commentators constantly forecast her resignation, a constant backdrop to her remaining time in office.

From the 2017 electoral setback to the end of the Brexit negotiations in March 2019, British public life appeared to be on hold. Urgent economic and social issues, health, education, the alarming state of prisons and the justice system were sidelined by the interminable conflict on Brexit, which dragged on throughout 2018 with no clear outcome. Citizens and families were divided. The first battle concerned the ultimate decision-making body that would ratify a deal on Brexit. The government's assertion, contrary to traditional beliefs on parliamentary sovereignty, that the issue would rest with ministers because the verdict had been decided by the referendum, was challenged by a private citizen in the high court, Gina Miller, well represented by David Pannick QC. The government was defeated there, and lost again, more importantly, in the Supreme Court by eight to three, several judges quoting Magna Carta in their judgements. They were crudely denounced in the right-wing tabloid the *Daily Mail* as 'enemies of the people'. So a government without a majority would stand or fall on the view of a deeply divided Commons, with the Lords being overwhelmingly pro-Europe.

The government's torment over Brexit was conducted on three levels, the negotiations with the EU, the situation in a hung parliament, and crises in a deeply divided Cabinet. With the European negotiators, there was an unexpectedly brisk start, with agreement reached early on over the so-called 'divorce terms', including a large payment in compensation to the European Union, much to the fury of Brexiters in Conservative ranks. Thereafter, there was a hard slog with little yielding on either side. It soon became clear that the hope of a concluding settlement being reached in a year and a half was remote, and a two-year 'transitional period' had to be agreed for 2019–21, during which EU rules and regulations in Britain would continue. Britain suffered from the casual style of its main negotiator, David Davis, and appeared to be arguing that it should enjoy the benefits of being in a Union while leaving the EU itself.

Apart from arguments over the single market and the customs union, there was deadlock over an issue that had scarcely appeared in the referendum debates—the border between Northern Ireland and the South, the only area where a part of Britain was physically contiguous to an EU country. There was a general view that a 'hard border' should be resisted to protect the peace process contained in the Good Friday Agreement years earlier. The EU demanded that Northern Ireland should join the customs union, while the pro-Brexit Northern Irish Democratic Unionists declared that in no way could the province be separated from the rest of the United Kingdom. There were two other extraneous problems—the fact that Northern Ireland had once again no government in post, after Sinn Fein ministers resigned, and the private pact made between the Democratic Unionists and Theresa May to prop up a minority British government. The British proposed technological methods to facilitate border movement of goods and people; the EU wanted a border to be created in the Irish Sea instead, which of course threatened the union of the United Kingdom. On most fronts there seemed very little meeting of minds. A document produced by the May government in September 2018, the 'Chequers plan', proposed 'frictionless' trade with the EU with 'a common rule-book' and a so-called 'backstop' arrangement to avoid a hard border for Northern Irish trade with the south and for the whole UK to remain part of the EU customs territory after Brexit. The other 27 countries of the EU dismissed it with contempt, and ministers resigned. Agreement, with a final settlement notionally only four months off, seemed improbable. The government now openly declared that 'no deal' was a distinctly possible outcome, which would leave the business world and the work-force apprehensive and in disarray. Government papers spelt out steps that would be taken if no deal resulted. Even though these were hypothetical circumstances, they illustrated the kind of problems the country faced. There were alarmist newspaper predictions of no planes in the sky between the UK and EU countries, Eurostar trains unable to travel to Paris, and a huge pile-up of heavy lorries in carparks in Kent around Dover while complicated customs checks were carried out.

The second complexity was the prospect of carrying a settlement through a hung parliament. This largely depended on swirling opinions within the Conservative, as torn over Brexit as it had been over tariff reform before the first world war. At times near-civil war in the party seemed to be breaking out. A hard-core group of backbenchers, the so-called European Research Group, numbering anything from 30 to 60, led by a vehement right-winger, Jacob Rees-Mogg, protested loudly against diplomatic compromise which appeared to go against the referendum result. The measure to proceed with Article 50 went through the Commons without trouble since the Labour Party chose not to resist the referendum verdict. Much more difficulty came with the European Withdrawal Bill (the original name, 'The Great Repeal Bill', was dropped). In the Commons Labour was now more resistant and supported a form of customs union. The strongly pro-European House of Lords was more hostile still and passed fifteen amendments again the government, most by large majorities. They covered a wide range of issues including the status of former EU law, the European Charter of Fundamental Rights, ministers' prerogative 'Henry VIII' powers, the prospect of Britain joining a compromise European Economic Association like Norway, the Northern Irish Good Friday Agreement, and what was meant by 'a meaningful vote' when the terms went before parliament. The government had many narrow escapes on the Lords' amendment, scraping through by majorities of between two and ten, and actually losing on a motion to keep links with the European Medicine Agency (which had decided in any case to move from London to

Amsterdam). On a European Trade Bill the government carried the day by three votes, helped by four Labour pro-Brexit votes and two Liberal Democrats (including their leader, Farron) missing the vote altogether. The prospect for a final deal getting through the Commons was obscure. In October, barely a month before the supposed day of settlement on 31 October, Halloween, the ten Democratic Unionists threatened to oppose the budget after further deadlock on the Northern Irish border.

The British position in negotiations over Brexit was made even more unclear through deep splits within the government. Boris Johnson vocally led them by condemning any deviation from a hard Brexit position. The point of collision was reached in early September when Theresa May put forward in Cabinet her so-called Chequers plan, which proposed some involvement in a customs union and a 'backstop' and a 'facilitated customs agreement' to preserve Northern Irish trade contacts with the EU. The complaints of Northern Ireland were matched by those of the Scottish Parliament and the Welsh Assembly, which both objected to the Trade Bill negotiations marginalising them and going against the thrust of devolution. The United Kingdom itself was now in peril. At this point David Davis, the EU treaty negotiator, resigned from the government, and called for Cabinet ministers to mutiny against May. Another major resignation was that of Boris Johnson, the Foreign Secretary, who now felt free to launch personal attacks on the prime minister and apparently promote his own claims to lead the country. The government staggered on regardless, but the forthcoming trial of strength in the lead-up to a finalized treaty agreement on 29 March did not bode well. Divided at home, assailed in Europe, marginalised in its relations with the United States after the election of the unpredictable nationalist President Trump, Britain's world standing seemed at a low ebb.

There were many commentaries on the state of British society during the years of the Brexit impasse. Many of them were bleak. The country continued to enjoy the external peace and relative internal tranquillity it had enjoyed since 1945. It moved on from the industrial crises of the 1970s and the Northern Irish troubles of the eighties. The prosperity of most citizens continued. Yet, from the turn of the century there was a growing picture of division and disillusion. Ever since the 1970s it had been accepted that social inequality, measured in terms of income, wealth or status had deteriorated. The IPPR Commission of Economic Justice, which included the Archbishop of Canterbury, Justin Welby, showed how Britain was being held back by years of falling living standards for working people, the worst rate of decline since the end of the Napoleonic Wars. Sociologists identified particular types of community in particular difficulty, smaller provincial towns and depressed seaside resorts amongst them. A harmful business culture was rampant, dominated by decades of short-term profit-taking, with weak levels of investment and low wages, which led to Britain slipping down the international tables for investment and productivity. With large-scale cuts in welfare, poverty grew rapidly. The Social Metrics Commission showed that more than half the families living below the breadline had at least one member suffering from physical disability.[2] With the introduction of Universal Benefit, government ministers admitted that the poorest in society, both those in badly-paid unskilled work and the unemployed, would suffer from serious cuts in what income they had up to the level of £2,000 a year, whereas the wealthiest continued to prosper.

Inequality became even more serious in the years of austerity after 2009, which led to benefits paid to the poorest falling by £37bn. It manifested itself in the food banks, rough sleeping, and a sharp rise in child poverty. At least 500 Sure Start centres for the young closed after 2010, along with over 478 public libraries which ministered particularly to the elderly. The social gulf in the country was alarmingly on display in 2017 in a terrifying fire in Grenfell Tower in Kensington, an area which contained many millionaires and had become a by-word for empty luxury homes

---

[2] Social Metrics Commission, *A New Measure of Poverty in the UK* (London, September 2018).

owned by a celebrity caste of international speculators and oligarchs. Seventy-four people, mostly poorer immigrants, lost their lives in Grenfell as a result of electrical faults, shoddy cladding and other poor materials being used in tower blocks, and inadequate provision for fire-prevention and basic safety. A society of two nations was on display to the world, and it cost many lives.

The Brexit referendum had also revealed a myriad of other social divisions, not necessarily based on class or wealth. Some saw it as a contest between those favouring an Open and a Closed Britain. There was, for example, division between generations, There was a relatively comfortable proportion of the elderly, 'grey power', who invariably cast their votes, usually Conservative. Brexit was largely the work of the retired. At the same time, the over-65s themselves suffered increasingly from an acute crisis in social care as a result of cuts in local government budgets. Conversely, there were struggling young people, finding it hard to get jobs, even armed with degrees, labouring under thousands of pounds of debt after their student days were over, failing to get on the housing ladder, and facing further threats to their employment prospects from Brexit. The young, especially the educated young, voted overwhelmingly for Remain. Indeed, the gulf in social outlook and lifestyle between the well-educated professionals and those with few educational attainments was a particular source of conflict. It was a delayed reaction against what Michael Young had described as 'the rise of the meritocracy' in the late 1950s. *The Economist* (22 December 2018) described 'The elite that failed'.[3] More generally, it seemed that most of those involved in productive work were not supportive of Brexit, from the Confederation of British Industries and the City of London down to individual members of the workforce.

There were also sharper regional divisions on display, a marked gulf in wealth and opportunity between cities and the

---

[3] The Elite that Failed: Britain's Political Crisis Exposes the Inadequacy of its Leaders. *The Economist*. 22 December 2018.

countryside, and between London and everywhere else. Indeed, London flourished now more as an international city, rather than a lynch-pin of the national economy. In the City, investment was outwards rather than inwards. Still, despite the high cost of house prices and services, the capital acted as a unique magnet for the young and was virtually a separate country. Attacks on the EU were targeted more against London than Brussels. In a way it rather resembled the Wimbledon tennis championship, an international arena of great distinction but in which foreigners usually won the prizes. Journalists questioned whether London was becoming a city-state on its own, while efforts made to shift major institutions to the provinces, such as the BBC relocating in Salford, had little effect. Proposals that a refurbished palace of Westminster should move from central London to central Hull did not find favour. Regions such as the North-East and East Anglia, along with South Wales and Clydeside in the Celtic nations, felt marginalised or excluded, resentful of a remote metropolitan elite who controlled their lives. Their reaction in a way was paralleled by Trump's nationalist voters in the US presidential election. The gulf between home-owners, even those hard-pressed to pay their mortgages, and renters of property formed another sharp social cleavage, as did the gap between in those who paid for expensive private health insurance and the majority, reliant on a crumbling National Health Service, another stark feature of the post-code lottery.

Britain in 2019 was a society far more obviously divided, almost at war within itself, than at any stage since before the relative solidarity of the immediate post-war years. New technical inventions made the division on all grounds far sharper. Social media such as Facebook could bring people closer together (as shown in the growth of grass-roots support for the Labour Party after 2015).[4] Others like Twitter could have the opposite effect. They commonly had a distorting effect on the presentation

---

[4] Alan Rusbridger, *Breaking News: The Remaking of Journalism and Why It Matters* (Canongate, London, 2018), pp. 213–27.

of unchecked, indeed uncheckable, fake news and dishonest journalism and other forms of communication. For individuals they encouraged a tone of greater aggression and confrontation. Digital media could be a force for immense unhappiness, from the bullying of young people, leading to a growth in suicides, to the unfair targeting of ethnic or religious minorities as public victims. This was reinforced by instances of anti-Semitism within the Labour Party, to which its leader, Jeremy Corbyn, seemed unable to respond effectively. He was to be attacked for this by the Chief Rabbi during the 2019 general election, while Islamophobia became more widespread in Conservative ranks. One effect of racial hostility was a rise in terrorist attacks. One cost the life of a policeman in the House of Commons, while there was a particularly horrifying atrocity at a pop concert in Manchester in May 2017 which killed 22, mainly young, people. The Brexit tensions fuelled these developments: far-right bodies like the English Defence League, a member of which had murdered Jo Cox MP, spread tension and aggression in many northern towns and cities, and foreigners felt themselves and their children to be at risk. Increasingly, once tolerant Britain was viewed as an angry country in which individuals reflected growing pessimism over their social and economic prospects. It was also, to a degree, a more violent country. Knife crimes by young men in London soared to almost 15,000 in the course of 2018-19, an increase of over 5,000 from 2015-16. At the start of 2020, it was recorded that 149 people had been murdered in the previous year, London's highest murder rate for over a decade.

Alongside this sense of division went a growing feeling of disillusion towards institutions and traditions deeply rooted in public awareness. In the view of right-wing nationalists this was fanned by the so-called 'flood' of immigrants who had entered Britain since the turn of the century. Parliament and the political system, where Britain had for long been seen as a land of stability and coherence, which had known no major internal crises since the civil wars of the seventeenth century, suffered a marked fall in prestige. During the Brexit debate, it was questioned whether

Britain embodied the sovereignty of parliament any longer. Books like David Marquand's *Mammon's Kingdom* (2014) expressed the lack of belief and trust in a system which had stood the test of centuries.

In the Churchill-Attlee period during and after the war, the British knew and respected those by whom they were led. Douglas Jay could write that 'the gentleman from Whitehall', the mandarin of centralist indicative planning, knew best. By the end of the seventies this faith was ebbing, perhaps inevitably so.. The rapid growth of the Scottish National Party demonstrated this sharply north of the border. After Brexit (mainly an English ideology), the challenge of possible Scottish independence again revived. Again, the House of Commons had discredited itself in a series of financial irregularities. It also seemed to be overridden by the popular sovereignty of the Brexit referendum and wide-ranging secondary legislation (often more primary in effect), and by the steady accretion of power to the executive through use of prerogative 'Henry VIII' powers. The revolving door through which senior politicians moved on effortlessly to well-remunerated business positions, exemplified by Tony Blair's and David Cameron's affluence in retirement, and by Nick Clegg's departure to California to work for Facebook, met with cynicism. The constitution, revered since Blackstone and Burke, was also under challenge from uncertainty over devolution, with the agreed reserved powers of the legislatures in Scotland and Wales threatened in the Europe Withdrawal Bill by a kind of centralizing colonialism at Westminster. The Union of the United Kingdom was no longer the totem it had been. The flying of the Union flag was less popular, including in England where an increasing nationalist mood saw the flag of St. George re-emerge from relative obscurity. The national anthem was heard less often in the Celtic nations. Republicanism was a minority view (perhaps 20 per cent support), but the monarchy retained its support largely through the personal regard for the long-serving monarch. The prospect of King Charles III, with his various controversial views, aroused longer-term concern for the monarchy. The marriage of Prince Harry to a divorced black American of progressive outlook was at first a popular event, but it later led to angry disputes and litigation between the prince and the tabloid press, and the couple left for California and forsook their royal roles and titles. Revelations about Prince Andrew's links with a convicted American paedophile led to damaging controversy, especially after a disastrous television interview. Overall, constitutionalists like Professor Anthony King pronounced the governmental system, for which Britain had long been renowned and admired, to be 'a mess', scarcely a representative democracy at all. A variety of populist challenges ranging from UKIP to the SNP seemed to illustrate the point.

Other established pillars of civil society, old symbols of 'Britishness', were also under fire. The Church of England continued mired in increasing decline, claiming the notional adherence of barely 10 per cent of the population, and these mainly elderly. Its internal divisions over women bishops and gay marriages (for which it was defeated) helped to discredit it further. Church disestablishment, however, which had occurred long ago in Ireland and Wales, was not strongly championed, mainly because interest in religious matters in a secular country was so tenuous. The nonconformist chapels of Wales and the north were shadows of what they had been, while the Roman Catholics were seriously damaged by claims of child abuse, long covered up. In Ireland the Church was in full retreat. The polls showed that fewer than half the population thought of themselves as religious believers; the only robust faith body being the Muslim. Again, universities had long been thought of as a glory of the nation. In 2018 Oxford and Cambridge were rated as the two strongest universities in the world, a rare instance of the pre-eminence of British 'soft power'. But the high cost of tuition fees led to some decline in their popularity amongst school-leavers as youth unemployment intensified, while their prestige was weakened by the rapacious concern of some vice-chancellors for their own remuneration. The small numbers of black students was much criticized. Famous innovations like the Open University, along with further education more generally, were in financial peril. Meanwhile a minister of education, Michael Gove, instructed the voters to beware of educated 'experts', out of touch with ordinary people. The BBC, esteemed since the Second World War as a unique and utterly reliable fount of truthful information, also lost ground, partly as a result of competition from the social media and commercial agencies. It was also under attack from feminists for the unequal payment of male and female broadcasters. The banks and the financial services in general had suffered a steep loss of esteem after the incompetence and greed revealed in the crash in 2008. In addition, as noted above, more than in most countries they were run from overseas.

The rule of law was also challenged by the Brexit process, and the representatives of the law suffered accordingly. Surveys of the judicial system painted a depressing picture of under-paid judges in shabby surroundings who felt unprotected under attack from the politicians and the tabloid press, 'enemies of the people' in the judgement on the Supreme Court in the inimitable *Daily Mail*. The members of the Lords Constitutional Committee were similarly abused by the same source. Sources of disquiet were numerous. Poorer offenders failed to receive proper legal representation because of serious cuts in legal aid. More widely, the nation's prisons were felt to be under-resourced and downright dangerous both for staff and the public. The rehabilitation of prisoners there was highly improbable while the probation service was run down under an inadequate, poorly-led Ministry of Justice. Ancient and inadequate institutions such as Swansea prison, whose work first began in 1845, were still in use. Britain as a law-abiding stable country no longer commanded the same esteem. Finally, the very concept of the United Kingdom, since 1707 one of the world's thriving and successful international associations, was seriously under fire after the nationalist challenge in Scotland and to a much lesser degree in Wales, where much of the sentiment was cultural. Unionism was thus another casualty of the time. The Brexit imbroglio sparked off a new interest in a unified Ireland with the advance of Sinn Féin. As elsewhere in Europe, notably in Catalonia, an established regime and social system were being weakened in much of their foundations. Commentators wondered whether Brexit would lead to some kind of rejuvenation of an ancient land or to its internal disintegration.

The later period of the political manoeuvres over Brexit between November 2018 and the destined settlement day of 31 October 2019 (later extended on EU insistence to 31 January 2020) were appropriately termed by one commentator 'the politics of Mayhem'.[5] There was further, prolonged shuttle diplomacy between Westminster and Brussels. In the first instance, they focussed mainly on the Northern Irish 'backstop', to which the Democratic Unionists were opposed. Then followed desperate attempts to prevent a no deal scenario', the worst of all outcomes which would leave Britain in a very vulnerable economic condition. On 14 November it was announced that Theresa May and the EU negotiators had finally reached agreement for the terms on which Britain would leave, but this was followed immediately after by the resignation of the newly-appointed Exit minister, Dominic Raab, from the government. A series of parliamentary defeats for the government followed. On 14 January 2019, when May put her version of the deal to the vote, the so-called Chequers plan, she suffered the humiliation of its being rejected by the Commons by no less than 230 votes, the largest defeat by any government in parliamentary history. The government soon suffered another defeat on the deal, by another very large majority.

The deadlock in policy was made worse for the Conservatives' minority government by unprecedented volatility in the Commons when the party system appeared close to collapse. A handful of Labour and Conservative MPs actually broke away from their parties to form a centrist Remain party, but it soon folded and its members mostly moved to join the Liberal Democrats in

[5] Tim Shipman, *Fall Out: A Year of Political Mayhem* (London, 2017).

campaigning for another referendum on the EU. There was the spectacle now, and bewildering to foreigners who thought of Britain, with its internal peace of having a unique tradition of strong and stable government of the Commons in disarray, a large Brexit group in the Conservatives, Labour in confusion and critical of its leader, Corbyn. British foreign policy seemed to be driven by rival groups of backbenchers totally unable to find a consensus on the way ahead. At one stage, the government had to urge its backbenchers to vote against their own motion. Unsurprisingly, the Commons did vote to accept a motion to delay article 50 coming into effect for at least several more months. It was typical of this chaotic period that on 27 March the Commons in effect tried to take control of foreign policy. The end product was that eight different proposals were put forward—and all eight were defeated. Things seemed to be falling apart. In central London meanwhile, a huge but good-humoured, peaceable crowd of over a million marched through the city demanding a so-called 'People's Vote', numbers last seen on the streets during the Iraq invasion in 2003.

Her policies in total deadlock, Theresa May resigned and an unhappy premiership came to an end on 23 July. Her successor, predictably, was the Brexiteer Boris Johnson, who defeated the ex-Remainer Jeremy Hunt with a two-to-one majority amongst party members. He announced his fierce determination to 'die in the last ditch' to achieve Brexit by 31 October; it would get done, 'do or die'. His premiership began with a series of parliamentary defeats. He responded with a daring attempt to abbreviate parliamentary opposition by trying to prorogue parliament for five more weeks. He was memorably defeated here too. On 24 October, a group of Remainer citizens, headed by Gina Miller again, took the case to the Supreme Court, which roundly demolished the government's argument by a majority of 11–0, The president, Baroness Hale, declared Johnson's action to be 'unlawful' and therefore null and void. She quoted a famous judgement in 1612 by Sir Edward Coke, criticising James I and strongly upholding the importance of the prerogative power giving way to the fact of parliamentary sovereignty. The rule of law was thus memorably restated; parliament returned the next day. The last attempt to suspend the legislature had taken place with the so-called 'Eleven Years' Tyranny' imposed by Charles I in 1629–40. And he had ended up also in Whitehall, but on the scaffold.

Johnson in the end, after several concessions, managed to achieve a controversial agreement with the EU on the terms of an exit. The customs border between Northern Ireland and the United Kingdom would indeed be located in the Irish Sea, while duties might be paid on goods sent from Ulster to the English or Welsh coast. This was approved by the Commons—but it then assumed control of the Commons timetable which removed Johnson's power to effect it. Johnson had met with further failure: the 'last ditch' of 31 October met with further delay, and 31 January became the new deadline. Deprived of any feasible alternative at home or abroad, Boris Johnson called for a general election on 12 December. The last December election since Stanley Baldwin's called in 1923 (which he lost), this might after three and half years of torment be the moment when Britain and Europe alighted on some form of separation, the break with Brussels being the most profound schism in the country's history since Henry VIII's breach with Rome.

The general election campaign in November-December 2019 was highly personalized and distasteful. When a young prison reformer was stabbed to death by a released terrorist, there was much partisan debate, led by Johnson, as to which party was responsible for the tragedy. Traditional party and class alignments were in disarray; for instance, a clear majority of working-class electors, many swayed by Brexit, voted for the Conservatives. The two main parties, especially Labour (who proposed spending a record £83 billion in their first year in power) tried to shift the argument towards domestic social and economic reform. After years of neoliberalism and austerity, the big state was back in vogue, including the nationalization of rail and other industries for the first time since 1951. But inevitably Brexit cast a huge shadow over the campaign, even if fundamental issues like the details of future trade and relations with the EU remained as vague as ever. Tactically, the Conservatives benefited greatly from the Brexit Party declining to oppose their candidates so as not to split the pro-Brexit vote. Tory Remainers were exiled. On the other hand, Labour, Lib. Dems, nationalists, Green and other Remain parties failed to reach any kind of common strategic position, while Labour suffered from the evasive outlook of Jeremy Corbyn who bewilderingly declared that he would be neutral if any further referendum took place. The dilemma facing pro-Brexit Labour voters in older industrial areas in Northern England, the Midlands and south Wales was thus laid bare.

The outcome was generally foreseen, even if significantly larger than estimated in the later polling before election day. It was an immense victory for Boris Johnson, who won 365 seats (44% of the vote),gained 66 seats and an overall majority of 80, their best result since the heyday of Margaret Thatcher in the 1980s The party made striking progress in the 'red wall' of previously Labour strongholds in the North-East of England, Yorkshire, parts of the Midlands, and in Wales, and captured large swathes of working-class communities, such as former mining areas, which had voted Leave in the Brexit referendum. Several industrial constituencies returned a Conservative for the first time. Conversely, for the opposition parties it was a total disaster. Labour's tally of seats fell to 203, a fall of 7.4% in their vote and 42 in their tally of seats, the worst result since the election of 1935. Only in the London area, with its younger, educated pro-Remain voters, did the party retain its strength, as it did in Manchester and other large cities. There seemed to be potential signs of a long-term decline of the party, in disarray over its policies, ideology and leadership, with Corbyn announcing he would shortly (though not immediately) resign. His elected successor, Sir Keir Starmer, the former Director of Public Prosecutions, was a centrist Remainer and immediately boosted Labour's standing in the opinion polls. For the strongly pro-EU Liberal Democrats it was near wipe-out: they fell from 12 seats to only

11, with their young leader losing her seat in Scotland. If the results confirmed the dominating influence of Brexit, it also reflected peril for the Union of the Kingdom. As in 2015, the Scottish Nationalists soared in the polls, winning 48 of the 59 Scottish seats and immediately calling for another referendum on independence which Scottish electors now seemed to favour. Johnson resisted this demand, and uncertainty and conflict within the British realm seemed certain to follow. In Northern Ireland there was also important change; the previously majority Democratic Unionists lost two seats and fell to just eight. Here again, the future of a basic component of the United Kingdom was in serious doubt, the forces of unionism in retreat.

A profound transformation seemed certain to follow. Brexit would surely come about after the disputes of the previous two and a half years. But if the parliamentary outcome was clearer, the broader future was anything but. The key underlying issues had scarcely been touched upon during a bad-tempered election campaign. Britain's trading relationships with the EU and the rest of the world, its robustness within a global economy, its collaboration with others on impending environmental catastrophe, defence arrangements, and the guarantee of domestic security, would lead to a complex and uncertain agenda for the prime minister, himself an unpredictable personality. The general election might have produced closure in parliamentary terms, but in a deeply divided land, facing unknown crises at home and overseas, so diminished from the imperial grandeur of former days, even from in 1945, the tensions and the uncertainty would surely continue.

What held the creaking structure of Great Britain together, many believed and hoped, was not its resilience in the face of contemporary challenges, but its attachment to its past, real or invented, even if it was a history that grossly underplayed the experience of the black minority. The importance of the slave trade in the commercial wealth of Bristol or Liverpool, for instance was usually overlooked. Boris Johnson's hero figure was evidently Winston Churchill, who rescued the nation in

1940 and whose life he had written in autobiographical vein. A series of commemorations of former glories gave the history of Britain renewed prominence. One, celebrated on both sides of the Atlantic, and also in France, was the eighth centenary of Magna Carta in 2015, still an inspirational and even romantic symbol across the globe. It was noticeable that the chairman of the celebratory committee was an American. This led to much scholarly and judicial praise of this unique declaration of the rule of law, and the liberty of the 'freeborn' citizen as against *raison d'état*. Lord Chief Justice Denning had seen it as the most important legal statement anywhere any time, a view shared by the great lawyer, Lord Justice Bingham. Another popular celebration of the past came with the centenary of the granting of the vote to women in the 1918 Representation of the People Act. It gave an opportunity to assess how the status of women had advanced over that hundred years. After all, there was a second woman prime minister in office in 2019—and also three women out of the eleven judges of the Supreme Court, including a doughty feminist as president in Baroness Hale, along with three female bishops. At the same time, the status of women was still restricted, sometimes through covert sexual harassment (attacked in the 'Me Too' protests), 'glass ceilings' in employment, and, less obviously, within the family. Women still suffered, but Mike Leigh's film epic to commemorate the bicentenary of the Peterloo massacre in 1819 was a reminder of the brutality confronted in winning the vote for working-class men as well. Significantly, the centenary of the even more savage slaughter by the British Raj of peaceful Indian Sikh demonstrators at Amritsar in 1919 was totally ignored by the British government. Not until 2020 did significant protests break out over the inequality and exploitation of Britain's Black minority. The statue of an eighteenth-century slave trader, Edward Colston, was pitched into Bristol harbour while that of the millionaire imperialist Cecil Rhodes, was, perhaps, to be taken down from the plinth in Oriel College, Oxford, as its counterpart was removed in the 'Rhodes Must Fall' campaign in the University of Cape Town.

More uncertain was the commemoration of the First World War. It could hardly be a celebration, but important works in print and on the screen reminded people of the sheer courage of British soldiers, sailors, and airmen in giving or risking their lives on behalf of a cause denounced by the poet Wilfred Owen as 'obscene as cancer'. It did remind the country how even in pre-republican southern Ireland thousands of men 'signed up' for the cause, although the widespread anti-war sentiment amongst working people and the ILP was given scant prominence. The centenary of the 1916 Easter Rising in Dublin, however, came and went without Anglo-Irish crisis. An Irish government representative laid a wreath at the Cenotaph on the centenary anniversary of the 1918 Armistice. So, too, did the German president while a joint Beethoven concert at Westminster Hall by the Parliament choir and the German Bundestag choir evoked a genuine spirit of reconciliation.

At the time of the 1918 Armistice Britain had been a massive global power. After the peace settlements of 1919–22, its imperial domain was even greater than before with a new dominance in the Middle East. Its prime minister, David Lloyd George, brought up in a shoemaker's cottage in Caernarfonshire, was then perhaps the greatest man in the world, comparable to Winston Churchill in 1940, even though the Welshman's name was largely an absentee in the 2018 centenary rituals. Remembrance Sunday thus paid annual tribute to a mighty but vanished heritage. Similarly, at Potsdam in 1945, Britain had been one of the 'big three', head of a worldwide Commonwealth which was now of little account; leading the sterling area, now obsolete, with the pound then a reserve currency following the Bretton Woods agreement of 1944; and financing a global defence structure that extended from Hong Kong to Belize. What one perceptive historian, David Edgerton, has called 'the warfare state' and the welfare state were intertwined, and both were struggling.

The country had after 1945 a strong self-contained economy, with its own energy and food supplies and massive manufacturing, for example in the car industry. Now, while major car firms on the continent like Renault, Volkswagen, Audi and Fiat were successfully run in their own countries, the British car industry, once pioneered by such giants as Lord Nuffield, had effectively perished. Overseas, after the war, Attlee's government even sought to take the lead in Europe in the guise of Western Union; in 1947 Ernest Bevin had signed the Anglo-French Treaty, symbolically, on the beach at Dunkirk. Now Britain was engaged in another, more extensive retreat.

It had become a marginalised power, perhaps in the second rank, which had cut back its armed forces, notably the navy, in a 'strategic shrinkage' since 2010, though maintaining its unused nuclear weaponry. Despite a damaging flourish in Iraq in 2003, the people had little appetite for overseas adventures. The Foreign Office was suffering from a crisis of identity and purpose, its influence much reduced by the loss of two key competences, international development (1997) and international trade (2016). Brexit made matters worse as the United Kingdom bowed out of centre stage. Britain decided unilaterally in 2013 not to follow the United States and France in engaging in the long-running civil war in Syria. It followed the dissentient isolationism of Keynes in 1919–22, when Bonar Law observed that 'we could not be policeman of the world'. In the Trump era, the 'special relationship' with the United States', now in nationalist vein, was exposed as the sentimental myth that perhaps it always had been.

Britain's pre-eminence as a country was popularly thought to reside in its culture, its 'soft power'. Many of those key cultural components were now regarded as being under threat. During the Brexit debate, a group of musicians, including world-famous conductors like Sir Simon Rattle and John Eliot Gardner, expressed their fears of Britain becoming a 'cultural ghetto', cut off from artistic stimulus from other lands. Distinguished filmmakers said much the same. Nobel prize-winners and other leading scientists complained of the 'corrosive effects' of Brexit potentially, with key research programmes in many areas undermined by the loss of EU research funding (of which Britain received 16 per cent) and research teams losing personnel crucial for research teams, including vital areas of life sciences and pharmaceuticals. So much for the land of Newton and Darwin. Britain still heeded and needed its history—for centuries it had been an inescapable component of its identity. But this history could be a burden as well as an inspiration, as in the unhistorical misuse of the 'darkest hour' view of the second world war, like Dunkirk, and the Blitz, during the Brexit debate ('We fought alone' was the celebrated, quite inaccurate, phrase). The romantic 'island story' view taught to generations of children over past decades could no longer serve. The United Kingdom was still a creative, civilized, peaceful country in which to live, but this view of its history needed to be revised quite frequently. Many of the challenged confronting Britain were man-made. But those coming from a ferocious climate, global warming, colossal droughts, floods and fires posed catastrophic world threats.

The destructive powers of the natural world were tragically illustrated by the sudden impact in February-March 2020 of Covid-19, a worldwide respiratory pandemic. Starting in central China, it raged throughout the world in just a few weeks. The United Kingdom was laid low like the rest of the world. Here was a natural disaster comparable with the Black Death of 1348 which had wiped out one third of the population of England in less than a year, more serious than the Great Plague of 1665 or earlier famines, fevers or cholera outbreaks because of its global impact. Some terrifying forecasts suggested a possible quarter of a million deaths. The response of the government was dramatic. The impact of the state on the citizen's liberties became more severe even than the 1915 Defence of the Realm Act, with people especially the elderly, told to stay isolated in their own homes, to keep their distance from others, and from shops, transport or places of work, if possible. The economy shrank by 35% in just three months, and lurched into the worst recession for 300 years. Unemployment soared, the Treasury responded by jettisoning any pretence of a balanced budget or controls on public spending, with a £350bn package of loans and grants to businesses and individuals crippled by financial collapse. Ethnic minorities suffered disproportionally. Public and private services, especially the National Health Service, and care homes were stretched to the limits after the recent austerity. The prime minister, Boris Johnson declared the country was on a war footing. It was another 1940; the Queen's message to the nation quoted the wartime lyric of Dame Vera Lynn, 'We'll meet again'. Johnson himself an erratic pilot in the storms, became a victim of the virus and spent some days in intensive care. He narrowly avoided becoming the first prime minister to die in office since Palmerston in 1865. Well over 100,000 British citizens died and the crisis illustrated the huge dangers of globalization and the inter-connectedness of mankind. It all suggested the prime urgency of international co-operation, Brexit or no. To recover, a tormented country would have to reunite, mobilize its talents, harness the state and the educated 'elite', and show its traditional solidarity in times of peril if 2,000 years of remarkable history were to leave a legacy worth inheriting. The chronicle of two millennia perhaps offered some confidence that it might do so, yet again.

SELECT BIBLIOGRAPHY

A comprehensive bibliography of the materials used for this book, written, oral, and visual, would run to many volumes. I list here only those most directly useful.

A. MANUSCRIPT COLLECTIONS

1. PUBLIC RECORDS

Cabinet: CAB 21 (Prime Minister's briefs)
CAB 128 (Cabinet conclusions, 1945–67)
CAB 129 (Cabinet papers, 1945–67)
CAB 130 (Cabinet committees: minutes and memoranda)
Colonial Office: CO 537
Defence: DEFE 4, 6 (Chiefs of Staff, 1945–58)
Foreign Office: FO 371
FO 800 (Foreign Secretary's papers)
Health: MH 77
Home Office: HO 45
Housing: HLG 102 (Miscellaneous files)
Labour: LAB 10 (Industrial Relations)
Prime Minister's Office: PREM 8 (1945–51)
PREM 11, 13 (1951–67)
Treasury: T 171 (Budget and Finance Bill papers)
T 225 (Defence Policy and Materials Division) T 227 (Social Services Division)
T 229–238 (Central Economic Planning Staff) T 247 (Keynes papers)

2. PRIVATE PAPERS

Lord Addison papers (Bodleian Library, Oxford).
A. V. Alexander papers (Churchill College, Cambridge).

C. R. Attlee papers (Bodleian Library, Oxford, and Churchill
College, Cambridge).
Lord Callaghan papers (Bodleian Library, Oxford).
Lord Cledwyn papers (National Library of Wales, Aberystwyth).
Lord Crookshank papers (Bodleian Library, Oxford).
Arthur Creech Jones papers (Rhodes House Library, Oxford).
Hugh Dalton papers (British Library of Political and Economic
Science, London).
Clement Davies papers (National Library of Wales, Aberystwyth).
Hugh Gaitskell papers (Nuffield College, Oxford).
Arthur Greenwood papers (Bodleian Library, Oxford).
James Griffiths papers (National Library of Wales, Aberystwyth).
Walter Monckton papers (Bodleian Library, Oxford).
Herbert Morrison papers (Nuffield College, Oxford).
Philip Noel-Baker papers (Churchill College, Cambridge).
Richard Stokes papers (Bodleian Library, Oxford).
George Strauss transcript interview (Nuffield College, Oxford).
Lord Woolton papers (Bodleian Library, Oxford).
Kenneth Younger transcript interview (Nuffield College, Oxford).

3. PAPERS OF OTHER ORGANIZATIONS

Committee of Vice-Chancellors and Principals.
Conservative Party (Bodleian Library, Oxford):
Conservative Research Department papers, 1945–64.
Director of Organization and constituency organization papers,
1951–64.
Executive Committee minutes, 1945–64.
Council for Wales (National Library of Wales, Aberystwyth).
Labour Party (Museum of Labour History, Manchester):
National Executive Committee minutes, 1944–79.
Policy Committee minutes, 1944–79.
General Secretary's correspondence.
International department, 1944–52.
University of Warwick Modern Records Centre:
MS 126 Minutes and Records, General Executive Council, Trans-
port and General Workers' Union.
MS 127 Reports and Proceedings, National Union of Railwaymen.
The Welsh Assembly, minutes 1999–.

B. NEWSPAPERS, PERIODICALS, AND REPORTS

1. NEWSPAPERS

Daily Herald
Daily Telegraph
Evening Standard
Financial Times
The Guardian (formerly *Manchester Guardian*)
The Independent
News Chronicle
The Observer
Sunday Times
The Times
Western Mail

2. PERIODICALS

Arcade
Bank of England Quarterly Bulletin
British Medical Journal
Contemporary Record
The Economist
Encounter
Foreign Affairs
Horizon
International Affairs
The Lancet
Lloyds Bank Review
Medicine Today and Tomorrow
The Music Maker
National Westminster Bank Quarterly Review
New Left Review
New Scientist
New Society
New Statesman
Oz
Planet
Private Eye

Proceedings of the British Academy
Political Quarterly
Political Studies
Prospect
Public Administration
Punch
Regional Trends
Social Trends
Socialist Commentary
Socialist Outlook
Spectator
Time
Time and Tide
Tribune
Wisden

3. REPORTS

Annual or quarterly reports of the following organizations:
Arts Council
British Academy
British Broadcasting Corporation
Committee of Vice-Chancellors and Principals
Confederation of British Industries
Conservative Party
Constitutional Unit, University College of London
Football Association
Historical Association
Institute of Welsh Affairs
Iron and Steel Board
Labour Party
Liberal Party
National Coal Board
National Union of Railwaymen
Plaid Cymru
Royal Society
Trades Union Congress
Transport and General Workers Union
Welsh Arts Council

C. BIOGRAPHIES AND MEMOIRS

Arranged in order of subject; place of publication London unless otherwise stated.

Acheson, Dean, *Present at the Creation: My years at the State Department* (1970).

Addison, Lord, *Portrait of a Progressive: The Political Career of Christopher, Viscount Addison*, by Kenneth and Jane Morgan (Oxford, 1980).

Ali, Tariq, *Streetfighting Years* (1987).

Attlee, Clement, *Attlee*, by Kenneth Harris (1982).

Atlee, Clement, *Citizen Clem*, by John Bew (London, 2016).

Barnett, Joel, *Inside the Treasury* (1982).

Beatles, The, *The Beatles' Progress*, by Michael Brown (1974).

Beaverbrook, Lord, *Beaverbrook*, by A. J. P. Taylor (1972).

Best, George, *Best: An Intimate Biography*, by Michael Parkinson (1973).

Benn, Tony, *Out of the Wilderness: Diaries, 1963–67* (1987).

Benn, Tony, *Office Without Power: Diaries, 1968–72* (1988).

—— *Against the Tide: Diaries, 1973–76* (1989).

—— *Conflicts of Interest, 1977–80* (1990).

—— *The End of an Era: Diaries, 1980–90* (1991).

Bevan, Aneurin, *Aneurin Bevan*, vols. i and ii, by Michael Foot (1962, 1973).

—— *My Life with Nye*, by Jennie Lee (1980).

—— *Nye Bevan and the Mirage of British Socialism*, by John Campbell (1987).

—— *The State of the Nation*, ed. Geoffrey Goodman (1997).

—— *Nye: The Political Life of Aneurin Bevan*, by Nicklaus Thomas-Symonds (London, 2014).

Beveridge, Lord, *William Beveridge: A Biography*, by José Harris (Oxford, 1977).

Bevin, Ernest, *The Life and Times of Ernest Bevin*, vol. ii. *Minister of Labour, 1940–1945* (1967) and *Ernest Bevin: Foreign Secretary* (1983), by Alan Bullock.

—— Ernest Bevin: Labour's Churchill by Andrew Adonis (London, 2020).

Bevins, J. R., *The Greasy Pole* (1965).

Blair, Tony, *Tony Blair*, by John Rentoul (new edn., 2001).

—— *Tony Blair, the Modernizer*, by Jon Sopel (1995).

—— *The Blair Effect*, ed. Anthony Seldon (2001).

Boyle, Sir Edward, *The Politics of Education*, by Maurice Kogan (Harmondsworth, 1971).

Brown, George, In my Way (Harmondsworth, 1971).

Brown, Gordon, *Gordon Brown: The Biography*, by Paul Routledge (1998).

Butler, Lord, *The Art of the Possible* (1971).

—— *RAB: The Life of R. A. Butler*, by Anthony Howard (1987).

Cairncross, Alec, *The Wilson Years: A Treasury Diary 1964–1969* (1997).

Callaghan, James, *Time and Chance* (1987).

—— *Callaghan: A Life*, by Kenneth O. Morgan (Oxford, 1997).

Cameron, David, *Cameron: Practically a Conservative*, by Frances Elliott and James Hanning (London, 2012).

Castle, Barbara, *The Castle Diaries, 1964–70* (1974).

—— *The Castle Diaries, 1974–76* (1980).

Churchill, Winston, *Winston S. Churchill*. vol. vii, *Road to Victory (1941–5)* and vol. viii. *Never Despair (1945–65)*, by Martin Gilbert (1986, 1988).

—— *Churchill*, ed. Robert Blake and William Roger Louis (Oxford, 1993). Cole, G. D. H., *G. D. H. Cole and Socialist Democracy*, by A. W. Wright (Oxford, 1979).

—— *Churchill: Walking with Destiny*, by Andrew Roberts (London, 2018).

Cole, Margaret, *Margaret Cole, 1893–1980*, by Betty D. Vernon (1986).

Cook, Robin, *Robin Cook*, by John Kampfner (1998).

Crickhowell, Nicholas, *Westminster, Wales and Water* (Cardiff, 1999).

Crosland, Anthony, *The Politics of Education*, by Maurice Kogan (Harmondsworth, 1971).

—— *Tony Crosland*, by Susan Crosland (1982).

Crossman, Richard, *Palestine Mission: A Personal Record* (1947).

—— *The Backbench Diaries of Richard Crossman, 1951–64*, ed. Janet Morgan (1981).

—— *Diaries of a Cabinet Minister*, 3 vols., ed. Janet Morgan (1975–7).

Cousins, Frank, *The Awkward Warrior*, by Geoffrey Goodman (1979).

Dalton, Hugh, *Hugh Dalton*, by Ben Pimlott (1985).

—— *Memoirs, 1945–60: High Tide and After* (1962).

—— *The Second World War Diary of Hugh Dalton*, ed. Ben Pimlott (1986).

—— *Political Diary, 1918–40; 1945–60*, ed. Ben Pimlott (1987).

Dash, Jack, *Good Morning, Brothers!* (1969).

Davenport, Nicholas, *Memoirs of a City Radical* (1974).

Douglas-Home, Sir Alec, *Sir Alec Douglas-Home*, by D. R. Thorpe (1996).

Deakin, Arthur, *Trade Union Leadership*, by V. L. Allen (1957).

Dell, Edmund, *A Hard Pounding* (Oxford, 1991).

Driberg, Tom, *Ruling Passions* (1977).

Duff, Peggy, *Left! Left! Left!* (1971).

Eden, Sir Anthony, *Full Circle* (1960).

—— *Anthony Eden: A Biography*, by David Carlton (1981).

—— *Anthony Eden*, by Robert Rhodes James (1986).

Elizabeth II, *The Queen*, by Ben Pimlott (1996).

Feather, Vic, *Vic Feather, T.U.C.*, by Eric Silver (1973).

Foot, Michael, *Michael Foot: A Life*, by Kenneth O. Morgan (London, 2007).

Franks, Oliver, *Oliver Franks: Founding Father,* by Alex Danchev (Oxford, 1993).

Gaitskell, Hugh, *Hugh Gaitskell*, by Philip Williams (1979).

—— *The Diary of Hugh Gaitskell, 1945–56*, ed. Philip Williams (1983).

—— *Hugh Gaitskell*, by Brian Brivati (1996).

Galbraith, John Kenneth, *Ambassador's Journey: A Personal Account of the Kennedy Years* (1966).

George VI, *King George VI*, by J. W. Wheeler-Bennett (1958).

Gladwyn, Lord, *The Memoirs of Lord Gladwyn* (1972).

Gormley, Joe, *Battered Cherub* (1982).

Griffiths, James, *Pages from Memory* (1969).

Hattersley, Roy, *A Yorkshire Boyhood* (Oxford, 1983).

Healey, Denis, *Denis Healey and the Politics of Power*, by B. Reed and G. Williams (1971).

—— *The Time of my Life* (1989).

Heath, Edward, *The Autobiography of Edward Heath: The Course of my Life* (1998).

—— *Edward Heath: A Biography*, by John Campbell (1993).

Henderson, Nicholas, *Mandarin* (1994).

Hill, Lord, *Behind the Scenes* (1974).

Hopkinson, Tom, *Of this our Time* (1982).

Horner, Arthur, *Incorrigible Rebel* (1960).

Howe, Geoffrey, *Conflicts of Loyalty* (1994).

Hurd, Douglas, *An End to Promises* (1979).

Jay, Douglas, *Change and Fortune: A Political Record* (1980).

Jenkins, Roy, *A Life at the Centre* (1991).

——(ed.), *European Diary, 1977–81* (1989).

Jones, Jack, *Union Man* (1986).

Jones, Mervyn, *Chances* (1986).

Keeler, Christine, *The Truth at Last* (2001).

Keynes, John Maynard, *Essays on John Maynard Keynes*, ed. by Milo Keynes (Cambridge, 1975).

—— *John Maynard Keynes. Fighting for Britain, 1937–1946.* By Robert Skidelsky (2000).

Kilmuir, Lord, *Political Adventure: The Memoirs of the Earl of Kilmuir* (1964).

King, Cecil, *The Cecil King Diary, 1965–1970* (1972).

Kinnock, Neil, *Neil Kinnock: The Path to the Leadership*, by G. M. F. Drower (1984).

—— *The Making of Neil Kinnock*, by Robert Harris (1984).

Lawson, Nigel, *The View from No. 11* (1993).

Lee, Jennie, *Jennie Lee*, by Patricia Hollis (Oxford, 1997).

—— *Jennie Lee: A Life*, by Patricia Hollis (Oxford, 1997).

Lee, Joseph, *Ireland, 1912–1985* (Cambridge, 1989).

Lloyd, Selwyn, *Selwyn Lloyd*, by D. R. Thorpe (1989).

Macleod, Iain, *Iain Macleod*, by Nigel Fisher (1973).

Macmillan, Harold, *Memoirs*, vol. iv. *Riding the Storm, 1956–1959* (1971).

—— *Memoirs*, vol. v. *Pointing the Way, 1959–1961* (1972).

—— *Memoirs*, vol. vi, *At the End of the Day, 1961–1963* (1973).

—— *Harold Macmillan*, 2 vols., by Alastair Horne (1988, 1989).

Major, John, *Major: A Political Life*, by Anthony Seldon (1997).

—— *The Autobiography* (1999).

—— *Too Close to Call: Power and Politics—John Major in Number 10*, by Sarah Hogg and Tim Hill (1995).

Maudling, Reginald, *Memoirs* (1978).

Mikardo, Ian, *Backbencher* (1988).

Miliband, Ed, *Ed: The Milibands and the Making of a Labour Leader*, by Mehdi Hasan and James Macyntire (London, 2011).

Monckton, Walter, *Walter Monckton*, by Lord Birkenhead (1969).

Montgomery, Field-Marshal Viscount, *Monty*, vol. ii, by Nigel Hamilton (1986).

Morrison, Herbert, *Autobiography* (1960).

—— *Herbert Morrison: Portrait of a Politician*, by Bernard Donoughue and G. W. Jones (1973, new edn., 2001).

Orwell, George, *George Orwell: A Life*, by Bernard Crick (Harmondsworth, 1980).

Ottey, Roy, *The Strike: An Insider's Story* (1985).

Owen, David, *Time to Declare* (1991).

Plowden, Sir Edward, *An Industrialist in the Treasury: The Postwar Years* (1989).

Prior, James, *A Balance of Power* (1986).

Redcliffe-Maud, Lord, *Experiences of an Optimist* (1981).

Rees, Merlyn, *Northern Ireland: A Personal View* (1985).

Rice-Davies, Mandy, *The Mandy Report* (1964).

Scargill, Arthur, *Scargill and the Miners*, by Michael Crick (Harmondsworth, 1985).

Shinwell, Emanuel, *Conflict without Malice* (1955).

Shuckburgh, Evelyn, *Descent to Suez: Diaries, 1951–56* (1986).

Silverman, Sydney, *Sydney Silverman: Rebel in Parliament*, by Emrys Hughes (1969).

Smith, John, *John Smith*, by Andy McSmith (1994).

Strachey, John, *John Strachey*, by Hugh Thomas (1973).

Swinton, Lord, *Lord Swinton*, by J. A. Cross (Oxford, 1982).

Taylor, A. J. P., *A Personal History* (1983).

—— *The Troublemaker*, by Kathleen Burk (2000).

Tebbit, Norman, *Upwardly Mobile* (1988).

Thatcher, Margaret, *The Downing Street Years* (1993).

——*Mrs. Thatcher*, by Kenneth Harris (1988).

—— *One of Us*, by Hugo Young (new edn., 1991).

—— *Margaret Thatcher: The Grocer's Daughter*, by John Campbell (2000).

Truman, Harry S., *Memoirs*, vol. ii. *Years of Trial and Hope* (1956).

Ward, Stephen, *The Trial of Stephen Ward*, by Ludovic Kennedy (1964).

Whitelaw, William, *The Whitelaw Memoirs* (1989).

Wilson, Harold, *Memoirs, 1916–1964: The Making of a Prime Minister* (1986).

—— *The Labour Government, 1964–70: A Personal Memoir* (Harmondsworth 1971).

—— *Final Term: The Labour Government, 1974–1976* (1979).

—— *Harold Wilson*, by Ben Pimlott (1992).

—— *Wilson: The Authorized Life*, by Philip Ziegler (1993).

Wright, Peter, *Spycatcher* (1986).

Zuckerman, Sir Solly, *Men, Monkeys and Missiles* (1988).

Biographical information may also be obtained from the *Dictionary of National Biography* (supplements for 1941–50, 1951–60, 1961–70, 1971–80, 1981–85, and 1986–90); *The Times: The House of Commons*, 1945–97; *Who's Who*; and obituaries in *The Times*, *The Guardian*, and *The Independent*.

D. OTHER PUBLISHED WORKS

Place of publication London unless otherwise stated.

Abel-Smith, Brian, and Peter Townsend, *The Poor and the Poorest* (1965).

Addison, Paul, *The Road to 1945* (1975).

—— *Now the War is Over* (1985).

Adeney, Martin, and John Lloyd, *The Miners' Strike, 1984–5: Loss without Limit* (1987).

Adonis, Andrew, and Stephen Pollard, *A Class Act* (1997).

Allsop, Kenneth, *The Angry Decade: A Survey of the Cultural Revolt of the Nineteen-fifties* (1958).

Alt, James E., *The Politics of Economic Decline* (1979).

Annan, Noel, *Our Age* (1990).

Ascoli, David, *The Queen's Peace* (1979).

Ashworth, William, *A History of the British Coal Industry, vol. v, 1946–1982* (Oxford, 1986).

Bacon, Roger, and Walter Eltis, *Britain's Economic Problems: Too Few Producers* (1976).

Bain, G., *The Growth of White Collar Unionism* (Oxford, 1970).

Bale, Tim, *The Conservative Party: From Thatcher to Cameron* (London, 2010).

Barker, Elizabeth, *Britain in a Divided Europe, 1945–70* (1971).

Barker, Rodney, *Education and Politics, 1900–51* (Oxford, 1972).

Barnes, Denis, and Eileen Reid, *Government and Trade Unions: The British Experience, 1964–79* (1980).

Barnett, Corelli, *The Audit of War: The Illusion and the Reality of Britain as a Great Power* (1986).

Bartlett, C. J., *The Long Retreat* (1972).

Batson, E. V., I. Boraston, and K. S. J. Frenkel, *Shop Stewards in Action* (Oxford. 1977).

Baylis, John (ed.), *British Defence Policy in a Changing World* (1977).

Beckerman, Wilfred (ed.), *The Labour Government's Economic Record, 1964–1970* (1972).

Beer, Sam, *Modern British Politics* (1965).

—— *Britain against Itself: The Political Contradictions of Collectivism* (1982).

Beveridge, Sir William, *Pillars of Society* (1943).

Bew, Paul, *Churchill and Ireland* (Oxford, 2016).

—— *Ireland: The Politics of Enmity 1789–2006* (Oxford, 2007).

Beynon, Huw (ed.), *Digging Deeper: Issues in the Miners' Strike* (1985).

Blackaby, F. (ed.), *British Economic Policy, 1960–74* (Cambridge, 1978).

Blake, Robert, *A History of Rhodesia* (1977).

—— *The Conservative Party from Peel to Major* (1997 edn.).

—— and John Patten (eds.), *The Conservative Opportunity* (1976).

Bogdanor, Vernon, *Devolution in the United Kingdom* (Oxford, 1999).

—— and Robert Skidelsky (eds.), *The Age of Affluence* (1970).

Booker, Christopher, *The Neophiliacs* (1969).

Boucher, David, *The Feminist Challenge: The Movement for Women's Liberation in Britain and the USA* (1983).

Boyce, George, *The Irish Question and British Politics, 1868–1986* (1988).

Bradley, Ian, *Breaking the Mould? The Birth and Prospects of the Social Democratic Party* (Oxford, 1981).

Brady, Robert, *Crisis in Britain* (1950).

Brandon, Henry, *In the Red: The Struggle for Sterling, 1964–1966* (1966).

Briggs, Asa, *Sound and Vision: The History of Broadcasting in the United Kingdom*, vol. iv (Oxford, 1979) and vol. v (Oxford, 1995).

Brittan, Samuel, *The Treasury under the Tories, 1951–1969* (Harmondsworth, 1964).

—— *Left or Right: The Bogus Dilemma* (1968).

—— *Steering the Economy: The Role of the Treasury* (1969).

—— *How to End the Monetarist Controversy* (1981).

—— *The Role and Limits of Government* (1983).

Brivati, Brian, and Tim Bale, *New Labour in Power* (1997).

Brown, E. H. Phelps, *The Origins of Trade Union Power* (Oxford, 1983).

—— *Inegalitarianism and the Origins of Inequality* (Oxford, 1988).

Brown, Gordon, *Where there is Greed: Margaret Thatcher and the Betrayal of Britain's Future* (1989).

Bruce-Gardyne, Jock, *Mrs. Thatcher's First Administration* (1984).

Burk, Kathleen, *The First Privatisation* (1989).

—— and Alec Cairncross, '*Goodbye, Great Britain': The 1976 IMF Crisis* (1992).

Burn, Duncan, *The Steel Industry, 1939–1959* (Cambridge, 1961).

Butler, David, *The British General Election of 1951* (1952).

—— *The British General Election of 1955* (1955).

—— Andrew Adonis, and Tony Travers, *Failure in British Government: The Politics of the Poll Tax* (1994).

—— and Gareth Butler, British Political Facts, 1900–1990 (1991).

—— and Dennis Kavanagh, *The British General Election of February 1974* (1974).

———— *The British General Election of October 1974* (1975).

———— *The British General Election of 1979* (1980).

———— *The British General Election of 1983* (1984).

———— *The British General Election of 1987* (1988).

———— *The British General Election of 1992* (1992).

———— *The British General Election of 1997* (1997).

—— and Anthony King, The British General Election of 1964 (1965).

———— *The British General Election of 1966* (1967).

—— and Uwe Kizinger, *The 1975 Referendum* (1976).

—— and Michael Pinto-Duschinsky, *The British General Election of 1970* (1971).

—— and Austin Ranney (eds.), Referendums: a Comparative Study of Theory and Practice (Washington, 1978).

—— and Richard Rose, The British General Election of 1959 (1969).

Butt, Philip Alan, *The Welsh Question* (Cardiff, 1975).

Butterworth, Eric, and R. Holman (eds.). *Social Welfare in Modern Britain* (1975).

Byrd, Peter (ed.), *British Foreign Policy under Thatcher* (Deddington, 1988).

Cable, Vince, *The Storm: The World Economic Crisis and What It Means* (London, 2009).

Cairncross, Alec, *Years of Recovery: British Economic Policy, 1945–51* (1985).

—— (ed.), *Britain's Economic Prospects Reconsidered* (1970).

—— *Managing the British Economy in the 1960s* (1996).

—— and Barry Eichengreen, *Sterling in Decline* (1983).

Cairncross, Frances (ed.). *Changing Perceptions of Economic Policy* (1981).

Callaghan, James, *A House Divided: The Dilemma of Northern Ireland* (1973).

Calvocoressi, Peter, *The British Experience, 1945–1975* (1978).

Campbell, Beatrix, *Iron Ladies* (1987).

Chester, D. N., *The Nationalised Industries* (1951).

Churchill, Randolph S., *The Fight for the Tory Leadership* (1964).

Clarke, Richard, *Anglo-American Economic Collaboration in War and Peace, 1942–1949* (Oxford, 1982).

Cockerell, Michael, *Live from Number Ten: Prime Ministers and Television* (1988).

Connolly, Bernard, *The Rotten Heart of Europe* (1995).

Coogan, Tim Pat, *The Troubles: Ireland's Ordeal 1966–96* (1995).

Cook, Chris, and John Ramsden (eds.), *Trends in British Politics since 1945* (1978).

Cosgrave, Patrick, *Thatcher: The First Term* (1985).

Cowley, Philip and Dennis Kavanagh, *The British General Election of 2010* (London, 2010).

—— *The British General Election of 2015* (London, 2015).

—— *The British General Election of 2017* (London, 2017).

Crewe, Ivor, and Anthony King, *SDP: The Birth, Life and Death of the Social Democratic Party* (1995).

Cronin, James, and Jonathan Schneer (eds.). *Social Conflict and the Political Order in Modern Britain* (1982).

Crosland, Anthony, *The Future of Socialism* (1956).

—— *Socialism Now* (1974).

Crossman, Richard, *Palestine Mission: A Personal Record* (1947).

—— *Planning for Freedom* (1965).

—— (ed.), *New Fabian Essays* (1952).

Crouch, Colin, *Class Conflict and the Industrial Relations Crisis* (1977).

Dahrendorf, Rolf, *On Britain* (1980).

—— *LSE* (Oxford, 1995).

Darwin, John, *Britain and Decolonisation: The Retreat from Empire in the Postwar World* (1988).

Davies, Christie, *Permissive Britain: Social Change in the Sixties and Seventies* (1975).

Davies, John, *A History of Wales* (1993).

Davis, William, *Three Years' Hard Labour: The Road to Devaluation* (1968).

Deakin, Nicholas, *The Politics of Welfare* (1987).

Dell, Edmund, *The Chancellors* (1996).

—— *A Strange Eventful History* (2000).

Devine, T. M., *The Scottish Nation 1700–2000* (2000).

—— *Independence or Union: Scotland's Past and Scotland's Present* (London, 2016).

Dockrill, Michael, *British Defence since 1945* (1988).

Donoughue, Bernard, *Prime Minister: The Conduct of Policy under Harold Wilson and James Callaghan* (1987).

Dorfman, Gerald, *Government versus Trade Unionism in British Politics* (1979).

Dow, J. C. R., *The Management of the British Economy, 1945–60* (Cambridge, 1964).

Durcan, J., W. McCarthy, and G. Redman, *Strikes in Postwar Britain* (1983).

Eckstein, Harry, *The English Health Service: Its Origins, Structure and Achievements* (Cambridge, Mass., 1959).

Edgerton, David, *The Rise and Fall of the British Nation: A Twentieth-Century History* (London, 2018).

Elbaum, Bernard, and William Lazowick (eds.). *The Decline of the British Economy* (Oxford, 1986).

Elsom, John, *Postwar British Theatre* (1976).

Epstein, Leon, *Britain: Uneasy Ally* (Chicago, 1954).

—— *British Politics in the Suez Crisis* (1964).

Floud, Roderick, and Donald McCloskey (eds.), *The Economic History of Britain since 1700*, vol. iii (Cambridge, 2nd edn., 1994).

Foote, Geoffrey, *The Labour Party's Political Thought: A History* (1985).

Ford, Boris (ed.), *The New Pelican Guide to English Literature*, vol. viii (Harmondsworth, 1983).

Foster, Roy, *Modern Ireland, 1600–1972* (1988).

Foulkes, D., J. B. Jones, and R. A. Wilford, *The Welsh Veto* (Cardiff, 1982).

Francis, Martin, *Ideas and Policies under Labour 1945–1951: Building a New Britain* (Manchester, 1997).

—— and Ina Zweiniger-Bargielowska (eds.), *The Conservatives and British Society 1880–1990* (Cardiff, 1996).

Freedman, Lawrence, *Britain and Nuclear Weapons* (1980).

—— *Britain and the Falklands War* (Oxford, 1988).

Fussell, Paul, *Wartime* (Oxford, 1989).

Fyvel, T. R., *Intellectuals Today: Problems in a Changing Society* (1968).

Gaitskell, Hugh, *Socialism and Nationalism* (1956).

Gamble, Andrew, *The Conservative Nation* (1974).

—— *The Free Economy and the Strong State: The Politics of Thatcherism* (1988).

Gardner, R. N., *Sterling-Dollar Diplomacy* (New York, 1969).

Geary, Richard, *Policing Industrial Disputes, 1893 to 1985* (Cambridge, 1985).

Gilmour, Ian, *Inside Right: A Study in Conservatism* (1977).

—— *Britain Can Work* (1983).

—— *Dancing with Dogma* (1992).

Glees, Anthony, *Exile Politics During the Second World War* (1982).

Glennester, Howard (ed.), *The Future of the Welfare State* (1983).

Goldthorpe, John H., David Lockwood, Frank Bechofer, and Jennifer Platt, *The Affluent Worker in the Class Structure* (Cambridge, 1969).

Goodman, Geoffrey, *The Miners' Strike* (1985).

Gould, Philip, *The Unfinished Revolution* (1998).

Gowing, Margaret, *Independence and Deterrence: Britain and Atomic Energy, 1945–52* (1974).

Grove, Eric, *Vanguard to Trident: British Naval Policy since World War Two* (Annapolis, 1987).

Gupta, P. S., *Imperialism and the British Labour Movement, 1914–1965* (1975).

Gwyn, W. B., and Richard Rose (eds.), *Britain: Progress and Decline* (1980).

Haines, Joe, *The Politics of Power* (1972).

Hall, Stuart, and Martin Jacques, *The Politics of Thatcherism* (1983).

Hall, Tony, *King Coal* (Harmondsworth, 1981).

Halsey, A. H., *Changes in British Society* (Oxford, 3rd edn., 1985).

—— (ed.), *British Social Trends since 1900* (1988 edn.).

Harrison, Martin, *Trade Unions and the Labour Party since 1945* (1960).

Harvie, Christopher, *No Gods and Precious Few Heroes* (1981).

—— *Scotland and Nationalism* (3rd edn., 1998).

Haseler, Stephen, *The Gaitskellites* (1969).

Hattersley, Roy, *Choose Freedom* (1987).

Heikal, Mohamed H., *Cutting the Lion's Tail: Suez through Egyptian Eyes* (1986).

Henderson, Nicholas, *The Birth of NATO* (1982).

Hennessy, Peter, *Cabinet* (1986).

—— *Whitehall* (1989).

—— *Never Again* (1992).

—— *The Prime Minister* (2000).

—— and Anthony Seldon (eds.), Ruling Performance: British Governments from Attlee to Thatcher (1987).

Hewison, Robert, *In Anger: Culture in the Cold War, 1945–60* (1981).

—— *Too Much: Art and Society in the Sixties 1960–75* (1988 edn.).

—— *Culture and Consensus* (1995).

Hobsbawm, Eric, *The Forward March of Labour Halted?* (1981).

—— *Politics for a Rational Left* (1989).

Hogan, Maurice, *The Marshall Plan: America, Britain and the Reconstruction of Western Europe* (London, 1987).

Hollingsworth, Mark, and Richard Norton-Taylor, *Blacklist: The Inside Story of Political Vetting* (1988).

Holmes, Martin, *The Labour Government, 1974–1979: Political Aims and Economic Reality* (1985).

—— *The First Thatcher Government, 1979–1983: Contemporary Conservatism and Economic Change* (Brighton, 1985).

Howard, Anthony, and Richard West, *The Making of the Prime Minister* (1965).

Howell, David, *British Social Democracy* (1976).

—— *The Politics of the NUM: A Lancashire View* (London, 1989).

Hutber, Patrick, *The Decline and Pall of the Middle Class* (1976).

Hutton, Will, *The State we're in* (1995).

Irving, Clive, Ron Hall, and Jeremy Wallington, *Scandal '63: A Study of the Profumo Affair* (1963).

Jackson, Brian, *Working Class Community* (1968).

Jay, Douglas, *Socialism in the New Society* (1962).

—— *After the Common Market* (Harmondsworth, 1968).

—— *Sterling* (1985).

Jeffery, Keith, and Peter Hennessy, *States of Emergency* (1983).

Jefferys, Kevin, *Retreat from New Jerusalem: British Politics 1951–64* (1997).

Jenkins, Peter, *The Battle of Downing Street* (1970).

—— *Mrs. Thatcher's Revolution* (1987).

Jenkins, Simon, *Accountable to None: The Tory Nationalization of Britain* (1995).

Johnson, Christopher, *The Economy under Mrs. Thatcher* (1991).

Joseph, Sir Keith, *Reversing the Trend* (1975).

—— *Stranded in the Middle Ground* (1976).

Kampfner, John, *Blair Wars* (2004).

Kavanagh, Dennis, *Thatcherism and British Politics* (Oxford, 1987).

—— (ed.), *The Politics of the Labour Party* (1982).

Keegan, William, *Mrs. Thatcher's Economic Experiment* (1984).

Kellas, James, *The Scottish Political System* (Cambridge, 1989 edn.).

Kelley, Kevin J., *The Longest War: Northern Ireland and the IRA* (Westport, Conn., 1988 edn.).

Kellner, Peter, and Norman Crowther-Hunt, *The Civil Service: An Inquiry into Britain's Ruling Class* (1980).

Kitzinger, Uwe, *Diplomacy and Persuasion: How Britain Joined the Common Market* (1973).

Kogan, David, and Maurice Kogan, *The Battle for the Labour Party* (1982).

Kramnick, Isaac, *Is Britain Dying? Perspectives on the Current Crisis* (1979).

Kynaston, David, *The Financial Times: A Centenary History* (1988).

Laski, Harold, *Reflections on the Revolution of our Time* (1943).

Leech, Kenneth, *Youthquake: The Growth of a Counter-Culture through Two Decades* (1973).

Leigh, David, and Ed Vulliamy, *Sleaze: The Corruption of Parliament* (1997).

Leruez, Jacques, *Economic Planning and Politics in Britain* (1975).

—— *Le Thatcherisme: doctrine et action* (Paris, 1984).

Lewis, Jane, *Women in Britain since 1945* (1992).

Linklater, Magnus, and David Leigh, *Not with Honour* (1986).

Livingstone, Ken, *If Voting Changed Anything, They'd Abolish it* (1987).

Lloyd, Selwyn, *Suez, 1956: A Personal Account* (1978).

Louis, William Roger, *Imperialism at Bay* (Oxford, 1977).
—— *The British Empire in the Middle East, 1945–1951* (Oxford, 1984).
—— and Roger Owen (eds.). *Suez, 1956: The Crisis and its Consequences* (Oxford, 1989).
Lowe, Rodney, *The Welfare State since 1945* (1993).
Lyons, F. S. L., *Ireland Since the Famine* (1973 edn.).
McCallum, R. B., and Alison Readman, *The British General Election of 1945* (Oxford, 1947).
McDonald, James G., *My Mission in Israel* (1951).
McIlroy, John, Nina Fishman and Alan Campbell (eds.), *British Trade Unions and Indusrial Politics* (Aldershot, 2 vols., 2000).
MacKenzie, Norman (ed.), *Conviction* (1958).
McKenzie, R. T., *British Political Parties* (new edn., 1963).
Macwhirter, Iain, *Disunited Kingdom: How Westminster Won a Referendum but Lost Scotland* (Glasgow, 2014).
Maddison, Angus, *Phases of Capitalist Development* (New York, 1982).
Mandelson, Peter, and Roger Liddle, *The Blair Revolution* (1996).
Margach, James, *The Anatomy of Power* (1988).
Marquand, David, *The Unprincipled Society* (1988).
—— *The New Reckoning* (1997).
Marwick, Arthur, *Britain in the Century of Total War* (1968).
—— *British Society since 1945* (Harmondsworth, 1982).
—— *Culture in Britain since 1945* (1991).
Maschler, Tom (ed.), *Declaration* (1957).
Matthews, R. C. O., C. H. Feinstein, and R. A. Odling-Smee, *British Economic Growth, 1856–1973* (Oxford, 1982).
Maynard, Geoffrey, *The Economy under Mrs Thatcher* (Oxford, 1988).
Michie, Alastair, and Simon Hoggart, *The Pact* (1978).
Middlemas, Keith, *Power, Competition and the State*, vol. i, *Britain in Search of Balance, 1940–61* (1986).
Middleton, Drew, *The British* (1957).
Miliband, Ralph, *Parliamentary Socialism* (1961).
Milward, Alan S., *The Reconstruction of Western Europe, 1945–51* (1984).
Minkin, Lewis, *The Labour Party Conference* (Manchester, 1978).

Moore, Richard, *Escape from Empire* (Oxford, 1983).

Morgan, Jane, *Conflict and Order: The Police and Labour Disputes in England and Wales, 1900–1939* (Oxford, 1987).

Morgan, Kenneth O., *Rebirth of a Nation: Wales 1880–1980* (Cardiff and Oxford, 1981, repr. 1997).

—— *Labour in Power, 1945–1951* (Oxford, 1984).

—— *Labour People: leaders and Lieutenants, Hardie to Kinnock* (Oxford, 2nd edn., 1992).

—— *Ages of Reform: Dawns and Downfalls of the British Left* (London, 2010).

—— *Revolution to Devolution: Reflections on Welsh Democracy* (Cardiff, 2014).

Nairn, Tom, *The Enchanted Glass: Britain and its Monarchy* (1988).

Neustadt, Richard, and Ernest R. May, *Thinking in Time* (New York, 1986).

Nicholas, H. G., *The British General Election of 1950* (1951).

Noble, Trevor, *Structure and Change in Modern Britain* (1981).

Nossiter, Bernard, *Britain: A Future that Works* (1978).

O'Malley, Padraig, *The Uncivil Wars: Ireland Today* (Belfast, 1983).

O'Rourke, Kevin, *A Short History of Brexit: From Brentry to Backstop* (London, 2019).

O'Toole, Fintan, *Brexit and the Politics of Pain* (London, 2019).

Ovendale, Ritchie (ed.), *The Foreign Policy of the British Labour Government, 1945–1952* (Leicester, 1988).

Owen, David, *Face the Future* (1981).

Owen, G. (ed.), *The Thatcher Years* (1987).

Panitch, Leo, *Social Democracy and Industrial Militancy* (Cambridge, 1986).

Parkin, Frank, *Middle Class Radicals* (Manchester, 1968).

Parkinson, Michael, *Liverpool on the Brink: One City's Struggle against Government Cuts* (1985).

Paxman, Jeremy, *Friends in High Places: Who Runs Britain?* (1990).

Pearson, Geoffrey, *Hooligan: A History of Respectable Fears* (1983).

Peden, G. C., *British Economic Policy, Lloyd George to Margaret Thatcher* (Deddington, 1985).

Pelling, Henry, *The Labour Governments, 1945–51* (1984).

Pittock, Murray, *The Road to Independence?: Scotland in the Balance* (London, 2014).

Pliatsky, Leo, *Getting and Spending* (Oxford, 1982).

Plowden, William, *The Motor Car and Politics* (1971).

Ponting, Clive, *Breach of Promise: Labour in Power, 1964–70* (1988).

Priestley, J. B., *The Arts under Socialism* (1946).

Pym, Francis, *The Politics of Consent* (1985).

Ramsden, John, *The Making of Conservative Policy since 1929: The Conservative Research Department* (1980).

—— *The Age of Churchill and Eden* (1995).

—— *The Winds of Change: Macmillan to Heath* (1996).

—— *An Appetite for Power* (1998).

Rawnsley, Andrew, *The End of the Party: The Rise and Fall of New Labour* (London, 2010).

Rentoul, John, *Me and Mine: The Triumph of the New Individualism?* (1989).

Renwick, Chris, *Bread for All: The Origins of the Welfare State* (London, 2017).

Reynolds, David, *Britannia Overruled* (1991).

Rich, Paul, *Race and Empire in British Politics* (Cambridge, 1986).

Ritchie, Harry, *Success Stories: Literature and the Media in England 1950–1959* (1988).

Roberts, B. C., *National Wages Policy in War and Peace* (1958).

Robertson, Alex, *The Bleak Midwinter, 1947* (Manchester, 1987).

Robinson, Colin, and Jon Morgan, *North Sea Oil in the Future: Economic Analysis and Government Policy* (1978).

Rock, Paul, *A History of British Criminology* (1988).

Rogaly, Joe, *Grunwick* (1978).

Rogow, A., and Peter Shore, *The Labour Government and British Industry, 1945–51* (1955).

Rosecrance, R. S., *Defense of the Realm: British Strategy in the Nuclear Age* (New York, 1968).

Rothwell, Victor, *Britain and the Cold War, 1941–1947* (1982).

Rusbridger, Alan, Breaking News: *The Remaking of Journalism and Why It Matters Now* (London, 2018).

Sampson, Anthony, *The Anatomy of Britain* (1962).

Samuel, Raphael, *Theatres of Memory* (1994).

—— *Island Stories* (1998).

—— Barbara Bloomfield, and Guy Boanas (eds.), The Enemy Within: Pit Villages and the Miners' Strike of 1984–5 (1986).

Sanderson, Michael, *The Universities and British Industry, 1850–1970* (1972).

Saunders, Robert, *Yes to Europe!: The 1975 Referendum and Seventies Britain* (Cambridge, 2018).

Saville, John, *The Labour Movement in Britain* (1988).

Schneer, Jonathan, Labour's Conscience: *The Labour Left, 1945–51* (1988).

Seldon, Anthony, *Churchill's Indian Summer: The Conservative Government, 1951–55* (1981).

—— and Dennis Kavanagh, *The Blair Effect 2001–5* (Cambridge, 2005).

Shanks, Michael, *The Stagnant Society* (Harmondsworth, 1963).

—— *Planning and Politics: The British Experience, 1960–76* (1977).

Shipman, Tim, *All Out War: The Full Story of How Brexit Sank Britain's Political Class* (London, 2016).

—— *Fall Out: A Year of Political Mayhem* (London, 2017).

Shonfield, Andrew, *British Economic Policy since the War* (Harmondsworth, 1958).

Simon, Brian, *The Politics of Educational Reform, 1920–1940* (1974).

Simpson, John, *The Independent Nuclear State: The United States, Britain and the Military Atom* (1983).

Sissons, Michael, and Philip French (eds.), *Age of Austerity* (Oxford, new edn., 1986).

Skidelsky, Robert (ed.), *Thatcherism* (1988).

Smith, H. L. (ed.), *War and Social Change: British Society in the Second World War* (Manchester, 1987).

Stead, Peter, *Film and the Working Class* (1989).

Stephen, Philip, *Politics and the Pound: The Conservatives' Struggle with Sterling* (1996).

Stephenson, Hugh, *Claret and Chips: The Rise of the SDP* (1982).

Stewart, Michael, *The Jekyll and Hyde Years: Politics and Economic Policy since 1964* (1977).

Strange, Susan, *Sterling and British Policy* (Oxford, 1971).

Studlow, Danley T., and Jerold L. Waltman (eds.), *Dilemmas of Change in British Politics* (1984).

Tanner, Duncan et al. (eds.), *Debating Nationhood and Governance in Britain, 1885–1939* (Manchester, 2006).

Tawney, R. H., *Equality* (1931).

Taylor, Andrew, *The Politics of the Yorkshire Miners* (1984).

Taylor, John Russell, *Anger and After: A Guide to the New British Drama* (1969 edn.).

Taylor, Robert, *The Fifth Estate: Britain's Unions in the Seventies* (1978).

—— *The Trade Union Question in British Politics* (1993).

Thompson, E. P. (ed.), *Out of Apathy* (1960).

—— *Warwick University Limited: Industry, Management and the Universities* (Harmondsworth, 1971).

—— *Writing by Candlelight* (1980).

Thorne, Christopher, *Allies of a Kind: The United States, Britain and the War against Japan, 1941–1945* (1978).

Tiratsoo, Nick, *The Attlee Years* (1991).

—— (ed.) *From Blitz to Blair* (1997).

Thurlow, Richard, *Fascism in Britain: A History, 1918–1985* (Oxford, 1987).

Timmins, Nicholas, *The Five Giants* (1993).

Titmuss, Richard, *Essays on the Welfare State* (1958).

Todd, Selina, *The People: The Rise and Fall of the Working Class, 1910–2010* (London, 2014).

Tomlinson, Jim, *Democratic Socialism and Economic Policy* (Cambridge, 1996).

Tooze, Adam, *Crashed: How a Decade of Financial Crises Changed the World* (London, 2018).

Townsend, Peter, and Dorothy Wedderburn, *The Aged in the Welfare State* (1965).

Toynbee, Polly, and David Walker, Cameron's Coup: How the Tories took Britain to the Brink (London, 2011).

Tyler, Rodney, *Campaign* (1987).

Tyrell, Jr., R. Emmett, *The Future that Doesn't Work: Social Democracy's Failures in Britain* (New York, 1977).

Uri, Pierre (ed.). *From Commonwealth to Common Market* (Harmondsworth, 1968).

Vaizey, John, *In Breach of Promise* (1983).

Verrier, Anthony, *The Road to Zimbabwe* (1986).

Walmsley, Roy, *Personal Violence* (HMSO, 1986).

Walters, Alan, *Britain's Economic Renaissance* (1986).

Wass, Sir Douglas, *Government and the Governed* (1984).

Watkins, Alan, *A Conservative Coup. The Fall of Mrs. Thatcher* (1991).

Watson, J. D., *The Double Helix* (1970).

Webster, Charles, *The Health Services since the War*, vol. i (HMSO, 1988); vol. ii (HMSO, 1997).

Weeks, Jeffrey, *Sex, Politics and Society* (1981).

Weiler, Peter, *British Labour and the Cold War* (Palo Alto, Calif., 1988).

Whitehead, Phillip, *The Writing on the Wall: Britain in the Seventies* (1985).

Whiteley, Paul, *The Labour Party in Crisis* (1983).

Wickham-Jones, Mark, *Economic Strategy and the Labour Party* (1996).

Wiener, Martin, *English Culture and the Decline of the Industrial Spirit, 1850–1981* (Cambridge, 1981).

Williams (Falkender), Marcia, *Inside Number Ten* (1972).

—— *Downing Street in Perspective* (1983).

Williams, Shirley, *Politics is for People* (1981).

Winter, J. M. (ed.), *The Working Class in Modern British History* (Cambridge, 1983).

Worswick, G. N., and P. Ady (eds.), *The British Economy, 1945–50* (Oxford, 1952).

——— (eds.), *The British Economy in the Nineteen-fifties* (Oxford, 1962).

Young, Hugo, *This Blessed Plot* (1998).

Young, J. W., *Britain, France and the Unity of Europe, 1945–51* (Leicester, 1984).

—— *Cold War Europe 1945–89: A Political History* (1991).

Young, Michael, *The Rise of the Meritocracy* (Harmondsworth, 1958).

Young, Wayland, *The Profumo Affair: Aspects of Conservatism* (1963).

Youngson, A. J., *Britain's Economic Growth, 1920–1966* (1967).

Zysman, John, *Governments, Markets and Growth: Financial Systems and the Politics of Industrial Change* (1983).

INDEX